ALEXANDER HERZEN
AND THE
BIRTH OF RUSSIAN SOCIALISM

ALEXANDER HERZEN
AND THE BIRTH OF
RUSSIAN SOCIALISM

By MARTIN MALIA

The Universal Library

GROSSET & DUNLAP

NEW YORK

UNIVERSAL LIBRARY EDITION, 1965

BY ARRANGEMENT WITH HARVARD UNIVERSITY PRESS

**TO THE MEMORY OF
MY PARENTS**

Preface

Since the subject — or subjects — treated in this book are such that they are less than usually well indicated by the title, a preliminary word of explanation is more than usually in order. The central core of what follows is a biography of Alexander Herzen from his birth in 1812 to the end of the reign of Nicholas I in 1855. I chose these dates because they delimit the period during which Herzen made his principal mark on Russian thought and, in particular, during which he developed his famous theory of Russian socialism founded on the peasant commune, a theory which furnished the ideological basis of the revolutionary Populism that inspired so much of the radical intelligentsia's activities in the last century, and indeed down to 1917. The study of Herzen's thought, however, inevitably led to the exploration of three problems which transcend his own career and which are crucial to early nineteenth-century Russian intellectual history in general.

The first of these problems is to account for the emergence of socialism in Russia as early as the reign of Nicholas I, at a time when what is usually considered to be the basis for such a development — an industrial proletariat — was an insignificant phenomenon. The second problem is to explain the extraordinary impact of post-Kantian romantic idealism in Russia under Nicholas and its relation to the origins of socialism, for Russian socialism, like Marxism, owed a pre-eminent debt to idealism. The final problem is to understand the ideological nationalism which appeared in Russia in the same period, a movement which drew much of its inspiration from idealism and which in turn helped inspire the theory of a specifically national form of socialism.

This book, then, is a study of ideologies much more than of politics. These ideologies, however, are not treated in the abstract, either in terms of the description and comparison of ideas *per se* or of influences and borrowings from other thinkers. Rather, I have tried to write in terms of what might be called the "social psychology" of ideas, that is, how ideological patterns emerge from, or express in transposed form, the social, political, and historical pressures of a given period. In particular,

I have sought to emphasize the psychological processes through which social pressures are reflected in ideologies.

Once this method was adopted, however, what began as a biography of Herzen inevitably turned into an attempt to produce a "sociology of ideas" for much of Russian thought under Nicholas. Moreover, since no intellectual development in this period can be understood independently of its European background, it was necessary to extend the same type of inquiry to kindred currents of thought in the West, particularly Germany and France. No doubt the cohesion of the book has suffered from the pursuit of so many ramifications, but I hope that this defect will be compensated for by some increase in understanding of the genesis of the extraordinary ideological politics of nineteenth-century Russia, which treated even in the simplest fashion would still make a more than usually complex work. In any event, what the reader will find will be less the story of Herzen's first forty-three years than an examination of the problems of idealism, socialism, and nationalism as reflected in his career under Nicholas I and as related to similar European developments.

This study began as a doctoral thesis in 1949–50. In that form it was exclusively devoted, in the scrupulous tradition of graduate-school training, to the verifiable description and delineation of Herzen's ideas, without reference to much of anything else. For this reason I felt it advisable to defer publication in order to permit reworking and amplification according to the method mentioned above. This latter enterprise, which in effect amounted to the composition of a very different study, occupied intermittently the years 1956–59. The book as it now stands is entirely the product of this second effort.

In both stages of this work, however, I had a single debt of intellectual gratitude — to Michael Karpovich, late Reisinger Professor of Slavic Languages and Literatures and Professor of History at Harvard University. It is no exaggeration to state that few in America in this century have known so much of Russian history, or have been so judicious in their judgments on it, as he; and none has matched him in command of Russian intellectual history, which, in fact, he was the first to introduce to the American university public. Without his knowledge to draw on, the beginning of this study would have been impossible; without his tempered criticisms as a guide matters would certainly have gone sadly awry *en route;* and without his encouragement they would hardly have reached completion, for, although I at times despaired of Herzen, Michael Karpovich had the kindness never to despair of me. Finally, the well-known liberalism with which he allowed his students to go their own way should exonerate him from all suspicion of responsibility for the errors which this book may contain or for the interpretations it sets forth.

In addition, I wish to thank most warmly Professor Hugh McLean

of the Slavic Department of the University of Chicago for the generosity
with which he gave of his time in reading the first half of the manuscript
and for his thoughtful criticisms, both of style and content. I wish also
to thank Mr. John Elliott of Berkeley, California, for his invaluable help
with matters of form and style throughout; Mrs. Helen Parsons and the
secretarial staff of the Russian Research Center at Harvard for their
patience and despatch in typing the bulk of the manuscript, often on an
unpredictable schedule which my erratic rhythm of production imposed;
Mrs. Miriam de Longpré of Berkeley, California, for the same virtues
amidst the same difficulties; and Mrs. Lee Ambrose of the Harvard
University Press for her unusually helpful advice and encouragement in
the final revision and editing.

Berkeley, California   Martin Malia

Contents

CHAPTER I

Introduction

I T IS a pious convention of Soviet scholarship to begin all studies of Russian history with a quotation from one of the masters of Marxism, an observance which will be respected here. In an oft-cited passage Lenin once declared that socialism "had grown out of philosophical, historical and economic theories worked out by educated representatives of the possessing classes." Therefore "the bearer of this science is not the proletariat but the *bourgeois intelligentsia;* contemporary socialism was born in the heads of individual members of this class." [1] With respect to his native land, however, it is possible to go Lenin one better. Russian socialism was born amidst a class more archaic than the bourgeoisie — the gentry or aristocracy (*dvorianstvo*), a class in which, according to all recognized canons in such matters, Marxist or otherwise, socialism ought not to take up abiding historical residence. But hereby hangs a problem, which is that of the present book.

No nation in history ever prepared its revolution longer or more self-consciously than Russia. Almost exactly a century before the event, in 1816, the first secret political society was formed, which in 1825 produced the conspiracy of the Decembrists. The movement of protest that prepared this development went back even further, to 1790 and Radishchev's famous *Journey from Saint-Petersburg to Moscow,* the first work in the language to openly attack autocracy and serfdom in the name of liberal, humanitarian values. From this time until the collapse of the old regime the problems posed by political absolutism, the absence of individual freedom, and the depressed condition of the masses (even though, after 1861, no longer serfdom) were to dominate Russian life with an obsessive consistency unique in modern history.

This, of course, is not intended to suggest any sort of historical teleology inexorably leading Russia to 1917, and of which the various movements of protest against autocracy and the servitude of the masses were the "logical" stages. If 1917 had not occurred, or if it had turned out some other way, these movements would have been the origin of something else. Yet they would be there none the less: they would still revolve around the same questions, they would continue to dominate nineteenth-century Russian history, and they would constitute the same historical problem as at present.

The movement of humanitarian protest in Russia was not at first revolutionary, and of course even less "socialist." Radishchev had no program of action, for action was impossible given the conditions existing under Catherine II. His book was simply a generalized cry of indignation thrown out into the air for want of a more effective means of attack. Nor were the Decembrists, although they attempted to act, revolutionaries in the fullest sense of the word. They were Guards officers who wished to stage a *coup d'état* in a manner which still had an air of semilegality about it at the time. The tempering of autocracy by armed intervention of the gentry to decide the succession had become by the beginning of the nineteenth century almost part of the "constitution." All Russian sovereigns — at least all who lasted — from Catherine I to Alexander I had either come to the throne or seen the conditions of their accession determined in some measure by armed gentry coup. The originality of the Decembrists was to attempt to turn these old methods to the new purpose of humanitarian reform.

These ends, however, were moderate when judged by the standards set later in the century by the radical opposition. Though far-reaching in the context of autocracy, the various programs of the Decembrists were no more than liberal, in the classical sense of that term, which though usually associated with a bourgeoisie is also appropriate when applied to a restive aristocracy. The abolition or constitutional limitation of the monarchy, the emancipation of the peasantry on more or less generous terms, and the greater or lesser democratization of society were the goals of the Decembrists.[2] They made no call for a mass uprising of the people and envisaged popular participation in the projected overturn only under the enlightened guidance of the officer elite. On the whole, the Decembrists, even the most radical such as Pestel, lacked that faith in the power of the "people" to achieve its own liberation which the full-blown revolutionary subscribes to even when in fact his methods are very elitist and "Jacobin." Moreover, the Decembrists lacked the cult of *Revolution* — the faith in some great historical catharsis which would regenerate the world, recreate mankind, and propel Progress to its ultimate conclusion. To be sure they had their ideals, and even their abstract idealism, but they did not go all the way to the creation of a millennial metaphysic, which just as much as the cult of the people is characteristic of the complete revolutionary.

The development of a fully democratic and apocalyptic ideal of revolution only came after the Decembrists, and as a result of their failure, in the reign of Nicholas I. At that time the opposition, or at least a part of it, first began to call itself "socialist," and to identify its cause with that of groups in the West employing the same name. Henceforth, revolution and socialism would be practically synonymous in Russia. And the creation of this revolutionary socialism, like the earlier, liberal forms of humanitarian protest, was the work of the gentry. It was the gentry, moreover, who first carried this development all the way to the creation of a metaphysic of revolution and its adaptation to Russian conditions. At least it did so on the level of theory, since in the thirty years after 1825 action again became impossible. Yet by 1855 and the death of Nicholas — in fact by 1849 — the theory of Russian socialism was complete in its essential outlines.

That this contribution was purely theoretical in no way diminishes its importance. A potent ideal was a necessary prerequisite to ardent action, bolder than that of the Decembrist, and mighty with the heroism, the unshakable conviction, and often the fanaticism which came to characterize the Russian revolutionary movement. The world could be moved only if there were first a vision. In following this priority the Russian development paralleled that of Western Europe: Marx too, after all, was only a theorist.

Moreover, the development of socialist theory, begun in the Great Revolution with the conspiracy of Babeuf and posed as an acute problem by 1830, was substantially completed everywhere during the Revolution of 1848. By this date Marx's position had been formulated in all its fundamentals in the *Communist Manifesto;* his later works, including *Das Kapital,* may fairly be considered as no more than immensely detailed elaborations. And Marxism was simply one, if also the most imposing, of the finished constructs. At the same time anarchism had emerged with Proudhon; Fourierism helped give impetus to the ideal of the producers' and consumers' cooperative; Louis Blanc had given a primitive version of the "welfare state"; Lamennais had laid the groundwork for a Christian socialism — and the list obviously could be lengthened. The contribution of the Russians in the wake of 1848 was peasant socialism, and the expression "Russian socialism" will be used throughout this book in the dual sense of simply socialism in Russia, and of an indigenous doctrine founded on a belief in the socialist future of the peasant commune (*obshchina*), or what came to be known under Alexander II as "Populism" (*narodnichestvo*).

After 1848 all over Europe, socialist thought turned from general theory to considerations of practical politics and strategy. Edward Bernstein and the various social democratic "revisionists" of Marxism are almost too obviously just that to mention; George Sorel's anarcho-syndicalism represents only a particular kind of anarchism; guild socialism is largely a specific application of the principle of "cooperation" and of syndicalism. The same is true in Russia, where the successive forms of Populism and Marxism were adaptations of first principles elaborated by Herzen, Bakunin, and again Marx. To be sure, these strategic revisions all had enormous practical importance, but they occurred within a framework of general doctrine which they themselves did not create, and outside of which they would have been impossible. The socialism of the various Internationals, of all the concrete movements since 1848, reaped what the visionaries of the *entre-deux-révolutions* had first sown.

Though these visionaries in Russia came primarily from the gentry, it would be a mistake to associate them with that class as a whole in any period of its history. As Lenin was perceptively aware, the socialist dream is always born in the heads of *individual* members of the possessing classes, or at least of some group above the "people." This emphasis is all-important. Although such individuals are *from* the possessing classes, they are no longer *of* them. They are socially or spiritually *déclassé* intellectuals, who in their alienation from their origins reach out for identification with the masses in some all-embracing democratic eschatology. In Europe such individuals sprang from almost every group in society: from the nobility, such as Saint-Simon; from the clergy, such as Lamennais; from among the industrialists, such as Owen; from the shopkeepers, such as Fourier; from the legal profession, such as Marx; or from the near-proletariat (but never quite the real thing), such as Proudhon and Weitling. As Lenin's thought was put somewhat cynically by a renegade from the cause: "The idea of socialism sprang, not so much from the physical distress of manual workers, as from the moral distress of mental workers." [3]

In short, the inventors of socialism did not come from any one class that can be defined in economic or social terms, but from what can only be called a moral or intellectual category, for which the Russians were the first to find an appropriate word — the intelligentsia. Nor was Russian priority in this discovery an accident. Here, as in so much else in modern history, Russia contained the extremes of phenomena common to the whole of Europe: to name only the most crucial examples, the extremes of authoritarianism and anarchism, of reaction and revolution, of actual backwardness and the cult of progress. In Russia, more clearly than in all other countries of Europe, the intelligentsia was unaccounted for by any possible economic or social classifications, which is why its existence was first noticed there.

A further extreme lies in the recruitment of the intelligentsia from the most conservative segment of society, the gentry, to a far greater degree than in the rest of Europe. Indeed, as the ultimate paradox, even one autocrat may be partially included — Alexander I in his early reforming years, when his dreams of a constitution and peasant emancipation were almost as radical as anything proposed by Radishchev or most of the Decembrists. To be sure, the term intelligentsia did not come into use until the *raznochintsy*, or commoners, took their place in significant numbers alongside the gentry intellectuals during the reign of Alexander II. But the "class" clearly existed under Nicholas, if not earlier, and almost all its prominent representatives were from the gentry. There were, of course, nongentry *intelligenty* such as Polevoi, Nadezhdin, and most notably Belinski, but such men were exceptions, and the vast majority of intellectuals occupied with forming public opinion until 1855 were from the gentry.

Furthermore, the Russian revolutionary movement and later the revolution itself developed the way they did primarily because of the intelligentsia's energies and ambitions. Here Marxist class categories only confuse the issue. The Russian revolutionary movement in its various phases was neither a "bourgeois," a "proletarian," or still less a peasant, phenomenon; it was essentially an "intelligentsia revolution." Of course, the intelligentsia eventually had an absolute need of proletarian and peasant discontent and even, to a certain extent, of middle-class restlessness, in order to make its revolution. But the revolutionary movement itself did not represent the interests, or often even the desires, of any of these groups. Instead it represented an ideal vision, of which the intelligentsia was the bearer.

This is perhaps not the place to attempt a definition, still less an explanation, of the intelligentsia in general or of the gentry *intelligent* in particular. The whole subject of the origins, composition, and nature of this peculiar but indubitably real "class" still awaits serious investigation.[4] What can be said here about its nature is best left to concrete examples in the narrative. Suffice it to say now, by way of a rough approximation, that the *intelligent* is any able, sensitive, and ambitious individual, from a more or less privileged group, who lives under an inflexible and "closed" old regime which does not offer adequate scope for his energies, and who consequently goes over to integral, as well as highly ideological, opposition to that regime. Moreover, the ideals which animate this opposition are derived by universalizing and absolutizing the values of independence and human dignity appropriate to the benefits of his greater or lesser privilege. In brief, the *intelligent* is a socially cramped individual caught in a contradiction between his immediate interests and his ultimate ideals, who in this conflict chooses the two birds in the bush over the one in the hand.

In Russia during the first half of the nineteenth century such individuals on the whole could come only from the gentry, since only that group had the privileges necessary to arrive at such ideals. This is why old-regime Russia could produce with relative regularity that type which Soviet historians, following Lenin,[5] refer to casually as a "gentry revolutionary" (*dvorianski revoliutsioner*), as if he were a generally prevalent and recognized species of radical, but who is in reality peculiar to Eastern Europe, and who, finally, stands in need of more searching explanation than his less aristocratic heirs have given him.

Under such historical circumstances the "birth of Russian socialism" is a subject which necessarily involves relatively isolated individuals, and hence also an extremely limited number of people. It concerns, in fact, exactly four major figures: Alexander Herzen; his ideological shadow, Nicholas Ogarev; Michael Bakunin; and, in a more indirect manner, Vissarion Belinski. These leaders, to be sure, were surrounded by lesser figures, such as the members of Herzen's university circle in the thirties and a slightly larger public in the forties, the most notable exemplars of which were the members of the Petrashevski circle. Nonetheless, the movement was confined to a tiny minority, a fact which explains much about its genesis and character. The subject of the origins of Russian socialism, then, is feasibly approached through biography. Indeed it is difficult to approach it in any other way, at least initially, for almost all we know about it is what we know of these four individuals and their immediate epigones.

Of these four figures that of Herzen presents certain advantages in studying the movement as a whole. Together with Bakunin he was the initiator of what was most specifically socialist in the activities of the group. Also, it is he who was the first socialist in Russian history, preceding Bakunin by a decade. Finally, it was Herzen much more than Bakunin who was responsible for the theoretical elaboration of socialism under Nicholas I, disseminating a specifically Russian adaptation of that doctrine and devoting his energies to revolution in Russia rather than to revolution in general. It would also be fair to claim that of the four leaders Herzen is intrinsically the most interesting, because he was the most complex, the most articulate and nuanced as an individual, as well as the only one who may lay claim to greatness as a writer. Beside him Belinski is a minor figure in the history of *belles-lettres*, however important he may be in the history of criticism; and Ogarev as a writer is no more than pleasant.

A final though no less significant consideration is that Herzen presents by far the best documented case of a "gentry revolutionary" on record, especially for the crucial formative years. There is relatively little direct information about the early years of Bakunin, Belinski, and Ogarev, although much can be inferred from what is known of their environments.[6] Herzen's evolution, however, can be traced almost from the cradle. Very early in life he decided that he was going to be an important historical personage and consequently that his example should be an open book for all the world to read. At the age of twenty-five he began writing his autobiography, an activity which continued, with interruptions, almost to his death. The first version, *Notebooks of a Certain Young Man*, was completed at the advanced age of twenty-nine.[7] The culmination was *My Past and Thoughts*, written over a period of fifteen years beginning in 1852, but entering exhaustively into the whole of its author's career back to childhood.[8]

My Past and Thoughts is Herzen's masterpiece as a writer and one of the great autobiographies of the nineteenth century in Russian or any language. With some plausibility it has been maintained that it is "worthy to stand beside the great Russian novels of the nineteenth century," and even that it is "comparable in scope and quality with *War and Peace*." [9] At all events, it is certainly the greatest single portrait of the generation which followed that described by Tolstoi, and which has gone down in Russian history with a distinctive name — "the idealists of the thirties and forties." Still more important, it is the most complete and frank confession we possess from any major figure of the reign of Nicholas I, since it is one of the rare memoirs of the period composed in freedom from censorship.

My Past and Thoughts, however, possesses all the vices of its virtues. As its literary standing would suggest, it is a guide to be used only with caution. Herzen was too good a story-teller to be also a good reporter. In addition his memoirs were intended as a political apologia, a circumstance which opens a further opportunity for the intrusion of romance into reality. Any study of Herzen, therefore, can only presume to be an attempt at rewriting *My Past and Thoughts*, as history if not as literature. This is fortunately made possible by the existence of a voluminous and introspective correspondence, the oldest portions of which go back to Herzen's sixteenth year, and of a number of highly autobiographical works of fiction composed from young manhood onwards. Taking all these materials together we are almost as well informed about Herzen's life while he was growing up as we are about the mature career of many a political figure. The story of these early years is worth following in detail as one of the rare cases in Russian history in which it is possible to witness the very birth of a revolutionary, for revolutionaries on the whole are born young.

In addition to telling us about the man, *My Past and Thoughts* chronicles the intellectual quest of the "generation of the thirties and forties" as a whole. An examination of Herzen's evolution leads inevitably to the exploration of the spiritual history of his age. More precisely, Russian socialism originated not in open politics but in the philosophic abstractions of a small circle of intellectuals. As in the case of Marxism, and of so many of modern Europe's headier visions whether of the Right or of the Left, the midwife at the birth of Russian socialism was German romantic idealism. This idealism, needless to say, was a phenomenon larger than Russian socialism, permeating almost the whole of intellectual life under Nicholas, radical, conservative, and nonpolitical. By the same token nothing in the period can be considered independently from it: idealism provided the primeval stuff out of which the theory of Russian socialism was made. Indeed, it will be necessary to speak at such length of this philosophic background that the present book might also have been called "Herzen and the age of Russian idealism."

The age of Russian idealism, however, like the period of the elaboration of Russian socialism, does not extend beyond the reign of Nicholas. Herzen's career, therefore, will be considered here only while he was occupied with the transmutation of idealism into socialism; after 1855, like the socialists of the West, he too was concerned primarily with political strategy. It is in the social and intellectual climate prevailing under Nicholas I that the explanation must be sought for what in Russia was a recognized type, but which in almost any other country or age would be a contradiction in terms — a "gentry revolutionary."

CHAPTER II

Family and Childhood

ERZEN's entrance into the world coincided with a great event in the annals of Russia and Moscow — a fact of which he was always proud — the Great Patriotic War of 1812. He was born in Moscow on March 25 [1] of that year, just a few months before the capture of the city by the French. The moment of his birth was appropriately chosen. The heroic year marked the apogee of old-regime Russia, and in particular of its most brilliant class, the gentry; the hearts of gentry and autocracy beat as one and the glory of the great year was equally the glory of both. But this date also marked the beginning of the decline of the old regime as well as of the gentry on which it was founded and which it in the first instance served. Within a decade this class produced the first active opposition to the autocracy, and after the revolt of 1825 nothing was ever to be the same with either gentry or regime again. If 1812 was the supreme achievement of old-regime Russia, it was also the beginning of its century-long agony of disintegration. Herzen was intimately involved in both facets of the great year: he was very much a product of the gentry in its flower and his life-mission was to be prophet and propagandist of its disintegration.

Herzen was the illegitimate son of a wealthy Moscow aristocrat, Ivan Alexeevich Iakovlev. While not among the most illustrious of Russian gentry houses, the Iakovlevs could trace their origins back to a boyar of Ivan III, at the end of the fifteenth century, and they had been vague cousins of the Romanovs before the latter's elevation to the throne.[2] For generations they had served tsar and emperor with honor if not with exceptional distinction. In the eighteenth century Herzen's great-uncle had been a brigadier-general and member of the Military College, or governing committee of the army. His grandfather, Alexis Alexandrovich Iakovlev, had been president of the College of Justice and director of the Imperial Mint. The Iakovlevs' economic position corresponded to their social status. They possessed over one thousand peasant "souls," together with several villages scattered throughout the central provinces around

Moscow. In short, they definitely belonged to the more opulent strata of the gentry, if not to the class of the great magnates.[3]

Herzen's grandfather is a rather shadowy figure, but what little is known of him suggests a typical military bureaucrat of the age whose interests were circumscribed by family and government "service." Born in the thirties of the eighteenth century, he was in his prime under Elizabeth and during the early years of Catherine. He represented, therefore, no more than the second generation of Westernization in Russia, when foreign manners and ideas served only to lend lustre to the life of the gentry but had not yet begun to undermine its unreflecting self-satisfaction. He belonged only to the first generation of the gentry's emancipation from the tutelage of the autocracy — the end of obligatory state service had been proclaimed as he was approaching middle age, in 1762 — a generation for which the habit of aristocratic independence and self-indulgence had not yet become second nature. He was all of a piece, a man of Russia's old regime while that regime was still young, and free from inner doubts about his place in the world.

His children present a rather different picture. Married to a Princess Meshcherskaia, like himself from the best Moscow gentry, Alexis Alexandrovich had four sons and two daughters. When both parents died relatively young, the main burden of the children's education fell to an unmarried sister of their mother. This aunt discharged her obligation by entrusting her wards to the care of French tutors, according to a practice just then coming into fashion.[4] The daughters turned out to be conventional products of their background, marrying well and raising children as conventionally aristocratic as themselves.[5] The sons were rather more interesting and atypical. Born in the 1760's and young in the palmiest days of Catherine, they took for granted what the generation of their father had only recently and imperfectly acquired. They were Westernized men of the world and self-willed aristocrats by nature and without effort.

Even so, the four brothers Iakovlev led strangely disjointed lives. They were, in fact, among the first representatives of a type characteristic of old Russia — the "superfluous man." Contemporaries attest to their great intelligence, their personal charm and the exceptional depth of their European refinement.[6] Most of them lived several years abroad, something by no means common among the gentry at the time. They read widely, and kept abreast of European fashions if only in a superficial manner. One brother in his old age even dabbled in the natural sciences, and "for want of anything better to do attended lectures at the university."[7] Yet nothing came of their talents or culture, neither exceptional careers in government service nor creative intellectual labor — not even satisfying personal lives of ease and refinement.

Like most noble Russians of their age, the brothers had been destined for military careers, the eldest in the Hussars and the others in the Iz-mailovski regiment of the Guards. Either from impatience with military discipline or from boredom with military routine, however, all four availed themselves of the gentry's recently won right not to "serve," and resigned their commissions young without advancing beyond the rank of captain.[8] After leaving military service, only one of the brothers, Lev (the Senator of Herzen's memoirs), continued to serve permanently in a civilian ca-pacity, and even there not brilliantly. In differing ways, the remaining brothers lapsed into self-destructive apathy and led violent, or frivolous, or simply empty lives. In *My Past and Thoughts* Herzen shortens, and especially softens, his portrait of the Iakovlev brothers, as if he wished to forget the painful circumstances of his origins. But the impact of their example on his development was sufficiently great to warrant our entering a moment into their careers. Fortunately Herzen had a cousin, by name Tatiana Passek, who supplies what he himself slurs over.[9]

The salient trait of the family's mores in the generation of Herzen's father was that all the brothers sired their children out of wedlock by women who lived in total servitude to them — a frequent consequence of the absolute power of the Russian landowner over his serfs and de-pendents. The eldest brother on leaving military service seduced a young Swedish governess, promised her marriage and installed her on his estate near Moscow. Although the promised marriage never took place the woman bore him three children and lived in his house for years, his wife in all but name. To insure the woman's dependence on him the eldest Iakovlev destroyed her passport, and she passed the rest of her days without any legal identity, completely at the mercy of his caprice. And cruelly capricious he was. Later in life he resumed government service for a time in the south, leaving his "family" behind. Aged and ill, and in need of feminine companionship, he carried off (or, according to other rumors, purchased) the wife of a subordinate official. On returning to central Russia he sent word to his former concubine to vacate his estate and retire to a nearby village. After thirty years of quasi-marriage such a *dénouement* was more than the poor woman could bear and she became mad.[10]

The second brother, after serving in the Guards and then on a diplo-matic mission abroad, was for a period in 1803 Procurator of the Holy Synod. His quarrelsome nature, however, first earned him dismissal from the procuratorship and subsequently banishment from St. Petersburg. He then retired to his estate in Tambov province, where his cruelty toward the peasants and his lechery with their daughters provoked a reaction from which he barely escaped with his life. Returning to Moscow, he passed the remainder of his life between his library and a harem of serf women, in loneliness, idleness, and endless lawsuits. One of his numerous natural children was Natalia Zakharina, later to be Herzen's wife. On his deathbed the old man married the serf mother of his eldest son (the "Chemist" of Herzen's memoirs) and recognized the latter as his heir, not, however, out of any love for either mother or son but simply to keep the inheritance from going to his younger brothers.[11]

The third brother, Lev, presents a somewhat less depressing spectacle. After service in the Guards, he was a member of various diplomatic missions to Western Europe during the Napoleonic wars, ambassador to the court of King Jerome of Westphalia, and, on his return to Russia in 1813, Senator, and curator of a hospital. Of a kinder and more social nature than his brothers, Lev was nonetheless an eccentric in his own way. His service as Senator and member of the governing boards of various philanthropic bodies was only nominal. He spent his time in an endless round of receptions, dinners, balls, plays — activity that busied without occupying him, and little of which served any practical purpose. Like his brothers, he never married, and like them he sired a number of servile bastards, who seem to have grown up in obscurity among his peasants as if they were not his children, but who at least escaped the more tragic lot of some of their cousins.[12] Although painted in softer tones than the family norm, the picture is nonetheless one of deep futility.

The fourth brother, and father of Herzen, Ivan Alexeevich, lived out in more subdued fashion the same frustrations as his elders. Born in 1766 and still a child at his parents' death, he was entrusted by his aunt to a French tutor, reportedly a relative of Voltaire, and entered active service in the Izmailovski Regiment in 1788 at the age of twenty-two. In the army, by virtue of a ready and sarcastic wit, he became the favorite and personal friend of the Grand Duke Constantine, second son of the Emperor Paul. Everything seemed to presage a brilliant career; then in 1797, for reasons that are unknown, Ivan Alexeevich, at only thirty-one, retired from the army, and indeed from all government service, for life.[13] In 1801 he went abroad and for ten years wandered about Europe in the midst of the Napoleonic wars, driven by what impulse it is impossible to say. In 1811, now forty-five and feeling that the best part of life was over, he returned to spend the remainder of his days in retirement in Moscow and on his estates in the country, occupied by nothing more than the care of his health. Of all the Iakovlevs he was most completely "the superfluous man."

What is the explanation for this strange failure of promise? Herzen himself concluded regarding his father's generation:

In Russia people subject to the influence of the mighty Western wind did not develop into historically meaningful individuals, but into eccentrics. Foreigners at home, foreigners abroad, idle spectators, spoiled for Russia by Western ideas, for the West by Russian habits, they were a kind of intelligent futility, lost in an artificial life, sensual pleasures and an insufferable egotism.[14]

But Herzen overgeneralizes. The Iakovlev brothers were atypical of their class and generation both in the extent of their Westernization and their negative response to it. They displayed only the destructive effects of the emancipation of the gentry. Their liberty was too complete and there was nothing to do with it. There were no challenges or obstacles to be overcome; and their cosmopolitan education led them only to reject participation in the life of their country without providing alternative outlets for their energies. They had come too soon in the modernization of Russian society, when the possibilities for meaningful activity, other than government service, were still too limited to absorb men of independent temper. They were the wasted first growth of modern civilization in Russia, who flourished to bear fruit, not in themselves, but in their still more independent and civilized sons.

The spectacle of his father's generation and, in particular, of his father's family, was to make a powerful impression on Herzen's mind. Many of his early writings, and to some extent his memoirs, are full both of their accomplishments and their misdeeds, and his reaction to his family and class heritage was correspondingly mixed. He was fascinated by their aristocratic elegance, the romance of their cosmopolitanism, and their haughty independence. Through them he had a vicarious historical experience going back to the glorious days of Catherine, when the gentry was great, free and self-confident in its independence; and this image he contrasted with the decadent subservience of the same class after 1825 when he himself was growing up. In spite of all their vices these were men — magnificent, anarchic individuals — and this was Herzen's ideal for himself and for the future.[15] Yet at the same time he was appalled by the barbarism that permeated so much of their way of life; and he never could forget the inhuman fate of all those — wives, children, serfs — who suffered from their aristocratic caprice. Later, in condemning the social order of the old regime he was first of all condemning his father's family. One of his later propagandistic efforts, an unfinished novel called *Duty Before All*, composed six years before *My Past and Thoughts* and much more frank about the gentry's mores, is little more than a portrait gallery of family horrors.[16] His own social ideals sprang largely from the contradiction between civilization and barbarism in the life of the Iakovlev brothers. In his more refined nature the family equilibrium burst asunder and led to his vehement rejection of barbarism in the name of civilization.

2

Like the other male Iakovlevs, Ivan Alexeevich never married, but he founded a family that was somewhat more conventional than the do-

mestic establishments of his brothers. Before his departure abroad he had
had a son, Egor, by a peasant girl on one of his estates. The boy was
rescued from serfdom and raised by his aunt, Princess Khovanskaia. Already half grown, he was presented to his father on the latter's return from
abroad: "The father, glancing at the boy, put his hand on his shoulder,
coldly kissed him, and, turning to his sister, expressed, in French, his
displeasure that she had taken on herself the education of the child without consulting him." [17] This unwanted son, who thereafter experienced
only persecution at his father's hands, was the original nucleus of Ivan
Alexeevich's "family."

Its principal members, however, were a young German girl and her
son Alexander. Henrietta Wilhelmina Louisa Haag, simplified for Russian usage to Louisa Ivanovna, had been born in Stuttgart, the daughter
of a modest functionary who later apparently settled in Kassel. For
reasons which are obscure, she was deeply unhappy in her parents' home.
Seeking relief, she often made visits of several days' duration to the house
of certain rich friends. There she met the Russian ambassador to King
Jerome, Lev Iakovlev, and his brother Ivan, who was stopping on his
wanderings through Europe. She was pretty, brunette, and young — only
fifteen. Learning of her plight, the brothers half-jestingly offered their
hospitality. Shortly thereafter, as a result of some unrecorded but final
crisis, Henrietta abandoned forever the parental roof and sought refuge
at the Russian embassy. The brothers granted her asylum and set her the
nominal duty of pouring their morning coffee. At the same time she became the particular protégée of Ivan Alexeevich. The latter soon left for
Italy and on his return found Henrietta pregnant. It was the end of 1811
and war was approaching between Russia and France. Ivan Alexeevich,
preparing to return home, proposed to leave Henrietta with her parents,
but this provoked such an outburst of despair in the girl that he consented to take her with him. Because of the danger of the time Henrietta
cut off her long hair and made the journey dressed in men's clothing.[18]

Shortly after the couple's arrival in Moscow, early in 1812, Louisa
Ivanovna (to call her henceforth by the Russian version of her name)
gave birth to a son. He was given the name Alexander, after his uncle
and godfather, the patronymic Ivanovich, thus indicating his father's
intention of adopting him as his *vospitannik,* or ward, and the last name of
Herzen, which he shared with his half brother Egor. The name Herzen
derived from the German word for heart, and was presumably chosen
to indicate the circumstances of his begetting.[19] Whether it was intended
by his father as a bit of dry humor or as a sign of affection is impossible
to say; either motive would have been consonant with his character. In
any event, by the time of his son's birth Ivan Alexeevich had decided, contrary to his original intention, to keep the child and his mother with him.

The first year of the new ménage, and the last active period in Ivan Alexeevich's life, was a trying one. Whether through accident or inertia, the household failed to leave Moscow before the arrival of the French and hence suffered all the rigors of the occupation and the great fire.[20] Finally, Ivan Alexeevich and his family were sent through the lines on a safe-conduct with a personal message from Napoleon to his "brother," Emperor Alexander, proposing a cessation of hostilities. The incident found its way into *War and Peace,* but otherwise nothing came of it.[21] By order of Alexander, Ivan Alexeevich was detained in semidisgrace in St. Petersburg, while his family spent the winter in straitened circumstances in a peasant hut on one of the Iakovlev estates. In 1813 Ivan Alexeevich was released and all returned to Moscow to establish themselves, together with the Senator, in the aristocratic quarter of the city along the Arbat, in a large old house which had escaped the fire. Ivan Alexeevich was now forty-seven and Louisa Ivanovna seventeen. They had come to settle permanently in "retirement" in Moscow.

The household in which Herzen was reared was a strange one indeed. Ivan Alexeevich installed himself in his own quarters on the first floor, Louisa Ivanovna with her son and Egor occupied one wing of the second floor, and the Senator occupied the other wing. Ivan Alexeevich lived in fastidious, hypochondriac withdrawal from Moscow society, and Louisa Ivanovna was acquainted with only a few of her compatriots in the city. The principal contact with the outside world was the Senator, who passed his time in frenetic, if empty, social activity. Even this element of sociability disappeared, however, when, toward Herzen's tenth year, the Senator moved to a separate establishment, apparently no longer able to bear the morose character of his brother. The family then moved to a more commodious dwelling, also off the Arbat, which Herzen later, doubtless reflecting a subjective impression more than an objective fact, remembered as having the aspect of a prison.[22] Mother and father continued to maintain their separate apartments, with young "Shushka" or "Sasha," as he was variously called, growing up somewhere in between.

The household was dominated by the misanthropic personality of Ivan Alexeevich. The old man's character — for even in his forties he was old — was mysterious. In his manners he was "the perfect man of the world,"[23] capable, when he wished, of great personal charm and an exquisite old-regime politeness. All accounts agree that he was highly intelligent and well read. By education he was a man of the French eighteenth century, to the end of his life writing more easily and correctly in French than in Russian. According to his son he never read a single Russian book. He once looked into Karamzin's *History of the Russian State,* having heard that the Emperor Alexander had read it, but abandoned it exclaiming: "All these Iziaslaviches and Olgoviches, who can be interested in that?" [24] His intelligence served only to feed a scathing sarcasm, which vented itself on all within his reach, even those dearest to him. He tormented his eldest son, Egor; he persecuted in innumerable petty ways the helpless Louisa Ivanovna; he harassed the servants and his peasants, who submitted to his whims when in his presence but who went their own way, cheating and deceiving him, as soon as his back was turned. He seemed to despise the whole world and to disbelieve utterly in his fellow men. Ridicule and irony were his answer to all problems. He appeared to believe in nothing more profound than a correct social bearing and a strict observance of *"les apparences, les convenances."* [25] Melancholic, irritable and withdrawn, he seemed to his son to carry some secret bitterness sealed in his heart which was perhaps the "result of the encounter of two such contradictory things as the [Western] eighteenth century and Russian life, in union with a third frightful stimulus to personal caprice — the idleness of the Russian serf-owner." [26]

The entire household was organized around his whims, and in particular around the exigencies of his supposed ill-health. The old man was approachable only at appointed hours of the day. Windows and doors had to be kept tightly shut for fear of drafts. Walks or drives in the carriage were undertaken only in fair weather and after due deliberation. The morning newspaper was brought to him after it had been warmed to dispel the chill of the damp pages.[27] As the years went by, friends gradually ceased calling, rebuffed by his constant complaints of a largely imaginary ill-health and by a more real ill-humor, and this abandonment only served to increase his irritability. Meanwhile, the heavy silence and the well-ordered boredom of the household grew apace.

Next to her husband, Louisa Ivanovna is a shadowy and colorless figure. She is almost absent from the pages of her son's memoirs, and only slightly less so from those of his cousin, Tatiana Passek. Herzen describes her (and Tatiana concurs) as exceptionally good but weak-willed, which seems to be a filial way of saying that she was not in any way remarkable. Given her modest background and her early "marriage," she could have had little formal education. In Russia she concerned herself with nothing but her domestic duties. It is doubtful that she maintained intimacy with Ivan Alexeevich after Sasha's birth. At least their relationship was unmarked by any show of affection, and she became simply a privileged dependent of her master — something more than a servant but much less than a wife. By the time Sasha was old enough to be aware of his surroundings, his parents' relationship had degenerated into a running war of small annoyances. His mother defended her wounded dignity by desperate resistance to the old man on innumerable small issues, but had surrendered to him on the main question of her status in his house; in turn, his father bent every effort to put her in the wrong and break her resistance.[28] Indeed, the main satisfaction Ivan Alexeevich seems to have derived from her presence was the pleasure of triumphing over her petty objections to his petty caprices. Why he never married her we are not told. Perhaps because of her plebeian birth; perhaps also because of the gratification he derived from her utter dependence on him. Why Louisa Ivanovna made her peace with this situation is equally difficult to determine. Her weak will may be invoked as an explanation. The fact that she had nowhere else to go and no means with which to provide for her son — if, indeed, she had been allowed to take him with her — may have had much to do with it. Of her compensations for an unhappy life we know equally little. She was a faithful, if only moderately pious, Lutheran. She appears also to have derived some comfort from her rise to the fringes of aristocracy, for she was a regular subscriber to the *Almanach de Gotha*.[29]

It was in the atmosphere of this household that Herzen lived, with almost no contact with the outside world, until the age of seventeen. With the exceptions of his cousin Tatiana and his friend Ogarev he had no companions outside of his family. He was educated entirely at home by private tutors, and although tutors were the rule among the wealthier gentry, such total isolation from the world was only the whim of Ivan Alexeevich. The old man's motives in so sheltering his son are nowhere given. We can only surmise that such complete control of his son's every act was the manifestation of an affection to which a gentlemanly distrust of "any familiarity" or "effusion" of emotion[30] denied expression in a more usual fashion.

The circumstances of Herzen's upbringing were extraordinary in other ways as well, for besides being brought up in the almost separate households of his father and his mother, he was also brought up in two separate cultures. Bilingualism, even trilingualism, was a common enough phenomenon among the Russian gentry, but the auxiliary languages, French and German, were usually acquired later than Russian and from teachers rather than the family. For Herzen German was almost as native as Russian. He was, of course, surrounded by Russians: the numerous servants, his nurse, Vera Artamonovna, his father, and the Senator. But the household was almost equally German: his mother, a second nurse, Mme. Proveau (who in spite of her name was quite *echt-deutsch*), and the Senator's valet, Kalo. When the Senator and Kalo moved away, there was a succession of German governors whose function it was "to supervise the health and the German pronunciation of their charge." Later there were French tutors, and by adolescence Herzen was almost equally proficient in all three languages.[31]

Although such trilingualism was not unusual, Herzen's precocity, and the situation this reflected, were. Herzen, in fact, was only half Russian.

That he was so by blood is of no importance; that he was so by family environment and education is of real significance. Two civilizations were sheltered under his father's roof — the one old-regime Russian and paternalistic, the other more Western, modern and individualistic. By one of his languages and a half of his environment Herzen was estranged, before he ever left his father's house, from the society into which he had been born. This estrangement went deeper than the mere access to subversive Western ideas which his facility with Western languages would later offer him. It was not the penetration of humanitarian ideas in themselves that set up tensions in the society of old Russia. Rather it was the progressive intrusion of a more humane way of life, beginning among the gentry, which made the social order of old Russia seem intolerable to the sensitive — a way of life which was different from that of the "bourgeois" West merely in that it was less widespread. It was only on such soil that humanitarian ideas earlier worked out in the West could take root; without it they could have "influenced" nobody. This conflict between the humane life of the minority and the inhumanity of the social system as a whole had been a growing force in Russian society since the emancipation of the gentry. But it assumed a more acute form in Herzen's life by virtue of the half-European nature of his surroundings, and the duality of languages simply served to symbolize and heighten the duality of life.

If old Ivan Alexeevich "sincerely and openly despised" [32] the mass of mankind, there was one exception, little Shushka. Unlike the unfortunate Egor, Shushka as a child was his father's delight, and spoiled by him extravagantly, with the entire household following suit. The child was surrounded by an army of adults whose first concern was his care and whose chief pleasure was catering to his every desire. He was the sole outlet for his father's repressed reserves of affection; he was all his mother had in the world; he was the favorite of the indulgent Senator; his Russian and his German nurses, his uncle's valet, Kalo, all had no other objects for their affections. *My Past and Thoughts* contains charming passages describing the elaborate surprises prepared for Shushka by Kalo, the expensive toys bought by the Senator, and the lavish attention accorded by all to the idol of the household.[33] The memoirs of his cousin Tatiana contain somewhat less charming passages describing tantrums when his will was thwarted in the slightest way, including the classic trick of spoiled children — pretending to be dead — a favorite means with Shushka for bringing the adults to heel.[34]

The principal expression of Ivan Alexeevich's affection for his son was an exaggerated concern for his health. Fearing colds, the old man kept the boy virtually confined to his room for the entire winter. On the rare occasions when he was allowed out for a stroll it was only after he had been enveloped in every conceivable under and outer garment. In order to prevent any possible stomach disorders Shushka was kept on a special diet, set by the old man himself. At the slightest sneeze the entire household was thrown into alarm, and Shushka, observing the commotion, "began to imagine that he was seriously ill and started to fuss so as to exhaust the patience of all concerned." The doctor was summoned, and "medicines were prescribed, which Ivan Alexeevich himself administered at the appointed hours." [35]

That all this was the reflection of the old man's own hypochondria, symbolized by a table laden with medicines permanently at his bedside and by three medical consultations a year,[36] made it no more appropriate as a way to raise a child who was not at all delicate, but, on the contrary, possessed of a lively disposition and inexhaustible energy. Its only result was to make Shushka an exceptionally self-willed child, to endow him with an overweening sense of his own importance, and to heighten in him the aristocratic temper he would in any case have acquired. During the first ten years of his life, he was the center of the only world he knew, and there he early learned to take for granted his position as an exceptional being. He had no friends or playmates, in part because his father did not want him to have any, in part also because his own imperious nature brooked no equals. As his cousin Tatiana wrote, "Sasha grew up alone, was unable to understand a refusal, did not know the meaning of a concession; he didn't like and was unable to play with comrades; the slightest opposition put him *hors de soi*." [37] His only playmates were the children of the household serfs, and these he commanded and coerced as the social inferiors they were.[38] In the opening chapters of *My Past and Thoughts* the frequentation of the household serfs — forbidden by his father — is described as one of the principal joys of his childhood.[39] Servants, Herzen later claimed, have the same simplicity and directness as children, which was why he found their company so congenial. He attributed his precocious hatred of tyranny to the outrages against their dignity which he observed in childhood and of which he gives a lengthy catalogue. Outrages there were, and those described in *My Past and Thoughts* were not invented after the fact, but Herzen was too much the little master in his relations with the serf children to feel any great indignation at the time. The action of their sufferings on his mind was by no means as direct as he later made out; he came to a realization of the humiliation of others only through the wounds dealt his own ego.

3

These wounds were not slow in coming as he approached adolescence. First of all, if Herzen was unusually pampered he was also unusually cramped and bored. The exclusive companionship of adults, the hovering

protectiveness of Ivan Alexeevich, and above all the absence of any
friends his own age built up a mounting sense of frustration. Moreover,
his father's attitude toward him changed. Around the age of ten Sasha
suddenly found himself, like the other members of the household, the
butt of Ivan Alexeevich's nagging and ridicule.[40] The passage of years had
undoubtedly further soured the old man; perhaps also he felt that the
permissiveness appropriate toward a child was no longer becoming when
directed toward a young man and future officer. In any event, after the
change Herzen was clearly afraid of his father, and at the same time
pained and mystified by the apparent loss of his affection. In reality,
the old man's affection was concealed rather than withdrawn. Years later,
at the time of his arrest in 1834, Herzen was amazed at his father's tears
of concern.[41] Yet in the crucial formative period which intervened,
Herzen was deprived of the love and approval which had been the balm
of his ego in childhood, a loss all the more devastating for seeming to be
capricious and unprovoked.

The old man had even more painful awakenings in store for his son.
It was inevitable that in time Herzen should learn the circumstances of
his birth. The revelation probably came sometime between ten and
twelve.[42] As he grew older he could not but become increasingly aware
of the antagonism which existed between his parents. According to the
account in *My Past and Thoughts,*

Until around the age of ten I noticed nothing strange or exceptional in my
position; it seemed to me natural and simple that I should live in my father's
house, that in his "half" I should behave correctly, that my mother should
have her "half" where I could shout and make mischief to my heart's content.
. . . Everything was as it should be, and yet certain things made me reflect.
Furtive remarks, unguarded words began to attract my attention. . . . The
domestic quarrels which at times broke out between my parents were often
the theme of conversation between Mme. Proveau and Vera Artamonovna,
who always took the side of my mother. . . . Once alerted, in a few weeks I
learned all the details of the meeting of my father with my mother. All this
I discovered without ever asking anyone a single question.[43]

The first consequence of this discovery was a "feeling of estrangement"
toward his father; the "scenes" between his parents and "the thought of
the sufferings" to which his mother was subjected because of him began
to "hang like a cloud over the bright fantasy of childhood." But realization of the domestic implications of his position was only the first stage
of awakening. Somewhat later Herzen discovered that his status brought
social disabilities as well. One evening two old regimental comrades,
including a certain General Bakhmetev, came to visit his father, and
Herzen overheard their conversation. Ivan Alexeevich spoke of preparing
his son for civilian service in the government. Bakhmetev objected that
"civilian service will do *your young man* no good. . . . He is clearly in a

false position; only military service can correct this and open a career for him." [44]

"Turning these lessons over and over" in his mind, "analyzing them for weeks and months in the total solitude" of the "monastic" silence of his father's house, Herzen came to certain conclusions. "From this time on the idea was deeply rooted in my mind that I was far less dependent on my father than are children generally. This originality, which I had thought up for myself, pleased me." [45] The knowledge that he had in a sense been robbed of his birthright did not, as it easily might have, lead to a sense of inferiority, but rather to a heightened sentiment of independence. "The result of my reflections on my 'false position' was . . . that I felt myself freer from society . . . that in essence, I stood on my own two feet, and with a certain childish arrogance, that I would 'show' Bakhmetev." [46] Writing some thirty years after the event, Herzen no doubt gave to his childhood reflections a clarity and consistency, as well as a liberal twist, that they hardly possessed at the time. Yet, in its main lines, his description rings true. His self-esteem did not collapse under the rebuff it had received. He was pained and outraged that he, the center of his little world, should be deficient or inferior in anything, that he should find such an unexpected obstacle, created by his father's callousness, in the path of his desires, as a limit to the expansion of his personality. He transmuted his hurt, however, into a new strength and a new self-affirmation. His reaction was to fight back, not to surrender. If a military career was only a means to wipe out an unmerited humiliation, then it too was a humiliation, and he wanted none of it. "I, who like all children had dreamed of military service and a uniform, so that formerly I had almost been in tears at the thought of being compelled by my father to follow a civilian career, suddenly grew cold to the idea of military service and . . . little by little uprooted entirely my love of epaulettes, aiglets and braid." [47] This was all the more painful since until that time he had fostered a passionate love of the uniform, to the point of secretly trying on before the mirror the resplendent trappings of a cousin visiting from cadet school. [48]

How deep were the wounds caused by this crisis? It would be too much to conclude that he became a rebel because an honorable position in society was denied him by his birth. As the position of the gentry was above the law in their dealings with their serfs, illegitimacy was a rather frequent phenomenon and, if the child happened to be brought up a son of the house, carried with it no particular stigma. To readers of *War and Peace* the example of Pierre Bezukhov comes immediately to mind. Aristocratic, unlike bourgeois, societies have always taken a lenient view of such matters. In fact, Herzen never suffered socially because of his birth, even though if he had wished a certain kind of public career, his illegitimacy would have made success slower, though by no means impossible. Nor were the numerous gentry bastards who really suffered, such as Herzen's own half brother or the half brother of Ogarev, conspicuous for the number of recruits they supplied to the ranks of radicalism.

Herzen's awareness of his "false position" worked in more subtle fashion. His cousin Tatiana records a scene which, although it must have occurred when Herzen was somewhat older, probably in his late teens, is nonetheless symptomatic of the conditions under which his whole adolescence was passed.

Once during dinner, when I was present, Ivan Alexeevich was in an especially acid frame of mind and finding no object on which to vent his spleen put on an air of misfortune and began to complain about his fate, his ailments, his helplessness, his abandonment.

"And here" — he finished his complaint, to which no one had responded by so much as a word — "And here I live completely alone; I only seem to have a family — but what is it: this woman and her son live in my house, and another ward — the gift of my sister the Princess."

Alexander didn't permit him to finish the speech. Furious, pale, he rose from the table and said with a trembling voice:

"I won't stand any more of your insults, neither for myself, nor for my mother. Your view of the situation and ours have nothing in common. Permit me to leave your house immediately."

Ivan Alexeevich was taken aback by this explosion. He tried to withdraw his remarks. His son continued to give vent to his indignation. " — 'Enough, stop, please calm down . . . forgive me' — said the old man, and with a broken voice began to sob." Overcome, he retired to his study, where he had a long conversation with Alexander. As a result the outward amenities of family life seem to have improved, but the basic tension remained.[49] Such behavior on the part of Ivan Alexeevich undoubtedly derived from his frustrated needs of affection, and was an expression of jealousy more than of hostility. In his desperation the old man was not above using the taunt of his son's "false position" to compel attention and instil a sense of dependency where he felt he could no longer command affection. But his son could hardly be expected to understand this; and the effect was to perpetuate and deepen the dual feelings of estrangement and independence which he had received from the initial shock.

Herzen says nothing of such scenes in *My Past and Thoughts*. Indeed, the account given there greatly minimizes the psychological impact of his illegitimacy on his development; in later life he chose to remember only his proud reaction to this first affront to his dignity. But in writings composed nearer to youth the scars left by the whole experience are more apparent, and his cousin's description is completely confirmed. One of the main themes of the already mentioned novel, *Duty Before All,* written in 1847, is gentry illegitimacy, the sufferings caused its victims and the latter's desire to escape to a more satisfactory world — in fact, to the Revolution of 1789 in France or that of 1830 in Poland.[50] Still nearer to youth, in 1837, he wrote to his fiancée:

Oh, I have never before spoken of all that I have suffered from the very minute I came into the world. . . . Completely *alien* in my father's house, and at every step affronts, *and what affronts* — enough to send an adult to the madhouse. Until June 20, 1834 [the date of his arrest] my father and I did not know each other. The hardness of his disposition created an impassable gulf. . . . And all those Golokhvastovs [his legitimate cousins] and company, *their benevolence,* their charity — ough, worse than the humiliation of the last governor [in exile at Viatka]. . . . *Insult and injury awakened in me a burning pride and an aspiration to power.*[51]

Here Herzen has revealed most of the mechanism of his reaction to his "false position." Initially, everything in his experience, especially his father's indulgence, fostered in him a self-willed aristocratic temper and a high sentiment of his own worth, indeed of his exceptional importance. Then by the single flaw of his birth, and a nagging insistence on it — both the fault of his father — his ego was brought low. Given the organization of the household and the patriarchal nature of Russian gentry life, his father, not his mother, had always been the important figure in his life. Hence Herzen's reaction was an explosion of anger against his father, and through him against all authority, and rejection of authority led to "a burning pride and an aspiration to power." Herzen's family circumstances made rebellion in the name of the dignity of the individual and of personal independence the center of his system of values long before he ever heard of the rights of man.

In his memoirs Herzen recounts how, during the silent family meals, "A large red earthenware bowl stood on the table beside my father, into which he himself put various morsels for his dogs; moreover, he fed the dogs from his own fork, which frightfully offended the servants, and consequently me. Why? It is difficult to say."[52] Forks are for men, but the whole Iakovlev way of life, with its aristocratic caprice, its contempt for inferiors and dependents, was a living denial of the very idea of humanity. By the circumstances of his birth Herzen was made to feel this to the depths of his being, and in his humiliation he developed a natural affinity for those still more humiliated than he, the household serfs, while awaiting the day when he would be able to generalize this sentiment into a self-conscious political protest. But he would not have felt all this had he not been both a Iakovlev and a Western European gentleman. "Although the relatives and friends of Ivan Alexeevich were very considerate of him, as of a legitimate son, he felt himself a stranger in their circle, where he had been placed, not by *right,* but by *circum-stances.*" [53] As a true son of his father he could not bear to be a human being by caprice only; this had to be his status by right.

It has become a commonplace to say that the hopelessly oppressed lack the self-confidence to revolt. It is only the somewhat cramped, but otherwise proud and even superior, who can summon the energetic indignation of rebellion. In Russia in the first quarter of the nineteenth century only the gentry was sufficiently humanized and yet still barbaric enough to produce such individuals in any numbers, and the relations of Ivan Alexeevich with his son represent these explosive potentialities of gentry life at their most acute.

4

Very early Herzen began to develop a series of ideal escapes from the family atmosphere. The first of these was an imaginative participation in the epic events stretching from 1789 to 1812. To have avoided hearing much about these events would have been impossible, but the young Herzen heard more about them than most Russian children of his age, and to the virtual exclusion of other tales of high heroism. *My Past and Thoughts* opens with an evocation of the burning of Moscow and the War of 1812, when he had been only a babe in arms, but to which the oft-repeated tales of Vera Artamonovna gave a living reality. Later he heard the same story with other details from old regimental comrades of his father, in particular Count Miloradovich (the same who later helped suppress the Decembrists), on their return from the campaigns in Western Europe. "Tales of the burning of Moscow, of the battle of Borodino, of the crossing of the Beresina and of the capture of Paris were my cradle song, my childhood romances, my Iliad and my Odyssey." [54] For Sasha this was first of all a marvelous adventure of which he was the hero, surrounded by emperors and resplendent marshals, in a tragic decor of winter, burning cities, and vast armies on the road.[55] It was also his first school of patriotism. The tales of 1812 brought Herzen into contact with the new and self-conscious nationalism of the gentry, awakened by the humiliations from Austerlitz to Tilsit, and matured by the triumphs of 1812–1814. "It goes without saying that in these circumstances I became a rabid patriot, dreaming of regimental life." [56] Though Herzen was soon driven to give up this military vocation because of his illegitimacy, his gentry nationalism was to remain tenaciously with him all his life.

At the same time young Sasha was made aware of the French Revolution through Mme. Proveau, who had lived out the great years in Paris, where her husband had been butler or janitor to a masonic lodge. She told of the horrors perpetrated by Robespierre, of "blood flowing in the streets," and of how her husband narrowly escaped hanging from a lamppost.[57] She told also of the macabre paraphernalia of the masonic rites, and Sasha "trembled like a leaf" as he listened. If there was any political content to her stories it was antirevolutionary; yet Sasha's curiosity was aroused, and the Revolution became an integral part of his childhood world of fantasy. For the moment it served only to sate his taste for drama and horror,[58] the reflection perhaps of resentment against the confining order of his father's house. At the same time, however, his attention was turned toward the political issues of the day. His childhood fantasies did not draw on the remote past: the legends of old Russia, princes of Kiev and tsars of Muscovy, or the lives of the saints of the Eastern Church. His heroes were contemporary and his epics were liberal, national, and revolutionary.[59] As the boredom of home grew he could look back to an immediate and *real* past, full of excitement and heroism, and find there a tradition and a spiritual refuge. There would be no need to destroy a childhood ideal of old Russia to become a liberal and a Westerner.

As Herzen grew into adolescence his principal release from boredom came to be wide and voracious reading. His father's library was well stocked, principally with French works of the preceding century. While Herzen was still a child Kalo used to spend hours explaining to him pictures in books of travel and natural history.[60] When he could read by himself his taste shifted to sentimental novels of adventure in exotic lands. The first books he remembered reading with emotion were two novels by Ducray-Duminil, a popular late eighteenth-century author of children's stories in the vein of Bernardin de Saint-Pierre: *Lolotte et Fanfan* and *Alexis ou la maisonette dans la forêt*.[61] Sensitive children like himself met with frightening and titillating adventures as castaways on desert islands or in the depths of idyllic forests. His taste for the exotic mingled with the horrible was even more gratified by *Les enfants de l'abbaye,* a translation in six volumes, by the abbé Morellet, of an English novel of Maria Regina Roche, an imitator of Mrs. Radcliffe.[62] He found similar sentimental fare in the German favorites of his mother, the novels of Lafontaine, and the plays of Kotzebue.[63]

When he was somewhat older he began to dip into the more adult items of his father's library. Dramatic literature was his passion, perhaps because of its close simulation of the life of action of which he himself was deprived. He devoured what he describes, no doubt with a certain exaggeration, as "some fifty volumes of the French *Répertoire* and of the *Russian Theatre.*"[64] His favorite was Beaumarchais' *Marriage of Figaro,* but not, strangely, for its accents of liberalism. "I was in love with Cherubin and the countess. Moreover, I myself was Cherubin; my heart stopped beating as I read. . . . How entrancing was the scene where the page dressed in women's clothes! I desired passionately to conceal in my bosom the ribbon of some girl and secretly to kiss it." [65] Another favorite was the noble, superior, and unappreciated Werther. "Half of the novel I did not understand and, skipping over it, hurried to reach the terrible conclusion, where I wept like a madman." The emotion was a lasting one; years later, in exile in Vladimir, chancing upon a copy of the book, he wrote, "I told my wife how I had cried as a boy, and began to read her the final letters [of the novel]. And when I reached the very same passage tears swelled from my eyes and I was obliged to stop." [66] Life in the imagination is the special gift of adolescence, but Herzen was compelled more urgently than the average to seek in fantasy the fullness of emotion denied him in reality, and it was not an accident that superior but frustrated heroes appealed to him most.

To appreciate the full impact of this reading on Herzen one has only to contrast his upbringing with the devout education of such Slavophiles as Khomiakov, the brothers Kireevski or the Aksakovs. Herzen's earliest spiritual nurture was secular and sentimental; religion was entirely lacking, at least in any orthodox or supernatural form. For Ivan Alexeevich religion was simply "one of the items in the culture of any well-educated man." It was necessary to believe in Holy Writ, but one should not reason or worry about it, since such matters were beyond reason. It was only proper "to observe the forms of the religion into which one was born"; but it was unbecoming to fall into excesses of piety, befitting only women and unworthy of a man. Once a year Ivan Alexeevich had his son confess and commune; the *mise en scène* impressed the boy for the moment, but only because it was dramatic, strange, and mysterious. Once he had made his Easter Communion and consumed a "few red Easter eggs," he did not give formal religion a thought for the rest of the year. [67]

He did, however, have some more meaningful contact with Christianity, if not with the church, and this is not without its importance for his subsequent development. After his fashion, he read, and knew well, the New Testament (although not the whole Bible, as he states in his memoirs). His mother was a Lutheran, "and consequently religious to a degree; once a month she attended Sunday service . . . and having nothing else to do, I went with her." From this he acquired a sentimental respect for the Gospels, which he read "frequently" and "with great love," both in Church Slavonic and in German. In spite of what he calls a "youthful Voltairianism" (by which is meant no more than a precociously acute eye for the ridiculous), he "never took the Gospels into his hands with a feeling of coldness . . . and each time their contents brought peace and humility to the soul." At least he knew the New Testament sufficiently well to impress a priest engaged by his father to teach him just enough "sacred learning" for the entrance examination at the university. The teacher was amazed not only by his pupil's general knowledge of the Gospels but also by his ability to quote long passages from memory.[68]

Yet this hardly constitutes a serious religious training, or even a real though amorphous religious sensibility. There was not a thought of such classical Christian notions as sin, repentance or redemption in Herzen's youthful "evangelicalism." The Gospels were no more than a collection of pleasant moral fables, a school of virtue and an exemplar of high sentiment. At most they gave an agreeable feeling of communion with the divine, which flattered the ego of the believer more than it magnified the glory of God. After the disappointments of the Revolution, the Age of Sentiment had come to discover in the Gospels beauty and warm emotion, where the Age of Reason had seen only superstition. Since the turn of the century, religion, if not always the churches, was back in fashion among men of good will. In spite of scriptural trappings this religion was often more that of Rousseau's Savoyard Vicar than that of St. Paul, and this was all Herzen derived from his unguided reading of the New Testament. For all his "warm love" of the Gospels, his education was essentially secular, in content if not entirely in form. Later, religion and the supernatural would not constitute obstacles, to be overcome by a painful inner struggle, to belief in the exclusive virtue of natural sentiment and reason.[69]

5

All this unguided reading was ruminated in solitude. In time Herzen acquired a companion and a confidante, a girl cousin two years older than himself and the granddaughter of his father's eldest brother, the already mentioned Tatiana. Her mother had died when she was very young and her father discharged his parental responsibilities by placing her for months at a time in various *pensions* or with different relatives. In this way she made long sojourns in the Moscow house of Ivan Alexeevich, with occasional summers on his country estate. From the time Herzen was ten or twelve until he was fifteen she was his only close contemporary. Her arrivals occasioned transports of joy; her departures brought on fits of melancholy. In her centered all his longings for a richer, fuller life. After one visit he wrote to her:

Was it a dream or did I really press your hand — tell me? For a long time I stared at the gate which had closed behind you; then I walked back and forth across the courtyard, deathlike and cold, as if I were searching for something. I returned to my room — but it was empty and cold. On everything lay the stamp of your recent presence, but you I found nowhere. Again solitude, again my books for my sole companions. I picked up a volume and tried to read, but was unable; I tried to think where you might be now.[70]

In the absence of any competing interest, Herzen magnified this unique affection to where it became something approaching love.

Tatiana fulfilled many functions for Herzen. First of all she provided relief from his father, whose moods shrank to less terrifying proportions once Sasha could discuss them with a sympathetic equal. With mixed fear and irony the pair took to referring to the old man as *"der Herr."* [71] More important still, Tatiana brought with her all the sentimental resources conferred by a solitary childhood, wide reading and long after-lights confidences in girls' boarding schools, and all this *sensibilité* overflowed onto Sasha. He participated vicariously in her slightly more mature emotional life by becoming the confidant of a deathless passion for a dashing but unresponsive hussar. [72]

Most of all Tatiana shared Herzen's reading and his dreams. Their reading consisted primarily in the analysis of sentiment and of all the delightful literary emotions with which they consoled their solitude. There was more Lafontaine, and in addition Madame de Genlis, Madame Cottin, some Scott, *The Vicar of Wakefield,* and Russian reflections of the same tradition, such as Ozerov's *Fingal* [73] — in short, a wide choice of the major and minor classics of that sentimentality which stems from Rousseau.

Later, in 1828, just before Herzen entered the university, the pair went to the source of the whole tradition, to Rousseau himself, an action which brought down a reprimand from Ivan Alexeevich. [74] Their favorite was the *Confessions,* "that testament of a martyr." They "suffered" together with "that energetic soul, struggling up through the workshop of a watchmaker, the livery of a lackey, through lust, through vice, to arrive at the highest stage of morality, at an all-embracing love of humanity." Herzen "worshipped Jean-Jacques, and at the same time his life, especially his poetic flight from men to Ermenonville, drew him to me more personally." Rousseau seemed to Herzen "a sacrificial lamb, bearing the afflictions of all of eighteenth-century mankind . . . and expressing all that was warm in the French philosophy of that century." In particular his appeal was greater than that of the more rationalistic Diderot, or the even colder Voltaire. One summer in the country Sasha and Tatiana baptized their favorite spot, a linden grove, with the name of Ermenonville, and Herzen proposed that they read together all the works of Rousseau in this retreat. They began with the *Social Contract* and the *Discourse on the Origin of Inequality,* both of which elicited their approval, and then went on to *The New Eloise,* which they found disappointingly old-fashioned and dull. [75]

Herzen, then, read most of Rousseau when he was young and impressionable, and yet his enthusiasm was aroused only by certain things. The properly political writings, the *Social Contract* and the *Discourse on*

Inequality, certainly provided a significant introduction to democratic and egalitarian sentiments, although Herzen seems to have retained little of Rousseau's arguments for equality through fraternal community or of his attacks on property as the origin of social discord. He also responded warmly to Rousseau's message of the virtue of natural, unfettered emotion. *The New Eloise,* it is true, left him cold (the *Emile* he seems never to have read) probably because it was too didactic and lacking in the Germans' idealized concept of love. But Herzen felt most thoroughly at home in the *Confessions,* where Rousseau is at his most anarchistic and egocentric; for he could see himself in this tale of the isolated, virtuous individual pitted against an immoral and "unnatural" world. If any single thinker was at the origin of Herzen's own philosophy it was Rousseau, and yet he absorbed him not so much as a theorist of political democracy but as the prophet of sentiment and sensibility.

One work in the sentimental tradition which made a particularly deep impression was Goethe's *Elective Affinities,* also read in the company of Tatiana. It tells of two couples who, discovering they are ill-matched, switch partners, and pleads for greater freedom and "naturalness" in human relationships. The novel is founded on an elaborate metaphysic of love which takes the form of an analogy between the sentiments and the laws of chemistry, a science then new and just beginning to arouse attention among the laity. The attraction of love was the law of the moral universe just as chemical affinity was the law of the material universe. In the same way that chemical affinity produced harmony and balance in nature, love was the source of universal brotherhood among men, and both were the reflection of God, the ultimate unity of all things. Herzen was deeply impressed by this cosmic and pantheistic doctrine of love, and he developed the theory somewhat on his own.

Egoism and love in our souls, since we are using the terms of the natural sciences, appear to me as mass and light. Egoism is dark, cold, concentrated all in the "I," as in a center of gravity — it is a point, a zero. Love is bright, fiery; it expands our being; like the sun, it illumines and warms. For egoism there is nothing in the world outside of its own "I," and for this reason it possesses no eternity. For love there is no "I"; there is *we, we* two — we, the whole of human kind — we the whole creation, and there are no limits to love in the finite world; it is a guest from on high.[76]

And it was Tatiana who, by her "love," had rescued him from the isolation of "egoism" and united him with a mankind and a world he did not know except through the exaggeration of his feeling for her.

From this it would be a mistake to conclude that Herzen was "in love" with Tatiana in the usual sense of the term. He gave that name to any strong and agreeable sensation he experienced. A more appropriate term, however, would be sentiment, in the meaning possessed by the adjective "sentimental." What he experienced has less to do with what Romeo felt for Juliet than with what Rousseau or Wordsworth felt for trees. In this connection it is worth pointing out that all the books which impressed Herzen in his youth were written roughly between 1760 and the end of the century. The literary histories classify this period as pre-romantic or sentimental, to distinguish it from those kindred tendencies after 1800 called romanticism proper. To the modern mind the sentimentality which inheres in both movements often seems exaggerated, self-indulging, false, and in the last analysis tedious. There is a fundamental disproportion between the expression of emotion, or the value attributed to it, and the real quality of the emotion itself. The most paltry quiver of feeling becomes a vibration in the mind of God and an event of cosmic significance, no matter how trivial its object or its cause. Every quiver of emotion is good, so long as it is sincere, for feeling is the voice of what Rousseau called "nature" speaking through "conscience," and the natural conscience is innocent of all error and baseness. It is ennobling and elevating, and thus richness of feeling is the sign of a superior soul and the mark of a higher destiny. Since this is so, the temptation is to cultivate feeling for its own sake: to invent it when it is not there; to magnify it out of all recognition when it is there; but always to indulge it uncritically. But indulgence of sentiment is indulgence of the self. Sentimentality is the glorification of feeling that knows no other origin but the self, or Rousseau's "conscience," just as it is the ability to ignore everything outside the self that conditions or contradicts the spontaneity of self-generated feeling. It means a lack of all sense of proportion about the relation of the self and its emotions to a disagreeable and intractable external world. It is a kind of emotional solipsism. Utterly lacking in lucidity about the character and implications of the emotions described, sentimental literature surrenders to these emotions in a gush of self-pity or self-glorification, unredeemed by so much as a velleity of self-analysis.

The persistence of this phenomenon for almost a century after Rousseau is, needless to say, no simple matter to explain. But one thing seems clear: the sense of personal importance of "les sensibles" was enormous. It was also, in one way or another, unsatisfied. There is something pitiful and lonely in the sentimental tone, and beneath it a wounded sense of personal dignity. It is the self-pitying cry of a frustrated ego constructing fantasies of gratification where reality itself is barren. It is an attempt to give importance and value to every particle of the self, because the self as a whole is denied the full expression of its possibilities and yet cannot accept this as inevitable. The sentimentalist glorifies emotion because emotion proceeds from the self alone and knows nothing of the frustrations of the external world. For all these reasons the literature of sentiment spoke words of consolation to Herzen's hemmed-in heart.

6

Despite all this, however, sentimental reading with Tatiana was too pale and subjective a thing to serve as a lightning-rod for all Herzen's energies. He required dreams which promised action in the great arena of the world, and he found them in the excitement generated by the events of the fourteenth of December, 1825. Herzen was not quite fourteen at the time. His reaction to the death of Alexander I was one of consternation, for his father had raised him in great respect for the emperor. Alexander, moreover, was the hero of the epic events of 1812, and a childhood idol, almost a friend and companion, at least in imagination. Once on a stroll he had actually seen the emperor, who returned his greeting with a smile.[77] Like everyone, Herzen expected Alexander's eldest brother, Constantine, to succeed to the throne. For Constantine, too, he had a boyhood cult, since the heir apparent had been the regimental comrade of his father. Tatiana tells us that Sasha bought one of Constantine's portraits, which were on sale everywhere in the shops, put it up in his room and summoned her "with a solemn voice" to bow down before it. "He is a great man," he said, which was no more than the oft-repeated opinion of his father.[78] A few days later the children were amazed by the news that there had been an uprising in St. Petersburg, which was all the more dramatic since the family friend, Count Miloradovich, had been killed in the fighting. From the shocked reaction of their elders they understood that something momentous had occurred, and the revolt, of which they grasped only the external drama, became the principal subject of their conversations.

During the following months the excitement continued. Herzen participated in the dismay that swept the aristocratic quarter of Moscow upon the arrest of sons of respected families. Among them were the brothers Obolenski, relatives of his aunt, Princess Khovanskaia. Then, in the spring of 1826, Ivan Alexeevich began to receive the visits of old comrades come to Moscow for the coronation. Their conversation centered inevitably around the revolt, the arrests and the fate of the guilty. In August there was the final excitement of the coronation. In the company of Tatiana Herzen witnessed the triumphal entry of Nicholas I into Moscow, attended the service of thanksgiving in the Kremlin for the delivery of the emperor from the hands of his enemies, and witnessed from afar the coronation and the accompanying public celebrations. For the children it was an orgy of pomp and patriotism, of which Ivan Alexeevich, with his habitual kill-joy attitude, disapproved.[79] Yet even the old man himself interrupted his routine, albeit reluctantly, to pay a visit to his friend Constantine in the Kremlin. Never before had the great world outside intruded so conspicuously into the closed universe of Herzen's childhood, and the vistas opened by the intrusion were vast and alluring.

In *My Past and Thoughts* Herzen claimed that his political awakening dated from these events. On the day of the Mass of thanksgiving, "a child of fourteen years, lost in the crowd . . . before the altar profaned by a bloody prayer, I swore to avenge the victims [the Decembrists], and dedicated myself to the struggle against that throne, that altar and those cannons." [80] In reality his evolution was much less rapid and direct. He was indubitably impressed by the revolt as drama; and he was equally struck by the dismay produced by the unexpectedly harsh treatment of the conspirators. His father firmly repeated that the death sentence was simply intended to impress the population, that it would not be carried out. "The inhabitants of Moscow could hardly believe their eyes when they read in the *Moskovskie vedomosti* the frightful news of the fourteenth of July." [81] The death penalty had been almost unknown since the time of Elizabeth. Moreover, the gentry, grown soft in the ways of independence, were no longer used to such treatment from their senior officer and emperor. If it was right to punish these insurgents because they had broken the tacit contract that bound autocracy and gentry together, to destroy them was nevertheless a breach of the decency and mercy to be expected from a father and a protector, qualities the great Catherine and Alexander, the gentry's own sovereigns, had always shown. In fact Nicholas was perfectly within his autocratic rights; the compact in question existed purely in the psychology and habits developed by the gentry during the sixty years since their emancipation. Nonetheless, the moral breach between the government and "society" — as the free and literate elements of the population were called — begun in the last reactionary years of Alexander, suddenly widened. The reaction of the aristocratic world of the Iakovlevs was one of hurt and bewilderment more than of anger. There was no thought of resistance, but there was a sense of estrangement. Although comprehending nothing of the political issues involved, Herzen made this sense of estrangement his own, for it corresponded only too well with the estrangement he felt in his father's house; and it corresponded equally well with his desire for action, for contact with the great outside. Here was something far more palpable and gratifying than weeping with Werther, or playing at Cherubin, or reading with Tatiana!

Herzen flung himself with ardor into his new dream. He was against the new emperor; he was for the insurgents, or at any rate for Constantine. For over a year he believed that the purpose of the uprising was to place Constantine on the throne (he adds "limiting his power," although it is doubtful that the concept of limited monarchy had any meaning for him at that time).[82] The result was an ardent cult for his new hero. In this, too, Herzen was adapting for his own purposes material he found around him. Constantine was a "great man" not only for Ivan Alexeevich. He was genuinely, if undeservedly, popular with the country as a whole, the people and the soldiers as well as the gentry; and this fact undoubtedly did not escape the notice of the quick boy.

Tales of the revolt and trial, of the sense of shock in Moscow, made a violent impression on me; a new world opened up, which became more and more the center of my moral being; I don't know how it came about, but understanding little — and that only vaguely — I felt that I was not on the side of the grape-shot and victory, of the prisons and chains. The execution of Pestel and his comrades definitively shattered the childhood sleep of my soul.[83]

This assertion from *My Past and Thoughts* can hardly be doubted. At fifteen the gifted and the sensitive are capable of immense emotional intensity in appropriating the sacred causes of their elders. Napoleon at the same age in the military academy at Vienne consoled his solitude and inferior social status with passionate dreams of the liberation of Corsica. There is nothing inherently implausible in Herzen's "childish liberalism," although its character should be kept clear. It did not mean that he was a liberal or a constitutionalist by intellectual conviction. It meant that from this time on the politics of revolt became the great theme of his daydreams, the foremost of his escapes from the house of Ivan Alexeevich and from everything in life that hemmed him in. This, of course, in no way diminishes the importance of his "liberalism," for it is on affective convictions of this sort that great causes are built.

Soon Herzen began to give more precise content to his political dreams. He had a whole army of private tutors: one each for Russian, mathematics, Latin, French, and German, and a priest for the "law of God." [84] In 1826 his French teacher was a certain Bouchot, a bourgeois of Metz, probably Girondist in politics, who had left Paris during the Terror but who had stayed long enough to witness and approve the birth of the Republic. Herzen's curiosity about the Great Revolution, which he knew only from the tales of Mme. Proveau, had been aroused by the Decembrist revolt. He had read a royalist history in the library of his father and had found it disappointingly negative, and so he decided to question Bouchot for further details. In the middle of a lesson Sasha asked, "'Why did they execute Louis XVI?' The old man . . . raised his spectacles onto his forehead . . . and said solemnly, 'Parce qu'il a été traître à sa patrie.' 'If you had been among his judges would you have signed his sentence?' 'With both hands.'" This lesson was "worth all the subjunctives in the world" to Sasha.[85] Bouchot, who until this time had been cool toward his unindustrious charge, suddenly warmed, and in the old man's tales Herzen was given the elements from which to construct a radical and heroic interpretation of the Revolution.

More important still was his Russian tutor, one Protopopov. Of humble (undoubtedly clerical) origin and bohemian appearance, he had prepared at a provincial ecclesiastical seminary before coming to study medicine at the University of Moscow.[86] A democratic breeze in the aristocratic calm of the old house of Ivan Alexeevich, he brought with him all the intellectual preoccupations of the youth of the university, and a "noble and vague liberalism which so often passes with the first grey hairs, marriage and a position in society." [87] It was to Protopopov that Herzen first confided his new concern for revolution and politics; and it was Protopopov who enlightened Herzen on the true nature of the Decembrist movement. The cult of Constantine was replaced by that of Pestel, Ryleev, and their comrades.

This new cult was rendered all the more attractive by a touch of the clandestine, for Protopopov placed in the hands of his pupil the first flowerings of a literary genre still new in Russia, the secret manuscript literature of opposition. The liberal fermentation of the last years of Alexander I which produced the fourteenth of December also spawned a subversive literature which, driven from the pages of the press, reappeared in manuscript copies circulating widely in "society." The writings of Ryleev, one of the executed leaders of the Decembrists, supplied the bulk of this literature; Pushkin, in his early years, had contributed a few items. Protopopov brought his charge "finely copied and tattered manuscript notebooks" of Pushkin's *The Ode to Freedom, The Dagger,* and *The Village,* together with Ryleev's patriotic-liberal fables in ballad form, the *Dumy,* and his short epic, *Voinarovski.*[88] In the latter, the hero, a nephew of Mazepa, and his wife suffer exile in Siberia for their revolt against the tyranny of Peter the Great in the Ukraine — as if in anticipation of the fate of the Decembrists and their wives. Herzen avidly recopied these verses and learned to recite whole passages by heart. As exercises in rhetoric, his tutor had him compose comparisons between Zenobia of Palmyra and Martha (*Marfa Posadnitsa*), heroine of "free" Novgorod in the Middle Ages, the subject of one of the *Dumy.*[89] A strong liberal patriotism, nourished on the mystique of the Decembrists and of 1789, had become Herzen's passionate reply to his father.

7

Protopopov acquainted his pupil with rebellion in literature as well as in politics. If romanticism had many intellectual guises, it had as many political uses. Although in Germany romanticism, in the narrow

and historically precise sense of the movement beginning in 1798 around
the brothers Schlegel, was conservative, or at least quietistic in politics
and oriented toward religion and the past, the French appropriation after
1820 of the name and of certain slogans of the movement carried very
different implications. In France romanticism, again if one takes the
term in the narrow sense of the movement centering around *Le Globe* and
acknowledging Hugo as its greatest representative, soon developed into
a conscious protest against the past in the name of the present and the
future. It struck out against the arbitrary "fetters" of classicism, as codified
by Boileau and popularized by Batteux and Laharpe, and for new and
"free" literary forms, and by extension called for liberation in matters
of feeling and love. Moreover, in its later stages it was openly on the
left in politics and consciously protested against the fetters of the Restoration in general. This French romanticism began to penetrate Russia in
the early 1820's, at the same time as its German cousin.[90] Ryleev himself
had produced an article in its defense.[91] Its principal exponent was the
rising journalist, Polevoi, in his review, the *Moscow Telegraph,* which
began to appear in the very year of the Decembrist revolt. The mission
of the new review was the propagation of Western ideas and of enlightenment in general; but more particular concerns were the defense of the
"new" literature and the vilification of the "old," and the popularization
of the ideas of French romanticism. This campaign was all the more
apposite in that it coincided with the years of reaction following the
suppression of the Decembrists. Energies that could no longer find expression in the struggle for liberalism in politics found a more subdued,
but not less subversive, expression in the struggle for liberty in art. It
was this radical French romanticism, the intellectual fare of the university youth of the mid-1820's, which Protopopov transmitted to
Herzen.[92]

Protopopov's function was to teach Herzen "rhetoric," or the art
of composition, according to the rules of French classicism, the accepted
model in Russia since the mid-eighteenth century. But the teacher himself believed in individual genius, not in the virtue of rules, as the unique
source of beauty in art. Protopopov's heroes were the leaders of the "new"
Russian literature, Ryleev, Baratynski, and especially Pushkin, who were
then scoring their first successes, and who were also the gods of the
Moscow Telegraph. The position of Pushkin between classicism and
romanticism is a moot one indeed, and if either label must be applied,
classic is perhaps the more appropriate. But at least he did break Boileau's
rules, and he was unmistakably a breath of originality after an era of
uninspired imitation of French classicism. What is more, he was reputed
to be a follower of the "rebel" Byron, and this was enough. Protopopov
subverted his lessons of classical rhetoric, turning them into a course

on the "new literature." His pupil was receptive in the extreme. The first cantos of *Eugene Onegin* had appeared in 1825; Herzen read with rapture each chapter as it issued from the press, carried them around in his pocket for weeks, learned them by heart.[93] Once, at a reception at the Noblemen's Assembly, from the gallery he and Tatiana saw with their own eyes Pushkin and Baratynski.[94] They also went to what they considered to be the source of Pushkin's inspiration, Byron, who had just been translated by Kozlov. "In all these people what an infinity of hopes, of burning and heart-felt aspirations there was!" [95]

The successor to Bouchot as tutor of French was a certain Marchal. In Herzen's characterization,

Marchal belonged to the race of those who from birth never knew burning passions, whose characters are luminous and even, to whom is given just enough love to be happy but not enough to burn. All such people are classics *par droit de naissance.* . . . He did not know, and felt no desire to know, the deeply spiritual art of Germany. He believed that after the tragedies of Racine it was impossible to read the barbaric dramas of Shakespeare, although there were flashes of talent in them. He believed that the inspiration of the poet could only pour itself out in the forms of Batteux and Laharpe, that the soulless poem of Boileau was the *corpus juris poeticis.*[96]

For Herzen, however, classicism meant rules and poverty of feeling, and he craved both freedom from rules and richness of feeling, which were the liberation of the self. The unfortunate Marchal, as the representative of constraint, became the whipping boy for Herzen's revolt against all constraint. In his exercises for Protopopov, Herzen "annihilated" the enemy classicism. He then translated these exercises into French and showed them to Marchal, proclaiming: "Here is how I respect your Boileau." [97] But in this battle of the tutors which Herzen fostered there was more at stake than literature. There was excitement in a life otherwise devoid of it; there was self-assertion, normal in all adolescents but exceptionally strong in the more than normally confined Herzen; finally there was the familiar cry of his cramped ego for self-realization, a cry so intimately connected with his cult of the Decembrists and the Great Revolution.

Herzen's restless search for an ideal led him in several directions simultaneously, notably to an interest in history, not just of Europe since 1789, but of Greece and Rome. Like budding radicals of the late eighteenth and early nineteenth centuries all over Europe he had a passion for Plutarch. This was supplemented by the universal history of Louis-Philippe Ségur, written at the beginning of the century, where antique heroes were cast in the mold of high heroism. The cause of this fascination for the antique is not far to seek. The protest of nascent liberalism, in the Russia of the 1820's as in the France of forty years earlier, lacked models in a tradition of its own; and ideal images of liberty were necessary to compensate for the poverty of the present as well as to supply an inspiration for the future. Herzen read his Plutarch and his Ségur, "not as a mirror of fact but as a novel," and saw himself as an actor "on the acropolis and the forum." Like the generation of the Jacobins or the Decembrists, Herzen found in antiquity a model of "civic virtue" and republicanism. But he added a touch proper to his own generation:

. . . ancient history . . . is an aesthetic school of morality. The great men of Greece and Rome have in them that astonishing, plastic, artistic beauty which engraves itself forever on a young soul . . . everything was so penetrated with the graceful that great men themselves resembled artistic creations. . . . The features of Plutarch's heroes are as wonderful, open, full of thought, as the pediments and porches of the Parthenon.[98]

For Herzen the heroes of antiquity were something more than the passionate yet stoically contained exemplars of republican virtue, in a very political sense, that they had been for the Jacobins or the Decembrists. They were already the prototypes of an aesthetic ideal of the human personality of a very different origin, more German than French and more literary than political. They are in fact *die schöne Seele* of Schiller decked in antique garb; and it was under the aegis of Schiller and the metaphysical Germans that Herzen completed the "sentimental education" begun with other epigones of Rousseau.

CHAPTER III

Schiller and Ogarev

I N TERMS of basic sensibilities and values most men remain all their lives what they become in adolescence, and for Herzen Schiller was unquestionably the greatest formative influence of this crucial period; or rather he was the catalyst of Herzen's deepest emotions, for men are never "influenced" by ideas they do not already hold in embryonic form. Schiller furnished the first ideological point of convergence for Herzen's youthful frustrations, and the most kindred articulation of his dreams. All his references to the poet, accordingly, are in tones of the most fulsome lyricism.

Schiller: I bless thee; to thee I owe the most sacred moments of early youth! What tears flowed from my eyes over thy poems! What an altar I erected to thee in my soul! Thou art the poet of youth *par excellence*. In thee is that same dreamy gaze turned only toward the future — *"dahin, dahin,"* the same noble, active captivating feelings; the same love of men and the same sympathy for all that is contemporary [i.e., liberal politics].[1]

Herzen never outgrew these youthful sentiments, although he moderated somewhat the tone in which they were expressed. In 1853 he wrote: "The poetry of Schiller has not lost its power over me; a few months ago I read *Wallenstein* to my son; it is a gigantic creation! Whoever has lost his taste for Schiller is either old or a pedant; he has grown stale or forgot himself." [2] In middle age Herzen recalled primarily a political Schiller. "From Möres [in the poem *Die Bürgschaft*], stealing with a dagger in his sleeve 'to free the city from the tyrant,' from William Tell, lying in wait for Gessler in the narrow pass of Küssnacht, the transition to the fourteenth of December and Nicholas was easy." [3] But in Herzen's earlier writings Schiller's significance appears more vast, and, in closer accordance with the real facts, he is presented as lighting the way to self-understanding at every step of youth. In the *Notebooks of a Certain Young Man,* Herzen records how he grew from the boy-like Moor to the "sombre, pensive" Wallenstein, and finally to the "proud virgin," the maid of Orleans, and the "wonderful mother," Isabella, in the *Bride of Messina,* both images of his wife Natalie. Schiller was "higher" than Goethe or Shakespeare, the very summit of world art. "Once I had taken Schiller into my hands I never left him, and even now [1838], in moments of sadness, his pure song is a therapeutic to my soul." [4] The importance of this influence for Herzen's political ideology is sufficient to warrant the closest examination of Schiller's message, even at the cost of digressing for a moment from the pursuit of Herzen's own career.

In his cult of Schiller Herzen expressed an intellectual fashion that was then new in Russia. Until 1825 French influence had on the whole dominated. "Advanced" elements, notably the Decembrists, had sought inspiration in the Enlightenment, or its spiritual heirs, French *"idéologues"* or English utilitarians.[5] Schiller receives an occasional mention from the Decembrists, but on the whole he is lost in the crowd of Frenchmen and *philosophes.* This is not to say that German influences, which for want of a better term we may call romantic, were unknown before 1825. With the help of Karamzin, and especially Zhukovski, German literature, in particular Schiller, had been gaining ground steadily since the beginning of the century.[6] The Germanophile "Society of the Lovers of Wisdom" was contemporary with the organizations of the Decembrists, and Odoevski's *Mnemosyne* championed the new Germanic "wisdom" against the old and superficial French "philosophy" at the same time that Ryleev's *Polar Star* was preaching civic virtue in the Gallic mode. Nonetheless, the dominant tone before 1825 was French and rationalistic; after 1825 it was German and "romantic." Before this date the Russians were "influenced" by the Germans; after it they grew up on them. Thus Herzen belonged to the first generation of thoroughly Germanized Russians.

Schiller was the John the Baptist of the new faith. The "men of the thirties and the forties" invariably began their German education with him, to be followed only later by Schelling and Hegel, the other great representatives of German influence in Russia. Rival Germans there no doubt were: Goethe, Jean-Paul Richter, Hoffmann, Herder, Fichte, and later Heine, and Herzen and his generation at one time or another paid their debt to all of them. In particular Herzen was attracted by the whimsical sentimentality of Jean-Paul and the fantastic revery of Hoffmann.[7] But it was Schiller, Schelling, and Hegel who were the structural ribbing of the edifice of German influence in Russia, and Schiller was the very head of the corner. His Russian public read him young, and he is an author best read in adolescence. Thus he reached the men of Herzen's generation when sensibilities were malleable and impressions indelible. Even when this same generation grew older it did not so much discard him as build on him, for Schiller in many essentials represents a poetic statement of attitudes later translated by Schelling and Hegel into metaphysics.

Schiller is conventionally considered a poet of liberty in the direct tradition of the Enlightenment, if not exactly of the Revolution. And there are undeniably liberal, Enlightenment elements in Schiller, such as the speeches on the "right of resistance" in *William Tell,* or the figure of Marquis Posa, who on his first entrance announces himself, like Anacharsis Cloots, as the "deputy of all mankind," or the title page of *The Robbers,* which bears the epigraph *In tyrannos.* Yet for a poet of liberty the political content of Schiller's dramas is surprisingly meager. Even in the early, more "radical" plays the concept of liberty is quite equivocal. The edge of revolt is always blunted by an ambiguous longing for reconciliation with authority, and in the end rebellion is invariably punished by failure. Schiller's only real anarchist, Karl Moor, finishes in submission and abject recognition of the virtues of order. The famous scene between Posa and Philip II in the third act of *Don Carlos* is as much a plea for enlightened despotism as a declaration of the dignity of the individual. William Tell, Schiller's only successful rebel, is not in revolt against the legitimacy of authority as such, but only against its abuse. Although not a "liberal" hero, Wallenstein is still a case in point, since he meets his nemesis by trying to be a law unto himself, heedless of all limitations on his ego. And the remaining plays, such as the *Maid of Orleans* or the *Bride of Messina,* are not about revolt at all. The liberal import of the plays is diluted even in their locales. Only two, *The Robbers* and *Love and Intrigue,* are boldly set in contemporary Germany; all the others take place in every country of Europe but Germany and in the remote past. There is something decidedly indirect and refracted about Schiller's concept of freedom. Indeed, if read carefully, his works are only a very conditional call to liberty, which has little of the political about it.

Schiller, in effect, represents the aspiration to individual dignity and independence of the Enlightenment transformed by the conditions of German princely absolutism together with the isolation of the tiny German educated class, hardly as yet a bourgeoisie and almost an intelligentsia in the Russian sense. He had been educated in what amounted psychologically to a barracks, the *Herzoglische Militärakademie* of the despotic Karl-Eugen of Württemberg, where he was surrounded every hour of the day by an unbelievably petty discipline, not dissimilar to that which Nicholas tried to impose on Russia on a national scale, or Ivan Alexeevich on the scale of his household. Release from this oppression was found in the enlightened Karl-August of Weimar, the great protector of German humanism, who respected the human dignity of his subjects and fostered the flowering of reason and artistic sensitivity in the few who were capable of it. And this solution completely satisfied

Schiller. He desired nothing more in the here and now, however much he might dream of a future freer and more glorious still for the whole of mankind. Indeed, when the French Revolution came he was at first indifferent to it and finally repelled by it. As artist and man it was difficult to be more timid and less revolutionary than Schiller.

The central theme of his works is not political liberty but something much more abstract and at the same time personal. It is the problem of the self-fulfillment of the individual, but considered largely in a social and political void. Self-fulfillment is found not in the practical world but in communion with beauty. The elements of political liberalism which do exist, especially in the earlier plays, are in the last analysis sublimated into this aesthetic idealism. It is only in the inner world of the spirit, in the development of a beautiful soul — *die schöne Seele* — that man is free and fully realizes himself. Such a soul is produced through the cultivation of noble and moral sentiment, moving naturally in harmony with reason. And sentiment is elevated and made moral by the action of beauty. Beauty refines the emotions and brings them into harmony with the moral law of reason so that the truly "beautiful soul" is reasonable, moral, and therefore free, without effort or constraint, in the spontaneous flow of sentiment. Reason and sentiment become one, which means that reason is swallowed up in sentiment and that the unfettered emotion of the individual becomes the supreme law of morality. This state, where man is moral, as it were, in an "aesthetic play" of the emotions, is the supreme plenitude of life and its "true" liberty. The beauty which produces this state is of course to be found in art, or the creative self-expression of the individual; it is also to be found in the nobler emotions — friendship and love. Through their combined action man arrives at the realization of his deepest potentialities. He thus comes to stand on the very threshold of the infinite and the divine, for in their upper reaches love and the beautiful tend to fuse with the holy and sacred, and reason begins to turn into a new religion. Art, friendship, and love, all three grounded in sentiment, are the ultimate values for Schiller and the only true path to liberty.[8]

There is much in this set of ideas which is reminiscent of Rousseau, who in fact had been the decisive influence in Schiller's early formation. Both deify "natural sentiment" and see freedom only in its unfettered expression. For both, morality and reason become simply following one's instincts or doing what one wants, which in practice means a cult of the individual will as its own authority and justification. But there are important differences as well. Self-realization for Rousseau lay in the cultivation of the whole range of human emotion; for Schiller it lay in the cultivation of aesthetic feeling and love in particular. Art, love, and friendship are activities either of isolated individuals or of a small elite. The "aesthetic play" of Schiller's utopia is a kind of private and personal anarchism.

The ego is immeasurably exalted, but it is placed in isolation where it can express itself only in fantasy. Rousseau's utopia is social: either a "state of nature" or civil society under the "social contract," in which the individual, although completely autonomous, is nonetheless related to other individuals and to society as a whole. The effect of Schiller's revision of Rousseau, then, was to preserve the latter's sentimentalism and individualism intact but to deprive them of all political consequences by administering an aesthetic anesthesia.

Most of Schiller's heroes are simply dramatizations of his gropings for this ideal. They are projections of his strivings for self-realization, and since the ego is cramped in the real world, it tends to become magnified to colossal proportions in its ideal projections. Schiller's heroes are titanic and sublime — either sublimely criminal, like Karl Moor, or sublimely virtuous, like Posa, or simply sublime in human force, either for good or for evil, like Wallenstein. For the same reason most of the plays tend to fantasy. Schiller's dramas are taken almost entirely out of his own mind. He once declared that in *The Robbers* he had attempted to portray people before he had ever seen any; but even after he had met a few it made no difference. His characters are not so much people as ideas, principles, or passions, and the drama is always played out between these idea-passions. The action, therefore, need have no relation to real life, nor adhere to any psychological or sociological verisimilitude. It can be pure daydream in which imaginary gratification for the ego is found in a world especially created for the purpose. It is for this reason — and not from any failure "to solve his dramatic problem" — that the happenings in Schiller's plays often appear so preposterous and unmotivated. These characteristics are more marked in the early works than in the later ones, but they are present to a degree in all.

Moreover, there is something very adolescent about all of Schiller's dramas, and it is not an accident that he is considered a poet of youth. Schiller never grew up, in the sense that he never experienced disillusionment with the ideals he held at twenty. His last play, *William Tell,* has the same adolescent simplicity as his first, *The Robbers,* and all his heroes are exemplars of the simple, direct and monolithic self-assertion, oblivious of the external world, which is the special illusion of adolescence. Essentially, Schiller's dramas are aesthetic fantasies of adolescent egoism, and by egoism is meant here not mere selfishness, but a state of mind in which the individual sees nothing but himself and views all external reality only as a function of self. The ego is exalted in fantasy and is made to seem great and sufficient unto itself by aestheticizing or "prettifying" all its passions and the rationalizations of its self-importance. This is not to say that there is anything Nietzschean about Schiller's exaltation of the ego. On the contrary, he is full of an eighteenth-century sense of the brotherhood of man, and all his heroes, even the bloody Moor, overflow with a lachrymose sympathy for the outraged dignity of the least of God's creatures. But both his humanitarianism and his egoism have a common origin: they are dual facets of an underlying self-pity, which expresses itself alike in direct, albeit imaginary, aggrandizement of the self and in tender compassion for others, the fraternal images of the self. It requires a more deeply wounded self-esteem than Schiller's to dispense with compassion for others and to seek self-affirmation at the price of the denial, even the destruction, of other egos. Schiller was not crushed by life; he was only highly cramped.

For Schiller liberty in the ideal was liberty enough, but the system he created was a highly unstable equilibrium between revolt and its sublimation. It momentarily took the radical sting out of Rousseau and the Enlightenment, yet at the same time incorporated almost intact their essential beliefs. In this it was a precursor of the whole of German idealism, that delicate tension of rationalism and mysticism, Enlightenment and Romanticism, of egoism and pantheism, whose general theme was the reconciliation of all conceivable opposites and progress through contradiction to some higher synthesis. Also like German idealism in general (notably Hegel), Schiller's "aesthetic humanism" was forever in danger of disintegrating into the opposites it sought to reconcile. In act it was "Right"; in potency it was "Left"; and it could be pushed either way with equal ease, for it was both a means to "reconciliation with reality," in Belinski's famous phrase, and a spur to revolt. It satisfied and made hungry at the same time.

Schiller, then, is not the poet of liberty *tout court;* rather he is the poet of liberty stripped of all its political and social contingencies. He is the poet of pure ego, of the limitless aggrandizement of self in fantasy, of that philosophical egoism which is the psychological kernel of the concept of liberty before any of the intellectual, moral, or political accretions occur which give us our practical theories of it — social contracts, bills of rights, or doctrines of checks and balances. Heine has remarked that while the French made their revolution in politics, the Germans made theirs in philosophy and art; and Marx wrote somewhere that the transcendental (to which we may add aesthetic) world of German idealism lay over the Rhine. It is not an accident that the concept of "alienation" was a German discovery; and Schiller's aesthetic ideal of liberty is "alienated" at several removes. He is the poet of people who, because of the situation of practical impotence in which they find themselves, are condemned to dream about liberty but never to live it, to seek it in ideal substitutes but never to realize it. Such were the Germans before the agitation of 1848; such were the Russians after 1825. The suppression of the Decembrists drove aspirations to freedom not so much underground as into the stratosphere — and into the arms of Schiller and all the other wonderfully spiritual Germans who had worked the whole thing out already in the years following 1789, when so much was happening in France and nothing was happening at home, just as it seemed that nothing would ever happen in Russia again after the fourteenth of December.[9]

2

Most of Herzen's contemporaries, such as Stankevich and his friends, used Schiller's cult of self-fulfillment through art, friendship, and love as a compensation for the lack of liberty in the real world. Herzen, already more to the "left" than the average of his generation, took it as this too, but also as a goad to his discontent. Schiller's heroes became the primary symbols for his own endless fantasies of self-fulfillment and emancipation. He began, quite logically, with the product of Schiller's adolescent confinement in the *Militärakademie*. When he was beginning to read Racine with his French tutor, the classicist Marchal, *The Robbers* first fell into his hands. "The band of Karl Moor carried me off for a long sojourn in the Bohemian Forests of romanticism." [10] At sixteen he wrote to Tatiana how on the family estate near Moscow he would throw himself under a tree, alone in the great sweep of nature, declaiming Schiller aloud and dreaming he was in the Bohemian Forest.[11] It was the fantasy of the defiance of his father and a confining world. He participated in Schiller's imaginary revolt of a band of students who take to the woods and brigandage in an anarchistic war against all the restraints imposed by society, driven by wrongs no more precise than an amorphous feeling of cramp and a revulsion from the moral ugliness of a philistine world. Herzen felt with Moor: "Am I to squeeze my body into stays, and straighten up my will in law? What might have been an eagle's flight has been reduced to a snail's pace by law. Never yet has law made a great man; 'tis liberty that hatches out colossi and extremes." [12] But the ideal of liberty is aesthetic, not political, and indeed very bookish.

I am disgusted with this age of puny scribblers when I read of great men in my Plutarch. . . . The fire of Prometheus is burned out, and now they substitute the flash of sulphur; a stage fire, which will not so much as light a pipe. The present generation is like rats crawling around the club of Hercules. . . . Mere milksop boys fish phrases out of the slaughter at Cannae and blubber over the victories of Scipio because they are obliged to construe them. . . . Fie! fie, upon this weak, effeminate age, fit for nothing but to ponder over the deeds of former times.[13]

But alas, such pondering is all that life offers in the present; man can be great and sublime only in books or dreams, or in some semimythical past, with the heroes of Plutarch, of the Great Revolution, or the Decembrists.

And the fantasy is only that; for in the end Moor is made to come out of the dream world of the Bohemian Forest and submit to authority and the laws of society.

Schiller also presided over the greatest personal event of Herzen's adolescence, and one of the greatest events of his life, his friendship with "Nick" Ogarev. Herzen had always intensely longed for and lacked a sympathetic friend — as he grew older there were too many important things that Tatiana simply could not understand. In 1827, at the age of fifteen, the dream of friendship came true. Nicholas Platonovich Ogarev, a distant cousin, entered his life, and the attachment was to last until death. In adolescence he was the light of Herzen's loneliness, the ideal of Schiller become flesh and blood.

Posa, Posa, where are you, youth and friend? . . . I needed a friend into whose embraces I could throw myself, in whose embraces I would be *liberated* and *free*. . . . He appeared, noble and young, as I had dreamed of him, as Schiller had painted him. We were drawn together by some mysterious attraction, as in a chemical solution two atoms of the same substance are drawn together by an affinity neither of them understands.[14]

That the Goethe of the *Elective Affinities* is here fused with the Schiller of *Don Carlos* is small matter; their ideas of affinity are akin, and it was the latter who incontestably molded the friendship of the two boys.

As a young man Schiller too had a friend, by name Körner, whose ideal affection had consoled the poet's isolation in an unsympathetic and philistine world. One of the monuments of this friendship was a short book called the *Philosophical Letters;* in it Schiller expounded his philosophy of friendship, or "love."

Egoism erects its center in itself; Love plants it beyond itself, in the Axis of the eternal All. Love intends unity; egoism is solitude. Love is the co-ruling citizen of a flourishing republic; egoism, a despot in a desolate creation. . . . The whole sum of harmonious activity, which exists together in the divine Substance, is isolated in Nature, the facsimile of that Substance, into innumerable grades and measures. Nature . . . is an infinitely divided God. . . . The existing form of Nature is the optic glass, and all the activities of spirits are only an infinite color-play of that simple divine ray. . . . The attraction of the elements gave to Nature its material form. The attraction of spirits multiplied and continued to infinity must finally lead to the abolition of that separation, or — may I utter it, Raphael? [Körner] — create God. Such is the attraction of Love. Then Love, dear Raphael, is the ladder on which we climb to a likeness unto God.[15]

"Love," or friendship, was not just the solace of human companionship; it concerned far more than the two individuals involved. It shattered the fetters of isolation in one great sweep which embraced all of nature, the cosmos, and God Himself. It gave a sense of meaningful relationship to everything that exists and conferred a feeling of "belonging," of security, of purposefulness and hope. It imparted a swelling sensation of self-importance, too, for it gathered the whole universe into the two friends and raised them to the level of the divine itself. "Love" was made to bear all the frustrations of life, and not just the need for sympathetic companionship. Only individuals who combine deep frustration with an equally profound belief in self need to construct such cosmic consolation out of the most ordinary human relationships.

This metaphysic of "love" became that of Herzen's friendship. Nick had been brought to visit by his German tutor. After sitting together shyly for a while, Herzen proposed that they read Schiller. "I was astonished by the similarities of our tastes; he knew by heart more than I did, and knew precisely those passages which appealed to me so. We put down the book and elicited, so to speak, sympathy from one another." The difference between Nick and the "empty lads" that Herzen had hitherto occasionally encountered was "striking." [16] As intimacy ripened they wished to use the familiar thou (*ty*), but did not even dare to use "the word 'friend,' giving to that word a vast and holy meaning." Little by little, though, the declarations of sympathy "came out obliquely." Ogarev wrote a note which he signed hesitantly: "whether or not your friend, as yet I do not know." [17] Just before parting for the summer Ogarev brought Herzen the *Philosophical Letters* and proposed that they read them together.

Ah, how my heart beat, how the tears flowed from my eyes. In vain we tried to hide them. "You have departed, Raphael, and the yellow leaves are falling from the trees; the haze of the autumn mist lies like a shroud over dead nature. Solitary I wander through the melancholy country; I call my friend Raphael, and suffer that he answers not!" I seized my Karamzin and read in reply: "Agathon is no more, my friend is no more." [18]

The declaration was made, "like inexperienced lovers marking out for each other passages in novels; indeed, we were *à la lettre* in love, and our love grew with each new day." Lest there be any misunderstanding, there was nothing the least bit Athenian about this "love." The hyperbole of expression in which it was enveloped was only a reflection of the fact that there was nothing else in the boys' dream-filled experience that was so unmistakably real, and where there was nothing else friendship became all.

3

A year younger than Herzen, Nick had had a very similar experience of life. Of more modest character than his friend, he was not given to writing periodic autobiographies, and we are relatively ill-informed about the circumstances of his early life. Yet the fragments of evidence which exist — the most important of which is an incomplete autobiographical sketch that we owe to the urgings of Herzen, always anxious to preserve the record of their extraordinary lives for posterity[19] — suggest a picture of loneliness and sensitivity not unlike that of his friend. Nick was the only legitimate son of a very rich serf-owner of Penza Province. His mother died soon after his birth, and, a rather sickly child, he was entrusted to the care of household serfs on his father's estate: pious, long-suffering peasant women and a semi-educated, doting and drunken *diadka,* or serf governor. These, especially the *diadka,* were the chief repositories of his affections, since his father, with little time for his son, was a distant and slightly terrifying figure. The old man in addition was a hard master to his serfs. His habitual answer to the *diadka's* somewhat inebriate remonstrances on the subject of Nick's education was a blow administered in the boy's presence. This treatment of the person Nick loved most made him "tremble with fear and indignation," and served to alienate him further from a parent already distant by virtue of the organization of the household.[20] When he was older he confided to Herzen that to his horror he could not help wishing for his father's death to clear the path of his future.[21]

Emotionally Nick grew up on the side of the victims of his father's world, and by the age of fourteen or fifteen this had produced the same cult of the Decembrists and of Schiller as in the case of Herzen. In 1820 he had been brought to Moscow and surrounded by the usual brigade of private tutors. At the time of the revolt he subscribed, like Herzen, to the cult of Constantine as "the man of freedom." [22] But his mathematics teacher, one Volkov, instructor in a Moscow gymnasium and later a tutor to Herzen, soon acquainted him with the real aim of the Decembrists and communicated the forbidden verses of Pushkin and Ryleev.[23] His teacher of French, Curie, formerly preceptor to the Decembrist Vasilchikov, reinforced these liberal sentiments. In this Nick was powerfully aided by the nearest thing to a mother he ever knew, and a close friend of his real mother, a Mme. Kashkina, whose nephew had participated in the revolt.[24] The cult of the Decembrists soon fused with that of Schiller. "Schiller for me was everything — my philosophy, my civics, my poetry." [25] By the time he met Herzen he had developed all the same defenses against an essentially similar situation,[26] and like Herzen there was absolutely no one with whom he could share his lofty dreams and ideal aspirations. Small wonder that their meeting ignited a flame which illumined the universe, and in which they detected the hand of a beneficent Providence working to assemble its elect that they might grow together in mutual inspiration for the accomplishment of the divine design of liberty.[27]

If the boys' dreams were identical, their characters were quite different, and on this mixture of similarity and difference the lifelong success of their friendship was based. Rather weak-willed and indecisive, Ogarev was an altogether more pastel version of his friend. Herzen speaks of Ogarev's "pensiveness" and "exceptional tenderness," [28] of his truly "feminine power of attraction." [29] Ogarev's writings bear out this description; the thick editions of his collected poetry make flabby reading indeed. The foremost student of his art has defined its essence, rather charitably, as unfulfilled aspiration, "a pure thirst for spiritual fullness in the abstract," unrealized in any concrete present.[30] Ogarev himself entitled one of his longer poems *The Confession of a Superfluous Man* — one of the first uses of this famous phrase in Russian literature — and the epithet is apt. There was something passive and dependent in Ogarev's nature, a lack of will and purpose of his own. He needed to be led and directed, and all his life he submitted gratefully to the tutelage of more masterful natures: his two wives, his friends and political associates — most notoriously Bakunin and Nechaev — and most of all Herzen himself. Such submissiveness, or receptiveness, complemented very happily Herzen's more decisive nature. Not that Herzen tyrannized over his friend. On the contrary, their relationship was a spontaneous dialectic of sentiment and ideas; but it was Herzen who constituted the more dynamic force. They could be allies without becoming rivals. It was the perfect formula for harmonious collaboration.

From the beginning it was tacitly conceded by both that Ogarev was the "dreamer" and Herzen the "activist," that Ogarev's special excellence was poetry while Herzen's was prose. In 1833 Herzen wrote to his friend:

Wonderful is my sympathy for you — we are different, very different. In you is a hidden, undeveloped, deep poetry — *involuta*. I have a poetry which is in a certain sense deep, but lively, luminous, an expansive poetry — *evoluta*. The essence of your being is contemplation — of mine propaganda. I am active, you are slothful; but your sloth is activity for the soul. And with all this there exists a wonderful sympathy which decidedly exists with no one else. Sympathy does not demand identity. A deep recognition of the qualities of one another, mutual complementary character — these are the principles of this friendship, strong above all circumstances.[31]

Mutual admiration was among the ties that bound them most strongly; and one of the sweetest boons of friendship for each was a heightened sense of his own worth, his dignity, and even superiority to the mass of mankind. "We respected in each other our future, we looked on each other as on chosen and dedicated vessels." [32]

Ogarev's unique moral superiority over his friend was that he took himself less seriously. This characteristic, although in origin an expression of self-doubt, was, paradoxically, the source of a certain strength. It made him more resilient in the face of catastrophe than Herzen, and capable of absorbing blows under which the more solid and less flexible ego of his friend crumbled. In his humility Ogarev was able to accept disasters, mistakes, and disappointments with a sad smile, where Herzen's pride found frustration intolerable. When stung, Herzen would react with irony, the humor of resistance, but Ogarev with whimsy, the humor of resignation.

It was to Ogarev that Herzen confided the trials deriving from his "false position." In 1837 he wrote to his fiancée: "O how often as a boy, pale and almost with tears in my eyes, I came to Ogarev and rested my head, boiling with inward injury, on his shoulder. And what would have happened if there had not been that friend? I awaited, like paradise, the minutes when I could tear myself away from home, which was turning into a hell. But decidedly no one but Ogarev ever heard these complaints." [33] Herzen's friendship for Nick was so intense because it was the only release from the humiliation, as well as the boredom, of his father's house.

4

Ogarev also shared, and stimulated, Herzen's ideal escapes from the same set of circumstances, and, as ever, under the aegis of Schiller. "A friendship, awakened under the blessing of Schiller, blossomed under his blessing; we identified ourselves with the characters of his heroes." [34] They lived in a world of fantasy created by Schiller, as if it were the real world. "The personages of his dramas for us were real personalities; we analyzed them, loved and hated them, not like poetic creations but like living people. More than this, we saw in them our own selves." They passed from the individual revolt of Moor, the hero of their solitude, to the universalized humanitarianism of Posa, the hero of their friendship. "My ideal was Karl Moor, but I soon betrayed him and went over to the Marquis Posa." [35] These sentiments fused with their devotion to the memory of the Decembrists. Indeed, the whole of Herzen's and Ogarev's youthful Decembrism soon came to be a fantasy adapted from *Don Carlos.*

The play is about two very young men, almost boys (Carlos and Posa), sensitive and noble but utterly alone in a world where only they have the courage to be independent individuals and where all others are the degraded slaves of the tyrant, Philip II. The play is as much about the redemptive powers of friendship, however, as about liberty, or rather the two themes are inseparably united. Schiller's own Körner had been the model for Posa, just as Posa was the symbol of Ogarev's friendship for Herzen. Carlos and Posa have pledged undying devotion, after effusively agreeing to call each other "thou." But above Posa there is the young Queen, an "angel of light, sweet saint," "the highest point of beauty," the symbol of the future, perfect humanity. She and Carlos are ethereally in love, and Posa participates in this love in a curious way through his friendship with Carlos, just as Herzen and Ogarev later felt that each should commune mystically in the love of the other for his wife. Yet, wed to the King (and hence legally Carlos' mother), she is an ideal beyond the possibility of attainment. The boys, moreover, have a very high opinion of their worth and of their mission in the world. They are to bring freedom and beauty of soul to all mankind; they are to make mankind like themselves. They have sworn an oath of friendship and of devotion to the cause of liberty "upon the sacred host," but they are aware that for the present they live in the "Middle Ages," and that their whole enterprise is premature, indeed hopeless: "a dream," no more than "a glowing vision which our friendship painted." In action, both Carlos and Posa are figures of impotence and frustration. They are driven to devious and trick plots, each one more unreal than the next — to spirit Carlos off to lead the revolt in Flanders, to win Philip to their side, or somehow to depose him, to liberate the Queen and free mankind. But they never have any real hope; the plots are presented as if they were not meant to succeed, as if the boys were playing. In the end Posa traps himself in his own deviousness and dies, while the King delivers Carlos over to the Grand Inquisitor for punishment.[36]

In their transposition of this fantasy, Herzen and Ogarev were the Decembrists and the tyrant was Nicholas I. "In a hundred ways I imagined how I would speak with Nicholas [like Posa in his famous interview with Philip] and how he would send me to the mines or execute me. It is strange but almost all our dreams ended in Siberia or on the scaffold and almost never in triumph." [37] There was also the same sense of a world-historical mission. "Life opened up before us triumphantly, majestically; we sincerely swore to sacrifice our existence to the good of mankind; we traced for ourselves an unheard-of future." [38] Modesty was never one of Herzen's virtues and numerous similar expressions of the greatness of his mission are to be found in all his youthful writings.

The consecration of their dedication to mankind and to Russia was their famous oath on the Sparrow Hills, which owes much to the oath of Carlos and Posa. It was in 1827 or 1828;[39] Sasha was at most sixteen, Nick fifteen. They stood appropriately on a series of low hills dominating Moscow.

The sun was setting, the cupolas gleamed, the city spread out in a boundless expanse beneath the hill, a cool breeze blew over us; we stood for a long time, leaning together and, suddenly, embracing, we swore, in the sight of all Moscow, to sacrifice our lives to our chosen struggle [for the liberty of Russia]. . . . From that day forward the Sparrow Hills became a place of pilgrimage for us; we visited it once or twice a year, and always alone.[40]

Years later Herzen still remembered the event with emotion. "This scene may appear very strained, very theatrical; nevertheless, after twenty-six years I am moved to tears at the memory; it possessed a holy sincerity — this our entire lives have demonstrated." [41]

Critics have doubted the reality of this famous oath on the Sparrow Hills.[42] However, if Herzen writing for public consumption many years later might have had reason to exaggerate the precocity of his revolutionary vocation, Ogarev, writing in 1833 and for the eyes of his friend alone, did not. On the contrary, he had every reason to moderate his language for fear the letter might be opened by the police. "For a long time I concealed my enthusiasm within me . . . but on the Sparrow Hills this enthusiasm was no longer weighted down by solitude, and you shared it with me. . . . When you come to write of the Sparrow Hills, tell how in that place the story of our lives unfolded." [43] Still later, in 1837, after exile had intervened to add a deeper significance to the Hannibal oath of boyhood, Ogarev wrote:

Friend! our path promises few joys, but much bitterness and many sufferings; yet which of us fears the crown of a martyr? And shall we complain of Providence? It has given us what few possess, a store of inexhaustible felicity. . . . Iskander [Herzen] do you remember that hill, that bank steep and high, under which flowed a quiet river, and beyond the river the city spreading out endlessly? O! I always remember it, when I am happy, and warm, sweet tears swell from my eyes. There we confessed our friendship, indissoluble to the grave, there we declared our best feelings, the best ideas of our youth.[44]

The ideas in question, of course, were their cult of the Decembrists, which caution forbade spelling out more unequivocally in a letter sent by the public post.

Yet, even without this confirmation, the romantic temper of the two conspirators makes the oath on the Sparrow Hills a logical gesture. In his memoirs Herzen undoubtedly exaggerated somewhat its conscious political content in the light of his later career; in Ogarev's letters the scene appears as much an effusive declaration of friendship as a dedication to revolution. But their friendship was indissolubly fused with the "great All" of Schiller. It was no paltry, everyday emotion, but had cosmic significance, linked with the future of Russia and mankind. Such friends could only be the heirs of the Decembrists.

That was the holy time of our friendship! . . . we felt in ourselves an extraordinary strength. . . . What a noble pride in this first sensation of ourselves! What a marvelous time, Herzen! Our friendship is a point of movement into the future, which we will fill with our existence. Sometimes these fifteen-year-old heroes seem funny to me, but at the same time I feel that they were magnificent: our whole life passed before my memory — that book all written over in the margin [the *Philosophical Letters*], and the room where we read it, and the door to the room closed. I look on us then as a work of art. Around us there were all those tedious people speaking nonsense; to us they were nothing. We are full of life, we determine our own future, we feel that we will not pass through the world along the same commonplace path as they. And through the window shines a little star. We loved it, we called it our lodestar, we believed.[45]

Alone, superior and glorious in their friendship, the two boys faced a philistine world armed only with their dream, like Carlos and Posa. The frustrations to their egos, the wounds to their self-respect were sublimated into a fantasy of self-fulfillment through "love," the wellspring of an infinitely creative beauty. Such self-realization also entailed unlimited freedom, and so they identified themselves with that great, stifled cry of liberty, the revolt of the Decembrists, generalizing their personal predicament into a universal principle, where their thirst for liberty rejoined that egoism which was its source.

5

It may seem excessive to linger over the daydreams of two green boys. In another place or time their antics would have been no more than somewhat curious excesses in a normal adolescent self-affirmation. Given the social and political structure of prereform Russia, their friendship and their Hannibal oath constituted a historic event. Nor was their conviction that some benign Providence had brought them together as extravagant as might appear. In 1828 there was hardly a handful of like-minded youths in the whole of Russia. The Westernized, "civilized" elements — in this period practically coterminous with the gentry — were a tiny minority, and Herzen and Ogarev were an infinitesimal minority within this minority. There were occasional plebeian Protopopovs and Volkovs, and there were the scattered gentry students whom the pair would encounter at the university, but this was all. The first growth of liberal protest had been flattened by the repression of the Decembrists, scattered in the wastes of Siberia, and lost forever. The majority of the rising generation, the Odoevskis, Aksakovs, and Kireevskis, the Stankeviches and the Botkins, even the Bakunins and the Belinskis, were turned exclusively toward aesthetics and metaphysics. Herzen and Ogarev were the first new shoots of humanitarian protest, and in this they were very near to what they thought themselves to be — the only link between the Decembrists and the future.

That they were boys makes their opposition no less serious. In circumstances of exceptional social tension youth is the natural breeding ground for the more desperate energies of protest, and politically speaking nineteenth-century Russia was one long succession of exceptional circumstances. Most of the Decembrists had been no more than in their early thirties; in 1825 Pestel was only thirty-one. The assassins of Alexander II were even younger, in their early twenties. The politics of youth are the politics of revolutionary innovation; St.-Just was a ruler of France at twenty-five, Napoleon at thirty. It is only British prime ministers, American presidents or Roman pontiffs who first attain political effectiveness in their fifties, sixties or later. Of course, Herzen and Ogarev never headed a Committee of Public Safety, staged a revolt, or assassinated a tsar. But they wanted to do something of the kind, or at least persuaded themselves they did, with the energy that is only given to the young, the energy of intuition more than wisdom, of enthusiasm more than knowledge. The Russian autocracy was to pay dearly for the opposition of youths such as these, first of all in the persons of Herzen and Ogarev themselves.

Herzen's youth is the key to his politics in still another sense. All his life he had a special tenderness for what he had been in boyhood. What he was then remained his ideal of what man in general should be. Both *My Past and Thoughts* and the *Notebooks of a Certain Young Man* contain numerous strictures on the amused condescension of adults toward the transports of youth. In both — written fifteen years apart — he takes exception to Sophia Pavlovna's dismissal, in *Woe from Wit*, of youthful enthusiasm as "childishness." For Herzen, " 'Childishness,' together with two or three years of youth, are the very fullest, the most beautiful part of life, the most intimately *ours*, and indeed almost the most important; it imperceptibly determines the whole future." In maturity man "belongs to himself far less, the lyrical element of the personality is weakened and in consequence feelings and pleasure — everything is weaker, except the mind and the will." [46]

In typical romantic fashion Herzen was acutely conscious of the loss of a certain kind of sensitivity that belongs only to youth and comes from the first awakening of adult potentialities, which once explored never have the same freshness again. All his life he lived in the lingering regret of this marvelous birth of the soul. "Smile, if you please, only tenderly, kindly, such as one smiles thinking about his fifteenth year. Or is it not better to grow pensive recollecting: 'Was I such, unfolding like a flower?' and to bless fate if you *had* a youth (mere youngness is not enough for that); and to bless it doubly if you had such a friend." [47] For Herzen's own youth, and his friendship with Ogarev, were the model of what all men and all human relationships should be, and what they would become, in a world and a Russia at last set aright.

Since he followed Schiller, this ideal was aesthetic rather than civic, and the master concept was the "human personality" (*lichnost*, a term Herzen often wrote underlined) rather than the citizen. The battle cry was freedom for the "flowering" of the personality, for the "expansion" of the individual, rather than any natural rights of man. It was in this

aesthetic guise that Herzen first understood the dignity of man, and not
in the sense of political rights. For this reason, his friendship for Ogarev
or the poetry of Schiller were on a level with the heroes of Plutarch, of the
French Revolution, or of the fourteenth of December as agents for the
liberation of mankind and heralds of the future. The beautiful, the great,
and the free are fused into an indissoluble unity. Herzen once wrote of
Napoleon:

Napoleon! whose corpse is not yet cold and whose colossal spirit is still so near
us that we may behold its presence. Boundlessly great is that man who began
our nineteenth century . . . that man who by his despotism helped the
revolution fly around half the world, who was the idol of the people he had enchained, who planted his shield on the walls of the Kremlin and on the Pyramids
of Egypt, and who finished out his life like those same Pyramids — on a lonely
cliff he lived, the mausoleum of his fame, erected in another world, from which
he ruled over a limitless steppe of waves.[48]

Herzen was unable to conceive of greatness of any sort in other than
aesthetic terms. The rebel in the name of freedom was particularly akin
to the artist. In an article written in 1834 he quoted with approval the
Danish imitator of Schiller, Oehlenschlager, to this effect.

> "Die Künstler und die Räuber, das
> Ist eine Art der Leuten. Beide meiden
> Den breiten, staubigen Weg des Alltagslebens." [49]

The artist and the brigand were the supreme exemplars of human dignity
and freedom because they recognized no law but their own unfettered
genius. It was this harkening to self alone which raised them above the
mediocrity of everyday life to the realm of the beautiful. This was the
very heart of Herzen's ideal of the "free human personality" and the
underlying principle of all his later political activity.

All liberal protest movements have need, in one form or another, of a
generalized ideal of man. Ideals of man differ, however, and in so doing
determine, or rather reflect, differing political situations. Thus people
who talk about man as an "artistic creation" do not have the same politics
as those who talk about his "natural rights." It has often been noted that
the farther east in Europe one goes the more abstract and general political
ideals become. The English agitated for the particular and historic rights
of Englishmen; the French for the universal and timeless rights of man;
the Germans sought freedom in the realm of the "pure" or "absolute"
idea. The generalization is no doubt overly simple, and yet, in its essentials, it is difficult to dispute, at least for the eighteenth and early nineteenth centuries. It is also roughly true that the farther east one goes, the
more absolute, centralized, and bureaucratic governments become, while
the middle groups between an ignorant peasantry and a military state
grow smaller and weaker. Moreover, the greater the pressure of the state

on the individual, the more formidable the obstacles to his independence, and the greater his social loneliness are, the more sweeping, general, and abstract are ideologies of protest or compensation. For where the entire order of the world, in every detail of its organization, is an affront to the dignity of the individual, the formulation of a specific set of grievances is impossible, and the cry of protest can only find expression in generalities. To be sure, even the most specific and limited political movements generalize their demands to a certain degree in terms of universal principles (even American political parties have a vague principle or two). But this ideal is at best in alloy with baser metals. With the Russians of Herzen's generation it was pure, and the aesthetic ideal of man is the most pure, abstract, disembodied, and lonely of all possible ideals — the human personality in and for itself, as a self-generating artistic creation — and the most remote from practical politics.

It is no accident that Herzen's political awakening occurred, not under the aegis of a Montesquieu or a Blackstone, or even a Voltaire or a Rousseau — all rather down to earth in their various ways — but under that of the "lofty" and "dreamy" Schiller. While west of the Rhine men were in fact destroying absolutism and proclaiming the concrete, political rights of the individual, the insignificant class of humanized and emancipated professional men of Germany sublimated their aspirations to independence into an ideal of self-realization through culture, thought, art, "noble" emotion, and the cultivation of the individual personality. Hence it was only normal that the even smaller minority of humanized and emancipated Russians, when their turn came to claim their dignity as men, should find German formulations of the problem of liberty more kindred than French or English ones.

As Herzen grew older, the aesthetic humanism of his youth merged ever more actively with politics. But politics which originate in aesthetics rather than in a quarrel over ship money, or a stamp tax, or different legal rights for nobility and Third Estate, always remain somewhat abstract and utopian. When Schiller's ideal of the beautiful soul is made into a program for the real world it can only lead to "total" political demands, and in the last analysis to the idea of revolution as the sole possible means for effecting so extraordinary a transformation in the state of man. However remote from politics it may at first appear, the aesthetic ideal of man is an education in revolutionary intransigence and the "maximalist" utopia. Moreover, it is an education in anarchism, that most extreme of libertarian protests, which will settle for nothing short of the complete emancipation of the individual personality from all external constraint. To speak the language of the Germans who created it, the absolute call to liberty of this aesthetic humanism is the dialectical antithesis of the absolute despotism under which it flourished. Such, in fact, was the origin of the revolutionary dream in Russia. Long before it was a threat to the established order of society, or even became a political movement, the Russian revolution was an ideal fantasy in the heads of few sensitive young men under Nicholas I, and first of all in the heads of Herzen and Ogarev, in their "little room closed to the world," or in their oath on the Sparrow Hills.

CHAPTER IV

University and "Circle"

IN 1829, at the age of seventeen, Herzen left his father's house for the first time to enter the University of Moscow. It was the beginning of his break with the pattern of life established for him by Ivan Alexeevich. The old man had enrolled his son while still a boy in the military chancellery of the Province of Moscow (called the "Kremlin Expedition"), presided over by a friend of the family, Prince Iusupov. In due course Herzen received the lowest officer rank, without, however, serving so much as a day, a favor normally accorded to the privileged. For the old man the matter was quite simple. His son was to serve the emperor as his forbears had done; and he was settled for life in a sinecure which wiped out the taint of his birth and conferred noble rank. In the way of education nothing further was needed than to attend a few evening courses at the university and to pass an examination especially designed to facilitate the advancement of the "lazy, the ignorant and the rich." [1]

But young Alexander had other ideas. He was not interested in an easy governmental career or in social position. For the accomplishment of his high mission for Russia and mankind he must eat of the fruit of the tree of knowledge itself and not of the dried peelings on which the military were nurtured, and thus he announced his determination to attend the regular university courses. Stormy scenes ensued, in which the old man denounced the caprice of the young and the teachers who filled them with absurd ideas. In the end, though, he gave way, in part because of Sasha's persistence, in part at the urging of a nephew, one of the "legitimate" Golokhvastovs. Not that the latter shared his cousin's radical aspirations; on the contrary he was quite integrated into gentry society and the bureaucracy of Nicholas, and in consequence was quite disliked by Herzen. But he was a man of culture (he later became assistant rector of the university under Uvarov), and he persuaded Ivan Alexeevich that advanced education was not incompatible with respectable "service" and a position in society. Privilege was again invoked, and Prince Iusupov

granted Herzen a three years' leave from military "service," which turned
out to be leave for life.[2]

2

Such a course was new among gentry sons at the time. Indeed, as
of 1825, higher learning itself was a recent phenomenon in Russian society. The oldest university, that of Moscow, dated only from 1755; all the
others had not been founded till 1803, and most did not begin functioning
in serious fashion until after 1812. Moreover, before 1825 all had served
primarily as training grounds for civil servants — bureaucrats, physicians,
or teachers. The students were children of the country's tiny professional
class, of commoners (*raznochintsy*) of various sorts, of priests or small
landowners. Gentlemen did not attend the university. Instead they entered
the Guards, after preparing with private tutors or in such distinctly class
establishments as the Corps of Pages and, a little later, the Alexandrovski
Lyceum. Their higher learning, insofar as they possessed it (which they
often did), was gentleman's learning, acquired by independent reading,
cultivated conversation, or travel abroad. In the generation of Pushkin
and the Decembrists the elite of the country, both socially and humanly
speaking, had almost invariably followed this course.[3]

After 1825 all this changed. The talented and the generous-minded,
the patriotic and the idealistic, largely deserted the army for the universities. If under Alexander most of the great names in Russian life had
been officers, under Nicholas they were civilians, trained at the universities. The uncritical obedience to emperor and government required by a
military career, which had appeared as the highest form of idealism in
the age of Austerlitz and Borodino, after 1825 carried with it a taint of
moral compromise, because it meant an abdication of the critical intelligence. The gulf between government and "society" which began to appear
in the last years of Alexander, and which was suddenly deepened by the
fourteenth of December, had much to do with this change. But its cause
was not just political. The new generation was more Westernized and
humanized, more sheltered and sensitive — in a word "softer" — than its
fathers'. It was civilian by temperament as well as by political conviction.
The humanization of the gentry, which had first produced the breach with
the government in 1825, was to widen it under Nicholas.

Of all Russian universities, that of Moscow was the most sensitive
to the new mood. It was the oldest, the most solid academically, and the
only one with a tradition. Moreover, it was set in a society whose mood
answered its own. If St. Petersburg was the capital of the government,
Moscow was the capital of the gentry and the focus of whatever sentiments of independence that class possessed. Not that Petersburg was

exclusively a bureaucratic city; because of the court, it was one of the preferred seats of the gentry's more aristocratic elements. But in Petersburg the gentry was overshadowed by the bureaucracy, whereas in Moscow it reigned without rivals and could indulge in the illusion of independence from a government which was nowhere visible. It could set the tone itself, and its tone was that of the independence natural to any aristocracy, as well as of a sublimated *fronde* against the autocratic turn of affairs in Petersburg since 1825.[4] After that date aristocratic Moscow gathered into itself all the feeble energies of protest which had survived the advent of Nicholas, and granted them asylum in its salons and in the lecture halls of its university.

One of the principal expressions of this change was the growth of the periodical press, which after 1825 flourished on a scale previously unknown in Russia. The reading public, of course, was slowly growing in size. Equally important, energies which had formerly found expression in political societies or in open discussion of reform now had no outlet but literature and the propaganda of ideas, certainly innocent enough in themselves, but "subversive" by the mere fact that they were ideas and hence denoted an independent public opinion. The thirties witnessed an outbreak of new periodicals of a novel sort — serious, intellectual, and proselytizing. The foremost among them was the already mentioned *Moscow Telegraph* of Polevoi, founded in 1825. In addition there were the *Atheneum* of Pavlov and the *Moscow Messenger* (*Moskovski vestnik*) of Pogodin between 1827 and 1830; the *Messenger of Europe* (*Vestnik Evropy*) of Kachenovski until 1830; the *Telescope* of Nadezhdin founded in 1831; and the short-lived *European* of Ivan Kireevski in 1832. All these periodicals had their seats in Moscow and, moreover, lived entirely off the subscription of the public, while Petersburg, save for a few exceptions such as Pushkin's *Contemporary,* was dominated by the so-called "reptile" press of Grech, Senkovski, and Bulgarin, either partially subsidized by the government or openly subservient to its interests.[5] Moderate as the Moscow press was, it represented "society's" effort to think for itself rather than to accept blindly the ideas handed down by the Minister of Education, Uvarov, through the "reptile" press. It further represented the principal avenue by which such Western ideas as could be discussed in print penetrated into Russia.

After 1825 the university was in constant osmosis with this press and the society that supported it. Pavlov, Pogodin, Kachenovski, and Nadezhdin were all professors at the university. Polevoi, although not of the university, was close to it. He polemicized with Pogodin in the pages of his review, while the latter carried into print the opinions he aired on the lecture platform. And aristocratic Moscow responded to the ferment of the university and the new press.[6] The retired Guards officer Chaadaev lived the philosophical and historical debates of the day as intensely as any professor, and published his epoch-making *Philosophical Letter* in Nadezhdin's *Telescope*. As early as the thirties the lectures of Davydov, a professor of literature with a philosophical bent, attracted a fashionable audience from outside the university;[7] a decade later the public lectures of professors Granovski and Shevyrev were major social events.

At the beginning of the reign of Nicholas the university had experienced a difficult period. After escaping the obscurantist attacks of the last years of Alexander, it was subjected to a brief but rude dressing-down at the hands of that advocate of a return to the sane simplicity of old Russia, Admiral Shishkov, then Minister of Education. Among other measures, he abolished the chair of philosophy as a useless, if not pernicious, foreign innovation. But this barracks regime imposed by Petersburg was short-lived. In 1828 Shishkov was replaced by Lieven and a new rector, Prince Golitsyn, was installed, who let the university go its own way in comparative freedom. It was under his lenient regime that Herzen was a student.

The university as yet was not a particularly good one; too many of the professors were either second-rate Germans imported early in the century or their poorly trained Russian pupils. But as the university became more important to "society" after 1825, standards began to rise. There was an infusion of fresh blood among both faculty and students, which produced an increased intellectual ferment and a new scholarly seriousness. After 1833, under the otherwise notorious Uvarov, the situation was improved still further by the introduction of numbers of well-trained younger professors, fresh from study in Germany, and by the fact that until the end of the forties the government on the whole let the university alone.[8] It was into this atmosphere of relative freedom and the intellectual excitement it engendered that Herzen entered in 1829. He was to live either in or near this university world until his departure from Russia in 1847. In a sense he was never to leave it. Together with the influence of his father's house it made him the personality he was to be all his life — a high-minded aristocrat and a Moscow intellectual of the thirties and forties.

3

Normally the university course took three years; for Herzen it in fact lasted five. In 1831 the university was closed for a year because of the cholera epidemic; and at the completion of his course Herzen lingered in the vicinity for another year, unable to break away from his circle of friends and the intellectual excitement of their companionship. These five years were perhaps the happiest of his entire existence. All through later life he remembered them with "gratitude" and "love." [9] Life at the university was as if his friendship with Ogarev had been multiplied a hundredfold and enlarged from a personal experience to a social one. For the first time he found full satisfaction of his desire for companionship and activity.

At last, the confinement of my father's house came to an end. I was *au large;* instead of the solitude of our small room, instead of quiet and semiclandestine rendezvous with my only comrade, Ogarev, a noisy family of seven hundred people surrounded me. In two weeks I grew to be more at home in it than in my parents' house from the day of my birth. [10]

Herzen, of course, continued to live at home, and his father attempted to perpetuate the old tutelage by flanking him with a lackey (and on the first day with two servants and a sleigh) who was to accompany him to and from the university, attending all lectures with him, making sure that he was warmly dressed and did not catch cold. But the parental spell was none the less broken. On the first day Alexander returned home bursting with joy. Tatiana reports that his excitement overflowed into an endless monologue in which he "described the professors, the students, the lecture-rooms, even the door-man . . . and gave summaries of the contents of the lectures," ending with satirical imitations of all the new people he had met. [11] Herzen quickly dispatched the lackey to the nearest alehouse before dispensing with him altogether, and during the hours he was away from home — which by his father's order were never to be later than ten-thirty — he was on his own. [12]

The university at that time, as throughout modern Russian history, was one of the few islands of democracy in the most unequal society of Europe. Its doors were open to all who could pass the entrance examination, gentry and commoners alike (although, of course, not to serfs). The testimony of contemporaries is unanimous that within its walls sons of great nobles competed on a footing of equality with children of village priests, impecunious small gentry, and merchants. Talent, personality, and energy were the sole criteria for success. [13] The university, in fact, provided the nearest thing which existed in Russia to that career open to talent which is perhaps the chief goal of all movements for liberty or democracy. Thus, by the mere fact of its existence, it was corrosive of the values of the surrounding world; no poorer school for adjustment to existing society could be found in the whole empire. Herzen as a young man, however, was aware of this only in the most theoretical way. He simply lived the democracy of the university until it became the very fiber of his being, until he could no longer adapt to the outside world of "unnatural" limitations on the freedom of the individual.

And Herzen made the most of his new freedom. For the first time his gregarious instincts, his wit, and his intelligence could operate in a

real social situation. The pent-up exuberance of seventeen years of isolation overflowed into a multitude of new friendships, endless conversations, and passionate "propaganda" of his own enthusiasms. He had
to meet everybody, like everybody, and have everybody like him.[14] His
energies once released, he swept like a whirlwind through the ranks of
his comrades. So much enthusiasm and personal warmth could not but
make a strong impression, and he quickly stood out among the students
by the very intensity of his personality. In fact he soon emerged as one
of the leaders in his new society. Endowed with talent and an exceptionally enterprising character, he rapidly discovered he could compete with
the best. Not only did the university provide friendship and freedom in
abundance; it furnished in equal measure a forum, recognition, and a
chance for leadership, which Herzen's not inconsiderable ego craved as
much as it did affection.

His first exploit as a public figure at the university was leadership in
a riot against an unpopular professor. Years later, in *My Past and
Thoughts,* Herzen still remembered the incident with deep satisfaction.
The victim was one Malov, professor of jurisprudence, whose arrogant
incompetence may or may not have been as great as Herzen states, but
who was unquestionably detested by the students. So they decided to
drive him from his lecture hall. Although not a student in the faculty of
jurisprudence, Herzen either was invited to attend the heckling at the
head of a band from his own faculty (as he claims) or decided to come
on his own, for the sheer pleasure of harassing the authorities. In all events
he appeared and played a leading role in raising a tumult which drove the
unfortunate Malov into the street, followed by howling students who
hurled his snowboots after him.[15]

To be a leader in such an action required greater courage or fool-
hardiness than might at first appear. The slightest insubordination to authority easily assumed major proportions in the eyes of the jumpy government of Nicholas, and serious consequences could have ensued for the
ringleaders if the case had fallen into the hands of the wrong bureaucrat.
The university authorities intervened quickly, however, and punished
the leaders by confinement, on bread and water, in the university deten-
tion-house, or *kartser.* Herzen later proudly reflected that the first nights
he ever spent outside his father's house were passed in prison.[16]

Ivan Alexeevich was appropriately horrified both by his son's conduct
and by his punishment, and immediately had the Senator and his nephew
Golokhvastov intervene to obtain "Sasha's" release on grounds of "weak
health." [17] When Herzen was informed that he could leave the detention-
house, but that his comrades must remain, he was outraged and declared
— to the boundless indignation of his father — that he would stay where
he was. Imprisonment for a just cause was an honor; indeed, it was a

pleasure, for Herzen liked being away from home. In addition, sympathetic students on the outside smuggled in wine, roast fowl, cheese, and cigars, and so the "prisoners" roistered all night and slept all day. Herzen had hardly ever been happier. The crowning vindication was the dismissal of Malov from the university. The whole affair no doubt was only a student prank, but it reveals in Herzen a more than average combativeness. Moreover, by his role in this incident — which he had sought out much more than it had been thrust upon him — he established himself as a public figure among his contemporaries, which was what his ambition most desired.

He was avid for academic honors as well. He took his studies seriously, first of all because knowledge was necessary for the accomplishment of his high mission in life, but also because he craved distinction. At the end of the university course he summarized his program for the future — "study, study, write, fame!" [18] While at the university, he wished intensely to impress his professors and to stand out among his comrades; and his bitterness at what he considered to be inadequate recognition of his worth is a measure of the force of this desire.

In particular he aspired to receive the first gold medal on graduation, but he received only the second silver one. Years later he still remembered this affront to his ego, as one remembers youthful disappointments, with a mixture of amusement and sympathy — but he at least remembered it. At the time his reaction was one of real pain and anger. He had set his heart on the gold medal months in advance, and putting aside everything else, had shut himself up with his dissertation — in reality only an essay of some twenty pages — in order to gain the coveted prize. He wrote to a friend: "I am giving my all and desire to have either the gold medal or — nothing." [19] The period of examinations and of waiting for the results was unbearable with expectancy. Then the initial satisfaction at receiving his degree (to which by no means all the students were admitted) was blighted by failure to obtain the gold medal. Herzen wrote his future wife: "I am a graduate, it is true; but the gold medal was not given to me; however, they gave it to such an individual that I would be ashamed to enter into rivalry with him. The whole university is astonished at this. I have a silver medal, one of three." And he added: "Graduation was today, but I didn't attend, since I don't want to be second when the rewards are handed out." [20]

The fault, of course, lay in the stupidity and ill-will of his professors. In May he had "blessed" the university for all it had given him[21] — sentiments to which, it must be said in justice, he would soon return. In June he wrote: *"pereat Academia! pereant professores!,"* and followed this general imprecation with a specific curse on the heads of almost all of his masters. The list included, rather unjustly, the celebrated Pavlov (characterized as "that Bombastus Paracelsus in miniature"), to whom Herzen owed more than to any other his formation at the university.[22] Herzen had originally been one of Pavlov's favorite pupils (of his influence more will be said later). Herzen, however, apparently impatient at being the submissive disciple of anyone, had once led the students in heckling the master in class, and he was convinced that his failure to obtain the gold medal was a piece of personal vengeance on the part of Pavlov.[23] Where the rights and wrongs of the case lie it is impossible to tell. Pavlov no doubt had his vanity; but Herzen even more certainly displayed an inclination, undue in one so young, to step into the master's shoes. The incident is minor, yet significant. Spoiled and vain as he was, Herzen reacted in exaggerated fashion whenever his wishes were thwarted in any way. A contemptuous, and often unjust, epithet was his readiest answer to all opposition. But, of course, intense democratic convictions are founded as much on personal ambition as on love of one's fellow man.

A similarly revealing incident also occurred at the university. According to *My Past and Thoughts,* one of the sweetest memories of Herzen's student days was a lecture he delivered before the students and professors of his faculty and the Minister of Education, Uvarov. The latter had ordered, as an educational experiment, that lectures be given by the best students in the various disciplines, and Herzen was chosen among them for his "well-hung tongue." He delivered his piece with a mixture of pride and terror: it was the first time he had ever spoken in public. The lecture apparently was a great success, and the satisfaction of having dominated an audience made an indelible impression on his mind, just as he never forgot his role in an amateur theatrical in Viatka a few years later.[24] It is no small part of the drama of Herzen's career that, born to seek the applause of a wide audience, these trivia should have left such a lasting impression, since they were his only appearances on a public platform in his native land.

4

Herzen found his principal satisfactions at the university, however, in a small group of close friends, which has gone down in Russian history as the "circle of Herzen and Ogarev." With its pendant and rival, the "circle of Stankevich," which included such figures as Belinski, Bakunin, and Constantine Aksakov, it was one of the two poles of attraction among the serious-minded students of the day. That the persons involved were very young in no way reduces the importance of the two groups. Between them they produced most of the philosophical- and political-minded talent of the thirties and forties, and they dominated the intellectual life of Moscow, and indeed of Russia, for the bulk of the reign of Nicholas.

The *kruzhok,* or "circle," in the period between the Decembrists and the Emancipation was much more than a casual grouping of comrades or like minds. Although without any formal organization, it constituted a true society, with all the cohesiveness and exclusiveness of a clan. It was founded on an ardent and idealized form of friendship, of the sort preached by Schiller and romantic Germany. Its members were brothers who communed in one another's "love" and mutual ideals as the faithful of a sect commune in its mysteries. They needed one another desperately, confided everything, judged one another's conduct and motives. Later, as we shall see, when they married, their choice of loves, by tacit consent, concerned the entire group and not just the individual immediately involved, because marriage was a bond hardly stronger than the brotherhood of the *kruzhok.* It was no more than appropriate that Herzen and Ogarev should become the moral center of such a society, since they were among the purest prototypes the age afforded of the exalted attachment on which the *kruzhok* was founded. The circle, as it were, was their friendship extended to the group.[25]

The basis of the circle's cohesiveness was the same as that of the attachment of the two friends — a sense of isolation. If during adolescence Herzen and Ogarev had felt that they alone in all Russia responded to the high message of Schiller and the Decembrists, at the university they were aware of being only slightly more, a mere ten or twenty, in a world that either did not understand or was hostile. The members of the *kruzhok* were young men of high ideals and a sense of mission, with a serious interest in ideas and a great ambition. There was not, however, a single periodical in the whole empire which echoed their preoccupations; there was no movement of opinion which shared their aspirations. They were thus driven to seek their intellectual nurture outside of Russia, in ideas and books that filtered through from Europe and which they had to digest as best they could alone, unaided by anyone outside their little band. Isolated, ignored and misunderstood, they were forced to draw all their intellectual and moral resources from themselves through mutual encouragement and comprehension.[26]

The circle consequently filled various functions of education and propaganda which in more liberal societies normally fall to the university, the press, or the political party. Belinski has aptly described the sociology of the phenomenon.

Our education deprived us of religion, the circumstances of life (the cause of which was the structure of society) did not give us a solid education and deprived us of the possibility of really mastering knowledge [contemporary Western thought]. With reality [society] we were at loggerheads, and by rights hate and despise it the same way it hates and despises us. Where then is our refuge? On a desert island which was our *kruzhok.*[27]

Under such circumstances youthful camaraderie turned into a metaphysical cult of the sanctifying action of friendship; and friendship itself became the foundation of something higher than the sum of the individuals involved — a dedication to Russia, humanity, the Absolute, or some other end of transcendent significance.

In his memoirs Herzen lingers tenderly over his university circle. It formed slowly, as Herzen, after his initial indiscriminate fraternizing was spent, gradually discovered comrades of like mind. The group of the elect eventually narrowed down to about ten. Among its important members was first of all Vadim Passek, the impoverished son of a Polish officer who under Paul I had been unjustly exiled with his family to Siberia. As the only member of the group who had personal experience of political oppression, Passek was an ardent liberal and for this reason, next to Ogarev, Herzen's closest friend at the university.[28] (This closeness later extended to Herzen's cousin Tatiana, whom Passek eventually married.) Next in importance was Nicholas Khristoforovich Ketcher, renowned in the circle for his ideological combativeness and the volume of his voice. Somewhat older than the others, he had already graduated from the Medical Faculty, but because of his interest in liberal politics and the life of ideas continued to lead a disorganized bachelor existence on the fringes of the university. His principal activity was less his service to the state as a physician than translating Schiller and Shakespeare.[29] Also close to Herzen was Nicholas Sazonov, by unanimous consent a young man of great gifts, and even greater vanity, who promised much but never produced, and after a life of futility died recanting in large part his radical opinions. Herzen later came to dislike him, because of this very futility, and gives him a bad press in *My Past and Thoughts;* but at the university he seems to have been the most considerable member of the circle after Herzen himself.[30] Close to Ogarev and Sazonov was Alexis Savich, a future professor of astronomy and a member of the Academy of Sciences, whose interest in politics and the fate of humanity ended with graduation.[31] Closer still to Ogarev (and later his brother-in-law) was Nicholas Satin, an amiable but rather ineffective individual whose devotion to liberty, though it never died, also never led him to active politics.[32] Finally, there was Alexis Lakhtin, the circle's only martyr to the cause of freedom, who died in his twenties, largely as the result of despondency provoked by his exile in 1834.[33]

Socially, Herzen's circle, like that of Stankevich, was rather variegated, and as such symptomatic of the growing democratization of intellectual life after 1825. Only Sazonov and Satin were, like Herzen and Ogarev, sons of large serf-owners, and none of them came from backgrounds quite as distinguished as those of many of the Decembrists. The other members of the group were of more modest origin. Passek and Ketcher were from the lower echelons of government "service," with either a small estate or none, which placed them only on the fringes of gentry society. Lakhtin and Savich appear to have sprung from the small landed gentry.[34] Still, none of the group came from below the gentry, as did Belinski and Botkin in the circle of Stankevich. And the group was dominated, both socially and intellectually, by its more affluent members, Herzen, Ogarev, and Sazonov. In its general tone, then, it may be described — using a favorite classification of Herzen's — as "middle gentry." It was "middle gentry" with a difference, though, both because the group included individuals whose primary association with this class was through their wits, and because almost all its members intended to pursue unaristocratic professional careers as professors, physicians, journalists or writers, and if possible, politicians. Only Satin, and for a time Ogarev, led the normal gentry life of a landowner. If one social description must be given of the group it can only be that of civilian and professionalized — hence alienated — middle gentry, which had largely cut itself off from its landed origins, and which at the same time maintained an opening for men of more lowly birth. This was the social formula for the budding intelligentsia throughout the reign of Nicholas.[35]

Herzen's group was fully formed into a "circle" only towards the end of his stay at the university. The year after his graduation was actually its golden age, "a continuous feast of friendship, an exchange of ideas, of inspiration, of revelry." After receiving his diploma Herzen gave no thought to the prosaic affairs of life or to a settled career, which could only have been "service" with the despised government. He lived on, heedless of the outside world, within the charmed enclosure of the circle. "A small group of university friends who had attended classes together did not separate after graduation but lived on united by mutual sympathies and dreams; no one gave a thought to his material position, to the arrangement of his future." [36] Such carefree, indeed irresponsible, divorce from the world around them was made possible only by their privileged position within that world; but most in the group were already too alienated temperamentally from their origins to come to terms with the everyday life of their class.

Ogarev's father possessed a large house in Moscow which his son usually enjoyed alone since the old man preferred to reside in the country, and it was here that the band gathered. In a first autobiographical fragment entitled, characteristically, *About Myself,* and written at the age of twenty-six, Herzen, from the solitude of exile, tried to recapture the glory of their gatherings.

Once toward the end of May 1833, in the lower story of a house on the Nikitski Boulevard a group of young men were roistering. The orgy was in full flame, in high brilliance. The wine, like bellows, fanned imaginations into a great tongue of flame. Ideas, anecdotes, lyric transports, comic imitations whirled and turned in a rapid waltz, raced on at a mad gallop.[37]

Twenty years later, in *My Past and Thoughts,* he returned to evoke the same scene in almost identical terms for many long, tender pages.[38] This "feast of friendship" and ideas was one of those "artistic creations" which were his constant ideal of the full life and the emancipated personality.

The deeper purpose of the circle, however, was not comradely revels. "The fundamental tone was not set by this; the diapason was too elevated. The pranks, the roistering were not our end. . . . We respected in one another instruments of the general welfare. Our end was faith in our calling." [39] This calling was the liberation of Russia. Herzen and his friends were convinced that their circle was in some way historically significant, perhaps even the nucleus of a secret political society, "a phalanx which would follow in the footsteps of Pestel and Ryleev." [40] This political purpose and sense of mission were certainly real; but they were equally amorphous, for active conspiracy was totally impossible under the conditions of the day. The practical significance of the circle, therefore, came to be something more modest: preparation for future activity by education and self-improvement, or what the group called "enlightenment."

Before proceeding to an examination of the contents of this "enlightenment," it should be stressed that the circle was an education in itself, by the mere fact of its existence. It was Herzen's introduction to society, and hence of crucial importance in the formation of his future social ideal, for the circle represented at the same time freedom for the "flowering of the personality" of each of its members, and full equality in fraternity among all of them. It hearkened back to the past, for it was like the anarchist band of Schiller's *Robbers* come to life; and it foretold the future, for it resembled the ideal image Herzen would later hold of the Russian peasant commune, which in spirit was little more than the circle generalized to the scale of the nation. In short, long before he heard of the word, the circle was his first taste of what he later called "socialism." Together with his friendship for Ogarev, and later his love for Natalie, it furnished him the vision of what life should be, and what it would become, in a better world.

Although all this would be the ultimate significance of the circle, for the present it meant primarily mutual education, not, like that of the Decembrists, in politics, but in a substitute — ideology — and first of all in German idealism.

CHAPTER V

Schelling and Idealism

IN *My Past and Thoughts* Herzen shows us the professorial lion, Pavlov: he "stood in the doorway of the Faculty of Natural Sciences and stopped the student with the questions: You want to know nature? But what is nature? What is it to know?" [1] These fundamental, eternal questions were those that most agitated the circle of Herzen and Ogarev at the university. If their purpose was preparation for their high mission for Russia and mankind, this meant first of all the acquisition of sure knowledge of the world they were summoned to change. This knowledge was something the generation called "science" (*nauka*), but which previous and subsequent ages are wont to term philosophy, or, even more narrowly, metaphysics. Specifically, "science" was post-Kantian German idealism, the great master of which in Russia during the thirties was Schelling. After an adolescence passed in the school of Schiller, a young manhood spent in tutelage to Schelling was the second step in the German education of the generation which grew up after 1825.

Yet the nature of the two influences was not quite the same, for the ideological Schelling inevitably provoked a more complex reaction than did the sentimental Schiller. Following a pattern common to most of his generation, Herzen began by absorbing much, though not all, of Schelling, and ended in a violent rejection of the whole idealist position. The positive phase of this development provides the chief key to his intellectual life during the ten crucial years from twenty to thirty, or approximately down to 1840, while the following decade is dominated no less pervasively by the negative phase. Ideas that men react against over many years mold their thought just as decisively as do ideas they accept. Every materialist is haunted by a repudiated idealism. Long after Herzen had consciously rejected Schelling and idealism, much of both remained in his fundamental habits of thought. Altogether, in terms of explicit ideology (as opposed to the more visceral values derived from Schiller) Herzen's intellectual make-up was largely determined for life first by his contact with idealism, then by his reaction against it, and in the last analysis by the combination of the two.

Since, therefore, nothing in his future development can be understood outside of the influence of idealism, the narrative must be interrupted here for an examination of what might be called the "social psychology" of that doctrine, an effort which may have the appearance of a digression but is in reality the heart of the story. Nor is it possible to adopt the too frequent evasion of intellectual historians and to say that at this point Herzen fell under the "influence" of Schelling, from whom he "borrowed" the following three, or five, or seven ideas, as if ideas were the discrete commodities of some mechanical ideological exchange. Ideas come in systems, or at least in meaningful relationships (even when they may be in logical contradiction); and intellectual "influence" involves nothing so simple as "borrowing." Rather it involves a complex correspondence of needs and emotions to total intellectual combinations. That the intellectual combination of German idealism is particularly intricate only makes it less possible to dismiss its impact in Russia by a catalogue of borrowings. Nor is the sociological significance of German idealism, in spite of the lip-service invariably accorded to its importance, so well elucidated by historical literature in English as to make superfluous an additional, if perhaps summary, effort. To characterize the influence of a Locke, a Rousseau, or a Marx it is often sufficient simply to refer to their names. However, in the historiography of Central and Eastern Europe in the English language, the German idealists, with the partial exception of Hegel, but certainly not of Schelling, are a rather different matter; and the significance of their influence where it existed cannot be taken for granted.

2

In their involvement with Schelling's idealism Herzen and his circle were poles apart from their chosen ancestors, the Decembrists. Here it is necessary to pursue further a theme already broached in an earlier chapter *à propos* of Schiller and the change of the intellectual climate in Russia following 1825. If the Decembrists had had some small contact with German romanticism in literature, they had had almost none with German idealism in philosophy. Their philosophy, in so far as they were concerned with such matters, derived from the empiricism and materialism of the French *philosophes*. The Decembrists, however, were not greatly interested in philosophy as such. Rather they were men of action whose formal thought was always no more than a prelude to some practical and immediate task. In this they were the true products of the simple eighteenth-century rationalism on which they had been reared. For them the problems of Russia were as clear as the eighteenth century had held nature to be in general; once understanding was achieved, appropriate action followed naturally and immediately.[2]

Such were the optimistic illusions of the beginnings of the liberal opposition in Russia, just as they had earlier been the illusions of a similar opposition in the West. Similarly, the defeat of the Decembrists in Russia provoked the same muddying of the intellectual waters that the disappointing outcome of the French Revolution had provoked in Europe as a whole. The generation of the aftermath in Russia, like that of a few years earlier in the West, was driven to seek the explanation of a reality no longer clear and simple in the sinuosities of metaphysics rather than on the straight highway of empiricism. In their search for an explanation of life they turned inevitably to the school of frustration, Germany, just as their predecessors had turned to the school of action, France.

German idealism, in fact, had begun to penetrate the more quietistic segments of Russian society before 1825. It made its first appearance early in the century, close on the heels of Schiller and German literature, in the scholarly world. By 1812 the professors Vellanski and Galich were preaching Schelling at the University of St. Petersburg, and somewhat later the professors Davydov and Pavlov introduced him at Moscow. But it was not until around 1825 that Schelling caught on in broader intellectual circles. The first symptom of the new movement was the formation in Moscow, shortly before the Decembrist revolt, of a "circle" known variously as the "Youths of the Archives" (from the fact that most of its members were young aristocrats who held sinecures in the archives of the Ministry of Foreign Affairs in Moscow) or as the "Lovers of Wisdom," the *Liubomudry*. The latter appelation was a literal translation into a pseudo-archaic Russian of the Greek roots for the word philosopher, and was chosen to indicate that the Wisdom concerned was of a higher sort than that associated with the term *"philosophe,"* debased by the vulgar empiricism of the eighteenth century. The group included many distinguished people: its animator, Prince V. F. Odoevski, the poet A. V. Venevitinov, the future Slavophiles A. Koshelev and the brothers Ivan and Peter Kireevski, and finally the future ideologists of "official nationalism" under Nicholas I, S. P. Shevyrev and M. P. Pogodin — in short the principal conservative talent of the coming reign. The group's mentor in philosophy was M. G. Pavlov, already a professor at the university, who was assisted as a purveyor of Schelling by his pupil, M. A. Maximovich. For a short time in 1825 the circle edited a review entitled *Mnemosyne,* contemporary of the equally short-lived Decembrist *Polar*

Star. After the fourteenth of December both group and review disbanded, lest their activities be mistakenly construed by the authorities as akin to those of the Decembrists.[3]

The "Lovers of Wisdom" during their brief existence were as voices crying in the wilderness, a minority overshadowed by the dominant Decembrists. But in the apolitical calm that descended over the gentry intelligentsia after 1825 their metaphysical preoccupations became those of enlightened society as a whole. The group dispersed, but its tendency triumphed. By 1830, among the Schellingians not only Pavlov, Davydov, and Nadezhdin, but also Shevyrev, Pogodin, and Maximovich held chairs at the university, and all of them, as did Ivan Kireevski, published or contributed to reviews. There was, to be sure, opposition to the new philosophy. Each Schellingian professor had at least one, and usually several, adversaries among his colleagues, who upheld a more empiricist position in natural science, aesthetics, history, or philosophy.[4] But these latter were now the voices in the wilderness. Protest as they might, conditions favored the new learning from Germany; it was to this alone that the serious youth hearkened. The "Lovers of Wisdom" had been the first swallows of a long metaphysical spring, which was to last well into the forties, and Herzen's formative years were passed entirely under its influence.

3

The German idealism to which Herzen and his generation were subjected marks a revolution in the philosophical tradition of modern Europe. One of the conventional ways to indicate its novelty is to point to certain characteristics which are on the whole nonphilosophical: a sense of historical becoming; a tendency to think of reality as organism; a feeling for the collective or social consciousness; ties with literary romanticism and a high evaluation of the aesthetic; and ties with the revival of religion following the French Revolution. German idealism is especially credited with discovering the nation in its historical particularity as opposed to the abstract, universal man of the eighteenth century. It saw, moreover, in art, religion and myth — all scorned by its predecessors as manifestations of the irrational — the essential expression of the nation's individuality. It saw in them also a means for understanding reality that was deeper than the formalized reason of the Enlightenment — in other words it rediscovered intuition. Thereby idealism rekindled the fires of emotion and imagination which the age of reason had damped, and by the same token exalted individual genius and the divine spark of inspiration.

Furthermore, idealism saw all these things in an organic structure.

There was a living link between art, religion and myth on the one hand and the political and social structure of any given age or collectivity on the other; all these elements were inextricably interrelated in a single whole expressing the spirit or "soul" of an epoch or a society. Idealism also saw an organic link between one age and another, with all ages and nations woven into one great chain of historical becoming, ever evolving from lower to higher cultural and social forms. Parallel to this organic view of history was a new and more poetic view of nature than that held by the empirical science of the eighteenth century; nature became animate, was endowed with spiritual force, and was looked upon as the prologue to history. At the same time idealism brought back, not exactly the old God of revealed religion, but Spirit — *Geist*, or the Absolute — which subsumed all of nature, history, and art in one unified whole. Finally, idealism declared this Spirit to be the highest form of reason, thereby reconciling philosophy with religion to the comfort of hearts disillusioned by the Enlightenment and the Revolution.

All these conventional attributes are undeniably characteristic of idealism; yet the list does not exhaust the originality of the movement, nor adequately account for its appeal. Nationalism, historicism (conservative or otherwise), romanticism, and a return to religion could and did arise independently of idealism, and could elaborate their doctrines without the help of German metaphysics. In France and England in particular all four movements made their appearance only slightly later than in Germany. Moreover, they ran their life's course without the aid of an elaborate philosophy, and with only occasional borrowings from Weimar and Jena by a Coleridge or a Madame de Staël. The wedding of these four currents of thought with idealism is, in fact, a phenomenon peculiar to countries east of the Rhine. The explanation for idealism's success, therefore, is not to be found in its accidents, which were common to the whole of Europe. Rather the answer must be sought in what was specific to the central and eastern portions of the continent, that is, in the movement's deeper character as a philosophy, and particularly in its idealist metaphysics, its pantheism and its dialectical "logic."

There had been idealisms and pantheisms before, and even hints of the dialectic, in the history of modern philosophy, but the form of each in post-Kantian thought was radically new, as was the combination in which the three were fused. Philosophical idealism can mean at least two different things. It can mean first of all a particular solution to the epistemological problem which holds that the mind can know only its representations of things and not things in themselves. In the language of Kant, with whose formulation of the problem German idealism began, we know only the phenomena of our experience and not the noumena of external reality, which forever escape our grasp although they are indisputably there. On the other hand, idealism can mean that the whole of reality is reducible to idea; that the mind comprehends in a unified system both the external and the internal world; that both are governed by the laws of mind; and that all reality finds its highest expression in the knowing consciousness.

It is in this second and vaster sense that the post-Kantians were idealists. Kant had meant his idealism chiefly as a solution to the specific problem of the character of knowledge, and not as an explanation of the ultimate nature of reality. For Kant all that man can know by reason is the phenomena of his own experience. There remain, however, many things in reality which are beyond the range of the mind's perception, both unknown by reason and unknowable to it — the noumena, God and even the deeper nature of the self. This caution and the limitations it placed on man's knowledge left unsatisfied Kant's successors, more impatient or ambitious than he. For them mind had to be able to grasp reality in its ultimate essence. Moreover, since they started with Kant's idealistic epistemology, the whole of reality, if it were to be completely permeable to man's mind, must be of the same nature as that mind. The mind of the knowing subject, or the self, and what the naïve would call external reality must be in some deeper sense one, fused into a unitary and indivisible whole. In this way the self could encompass the entire universe, since the universe would be identical in structure with mind. Because of this identity the following two notions were also valid: in knowing itself, the mind likewise knew the universe; and in knowing the universe the mind at the same time discovered itself. Thus for the post-Kantians the essence of reality was idea, and all knowledge came to be self-knowledge.

In effect, the limited transcendental world of Kant's phenomena had retained its radically idealistic character but had been expanded to include the whole of noumenal, "objective" being. This seamless garment now encompassed the external world of nature; it embraced the deeper essence of the knowing self; it was the common ground of all individual selves and their unity with everything that at first glance appeared alien to them; and, if one held to such a notion, it could also be God. It was, in a word, the All, or the Absolute. Moreover, since reality was both unitary and of the same nature as mind, the Absolute too in its deepest essence was idea: indeed it was *the* Idea. To pursue this essential tautology further, the Absolute could know itself, or attain to "self-consciousness," not in the material life of the universe, but only in the realm of ideas — in other words in the mind of man. Thus the mind of the species became the self-consciousness of the Absolute.

Conversely, since for idealism all knowledge is self-knowledge, the mind in knowing itself also knows the Absolute. In a sense, mind even constructs the Absolute out of itself, or at least out of its perceptions, since apart from mind the Absolute has no existence. Just as mind is the culmination of the life of the Absolute — its self-consciousness — so the Absolute is the projection of mind. No post-Kantian would have put the matter quite so baldly, but the identification of mind with the Absolute is so complete in romantic idealism that for all practical purposes the self comes near to creating its own universe. Thus the original idealism of Kant, rationalistic and empirical in spirit after the manner of the Enlightenment, has become a radically different thing in the hands of his successors. Idealism is no longer merely a solution to the epistemological problem; it is a metaphysical doctrine in which reality is seen as conforming completely to the structure of mind, in fact identified in its deepest essence with mind, or the self.

Furthermore, romantic idealism has become a radically secular pantheism. Older pantheists such as Spinoza (of whom the post-Kantians were so fond and whom they so largely misread in the spirit of their own doctrines) had viewed both nature and the soul, or mind, of man as finite modes of a God greater than any of his individual expressions. For the post-Kantians the Absolute (which included the idea of what old-fashioned religion meant by God) is no more than the sum of its finite expressions in nature and in mind. It does not exist over and above them; it is purely immanent in them. The Absolute is indwelling in nature, and especially in the mind of man, whereas in older, less anthropocentric pantheisms things had been the other way around: nature and man had been indwelling in God. Thus the mind of man, as the culmination of the Absolute, is the center of the system; and through a synthesis of pantheism with idealism it comes to occupy a position formerly accorded only to God. The human mind, no matter how much the post-Kantians hedge in their formulation of the point, has in effect been elevated to the rank of soul of the universe, for the Absolute knows no fuller self-expression than the consciousness of man.

The notion of the dialectic and the extraordinary importance accorded to it by the post-Kantians derive rather logically from this fusion of idealism with pantheism. As we have seen, the knowing subject, or mind, and the known object, or the world external to the self, are in their deepest essence one in the Absolute. This was a necessity for idealism if mind were to grasp the whole of reality and not be shut up in a closed world with the phantoms of its own perception, which was where Kant had left it. Yet at the same time, mind and the external world must to a certain degree be separate and distinct, or otherwise the same unfortunate result would occur: the mind would know not reality but the phantoms of its own ideas. Mind and the external world, subject and object, then, had to be both the same and yet different, one and yet many.

The necessity of the dialectic springs directly from this paradox. In terms of traditional logic such a combination of identity and separation was an impossibility. But if the relation between subject and object were conceived not as something static and fixed, but as an organic or a dynamic process, all would be saved. Then the subject would develop into the object and vice versa; they would be united by a dynamic tension, in which they were at the same time separated by the opposition between them yet united in the process of struggle which embraced both. Such was the dialectic. Mind and the external world, subject and object, were united but at the same time enabled to maintain their separate identities by an antithetical interplay between them. The structures alike of mind, nature, and the Absolute were dialectical, in a process of perpetual becoming and growth, whereby one thing was constantly turning into its opposite, and where all things preserved their individuality and yet lost it in the unity of the Absolute Idea.

The adoption of this device radically transformed the relation between subject and object from what it had been before the advent of post-Kantian idealism. The relation of the mind — or self — and the external world — or all that is not the self — is no longer a relation of cognition or perception. Instead it has become a relation of struggle and tension, whereby the ego seeks to overcome the external world, or to comprehend it in a single whole with itself by a union through opposition. Beginning with Fichte the relation of subject to object is seen in terms of action and will rather than knowledge. Thus the epistemological problem with which Kant began is once again transformed into an ethical or metaphysical one, and idealism turns to exploring the relation of the individual to the world in terms of value or destiny rather than of understanding. At the same time, the dialectic becomes a dramatic image of the individual pitted against a hostile world and striving to overcome it, or in some way to identify himself with it by transcending conflict in a higher harmony.

A final characteristic of idealism must be mentioned. The post-Kantians considered themselves to be in the modern rationalistic tradition. In practice, however, their method opened the door to the widest use of what can only be called personal, poetic intuition. This use of intuition as a form of "reason" flowed alike from their idealism and their dialectical "logic." Since all knowledge is self-knowledge, and since mind is the mirror of the universe, for practical purposes whatever the self thinks or feels acquires the validity of absolute truth, and strict objective guarantees such as vulgar empiricists demand are not required. Moreover, since reality is dialectical, founded on paradox and contradiction, there are in practice few limits to the diversity of normally incompatible propositions that may be entertained as "true" at the same time.

For idealism, then, neither empirical evidence nor the ordinary rules of logic needed to be taken very seriously in deducing the Absolute from the self. Not that the idealists explicitly rejected empirical evidence or logic; but they claimed to have surpassed what their simple-minded predecessors had understood to be the uses of both. Empirical evidence had to be interpreted in terms of the laws set by mind, that is, by intuition; and logic was much more complicated than had previously been thought — it was dialectical, or contradictory. The result was that the individual could allow free play to his poetic intuition and still call the result "science," and that the philosopher could almost make up the world he wished, at least in the "Idea." [5]

These, then, were the basic tenets of idealism; but what was their psychological appeal? First of all, it is evident that the salient characteristic of idealism is an unbounded egocentrism. God, the Absolute, nature, and the whole of world history come, in effect, to focus in the self. The ruling principles of the universe are idea and mind — the most intimate properties of the self. To be sure, the self in question is, technically speaking, not the same as the ego of any individual; but for practical purposes this distinction tends to disappear, and the idealist philosopher feels free to speak in the name of the Absolute. In addition, idealism's emphasis on what is in effect a form of poetic intuition, and its scorn for empirical evidence without the illumination of the idea, only enhance this egocentrism. The universe in effect becomes what the self feels in its heart the universe should be.

Combined with this colossal individualism, though, is an equally colossal effort to unite, even to the point of identity, with collective wholes larger than the self: the community of all human minds in history, the spirit of the age, the world-spirit, the organic life of nature, or the Absolute. This indeed is the great paradox on which idealism is founded. Idealism's affirmation of the individual's selfhood is matched by an equally strong yearning to belong, to participate meaningfully in collectivities which transcend the self. Idealism exalts at one and the same time the individual and the collective — nature, history, the *Volk*, or society — by making both necessary for the full expression of the Absolute. The universal pantheism of the system is as essential to its appeal as is the egocentric idealism.

Still, talk as he might of the Ego and the All, the idealist did not lose entirely the common-sense perspective, and he could not but know in his heart that he was caressing an illusion. In the last analysis his luminous universe was achieved only in idea or the mind — in other words, in imagination — and the whole enterprise was largely one in wishful thinking. But idealism came to meet even this awareness of illusion, and here lay the psychological significance of the dialectic. In intent the dialectic was a device to bridge the gulf between the mind and external reality by making opposition itself a bond. In this it paralleled the function of the pantheism of the system, for it provided a sense of unity, however illusory, between the isolated ego and the external world. Yet at the same time the dialectic expressed an acute awareness of tension, conflict, and hostility, and as such it was the sign of what the age itself called "alienation," or an immense desire to belong, aroused by a feeling of not, in fact, belonging. Thus the dialectic, forever paradoxical, at the same time expressed and partially assuaged the sense of the isolated ego's opposition to an alien world.[6]

4

The nature of idealism's appeal will perhaps be more precisely elucidated by an examination of the first fully developed system of the movement, the early thought of Schelling. If some repetition is involved, it might be pointed out that the piling of Ossa on Pelion was a favorite expository technique of idealism itself; the movement sought to convince as much by weight of mass and the creation of mood as by argument. Strictly speaking, it is impossible to talk of Schelling's "system." He refused, on philosophical principle, to have one; or rather he had a new one with each year and each new book. But he did have a set of underlying attitudes which stood in fairly constant relation to one another. This is particularly true of his Jena period, around the turn of the century, and in such works as the *Philosophy of Identity,* the *System of Transcendental Idealism,* and the *Philosophy of Nature,* which were what filtered through to Russia in the twenties and thirties.

Fundamentally Schelling's position is that of idealism in general, namely, what he called the "identity" of the unconscious world of nature and the conscious life of mind in the common *Grund* of the Absolute, of which man's intellect was the highest self-realization. The Absolute, moreover, was structured dialectically, or according to what Schelling called the laws of "polarity," taking an image from recent discoveries in magnetism. Within this general framework, however, he had certain emphases which were his own, and which are significant for understanding his impact. First of all, he insists more on the "identity" of nature and mind than on their separation; nature in effect becomes almost a projection of the self, just as the laws of its development are the unconscious forms of the life of mind. His notion of the dialectic, the laws of polarity, is as much a notion of complementarity or correspondence as of conflict. The correspondences between the ego and the external world are accented more than the antitheses which render them distinct. The effect of these emphases is to make his thought more "mind-centered," or subjective, than that, for instance, of Hegel. The center of gravity of his speculations is the knowing self, and both nature and the Absolute are considered primarily in their function as mirrors, almost extensions, of the self.

Concretely, for Schelling the whole of reality, or the Absolute, is analogous to a gigantic organism in a perpetual process of development from unconscious to conscious forms. Its life begins in the muteness of inorganic matter and rises upwards, by a process of struggle, tension, and self-transcendence, through organic nature to the pinnacle of all, man, in whom the entire process at last attains its goal of complete self-consciousness. The collective mind of mankind is in effect the mind of the universe, the conscious upper reaches of the whole constituted by nature, history, and the individual together. By the same token this collective mind is the consciousness of the Absolute, since the latter subsumes the life process of the universe. As for the precise nature of that elusive entity, the Absolute, it is greater than any individual mind, and in a rather mysterious way greater than the sum of all minds; but it is not over and above them, their creator and sustainer, as the God of traditional theism is the creator and sustainer of souls. Rather, the Absolute is completely immanent in mind and nature, since it is both the "identity" of the conscious and unconscious life of the universe and, in a more obscure manner, the "identity" of all individual minds. In reality, the Absolute is what mind throughout its entire Odyssey of self-realization in nature and man has been striving to become. Put in more simple language, for Schelling the highest value in life was self-consciousness, and the Absolute attained this, its fullest expression, only in the mind of man, whether collective or individual.[7]

This general view of the universe led to two major elaborations and one minor one. The first was the philosophy of nature, the *Naturphilosophie*, in the propagation of which Schelling was seconded by his contemporary Oken. Since nature was in effect a projection of mind and governed by the same laws, it was like a mirror in which the ego saw itself reflected. In fact the mind understood itself most easily, not in itself, but in its "identity" with nature. Thus the understanding of nature was the first form of self-consciousness for man, as well as the initial revelation of the Idea. The study of natural science, therefore, in the poetic and analogical sense understood by Schelling, was the cornerstone of all knowledge, and the first step on the way to the mind's identification with the Absolute.[8]

The second major elaboration of Schelling's thought concerned the highest form of knowledge, the mind's direct knowledge of itself, where the ego attained to full realization of the Absolute. Religion and philosophy were obvious forms of this knowledge, but the highest form of all was art, in which the individual subsumed the life of his nation or age. Such total self-realization was not given to everyone, however; it was accessible only to rare spirits, the elect of the Idea, called geniuses. Genius, manifesting itself in the act of artistic creation, was the highest self-realization both of the Absolute and of the individual ego, and the supreme sacrament of the Schellingian pantheism. The genius was a very God, and the act of artistic creation the Nirvana of the new religion. Yet artistic creation should not be understood too literally as achievement in poetry, music, or painting only. These indeed were its highest forms, but any great act of self-realization — a magnificent deed, a great idea, a noble friendship, a lofty love — was also an artistic creation. Friendship and love in particular were akin to art. As Dante had his Beatrice, Schelling had his Caroline Michaelis, and his love for her was almost as great a realization of the Absolute as was his philosophy.[9]

Finally, history, as the cumulative record of man's self-consciousness, was a mirror of the Absolute. It was the collective life of the species struggling upwards from ignorance and barbarism to self-knowledge in philosophy and art. It was also the collective life of nations, each with its own individual word of genius to speak. This third aspect of his thought Schelling emphasized much less than the other two.[10] But this was not so of his Russian disciples. The philosophy of history was elevated by them to an equal rank with the *Naturphilosophie* and the philosophy of art, and it was in these three forms together that Schelling's thought dominated Russian intellectual life in the thirties.

Psychologically, Schelling presents a particularly egocentric and facilely optimistic statement of the general position of idealism. No other modern philosopher (save of course Fichte) goes farther in exalting the importance of the individual. The whole of external nature has in effect become a projection of the self; the Absolute itself is no more than the highest manifestation of the creative ego. No matter how far the ego ranges in its voyage of auto-affirmation it is forever brought back to itself, the alpha and omega of all reality.

Yet at the same time few individualisms are more abstract and lonely. If all reality finds its focus in the ego, by the same token the ego realizes itself alone, in its own mind, which in the last analysis means in fantasy. It is significant that Schelling saw the highest forms of contact with the Absolute in actions that the self can perform alone, through imagination — the "pure" thought of philosophy and the artistic creation of the individual genius. The summits of "identification" with the Absolute are solitary ones, where the ego breathes the rarefied and dizzying atmosphere of its own dreams. And this is true even though in Schelling's system the individual genius was conceived, formally and technically, as no more than the oracle of some collective consciousness, whether of a people, a nation, or a civilization. But the anthropomorphism of the "objective" *Grund* that Schelling gives to the self is most tellingly revealed in his principal effort to break out of isolation, the *Naturphilosophie*. Even in this domain which, more ostensibly than art or philosophy, relates to a reality outside the self, Schelling's sense of estrangement from the external world is betrayed by the extravagance of his protestations of harmony with it, which again are pushed to an assertion of identity. The self seeks simultaneously to divine the pattern of nature by exploring the structure of mind and to discover the key to its own identity by probing the structure of nature. Thus nature is not only related to the self, it is virtually annexed to it. But since this feat is achieved quite "transcendentally" — or, in the language of an empiricist, through the imagination — the ego is once again thrown in on itself and remains as isolated from the real world as before.

Needless to say, there is much in common psychologically (although by no means doctrinally) between Schelling's idealism and certain forms of religious mysticism. Neither is concerned with *knowledge* as an end in itself; rather, for both knowledge is a means to what the mystic would call "beatitude," and the idealist "harmony," "identity," or in Russian "reconciliation" (*primirenie*). Hence the relative indifference of the idealist to problems of epistemology: these had been taken care of once and for all by Kant. So the post-Kantians dispensed with any searching into the conditions of man's knowledge and proceeded immediately to metaphysical construction. It may be noticed from the above that their doctrines are involved almost exclusively with metaphysics and in general with those parts of philosophy which are the nearest to the questions of religion, and almost entirely unoccupied by epistemology and those parts of philosophy which come the nearest to the concerns of science. In effect, idealism tends to be a secular answer to needs more usually met by faith than by philosophy; or it may be considered a school of an Alexandrine or Neoplatonic sort far more than a rationalism in the main line of modern speculation from Descartes to Kant.

The parallel between idealism and religion, however, should not be pushed too far. Although idealism attempts to meet many needs of the religious temperament, it is, after all, founded on the concept of a divinized man rather than of a transcendent God, and this mixture of similarity with and difference from religion is both a strength and a weakness. The strength of idealism is that it offers not mere knowledge but communion with the cosmos; it pretends to satisfy the needs of the whole man, not just of his mind, by making mind the essence of the universe. The weakness of idealism is that it is a supposedly rational explanation of a purely this-worldly reality, and hence exposes itself to logical criticism and empirical verification in ways that religion does not. Its promises can be revealed by experience to be true or false, whereas those of religion are invulnerable to the same test; nor is human wishful thinking so strong an armor, psychologically, as supernatural hope. Metaphysical Absolutes, therefore, are not as long-lived as real Gods; and in the last analysis, idealism has the worst of two possible worlds. By attempting to provide the satisfactions of both it very quickly falls somewhere between the two, for it offers neither the certitude of positive science nor the serenity of religious faith. Yet for a time, given particular kinds of frustration, it can bring solace indeed to distraught intellectuals for whom neither straight religion nor straight science is enough.

To this must be added what has already been said above regarding Schelling's egocentrism. The self-importance he accorded the individual was too great to withstand the slightest shock administered by reality; and his sense of identity with the external world was equally vulnerable to the same menace. Both were illusions which could flourish only in a hothouse, such as a German university, or a more provincial Russian version of the same. But even there they could not flourish for long. If a harsh world did not intrude to destroy them, in the end they would fail, by their very unreality, to satisfy creatures of flesh and blood. Only the excessively cerebral, or the young and untried, could find comfort in such self-generated gratification. By its very nature Schelling's idealism could be no more than a flower of the May; but while climatic and other conditions were right, it could be consoling indeed.

5

The climate which produced post-Kantian idealism, as well as the romanticism closely allied with it, was that of the German university world and its literary fringes between 1794 and 1806, that is, between the height of the French Revolution and the battle of Jena, or, in terms of intellectual history, between Fichte's *Grundlage der gesamten Wissenschaftslehre* in 1794 and Hegel's *Phenomenology* in 1807. Without exception all the essential innovations of romanticism and of post-Kantian idealism date from this period, although in numerous cases, notably Schelling and Hegel, the productive career, as well as its influence, continued much longer. The whole of Europe was in a turmoil of activity greater than any that recent history had known; only in Germany was there no other outlet for talent, energy, and ambition than in thought or art. Nor was any class of intellectuals in Europe smaller or less integrated with society than that of Germany. These intellectuals might have the universities and an occasional princely court, but their influence stopped where the world of action began. Society was neither democratic nor fast-changing enough to provide opportunities for achievement in the world at large. In London the penniless and pushing Fichte might have risen to significance in a bank or in political journalism; in Paris he might have become a tribune of the people or a prince of the empire; but in Germany the only market place was the market place of ideas, and the only battlefield that of the schools. He and his kind were driven to seek there what self-realization they could, and to sublimate their remaining longings into a philosophical view of the individual which accorded those gratifications the real world denied.[11]

This situation had, of course, existed in Germany before the Revolution. The primacy of thought, art, and the inner life was dogma for Goethe and Schiller long before idealism and the brothers Schlegel. Nor had pantheism as a device for achieving harmony with the world outside the study walls waited for Schelling. Both Goethe and Schiller express strong pantheistic sentiments; indeed they prepared the way for what came after 1795. But the Revolution heightened the German intellectual's sense of alienation from the world of action. It rendered more imperative the creation of ideal consolations for the barrenness of life, and it increased the need to declare these substitutes absolute, to claim for them equality with, indeed superiority to, satisfactions in the world of matter and fact. Thus, after 1795 the German intellectual was led to systematize what had previously been a literary attitude, and to turn into a conscious metaphysic what had only been a state of mind. Post-Kantian philosophy is largely the aesthetic pantheism of Goethe and Schiller pushed to its ultimate conclusion and abstraction. Nor were the contemporaries entirely unaware of what they were doing. In a famous phrase of Jean-Paul Richter, the French had the empire of the land, the English the empire of the sea, and the Germans the empire of the air. But the empire of the air, as Hegel says somewhere, is a world where men appear to walk on their heads; to which it might be added that they *do* in fact walk on their heads, inverting the common-sense order of the universe so as to make the mind of the self the axis of the All.

These considerations make it now appropriate to attempt an answer to certain questions with which this chapter began: why in Central and Eastern Europe should idealism become the vehicle of movements, such as nationalism, which elsewhere did without it? In the static and authoritarian societies of these lands men were not only alienated as individuals, they were frustrated as classes and nations as well. More often than not they longed for self-affirmation, either as a group against groups that stood over them or as a nation against neighbors who were politically more powerful or culturally richer than they; and frequently they longed for both things at once. Hence their primary desire for individual self-realization could easily fuse with an aspiration to belong to a class or a nation that was in some way exalted. That is, their social or national consciousness was simply another, more generalized, form of their frustrated desire for personality. And the spectacle of the combination of individuality with "belonging" that was in the process of achievement across the Rhine only made these desires all the more acute. Consequently, the pantheism of their philosophy, born originally of their alienation as individuals, could also become the vehicle for a cramped nationalism or an irritated social consciousness. Both these urges, since they were frustrated in the present, could find expression only in contemplation of the march of history, in past and future alike — in other words, in historicism. Thus idealism logically became the ideology both of nationalism, as the cult of the organic community of the "people" (whether defined conservatively or radically), and of historicism.

Furthermore, all these aspirations converged on the Absolute. It was because men felt isolated as individuals that they first had need of an all-embracing Absolute which would realize their every hope. But since they also felt weak as classes or nations this need was vastly increased, and the Absolute became a kind of historical Providence, either social, or national, or both, which would accomplish for them what they could not accomplish themselves. Since the Absolute was very near to the idea of God, it could also lend comfort to a revival of religion, a task in which it was aided by idealism's strong emphasis on intuition. Finally, because of this same apotheosis of intuition, idealism could lend a helping hand to poetic inspiration — the speaking of the inner voice of literary romanticism — and German romanticism was certainly more extreme than French or English. In short, idealism was ready-made to receive the accretions of romanticism and of a return to religion no less than of historicism, nationalism, or a sense of the collective. Thus, everywhere east of the Rhine each of these movements came to reinforce, and was reinforced by, the lonely ego's self-affirmation in the ideal, which was the philosophical core of the movement.

Emphasis on the accretions to idealism, however, especially the coupling of religion with nationalism and historicism, can give the movement too conservative a cast. In conclusion to this discussion a word must therefore be said about the politics, or rather the political implications, of idealism. One of the commonplaces which Marx introduced into circulation (though he did not invent it, since it was the general property of Left Hegelianism) is the notion that idealism is an ideology of the Right, or at most the Center, either reactionary or highly moderate in its political uses. For Marx idealism is an "ideological" obfuscation of real issues, designed, whether consciously or not, to divert man's attention from the world of fact to an imaginary world of ideal essences, and hence blunt his will to change. It is a sort of opium of the intellectuals, just as religion is the opium of the masses.

Although this is largely true for the idealism of which Marx was chiefly thinking, namely that of Hegel's Berlin period, it is much too simple a generalization when applied to German idealism as a whole. Kant, if he is to be included in the genealogy at all, was distinctly on the "left" of his age and a proponent of progress and enlightenment. As we have seen, Schiller, so important for the psychological preparation of post-Kantianism, was a would-be liberal turned pantheist *faute de mieux*. Even more clearly Fichte was a hyper-individualist and a conscious political liberal who expressed himself in metaphysics for want of a more satisfactory outlet, and the early Schelling was in much the same category (though in later life he fully merited Marx's strictures against ideology in general). Though Schelling never concerned himself directly with politics, the writings of his Jena period can only be understood as the apotheosis of the value of the individual, and hence as the projection of an intense but submerged desire for personal freedom. This individualism is, to be sure, transferred to the plane of metaphysics and the ideal; but by comparison with Hegel's strong emphasis on the collective, the objective and the "general" — in a word, society — it approaches sedition. Idealism can be sublimated liberalism, founded on an almost anarchistic individualism, just as easily as it can be a conservative rationalization of the status quo.

Sublimated liberalism, however, is not the same as the real thing. Like Schiller's aesthetic utopia, it is an alienated, and hence a highly equivocal position. The individual seeks self-fulfillment in a purely cerebral existence and not in the real world. Thus the danger is ever present that life in the ideal may become positive acceptance of the world as it stands. In fact, this is what happened to German idealism by the time of Hegel, and, indeed, what eventually became of Schelling himself. But before this occurs an important difference remains — important at least when one is close to the phenomenon, for in the world of idealism, where from afar all seems black, it is essential to distinguish shades of gray. On the one hand, the early Schelling's encomiums to "genius" and the ego's free creativity do not correspond to a mood of quietism, as does Hegel's emphasis on the necessary, objective order of the universe. But neither do they fit a mood which might make barricades rise tomorrow. Rather, Schelling is a way-station where frustrated yet optimistic souls may find temporary sustenance while awaiting something more real and nearer the heart's liberal desire — either that or giving up in despair.

To adapt a pair of terms from the history of Hegelianism, Schelling lent himself to both a "Left" and a "Right" construction; in content he was radical, in form he was quietistic, and his doctrine could evolve in either direction with equal ease. Like the whole of idealism he was ambiguous — or dialectical — either Right or Left, or both, all at the same time. And this ambiguity was the faithful mirror of men's confused aspirations in that realm *par excellence* of what Hegel called the "Unhappy Consciousness" which begins at the Rhine.

6

In Russia after 1825 the gentry elite and the university intellectuals found themselves in a situation similar to that of sensitive Germans just after the French Revolution. They experienced the same isolation, the same lack of an organic tie with society, and an identical inability to influence the world of action. Their situation was, if anything, even more desperate. Their numbers were smaller and, unlike the Germans, they had dared to act but failed. At the same time they lacked an intellectual tradition of their own to furnish answers to their dilemma. So they threw themselves on the consolations offered by Schelling in order to maintain faith in their worth as individuals, and to gain a sense of belonging to the Absolute if not to the Russia of Nicholas I.

Turgenev, who knew of what he spoke since in youth he had lived through the idealist dream, described its effect in *Rudin*, with Bakunin undoubtedly in mind as his hero.

When we heard Rudin for the first time we thought we had at last got a hold of it, that general link — we felt the curtain was raised at last. Of course, they were not his ideas — what matter — at least a harmonious system began to reign over all that we did know; all that had been higgledy-piggledy was reassembled, harmonized, and before our eyes grew like a building; the world was a lighter place, there was a spirit abroad. Nothing was any longer senseless or fortuitous; in everything there showed a rational indispensability, a reasonable beauty; everything acquired a lucid sense which was at the same time mysterious; every individual phenomenon in life rang harmoniously; and we ourselves, infused with what I might call a religious awe of wonder, our hearts fluttering sweetly, felt as it were living vessels of eternal truth, its instruments, directly connected with something tremendous.[12]

Ogarev, after his graduation from the university, worked long at something he called his "system," but which in reality was simply a recast of Schelling. The chief monument to these labors is a document written in French and entitled *Profession de foi*, undoubtedly in memory of Rousseau's Savoyard Vicar. It concludes with an item called "Ma prière."

Etre absolu! Gloire à toi! parce que tu es.
Gloire à toi parce que tu es dans l'univers et l'univers en toi!
Gloire à toi parce que tu es dans l'humanité et l'humanité en toi!
Gloire à toi parce que tu es en moi et moi en toi — et je tâcherai de
marcher dans tes voies et d'accomplir ce que tu m'auras ordonné.
Gloire à toi! Amen! [13]

The self, humanity, and the universe are fused in a single harmonious
whole, of which the self is obviously the highest expression. This is the
idealist formula at its nearest to religion — though for Ogarev it was
still also "science" — and he has quite rightly framed the conclusion
of his system as a prayer rather than a proposition. The list of such
examples could easily be lengthened by quotations from such figures
as Bakunin, Stankevich, Belinski, Constantine Aksakov, or indeed most
of the important intellectuals of the thirties.

In such an atmosphere Herzen could hardly have escaped contamina-
tion; yet this is very nearly what he claims. Later in life, whether deliberately or through forgetfulness, Herzen greatly played down the
role of Schelling and idealism in his early development. He was either
ironical or silent on both subjects. In *My Past and Thoughts* he set his
circle in sharp contrast to that of Stankevich. "They did not like our
almost exclusively political orientation, we did not like their almost
exclusively speculative orientation. They considered us *frondeurs* and
Frenchmen, we considered them sentimentalists and Germans." [14] The
dichotomy is far too simple; Herzen, as so often in his memoirs, is no
doubt trying to make himself look redder in youth than he really was.
Yet his words have been taken up by many commentators and the general
histories, and Herzen is often presented as an exception to the idealism
of the period, with his interest in politics, socialism and the natural sciences.[15] Differences there were between the two circles, and mainly over
politics, but they existed within a common framework of Schellingian
idealism and German "sentimentality." To take due account of both the
similarities and the contrasts between Herzen and his contemporaries,
one may best situate him on the far Left of Russian Schellingianism,
though still well within the movement as a whole. It will be the task of the
remainder of this chapter, as well as of most of those immediately following it, to reconstruct the role of idealism during his young manhood.[16]

7

Herzen first became acquainted with Schelling, at least in a vague
way, a year before entering the university. In the fall of 1828 he wrote to
Tatiana that one of his tutors, a graduate of the university, had brought
him Schelling: "He [the tutor] holds him in high regard, but understands

little, believing mostly on the word of Michael Gregorevich Pavlov." [17]
What work of Schelling Herzen first read we are not informed; but
given the interests of Pavlov — obviously the tutor's source — it was
most probably the *Naturphilosophie*. Nor should we be deceived by
Herzen's scorn for taking things second hand. Although with his excellent
knowledge of German he undoubtedly looked into Schelling at this time,
most of his early information probably derived from popularizations:
either those of Pavlov and his colleagues in their various periodicals, or
Victor Cousin's simplified adaptations of idealism, which were readily
available and very popular in Russia, both in the original and in translation for the highbrow Moscow journals.[18] Whatever his source, on entering the university Herzen was already something of an adept of Schelling's philosophy of nature.

This orientation was more than a question of influence, however, for
Herzen came to Schelling already an idealistic pantheist in spirit. In the
summer of 1828, before he made any mention of reading Schelling or his
adaptors, Herzen wrote to his cousin.

Sometimes I lie with a book on a hill, and how free I feel myself there! Before
me stretches out an infinite expanse, and it seems to me that this distance is
my body, and I hear its pulse, as in a living organism. Sometimes I seem to
myself to be completely lost in this infinity, a leaf on an enormous tree, but
this infinity does not oppress me. Is it possible that the sun's ray, that glance of
love of God the Father on the Son, is dead? Is it possible that this river, moving
with each ripple, is dead? And has not life raised up the mountains, and did it
not furrow the valleys with ravines, with trees; has it not striven to raise itself
ever upwards, like a butterfly taking flight from the earth, and does it not come
to contemplate itself in me? Great Spirit arraying itself in flesh, I pray to thee
warmly and passionately! [19]

Herzen was only sixteen when these lines were written and certainly a
novice in formal philosophy. Yet the essence of Schelling's egocentric
pantheism is here, and not merely as an intellectual conviction, but as
a deeply felt attitude towards his relation to the world. Schiller's *Philosophical Letters,* Goethe's *Elective Affinities,* perhaps some articles in the
Moscow press or conversations with his tutor, had undoubtedly prepared
him for such ideas. But his sentiment of union with the cosmos and of the
indwelling of the Great Spirit in himself derived first of all from his own
need for release from the emptiness of reality. Schelling soon aided in
articulating this mood, thereby reinforcing it; but he did not create it in
Herzen.

At the same time that Herzen first came in contact with the *Naturphilosophie* he was subjected to a diametrically opposite influence. This
influence was exercised by a cousin, Alexis Alexandrovich Iakovlev, called
in Herzen's memoirs "the Chemist." Like Herzen he was an illegitimate

son, the offspring of the second Iakovlev brother by one of his serfs, and, as has already been noted, he had been adopted and made his father's sole heir when the old man was on his deathbed, in order to cheat the remaining Iakovlev brothers of their expected inheritance. After his father's death, the Chemist lived in retirement in his Moscow mansion, with his aged peasant mother as his only companion, and devoted himself to the study of the natural sciences, particularly — in spite of his nickname — biology. Misanthropic and eccentric, he lived in solitude and disorder amidst his scientific instruments, having no interest in life but the study of nature.[20]

Herzen was no doubt first drawn to his cousin as a fellow sufferer from Iakovlev caprice. This feeling of kinship was increased when the Chemist lightened the burden of his serfs by cutting in half the *obrok*, or money dues, they owed their master. But Herzen did not find in his cousin a fellow liberal; instead he encountered an exclusive dedication to science and a scorn for all politics. The pair could still meet on the common ground of science, however, for which Herzen too was beginning to develop an enthusiasm, inspired by the *Naturphilosophie,* even though this was not the science of his cousin, who was a convinced materialist and an empiricist after the manner of the later Enlightenment. But because the Chemist felt that Herzen's interest in science was serious, he took his young cousin in hand and tried to save him from his idealistic misconceptions. Long and lively debates ensued. The Chemist urged Herzen to abandon the "empty" study of literature and his "uselessly dangerous" interest in politics. He castigated religion and attacked all philosophy as "twaddle." In particular he poured scorn on the new idealism; he considered the transformationist biologist and one of the saints of the *Naturphilosophie,* Geoffroy-Saint-Hilaire, "a mystic," and felt that Oken was "simply mad." The only sound view of the universe was the materialism of late eighteenth-century France; human impulses were entirely an affair of "organization, circumstances and in general of the nervous system"; and the Chemist was fond of citing Laplace's famous remark to Napoleon that in science God was an unnecessary hypothesis.[21]

Herzen was both shocked and fascinated by such views. There was much in the Chemist's castigation of mysticism and metaphysics that was congenial to him, and it was a position which would one day be his own. But he was too deeply committed to idealism for reasons that had nothing to do with science to allow himself to be convinced. Although he accepted his cousin's "personal guidance" and his books, the "speech of Cuvier on geological change and the book of Candole on vegetal organography," and made use of his "excellent collections, instruments and herbarium," [22] he could not bring himself to accept his cousin's hard-headed philosophy, though he constantly came back for more and seemed to enjoy being disturbed by such a bold materialism.

Nonetheless, the Chemist made his point, at least in part. His influence, added to that of the *Naturphilosophie*, "determined" Herzen's choice of the Physico-mathematical Faculty (the faculty of natural sciences) at the university in spite of the fact that, according to Herzen's own admission, he never possessed any great ability for mathematics.[23] With his talents a more likely choice would have been the Faculty of Philology and History, where most of his friends, including Ogarev, were enrolled. But the challenge presented by the Chemist had convinced Herzen that the study of nature alone provided a sound method for answering the great questions of life. At the same time, in true idealist fashion he believed that the study of nature was also the study of man, of history and the Absolute. Nevertheless, however ambiguous, this involvement in science from the beginning gave Herzen's idealism a more down-to-earth character than that of the majority of his contemporaries. Though he could not but be an idealist, he at least had to grapple with the problem of understanding the world in its most concrete form, where the fantasy of idealism was counteracted in some measure by the rigor of scientific observation. When the time came to cast idealism off he could be more lucid about its defects than most of his peers, and he would have another training to fall back on. In this too the Chemist had made his point, if only for the future.

Once at the university, Herzen fell completely under the influence of the *Naturphilosophie*. The great personality in the Faculty of Natural Sciences was Pavlov, who, though technically professor of "physics, mineralogy and agriculture," in fact taught philosophy. The chair of philosophy proper had been abolished shortly after the accession of Nicholas, but Pavlov, together with his Schellingian colleagues, Nadezhdin, Davydov, and Pogodin, more than made up the lack in their courses on other subjects. Pavlov used his lectures on science as a vehicle for metaphysics, and as an exponent of the *Naturphilosophie* was a master, explaining his foggy subject with "a plastic clarity" not native to it but which was admirably suited to making it comprehensible to novices.[24]

In later life Herzen passed over his relations with Pavlov in almost total silence. While at the university, though, he wrote that he "studied assiduously" with him,[25] and their closeness was such that Pavlov published an article by Herzen in the *Atheneum*.[26] More important still, everything Herzen wrote at the university is thoroughly in the spirit of Schelling, as preached by Pavlov, who expounded a somewhat simplified and more coherent version of the original. It is probable that Herzen continued, as before the university, to get his Schelling largely second hand, whether from Pavlov or from Cousin's *Introduction à l'histoire de la philosophie* and his *Fragments philosophiques*.[27]

8

Herzen's university writings are concerned primarily with the theme of biological becoming, the universe as organism. They include his dissertation, *An Analytical Exposition of the Solar System According to Copernicus,* and several articles published in university journals, of which the most interesting are *On the Indivisible in the Vegetable Kingdom* and *On the Place of Man in Nature.* In all of these writings Herzen displays a good knowledge of the serious scientific literature of the period in natural history, especially works which announced the idea of evolution. He went more deeply into books first revealed to him by the Chemist: Cuvier's *Discours sur les révolutions de la surface du globe et sur les changements qu'elles ont produit sur le règne animal* and Candole's *Traité sur l'organographie des plantes.* He knew his Linnaeus; he had some familiarity with the writings of Erasmus Darwin, the grandfather of Charles and to a point his ideological predecessor; and had read the less reputable Oken.[28] He was abreast of the debate between the followers of Cuvier, who held to the immutability of species, and Geoffroy-Saint-Hilaire, the transformationist or evolutionist; and of course he took the side of the latter, since the idea of continuous evolution was necessary to illustrate the progressive unfolding of the Absolute.[29] In short, Herzen's scientific training lay essentially in the raw materials for the biology of the *Natur-philosophie.*

On a more general level he indulged in all the school's clichés about the organic development of the universe from inanimate matter through animate nature to self-consciousness in man. The eighteenth century, with its "cold" materialism, its "narrow" empiricism, and the evil authors of all these things, the French, were castigated in the best romantic fashion. "Only look at nature as it came forth from their hands. It is no longer true nature, full of life and beauty, breathing freedom, manifesting the idea of God: in a word the nature of the mountains and the ocean, the nature of storms and the beauty of maidens. No, it is a cold, dead corpse, cut up on the anatomist's table." [30] And man, "what did they make of man? An animal!" [31] "In what manner is man distinguished from the animals? *Self-knowledge, thought. Cogito, ergo sum!* said the great forefather of modern philosophy." [32] Mind, consciousness, the idea, were the principles of all being and the culmination of nature's development. Herzen carried the attack over into method. Empiricism, in spite of the wonderful results it had produced since it was first advocated by Bacon, was incomplete. To give true knowledge it must be wedded to imagination, insight and a

philosophic sense of the deeper meaning of things. ". . . it is a mistake to
consider empiricism and idealism as different methods: they are but the
extremes of one unitary method, which do not exist in separation one from
another. . . . They are but parts of a unified system of knowledge." [33]
It is only in this unification that "natural history rises to the high level of
science." [34]

Derivative as all this is, it is crucial for the development of Herzen's
mentality. First of all, though he never seriously occupied himself with
natural science in later life, the idea of the world as biological becoming
remained, in one form or another, a cardinal component of his thought
for most of his career. What is even more important, he carried into all his
subsequent thinking on politics and history the method of thought developed in contact with the *Naturphilosophie*. He always looked on his
political and historical thinking as "scientific" in the same way that he
considered the *Naturphilosophie* "scientific." It was "science" of a very
special sort, of course. The word *"nauka"* (science) was always used by
Herzen and his generation to mean both positive science and metaphysics.
German idealistic philosophy was almost invariably referred to as German
"nauka," and was considered to be the crowning achievement of all individual sciences. Moreover, this kind of *"nauka"* was not different in nature from the established branches of natural science it sought to syn-
thesize. Schelling and Hegel were *"nauka"* no less than Newton and
Laplace; indeed they were *"nauka"* of an even higher sort. And what
Herzen called the "method of idealism," but which is more accurately described as intuition, was just as valid a part of "scientific"
method as what he called "empiricism," or what is more usually understood to be the method of the natural sciences.

Specifically, belief in "idealism" as a part of "scientific" method meant
an education in wishful thinking. It has been said that Schelling was the
first school of logic and systematic thought for Russian minds.[35] Logic,
however, is not quite the right word. Schelling was certainly the first
school of abstract philosophy for Russians; but the result of his teaching
was facility more in the construction of resplendent visions of the meaning of it all, or pseudo-rational utopias, than in logic. There was a logical
illusion, of course, in the neatness with which the ideal construct was
endowed and with which all the scattered parts of experience were assembled in one harmonious whole, but in reality Schelling's "logic" was
the arbitrary stringing together of whatever ideas the thinker wished, or
needed, to believe in. This was only natural in a system where each
"genius," so to speak, created his own universe. Heine, with his customary
lucidity about the romantic mists in which he was raised, wrote:

Schelling himself tells us it was only a school such as existed among the
ancient poets that he desired to found, a school of poetry in which no one was

bound to accept a particular doctrine or to submit to a special discipline, but one in which each was to obey the Idea and to manifest it in his own manner. He might also have said that he wished to found a school of prophets, where the inspired should begin to prophesy as fancy moved them, and in whatever dialect they pleased . . . and philosophy had its great day of Pentecost.[36]

The law of "logic" underlying these prophecies was in effect thinking by poetic analogy, and this is what gives the illusion of "science" to idealism as a style of thought. Again to have recourse to Heine:

It seems to me often necessary, in reading his [Schelling's] works, to distinguish where thought ceases and poetry begins . . . for he lives in a world of intuition; he does not feel at home on the cold heights of logic; he stretches forth eager hands towards the flowery valley of symbolism, and his philosophic strength lies in the art of construction.[37]

Nothing is easier for novices in abstract thought than thinking by analogy; nor does any device make the universe seem easier to comprehend. It is a "method" that admits of no permanent enigmas, which leaves no areas of uncertainty or doubt. It is, in short, a device for people who cannot afford to face reality as it is and yet who are in a hurry to make the world over in the image of the heart's desire, a short cut to understanding and to an illusive feeling of mastery over experience. It was this habit of thought which was Schelling's and idealism's ineradicable legacy to Herzen.

9

There were, however, limits to his acceptance of Schelling, as well as important nuances in his approach to the master, which set Herzen off from the average idealist of the thirties. First of all, though he accepted most of Schelling's doctrines individually, and even the general spirit of his thought, Herzen could never quite bring himself to accept these doctrines as a formal system; and he never called himself a Schellingian. In particular, at least during this period, he always refused to include God and the idea of religion among the components of the Absolute; he wished his idealism to be as naturalistic and as rational as possible. Nor at this time did he overflow in "prayers" to the Absolute, as did Stankevich, and even Ogarev. Rather his position was that of the unbaptized believer. He needed idealism, for there was nothing else to give coherence to life; yet at the same time he obscurely felt it was a trap, a refusal to face the real world. But this ambiguity is the essence of what has been called here "Left Schellingianism."

When in 1833 Ogarev announced his full adherence to Schelling Herzen answered:

You have become a Schellingian. This, indeed, is not bad, but only in part, for some sort of [practical] application is necessary. . . . Schelling is a great poet; he understood the needs of the century and created, not a soulless eclecticism [i.e. Cousin], but a living philosophy, founded on one principle, from which everything harmoniously develops. Fichte [i.e. individualism] and Spinoza [i.e. pantheism] — these are the extremes united by Schelling. But we must go farther, modify his teaching, throw out the *ipse dixit* and accept only the method. The cause: Schelling ended in mystic Catholicism, Hegel in despotism! Fichte, that *régime de terreur* of philosophy (as Quinet calls him), at least understood the worth of man.[38]

The philosophical level of this pronouncement is obviously not high, and Herzen is, as so often, speaking with an authoritative air of things about which he knew very little. He most certainly had read no Hegel, almost certainly no Fichte, and by no means all of Schelling; the reference to Quinet indicates once again how dependent he was on popularizations and the climate of the age. Nonetheless, the judgment expressed is significant. Herzen was suspicious of philosophies which led to conservative political conclusions, however much he might be attracted to idealism as a method. This, more than anything else, left him with a residual suspicion of Schelling which the apolitical thirties as a whole did not share.

As we shall see, it was only after the university and under the pressure of exile that these reticences for a time disappeared. This is the period when Ogarev went over to Schelling completely and developed the "system" previously referred to. At the same time Herzen went almost as far. In 1839 he wrote to a friend: "Schelling I read himself. . . . What enchanted me most is his Pantheism — his Tri-hypostatic God — as Idea, as Mankind, as Nature. As possibility, as object, as self-knowledge. What cannot one construct out of such a principle!" [39] Indeed, one could construct whatever one wished, a different thing every day, and it would all be "science." Here Herzen is at last speaking in the pure idiom of Stankevich. Even at this, his fullest acceptance of idealism, however, he never construed it in a politically conservative sense, as did most of Stankevich's friends. Herzen remained on the Left of Russian Schellingianism in all phases of his involvement with the movement.

But "Left Schellingianism" was not just a question of politics or religion; it was also a question of ideological emphasis within "science" itself, and here too Herzen found a tone of his own among his contemporaries. One example of this we have already seen, in his attraction to the philosophy of nature. In the jargon of the day, this was the most "objective" side of Schelling, or that which most strongly called attention to a reality outside the self; and it is significant that Herzen first approached Schelling from this side. In this he offers a significant contrast with the circle of Stankevich, which emphasized the more "subjective" aspects of Schelling — ideas in themselves, the philosophy of art, and inner perfection.[40] From the beginning, Herzen's constant effort was to make of idealism, insofar as possible, a fermentation in the real world, and not just to seek in it a refuge from reality.

Another indication of Herzen's "Left" construction of idealism was his interest in the philosophy of history, again a study directed toward a more "objective" and concrete manifestation of the Absolute. The philosophy of history or culture was, of course, one of the possible divisions of self-knowledge for Schelling, but he left it more as a suggestion than as an elaborated doctrine. The cultivated minority of Russia, however, concerned for their identity as a group no less than as individuals, seized on this suggestion and exploited it as one of the principal branches of philosophy.[41] This task began with the introduction of Schelling into Russia, in the days of the "Lovers of Wisdom." By the time Herzen entered the university "historiosophical" speculation about the destiny of mankind, and of Russia in particular, had become an accepted philosophical occupation. In 1832 it bore its first significant fruits in Ivan Kireevski's review, *The European*, and his famous article, "The Nineteenth Century" (which brought about the closing of the review by the censorship after only two numbers), the first original inquiry into Russia's historical destiny inspired by the new idealism.

Herzen in adolescence had been an avid reader of history, and at the university, in spite of his preoccupation with science, this interest continued. By the end of his course, in 1833, his letters contain enthusiastic references to Michelet, Augustin Thierry, Jean-Baptiste Say, Malthus, Montesquieu, Speranski's *Historical Inquiry into the Code* (*Istoricheskoe issledovanie o Svode*) — which led him "to look into Bentham" — works on Roman history and law, and, perhaps most significant of all, Vico and Herder.[42] How much of all this Herzen actually read, or how thoroughly he read it, it is impossible to say. Given his tendency to display his learning he probably read less than he implied in his letters. Whatever he did read, however, he immediately worked into an all-embracing metaphysical scheme of history. Indeed, by his last year at the university, discovering the key to the meaning of history became his principal "scientific" occupation, largely replacing the study of nature, however much he continued to revere the latter as a school of method.

His first essay in "historiosophy" represents an application of Schelling's categories to the problem of Russia's national destiny, and in particular to the question of Russia's relation to Europe. In substance and approach it is close to Kireevski's article of the previous year.[43] Though there is no direct evidence that Herzen read "The Nineteenth Century" at this time, it is highly probable that the relatively momentous police action it called forth attracted his attention, and in the small world of intellectual Moscow, once his attention was aroused he could hardly fail to learn of Kireevski's ideas, if only at second hand. In any event, his own article represents a more juvenile version of Kireevski's, and as such is one of the first crude attempts of Russian idealism to work out a national philosophy of history.

Herzen's article, written in 1833 but never published, was entitled "28 January," after the anniversary of the death of Peter the Great. Its purpose was to define the laws of history in general and to determine their application to Russia in particular. The laws of history turn out to be the same as those of nature and, like them, a reflexion of the harmony of the divine Idea underlying all being. *"That which is manifested in the boundless expanses of the heavenly systems is repeated in the development of humanity, whose orbit is also calculated."* [44] Herzen drew this proof by analogy from the reading in astronomy he was then doing for his dissertation on Copernicus. Though he was somewhat disturbed by what this sweeping assertion did to free will, in which as a libertarian he also felt it necessary to believe, he was even more enraptured by the majesty of human destiny developing logically through the ages. "Though the human will is not enchained in mathematical laws, it is difficult here to admit arbitrariness, while observing the harmonious development of humanity, in which each individual will, so it seems, is swallowed up in the general movement, exactly as the movement of the earth carries along with it all the bodies located on it." [45] But in the end he has the satisfactions of both free will and historical pattern; for in history, as in nature, there are comets — grandiose exceptions to law which nevertheless move against a background of logical order. "The development of humanity demands, nay more, consecrates certain people for the lofty task of leading progress. Let us bow before them, but let us not forget that they are the instruments of ideas, which even without them — perhaps in another fashion, perhaps later — would have developed just the same." [46]

Such a historical "comet" was Peter the Great, and the "idea" he embodied was the integration of Russia with Europe. Even before Peter Russia was potentially a part of Europe. This was true because the Slavs were heirs of the Roman Empire, albeit of its Eastern half, and, even more important, because they shared "the common bond of Christianity." [47] Furthermore, Europe was one "living organism, having its own life, its own end." In other words, Russia, though seemingly backward and benighted, was, underneath, of the same essence as Europe and potentially capable of equaling the freer, more civilized nations of the West. The common "end" of Russia and Europe, moreover, was the development of the "civic virtues" inherited from Greece and Rome and of the "lofty principles of Christianity," [48] both of which meant, in more direct language, personal dignity and freedom. Thus the historical march of the Idea furnished the hope for Russia's future which current politics could not provide. It was a line of argument, and a set of historical examples, which Herzen, and later the Westerners in general, were to use over and over again.

In addition, the life principle of the historical "organism" was "opposition" and conflict, or the dialectic, though Herzen does not use the word at this time. Progress had come about in the West through a series of struggles, beginning in the immobile Dark Ages, gathering motion in the Reformation, and culminating in the fully conscious liberation of the French Revolution, just as in nature the Idea develops from the bondage of unconscious matter to the freedom of self-understanding in man. All this time, "Asiatic stagnation overlay Russia," who failed to realize the promises of her heritage because she lacked the vital element of conflict.[49] But then: "Peter appeared! He placed himself in opposition to the people, expressed Europe in his person and took upon himself the task of introducing Europeanism into Russia." [50] By setting up the Western historical dialectic in Russia the way at last was opened for progress and humanization. Yet Peter had by no means completed this development, or even expressed its full essence. "Peter like all revolutions was the exclusively one-sided extreme of a single idea and he developed it by using any means, even going to the point of cruelty, just as the Reformation or the French Convention did." [51] Much remained to be done; and, since progress would continue to be dialectical, there is the strong implication (though Herzen does not spell it out) that further advance would not be through the "one-sided" autocracy of Peter but by means in opposition to it. Thus Herzen was able both to admire autocracy in the past and to reject it in the present, to take pride in the accomplishments of Russia and yet remain in the opposition — but of course the dialectic had been developed precisely to express such ambivalence.

National pride is indeed strong in this essay. Peter was a man of destiny — like Alexander, Caesar, or Napoleon, one of the chosen instruments of the Idea. But he was greater than any of these, for he found his strength in his individual will alone, unaided by precursors or external circumstances; "lighthouse-like" his self-chosen end illumined the path of his firm advance.[52] Peter in himself was a phenomenon comparable to the Reformation or the French Revolution: *"Et la révolution se fait homme,"* were the words of Victor Hugo chosen as epigraph to the essay. Russia in the past, through Peter, had accomplished things as great as any nation of Europe; thus Peter was the pledge that Russia possessed the resources for even greater accomplishments in the future. Also, he was the guarantee of the final success of "Europeanism" (or liberalization) in Russia, a mission which Herzen and his friends had currently taken on themselves. In the image of Peter reforming Russia by his own unaided will Herzen saw himself struggling in isolation against the stagnation of Russia under Nicholas. National pride and personal egoism fused into a single whole, guaranteed by the sure, "scientific" knowledge that the Absolute and history were on the side of both.

Such were the multifarious consolations furnished by idealism to Herzen and his little circle in their alienation from surrounding society. Through "science" they passed from isolation to a feeling of harmony and identity with the cosmos, to an assurance of their own high worth as individuals, and to participation in an idealized nationhood. The drabness and poverty of the present were conquered by a bright vision of hope in the future and by communion in the ideal. They could be certain that one day their lives, and the life of Russia, would in fact see the full revelation of the Absolute, whose spirit they felt within them.

CHAPTER VI

Saint-Simon and Socialism

GERMAN idealism gave Herzen much at the university, but by no means all he craved. In particular it could not provide a properly political goal. It could do no more than furnish a philosophy of history which, to be sure, demonstrated the inevitability of progress in Russia, but only in the most general terms. And Herzen's interest in history, even more than in "science," was sublimated politics. He no more cared for history as the *understanding* of the past for its own sake than he cared for "science" merely to understand nature; his interest in both was to grasp the meaning of man's destiny in order to *act* upon that destiny. Thus his attention was always directed as much toward the present and the future as toward the past. Throughout his life all his schemes of history were addressed more to the question, "Where are we going?" than to the question, "Where have we come from?" Idealism's answer, in terms of the progress of the Idea to self-knowledge, enlightenment and inner freedom, was consoling as far as it went, but Herzen, unlike most of his generation, required something more. He found it at the end of his university course in the teaching of the Saint-Simonians. The date is a momentous one; if any date marks the birth of socialism in Russia, it is the espousal of Saint-Simonism by Herzen, Ogarev, and their circle.

In their first years at the university Herzen and Ogarev never abandoned their interest in politics nor their cult of the Decembrists. Sometime during this period Herzen acquired a copy of the report published in 1826 by the investigating committee that had "tried" the Decembrists, which gave a partial record of the hearings and a list of the condemned — a veritable calendar of martyrs.[1] At the same time he became rather well acquainted with two members of the conspiracy: the friend of Pushkin, M. F. Orlov, and an individual identified only as V.[2] Both, though arrested for membership in the secret societies, had escaped major punishment and were allowed to reside at liberty in Moscow. In *My Past and Thoughts* Herzen speaks of their "tricolor" liberalism with due socialist condescension; at the time, though, he no doubt revered them as heroes who not only dreamed of liberty but had once acted in its cause. This Decembrism probably remained Herzen's political ideal down to 1832 or 1833. It is at the end of 1832 that the first reference to a "socialist" author occurs in his writings; indeed, it is the first mention of a "socialist" work in Russian history. The reference is a quotation from *La religion du St.-Simonisme* by Eugène Rodrigues,[3] one of the earliest disciples of the master. In itself this quotation is innocuous enough, being no more than a conventional idealist attack on the "cold empiricism" of the eighteenth century, and it is only in the following year, 1833, that Herzen's interest in Saint-Simonism as a social and political doctrine becomes explicit.

In *My Past and Thoughts* Herzen explained this evolution by the impact of the July Revolution in France and the Polish revolt of 1830–31. Herzen claimed that he and Ogarev, mere

eighteen-year olds . . . followed each event step by step . . . loved all the radical leaders, and kept their portraits with us, from Manuel and Benjamin Constant to Dupont de l'Eure and Armand Carrel. Then, in the middle of this conflagration, suddenly, like a bomb exploding alongside, the news of the Warsaw insurrection deafened us. This was no longer far away, this was right at home, and we looked at each other with tears in our eyes, repeating over our favorite: *Nein, es sind keine leere[n] Träume!* [4]

This description is undoubtedly true in its main outlines: given their cult of the Decembrists and the French Revolution, Herzen and Ogarev could not have failed to respond to the events of 1830. But the conclusion he claims they drew from the disappointing outcome of these events is of more doubtful veracity.

The period following on the crushing of the Polish revolt rapidly educated us. We were not only tormented by the fact that Nicholas had fully consolidated his power and grown in cruelty; we began to perceive, with inward horror, that in Europe, and especially in France, whence we expected the initiative and a slogan in politics, things were not going smoothly — our theories became suspect to us. The childish liberalism of 1826, which we built up little by little on the French model, which Lafayette and Benjamin Constant had preached, and Béranger had sung, lost for us its captivating charm after the ruin of Poland.[5]

This disillusionment with political revolution and liberalism is too clear-cut for such novices in politics as were Herzen and Ogarev at the time. The same applies to the interpretation Herzen gives of their consequent conversion to "socialism," though the factual basis of his assertion is true enough.

In the midst of this fermentation, of these surmises, of these efforts to understand the doubts that frightened us, the pamphlets of the Saint-Simonians, their sermons, their trial, fell into our hands. . . . A new world knocked at the door; our souls, our hearts opened to it. Saint-Simonism became the foundation of our convictions and in all essentials has constantly remained so.[6]

In short, the experiences of 1830 convinced Herzen and Ogarev that the political revolution was not enough and that a social revolution was necessary for the true liberation of Europe. This is one of the classic arguments for the necessity of socialism. It developed soon enough in France after 1830, but it did not gain currency in Russia until the forties; at least it appears nowhere in such clear-cut form in the writings of Herzen and Ogarev, who were the whole of Russian socialism at this time. Nor is it consonant with what is known with certainty of their youthful politics. In their Decembrist phase they were hardly political liberals in any mature, let alone doctrinaire, sense; they stood vaguely for liberty and revolt, but lacked any precise program. And their early "socialism," as will appear below, was no more precise. Hence the sharp contrast between the two which Herzen draws in *My Past and Thoughts* is hardly probable. It is in fact a projection into the past of the more distinctly formulated opinions he held on the eve of 1848. An even clearer anachronism appears in what he claims he discovered in Saint-Simonism: "On the one hand, *the liberation of woman,* a summoning her to a common task, the giving over of her fate into her own hands, union with her as with an equal. On the other hand, the justification, the redemption of the flesh, *la réhabilitation de la chair!*" [7] Both these points, of course, were doctrine for the Saint-Simonians, but Herzen noticed them only in the forties, under the influence of George Sand and of his own marital difficulties. There is none of all this in the sources which have survived from his youth, but there is much else. Though all the details are not clear, what probably happened was the following.

Herzen was always more influenced by events than by ideas. Ideas reached him as embodiments of a living situation — either a political movement, a campaign of propaganda, or a polemic. He responded to ideas as expressions of practical problems, not as abstract questions of understanding. And however intellectual he was, he was hardly a disinterested scholar; rather he was a political journalist and moralist, who was compelled to live a life of reflection because more natural avenues of expression were closed to him. His conversion to Saint-Simonism is to be understood only against this background — not as the result of a reasoned analysis of the events of 1830, but as an elemental reaction to their drama.

The July Revolution and the Polish revolt were the first significant political events since 1825; their effect was undoubtedly to give Herzen hope for imminent change, perhaps even revolution, in all of Europe. This hope must have been all the more vivid for the fact that for the second time in five years the autocracy had been challenged, arms in hand, within

Russia itself. The world became alive as it had not been since the fourteenth of December. Even the crushing of the Poles did not extinguish Herzen's hope, for the agitation in France continued: there was a revolt of the Lyons silk workers in 1831 and a republican uprising in Paris in 1832, and there would be further revolts in both cities in 1834. France was in effervescence, as if on the eve of another 1789, and the echoes filtered through to Moscow with each package of newspapers from abroad. One of the more exciting items connected with the Paris uprising of 1832 concerned a group of extraordinary young men called Saint-Simonians. The group preached a more "advanced" creed than any heard of in Moscow before, known as the "New Christianity." Their trial in August of 1832 (called the trial of Ménilmontant after the street where the sect had its headquarters) was widely reported in the international press. This public prosecution caught Herzen's imagination and sent him to the pamphlets and periodicals published by the martyred group.[8] But he and Ogarev were drawn not only to the Saint-Simonians, as the account in My Past and Thoughts implies. Anything that came out of the fermentation in France was worthy of reverent attention: the exciting idea of a palingénésie sociale put forth by a certain Ballanche, as well as a système d'association by one Fourier.[9] Herzen's and Ogarev's first allegiance was not to any particular doctrine but to whatever was new and radical in France, as the only place in Europe where anything significant was happening. (England was outside their ken and the Reform Bill of 1832 passed unnoticed by them.)

Their first reason, then, for turning to "socialism" was the lure of novelty; such automatic allegiance to whatever was new on the Left was psychologically necessary to being progressive. Of the social issues to which the new movement addressed itself, Herzen and Ogarev initially had no more understanding than they at first had had of the Decembrists. Thus the immediate cause of the spread of "socialism" to Russia was simple coincidence in time between the appearance of the new doctrine in Europe and the growing restlessness of the nascent Russian Left. Yet this is hardly enough to explain the persistence of the socialist ideal in Russia, and particularly in the thinking of Herzen and Ogarev. Beneath the initial coincidence there lay a deeper affinity which made the new ideas from France, at first received only superficially, stick for life.

To explain the nature of this affinity, however, it is necessary to make a further digression from the main line of the narrative. The problem of the deeper contact between Herzen and the Saint-Simonians is the same as that of the meaning of Russian socialism in general; and the solution to both, once again, is too often presented in terms of mere coincidence, "influence" and "borrowing." [10]

2

So accustomed are we to associating the idea of socialism, even utopian, with industrialism that at first glance it seems slightly incredible that the movement could have existed in any meaningful sense in nine-teenth-century Russia, at least before the industrialization of the 1890's. It seems especially incredible that it should have appeared among the serf-owning gentry under Nicholas I, in fact just seven short years after the failure of Decembrist "liberalism." Under such conditions, the Popu-list phase of Russian socialism, extending from Herzen to the advent of Marxism in the 1890's, would appear to have little in common with Western socialism but the name. Yet on the other hand, it would be even more incredible that so many generations of Russian Populists should have lived an illusion, and that they were not in fact representatives of "real" socialism.

A good part of the problem obviously lies in defining what is meant by "socialism." Given the great diversity of movements that at various times have claimed the name and its consequent ambiguity, especially in its non-Marxist uses, the establishment of the lowest common denomi-nator of all socialisms is a task which most writers prudently prefer to avoid.[11] Yet it must be faced here, for Russian Populism adhered to socialism in its essence and in little else. In particular, it must be faced for the seedtime of socialism between 1830 and 1848, especially in France, whence the Russians derived the inspiration which lasted them until the 1890's. Consequently, the socialism with which the following discussion will be concerned is not so much that represented by the British Labor Party or the Second International as by the more visionary or chiliastic forms, both peacefully utopian and violently revolutionary. Nor is the question of definition an academic one; it is the same as the problem of the origin and character of Russian socialism itself.

The most obvious — and superficial — way to state the essence of socialism is in formal, programmatic terms. Socialism is what its name suggests: advocacy of some form of socialization or collectivization of wealth and the abolition of private property. This program is indispen-sable to all meaningful ideas of socialism; without it any system is fairly open to the suspicion of not being "real" socialism, but, as Marxists would say, simply a camouflaged "bourgeois-democratic" reformism. Sooner or later all socialism worthy of the name must demand some measure of collectivization of wealth. Even so, socialism does not necessarily begin with this demand. In particular, none of the three men generally recog-nized as its first prophets — Saint-Simon, Fourier, and Owen — consistently advocated the abolition of private property (though their predecessor Babeuf did), nor did such prominent members of the second generation as Pierre Leroux and Proudhon. Indeed, two of this group, Fourier and Proudhon, were distinctly hostile to the idea, though all, to be sure, insisted on the socially responsible use of wealth and called for institutionalized measures to insure this. Such diversity of opinion at the outset indicates that collectivization of wealth is not the essence of socialism, but the means, if ultimately indispensable, to an end more basic still.

The same is true of other conventional statements about socialism. The most important of these is that socialism means a doctrine of economic as opposed to purely political reform, and hence does not remain on the surface of problems, as does liberalism, but goes to their very heart. Another characterization is that socialism means essentially that political liberty has no meaning unless supplemented by economic equality; or that the legal republic is a sham unless transformed into the social republic. There are further definitions still more economic: that socialism means fraternal cooperation and security as opposed to the individualistic competition of *laissez-faire* capitalism; or that it is economic planning, as opposed to the irrational profit motive and the business cycle; or that it means abundance for all and full employment, as opposed to "Malthusianism." Finally, for its enemies, socialism means "collectivism" and regimentation as opposed to "individualism" and freedom. Though there is undoubtedly truth in each of these descriptions, once again they are all fairly external and formal. Moreover, they all refer to means rather than essential ends. Indeed most of them (except of course the last) first appeared as slogans of the movement in Western Europe between 1830 and 1848, and reflect largely the local conditions of a primitive factory system and "censitary" liberalism based on a property suffrage.

None of these definitions, however, has any application in Russia until the end of the century. That country hardly suffered from "mere" political liberty, anarchic competition, or unbridled individualism. Nor were Russian radicals concerned with such economic problems as the business cycle, the profit motive, "wage slavery" or insecurity of employment. They were not even primarily concerned with the overthrow of private property, though, of course, they always made this a part of their program. Rather, the real problem in Russia was the liquidation of the old regime in its simplest and crudest expression: political autocracy and, at least until 1861, the most naked form of social inequality, legal serfdom. In short, the problem by rights should have been that of the "bourgeois revolution." Yet, beginning with Herzen and Ogarev, Russian radicals chose to think of their aims as "socialist" rather than merely liberal. Thus none of the conventional characterizations of socialism can capture its essence, if it is to have meaning for Russia.

Another approach to the definition of socialism goes deeper than programmatic considerations and touches on the sociology of the subject. Following Marx, and indeed most Western theorists, it is generally assumed that socialism, or at least "real" socialism, is the class reaction of an industrial proletariat against a capitalistic bourgeoisie. But again, however close this comes to fitting many phases of the Western development, it does not apply to nineteenth-century Russia, where industry and the proletariat were insignificant and where socialism, until the nineties, was the affair of a few intellectuals. These intellectuals' solicitude, moreover, was directed almost exclusively toward a peasantry which, unlike the Western proletariat, had no notion of what socialism was about. But who, in the mid-twentieth century, would presume to claim that this aberrant Russian doctrine was less significant than that of the West, or to make of the latter the universal standard of "genuine" socialism? Nor does the role of Marxism in Russia after industrialization in the 1890's invalidate this contention; for Bolshevism, with its reliance on an elite party (practically speaking, the intelligentsia) and its willingness to exploit peasant anarchism, owes as much to native Populism as to Marx.

The apparent aberrance of the Russian movement, especially the priority of its triumph, has led to still another view of the deeper nature of socialism in general: namely, that it is the product, not of a mature capitalism, but of economic backwardness. Since 1917 events all over the world have made it increasingly evident that revolutionary socialism is effective in inverse proportion to the development of capitalism, and not the other way around, as the nineteenth century thought. By now it has become almost a truism that socialism, at least in its more millenarian guises, is the expression of proletarian alienation in the early stages of industrialization or in an imperfectly industrialized society.

To dwell for a moment on the obvious, socialism first appeared in Western Europe, in both its utopian and Marxist forms, during the initial and harshest phases of industrialization in the first half of the nineteenth century. During the same period the most advanced capitalism was to be found in England, whereas the most self-conscious socialism was to be found in France and a little later, as well as in a more theoretical form, in Germany. It scored its greatest triumphs in Russia, both in its Marxist and Populist versions, only after the industrialization of the 1890's had created conditions similar to those of the early nineteenth-century West. And it spread to the underdeveloped countries of Asia in the period following the two world wars. In countries of advanced capitalism socialism either has hardly existed at all, as in the United States, or it has gradually abandoned dreams of the millennium and settled down to peaceful and piecemeal reform, as in most of Western Europe since the Second International, notably in England and Imperial and post-

World War II Germany. Finally, apparent exceptions to this generalization really confirm it. In such countries as modern France and Italy, where socialism has continued prominent in its more virulent forms, first as anarchosyndicalism and later as communism, a truly modern capitalism has never become dominant in spite of important islands of large-scale industry.[12]

To this should be added the oft-repeated observation that the greater the development of political democracy, either the less there is of socialism or the less virulent are the forms it assumes. Universal suffrage, government responsible in some measure to a parliament, freedom to organize trade unions or parliamentary socialist parties, and freedom to strike and to agitate openly for reform almost invariably take the millenarian tinge out of socialism. Under such conditions, though much of the old ideology may remain, the movement in fact becomes pragmatic, reformist and gradualist, and not too different from the more thoroughgoing forms of liberalism. This is what happened to most of European socialism under the aegis of the Second International. There are, to be sure, exceptions to this, such as the communist movements in Weimar Germany or modern France, but these are to be explained largely by temporary catastrophes such as war and major economic collapse or, as indicated above in the case of France, relative economic backwardness.

Finally, it is once again obvious that the triumph of political democracy in Europe during the last third of the nineteenth century coincided with the maturity of industrial capitalism (the United States is the only important case where political democracy preceded industrialization). Nor is it necessary to be a historical materialist to maintain that industrialization was the root-cause of this democratization in Europe. So again we are brought back to the notion that the intensive development of capitalism leads to the domestication of socialism, rather than the reverse. Needless to say, in stating this position fully it would be necessary to introduce nuances not given here; yet the general relation between the revolutionary strength of socialism and the timing and intensity of industrialization is too clear to deny.

Explanation of this set of correlations, however, is somewhat more complex. One approach to the relation between socialism and industrial backwardness tends to emphasize the economic. Socialism is viewed as a reaction, not just to liberal capitalism, but to industrialization itself. Yet it is a dual or ambivalent reaction — an ideology both of resistance to industrialization and one of adaptation to it. It embodies the protest of a peasantry turned into a proletariat and caught up in the discipline, the insecurity, and the competition of early industry, without any legal, peaceful means for redress of grievances. At the same time it promotes adaptation to the new industrial conditions, for it extols the productive power of an organized and "rational" economy and promises the worker eventual security, abundance, and status within it. Saint-Simonism, Louis Blanc, Fabianism, and in general the reformist types of socialism place the major emphasis on adaptation. Blanquism, syndicalism, and in general the forms of anarchism stemming from Proudhon and Bakunin are pure protest. Finally, Marxism represents an even combination of the two; this is why it has been able to appeal so universally, functioning simultaneously as the inspiration of an insurrectionary conspiracy and of a trade-union reformism or as the ideology of an anarchic revolution and of an authoritarian, technocratic state.[13]

Still, pertinent as all this is to most socialism, it is not of direct relevance in explaining Russian Populism before the 1890's or the role of gentry intellectuals, to whom the pressures of industrialization were utterly foreign, in launching it. For this it is necessary to broaden the concept of backwardness from an industrial, or even an economic, one to a more general view; at the same time it is necessary to pursue further the line of reasoning broached above in discussing the relation of socialism to political democracy. The primary pressure of backwardness in certain situations may be social and cultural in a general sense, and more especially political. To be sure, these factors are not unrelated to the economic; but in a preindustrial situation men are hardly aware of the relation, for it is only the development of modern industry which has given us a full sense of economic forces in molding a culture. Before this, men reacted consciously mostly to social and political pressures; and it is this conscious reaction that counts in explaining their motivation and the nature of their doctrines.

Specifically, political and social backwardness in modern Europe means first, an absolute monarchy; secondly, government by bureaucracy designed chiefly to support a military machine; and, finally, a legal class hierarchy defined in terms of duties to monarchy and state. (In addition, it is obvious that such a situation is incompatible with modern industry, and hence includes the idea of economic backwardness, though this is the last rather than the first objection to such an order by the people who live under it.) In short, such a society is what men after 1789 came to call an "old regime." Old regimes, moreover (as has already been noted), become progressively more clear-cut in structure, more all-embracing and rigid, as one proceeds from England to Russia. The Russian was the simplest and most brutal of all, for autocracy and serfdom are the crudest forms of authoritarian monarchy and class inequality. By comparison, pre-1789 France was liberal and pre-1832 England anarchic.

Thus the end of the eighteenth and the beginning of the nineteenth centuries in Western Europe, and a period down into the twentieth century farther east, were occupied not only with the beginnings of industrialization but also with the destruction of the old regime. The trans-formation everywhere was in the direction of greater liberalization of the social structure as a whole and of equalization of legal conditions within it — in a word democratization. To be sure, this development occurred under the pressure of economic changes of a capitalistic sort: the slow expansion of private commercial and "manufacturing" enterprises inde-pendent of government tutelage, and later the pressure of more advanced economies on backward ones through the international market. The breakdown of the old regime would have been impossible without these economic changes, but, again, men were at first largely unaware of their effect. Outside of England, moreover, intensive industrialization, involv-ing mechanization and a factory system, was not prominent until relatively late. The first frontal assault against the old regime, the French Revolu-tion, occurred in a society which was largely preindustrial. In Russia pres-sure for modernization began to build up as early as Alexander I, when even the least modern forms of capitalism were an insignificant force.

It was in this atmosphere of general democratic attack on the old regime, as much as in the world of nascent industrialism, that socialism was born. In its deepest nature, then, socialism may be viewed as the *nec plus ultra* of democratic protest against an old regime, of which the proletarian reaction against early industrialism, where it existed, is only a part. Hence the lowest common denominator of all socialisms may be fixed at the demand for integral democracy. Socialism is a call for a total change from the old regime, at once and without compromise, a change that will not remain on the surface but will embrace the very structure of things — the "social," from which the movement derives its name. Here, at last, is a definition broad enough to include the Russian phenomenon and to link it meaningfully with that of the contemporary West.[14]

At first glance this idea may seem too self-consciously contrived to in-clude Russia, for is not "bourgeois" liberalism the revolutionary response to an old regime, and socialism the revolutionary response to liberalism? It would be a mistake, however, to assume that 1789 had fully liquidated the old regime and replaced it by a modern liberal-democratic society. Looking back on the eventual triumph of such an order in most of Western Europe after 1870, it is only too easy for us to forget how pro-foundly undemocratic and old-regime early nineteenth-century Europe still was, even in the most advanced nations such as England and France. What is more important, since we know that the demise of those elements of the old regime which had survived 1789 was a foregone conclusion, we tend unconsciously to minimize their immense impact while they lasted.

To insist once again on the obvious, nowhere in Europe was there anything approaching universal suffrage and equal political rights for all; nowhere was there even real equality before the law (for instance in most places labor could not organize); nowhere was it the normal expectation that any man, through universal education and equality of opportunity, could rise to become a full "human being" and citizen. Though no longer divided into estates, society was still separated into fairly rigid classes by unequal civil and political rights, and not just by inequalities of wealth. Nor was it only the masses who suffered from this lack of equality. In the West large segments of the bourgeoisie were excluded from full participation in the national life. Neither in France after 1830 nor in England after 1832 was more than a part of the middle classes enfranchised; and in both countries this portion had to share its power extensively with more ancient, aristocratic groups. East of the Rhine, of course, no one was enfranchised, not even the aristocracy, and everywhere a monarchical executive or its cabinet, responsible only to a very limited body of opinion, if indeed to anyone, remained supreme.

At best the old regime lived on in subtler, attenuated forms; at worst it became more rigid, as in Eastern Europe after 1815, and particularly in Russia under Nicholas. The events of 1789 had only begun the "bourgeois" revolution; Western Europe would not see it finished until near the end of the century, and Eastern Europe not until after 1918. Thus, socialism in origin, and in its revolutionary and apocalyptic forms, is not the phenomenon of a society that has made its "bourgeois" revolution too well, but of a society that has not made it well enough, or has not made it at all. That socialism acquired its greatest mass following only after the triumph of political democracy does not change this situation in the least. The pressure for greater democracy is a continuing one, for new inequalities and alienations arise with each economic and social change in the modern world, and the goal of total democracy is never realized. Even after the old regime has disappeared, socialism in reformist guise remains as a symbol and a goad. But the old literalness is gone. To the politicians of the Second International, though they kept the former slogans and ideology, preoccupation with the millennium was not a serious concern. By 1914 it had become amply apparent that the Western Social Democrats by no means meant all they said about revolution; by the mid-twentieth century it is clear that they do not even mean all they say about property. For the men of 1830–1848, however, preoccupation with the millennium was a very serious concern, and all their declarations were meant quite literally.

Under the conditions of the early nineteenth century, pressure for liberalization could originate in any group, from an aristocracy to a proletariat, that felt it was denied its full measure of freedom or of equality with other groups. Thus, opposition to the old regime quickly developed a whole spectrum of alternative programs. It began with the most moderate, "censitary" liberalism, which wished to preserve the monarchy and admit to a share of power only groups with a vital, or propertied, interest in "order." It extended to liberal democrats, who wished full civil and political rights for all, such as Jacobins and republicans in France or "radicals" in England. It culminated in the integral democrats, or socialists, who wished not just political and institutional changes but a total reformation of society, since the abolition of private property and the collectivization of wealth are simply the logical extremes of democratic, egalitarian demands. Moreover, these varying degrees of protest existed simultaneously, rather than successively, throughout the early nineteenth century. It would not be an exaggeration, then, to say that liberalism and socialism are, respectively, the "minimalist" and "maximalist" wings of one broad movement of protest against the still tenacious remnants of the old regime.

It would, however, be a mistake to draw too sharp a line between these protests on the basis of class interest. Interest, of course, was the first basis for the various positions; each social group tended to demand, at least with insistence, only just enough liberty and equality to include itself among the body of full citizens. And the lower down one was in the social hierarchy (and there were many groups, not just aristocracy, "bourgeoisie" and "people") the more real was his interest in demanding greater democracy, while the proletariat obviously had the most solid interest of all. Yet the psychology of frustration was almost as important in determining the intensity of democratic feeling. When pressure for reform became strong enough, or when it was founded on an extreme sense of injury or injustice, it could be generalized far beyond the immediate interests of the group or individual concerned into a demand for universal democracy; it could embrace Philippe Egalité, cramped only by the elder branch, at the same time as Babeuf, cramped by all property owners. If this demand were frustrated long enough or vitally enough in an individual from any group, it could go the lengths of a self-conscious socialism; it could become either revolutionary and apocalyptic or utopian and metaphysical, or both at once. Early socialism is largely no more than the demand for democracy made shrill and insistent through frustration. And the Russian intelligentsia affords the purest example of a socialist commitment founded on general frustration rather than on any specific class interest.

Under such conditions, early nineteenth-century socialism was not the protest of a single class; it represented a congeries of protests, coming from any social element or individual who felt angry enough about the state of society. Saint-Simon and his school, for instance, were hardly protesting against too much capitalism; rather they were protesting against too little. Their war was against the obstacles to industrial progress created by an archaic society; as an interest group they represented technocratic engineers and entrepreneurs frustrated in their grandiose plans for economic development by parasitic, landed aristocrats, *rentiers*, politicians and courtiers. Yet they are fairly considered "socialist" both because they generalized their desire for a free scope for themselves into a dream of progress for all mankind and because they demanded, albeit peacefully, the complete renovation of society.[15]

Similarly, Fourierism hardly represents a proletarian protest. Though, unlike Saint-Simonism, it is anticapitalistic, it is not so from a working-class point of view. Rather, Fourierism is best understood as the protest of the petty-bourgeois consumer, the small employee or artisan, both against the absence of means for insuring his security in the existing undemocratic order and against a nascent capitalism. Caught up in a productive machine which controls his destiny and yet which is so vast that he cannot affect it in any way, the "little man" of Fourierism imagines the phalanstery as the panacea which will simplify the machine by abolishing the distinction between consumer and producer and organizing society into manageable, self-sufficient units (like the old village), where each man will work only at what he pleases, in "harmony" and security, not competition, with his fellows. Thus Fourierism is a democratic glance backward to an idealized agrarian order as much as a glance forward to the problems of modern industry; in this it bears the unmistakable imprint of conditions that are still largely old-regime.[16]

The list of nonproletarian "socialists" in the period 1830–1848, of men concerned largely with problems posed by survivals of the old regime, could easily be lengthened and the question of "socialist" motivation correspondingly complicated. To mention only the most prominent, the former Saint-Simonian and mystic humanitarian Pierre Leroux, the Saint-Simonian and Catholic democrat Buchez, or the former Catholic and still religious Lamennais — all concerned largely with "modernizing" Christianity — are just as characteristic of the birth of socialism as are more proletarian-minded thinkers such as Louis Blanc, Cabet, Blanqui, Barbès, or, a little later, Proudhon.[17] What all have in common is a frustrated desire for democracy pushed to the point of demanding the total reorganization of society.

This diversity of group or class motivation among early socialists and their overlapping with "bourgeois" liberalism in fact can be traced back further, to the very moment when protest against the old regime became fully democratic in the theories of Rousseau. It is not an accident that most histories of political thought are somewhat embarrassed whether to classify Rousseau as an extreme democrat or a forerunner of socialism, since at times he makes property the origin of inequality. In reality he is both, for he represents a moment in the reaction to the old regime when radical liberalism and socialism had not yet become distinguished. It would be difficult to deny to the *Discourse on the Origin of Inequality* and the *Social Contract* a radically leveling and "social" strain that transcends the merely political in its implications. Moreover, Morelly and Mably, both before 1789, made this explicit by recommending collectivization of wealth as necessary to full democracy.

The Revolution itself was just as ambiguous. Historians have been able to dispute about the "socialist" nature of certain measures of the "bourgeois" Jacobins such as the *maximum* or the "decrees of Ventôse," not to mention the widespread rumors at the time of an equal distribution of land among the people, the *loi agraire*. What is more important, the first organized movement for the collectivization of wealth which all authorities would call "socialist" without qualification, Babeuf's "Conspiracy of the Equals," was an offshoot of the Revolution. To be sure, all these phenomena were exceptions in their time; nonetheless they indicate that the logical conclusion of both Enlightenment and Revolution was that integral democracy which later was called "socialist." To return to "socialism proper," its first significant theorists, who both began to publish immediately after 1800, were Saint-Simon, by upbringing a figure of the late Enlightenment, and Fourier, who developed his ideas under the immediate impact of the Revolution.

Nor is there a clearer break between the "bourgeois" revolution and socialism in ideology than in history. Essentially, the socialist dream is no different from that of the more radical phases of the Enlightenment and the Revolution. All the novel proposals put forth from Saint-Simon to Marx, the "New Christianity," the phalanstery, "association," the "organization of labor," the "classless, stateless society," etc., are ultimately reducible to the commonplaces of the *philosophes* and the Mountain. Put in the most general possible terms, what the early socialists wanted was a completely just, humane, "rational" and "natural" society — or liberty, equality and fraternity for all. They gave, however, a redoubled urgency to the words of the original promise. They insisted that society must at last become *completely* rational and humane; that *all* men, and not just some, must in *fact* and not only in form enjoy total liberty in full equality and true fraternity. They were, so to speak, the "ultras" of the Enlightenment; they were the intransigents, as opposed to the compromisers, of the tradition of 1789.

To this perhaps should be added that socialism in intent is not "collectivistic" or anti-individualistic in a way that would now be called totalitarian or authoritarian. On the contrary, early socialism was inspired by a reverence for the sanctity of the individual that was, if anything, even greater than that of contemporary liberalism; its emphasis on the "collective" was simply an insistence that *all* men must have the right to become complete human beings. Reform must be universal in order to give each and every individual a decent, humane life and freedom for the full development of his personality, since the emancipation of no man is complete without the emancipation of all men. Viewed in terms of goals rather than institutional means, socialism in fact represents the individualism of the Enlightenment and Revolution carried to its logical extreme and generalized to the whole of humanity, because of disappointment with the results of 1789.

Indeed, disappointment with all assaults on the old regime since 1789 is another essential characteristic of early socialism. The Jacobins, too, had been intransigent in their pursuit of the dream of the Enlightenment, but they were not socialists. To produce socialism as a distinct movement among the currents of protest proceeding from the Revolution, an accumulation of frustration was necessary. The mounting sense of frustration after 1789, as the old regime continued to survive under other forms in spite of so many attacks, and worse still when it was partially restored in 1815, is fully as important to the genesis of socialism as the new proletarian class interest created during the same period. The socialists were those who would settle for none of the compromises produced by the Great Revolution, even at its best, and still less for those produced by 1830; they wanted the whole ideal and not just a part. Moreover, they wanted it right away, without temporizing or delay; they would not listen to appeals for gradual, piecemeal progress. In their eyes the willingness of mere liberals to accept only partial implementation of the ideal, or to wait more or less indefinitely for its full realization, was not only immoral and the sign of an underlying hypocrisy, it was also self-defeating, for it created new privileged interests in the place of the old to block the road towards full democracy.

Specifically, the disenchantment of the socialists was twofold. First, the series of failures between 1789 and 1830 to effect a fundamental change of society revealed the existence of a large group of compromisers who mouthed all the great slogans but who in practice were ready to sell the ideal short for their own particular profit. Secondly, these same failures gradually made the idealistic realize that the problem of creating the perfectly rational society was much more complicated than had originally been thought. The exclusively political means advocated by the first generation of democrats seemed paltry and inadequate to the second. So the idea was born that all the changes from 1789 to 1830 had been necessary but only negative; there had to be a second, creative change to produce the longed-for new world. Furthermore, this result could be realized only by totally new means, infinitely more radical than any previously used. In short, there had to be a second coming of the Revolution, not necessarily in a political form on the model of 1789, but in some form, either a violent upheaval or a moral reformation, which would regenerate society from top to bottom. Nor did this line of reasoning affect only France; once 1789 had occurred nothing could ever be the same again anywhere within the European cultural orbit.

The idea of a more thoroughgoing 1789 became completely clear only in the wake of the expectations unleashed — and immediately disappointed — by 1830. Before this there had only been tiny groups, such as the conspiracy of Babeuf, or isolated individuals like Saint-Simon and Fourier, to pursue the idea of democracy to its logical conclusion. The shock of 1830 made socialism a movement; the clusters of disciples around Saint-Simon and Fourier mushroomed into schools, and new groups sprang up alongside. By 1840, as frustration and repression continued, the term socialism came into general use to denote any doctrine that viewed reform as the total transformation of society and not just of certain institutions. Shortly thereafter the word communism became current to signify more precisely the radical equalizing of wealth,[18] although in fact the distinction between the terms was not sharp, and socialism was the more widely used, as well as the more inclusive, of the two. It was the word socialism which caught on in Russia under Nicholas, precisely because of its more general, less property-conscious character.

Another distinction between the terms socialism and communism regards the means for achieving social change, regardless of ends. On the one hand there was an insurrectionary communism, hearkening back to Babeuf, and owning Blanqui and Barbès as its most prominent representatives; on the other hand there was what Marx called "utopian" socialism, which hoped to transform society by the propaganda of ideas, the appeal to universal reason, moral reformation, or the peaceful adoption of some great scheme for the reorganization of things, such as Saint-Simon's New Christianity or Fourier's phalansteries. Of the two tendencies the latter was certainly the more prevalent, for, if early socialism was uncompromising in its insistence on *full* democracy, it was not yet so embittered as to rely primarily on force or a hard-bitten class interest. Though it called for a second coming of the revolution, its revolution was a vague thing, ranging from actual barricades to a moral, even a religious, regeneration. This catholicity — or ambiguity — of means was also very appealing in the Russia of Nicholas I, where men desired something radical and sweeping, but where insurrection could only be a dream.

At the same time the new socialism had a particular solicitude for the most dispossessed of classes, the workers or proletariat, again a new word in common usage. In the wake of 1830 the effects of industrialization were beginning to be unmistakably apparent in France. This dramatized the inequalities of the existing order and for the first time furnished a reasonably cohesive and semiorganized force to use against it. Hence the inevitable association of socialism and proletariat in the West. But this is simply a local expression of a more general principle. As an aspiration to total democracy, socialism is directed, not just to the proletariat, but to an entity much vaster and more vague: what Saint-Simon called *la classe la plus nombreuse et la plus pauvre,* and what a little later came to be known as the "people," the masses. The "people" can mean a peasantry, or simply the humble of any sort, as easily as an industrial proletariat, depending upon the social situation wherever democratization is an issue. In particular the Russian word for "people," or *narod,* in radical usage came to mean at the same time the masses in general and the peasantry.

Yet the new socialism was not the creation of the people, or even of the proletariat; nor was either its principal carrier. Lenin was more shrewd than Marx when, in a famous phrase, he observed: "The history of all countries bears witness that by its own resources alone the working class is in a position to generate only a trade-union consciousness." [19] In other words, the protest of the workers (and indeed of the peasants or the bourgeoisie) is always specific, and ultimately reformist in nature. It is a protest which remains near to concrete grievances and precise remedies. The masses want the right to organize and strike or otherwise protect their interests; they want full reward for their labor and security of employment; they want access to education and complete equality before the law; later, they want the vote in order to protect these gains; and if the masses are a peasantry they want emancipation from serfdom and partition of the large estates. But in all these cases the masses want primarily to live, to achieve security, and ultimately to advance in terms of the situation in which they find themselves. Like everyone else they are most vitally concerned with their own lot rather than with that of *all* mankind. It is only in moments of extreme crisis or desperation, when the frustration of their specific demands becomes intolerable, as in 1848 and 1871 for the French worker or 1917 for the Russian worker and peasant, that the masses actively and literally desire the fullness of socialism, or a totally new order, and are willing to follow to the end leaders who proclaim this goal. But the rest of the time, for the people socialism is the symbolism of protest, the extreme projection of discontent, rather than an immediate program.

The fullness of socialism — the demand for ideal, integral democracy and a total reformation of society — is primarily the preoccupation of the intellectual. (The intellectual, of course, on occasion can come from the people, such as Proudhon or Weitling, but in such cases he is no more typical of his background than is an aristocratic socialist of his.) Again,

however, his tendency to ideology is not just a question of better education or greater knowledge; it is fundamentally a question of the quality
of the intellectual's frustration. The desire to know the truth and expound
it, to be a moral authority and point the way to reform, is also a desire
for leadership and power, however consciously disinterested the intellectual may be. Such urges denote a more sensitive ambition, a more
intense self-importance, than does the worker's or peasant's desire to have
money or land enough to live. The same is true of the intellectual's
striving for the fullness of life — aesthetic, affective, and cerebral — or
as Herzen would put it, "the full flowering of the human personality."
Or perhaps all these things are the expression of frustrated ambitions of
a more mundane sort, for people who actually live the "fullness of life"
do not need to talk about it.

At all events, in the rigid and narrow structure of an old regime,
even one in disintegration, places of importance and influence are few,
whether in business, government, or the professions, and most of them
are occupied by a small group of the self-perpetuating privileged. In
other words there is inadequate "social mobility," "circulation of elites,"
too few careers open to talent. Thus the intellectual's desire to realize
fully his potentialities are frustrated — or people who are frustrated in
this desire become intellectuals. This frustration, moreover, is felt most
acutely by men near enough to privilege to know what full freedom
can mean, by those cramped enough to be angry but still hopeful enough
to protest. It is this group which furnishes the radical intelligentsia with
the bulk of its recruits; and, of course, depending on the time and country, they can come from very different social classes. In its alienation
this intelligentsia generalizes its discontent into the demand for the
total renovation of society, and for the full liberation, not just of itself,
but of all men. Through frustration its protest becomes universal, absolute, uncompromising, and perfectionist.

Thus the protest of the socialist intellectual is not just specific, like
that of the worker or peasant; it is also, and fundamentally, general. The
socialist intellectual is against the whole "old world" of existing society
and for a totally "new world." His ideal is always framed as an apocalyptic contrast: for Owen it was the immoral present and the "New Moral
Order"; for Saint-Simon the second term was the "New Christianity,"
and for Fourier "Harmony." For Marx the contrast was made more
complicated and intellectually rigorous by his training in German
philosophy, but essentially it was the same: the present world of "alienations" and "internal contradictions," expressed concretely as class exploitation and state oppression, would give way to the full equality of
a classless society and the full freedom of a stateless one, where man at
last would come completely into his own.

The socialism of the intellectuals always contains this eschatological element, this vision of the final end of things. To be sure, it also contains specific, programmatic demands, reflecting the grievances of one or another social group, but these are not its essence. Its essence is a vision of a "new world" to which all specific demands are related. Its origin is a state of mind which will settle for nothing less than a really new order, and will have no truck with merely patching up the old. The socialism of the intelligentsia, no matter how hardheaded it may become about questions of power, is always in some significant degree visionary, idealistic, millenarian, chiliastic, or any of the other terms usually employed to indicate an intransigent, all-or-nothing mentality. By the early twentieth century in Russia, where experience of this phenomenon had been particularly long and deep, men took to designating such a mentality as "maximalism." And if the programmatic essence of socialism is integral democracy, its psychological essence is maximalism, or intransigence in pursuit of this end.

Thus the quintessential socialism of the intellectuals, since it is not a specific program but the most generalized democratic idealism, is so readily exportable beyond the confines of the conditions which produced it. In this it differs from the more concrete and somewhat drab doctrines of liberalism, which can easily seem paltry to the impatient, since their consequences are so predictable and limited. The program of the liberal can be described quite precisely, from its electoral law to the last article of its bill of rights. But there is magic in socialism, which promises an infinity of nameless bliss, for aside from certain very general recommendations, it offers no one set of institutions, but an ideal alternative to all existing institutions — which may be liberalism and capitalism, or autocracy and serfdom, depending on the time and place.[20]

Under such circumstances early socialism was seldom primarily an economic doctrine. Most early socialist systems were first of all moral doctrines, in which, to be sure, economic ideas played a large part, but in which they were always inextricably mingled with less material considerations. Early socialist systems, therefore, including partially that of Marx, lean strongly to metaphysics and a sort of ethical idealism. Because the protest of socialism is general rather than specific, it tends to sweeping eschatologies as the only expression adequate to frustrations — and aspirations — so vast. This tendency towards abstraction, which Marx called "utopianism," is most evident among the first generation of socialists, that of Saint-Simon and Fourier, and it dominated the movement as a whole through the thirties. As the century advanced and experience with practical politics increased, the programs of the various branches of socialism grew increasingly precise. But until 1848 (and down to the present in many of the more backward areas of the world) no form of socialism, including Marxism, could do without a grandiose meta-physic of progress.

Specifically, the early forms of socialism tended towards a philosophy of history combined with a philosophy of religion. Progress was viewed as a sort of secular providence guiding man's ascent from barbarism to a future of harmony and brotherly love. This was the essence in particular of Saint-Simon's New Christianity, but it extends to most other early socialists as well. Fourier, Pierre Leroux, Buchez, Lamennais — in a word, almost all the social prophets of the thirties — not only believed in God, but considered that some form of religious cult was necessary to the complete man. They conceived of socialism as the final historical fulfillment of Christianity's original promise of universal brotherhood and love. Religion thus became the key to the development of mankind's ethical aspirations through the ages. It is indeed strange that much of radical democracy in the early nineteenth century, and especially during the thirties, should garb itself in a secular mysticism and a poetry of high sentiment in order to promote "enlightenment." The reactionary conditions which prevailed, however, or at least the impossibility of immediately affecting the real world, made a more down-to-earth state-ment of hope difficult; the "new world" of reason and humanity bore such little relation to the present that one could speak of it only in figurative terms. Of course, in all this there is much that relates early socialism to the more cerebral utopias of idealist philosophy. Both were "rational" mysticisms and both were philosophies of history. In the new socialism, as in idealism, a theory of history backed by a feeling of religious urgency was necessary to demonstrate in the teeth of a dis-appointing present the inevitable triumph of the divine idea of reason, humanity and brotherhood.

When socialism is presented in this aspect, it not only is unsurprising but indeed logical that it should have caught on in Russia almost as soon as in the West. Since socialism, when stripped of all programmatic contingencies, is quintessential democratic protest against an old regime, it is only natural that it should appear under the most quintessential of old regimes — that of Russia; and among the only class allowed the luxury of idealism and a sense of human dignity by so brutal a society — the gentry. In Russia after 1825 it was meaningless to think in terms of specific changes, whether a reform bill or an insurrection, since no gesture of conciliation could be expected from the government and no action from the masses. Since under such circumstances democracy could not be realized by any conceivable concrete institutions, to approach politics pragmatically was in effect an abdication of hope, if not downright collaboration with the existing order. Therefore the only thing left to do was to think in terms of general principles; and principles, the longer one lives with them, without any possibility of application, become increasingly pure, ideal, sweeping and, most crucial of all, uncompromising. The reformer turns intransigent and will settle for nothing less than the complete destruction of the "old," corrupt world and the creation of a totally "new" one, or socialism.

Thus socialism could appear in Russia among the circle of Herzen and Ogarev almost at the moment it emerged as a significant movement in the West in the wake of 1830, and after only seven short years of the frustration induced by the catastrophe of gentry liberalism and limited reform with the Decembrists. It appeared, moreover, in its most generalized, abstract form as total protest against the old regime, without any of its Western industrial applications, which had no meaning either to Russia in general or to the gentry in particular. Yet if Herzen and Ogarev could take nothing in the way of a precise program from the new socialism, they could enter fully into its psychological essence: its intransigence, its maximalism, and the historical and pseudo-religious metaphysics which derived from such a mood.

3

Evidence about Herzen's and Ogarev's recourse to Saint-Simonism is limited: there are a number of letters on both sides, all produced during the summer vacations of 1832 and 1833 when the two were separated; and there is the record of their interrogation after arrest in 1834. But much of what they wrote at the time — further letters and "articles" mentioned in their trial — has been lost, and what has survived gives a somewhat fragmentary picture of their evolution during these two years. Nonetheless, it is sufficient to sketch the main lines of their development.

We last left the narrative amidst the expectation and frustration of 1830. The pair soon turned to the only available substitute for politics, speculation about the mystery of the future, or the philosophy of history. In particular, under the influence of German idealism, they were preoccupied with the historical significance of Christianity. It was in their search for a philosophy of history and of religion that they first noticed the Saint-Simonians, whose existence was dramatized by the trial of Ménilmontant in 1832. It was shortly thereafter that Herzen first referred to a work of the sect, the *Religion du St.-Simonisme* of Eugène Rodrigues mentioned earlier in this chapter. It was only after a number of false starts, however, and over the course of the following year, that the pair absorbed the essentials of the New Christianity.

The way seems to have been led by Ogarev, who appears to have begun his search in 1832 with the discovery of Lamennais. His source was a chapter on the latter in a book entitled *Histoire de la philosophie au XIXe siècle en France* by a minor eclectic philosopher, Jean Philibert Damiron.[21] Lamennais, in a fashion to which Ogarev had been habituated by German idealism, divided the history of religion into three stages: a pre-Mosaic phase of pantheism where God was outside of man, in nature, which was a rather primitive and debased notion of God; a stage of Mosaic theism, where God was separated from both man and nature, and thereby became more exalted but also very remote; and, finally, the age of Christianity, in which religion was humanized, where "moral aspirations" were paramount and man at last was able "to draw near to God." In short, what Ogarev found in Lamennais was the familiar notion of German idealism, stated in more theistic terms, of man's ascent through history from the "alienation" of unconscious nature to intelligent union with some Supreme Being conceived of in humanized rather than transcendent terms.

Ogarev was much impressed with this scheme of progress so far as it went, but he felt it did not go far enough. He added his opinion that the development of humanity did not stop with traditional religion and its "mystic-moral, dreamy, unclear truth, perceived as through a fog."

Our times have become sufficiently positivistic so that we can accept only what is demonstrated by reason; thus we must await a poetry in which the idea of the deity will be developed clearly by rational conviction, or such a religion that will merge with philosophy or, it is better to say, will disappear into philosophy; i.e., faith in God will turn into a knowledge of God.

The development of such a religion was "pregnant with the final perfecting of mankind." [22] In other words, Ogarev hoped for a philosophic idealism, with a "rationally" deduced Absolute or God, which would not be just abstract truth but a force for the regeneration of society.

At the same time he found a hint of this new social religion in the *Philosophie du droit* of one Jean-Louis Lerminier, a half Saint-Simonian, half liberal popularizer of the German historical school of law. Ogarev recorded his impressions for Herzen:

The last four chapters sent me into transports. Friend! Read them, read them without fail. I caught fire from them, *innere Fülle* began to rage within me, I wanted to create something, and with chagrin and horror see that I am eighteen and in the country. But suddenly I remembered you, my friends; I compared what Lerminier said with ourselves, and something very sweet spoke to my soul — the future, the magnificent future! So many hopes and expectations! Friend! "Thus a momentary joy of the soul from time to time visits the suffering prisoner in his narrow cell!" [Pushkin] And this joy is the future! — and I am convinced, convinced that this is not *Knabengedanke*. . . . But how, what and when? Let us forget this question now, let us take pleasure in our hope for the future! Herzen! read the last four chapters, and your soul will ascend to such a state of thirst for action that all your muscles will move involuntarily, as if you were doing something, accomplishing something, creating.[23]

The feverish expectancy of this letter, its emphasis on hope and conviction as the equivalents of, or at least adequate substitutes for action, are as much a part of Ogarev's nascent socialism as any ideas he might have gleaned from Lerminier.

Herzen, when he eventually came to read the latter, was much less impressed than Ogarev, no doubt because the *Philosophie du droit* seemed too moderate.[24] Herzen, moreover, in 1832 was less concerned with religion than was his friend. Together with Vadim Passek, who was training to be a historian, and his brother Diomed, Herzen was looking for the key to man's destiny in secular history,[25] and in more concrete directions than the eschatologies attractive to the poetic temperament of Ogarev. The principal expression of this interest was the article on Peter the Great, discussed in the preceding chapter. At the same time Herzen cast a glance at the recently founded United States. He read the books of Achille Murat, a son of the king of Naples who had long resided in America. A discussion with Ogarev on the merits of the new republic ensued. Their conclusion was that, though the political liberalism of America was more impressive than anything of the kind produced by Europe, and indeed an accomplishment worthy of some admiration, it was still not enough. In particular there was too much money-grubbing in America, too much self-complacency and most of all not enough of that "conflict" from which springs "truth," the "rapid" progress of society and "public enlightenment." There was much more of such conflict, with a resultant high excitement over ideas, in Europe; hence it was there that real hope for the future lay.[26] Without quite realizing it, in failing to respond to America, Herzen and Ogarev were in effect rejecting liberalism for vaster schemes more adequate to their exalted hopes. Nor, it must be said, did the American experiment offer much that was relevant to the problems of Nicholas I's Russia.[27]

In 1833 the pair's search culminated in the espousal of Saint-Simonism. In the summer of 1833 Herzen answered some now lost exhortation of his friend, obviously impressed, but also a little piqued that Ogarev — and indeed Saint-Simon — should have anticipated him in anything.

You are right, *Saint-Simonism* merits our attention. We feel (and I wrote you this two years ago, and then it was original with me), that the world is awaiting a rebirth, that the revolution of 1789 destroyed and did only that, but that it is necessary to create a new *palingenetic* epoch, it is necessary to give other foundations to the societies of Europe; more law, more morality, more enlightenment. Here is an attempt at it in Saint-Simonism. I am not speaking of its recent fall, as I call its religious form (P. Enfantin, etc.). Mysticism always takes hold of a young idea. Let us take the pure foundation of Christianity. How fine and lofty it is; then look at its adherents — a dark and gloomy mysticism.[28]

Herzen was suspicious of the mysticism of the Saint-Simonians, just as he had been suspicious of that of Schelling or of Ogarev's tendencies

in the same direction. Nonetheless, he was impressed by what he took to
be the central idea of the Saint-Simonians: the necessity of a new, constructive 1789 which would be a moral rebirth for mankind, continuing
in secular, "enlightened" form the regeneration of the world first proclaimed by Christianity. The term "palingenesis," or rebirth, he owed
to the theocratic yet democratic Catholic, Ballanche — another of the
numerous cases of that osmosis between ideologies of the Right and of the
Left so typical in early nineteenth-century thought and of which
so many examples will be given in these pages. Herzen probably gathered
this resounding neologism at second hand from some Saint-Simonian
periodical, for Ballanche was looked upon by the school as a forerunner
of the New Christianity. Herzen's letter ends on an even more eclectic
note. "There is also a *système d'appropriation* [a mistake for *association*]
by Fourier. You can read it in the [Saint-Simonian] *Revue Encyclopédique* for February, 1832. Its purpose justifies its strangeness." This
remark was no doubt included to indicate to Ogarev a doctrine of
"palingenesis" less involved with religion than Saint-Simonism. Somewhat wary of mystical excesses, Herzen still held off from complete
commitment to the New Christianity.

A few days later Ogarev returned to the attack in an even more
exalted mood. He declared that the philosophy of history, "the greatest
subject of our times," must be integrated with the philosophy of religion,
the philosophy of nature, and ontology: in other words, idealism and the
New Christianity must be integrated into one, unified system (an effort
which eventually culminated in Ogarev's *Profession de foi*). Particularly
important is the study of "how religious thought developed in mankind:
before Christianity, pantheism; after Christianity, deism"; and at the
end of this evolution of religion into philosophy, the hoped-for "regeneration" of mankind. In his enthusiasm for this new synthesis Ogarev announced his conversion to belief in a Creator, at the same time pleading
with Herzen, who remained hostile to such an idea, not to treat his belief
"coldly." Then the tone of the letter changes, revealing the despondency
that lay beneath his new hope. "In a moment of bitterness, disappointment and hate" he had reread Schiller's *William Tell*, that play of a
"period of crisis," so like his own age. "But all this is the thought of
destruction! I already wish to create; out of the general principles of my
philosophy of history I must deduce a plan of association [the term of
Fourier]. Fourier I have not yet read, but will read, perhaps today." The
frustration of inaction, however, is again overcome by hope in the ideal,
and the letter closes with a poem written at sunrise on a wonderful
morning, after a sleepless night of "visions," "secret dreams," and "fiery
reflections" — the "children of the soul's fullness." As the sunlight spreads
over the woods and glades, Ogarev's heart is buoyed up by the conviction

that some great spirit dwells in all; suddenly his thought is illumined, "everything is filled with the secret of the divinity, and the world seems to grasp the soul of the universe." [29] Schelling, Lamennais, "socialism," Christianity and his own nameless longings are fused in a compound of sadness and joy, of the desire to destroy and the desire to create, of frustration and expectation.

Herzen answered disapprovingly of this excess of Schelling and mysticism; at the same time he announced that he had embarked on a more positive program of study, comprising history and political economy, under the guidance of a law professor at the university.[30] Nevertheless, the result of these endeavors, revealed in a letter to his friend a few days later, was a version of the New Christianity only slightly less mystical, and no less metaphysical, than Ogarev's own. Herzen first of all recognized that he had insufficiently appreciated the "poetry" of Christianity. He then proceeded to give a sketch of its historical significance, largely in the spirit of Saint-Simon, but with appropriate borrowings from other sources. The general tenor of the sketch betrays a debt to the "World Spirit" of Schelling and idealism, and many of the specific historical judgments derive from Michelet's *Roman History*, from Augustin Thierry, and especially from Guizot's *Histoire de la civilization en Europe et en France*, a favorite mine of ideas and information in Russia at the time.[31] This letter, the principal statement of Herzen's Saint-Simonism, deserves comment at some length, however cumbersome it may be to render its "historiosophical" jargon into English.

Essentially, Herzen's speculations reduce to a commonplace of the historical literature of the Restoration, both in France and Germany, and hence also in Russia, where it was repeated in different forms by such writers as Ivan Kireevski, Polevoi, and Pogodin;[32] in fact, Herzen himself had already touched on it in his article on Peter the Great earlier in the year. This commonplace was that contemporary civilization was founded on a classical and a Christian heritage, and that European history since antiquity had consisted in the development of the principles of humanitarianism, individuality, and freedom implicit in both inheritances. Specifically, Herzen's sketch of this theme went as follows.

In the ancient world, before Christianity, the development of the "civic spirit" was "one-sided" and man was swallowed up in the city. Moreover, the human quality of all men was not recognized, since slavery was an accepted institution even for the most enlightened, such as Aristotle; nor was there any idea of human betterment and progress. Imperial Rome represented the final consequences of this "one-sidedness"; once the world was at their feet, the Romans became no more than "slaves in republican dress; Rome simply began to rot." In short, the ancient world developed the idea of man as a citizen, but not as a complete individual, and this limitation on its creative powers was the cause of its decay. This "one-sidedness" also caused the rise of a dialectical antithesis, or rather, of two of them. On the one hand, "the Cimbri and the Teutons appeared — the virgin peoples of the north began to pour forth into Italy — pure and virtuous"; on the other hand, "in Nazareth was born the son of a carpenter, Christ. To him (so speaks the Apostle Paul) was granted the destiny of reconciling God with man. . . . 'All men are equal,' says Christ. 'Love one another, help one another' — here is the incommensurable foundation on which Christianity is based." Christianity and the barbarians together represented the "rebirth" of the "dying" classical world and the origins of modern Europe. They were able to fulfill this function because both contained in germ the idea of the sanctity of the individual and the equality of all men; and this was especially true of Christianity.

For centuries, however, the democratic implications of Christianity remained largely an unfulfilled promise. ". . . men did not understand it. Its first phase was mystical (Catholicism) . . . The second phase was the transition from mysticism to philosophy (Luther). Now the third, *true, human* phase is beginning, the phalansteries (or perhaps Saint-Simonism? ?)" The promise of Christianity would be fulfilled only when it became a secular, social doctrine founded on "reason." Since this process had only recently begun, though, there remained two conflicting strains of thought in the world. One was "still mystical," that is, all the forms of religion that had survived from the Middle Ages; the other was "purely philosophical: Voltaire, Locke, the sensualists." Herzen added fondly: "I thought this idea was completely new and my own, and I cherished it"; he was chagrined to discover it in a certain Charles Didier, a minor contemporary radical whose works were discussed in the Saint-Simonian *Revue Encyclopédique*. Nonetheless, he agreed that this "sensualism," or the rationalism of the Enlightenment, "had an effect on the political world analogous to that of Christianity." [33] In other words, early Christianity, the Reformation, the Enlightenment, 1789, and the future social revolution were successive and interrelated stages in the historical development of the ideas of the supreme worth of the individual and of human freedom. This, in its essence, is the metaphysical scheme of the New Christianity, though it is also near in spirit to Fourierism and other radical social philosophies of the thirties, as Herzen himself sensed when he claimed to hesitate between the phalansteries and Saint-Simon.

Yet, still distrustful of so much emphasis on religion, Herzen was careful to disentangle himself from the Saint-Simonians' residual admiration for Rome. The Pope was not, as he was for Didier,

the highest manifestation of Christianity, its expression in one person. No, to me (and this thought is really my own) the Pope is explained by the South. The

South is sensualist and sensuous: the ardent nature of the South, its torrid sun, makes it nearer to the earth, and this is why the immaterial religion of Christ, born among the dying Semitic tribes, *a religion not native to Asia, a religion in essence of the Germanic and Slavic tribes, realized itself in the South in the Pope.* What was Rome? A peasant with strong fists. And the Rome of the Popes was the material side of Christianity, and decidedly not its idea.[34]

Though this theory of the Papacy is not important in itself, since Herzen was not to return to it, it is noteworthy as an example of the method of "proof" by poetic analogy he had first derived from Schelling. Just as significant is his judgment on the essence of Christianity. The German romantics had already decided that Christianity, the "religion of freedom," was really more native to the North than to the Mediterranean, and that its libertarian implications were fully developed only in an evolution running from the barbarian *comitatus* through Luther to idealistic philosophy (or at times to Anglo-Saxon political institutions). Here Herzen has extended this privilege to the Slavs. His purpose was primarily, as in his essay on Peter the Great, to include Russia in the main stream of European civilization and hence to assert her historical right to eventual freedom on a footing of complete equality with the West. Yet at the same time, like the Germans, he has given his native land a special relationship to the "religion of freedom." From the beginning Herzen's socialism was not without a tinge of nationalism, if for the moment only ever so faint.

This set of ideas was the essence of Herzen's youthful Saint-Simonism. He is a little more political and a little less supernatural in his use of Christianity than Ogarev, but basically his position is the same. His socialism was a theory of progress that is primarily ethical, since religion is only a poetic expression of true humanism, and secondly idealist, since the evolution of ethical concepts, or "enlightenment," constitutes the universal impulse to progress. This was to be the whole of Herzen's "socialism" down to 1840, and a large part of it thereafter.

Moreover, the specific applications given here to these general concepts were to be repeated endlessly over the years. By the age of twenty-one Herzen had developed his permanent arsenal of "historiosophical" arguments. First, there was the parallel between the "death" of the ancient world followed by its "rebirth" in Christianity on the one hand, and the present crises of the "old world" to be followed by its hoped-for rebirth as a "new world" of socialism on the other. Secondly, there was the analogy between nations and organisms, which held that peoples can be "young" and "virgin" or that they can "grow old" and "die" — with the obvious advantage this conferred on such recent arrivals in history as the Slavs. Finally, there was the idea that all changes from Luther to the French Revolution had been only negative or destructive, that despite all attacks many old superstitions and shackles still remained, and that a truly rational society was yet to be built. The Great Revolution was a beginning and not an end, while the final "palingenesis" was still to come. Herzen himself was aware that these ideas expressed his deepest aspirations: "Don't tear up this letter, save it, maybe I will need it someday, for at present I am in a great state of exaltation over your letter and in a cool mood I won't be able to reproduce these thoughts." [35] The admonition was quite superfluous (though it is consistent with Herzen's sense of self-importance), for the same thoughts were to reappear in endless variations in all his writings.

The nearest that Herzen came during his Saint-Simonian period to a programmatic statement of his "socialism" — in the sense of a conscious opposition to liberalism — was in a letter to Ogarev written a few days later. In this declaration Herzen expanded the idea that all previous revolutions had been only negative. "The century of analysis and destruction begun by the Reformation was finished by the Revolution. France expressed it in all its *completeness*." To this principle of Saint-Simon Herzen adds a bit of Schelling. "Each separate people expresses one idea, and France expressed hers in this century of criticism, which gives rise to the question: will regeneration come from France? It would seem not, in theory, and a factual analysis leads to the same conclusion." The French nation was "in the grossest ignorance" — by which Herzen meant ignorance of the new German "science." Moreover, France had participated in the "corruption of the eighteenth century, she is impure" — which meant that France was capable of destruction but not of the "new, enormous task of reconstruction." Where, then, would this occur? "In England? No, her motto is egoism [individualistic liberalism], her patriotism is egoism, her Tories and Whigs are egoists, they have no sense of community [with the other peoples of Europe], no foundation in breadth. The Normans gave the English Magna Carta, and Europe did not participate; Cromwell appeared and Europe remained aside." Translated still more plainly into the language of the nation under discussion, the English were neither democrats who believed in the people, nor internationalists who believed in the brotherhood of all men; they were selfish, aristocratic individualists and narrow nationalists, with none of that breadth of vision required to produce the rebirth of Europe.

Whence, then, will regeneration come? "I boldly answer: in Germany, yes in the land of the pure Teutons, in the land of the vehmic courts, in the land of the *Burschenschaft*, and the rule *Alle für Einen, Einer für Alle*." Germany was still "young," she had not yet played her full role in history, and she possessed a sense of democratic fraternity and mutual help — in short, of the "social." These are precisely the qualities that Herzen would later find peculiarly Russian. The outlook in Russia at this time, however, both political and intellectual, was too bleak, and the prestige of German "science" too great, for Herzen to claim the supreme, "palingenetic" honor for his native land. Therefore, regeneration could only come from Germany. Why, then, does Germany not take a "clearly contemporary," that is, radical, direction? Because for the moment a "contemporary direction" is *une transaction entre la féodalité et la liberté*, a contract between the lord and his servants." In these words, made somewhat obscure by a long frequentation of abstract terminology, Herzen is castigating political liberalism and "one-sided" individualism, without any sense of the social. Rather than accept the compromises of mere liberalism, as France had done in 1830, Germany did far better to concentrate on the true foundations of the coming regeneration, the revolution in men's minds. "Enlightenment — there is the answer!" And Herzen concludes, in enigmatic tones, that when he speaks of Germany he does not mean reactionary Prussia, but "a certain part" of Württemberg (no doubt because it was the birthplace of Schiller) and Weimar, the center of idealist humanism. "Here I stop. You will understand my thoughts. I will work them out in an article *for friends*." [36] The article, if it ever was written, unfortunately has not survived.

This was the full extent of Herzen's and Ogarev's youthful Saint-Simonism. It should be noted first of all that it derived not from Saint-Simon himself but from the Saint-Simonian "church," such as it existed after the master's death and particularly after 1830. At no time do Herzen and Ogarev seem to have read Saint-Simon himself — except perhaps his last work, the *New Christianity* — with his technocratic rationalism and emphasis on economics. Instead they seem to have studied only his disciples — Enfantin, Leroux, Buchez, the brothers Rodrigues, and Bazard — all of whom, with the partial exception of the last, heavily accented the mystical and ethical aspects of the doctrine. Even in this reading, however, Herzen and Ogarev completely overlooked what the disciples retained of Saint-Simon's remarkable insights into the effect of economics on the workings of society. Instead they seized on three aspects of the system: its ethical mysticism, or the New Christianity; its philosophy of history, which explained the progress of mankind from the "old world" to the "new"; and the vague rejection of merely political reform in favor of some deeper regeneration, which was conceived of as an ethical and ideological change as much as a social one. Thus they adopted from Saint-Simon what was most general and abstract and hence nearest to German idealism. Indeed, all that they took from the Saint-Simonians could be, and was, fitted into the biography of the Absolute as written by Schelling, and fused with the half-religious, half-aesthetic ideal of man derived from Schiller. They had taken only the first, and purely ideological, step toward the democratic and rationalistic maximalism that is socialism.

4

What did Herzen and Ogarev propose to do about their new convictions? There was little they could do but hope in the future and in the meantime feed the flame of expectation by intense reading, questioning and writing. In short, they could further the cause of "enlightenment," and first of all in themselves, for it was on this that the realization of the "new world" depended. There is every evidence that the years 1833 and 1834 were spent in feverish speculation, conversation and correspondence, for the two were convinced that the salvation of Russia depended on their work of self-enlightenment. Herzen had his program for the study of world history. Ogarev was busy with the construction of his "system" uniting the philosophies of religion, history and nature, or Schelling with Saint-Simon. The activities of both combined with similar efforts by other members of the group. Herzen found in the Passek brothers, Vadim and Diomed, a common concern with history, while Ogarev conducted an involved correspondence with Lakhtin on the philosophy of history and religion.[37] Numerous "articles for friends only" seem to have been written, or at least planned, though few have survived. Herzen composed an article on a work called *Introduction à la science de l'histoire ou science du développement de l'humanité*, by the Catholic socialist Buchez. It also seems that he was "publishing a book" — of which absolutely no trace has survived — "on the present state of enlightenment in Germany," a project that, given his views on the ultimately revolutionary significance of "enlightenment," had obviously political overtones.[38] In his letters Ogarev speaks of numerous articles, which, more often than not, appear never to have seen the light of day.

The use of the term article rather than essay is no slip of the pen. The group did not wish to keep its enlightenment to itself, but dreamed constantly of carrying it to the nation. To this end Herzen for a time thought of preparing himself for a professorship in natural history at the university. But the real hope of the group was journalism. The vaguely liberal *Moscow Telegraph* of Polevoi was inadequate to their new demands: it was too timid in tone, too ignorant of the new German "science," and would have nothing to do with Saint-Simonism. According to *My Past and Thoughts*, Herzen broke with Polevoi over the question of Saint-Simonism, which the latter denounced as "madness, an empty utopia, hindering civic development." [39] Either as a result of this quarrel or from a desire for activity broader than speculation within the confines of the circle, the group planned, or at least dreamed of, its own review, more enlightened than the *Telegraph*.

The participants in the proposed enterprise were Herzen, Ogarev, Sazonov, Satin, Ketcher, and Lakhtin. The program, as drawn up by Herzen, was Schellingian in inspiration, with such intimations of Saint-Simonism as it was hoped the censorship would allow. The purpose of the review was: "To follow humanity in the principal phases of its development, and for this to turn at times to the past, to explain certain moments of the marvellous biography of the human species and to deduce from this our own position, to turn attention to our own hopes." The first form of the study of mankind was literature, or more generally, aesthetics:

Mankind develops in two directions: in the civic world and in the aesthetic world, in the world of the *deed* and the world of the *word*. But these two branches, like those currents which wash the bright valleys of paradise, take their rise from one source, from the place of the creation of man, and flow into one holy Ganges. For this reason literature and the political world seem to us inseparable. The civic condition is the *incarnate word*, and conversely literature, as the word of the people, is the expression of its life.[40]

Since for Herzen and his circle, however, there could be no "world of the deed," the "world of the word" had to bear the psychological burden of both; the immaterial voice of enlightenment became tantamount to a political act. The same mystical "identity" that existed between man and art also bound man to nature; "consequently, in order to understand man it is necessary to understand nature." So the review would have a section devoted to the natural sciences, in particular to those which show most clearly how man emerges from nature — "the geological, physiological and psychological" sciences.[41]

The most important place in the review, however, would be occupied by history, the nearest to actual politics among the various substitutes for it which the circle pursued. "The subject of history is the life of mankind. And that life is nothing other than the process of elevating the form to the idea" — which was simply an abstract way of saying that the life of man is progress through enlightenment to full personality.[42] The threefold division of Schelling's thought into the philosophies of art, nature, and history is faithfully reproduced, but the whole system has been given a more social, less metaphysical bent. The philosophy of art has lost, and the philosophy of history has gained in importance, and under the philosophy of history have been included vague ideas of a social "palingenesis" after the manner of the Saint-Simonians. It was this fusion of idealism and socialism which constituted the "enlightenment" which Herzen, frustrated of more concrete activity, wished to make the vehicle of his mission for Russia. Yet even this modest measure of self-expression was denied him by the police of Nicholas: the review was nipped in the bud by the group's arrest before the first steps had been taken towards its creation.

Indeed, Herzen and his circle had not really thought they would be allowed to speak their "word" of enlightenment. Their dreams were less of victory than of martyrdom. Whatever Herzen tried to imagine himself doing, he always saw it ending in defeat, like the activities of the Decembrists. This is indicated by his first love affair, which occurred during his Saint-Simonian period. The object of his sentiment was a sister of the Passeks, Liudmila, the "Gaetana" of *My Past and Thoughts*. On Herzen's side the affair did not go very deep, and seems to have been conducted more as an experiment in testing his power to attract women's hearts than as a serious relationship. The effort proved gratifyingly successful, indeed, too much so, for it turned out — to Liudmila's great misfortune — to be the love of her life, whereas for Herzen it was no more than a passing idyl. Yet it has its significance for Herzen too, which lies in the elevated and civic tone in which it was conducted.

The pair imagined themselves as the hero and heroine of a melodramatic novel called *The Maimed One* by a French writer, Saintine, from whom they took the name Gaetana. Liudmila nobly recognized that she must not let herself stand in the way of Alexander's mission for Russia. She knew he must fight for the truth, either from a chair at the university or through the printed word, until Nicholas at last cut him down, while he knew this martyrdom would be the only blow he could strike for Russia. On the model furnished by Saintine, the two imagined in vivid detail Herzen's self-sacrificing struggle against the "monstrous force" of autocracy, his inevitable failure, "the exile and the dungeons" and "how she would accompany me to the Siberian mines" — just like the Decembrists and their heroic wives.[43] As in boyhood, when he had played at a Schilleresque Decembrism with Ogarev, Herzen was defeatist because he knew in his heart, in spite of all his brave visions, that in the real world he was powerless to change anything. So, just as in boyhood, his politics tended to literary daydreaming, only now the dream, in addition to the presence of his Gaetana, was enriched by the complexities of idealist and socialist metaphysics. The poetic symbols of Schiller had been transformed into the symbols of a philosophy of history and of religion. But the new symbols, like the old, remained disembodied abstractions, for anything more concrete was still impossible.

5

Herzen and Ogarev gave no more precise statement of their new faith than such abstractions. Is this enough, then, to call the pair "socialist"? They did not mention the most obvious programmatic demand of socialism, the abolition of private property; nothing in their situation made them feel that property was the cause of their oppression, or of that of the masses. In a more general way, they had no notion of the economic aspects of inequality, or of economic factors as a force influencing politics. Nor, aside from a general opposition of "egoism" to "love," a notion long ago derived from Schiller and Goethe, and a vague idea of "association," did they have any concept of a "collective" organization of society. Even their sense of "the people" was very weak. Their "socialism," then, consisted only in the general idea that political change was not enough, but that some universal or "social," change would be necessary to root out all the old, bad things and inaugurate the new world.

With regard to the institutional aspects of this change they were vague almost to the point of silence; still, certain things may be inferred with certainty. The launching of the "new world," of course, would be accompanied by the end of autocracy and serfdom together with the establishment of all the usual political freedoms. It would also probably take the form of a revolution, since the pair inevitably associated progress with action in the tradition of 1789 or of the Decembrists, as the only forms of protest they knew. But they seemed never to have asked whether the revolution would be made by the masses or by an elite, since the possibility of change in Russia was so remote as to deprive this problem of practical significance. Action by an elite, however, on the model of the Decembrists, was certainly what suited them best psychologically. It fitted their sense of personal mission, their self-image as the vanguard of "enlightenment," their aristocratic tempers, and their position as an isolated minority lacking contact with the masses. Also, they worried little over means because they thought of the revolution less in national than in European terms, eagerly scanning the western horizon for help from outside, either from the "science" of Germany or the political agitation of France.

The most fundamental reason, however, why they were so little concerned with institutions or means was that they looked on the coming change primarily as a revolution in men's minds. After his arrest Herzen declared to his interrogators: "In the ways of thinking and living (*v nravakh*) of Europe there is much that is obsolete, that no longer has the same meaning as formerly; these hangovers from the past must be replaced by ways of thinking and living derived from new principles, with a purer morality." [44] When due allowance is made for the fact that Herzen was trying here to make his interest in "regeneration" seem as unpolitical as possible, this is still an accurate statement of what he held the essence of the coming revolution to be. This philosophy of his twenty-first year was to remain substantially his position for the rest of his life.

In drawing the lesson from the failure of the Revolution of 1848 to "regenerate" humanity, he wrote:

> Ordinarily men think that socialism has as its exclusive end the solution of the question of capital, unearned income and wages, i.e. the abolition of cannibalism in its cultivated forms [an expression of Blanqui]. This is not exactly so. The economic questions are extremely important, but they constitute only one side of the concept of socialism, which aims, on a par with the destruction of the abuses of property, at the destruction of everything monarchic, everything religious — in the courts, in the government, in the whole social structure, and most of all — in the family, in private life, around the hearth, in the conduct of the individual, in *morality*.[45]

In conceiving of socialism in this ethical and idealist manner Herzen and Ogarev reflected the frustrations of their position as an insignificant and impotent minority. They began by desiring freedom from an absurd, confining world, freedom to become the full, creative individuals they felt themselves potentially to be. But since they lacked concrete means to achieve this liberation they were forced to seek it in ideal constructs — universal "reason," the sweep of history, the "idea" of religion, or an apocalyptic struggle between the "old world" and the "new." For want of anything firm to grasp hold of, to agitate for, abstraction was the only refuge: either the conquest of an ideal independence through self-consciousness as preached by German "science," or the more disembodied aspects of French socialism, the philosophies of history and religion and the pure principles of enlightenment, progress, and humanity.

This tendency to generalities was all the stronger since the whole existing order in Russia, and not just certain aspects, was odious to them. Partial reform was not a solution, since there was nothing they wanted to keep. Piecemeal change might satisfy Englishmen, and even a majority of Frenchmen, in spite of the agitation of a radical fringe. But as things stood under Nicholas, the choice for humane, sensitive Russians was literally all or nothing. Even if there had been something worth keeping, the government's attitude made partial reform an unreal issue. So the only recourse was to demand a *totally* rational and just society, without compromise — or the "new world" of socialism. Yet, since for this too the practical means were lacking, the demand for revolution could express itself only as "hope in the future" and as a mystical certitude that the Absolute, History, the Idea and the logic of enlightenment, rather than mere men, were working for "regeneration." An infinitesimal minority, Herzen, Ogarev, and their friends had to trust to forces larger than themselves, forces that were necessary and inevitable. They had to exalt these forces to the level of the divine, to turn them into a secular religion, and to surround them with all the power of emotion and sentiment, since there was so little pragmatic ground for belief that their dream would come true.

Of course, all these far-flung fantasies were in reality a projection of themselves. They had generalized their own frustrated desires into a demand for the liberation of all men. Their feeling for equality and their solicitude for the "people," in the very abstract way that Herzen and Ogarev entertained such sentiments at this time, originated in a heightened awareness of their own worth. Most of all, they had generalized this awareness into an eschatological March of History, and at the beginning their "socialism" meant this much more than any conscious concern for the "people." As they grew older their socialism moved gradually from the general to the particular, from History to concrete men. But its origin was in a grandiose "historiosophical" projection of themselves, compounded with Saint-Simon and Schelling and with all the magnificent visions of progress and "palingenesis" that similarly cramped souls in the West had invented.

Thus, sensitive and proud gentlemen, hyperconscious of their value as individuals and impatient of all restraint on their wills, in demanding their own liberty were led to demand the destruction of the existing order and a total, democratic "regeneration." It was in this manner that "socialism" was born in Russia in the heads of a few members of the aristocracy. And this is no paradox if "socialism" is regarded not as the class consciousness of a proletariat, or a demand for the equalization of wealth, or a sense of the economic as opposed to the political, but as the "maximalist" wing of the opposition to a paternalistic and authoritarian old regime. Such in fact was the origin of the movement in Russia among the circle of Herzen and Ogarev.

CHAPTER VII

Arrest and Exile

THE ARREST of Herzen, Ogarev, and most of their circle came about in an accidental and unforeseen manner. Ever since the Decembrist uprising, and especially since the Polish revolt of 1830, a jumpy government tended to see plots everywhere. The University of Moscow, in particular, was an object of its suspicions; between 1825 and the affair in which Herzen was involved there had already been two "conspiracies" uncovered among the students. The first, known as "the affair of the Kritski brothers," had occurred in 1827. The participants were accused, rather fancifully, of organizing a secret society with an eventual view to overthrowing the government, and, more realistically, of spreading the forbidden verses of Pushkin, Ryleev, and Polezhaev. Polezhaev, himself a former student of the university, had only the year before been sent into the army by Nicholas in punishment for a satirical poem that displayed sympathy for the Decembrists. All those involved in the Kritski affair received heavy sentences, either prison or service on remote frontiers as privates in the army.[1]

The second affair, that of the so-called "secret society of Sungurov," occurred in 1831, after Herzen's arrival at the university, and several of the participants were known to him personally. These men seemed in fact, and not just in the imagination of the police, to have formed a loose organization, and looked on themselves as the continuators of the Decembrists. Even more subversively, they were in close contact with certain Polish officers then resident in Moscow who were preparing to join the revolt at home. After spending a year and a half in prison awaiting sentence, Sungurov and his friends were dispatched to hard labor in Siberia or to the ranks of the army.[2] Memories of Polezhaev, the Kritski brothers, and especially Sungurov were still fresh at the university in the time of Herzen and Ogarev. The long tradition of Russian revolutionary martyrology was being created under their eyes.

It was through a show of sympathy for Sungurov and his friends that the circle of Herzen and Ogarev first drew the attention of the police to itself. Sungurov and his companions were without money or adequate clothing for the long journey east, and Ogarev took up a collection for them among his and Herzen's friends. The beneficiaries wrote their thanks from Orenburg, but the bearer of their letter turned out to be sufficiently anxious to demonstrate his loyalty to the emperor to turn it over to the authorities. Herzen was not mentioned in the incriminating missive, but Ogarev, Ketcher, Satin, and Vadim Passek were. They were called in by the police, reprimanded, and told that henceforth they would be kept under "strict surveillance." The warning had no effect, however. The group went about Moscow flaunting tricolored scarfs and berets à la Karl Sand.[3] Ogarev in particular kept dubious company, which included a fellow poet, V. I. Sokolovski, who had been in government service in Siberia, where he had known some of the exiled Decembrists. Under their influence, he had composed a number of unpublished, and unpublishable, political verses. According to a police report of December 1833, he and Ogarev had been observed on the steps of the Maly Theatre "in an excessively unsober state" singing the "French aria, *Allons enfants de la patrie*" — in those innocent days still a subversive hymn.[4]

The crisis came in connection with a series of mysterious fires which ravaged Moscow for a period of several weeks in 1834. Under conditions where a legal right for the redress of most grievances did not exist, a favorite outlet for social discontent was arson. The famous Petersburg fires of 1862 — started either by radicals, or by the Right in order to discredit the radicals — were only the most celebrated examples of this phenomenon. In 1834 in Moscow, as fire after fire broke out in the largely wooden city, the population was thrown into a panic and both the local administration and the central government were deeply alarmed. Numerous arrests were made, in part to allay the authorities' feeling of helplessness, in part to terrify whoever might be responsible. The real culprits, however, remained undiscovered. In the midst of this panic an individual described as a "mechanic" came to the police and denounced certain drunken young men who wandered the streets at night singing seditious songs — with the implication that there was a connection between these activities and the fires. The mechanic was instructed to set himself up as a *provocateur,* and on July 8, with police funds, he arranged a drinking bout in his quarters at which the incriminating songs were sung with the *Oberpolizeimeister* of Moscow listening behind the door. Neither Herzen nor any of his friends was present at this gathering, but one of those arrested, in order to ease his own lot, denounced the seditious opinions of Ogarev and another member of the circle, I. A. Obolenski. As a result, Ogarev was taken into custody, and when the police found in his papers certain letters from Herzen (most of which were quoted in the previous chapter), on July 21 he, too, was arrested. A few days later

Satin and Lakhtin were apprehended by a similar process, although none
of the group except Ogarev had known directly any of the participants
in the affair. As a final display of logic, Sokolovski, who all the time had
been in Petersburg, but some of whose verses had been sung at the party,
was arrested as "the chief participant in the affair." [5]

The matter was submitted to Benkendorf, the chief of the Third
Section of His Imperial Majesty's Own Chancellery (the political police
established by Nicholas after 1825). Benkendorf placed the affair before
the emperor, and the latter ordered the establishment of a special investigating commission, similar to that which had "tried" the Decembrists.
The prisoners were incarcerated separately without the right to com-
municate with one another. There was, of course, no counsel for the
defense, and the proceedings were strictly administrative and secret.
Herzen initially was placed in an ordinary prison in Moscow. Although
as the son of a noble and a political offender he was lodged in a separate
cell, he had occasion for the first time to observe, in the treatment of
numerous suspected arsonists from the lower classes, the full brutality
and arbitrariness of imperial "justice." The spectacle brought home to
him how the capricious oppression from which he himself suffered was
multiplied a thousandfold and as a daily occurrence for the defenseless
masses;[6] the rather abstract sympathy for the people derived from his
own frustrations began to acquire a more real content. In September he
was transferred to a solitary cell in a former monastery near Moscow,
where he remained until the end of March, 1835. All told, he passed ten
months under interrogation and waiting to be sentenced. The regimentation to which he was subjected was not particularly severe. He
could have books and small luxuries such as wine, and he was permitted
to correspond with his family although not to receive visits. Several of
the prison officers, young noblemen like himself who were uneasy in exe-
cuting a punishment they felt was excessive, cooperated beyond the letter
of the law to make life as bearable as possible.[7] Still, the shock of his
confinement was a severe one and an unexpectedly harsh sequel to his
romantic and purely cerebral *fronde* against the regime.

The intention of the government was to establish that the miscellaneous assortment of people apprehended constituted a secret society engaged in a conspiracy against the state. The investigation failed to bear
this out, but Nicholas and the representative of the Third Section on the
commission, Prince A. F. Golitsyn, insisted nonetheless on severity. The
accused were divided into three groups. First there were the authors of
the objectionable songs, including Sokolovski, and those who had participated in the singing; their position was the most serious since the government did have evidence, however trivial, against them. Secondly, there

was a miscellaneous group of persons who had been implicated in the affair only through the excessive zeal of the police. Finally, there were Herzen, Ogarev, Satin, and Lakhtin (the rest of the circle had escaped notice, an indication of the fundamental inefficiency of Nicholas' gendarmes). The commission recognized that Herzen and his friends had nothing to do with the "pasquinades" and that, moreover, they were without any intent to act, their ideas being no more than "the mere dreams of a fiery imagination." [8] Nonetheless they were held to be potentially if not actually dangerous; from their correspondence the commission described Herzen as "a bold free-thinker, exceedingly dangerous for society" and Ogarev as "a stubborn and covert fanatic." [9] The interrogation revolved around this "free-thinking," as exposed in their letters, and in particular around their interest in Saint-Simonism, for the trial of the Saint-Simonians in 1832 had brought their doctrines to the attention even of the police of Nicholas I.

In *My Past and Thoughts* Herzen somewhat exaggerates the carefree boldness of his replies to the judges; he even relates how he twitted a worthy but not very learned member of the commission for having in his library the *Memoirs* of the *Duke* of Saint-Simon.* [10] The transcript of the interrogation gives a somewhat different picture. Herzen and Ogarev tried as best they could to give innocuous explanations of the more embarrassing passages in their letters, emphasizing the theme of religious and moral regeneration divorced from all politics.[11] Still, they did this in a manner compatible with their dignity; they omitted or soft-pedaled certain things they did believe but subscribed to nothing they did not believe. In particular, they made no display of remorse and owned to no guilt. This, more than anything else, made their cases seem grave to the commission. In part through the intercession of Herzen's father with influential friends, and in part because of standing policy, they were offered a light sentence if they would admit their guilt, denounce other individuals, and promise to reform. The government was as much interested in winning over to the throne culprits so young and malleable as in punishing them.[12] But Herzen and Ogarev, as well as the other members of their circle, refused to capitulate, unlike some of the smaller fry caught in the police net. This action gave Herzen a pleasing sense of heroism, but it also called down the full rigor of the government's wrath. Herzen was sentenced to exile for an indeterminate period in the remote provincial city of Perm — which was almost immediately changed to nearby Viatka — where he was to serve as a government clerk. Ogarev was sent on the same terms to Penza, his native province, a favor granted

* The memorialist of the court of Louis XIV; Herzen's Saint-Simon, of course, was only a count.

only because his aged father lay paralyzed and dying at home. Those who repented got off with little more than a reprimand. The chief culprits, Sokolovski and two others, received the heaviest sentences — confinement in the dread Schlüsselburg fortress for an unspecified period, from which two of them emerged broken men and one never emerged at all.[13]

The whole affair was typical of the moral tone of Nicholas' rule: the trappings of a benevolent paternalism vainly attempted to conceal an arbitrary exercise of power which recognized no rights for the individual independent of the needs of the state and the will of the emperor. That there was no law in Russia but his will, and no appeal from the brutality of his agents would have been bad enough if displayed frankly; it was made doubly unbearable by a hypocritical solicitude for the lost sheep, and the mingling of arbitrary punishment with arbitrary favors. Autocracy in itself was odious, but Nicholas' personal style of autocracy was particularly loathsome, since he wished to play father to the nation precisely at the moment when the growing children desired to strike out on their own. The exaggerated suspicion of the government, going to the point of imagining conspiracies where none existed, its inability to distinguish any shades of opinion between abject servility and sedition, only made the situation more intolerable.

Herzen had known about all this before. It had been manifested in Nicholas' treatment of his various wayward sons from the Decembrists to Polezhaev; it was present in the very air of Russia after 1825, in the suppression of the chair of philosophy at the University of Moscow, in the capricious closing of periodicals, such as Kireevski's *European* in 1832 or Polevoi's *Moscow Telegraph* in 1834; but most painfully of all it appeared in the perpetual necessity for caution and subterfuge in expressing one's most essential thoughts — or simply in being oneself. It was only his arrest on the most absurd of pretexts that brought home to Herzen for the first time the full force of what it meant to be an independent, thinking individual, or simply an individual, in Nicholas I's Russia. Until then his radicalism had been as much directed against the ways of Ivan Alexeevich as against the regime. It was, to be sure, still very immature: part adolescent pose, part the flexing of young muscles, part youthful seriousness for generous principles. But active persecution by the government began to harden this *fronde* into a real radicalism. Until then Herzen and his friends, in spite of what they knew had happened to others, hardly realized the degree to which they were playing with fire in baiting Nicholas. If they had been only a little more imprudent they could easily have experienced the fate of Sokolovski or Polezhaev, or later of the Ukrainian poet Shevchenko or the Petrashevski circle — years of confinement in a fortress or degrading servitude as privates in the army — and life in effect would have been over.

2

As it was, they hardly got off lightly. After ten months in prison, from July 1834 to April 1835, Herzen spent five more years in exile in remote provincial towns: almost three years in Viatka, from 1835 to the end of 1837, and another two years in Vladimir, until early 1840. Viatka was by far the heavier punishment of the two. Situated a thousand versts from Moscow in the northern reaches of European Russia, almost on the Siberian frontier, it was bleak, backward and poor, and the very end of the earth for the young aristocrat from the capital. Vladimir, only two hundred versts from Moscow, was much more civilized, although still provincial. Still, near or far from Moscow, Herzen remained cut off from the social amenities, the companionship, and the life of ideas that had been his world until then. For five long years he was out of circulation, thrown inward on his own resources and surrounded by a reality harsher than any he had ever known.

This isolation was the principal suffering of exile, for in all other respects he was reasonably comfortable. He knew none of the horrors experienced, for instance, by Dostoevski, under the grimmer forms of banishment which Nicholas had at his disposal. Except for the fact that he could not leave his province of residence or resign from government service, Herzen lived a normal civilian life. He even departed from Moscow accompanied by a German valet, an old retainer of the family named Karl Ivanovich Sonnenberg, charged by Ivan Alexeevich with looking after the young master, and in particular with arranging for his physical comfort. In Viatka Sonnenberg rented and equipped a house, and purchased three horses, two for Herzen and one for himself.[14] Money was never wanting, since Ivan Alexeevich was as large with his purse as he was small with less palpable manifestations of his affection. Materially the old life of ease continued, if on a provincial scale. It is true that for two years in Viatka Herzen served a hard master, the Governor Tiufiaev (of whom more will be said later); Herzen had several collisions with him which could have resulted in further banishment to some remote village of the province had Tiufiaev not been disgraced in time. Yet, with this one exception, Herzen was never harassed by his superiors, a fact of which he characteristically makes much less in his memoirs than of Tiufiaev's persecutions. Indeed, after the fall of the latter, Herzen, as a cultivated young man of good family, was accorded privileged treatment, and in particular, relief from the drudgery of bureaucratic work, by the successive governors under whom he served.[15] For all this, exile was nevertheless exile, and the shock was a severe one which upset his spiritual equilibrium and deflected his intellectual development for most of his young manhood.

Externally, at least, he was kept occupied. For the first months in Viatka he worked as a subaltern clerk in the provincial chancellery, a cruel descent for one whose ambitions and self-esteem were pitched so high. Then he found some relief. The government issued orders for a statistical survey of the empire by provinces, and the survey for Viatka was entrusted to Herzen, as the only well-educated functionary of the chancellery. Moreover, by a special dispensation from the governor he was allowed to work at home, away from the depressing company of the other clerks. In the spring of 1837, for a visit of the Crown Prince, his learning was called on once again to arrange an exhibition of the products of the province. In the last months of his stay in Viatka he participated in a commission investigating embezzlement in the administration of state property. In Vladimir his duties were significantly lighter and somewhat more interesting. In 1839 the government ordered the administration of each province to establish a newspaper for the enlightenment and instruction of the population, and Herzen was made one of the two editors of the *Vladimir vedomosti,* a task neither exacting nor time-consuming.[16]

These occupations gave Herzen for the first time in his life a chance to learn something of the realities of Russian government. Unfortunately we are not as accurately informed as might be desired of the impressions he received. There is a voluminous correspondence for the years of this exile, but except for occasional letters to members of his circle who had escaped arrest, all of it is addressed to his future wife and tells of little but his love. *My Past and Thoughts,* as usual for the earlier years, speaks only of what Herzen in later life cared to remember of his experiences, and on the subject of the Russian government all that he wished to remember was negative. The few letters to friends which have survived, though, give a somewhat more complex picture. He was struck for the first time by the role of the government as a force for progress and enlightenment, something he had always associated with the autocracy of Peter but which he had never been prepared to concede to the autocracy of Nicholas. The provincial administration was "on the whole incomparably better" than he thought; he was impressed by "the work of the Ministry of Internal Affairs for the material welfare [of the country], and even more by the impulse toward progress communicated by the Ministry, which is far in advance of the understanding and the demands [of the people]." He was staggered by the number of periodicals sent to the provinces by the Ministry and the quantities of instructions regarding the founding of libraries and reading rooms: "and who is to blame if [these publications] remain uncut till some Herzen decides to cut them?" He even has a kind word to say for the educational work of the clergy, which has "not yet lost its true and high vocation — to enlighten." The statistical committees were an excellent idea, with "a high and real usefulness," but unfortunately the means necessary for carrying out their task were lacking.[17]

In a short essay of 1836, entitled *Miscellaneous Remarks on Russian Legislation,* he goes even further in singing the praises of progress through autocracy, even that of Nicholas. "In the social sphere . . . the progressive element is the government, not the people. The government is the formula of movement (*du progrès*), the expression of the idea of society, its historical form. . . . Nowhere has the government stood so far ahead of the people as in Russia." The best proofs of the autocracy's desire "to raise" the people were two: the collegial principle in the central administration and the elective principle in the management of the affairs of the nobility and the incorporated cities, the first introduced by Peter and the second by Catherine. Both of these devices Herzen interprets rather unhistorically as efforts towards a division of powers and popular participation in government, efforts "so vast that other nations with a long judicial development have not yet attained them . . . the highest development of autocracy based on popular foundations." The notion of a progressive autocracy is even applied to the reigning sovereign. "In the laws of the Emperor Nicholas is seen a strongly positive character which was lacking previously — the character of the inward strength of the state, which feels its full might." In particular, the code of 1833, the first such systematization of Russian law since the seventeenth century, came in for praise. "The code of the Emperor Nicholas is a gigantic juridical fact; it fixed the judicial life of Russia and, showing all that she has accomplished, all that the government has done, has indicated the individual works which now must lighten the task of the government." These individual works of enlightenment presumably would be accomplished by advanced citizens such as Herzen himself, but in collaboration with the government, rather than in opposition to it.[18]

At first glance these seem like rather strange sentiments in one who had just suffered exile at the hands of this same government for the too "individual works" of Saint-Simonism. Actually, though, Herzen had not reversed his stand. The problem of the early nineteenth-century Russian radical was twofold: the arbitrary power of the autocracy and the appalling ignorance and poverty of the masses. When the would-be reformer allowed his attention to concentrate only on the latter problem, the difficulties to be overcome seemed so overwhelming that the temptation inevitably existed to think that nothing short of the absolute power of the autocracy would be adequate to the task. Had not all impulses to progress come from the autocracy in the past, under Peter, under Catherine, and even as recently as the early years of Alexander I? If only Nicholas or his successor would cooperate with the enlightened minority that the autocracy itself had raised up, what wonders might be accomplished! The change in the autocracy's role from a progressive to a conservative political force, which occurred only after 1812, was still so recent that the hope that it was not permanent was still possible. In spite of thirty years of political reaction under Nicholas, this possibility remained an open one for the aristocratic radicals of Herzen's generation. Bakunin after 1848 actively considered it.[19] Belinski at the very end of his life was attracted by the idea of a second Peter.[20] Herzen, on the accession of Alexander II, at least had hopes. The first generation of "socialist" radicals was not sufficiently hardened by a long experience of rebuffs and disappointments, and by the hardening of the autocracy itself, to take a definitive stand of no compromise with the enemy. This occurred only in the next generation, born under Nicholas, and made intransigent by his intransigence. But when Herzen was in Viatka things had not yet reached this pass. Nicholas had been on the throne only a decade, and Herzen's radicalism had by no means hardened into complete intransigence, while his first close look at the enormity of the task of "enlightenment" in Russia gave him pause. This was the nearest he ever came to a reconciliation with the autocracy under Nicholas, and despite appearances, it was not very near, for it was based on a misunderstanding, both of the "democratic" exertions of the autocracy in the past and of its willingness to let "enlightened" individuals take up its burden in the present. Nicholas would very soon disabuse Herzen; but for a moment at least the latter had known the ever-present temptation of power to the impatient Russian radical.

Connected with this temptation was a new sense of the greatness of Russia as a nation. Herzen, like all educated Russians after 1812, was a patriot if not an exclusive nationalist, and acutely aware of the differences between his native land and the rest of Europe. For conservatives of varying shades these differences were easily rationalized as superiority to the West; for men of the Left the problem was far more difficult. They loved Russia no less than the conservatives, and were no less concerned to define the national essence *vis-à-vis* Europe, but since they rejected the traditional Russian values of autocracy and Orthodoxy in the name of enlightenment and found the differences from Europe a scandal more than a consolation, they were rather hard put to arrive at a concept of the national essence compatible with both their patriotism and their progressivism. "Hope in the future of Russia" was the standard solution to this dilemma. Abstract hope without specific reasons for hoping, however, is a rather barren and unsatisfactory thing, and the need was felt to find more concrete "seeds of the future" in the present. While at the university, Herzen found some consolation in the contemplation of the one-man revolution wrought by Peter and in the idea of a Saint-Simonian Christianity as the religion of the "young and virtuous" Slavs and Germans. But both these "seeds" were rather abstract. The trip east through Kazan, Viatka, and Perm offered more tangible reasons for hope. Herzen was fascinated by the mingling of Asia and Europe that he first encountered in Kazan, a mingling that seemed to him unique to Russia and portentous of a great future. The monument at Kazan to Ivan the Terrible, who had conquered the region from the Tartars, filled him with a sense of the grandeur of the nation's historical mission. "Here the Terrible accomplished something great; here he was a hero and the precursor of Peter, with the force of arms carving out a space to give scope to his ideas, to give full play to the Russian spirit." The kremlins of Nizhni Novgorod and Kazan, the "younger brothers" of the Moscow Kremlin, reminded him of the wide spread of the national, Orthodox culture, and he spoke in more conventionally patriotic tones than ever before of "our Russia, holy Russia" (*Rus*) and of how "the Greek faith and Byzantine architecture had deeply implanted themselves in the life" of the nation. "Gazing on our cathedrals and kremlins it is as if one heard the native melody and the maternal speech" — sentiments worthy of the most ardent Slavophile.[21]

More concretely, Herzen was impressed by the sheer size of Russia and the vastness of her potentialities. In Kazan he quoted a letter of Catherine the Great to Voltaire written from the same place: "I am in Asia! . . . [here] it is necessary to create an entire world, unite it, maintain it." Herzen comments: "The great Empress understood much, embracing with a glance of genius one corner of Russia, that which Peter the Great called so rightly a whole *part of the world.*" Nevertheless, Herzen did not view this extraordinary national destiny in exclusively Great-Russian terms. He was highly impressed at Kazan by the multinational, indeed Asiatic, character of the population, and by what he took to be the power of Russian Orthodox culture to assimilate without crushing the backward men of the East. Kazan symbolized Russia's mission to bring Europe and civilization to Asia, and to acquaint Europe with Asia, "as Peter had foreseen." [22] Here indeed was a noble destiny not granted to other peoples! Nor was this new sense of Russia's imperial greatness unrelated to Herzen's simultaneous respect for the progressive role of the autocracy.

At the same time Herzen was drawn by what he conceived to be the democratic potentialities of Siberia, which he never visited but of which he heard much in Viatka.

But what is Siberia? . . . a completely new land, an America *sui generis*, precisely because it is a land without an aristocratic past, a land which is the daughter of the Cossack, the robber who does not remember his birth, a country in which appear regenerated people who have closed their eyes to all their past life. . . . There life is gay, there one finds enlightenment and most of all freshness, newness. All that has been settled in recent times possesses the impulse toward progress.[23]

Here is the first recorded appearance in Herzen's thought of the twin concepts of the "broad nature" of the Russians and of the advantages conferred on them by historical youth and freshness — concepts which after 1848 were to be main components in his theory of Russian socialism. These rationalizations, of course, were adapted from German romanticism, and Herzen had begun to apply them to Russia while at the university, but never so clearly as here. Still, all this is only a rough draft of a progressive patriotism. The consolation provided by contact with the eastern reaches of the empire was real but in the last analysis slight; and Herzen concluded his exile pretty much on the old note of bright but amorphous hope. It would not be until after the Revolution of 1848 that he would find a more concrete basis for his patriotic optimism.

3

The main revelation of exile, however, was not the greatness of Russia's future; it was the inhumanity and barbarism of Russia's present. There are few expressions of this in his correspondence for the period. This silence was due in part to prudence before the censorship, in part to absorbing preoccupation with the progress of his courtship. But the corresponding chapters of *My Past and Thoughts* present one long succession of tragic incidents, which he had either observed himself or heard about from firsthand witnesses. Though these bulked larger in his reminiscences than they did in his life at the time, there is no reason to doubt that they constituted a substantial part of his contemporary impressions. His expressions of respect for the progressive role of the autocracy and his praise of the code of Nicholas date from the early months of his exile; this respect does not seem to have survived close contact with the workings of both autocracy and code in practice. The final judgment on the Russian government for the years of his exile was negative and was to remain so for the rest of his life.

All of the stories Herzen relates turn about one theme: the lack of a just and orderly process of law, and consequently of adequate protection for the rights of the individual against arbitrary power. Russia was a society where the higher authorities were despotic and capricious and the lower ones venal, ignorant, and corrupt. Herzen was aware that the wealth of the country belonged to the few, and that the many went without. His main indictment of the regime, however, was the absence of civilized law, of due process. In other words, his objection to the regime was legal and political, not social or economic; it was the objection one would expect of a "liberal" and not of a "socialist." This was, of course, in keeping with the general character of his "socialism" as an extreme form of libertarian protest, born of the complete lack of guarantees of liberty for anyone under Nicholas.

Herzen attacked first the despotic power of the provincial governor, an attack which by implication extended to the central government which created it. Immediately on arriving in his first place of exile, Perm, he noticed that "everything in the province turns on the governor, is understood only through him; he is the center and all the rest is a periphery, he is the sun and all the rest are satellites." [24] This unqualified subordination of all to the absolute power of one was deeply scandalous to Herzen in itself; it was doubly so in the person of the governor of Viatka, Tiufiaev. Tiufiaev had risen from poverty and obscurity to power as a protégé of Arakcheev, the notoriously tyrannical minister of the last years of the reign of Alexander I. With the power-consciousness of the parvenu, made vengeful, moreover, by his early humiliations at the hands of the mighty, he played the absolute despot in his domains, a little Nicholas on a provincial scale. "The power of the governor in general grows in direct proportion to the distance from St. Petersburg, but it grows in a geometric proportion in those provinces where there is no gentry, such as Perm, Viatka, and Siberia. Such a province was necessary to Tiufiaev." [25] "Debauched," "coarse," "intolerant of any objections," he seemed to love power primarily for the opportunity it gave to make others grovel before him. "In him Byzantine slavishness was combined unusually well with a chancellery-bred sense of order. The effacement of self, the abdication of his own will and thoughts before higher powers, went inseparably with a ferocious persecution of subordinates." [26]

The abuses of power that Herzen attributes to Tiufiaev are too numerous to recount, but one of the more characteristic is the following. The brother of one of the governor's mistresses had objected to his sister's enforced concubinage and threatened to appeal to the central government. Tiufiaev, in answer, terrorized the medical and police authorities of the province into committing the brother to an asylum for the insane where he died under mysterious circumstances, most probably murdered at the governor's order. [27] Indeed, Tiufiaev was so bad that even the government could not help noticing his malfeasances; on a visit of the Crown Prince to Viatka in 1837 the complaints became so loud that he was deprived of his governorship — and retired from service with a life pension! [28] For Herzen he simply represented in more blatant form than the government which punished him the evils of an absolute power from which there was no appeal — the barracks autocracy of Paul, Arakcheev, and Nicholas in microcosm.

If Tiufiaev was odious in himself, he was even more odious in his effect on others. The fear of his power translated itself in those around him into a slavishness which destroyed all human dignity. Herzen declared with some pride: "What he could not stand in me was a man who bore himself independently . . . he sought not just subordination but the *appearance* of an unconditional subjection. Unfortunately, in this he was national." [29] Tiufiaev used to delight in giving great, "greasy Siberian dinners," which his subalterns were obliged to attend.

Tiufiaev knew his guests through and through, despised them, showed them from time to time his claws, and in general treated them as a master treats his dogs: either with excessive familiarity or with a coarseness which passed all bounds — and yet he invited them to his dinners, and with trembling and joy they came, humiliating themselves, slandering [others], fawning, flattering, smiling, bowing.[30]

When Tiufiaev fell from power these same functionaries exulted "disgustingly" in triumph. Perhaps more than anything else it was this destruction of human dignity, both in the wielders and in the victims of power, which Herzen could not forgive the system.

In his memoirs he records an incident which occurred as he was leaving Viatka for Vladimir. His sleigh had stopped at a post station for a change of horses, to which, as a government functionary, he was entitled. The driver entered the station to demand the horses and received a flat refusal. Herzen in anger then went himself and found that the refusal came from a police officer whom he had known in Viatka. The officer sat in a half drunken state dictating a memorandum on an alleged murderer, a peasant who lay bound on the dirt of the floor. Since Herzen had been shown favor during the Crown Prince's visit, he was now a personage to be feared, and the police officer when he recognized him fell into a state of panic. His autocratic arrogance changed instantly to slavishness. " 'I'm guilty, I'm guilty, I know it, but I hope you won't tell his excellency about this, don't ruin an honest man.' With this the police officer *took my hand and kissed it,* repeating each time, 'For the sake of God, don't ruin an honest man.' " Herzen, more out of contempt than of pity, spared the man and his career, only to encounter him several years later in high function in the Ministry of Internal Affairs in Petersburg, once again impressing his power in lordly fashion on his underlings.[31] Under autocracy, the dignity of the individual was a function of power and rank, and not of the intrinsic worth of a man, and this more than anything else was what Herzen could not pardon in the regime of Nicholas.

Equally repugnant was the bureaucratic machine bred of autocratic power — "one of the saddest results of the Petrine revolution." This machine produced "an artificial, uneducated class, able to do nothing, except 'to serve,' knowing nothing but bureaucratic red-tape . . . and sucking the blood of the people through a thousand hungry, unclean mouths." [32] Herzen depicts his colleagues at Viatka in the blackest terms.

In the chancellery there were some twenty clerks. For the most part they were the children of clerks and secretaries, without the slightest education or morality, accustomed from the cradle to the grave to consider government service as something to be exploited, and the peasant as dirt, fertile with revenue. They sold documents, accepted every conceivable coin, engaged in deception for a glass of wine, degraded themselves, engaged in all sorts of baseness.[33]

And he goes on to paint the classic picture of Russian bureaucratic venality, so familiar since Gogol's *Inspector General,* but he paints in tones much harsher than those used by the average of his contemporaries. The clerks, the police, and the whole army of functionaries lived off the ignorance of the peasants and their fear of "the authorities" (*vlasti*), that congeries of administrative powers to which one must submit blindly and from whose caprice there was no appeal. Before "the authorities" no one had rights; there were only favors or graces, and these were conceded only through fear of a higher "authority" or for money. Law did not exist in Russia; justice was administered either by favoritism or by bribery. The rich and the powerful had the former as their defense, but the poor and humble could only sell their meager possessions, pay and hope, and if they could not pay, suffer.

Herzen recounts numerous examples of injustices he witnessed while in Viatka. Peasants were deprived of their lands by decree from Petersburg in order to create an estate for the relative of a minister. Other peasants were menaced with lashes and Siberia by one official for having offered the bribes solicited by another official. Wandering gypsies were forced by the troops to settle down; all the adult males among them who were fit for military service were sent off to the army, and all male children taken away from their mothers and entrusted to the aged poor who were maintained at the state's expense. The heathen Votiaks and Cheremisy of the region were forcibly converted to Orthodoxy by a drunken, career-minded priest and a helper from among the Muslim Tartars, who received the Cross of St. Vladimir for his efforts on behalf of the Gospel! Other villages of Votiaks and Cheremisy were visited yearly by the police or the priest, or both together, and allowed to buy their way out of baptism, or out of the imaginary crimes charged against them for this very purpose (these tribes were more docile and defenseless than the Russian peasants). On one occasion Herzen saw a horde of Jewish children, aged eight to fifteen, forcibly taken from their parents and driven in the winter on foot over the wastes of Perm and Viatka for eventual service in the fleet — that is, those who survived the march.[34] On another occasion he witnessed, on a cold dawn, a file of prisoners, fettered, in carts and on foot, on the road to Siberia, a sight which "remains in the memory for life." [35]

The entire system, from top to bottom, was rotten, immoral, and inhuman.

The serf-owner says to his servant: "Shut up, I won't stand for you to answer me." The head of the department remarks, growing pale, to the functionary who has dared a rejoinder: "You forget, you know, *with whom* you are speaking!" The Emperor *"for opinions"* exiles men to Siberia, for *verses* starves others to death in dungeons, and all three are sooner ready to forgive thievery, bribery, murder and brigandage than the insolence of a sense of human dignity and the audacity of independent speech.[36]

Herzen then utters a curse upon the whole regime. "What monstrous crimes are obscurely buried in the archives of the villainous, immoral reign of Nicholas! We have become accustomed to them, they have become daily affairs, become normal, noticed by no one, lost in the frightful distances, silent, stifled in the mute back-waters of chancelleries or suppressed by the police censorship." [37]

The only wholly admirable people Herzen met in his years of exile were a few Poles, banished to Perm for the revolt of 1830. This was his first contact with martyred Poland, a country which was later to play such a large role in his own political activity; indeed it was his first contact with live heroes of the armed resistance to Nicholas, of the sort that had filled his dreams from boyhood. The encounter produced a considerable impact. In Perm one Pole in particular, by name Cechanowicz, caught his sympathy. Herzen was impressed by his courage, his self-abnegation and his calm acceptance of suffering in a just cause. Living in the direst poverty, separated from wife and family, he had lost everything in the struggle for the liberty and national dignity of his people. Herzen listened to the tale of "the sufferer" with admiration, and at the same time with embarrassment as a member of the persecuting nation. His chief concern was to demonstrate by his sympathy that the love of liberty dwelt in Russian hearts too, and that oppressed Poland had a brother in young, enlightened Russia. Cechanowicz responded to Herzen's attempts. In parting, they exchanged "sacred tokens" of sympathy and devotion to a common cause.[38]

4

The impressions of exile recorded above are those of Herzen's Viatka and Vladimir years, but the tone of their formulation is that of the fifties, a tone he began to acquire only after 1840. Although he was certainly struck by all the horrors he relates in *My Past and Thoughts*, his reaction at the time was less violent than it became after many more years of bitter experience at the hands of Nicholas. In reality, during his exile, his attentions centered more on his own sufferings than on the sufferings of the people. His rejection of the world as it stood remained personal more than social, and his rebelliousness a generalization from his own frustrations rather than from the frustrations of others. In all this he continued the pattern of his earlier years.

Much of his suffering in Viatka derived from the offensiveness of provincial life to his aristocratic and idealist sensibilities. If he was appalled by the absence of law in Russian life, he was at least equally, if not more, repelled by the absence of spiritual beauty, of that *Schönseeligkeit* which Schiller had taught him to prize so highly. He looked on himself as a superior being, dragged down and compelled to a frightful waste of his noble energies by a base and ugly world. The chancellery of Viatka was simply the worst instance of this: "not that the material work was excessive, but the stifling atmosphere of that mouldy environment, like a dog's burrow, and the frightful, stupid waste of time — this was what made the chancellery unbearable." Only the director, who had studied at the Kazan Gymnasium and consequently was respectful of a graduate of the university, was close to a human being, in fact "rather polite." The rest of life was composed of "trivial conversations, dirty people, base ideas, vulgar feelings." [39] There are many references in Herzen's writings, both during his exile and later, to the "crowd," which "besmirches, like coal, all that is holy." [40] Knowledge "appears inaccessible only to the lazy crowd"; he, Herzen, on the other hand, had learned Italian in two months in prison and architecture in the same length of time in Viatka.[41] "True, it is painful to me that I have brought so much grief to my parents . . . although I cannot be blamed that God has given me a soul higher than the crowd, talents greater than ordinary people — and in this is all my guilt." [42] Such an attitude was hardly calculated to make him enter deeply into the sufferings of the peasants, nor was his attitude toward wealth. At one point he chides the idealism of his fiancée: "You repudiate wealth completely — this is unjust. In me there is no cupidity, no attachment to luxury; I am ready to sacrifice wealth for a friend, for a cause, but I do not spurn it. You do not know life; wealth is freedom; freedom in the first place to do what one wants, to live as one wishes, freedom from concern with *material affairs*, for material affairs smirch with grease." [43] It would be difficult to take a more aristocratic, individualistic, and "unsocialistic" attitude towards wealth — or towards freedom, for that matter.

It was affronts by the "crowd" to his aristocratic individualism which most rankled in Herzen's life at Viatka. He even "heartily" missed his Moscow cell: "There at least I was free, did what I wanted; no one disturbed me." [44] This kind of freedom — the absolute right to dispose of oneself, subject only to the voice of conscience (which again is one's own voice) — is a sense of freedom that is given only to the very secure, which in Russia meant the gentry. But it was not the absence of such freedom, nor the pall of "vulgarity" and "ugliness" that overlay Russia, which troubled the mass of the population about the existing regime. In spite of all he saw during his exile of the real grievances of the people, Herzen had not yet succeeded in identifying his own frustrations very closely with theirs. He remained a democrat in idea much more than in sentiment, and what he saw of the people's sufferings was largely stored up for the future. For the present he continued to think his opposition to the regime in terms of his own personal relation to it, and of the relation of his class and type, as indeed he was always to do in some measure, even at his most authentically democratic. In the most profound way, the style and psychology of his protest against the existing order was, and would remain, very much that of the "gentry revolutionary." [45]

CHAPTER VIII

Love and Religion

TRUE to the aesthetic individualism of his period and class, Herzen's greatest experience in exile was not public and political but personal and inward. Under the shock of banishment he passed through a crisis of the first magnitude, which led to a form of religious conversion and to a love affair that was one of the more extraordinary produced by the age, and quite the equal of anything imagined by the most resourceful romantic writers of Germany. Nevertheless, these personal adventures are not devoid of a wider social and historical significance. The second half of the thirties, the period of his exile, was the height of Russian idealism and romanticism, and Herzen's conversion and love represent his heaviest tribute to both, his farthest retreat from the real world into the realm of the purely inward life. They are the culmination of all the idealistic and sentimental tendencies of his youth, and of his long German education under Schiller and Schelling.

While in prison in Moscow, Herzen's morale held up quite well. Perhaps not fully realizing the dangers of his situation, he derived a certain satisfaction from the drama of his plight. Real suffering at the hands of the tyrant elevated him to the level of the Decembrists not just in fantasy but in fact. Looking back a year later, he wrote to his fiancée: "That was a magnificent time for my soul! There I was great and noble, there I was a poet, a great man. How I despised oppression, how firmly I resisted my inquisitors! That was the best period of my life; it was bitter for my parents, for my friends, but I was happy." [1]

He was able to work. He produced a political article in the form of a tale called *The German Traveler*,[2] who in reality was an image of himself. The traveler was cultivated, cosmopolitan and, like Eugene Onegin or the heroes of Byron, somewhat weary of soul. He had lived through all the great events from 1789 to 1815 and, having "said goodbye to Europe forever," was traveling to the young lands of the east "to rest" from the old world. A German, he had lived in France during the early years of the Revolution as a protégé of Anacharsis Cloots. This choice of nationality for Herzen's projection of himself into a world of revolution was not the result of chance. He felt akin to the lone outsider from the east who approached the great event more as a spectator than a participant, and identification with the cosmopolitan Cloots served to render the Revolution more European in significance, and hence more meaningful for Russia, than would fantasies centering around French heroes.

In 1792 the traveler encountered Goethe in the army of the Duke of Brunswick, a meeting which gave Herzen a pretext to express his views on German romanticism and idealism. For Herzen the individual life of the spirit was all very good and necessary, but it should not become an escape from one's duties as a citizen. "I am ready to bend the knee before the creator of *Faust,* just as I am ready to turn my back on the counselor Goethe who writes comedies on the day of the battle of Leipzig and doesn't busy himself with the biography of humanity because he is perpetually busy with his own biography." Herzen adds that the civic attitude of Schiller was infinitely to be preferred — a favorite contrast for Russian radicals during the period, notably for Belinski after 1840. There can be no "pure" art or "pure" idealism, for we all "live of the common life of humanity"; therefore, away with all "mystification" and "egoism." Herzen concludes with a concrete illustration of his moral: "Do you know how Lord Hamilton finished, after having spent his whole life in search of the ideal of the beautiful among pieces of marble and stiff canvases? He found it in a living Irish girl."[3] Under the pressures of exile, however, Herzen was to fall into all the sins he castigated here: mysticism, an exclusive absorption in self, a pure idealism divorced from any civic concerns, and abandonment of the "living girl" for the "heavenly maid."

Religion already permeated the atmosphere around Herzen. As we have seen, in 1833, before the pair's arrest, Ogarev had accomplished his conversion to integral Schellingianism and belief in a Creator. In prison Herzen's own reading began to change. After writing *The German Traveler* he abandoned the political and historical fare which had occupied the last year before his arrest. He turned to Pascal, and he reread the Gospels.[4] Prompted by a romantic longing for a luminous and carefree south, and in search of a substitute for the long desired voyage to Europe, which now, it seemed, would never take place, he set to learning Italian with the aid of a grammar and a copy of Dante, and Dante too turned his thoughts toward religion.[5] At the same time, "with transports" he read the great collection of the lives of the Eastern saints, the *Cheti-Minei,* and found his own fate mirrored in the tales it told. "There were divine examples of self-sacrifice; they were men!"[6] Simultaneously, and for the first time in his life, he came to believe, not exactly in God, yet in something more personalized than the Absolute of Schelling, something which he called Providence. ":.re we [Ogarev and himself] destined to perish? And to perish in what horrible fashion — mute, deaf, and no one to know about it? Why did nature give us these fiery souls, aspiring to action and fame? Can this be only a mockery? . . . But no, here in my breast burns a strong, living faith: there is a Providence." [7] In the absence of any concrete reasons for optimism Herzen had need of a force more powerful than himself or than Nicholas to sustain belief in his mission, just as earlier the inevitable march of the Idea had been necessary to redeem a barren present which the individual was impotent to change.

The result of these meditations was a second tale, written at the end of his confinement and reworked in exile, *The Legend of St. Theodora*. Herzen's theme was no longer, as in *The German Traveler*, the Great Revolution, but what according to Saint-Simon was its counterpart in the past, the death of the ancient world and the "rebirth" of humanity in Christianity. The subject was from the *Cheti-Minei* and concerned a profligate lady of ancient Alexandria, who abandoned the "old world" into which she had been born for a life of sacrifice and eventually sainthood in the fraternal community of the new Christians. Theodora — another of Herzen's fictional self-projections — was a creature in whom the natural passions were strong; and in her person he was grappling with the problem of how the earthly may be transmuted into the heavenly, the vulgar into the ideal, or in the jargon of the day "egoism" into "love." In contradiction to both his own habitual glorification of the natural man and the Saint-Simonian "rehabilitation of the flesh," he concluded in favor of asceticism and immolation of the ego on the altar of the ideal. It was another psychological device for turning defeat into victory. By making mortification of individual desire an ideal Herzen not only came to accept his imprisonment, but was even able to construe his impotence as a pledge of future victory.

The main spokesman for Herzen's new hopes is the abbot of the monastery where Theodora has taken refuge, and whose cherished disciple she is, a relationship which puts Herzen-Theodora in the position of being the elect of the prophet of the "new world." Oppressed by the "rotten" atmosphere of the old world of Rome, and after many years of anguished searching, the abbot finds consolation in the "colossal aim" of the Christians "to recreate human society, to recreate man himself, to lead him back to God, and through him the whole of nature." In the monastic community he discovers a sort of phalanstery, a marvellous wedding of "two ideas, in appearance hostile — hierarchy and equality, at the very time when the political history of humanity showed a single, ceaseless effort toward this harmony, a vain effort, for the means employed are poor and petty" — by which Herzen meant purely political reform of any kind, or in his own day, constitutions. The monastery is the promise that one day all of humanity would live as had the first Christians, "one family, with one heart, where there was no property, where everything was in common." This is more "socialist," programmatically speaking, than the historiographical generalities in which Herzen had indulged before his arrest. But it is also more poetic and religious. "The day has struck for humanity to go out of the land of Egypt. The way is difficult: deserts, hunger and heat, but once again Jehovah will separate the Red Sea for us and will lead us into the Promised Land." Herzen then alludes to his own fate. "We perhaps will perish on the way, but [our heirs] will pass. Is not this one thought enough to appear before the Judge with a sweet hope, having fulfilled our duty? Long must we wander still, and frightful is the present situation." [8] Eventually the cause for which his generation must sacrifice itself will triumph, and God will bring to pass what they themselves have been unable to accomplish. Mankind would one day see the full realization of the divine promise.

The earthly world will perish, a heavenly universe will emerge. What a triumphant day when the world for the first time echoed to the word of the Gospel! A world torn with war heard the word of peace; a world trampled down in slavery heard the word of freedom; a world of hate, the word of love; a world of unbelief, the word of faith. The Gospel spoke to all: tribes and castes disappeared. . . . Greek and Jew were received together. All were summoned to the bosom of the Lord, all into the embraces of brotherhood. . . . And can man remain deaf to the apostolic call — never, never! [9]

This is, as yet, hardly religion of a very supernatural sort. In the *Legend* there are a few words about sin, redemption and grace, drawn largely from Dante, but for the most part the abbot speaks like the more exalted followers of Saint-Simon, such as Enfantin. Nonetheless, the change from the version of the New Christianity to which Herzen had subscribed before his arrest, or even since he wrote *The German Traveler*, is striking. Then he had explicitly rejected the "mysticism" of Enfantin, just as he had rejected the religion of Ogarev. In the *Legend*, however, the shock of ten months of prison was beginning to produce its effects. As life itself became bleaker, in order to maintain belief in his star he had to fall back on more poetic and less real expressions of his desires. As rational reasons for hope diminished, he retreated more into symbolism to maintain what self-confidence he could.

In Viatka this process reached its culmination. Under the pressures of provincial isolation and provincial vulgarity Herzen's morale went completely to pieces.

After sitting all day in that galley [the chancellery] I would come home in some sort of torpor of all my sensibilities, would throw myself on the divan, exhausted, humiliated and incapable of any work, of any occupation. . . . And when the thought came into my head that after dinner I would have to go back, and then again the next day, immediately fury and despair would seize me and I would drink wine and vodka for consolation.[10]

In a desperate search for some sort of release Herzen threw himself on Viatka society with the same hunger with which he had once thrown himself on the university. The society of Viatka, though, was not that of the university; heavy drinking, cards, and wild nights in the company of the sons of local merchants were a sad anticlimax to the elevated revels of his Moscow circle, and they brought not consolation but disgust at the vulgarity of his companions, and of himself. He soon found it necessary to offend everyone by the withdrawal of a friendship too hastily and too widely given, a result which simply increased his sense of isolation.[11] He retreated into melancholy brooding and long bouts of daydreaming, a process already begun in prison. "I read for a long, long time something good, then, throwing aside the book, I transport myself there, into the world of that book, and for hours on end I can live completely in another century, with its ideas." And he adds, half in irony, half in real alarm: "Pleasant, very pleasant; and if this is the first step of madness, then I have no objection to going out of my mind." [12] This mood returned intermittently all through his stay in Viatka. He felt his faculties growing dull with disuse. In the company of a fellow exile, he studied the history of architecture, and with visions of Greek temples and Gothic cathedrals he mentally "migrated to a time when men were not afraid of greatness" and dreamed of escape to Italy, to the sea, bright sunlight and joy.[13]

2

His desperation was increased by the failure of his principal attempt to break out of isolation: a liaison formed during his first months in Viatka. Prior to this he had had little experience with women. He had, it seems, sampled those pleasures which a well-furnished purse could procure in Moscow, though, in spite of references in his correspondence to "mad Bacchanalia," these appear to have consisted of no more than the infrequent satisfaction of youthful curiosity. Then there had been his fleeting love for Liudmila Passek,[14] who by the time he got to Viatka remained in his memory only as a reproach, since he had come to feel that he had let her down rather shabbily.[15]

The affair in Viatka was altogether more serious. Its object, named Praskovia Medvedeva (the P. of his memoirs), was the young and handsome wife of his next-door neighbor. Then twenty-five, she was slightly Herzen's senior. At fifteen she had been married to an elderly functionary, to whom she had since borne three children, while her husband had become an incurable and cantankerous invalid and a blight on her young and loveless years. Herzen's heart went out to her in her loneliness, and only a few months after his arrival in Viatka they had arrived at the last degree of intimacy. Herzen's motives seem to have been mixed. On the one hand, this was his first mature conquest, and his ego drew pleasure from the fact; on the other hand, Medvedeva represented consolation of a very concrete sort and a loneliness answering his own. He allowed himself to be carried away and said more than he really felt. Then, catastrophically, his only protection in this game, the husband, died; Medvedeva was free to marry and Herzen was confronted with a situation of alarming seriousness. Simultaneously he discovered that his infatuation had cooled. As a result he was plunged into a despair deeper than that which had marked his first months in Viatka.[16] He was seized with remorse at the suffering he had caused Medvedeva; still worse, his belief in the nobility of his motives in all things was shaken. The values necessary to preserve his moral equilibrium in the face of adversity were suddenly undermined.

Salvation came from the purer love of another woman, a young cousin back in Moscow, named Natalia Alexandrovna Zakharina. Like Herzen she was an illegitimate child, the daughter of the second Iakovlev brother and one of his serfs, and hence a sister of the "Chemist," though by a different mother. On her father's death, her brother had been about to send her back to the village, along with the rest of the paternal harem and its offspring. Her father's widowed sister, Princess Khovanskaia (the same who had rescued Herzen's brother Egor), however, was attracted by the eight-year-old girl's "sad, pensive look," and decided to raise the child as her ward, for the princess seems to have been given to rescuing her brothers' unwanted children to gratify maternal instincts frustrated by the death of her own daughters. But her affection could be withdrawn as capriciously as it was granted, for she was too old to sustain interest in small children. She tired quickly of her new role, and Natalie — as she was called familiarly — grew up neglected and unloved by her aunt and harassed by the latter's still more disagreeable *dame de compagnie,* who spent her time reminding the young girl of the gratitude she owed her "benefactress."[17] As she herself later characterized her early life:

My childhood was the saddest and bitterest possible; how many tears I shed, seen by no one, how many times at night, not yet understanding what prayer was, would I get up secretly (not daring to pray openly at any time but the appointed hour) and beg God that someone would love me, caress me. . . .

Around me everything was old, evil, cold, dead, false; my education began with reproaches and insults; the consequence of this was an estrangement from all people, mistrust of their caresses, aversion to their sympathy, withdrawal into myself.[18]

In this situation Natalie soon developed a set of intensely emotional compensations. Unlike the fantasies of Herzen's boyhood, however, Natalie's dreams were directed to the next world rather than to this, for she was too crushed by life to have any hope in it. Her only friend was a household serf-girl of her aunt. In the company of this friend, and under the influence of a poor but devout priest hired at low rates to be her Russian tutor, she developed a lachrymose and ecstatic piety. The two girls would often rise early while the rest of the house still slept; they would read the Gospel and pray in the courtyard, "under the pure heaven," for the princess and her companion, "beseeching God to open their souls." They invented penances for themselves, went without meat "for whole weeks," and "dreamed of the convent and of life beyond the grave." "The orphan" and "the slave," moreover, were devoted to each other with a passion no less feverish than their love for God.[19] Each was all the other had in the world and their mutual attachment was correspondingly desperate and exalted. In short, Natalie as a girl lived through all the sentimental compensations for a cramped and frustrated existence so common to her generation, but she experienced them in their most extremely ideal, morbid, and unreal form.

As she grew older, her need for affection, and the concomitant need to worship and adore, were transferred to her dynamic cousin Alexander, a process which, according to her own admission, seems to have begun when she was still very young.[20] Herzen, however, while at the university, took no notice of her; he was too busy with his friends, with politics and philosophy, and with "Gaetana." Natalie in his eyes was a mere child, fully five years his junior, and for a long time she pined in silence. It was at the time of his arrest that he first really noticed her. He encountered her by chance in the melancholy atmosphere of a cemetery just after he had learned of the arrest of Ogarev, and on the eve of his own apprehension. Natalie displayed appropriate tenderness and compassion. It was the nineteenth of July, 1834, and the first "sacred" date of their love: she was not yet seventeen and he was twenty-two.[21] For the moment Herzen felt no more than gratitude for sympathy offered at a time when he needed it greatly. On the basis of this feeling an extensive correspondence between the two developed while he was in prison; since he could not live withdrawn within himself, Natalie became the confidant of his most intimate thoughts. It was in part under her influence that he turned for consolation to the Gospels, the *Cheti-Minei*, and the idea of Providence; and it was partly for her that the *Legend of*

St. Theodora was written. He saw her only once in prison, on the eve of his departure into exile, which was the ninth of April, 1835, and the second "sacred" date of their love. (Subsequently these dates were usually underlined in correspondence between the two.) For the first time, in her look of desperate affliction and sympathy, he began dimly to understand the true nature of her feelings, the depths of which she herself by no means realized. No word was spoken, though, and they parted as "brother" and "sister." [22]

It was under the impact of the frustrations of Viatka that Herzen's sympathy ripened into passion. From the depths of her loneliness Natalie deluged her cousin with protestations of "sisterly" affection and promises of eternal devotion to "Alexander alone," protestations which revealed far more than she herself was aware. The tone of her letters was feverish and painfully "exalted"; key words — "friend," "brother," "you," "soul," "divine" — were underlined, repeated at least twice, and followed by exclamation points. At first Herzen did not respond in kind; he was too absorbed by the initial shock of life in Viatka and by his affair with Medvedeva. As the dreary months of exile dragged on, however, he grew more and more sensitive to his cousin's ecstatic devotion, and to her invocations of a beneficent Providence presumed to be watching over them. With distance and time, the dates of their two final meetings began to acquire a sacred luster. Finally, at the height of his affair with Medvedeva, and driven by the contrast between the carnality of his relations with the latter and the purity of Natalie, Herzen declared himself to his cousin. He wrote in enigmatic tones of a *"feeling between earthly love and friendship"* and asked Natalie whether she believed that the feeling which existed between them was *"ONLY FRIENDSHIP,"* adding that he himself did not believe that it was.[23] Natalie at first did not understand. She answered:

I believe, I believe that we are united by friendship, the very loftiest friendship for which there is no precedent. There is no being on earth dearer to me than you. I love you more than all others on earth. If this feeling is more, is higher than friendship, then I am unable to give it a name, but I believe in it. Never, never will I love, never will I allow any feeling in my soul to stand higher than the feeling I have for you. . . . In my soul there is only one feeling higher than love of you — love of God; but these two feelings are so close, so united that without love of God I cannot love you, without love of you I cannot love God. If friendship is unable to unite two beings, is unable to raise itself so high, then let what we feel be a feeling *between earthly love and friendship*.[24]

Herzen returned to the attack, explaining "that what you understand, my angel, by the word friendship, is not friendship";[25] and Natalie, compelled by the weight of evidence, came at the beginning of 1836 to accept his diagnosis.

The love which each at last agreed to call by its real name was, however, no mere "earthly" passion. It had a profound religious significance, which far transcended what the vulgar understood by love, and which united the two in God. In this Herzen submitted to the values of Natalie, to the mysticism of her childhood, where the divine was interpreted, not in the half-metaphorical sense of Schiller and German idealism — to which he already subscribed — but in the literal sense of traditional Christianity. Under Natalie's influence the vague notion of Providence Herzen had entertained in prison ripened into belief, or what he thought was belief, in a transcendent God and into acceptance of all the mysteries of the Orthodox Church. At first Herzen resisted the piety of his cousin, just as he had at first tended to see in their love something not too different from an ordinary "earthly" attraction. But in the end he succumbed, and at that rather quickly, both to her religion and to her estimate of the quasi-sacramental significance of their passion.

One of the principal agents in bringing about this transformation was remorse over his conduct toward Medvedeva. Herzen cooled to his mistress at the same time — the end of 1835 — that he first declared himself to Natalie. Medvedeva remained in Viatka two years more, friendless, impoverished, and a living reminder of his capitulation to the vulgarity of the "crowd." In addition, she soon came to be in need of protection from the attentions of Tiufiaev. For all these reasons Herzen felt it was impossible to abandon her to her fate. Yet, in his guilt, he pushed solicitude to the point where it became in effect cruelty. Out of a misplaced pity he did not dare crush her hopes with a clear refusal of marriage, and thus for almost two years he maintained what was hardly a courageous silence, hoping that she would understand without demanding from him the humiliation of an explicit repudiation of his previous affection. Nor was it easy to tell the truth to Natalie. Herzen was tormented by feelings of guilt — insofar as his basically tenacious self-esteem allowed such feelings — toward both women. Still, Natalie offered the safer haven of the two and so he turned to her to "redeem" him and to restore his self-respect. Forgiveness from her would release him from his "sin," if not exactly abolish its consequences, and restore his pristine greatness of soul.

At first in his letters he only hinted darkly at his "fall": "What traces, what scars, corruption leaves in the heart. Alas!

> Une mer y passerait sans laver la tache.
> Car l'abîme est immense, et la tache est au fond." [26]

Furthermore, in spite of frequent direct references to Medvedeva, Natalie in her innocence did not understand. She construed her Alexander's expressions of remorse as the sign of an exceptionally sensitive nature, and his references to Medvedeva's sad fate as the product of a noble charity. Therefore, after several more months of torment, Herzen was driven to direct confession. He reproached himself with acting out of "self-love, vanity and the pride of conquest." But he excused as much as he accused. Medvedeva was "a young flower plucked, not to be a bride, but for the grave; a creature far from lofty, ideal, but in whom misfortune had instilled a certain poetry. . . . Little by little I began to show indifference to her; I became sure that her soul was not deep enough for a true love to take root in it; she will forgive me." As for himself, Natalie had saved him from "the passion" of his "baser nature." "I pushed aside all these monsters with serpents' heads to which I had given myself, and I was resurrected by my love for you." [27] Natalie alone could forgive him, because she alone, through the "loftiness" of her nature, could appreciate that one "fall" had not basically impaired his own "loftiness." Besides, the fault lay only partially with him.

I know that the *crowd* will not condemn me, it will call my act a prank, levity, quite pardonable, but I must not judge myself by the rules of the crowd. I repeat, I am convinced that her passion will soon pass, and in conclusion I add that half the guilt I throw on those who urged me on. The crowd! Once I gave myself over to you [the society he had frequented in his first months in Viatka], impure people, you used this in order to defile me. Natasha, Natasha! have pity on Alexander and, if your heart is full enough with the highest goodness, forgive me. [28]

Secretly Herzen half shared the "crowd's" opinion that his act was only a prank, indeed that it was somewhat to his credit since it demonstrated a rich, fiery nature. Yet, to abandon the lady so unceremoniously was in painful contradiction with the high estimate he entertained of his personal qualities. Such an abandonment could be made compatible with this esteem only if the object of his new affection were exalted to the highest plane of loftiness and endowed with the power to forgive his sin, thereby transforming it into a new form of nobility. Hence his need both to deify Natalie and to abase himself before her; it was after all much less humiliating to ask forgiveness from Natalie than from Medvedeva. Thus, in the abjection of his repentance, Herzen contrived to perform the rather extraordinary feat of reviling himself without in any way undermining his self-esteem, indeed with the result of increasing it. In the process, however, the wrong done to Medvedeva paled into insignificance beside the menace it presented to Herzen's conviction of superiority; the emphasis of his repentance was not on her misfortunes but on his wounded pride. This feeling of superiority was absolutely necessary to continued belief in his system of values. His mission above the crowd, his politics, and his enlightenment were all one with his ego, and any menace to his self-esteem endangered the whole structure of life that he had fashioned for himself since boyhood. His breast-beating over Medvedeva was consequently exaggerated and protracted. He had abandoned Liudmila Passek, whom he had made almost as unhappy as Medvedeva, with only a fleeting moment of remorse; and he was to treat later falls from virtue, after his marriage, with an indifference almost worthy of his father. But repentance for Medvedeva occupied him unceasingly for three years, from 1835 until his marriage early in 1838, and long after the end of the affair his letters constantly returned to the subject.

Herzen even pushed his desire for self-vindication to the point of eliciting from his old love a blessing on the new. When he first began to hint at the true nature of his "fall" to Natalie, she replied in her evangelical zeal to "save Medvedeva." Herzen immediately took up the suggestion, which he had no doubt hoped his avowal would produce,[29] for the task had flattering implications for his own superior virtue. He set about intimating gradually to the poor "plucked flower" the exigencies of his loftier passion for Natalie. After his full confession, and at his own suggestion, Natalie even wrote to Medvedeva in sisterly tones explaining that she bore her no ill will and expressing the greatest compassion for her plight. Medvedeva at last succumbed to this pⅼessure and replied in kind.

Cara sposa, here are two letters for you from Medvedeva. Oh, she is worthy to be your sister — higher than this can I place no mortal; here is the proof that she was capable of sweeping your Alexander off his feet, because in her is a strong soul. . . . Her complete cure is much more important to us than over-coming parental objections [to their marriage]. Perhaps it would be possible to invite her to meet with us, but, all the same, this would demand more than human strength.[30]

The meeting, no doubt wisely, did not take place; the two women limited their sisterly contact to an exchange of portraits sketched especially for the purpose.[31] There seems also to have been a money settlement, for Medvedeva was utterly without financial resources. (At least Herzen's family maintained contact with her for the rest of her life and it was Herzen's brother who buried her when she died in 1860.) [32] With these acts Herzen considered that he had done his duty and that Medvedeva was "cured," leaving him to enjoy his Natalie in peace. And Medvedeva was cured, at least to the extent that, on the surface, she consented to regard both Herzen and Natalie as "friends," in the most sacred sense of that word. Although this time the triangle of "friendship" and "love" worked out relatively well for Herzen, it was the adumbration of the much more tragic events in which he later became involved, first with his own Natalie and the German poet Herwegh and then with Ogarev and the latter's second wife.

The final testimonial to Herzen's remorse over Medvedeva was a long story, entitled *Elena*, composed shortly before his marriage. Among all Herzen's writings it is unquestionably the worst, and the most blatantly a fantasy of self-justification and self-pity. In it Herzen imagined himself as a young nobleman of the time of Catherine II, a period when the gentry was still great of soul and free, brilliant and cosmopolitan, so unlike the degraded underlings who served Nicholas. Herzen's young nobleman represents the qualities of his class at their most glorious. He is, moreover, the darling of the great empress, but his own "fiery" nature and the jealousy of certain old lords of the court bring down upon him an unjust exile. Just before his departure he meets and is loved by a noble maiden with all the heavenly qualities of Natalie. In the despair of exile, however, amidst a vulgar society that provides no outlet for his vast energies, he accepts the consolation of a loving soul, Elena, noble to be sure, but not quite so noble as his first love. "But am I guilty that instead of blood, fire runs in my veins?" They have a child. Then he is pardoned and returns to the court and to his first love, whom he marries. The parting with Elena is bitter; he heaps reproaches on himself, but he must obey his higher destiny. Elena, her spirit broken, dies. The nobleman, when he learns her fate, is seized with a return of his old remorse. He suffers indescribably, falls into hallucinations and macabre visions. All through his sufferings his wife is an angel of mercy; in the hope that he can be cured she even goes to pray on the grave of Elena. Love and compassion for the unfortunate girl are in her soul: "You are right Elena! to whom else could you have given your soul but to him — vast and deep as the ocean?" But heaven does not answer her prayer; the nobleman must suffer still more, and his powerful personality disintegrates in insanity. Yet his faithful angel does not despair; she becomes the abbess of the Convent of the Virgin where Elena is buried, and every day she prays on her grave for the celestial redemption of the two sufferers.[33] Natalie, on reading the story, wrote Herzen: "When the princess begged reconciliation with Elena on her grave, I could no longer contain myself, I burst into tears and threw myself on the ground; I thanked God that I can bend my knee before Elena alive, beg her hand in reconciliation." [34]

3

The essence of Herzen's religion, however, was not a sense of sin originating in his conduct toward Medvedeva, but a frantic striving for self-assurance centering in Natalie. In his correspondence with her (which, on both sides, runs to over six hundred closely printed pages for a period of only three years and every letter of which was preserved as a sacred relic), he never tired of rehearsing the history of his conversion, and he makes it abundantly clear that this conversion was the combined product of his isolation and his growing love for her.

Do you know that before 1834 I never had one religious idea; in that year, which begins a new period in my life, first appeared the idea of God. The world which was soon to punish me came to seem to me incomplete, insufficient. In prison this thought grew stronger, and I experienced a great need to read the Gospels; with tears in my eyes I read them, but I did not completely understand. . . . Here in Viatka I went further. . . . I saw with horror that the whole world is merely a "vanity of vanities"; I began to seek a fatherland for my soul and a place of rest. My first inspiration was the apostles and the saints; in them I saw that very peace which was lacking in my soul. . . . Then the ninth of April was sent to me. That revolution was enormous. It may seem strange to you that I, a strong, grown man in your eyes, was completely regenerated by you in a few hours, during which you did not speak a single word, yet this is so. But my body lagged behind my soul; I slept and my sleep was my miserable life in Viatka, my last tribute to vice. Awakening I looked on nature, on man, on God with different eyes; I became a Christian and my fiery love for you increased out of gratitude.[35]

Indeed it is only through his love for Natalie that he has come to love God. "The one link with heaven is love. Man is a fallen angel, Lucifer; for him the one road to heaven, to the earthly paradise, is love; this is the self-humiliation of two in one soul: this is what you have revealed to me, angel; you, worthy to reconcile God to man." He has been "cleansed" by her love, purged of the "leprosy" of "egoism," "the remains of the fall . . . of Lucifer." [36] In Herzen's theology love takes the place of grace and Natalie that of all the saints, of the Virgin, and almost of God Himself. "I will pass this year in an entirely different manner. I will remain at home constantly, and like the anchorites of former years who passed their time in prayer to the Virgin, so I will pass my time in prayer to you." [37] The language of the liturgy is adapted with an idealist twist to glorify the power of Natalie's love. "The rights of the idea are imprescriptible, and as the Christian worships God in Christ, so I, through you and through Him, in you and in Him, understand, feel, the holy, the beautiful." [38] Herzen himself is inflated to supernatural proportions. He is "like a medal, on one side of which is the Archangel Gabriel, and on the other Lucifer." On another occasion the comparison is Christ and Judas Iscariot, but in neither case does he sink below angelic or apostolic rank. Natalie can restore him to his pristine glory so easily because, although slightly "fallen," he is still basically of the same angelic stuff as she.

I know that I cannot fall deeply. I know that my moral sense will outweigh my passions, but I also know that it is not I, but you, you, who have made me moral. My pride does not suffer from this thought — no, for you and I are inseparable, one, and what is bitter is that I look on you as heaven, and understand that I am not worthy of you, that I am worse. And what audacity to wish to bring you down to earth! Such is man, Natasha! To redeem him God sent Christ and he crucified Him. But Providence has already decided. Be my support, save me from myself. To you I give over my entire being.[39]

Natalie responded in kind. Alexander was "angel" and "redeemer" for her no less than she for him; indeed it is with Natalie that the whole mythology originated.

Among Herzen's favorite comparisons for his love was the imagery of the *Divine Comedy,* one of his preferred books ever since prison. Exile in Viatka was his Inferno (or Purgatory, it is not clear which), and he tirelessly repeated, with reference to his situation, the famous lines placed over the entrance to Hell:

> Per me si va nella città dolente
> Per me si va nel eterno dolore . . .

Almost as appealing was the dramatic invocation, in Provençal: "Sovenha vos à temps de ma dolor." [40] God had sent salvation, however, in the form of "friendship" and "love." "When Dante became lost in everyday life, Virgil appeared to him and led him through a series of tribulations to Purgatory; there Beatrice descended and led him into Paradise. This is my story, this is Ogarev and you." [41] The comparison with Beatrice was taken with immense seriousness and literalness. In Viatka he had a friend named Witberg (about whom more will be said below), who at times shared with Ogarev the honors of the role of Virgil. For Witberg's birthday in 1837 Herzen staged a series of *tableaux vivants* for friends. The first scene showed Dante, played by Herzen attired in a medieval costume which he claimed "lent a special expressiveness to my face." Dante was "weary with life, tormented, extenuated"; then the shade of Virgil — Witberg — appeared and pointed out the path of light. The second scene showed Beatrice on a throne flanked on one side by the "light of poetry" and on the other by "heavenly grace"; Dante, dazzled by the brilliance, threw himself on his knees before her; "tears were in my eyes . . . I thought of you my angel." In the final scene an angel stood holding an open book in which was written "the text from the Agony in the Garden of Gethsemane: May this chalice pass from me, but if thou wilt . . .", and here Herzen thought of his own sufferings. The success of the spectacle was tremendous; the audience demanded an encore, which was cheerfully accorded. "For the first time from a public stage I heard applause for myself. . . . Afterwards Witberg sat me on Beatrice's throne and placed a laurel wreath upon me." [42] The whole experience was gratifying in the extreme.

In the same way Natalie was mingled with all the sacraments of the church. Even at the height of his religious fervor Herzen had difficulty in bringing himself to participate with conviction in the rites of the church. "Our entire education, our entire life are so opposed to these rites that rarely do our hearts participate in them . . . perhaps it is necessary to possess a simpler soul. The outward forms act more efficaciously on the people. They are crushed by them, and not seeking any further, not understanding, they can pray fervently." [43] He found it particularly difficult to pray, a solace which Natalie constantly urged on him. "I am still far from prayer; prayer comes sometimes, like lightning, momentary and bright, in instants of deep affliction, in minutes of strong rapture — but most of the time I feel no need to pray. Pray in my stead, angel, pray." [44] It was only by making the sacraments of the church into sacraments of his love that he could enter into them with fervor.

Today, *for the first time in my life*, I confessed. In a cold, uninspired mood I arrived at the church, coldly I approached the altar. The first thing that moved me was the beautiful visage of the priest. "Do you believe in God?" I believe. "And what does it mean to believe?" asked the priest, glancing at me quickly and keenly. My soul opened up; I answered ardently, and his soul abandoned its formalism. A conversation of father and son, full of love, came out of my confession . . . he turned his glance toward heaven and said: "Oh Lord, strengthen your servant Alexander!"; we parted almost with tears in our eyes. . . . [The next day], as I am about to receive communion, behind me is a pretty little girl; when her mother held her up she pronounced her name — Natalie. I remained in my place, did not move back and gazed up to heaven in rapture. . . . Why was it that out of two hundred names which one hears constantly I met with Natalie at the communion table — that name with which I pray, your name . . . the communion table is of metal, it is of the earth, crude, but when it is covered with holy blood it becomes holy; thus am I, a vessel of earth, but I will be holy when the grace of God through Natalie enters into me.[45]

In another letter he declares: "your life — I fear to express my complete thought, but it is so — is higher than the Gospels for me." [46]

It need scarcely be pointed out that this is hardly an orthodox form of Christianity, however wide one is willing to stretch the definition of orthodoxy. It barely deserves the name of religion, however amorphous, for there is no clear idea in it of a God distinct from the lovers. In reality Herzen worshiped not God but Natalie; and since he and Natalie were one, through her he worshiped himself, or at any rate his ego as he idealized it. God was not the transcendent being of the church, to which by a misunderstanding Herzen considered that he belonged; the deity was completely immanent in Natalie and himself, and their love was the fullest possible realization of the divine essence. In short, Herzen's religion was simply another fantasy of self-aggrandizement, along the lines of Schiller's aestheticism and Schelling's idealism. But it was a much more extreme and alienated fantasy precisely because it was constructed out of symbols taken from transcendent religion instead of being presented frankly as a secular sentimentalism. The degree of illusion, and of self-delusion, is much greater in confusing oneself with God than in poeticizing one's really existing sentiments.

Herzen himself was at least partially aware that his religion and his love were a more exaggerated form of the Schilleresque cult of friendship of his youth. Indeed, the comparison of his feelings for Ogarev and for Natalie constantly comes to his pen, in a tireless litany of "*him*" and "*thou.*"

My whole life shows me only two emotions, two aspirations. It was they which formed me and gave me the strength to endure so much. I was still a child . . . people met me *with insults, affronts!* [because of his illegitimacy]. Wherever I turned I encountered only stone, coldness. . . . Then I might have perished, but Providence judged otherwise: it gave me Ogarev. And how triumphal was the moment when we, youths, children, embracing each other realized how kindred were our souls! That was in 1826 on the Sparrow Hills. . . . Oh how joyously beat our hearts. *This, my first emotion, was friendship,* it saved me, preserved me. . . . Bitter fate again touched me with its cold hand: 1834, my soul, again turned in on itself, was breaking, its very firmness prepared its fall, and you my angel of heaven appeared to me on the ninth of April, and I stretched out my fettered hand to you, and drank in that light which poured from your eyes, and I was saved, — this *second emotion was love.* And after this how is it possible not to believe in Providence, when it is so clearly leading me? There is no place in my breast for a third emotion: all the rest is petty, weak, and depends on these two. But you will say: truth! the beautiful! But do not both of these have their home in you? [47]

This is no more than Schiller's theory of redemption through love rendered more exalted and hysterical by its identification with the symbolism, if not the substance, of revealed religion.

Under Natalie's influence Herzen for the first time arrived at a comprehension of Schiller's heroines. The women of Schiller's dramas play a very particular role. They are all the same, and they represent not so much real women as the principle of the divine action of love. They are all beauty of soul unalloyed and the inevitable epithet used when addressing them is "angel." Moreover, they all exercise a distinctly uplifting effect on their men — Amalia on Moor, the Queen on Carlos and Posa, Thekla on Max Piccolomini in *Wallenstein,* Isabella in the *Bride of Messina* and, most of all, the Maid of Orleans on everyone concerned. It was in the "loftiness" of Schiller's women that Herzen found the most adequate model for his own Natalie. At the beginning of the courtship Natalie knew neither German nor Schiller; Herzen urged her to study both. "If you could read Schiller there you would find our love. Indeed, it is only in Schiller." [48] Natalie soon set about reading him.

With raptures I saw in your last letter excerpts from Schiller's *Joan* [*The Maid of Orleans*]; if you can read *Joan*, even only with difficulty, then progress has been made, and I will send you all. Read, read Schiller — all his life he dreamed of a maid who would be part Joan and part Thekla; all his life he called to heaven for an angel, he did not belong to this world; but the angel never flew down to him, and a sad cry closed his life of dreams (*Resignation*). . . . I demanded no less — oh no! and I found in you more, much more than I demanded.[49]

Natalie came to Herzen like the "white dove" of the Almighty descending on Joan or like the celestial *Mädchen aus der Fremde,* who, "by her worth, by the loftiness of her nature drove away everything that was earthly." [50]

All the essential points of Schiller's ideal of love, as expressed in the *Philosophical Letters,* reappear in Herzen's religion. The doctrine of the Redemption itself is construed as the progress from the isolation of "egoism" to harmony with the cosmos through "love." "Does not the life of humanity consist in the effort to express itself in one man, one creature, one soul, one will? And this unified humanity is Christ, it is the second coming, the return of God." "Egoism," the great sin of "earth," had been the essence of Herzen's "fall"; Natalie had been able to redeem him from it because, like Christ, she represented the heavenly principle of love and unity. Thus their love prefigured the redemption of all mankind in love and unity through Christ. Herzen constantly returned to this idea. "Thus you will express the untarnished, pure principle in man, and I, earthly man; together we are angel and man. Just imagine to yourself all of humanity, united intimately by love, men giving their hands and hearts to each other, complementing each other — and the great thought of the Creator and the great thought of Christianity reveals itself before you." [51] Herzen's hope for the "regeneration" of mankind, which formerly had been social, now becomes purely personal, and concentrated entirely in Natalie and himself. Once on returning from church he wrote: "I was so carried away by the poetry of the liturgy that I embraced all the priests from the depth of my soul, as a son would a father. Oh, this is how Christ wished humanity to be, so that the whole of mankind would embrace and cling to His incommensurable heart! The whole of mankind should love one another as I and Natasha love." [52]

The love of two "beautiful souls" is indeed the supreme sacrament of Herzen's religion, the be-all and the end-all of life.

Love is the highest of emotions; it is as far above friendship as religion is above philosophy, as the rapture of the poet is above the thought of the scientist. Religion and love do not seek a modest corner in the heart: they demand the whole soul: they will not share it: they intersect and mingle. And in their fusion is the full human life. There is the highest poetry, the rapture of the artist, the ideal of the beautiful, the ideal of the holy. Oh Natasha! Through you I came to know all this.[53]

And love is one with beauty just as it is one with God.

In the first place there is poetry (religion is inseparable from it). Then history; history is a great poem, created by God, it is his epic . . . for us everything will be a poem — both we and nature, and Schiller, and the Mass, and winter evenings in a cold room and summer nights, oppressive like a threatening premonition. Oh God what a prayer will pour forth then from our one soul! [54]

Herzen's religion, in effect, was no more than an exaggerated poeticizing of his love, the aesthetic idealism of his youth developed to ultimate intensity by the isolation of exile.

4

All these tendencies were reinforced by the influence of Herzen's Viatka "Virgil," Alexander Lavrentevich Witberg. An architect, Witberg had been commissioned by Alexander I to design and build in Moscow a great cathedral to Christ the Saviour in commemoration of the Russian victory over Napoleon. He had also been a freemason, a product of the movement that had flourished under Catherine and Alexander. At the Academy of Fine Arts in Petersburg he had been the protégé of Labzin, the friend of the celebrated Novikov and the editor of the masonic *Messenger of Zion* (*Sionski vestnik*). Witberg himself had known Novikov and was steeped in the mystical lore of masonry — Jacob Boehme, Swedenborg, Saint-Martin, Eckartshausen, Jung-Stilling — which Novikov and Labzin disseminated through Russia. The church which Witberg designed for Alexander, at the time just after 1812 when the latter was inclined to mysticism of an unorthodox sort, was a vast architectural anagram of the themes of masonic spiritualism. The project, in Herzen's description, was "colossal . . . full of religious poetry . . . a work of genius, frightening, insane (*bezumny*)!" [55] After having designed this temple, Witberg, inexperienced in practical affairs, unwisely undertook to direct its construction. The execution advanced slowly and inefficiently. Then, with the change of reigns, masonic mysticism together with all the deviant spirituality that went with it fell from favor, and the government returned to the exclusive support of Orthodoxy. Witberg's project was abandoned and its author exiled, unjustly charged by Nicholas with mismanagement of the funds allotted for construction of the cathedral.

For over two years Herzen lived in the same house with Witberg. In spite of the difference in age (Witberg, then nearing fifty, was a quarter of a century older than Herzen), they became close, if not intimate, friends. Witberg was the only man in Viatka whose mind and

moral qualities Herzen respected. He became a spiritual counselor to
Herzen in his "fallen" state, a prop to his morale in the spiritual wastes
of exile, and a Virgil to Natalie's Beatrice. Herzen admired Witberg as
a noble sufferer from the barbarism of Nicholas, and he participated
in these sufferings to the extent of aiding Witberg in the composition of
a lengthy biographical apologia.[56] He also studied the history of architecture with him, in a half-masonic, half-idealist version in which changing artistic styles were at the same time symbols of the progressive
revelation of God to man and embodiments of the Absolute's successive
manifestations in history. For the rest of Herzen's life Witberg remained
the model of the artist, after the German romantic concept of the inspired
prophet, the priest of the ideal: "Rapturous, eccentric, given over to
mysticism . . . day and night the young artist roamed through the
streets of St. Petersburg, tormented by a persistent thought." [57] Most
important of all, Witberg introduced Herzen to masonic mysticism. The
apologia which they composed together contains a very complete exposition of the doctrine; Witberg's letters to Herzen after the latter had
left Viatka are full of spiritual advice in the same vein;[58] and Herzen's
own letters echo the whole. We are confronted with the spectacle of the
Herzen who had once been suspicious of the "mysticism" of Schelling
requesting his friends to send him Swedenborg, Paracelsus, Eckartshausen, and Neoplatonic writers "of the time of Apollonius Tyanus." [59]
He wrote to Natalie that religion was above philosophy just as poetry
was above science, and to his Moscow friends that "all our theories of
humanity are nonsense. . . . We wished to arrive at a formula of being
all by ourselves and we only arrived at an absurdity (eclecticism)" [60] —
by which he meant not only the philosophy of Victor Cousin but all
"rationalisms," whether German idealism or French socialism.

The doctrine for which Herzen thus deserted his former masters was
founded on a belief in the Bible as a symbolic representation of the
destiny of man. Created as a being of light and harmony, man had fallen
from this blessed state. He could return to it only by an effort at self-
improvement, the chief agent of which was love; through the action of
love man recreated in himself Christ, who had been sent by God as a
figure of redemption. In his fall man had also dragged down nature,
which was both humanity's place of exile and a great book of symbols
in which the divine was manifest. Moreover, nature, man, and God were
linked together in one great chain of being, developing in a hierarchical
progression from baser to purer forms of being, and all these forms
spoke in mystical correspondences of their author and sustainer; God
could be read everywhere in his creation. The supreme key to the life
of the universe was the Trinity. The trinary pattern is present in all of
physical nature: on the level of the divine it is expressed in the Incarna-

tion, the Transfiguration, and the Resurrection of Christ; in man it corresponds to the body, the soul, and something known as the "spirit," which was a particle of the divine lodged in man himself. God was in man and man in God, and salvation was to rise through love to the life of the "spirit," to union with God. Witberg's temple was intended as a representation of this theosophy in stone: constructed in three superimposed parts, it was to symbolize the ascent of man from the body through the soul to the life of the "spirit" and God.

Herzen recapitulated the same ideas in his own Schilleresque jargon for the benefit of his Moscow friends.

Mankind is a fallen angel; revelation has told us this. . . . All those who have understood have believed in a lost paradise — Vico, Pascal. And what remains for us? Two contradictory tendencies drag us down, poison us by their struggle: *egoism*, which is gravitation, darkness, contradiction, the direct inheritance of Lucifer; and *love*, which is light, expansiveness, the direct inheritance of God. One draws us to the annihilation of everything except the ego, toward matter; the other is the palingenesis beginning with the pardon of Lucifer. Dante saw much when he represented all the vices dragging us down to Lucifer, into the center of the earth; this is a hieroglyph. I do not disagree, but where can we find words in our language which would replace the hieroglyph? [61]

Herzen made the most of the obvious points of contact that exist between masonic theosophy and the *Naturphilosophie*. For example, in Dante, whom he read as a masonic text, he "found an important and wonderful thing": "*Del Purgatorio Canto XXV* on the origin of man. This is *le dernier mot* of present-day philosophy — zoology; it is the whole theory of Geoffroy-Saint-Hilaire [the biologist], even more complete than in the latter, for he [Dante] has extended it to the vegetable kingdom." [62]

As time went by the scientific trappings of his new religion gave way to a purer poetry.

Look at the heavens: in them the sun is luxuriant and warm — this is the love of God, the glance of the Father. Look at these mountains, these cliffs, these scattered stones — these are the exhausted body of the rebellious Son; but look, from everywhere life aspires to the glance of the Father, the trees, the moss, and that effort of life which culminates in the flower — in the flowers the stamp of despair has already been effaced: in them is the joy of life. And between the glance of the Father and the body of the Son who is being resurrected is thought and feeling, entrusted in the light of God to the fallen angel — Man. To him is given to know all the beauty of the universe; he is able to rejoice in the heavens, the sea, the look of his beloved, and he is fated not to leave the earth until he has attained to all the beauty on it. [63]

The *Naturphilosophie* of Schelling and the aestheticism of Schiller have been fused with the universal correspondences of illuminism, and the mixture was Herzen's theology far more than the doctrines of the church.

This position is somewhere between a real theism and the pantheism of German idealist philosophy. Illuminism inclines to traditional theism in that it conceives of God as a partially transcendent being, the creator of the universe and in some degree, at least, separate from and superior to his creation. In other words, its God is supernatural, like the God of revealed religion, and not a purely natural deity, like the Absolute of idealism. In addition, illuminism holds that God is known, not by reason, but by revelation, and that He can be approached only through means which are nonintellectual, or mystical. On the other hand, in spite of its formal belief in God as a transcendent being, illuminism has so involved Him in the fabric of nature and in humanity that He approaches very closely to the immanent Absolute of idealism and becomes almost identical with the universe. There are further points of contact between the two positions in the matter of man's cognition of God or the Absolute. Unlike the revelation recognized by illuminism, idealism knows only "reason," or at least purely natural faculties, such as aesthetic intuition or metaphysical speculation. This natural reason, however, because of its emphasis on intuition, is in fact very near to the individual illumination of masonry. In short, both doctrines are pantheisms founded on intuition, with the difference that the pantheism of illuminism is supernatural and that of idealism natural. But the similarities are perhaps more important than the differences. The essential points of contact are two: the idea that the Supreme Being dwells in man and nature, and the belief that this fact is perceived undogmatically by the individual alone, through his powers of feeling and insight. It is this pantheism, together with the rejection of any principle of divine authority external to man's mind, which sets both doctrines apart from theism and orthodox Christianity.

Of the two, illuminism is by far the cruder and the less rigorous intellectually. It is more emotional, more obviously based on the feeling that things must be the way the heart wants them to be. It is less rational, less concerned to find a justification in objective, verifiable evidence. It is blatantly a structure of symbols and images, of pleasant poetic correspondences which unlock all the mysteries of the universe without effort. Idealism, on the other hand, presents itself as a logical structure, and is at great pains to find support in the evidence of science and history, however much this endeavor may in fact be determined by wishful thinking.

Illuminism, in short, is a less mature, more primitive and "alienated" expression of the urges which lay behind idealism. It represents the same effort, but less related to reality, to overcome isolation and helplessness through identification in fantasy with the external world and the superior powers that rule it. But, by its more literal attribution of divinity to the individual — the indwelling of God in man's "spirit" —

it reveals a greater desperation and lack of self-confidence than does idealism. If in the frustration of the years before his arrest Herzen had need of the consolations of idealism, in the more crushing frustration of exile he had need of the headier consolations of illuminism. Only this can explain the abdication of his considerable intelligence in the puerile imaginings of masonic theosophy.

5

It is only by the same desperation that one can explain the fantastic mythology surrounding his passion for Natalie. In a personality normally as self-assertive as Herzen's it is strange to behold self-effacement so complete before anyone, no matter how beloved. Natalie was only seventeen at the time of his arrest and only twenty-one at the time of their marriage in 1838. All through their epistolary courtship she remained a morbidly sentimental schoolgirl, in every way his inferior — in intellect, in education, in imagination, and in the range of her interests. He scarcely knew her, let alone loved her, before his departure into exile. His passion in no way derived from daily contact, common interests, or knowledge of a real being; it was spun entirely out of his brooding isolation in Viatka and of the image of a redeeming angel *aus der Fremde,* who deluged him with exalted, lachrymose, and desperate letters which answered so wonderfully his own mood.

His subjection to her, moreover, went to lengths which, in terms of the rest of his career, are incredible. Herzen by nature could not live without other people and public activity, and fame in the service of mankind and Russia had been his dream since boyhood; yet all this he was prepared to renounce for his love.

I see that I must root out my love of glory, it is the highest degree of egoism . . . but who could shake my old dream of fame, that dream which troubled me as a child, which would not let me sleep nights, which made me work at the university, gave me the strength to bear sufferings? This thought was the Holy of Holies of my soul; you with a single word, a single line have shaken this altar of pride to its foundations, I will cure myself of it. . . .[64]

The cure was soon effected. "Little by little everything died in me and my soul was transformed into an altar to you, Natasha; before this feat everyone must bend the knee. The whole of mankind never could have worked this change in me — but you have done it, maid and angel!" [65] The invincibly gregarious Herzen even maintained that the society of his fellow men was no longer necessary to him. "Every day I grow more and more withdrawn, men are becoming such strangers to me, so alien, that I fly wherever there are any number of them together. . . . Men have lost greatly in my esteem since 1834 . . . all my feelings for them have become concentrated around two ideals of godlike sanctity: around *you* and Ogarev. In you two I love men and love myself." [66] As often as not, though, his love for humanity was concentrated in Natalie alone. The days before his marriage were a crescendo of renunciation and self-abasement. "My literary mission is nonsense . . . you are my mission." [67] "I am writing to everyone: Friends, I do not wish to deceive you, I am not yours, I do not need you, go your own way; my life is full, it has its course and aim, it is higher than your life; my life is to live for Natalie, her life is life enough for us two." [68] It was as if the oath on the Sparrow Hills and his dedication to mankind had never existed.

The same uncharacteristic renunciation of the world is to be observed in the ascetic ideal of marriage he for a time entertained. At the beginning of their courtship Natalie announced the idea, rather logical for "angels," that marriage would be an unnecessary, indeed an unthinkable, consummation of their love. Herzen for the moment still had enough of the old Lucifer in him to find this excessive. As his passion grew "loftier," however, he came around to the idea of a marriage made only in heaven. "Do you know that even now I cannot think of marriage without recoiling from the thought? You my wife! What degradation: my holy one, my ideal, my heavenly one, this being united with me in the sympathy of heaven, this angel — my wife! . . . Closer to one another we cannot be [than now], for our souls have fused, you live in me, you are me." [69] Yet if a formal, "earthly" union should be necessary, "I by no means consider this a particular happiness; it is a sacrifice to civil society, an official acknowledgment that you are mine, nothing more." [70] At the first sight of Natalie after his release from Viatka these sentiments, of course, evaporated instantaneously, and the pair made the necessary "sacrifice" to the demands of society with no undue display of reluctance.

All this is quite aberrant in Herzen, who by nature was anything but an ascetic or a recluse. It is much more than the result of the overpowering effects of love, the explanation he himself later gave of his extraordinary behavior during this period. He was no doubt in love, but by no means obsessively. Natalie did not offer enough resistance for that; and he became bored with her too quickly after their marriage for his passion ever to have been as deep as the imagery surrounding it would imply. His love went to the metaphysical lengths it did because of what was grafted onto it by the frustrations of exile. Hence the association of Natalie with the idea of Providence, God, the angels, heaven, and all other conceivable occult powers necessary to save him from despair in the face of adversity. Perhaps the most preposterous aspect of the whole affair is the solicitude attributed to Providence for the welfare of the inestimable Alexander.

For Natalie's twentieth birthday Herzen composed a little fantasy entitled *It Was the Twentieth of October 1817* (the date of her birth). The five-year-old Herzen is sitting by his window. "The pale color of his face, his short height, the tenderness and frailty of his limbs denoted a weak, sickly constitution; but the features of his face were sharp, and his childish eyes sparked fire." Looking at him one might easily predict that "suffering" would "break this tender vessel — this vessel of powerful thought and powerful emotion . . . if God did not extend to him the hand of help." But God would surely do so, "because the whole material world is nothing other than the hand of help to the fallen angel." The Spirit of life looked down on the boy; he was moved that such a "little body" should enclose such a "great soul," and he felt pity for all the sufferings the boy would endure because of his "fiery nature" and his "proud thought." A swarm of angels surrounded the great Spirit; one of them, "exuding a benign and tender radiance," looked down on the child and perceived "on his brow the stamp, which had not yet been effaced, of the beauty of Lucifer," and the angel volunteered to be his savior. The boy then saw a bright star fall from the heavens; in the morning his mother came to tell him that a little girl cousin had been born to him.[71] From the whole tone of the correspondence one gathers the impression that the chief, if not exactly the exclusive, concern of Providence was to look after Herzen's destiny.

Such puerility is not the automatic result of a strong love. Natalie was of course necessary to this mythology, but she is by no means a sufficient explanation. Herzen's pretensions to divinity derive from a desire to escape, if only in imagination, from the impotence of exile. In his letters, the reiterations of faith in the saving hand of Providence are accompanied by despairing reflections on his inability to affect his destiny in any way.

Strange, very strange has been my education by Providence; I bear practically no responsibility for my life. . . . A force independent of me, not directed by me, has ordained, impelled, disposed — and in that prison you appeared . . . finally, my present position is stranger than anything in the past . . . on the one hand *perhaps* I will live on here another year, *perhaps* I will be transferred to some neighboring province; on the other hand *perhaps* in a month I will be clasping you to my breast, *perhaps* within a month I will be in some ministry [in Petersburg]. And note, above all, that in all these *possibilities* my will is for nothing; like a boat cast away upon the sea I do not even have the strength to wish this or that, I must wait to see how, and with what, fate will resolve the story of my life. So let us submit ourselves to the finger [of Providence].

Yet from this very impotence Herzen extracts reasons for continued belief in his star. "Not everyone is led by such steep paths, for not everyone is worthy. Look at others: they dispose of their lives, like property, . . .

but their march, with all its freedom, is not their march, but the march of the multitude, of the crowd; yet my course, for all its unfreedom, is my own. Natasha, it is to such a man that you must belong . . . and for him you will be the extension of the finger of the Lord." [72]

The idea of Providence working through the love of Natalie was necessary to Herzen to rationalize the uncertainty of his existence into a higher certainty, his bondage into a higher freedom, and his impotence into a loftier strength — all safely beyond the contingencies of real life. In imagination, everything that had happened to him was made to seem the opposite of what it was in fact. The waste of five years and the capricious decrees of the government became a meaningful pattern of destiny. Isolation became union with God, and frustration self-fulfillment. Despair became hope, and pessimism optimism. In short, an absurd lot was transfigured into a higher glory. Nor was the fact that Providence should choose to act through love an accident. There were few enough outlets for independent energies under Nicholas I: either the life of ideas in literature, journalism, or the university, which had been Herzen's initial choice; or personal relationships, "the circles," friendship and love, on which he had also always relied heavily. By his exile Herzen had been cut off from all of these activities except love, which therefore had to bear the entire burden of his energies. His whole life contracted into his love for Natalie; she became his Goddess, and their love the salvation of all mankind. All other aspirations he must renounce, for only through her could he save himself, since she in fact was all he had in the world.

The exile system of Nicholas had done its work well. Herzen was subjected to it for five years, and he passed only two and a half of them in the "Hell" of Viatka; if he had remained another five years in the provinces, or if he had suffered the worse fate of Schlüsselburg, or the army, or Dostoevski's "House of the Dead," there would have been little left of him with which to discomfit the regime any further. One classic result of exile in Imperial Russia was a form of religious conversion, or at least a retreat into a facile variety of mysticism, often accompanied by repentance for "sins" against God and emperor and by submission to "fate." This was the path of a goodly number among the Decembrists, of Dostoevski, and of many others. Herzen himself went at least halfway along this path. And in a sense Natalie did "save" him. Although not an "angel" she was at least real, a lightning rod for his abstract fantasies and a bit of concrete substance behind the phantasmagoria of his ideal escapes. She was something to live for, something in which he could realize himself, however inadequately. If she (and perhaps also Witberg) had not been there to sustain his belief in himself, it might well have snapped definitively under the strain of exile.

6

Seen in this light Herzen's love is more than a fact in his personal biography; it is a fact in the spiritual history of the age. Almost all the "idealists of the thirties" lived through similar experiences which mingled the sentimental and the supernatural. Stankevich, in his circle, was the high priest of a romantic and religious cult of love no less extravagant than that which Herzen held for Natalie.[73] Bakunin's role in maintaining a high level of passion among his friends is even better known. Belinski tried to live his affairs of the heart in the same way, and it was not his fault that he failed.[74] But it was Ogarev who, in his exile in Penza, had an experience which was most nearly identical with Herzen's.

Ogarev's conversion to religion began even before his arrest, and in the provinces developed to the same extremes as did his friend's. The only difference was a minor one: instead of masonic mysticism Ogarev turned to a theistic elaboration of Schelling, in which the Absolute was construed as a personal God; it was in response to this stimulus that he developed his "system" and composed his *Profession de foi*. For Ogarev, too, Providence demonstrated its solicitude by sending an "angel," named Maria Lvovna, to redeem him, and through them to effect the salvation of all mankind. A few days before their marriage Ogarev wrote to his bride in an ecstatic mood at four o'clock in the morning.

If I have enough soul to love you then I certainly have enough strength to follow in the steps of Christ — for the liberation of mankind. For to love you means to love all that is noble, God, the universe, because your soul is open to all good and capable of encompassing it, because your soul is all love. . . . Our love, Maria, contains in itself the seed of the liberation of mankind. . . . Our love, Maria, will be retold from generation to generation, and all future generations will preserve our memory as a relic. I predict this to you, Maria, for I am a prophet, for I feel that the God living in me has sketched out my fate for me and rejoices in my love.[75]

All the mythology which surrounded Herzen's passion was reproduced to the letter in the romance of Ogarev. Contrary to what Herzen implies in *My Past and Thoughts,* the pair went completely the way of their brother idealists of the circle of Stankevich into metaphysical and mystical fantasy.

The universality of such a mood, nevertheless, is much more than mere coincidence or the curious and amusing behavior of an eccentric age. If the first fifteen years of Nicholas' reign, together with the years just after 1848, were the bleakest for men of independent mind, the second half of the thirties were among the most oppressive of all, a time when the "opposition" in effect ceased to exist. The mildly liberal reviews, such as

Polevoi's *Moscow Telegraph* and Nadezhdin's *Moscow Telescope,* had been suppressed in 1834 and 1836, respectively, and they were to find no successor until the emergence of the *Annals of the Fatherland* after 1840. The only public dissent of the period was Chaadaev's *Philosophical Letter* in 1836. Yet even this was framed in "alienated" religious terms, and not as a direct political protest; for to Chaadaev the root of Russia's troubles lay not in her political and social structure but in her religion — the choice in the tenth century of Greek Orthodoxy rather than Roman Catholicism as the national form of Christianity.[76] But what was most shocking of all, two of the greatest radicals of the age, Bakunin and Belinski, had temporarily foundered in political conservatism, for this was the time of their famous "reconciliation with reality." At the end of the thirties the tensions between the ideal and the realities of Russian life were enough to break even the strongest. It was the dark night of the soul for all of Russian enlightenment, a period of demoralization, resignation, and withdrawal.

The mystical loves of Herzen and Ogarev were only one phase of this rout; they represent their particular form of "reconciliation with reality." Yet Herzen and Ogarev managed to save somewhat more from the wreckage than most. Although they withdrew almost completely into the ideal, they never became political conservatives; and, though alienated from reality, they at least lived their alienation through the medium of existing creatures of flesh and blood and not exclusively in ideal constructs as did Stankevich, Bakunin, or Belinski. As in the first half of the decade, Herzen and Ogarev were on the left of idealism, where some effort, no matter how limited, was made to bring the ideal to bear on the real. More particularly, Herzen and Ogarev at least got married, something which idealists such as Stankevich or Bakunin consistently feared to do, lest the ideal be diminished by too close contact with the material.[77]

7

Herzen's marriage was made possible by a providential transfer from Viatka to Vladimir. The form in which Providence manifested itself was a visit of the Crown Prince and his tutor, the poet Zhukovski, to Viatka at the end of 1837. Herzen, who acted as cicerone during a portion of their stay, made a favorable impression on Zhukovski by his education and talents. The latter promised to intervene with the emperor, and as a result Herzen was in Vladimir by January of 1838.[78] His romance was approaching a crisis; both Princess Khovanskaia and Ivan Alexeevich disapproved of the match, from what motives it is not clear, but the sheer pleasure of being disagreeable is not to be excluded. As an alternative the family pressed one unwelcome suitor after another on Natalie, most of them wealthy if not always young and handsome. To complicate matters further Herzen's half brother, Egor, a chronically ill and tragic figure, had developed a consuming passion for Natalie and was besieging her with his affection.[79] Herzen was understandably in a state of great anxiety; he advised Natalie to resist and, as a gesture of defiance, to "read *Don Carlos* openly, and let come what may." [80] Then the temptation of the proximity to Moscow became too much for his "fiery" and "impulsive" nature to resist; with the help of his friend Ketcher, on the third of March (another "sacred" date) he stole off to Moscow for a secret rendezvous with Natalie, the first time he had seen her in three years. The act was indeed foolhardy. If the Third Section had gotten wind of it, it could have meant Viatka again, or even worse, but after three years of waiting Herzen was, understandably, not in a reasonable mood. The risk was repeated in May, this time for higher stakes; helped by the same faithful Ketcher, Herzen returned to carry Natalie off, marry her, and confront the family with a *fait accompli*. With the benevolent aid of the governor of Vladimir the ecclesiastical authorities of the city were brought to contravene established custom, if not the actual law, and Alexander and Natalie were at last united, on the tenth of May — another bead in their rosary of sacred dates.[81]

Their life of solitude and love began, and lasted a little over a year, until Herzen's pardon by the emperor in July of 1839. It was a blissful year, and the first period of real satisfaction he had known since the university. The angelic pair seems to have made the adjustment to the exigencies of earth quite effortlessly, for Providence blessed their union with a son on the thirteenth of June, 1839, the last of the sacred dates to which their hearts were to beat as one.[82] In the course of this year of bliss Ogarev came to visit with his Maria Lvovna; it was the first time that the two friends had seen each other since 1834, and the first time each met the other's wife. The result could only be the spiritual union of the four, the mystic marriage of friendship and love. As Herzen described it at the time:

I had kept a Crucifix that Nick had given me when we were parted. And there the four of us threw ourselves on our knees before the Divine Sufferer, prayed and blessed Him for that happiness which He had vouchsafed us after so many years of suffering and separation. We kissed His nail-pierced feet, and kissed each other, saying, "Christ is risen." [83]

It was "one of those highest moments in life, in which it would be a blessing for men to die." [84] After the newlyweds' return to Moscow a few months later, Natalie was initiated into the mysteries of the shrine of "friendship" on the Sparrow Hills, which until then had been reserved for Herzen and Ogarev "alone." [85]

There is good precedent for all this in Schiller's concept of love. Just as the spouse was "sister" as much as wife, so too each friend communed mystically in the love of the other, like Posa in the love of Carlos for the Queen. Hence each friend had to pass on the other's marital choice, and for the wife of one to be judged insufficiently "lofty" by his friend was a catastrophe that might shatter the very fabric of their lives, and indeed of the cosmos itself, since friendship and love were interwoven with the life of God and the salvation of mankind. With so much at stake the friends were understandably nervous in presenting their loves to one another, and the effusions of tears and the quadruple embraces were necessary to give the desperately required assurance that approval was mutual. Natalie was only too glad to oblige, for the incident was in her native manner. But Maria Lvovna, though she submitted because she was outnumbered, inwardly felt the scene was "strained and childish," as she later confessed to Herzen. At the time Herzen noticed her "amazement," but suppressed awareness of it out of deference to Ogarev; only later would he hold it against her.[86] Nonetheless, the seeds of the dissolution of the union between friendship and love were sown at the moment of its seeming triumph, just as seeds of discord were present in Herzen's excessive idealization of his own marriage. For the moment, however, none of this was apparent, and it was possible to live in the dream of four beautiful souls united in love, God, and the cosmos, a beacon for the regeneration of mankind and the highest realization of the life of Providence, the Absolute, Christ, and of the Great Spirit of the world that dwelt within them.

8

This was the last time Herzen would find consolation so easily in an ideal fantasy, his final tribute to "romanticism for the heart and idealism for the head," as he later ironically dismissed his youthful excesses.[87] But much was always to remain of an experience so prolonged and deep. It remained first of all in his style, both as a man and as a writer. Herzen has often been called the "Russian Voltaire," because of his gift for satire and his later hostility to metaphysics and mysticism, to all "superstition" and intolerance. It is these qualities which make the writing of his mature years, and in particular *My Past and Thoughts,* great. Even at his most Voltairian, however, there is a strange ambiguity in Herzen's style. Alongside passages of mordant satire, including more than one famous thrust at the idealism of the thirties, are passages of the most maudlin sentimentality. In particular, the account of his friendship and love in his memoirs shows little gain in common sense over his youth. And the manner is the same whenever he comes to speak of his hopes for the "future of Russia." This duality of tone goes back to Herzen's earliest years; one of his earliest surviving letters, written at sixteen, gives excellent satirical portraits of his various tutors, annunciatory of his later manner and in apparent contradiction to any tendency to exalted reverence or poetic idealization.[88] Even his worst romantic stories, such as *Elena*, contain penetrating bits of social description, roughly in the manner of the Russian realistic novel.[89] Yet this is only half of Herzen. No one who had received a sentimental education as thorough as his could ever qualify as a full-fledged Voltaire, no matter how hard he might try in later years. Nor should we let the pose of critical lucidity so impressively struck in most of *My Past and Thoughts* obscure what Herzen had really been for the first half of his life.

Herzen's love and religion marked more than his style; they marked his political and social ideals as well. Like his friendship for Ogarev, his love for Natalie always remained more than a personal experience for him: both relationships anticipated the ideal future of humanity. Herzen was forever writing his autobiography; the earliest versions (largely lost) go back to his exile in Viatka; most of his stories and his two novels are thinly disguised self-dramatizations. One of the chief purposes of these efforts was to place himself before the world as a model. And the most wonderful part of his destiny was his youth — his "friendship" and his "love." In his first surviving autobiography, composed shortly after his marriage, he wrote: "Whoever has lived with his mind and heart, whoever passed a burning youth, whoever humanly suffered his every affliction and deeply felt his every rapture, whoever can point to *her* and say, 'Here is my beloved,' and to *him* and say, 'Here is my friend' — that man *has accomplished something*." [90] The work of his mature years, *My Past and Thoughts,* is dedicated to the same ideal. "This book speaks most of all of two persons. One is no more [Natalie]: you [Ogarev] still remain, and therefore to you it by right belongs." [91] In spite of all the disenchantments of later years, and the betrayals of both "love" and "friendship" by all parties concerned, this ideal remained sacred to the end, the figure of the fullest perfection to which mankind could aspire, and thoroughly "socialist," in the ethical and aesthetic sense Herzen always gave to that term.

CHAPTER IX

The Quest for Reality

WITH his transfer to Vladimir and his marriage, Herzen began a slow return to earth from the lofty heights of his love and his religion. The return was in several stages and spread over four years, from the beginning of 1838 to 1842. First in Vladimir, then in Moscow and Petersburg, he progressively sloughed off his youthful romanticism; finally, during 1841 and 1842 in Novgorod, he arrived at the formulation of a new position. It is to the first phase of this process that the present chapter is devoted, reserving the second phase for separate treatment in the sequel. During this period Herzen continued to live for the most part removed from his native soil in the Moscow circles. Yet the spiritual isolation of Viatka was broken, for he was once again seeing and corresponding with his friends, reading the same books as they, concerning himself with the same problems, and, finally, pouring forth his ideas in numerous articles and tales.

Under the influence of this new life, Herzen's opinions underwent a transformation as profound as any in his career, and no less radical than that, better known, marked by the Revolution of 1848. The change was from the idealism of his youth to a position which Soviet historians call "materialism," but which is better described as a form of positivism, in the general rather than the specifically Comtean sense; even more precise is the term Left Hegelianism. All these labels, though, are really too philosophical and make of the change too exclusively an intellectual matter. At bottom it was temperamental and political, even though it was expressed largely in the language of metaphysics; the best single name for it would be a more noncommittal term drawn from changes in the literature of the day — realism. This does not mean, of course, that henceforth Herzen saw the world only as it "really" was, for much of his thought after 1840 would fail to qualify as "realistic" by any exacting standards. But his new position does show an attempt to overcome what he felt to be the idealistic illusions of his youth and to attain a greater contact with the realities of the Russia around him.

The term "realism," therefore, as applied to his development should be understood to denote effort and intention more than achievement — or at least achievement only relative to his previous opinions.

Concretely, this realism involved first of all a rejection of idealism in the loose sense of a mental flight into a world of "ideal" perfection. Philosophically, this entailed the rejection, not of idealist metaphysics (for this Herzen did not really do), but of revealed religion, which was replaced by a thoroughgoing rationalism. In politics it meant a greater readiness to face the realities of Russian life in all their unpleasantness and to struggle with them in the concrete rather than in the abstract. In literature it meant the abandonment of a romanticism which situated its productions in a world of fantasy for a "realism" which depicted the life of contemporary Russia. Most basically of all, the new outlook of Herzen and his generation meant the rejection of pure philosophy, pure art, and pure love for more socially responsible versions of all three. And this meant propaganda and public "enlightenment" — in short, the nearest thing to political agitation that the situation permitted. By 1842 Herzen was a convinced atheist, an aggressive rationalist and, in spite of his youthful Saint-Simonism, for the first time a serious social radical.

The causes of these changes, of course, are to be found in large part in Herzen's personal experience during these years, but they do not lie there alone. The turn from the thirties to the forties marks a watershed in the intellectual life of the whole of "Young Russia," and indeed of most of "Young Europe," for whom the imposing structures of pure romanticism and idealism began to crash everywhere. They had crumbled first in France, as an aftermath of the Revolution of 1830; but France was the continental country where conservative romanticism had most recently taken root, and where idealism on the German model had never found more than a pale reflection. In the absolutist lands farther east, in particular Germany, the structure was sturdier and the crash came a decade later. In 1840 Frederick William IV, in whom those restless for change had mistakenly placed their hopes, ascended the throne of Prussia and the open fermentation of ideas which was to lead to the outburst of 1848 began. The old literature of dream and the inner life was cast aside by a new generation under the inspiration first of Heine, and later of such figures as Herwegh, a generation which was perhaps no less romantic than its predecessor, but which at least carried its romanticism over into politics. The conservative and religious idealism of the later Schelling was largely ignored, while the much more influential but equally conservative idealism of Hegel was progressively transformed into an atheistic and radical creed by such Left Hegelians as David Strauss, Bruno Bauer, Max Stirner, Arnold Ruge, and Ludwig Feuerbach. Among the bolder spirits this fermentation was beginning to develop into an assault on absolutism. Intellectual Germany, which since the end of the eighteenth century had on the whole been Francophobe and had rejected successively classicism in literature, empiricism in philosophy, and revolution in politics, now for the first time in fifty years was becoming Francophile. Francophilia meant at least liberalism, while in the more advanced circles it was beginning to mean socialism.

Russia, especially sensitive, as always, to happenings in Germany, could not but be affected, and the beginning of the first real radicalism in Russia since the Decembrists synchronized exactly with the change of climate in Germany. The youthful Saint-Simonism of Herzen and Ogarev, the only exception to the apolitical character of Russian thought in the thirties, had indeed been child's play with no general significance, however symptomatic it was for the future. Their radicalism after 1840 was both more serious in itself and a part of a growing movement. In 1840 the coryphaeus of Russian idealism, Stankevich, died, and the revolt against metaphysics by two of the most important members of his circle followed shortly; Belinski and Bakunin both abandoned conservative Hegelianism for radicalism between 1840 and 1842. The motive for the change in both cases was the same, weariness with a life of pure cerebration. As Bakunin explained later to a friend: "I then definitively renounced all transcendental science — *denn grau ist alle Theorie* — and, head lowered, I threw myself into practical life." [1] Even Stankevich's more moderate friend, Granovski, returned from Germany in 1839 at least sufficiently Left in his Hegelianism to interpret the dialectic as a law of change impelling Russia along the path of progress, an application of philosophy Stankevich would not have dreamed of making.

At the same time Russian literary romanticism, never too sturdy a growth, withered away, to be supplanted in the course of the forties by a movement soon baptized the "natural school" (*naturalnaia shkola*), but which is more conveniently referred to as "realism." By an accident of fate, the leading representative of Russian romanticism, Lermontov, was killed in 1841. To be sure other romantics remained, such as Tiutchev, who continued to produce verse of a mystical and metaphysical sort until well past the death of Nicholas, but their work was largely ignored by the public. As far as society was concerned romanticism as a phase of the spiritual development of the nation was over by 1840. Indeed, with the deaths of Pushkin (1837) and Lermontov, for the general public the age of poetry was over and the age of prose had begun. The first great monument of the new period, Gogol's *Dead Souls*, appeared in 1842. Whatever reservations one may justifiably entertain about qualifying this production as "realistic," because of both the lyricism of its style and the religious message of its author, the fact remains that *Dead Souls* (even more than Gogol's slightly earlier *Inspector General*) was the first major literary work in Russia to be built on the description of contemporary national life, free from the more conventional aestheticizing of earlier romanticism. Furthermore, the book, in spite of the author's description of it as a poem, was unmistakably in prose. Its impact on the literary sensibilities of the period was immense. That "society" largely misunderstood Gogol's intention by interpreting *Dead Souls* as a work of social criticism is, in a sense, beside the point, for never again would it allow literature to retreat into a world of private fantasy. Literature would henceforth have to deal in "realistic" terms with current Russian life, or society would not read it, and it had best be in prose.

In advocating such social literature throughout the forties Belinski was reflecting, as much as fostering, this new aesthetic trend. During this decade most of the classic writers of Russian prose were launched before the public. S. T. Aksakov, the father of the Slavophile brothers, had been awakened to literary activity by Gogol and had given the first realistic description of gentry life. Soon after, Grigorovich introduced the peasant as a respectable subject for fiction with *The Village* and *Anton Goremyka*. In the middle of the decade Turgenev turned from poetry to prose and began to portray the Russian countryside, and once again the peasant, in the *Sportsman's Sketches*. By the end of the decade Dostoevski had described the *Poor Folk* of the towns and Goncharov had published the first version of *Oblomov*, applying a psychological realism to the mores of the gentry. Finally, before the end of the reign Ostrovski had begun his dramas of merchant life and Tolstoi had entered the scene with the publication of his first stories. The last fifteen years of the reign of Nicholas, then, witnessed the emergence of all the principal representatives of the golden age of Russian fiction, and the years before 1848 in particular were the decisive turning point. It is against the background of this trend of a whole society towards "realism" in one form or another, literary as well as philosophical, and international as well as national, that Herzen's own turn to realism is to be understood.

2

At this point the Soviet historian invariably interrupts with the appropriate economic explanation of these intellectual changes. He points to the "developing crisis of serf-based agriculture" under Nicholas, to "the intrusion of capitalist relationships" in the social structure and to the resultant "intensification of the class struggle." As the reign of Nicholas progressed, the crisis of serfdom proceeded apace, to break out into the open as soon as he was dead. The coming of the railroad and the steamship, the repeal of the English Corn Laws in 1846, the increasingly stronger ties that bound Russia to a world market dominated by an increasingly industrial Europe, all these things made Russian agriculture, and the Russian economy in general, more capitalistic and by the same token made serfdom more of an anachronism. Under Nicholas the social fabric of the old regime was slowly crumbling behind the façade of changeless order imposed by the government.

While all this is certainly true, the Soviet historians are rather less helpful in revealing the transmission belts which connect the economic changes of the period with the revolt against idealism. What they say amounts to no more than that the radical intellectuals, speaking out ever more boldly against the old order, somehow represented the swelling anger of the masses. The intellectuals, however, knew precious little about the peasants, and they displayed even less awareness that "capitalism" was gaining ground or that serfdom, as an *economic* institution, was in a state of crisis — the changes in Russian society were too slow and small to recognize that. They were aware of a *moral* crisis bred by serfdom, but the economic changes of the period acted only in the most indirect way to produce this awareness and the ideological shift accompanying it.

One of the more obvious links between social change and ideas under Nicholas was the slow increase, both in numbers and independence, of the small group situated between the government (together with its supporters among the gentry) and the masses — people who in the next reign would receive the name of intelligentsia. The slowly growing complexity of the nation's economic life was one of the pressures responsible for this development. But the autocracy also contributed, by fostering the professional skills necessary to maintain an expanding bureaucratic machine. One of the best known examples is also one of the most typical: that of Belinski. His grandfather had been a village priest; his father had risen in society through a career as a military doctor; the son aspired to total independence from all service to the government. Dostoevski attained the same free-wheeling status from a similar family background of medical service in the army. Paradoxically, the reinforcement of autocracy under Nicholas further contributed to this development. It did so in part by expanding the bureaucratic apparatus in order to implement the emperor's policies of tighter centralized control over the country. It did so also by spreading and improving education, through the energies of Uvarov, in order to secure more competent personnel for government service. By the forties the products of this dual effort were already furnishing the readers for the social literature of the Belinskis, the Dostoevskis, and the other "realists" who emerged during the decade. At the same time this group of professional and clerical origin was beginning to fuse with the older group of humanized gentry which had become prominent in the previous reign.

Meanwhile the contingent of the disaffected from this latter class increased, for as the gentry declined economically it thought less and less as a unit, believed less in its future, and consequently felt decreasingly at one with the government. In the forties the Russian intelligentsia, in gestation since the eighteenth century, first emerged into the full light of day. Certainly this development is one of the main differences between the country in 1840 and at the beginning of the reign.

Another of the conventions of Soviet historiography is to document the approaching demise of the old order by citing police figures on peasant disorders, which increased ominously as the reign of Nicholas advanced. Such figures are taken to indicate "the deepening crisis of serfdom." Given the policies of the emperor, however, they might also indicate simply that police records were better kept than under his predecessors. Indeed, there is little demonstrable relationship between peasant discontent and the crisis of the old order. By the time of Nicholas serfdom had existed for fully two centuries, and it had never ceased to provoke peasant violence nor to require for its defense government force. Moreover, the worst crises of serfdom, the revolts of Razin and Pugachev, were far in the past; the last years of the institution were in fact among the quietest of its existence. Leaving aside the economics of the problem, there is no reason why serfdom, having survived Pugachev, could not have continued to exist indefinitely if the government and the gentry had continued to be willing to use repressive force. The point is that they were not, or rather that they were increasingly apprehensive about maintaining a situation where they might have to make the disagreeable choice. It is doubtful that public opinion would have stood for another *pugachevshchina,* and one of the principal reasons for this was the growth of the intelligentsia.

The old order in Russia was corroding, not so much at the bottom, as at the top. The most important revolutionary statistics of the reign are not those for peasant disturbances but those for the circulation of periodicals. The subscribers to the principal liberal journal of the early thirties, the *Moscow Telegraph,* numbered 1500; those of the principal crypto-radical journal of the forties, the *Annals of the Fatherland,* totaled 4000 at its peak in 1847.[2] In large part because of the situation revealed by these figures, after 1825 a frightened and ruthless government had easily cowed the enlightened minority, and the ideal consolations of their brethren in frustration, the Germans, had seemed the most that they could hope for. By 1840, however, the members of the intelligentsia, deriving confidence from their growing numbers, for the first time since the beginning of the reign could afford to find the consolations of idealism less necessary. Their attention turned, with a critical gaze, from the empyrean of the abstract to the Russia before their eyes, with all its imperfections.

One cause of this change lies in the nature of idealism as a secular substitute for religion. The psychological weakness of idealism is that its Absolute is immanent, realizing itself wholly in the institutions of existing society and in the art and thought, the friendship and love, of this world. Its promises can be checked against experience, and it is difficult for one with knowledge of the world outside of his study walls to believe indefinitely in the divinity of his loves and of his artistic outpourings, or in the idea that the life of the universe culminates in his thought. Any of the usual disappointments of life, from an unhappy marriage to a professional failure (or, under absolutism, unjust imprisonment) are enough to shatter the dreams of idealism. The mere process of growing up is enough: what looks like a reasonable expectation at twenty appears as an extravagantly inflated dream at thirty. Idealism, like all forms of life in fantasy, is the special gift of untried youth, when the individual stands with his whole life before him and any wish seems possible of fulfillment. A part of the change in the intellectual climate of Russia around 1840 occurred simply because, as individuals, the idealists of the previous decade were entering middle age. It was only in Germany, where the reaction against the Enlightenment had come earlier and where the pressures which sustained it lasted longer, that, more or less contrary to nature, men had been able to grow old in the idealism of their youth.

The numerous intellectual ties between Russia and Germany under Nicholas I, then, should not obscure differences which are equally significant. It was the Germans, after all, who invented the great ideals; the Russians merely borrowed them, and these ideals were never as native in the land of their adoption as in that of their creation. If Russia was the only major nation to participate deeply in the life of German idealism, its timetable of patience with stagnation was very different: only fifteen or twenty years, or roughly from 1825 to the beginning of the forties, as compared to some fifty in Germany. Literary romanticism in Russia was even less hardy, flowering as it did only for a precarious spring between the "classicism" of the Pushkin Pleiad and the "realism" of Gogol.

Nor did the Russians dream their dreams in the same way as the Germans. The Russians produced no creative philosophers, indeed, no philosophers at all. Except for a few individuals such as Stankevich, and, for a short period, the other members of his circle, the constant effort of the Russians was to make the ideal impinge on the real and not just to take refuge in it from a harsh world. They all tended to interpret the

ideal literally and practically, applying it boldly to contemporary problems, something the first generations of German idealists, less naïve but
also more timid, scrupulously refrained from doing. But then the
Russians were in a very different position from the Germans. The pressure
of the numerous petty German absolutisms, confining though they were,
in the last analysis was not crushing, if only because there were so many
of them. Karl-August of Weimar was really quite an understanding
patron of outstanding personalities, and there were chairs aplenty and
freedom of thought, for the few at least, in nearby Jena. The monolithic
Russian autocracy, with no islands of relief, was a far different matter.
The sensitive and humane Russian was too oppressed, too outraged in
his sense of human dignity to find consolation for long in the ideal
alone. A highly unpleasant reality, often in the crude form of the police,
was ever more ready in Russia to intrude into the comfortable world of
the ideal. So the Russians took what consolation they could from the
Germans, and they took much; but far more quickly than in Germany
it proved to be inadequate, and they demanded more virile stuff promising action in the real world.

3

The change in Herzen's opinions began almost immediately after he
settled in Vladimir. He now received visits from nearby Moscow — his
brother Egor and old friends from his circle at the university, such as
Ogarev and Ketcher. News from the capital reached him more quickly;
books and periodicals could be ordered almost as fast as they appeared
in Moscow or arrived from abroad. To occupy his energies he was thrown
less in on himself and on the meager resources of provincial society.
Most important of all he had the consolation of domestic happiness. No
longer was he yearning after a semimythical maid far away on the
horizon; he had at his side a real woman of flesh and blood. These
circumstances had a tranquilizing effect on nerves frayed to the breaking
by the isolation of Viatka. His situation no longer seemed so desperate,
and the need to seek salvation in fantasy correspondingly declined. He
could wait with greater patience for the pardon he now knew would
come eventually.

At first he found it easy to keep to the intention, formulated in Viatka,
to live only for Natalie. What was exile to him now? "A corner of paradise,
and if man needs an earthly resting place, it is all the same whether it
be on the Kliazma or the Elbe." [3] As late as eight months after his
marriage he was still writing: "Now . . . I am pure: I have driven the
crowd far away, I am eternally at home, eternally with her and with
my peace." [4] Yet, at the same time his "soul was still as stormy, as

impetuous as ever," it had "grown even younger, all the former passion, hopes had returned." [5] Such bursting energies could not long be contained within the narrow confines established by Natalie's love. A purely personal joy was glorious, but it was difficult to make a life career of it. As early as five months after his marriage he was already writing: "I am happy; however it is time to abandon the provinces: enough for the heart, the mind too desires activity." [6] Before the year was out he was off again awhoring after his old loves — fame and politics.

The politics in question hardly constituted a very direct menace to the regime; they were a return to the religious and "historiosophical" socialism of his days at the university. The literary sources of this revived interest in the social were even very close to those of his earlier Saint-Simonism. The supply of books and reviews fed to him from Moscow by Ketcher brought him up to date on intellectual developments in France and Germany during his isolation (there was, alas, as yet nothing of any note occurring at home). One of the more exciting new items was the *Encyclopédie Nouvelle* of the former Saint-Simonian, Pierre Leroux, whose particular contribution to the continuing socialist fermentation in France was the elaboration of the more spiritual aspects of the master's teaching. In August, 1838, Herzen wrote: "I am in transports over the *Encyclopédie* of Leroux — what a wonderful monument to the enlightenment of the nineteenth century!" [7] Only shortly after, at the beginning of 1839, he made a discovery equally wonderful: the novels of George Sand. The work which first caught his attention was a product of her "Christian" socialist phase, entitled *Spiridion*, composed under the inspiration of Leroux. It had just appeared, in 1838, in the *Revue des Deux Mondes*, a periodical read by all Russians with any pretensions to European culture and one of the first items Herzen requested from Ketcher after his marriage.[8] By February, 1839, he was impatiently demanding the issue containing the ending of *Spiridion*, and placing its author at the summit of contemporary French literature, even ahead of Victor Hugo.[9] A few weeks later the request was repeated with redoubled urgency, since the appropriate numbers of the *Revue* "must be in Moscow." [10]

Under the influence of these new prophets Herzen made a mental return to the enthusiasms of his university days. "Remember the time of the Restoration, when the new historical, philosophic and poetic school was printing the most wonderful works. Remember even the time just after the July Revolution, . . . and what enthusiasm there was then: Enfantin appeared as some John of Leyden and Bazard as Savonarola [prophets of the forthcoming social Reformation]." [11] The situation in France was no longer so brilliant, but at least Leroux and Sand carried on the tradition of divine discontent. From them Herzen derived a reaffirmation of his old faith in Saint-Simon's New Christianity. As George Sand's far-seeing medieval saint, Spiridion, revealed, Christ was not some abstract deity but a figure for the free and fraternal humanity of the future; the official churches had betrayed their calling by making Him the remote God of supernatural religion. The task of the New Christianity would be to restore His human image, and to regenerate mankind through a religion no longer otherworldly and mystical but social and terrestrial.

The impact of this message was reinforced by kindred German influences. The great intellectual novelty in Russia since Herzen's disappearance into the wastes of Viatka was Hegel. Herzen as yet had not read him, but he had heard rumors and he was highly curious to know more.[12] In letter after letter he asked Ketcher to send him Hegel,[13] but in vain; he was not to read the new philosopher until two years later, in 1841. In the meantime he had to content himself with secondary accounts. The principal of these was a *Histoire de la philosophie allemande,* by a certain Barchou de Penhoën, one of the principal contemporary popularizers of German idealism for the profane. Herzen complained of the inability of Barchou, and in general of the French, to write on the high level of German "science": they produced no more than "bad lithographs from which it is possible only to guess at the thought of the artist." [14] Nonetheless, the lithograph "strongly fascinated," even though it "did not satisfy." [15]

What Barchou gave Herzen was a rationalistic and humanistic interpretation of religion. "Present-day German philosophy (Hegel) is very consoling; it is a fusion of reason and revelation, of the outlook of idealism with the theological outlook." [16] Every item of news about this development was precious to him. Early in 1838 an acquaintance of Ogarev, a German clergyman named Zederholm, who was also a minor writer and historian, passed through Vladimir. From him Herzen "learned much that was new about German literature, for example that the young generation no longer looks on Goethe so humbly, that rationalism in religion, which has become almost completely philosophical, has grown to be preponderant over pietism [mysticism]." [17] Indeed, the good pastor was so upset over the "harm" done by Hegel that Herzen concluded, with a self-assurance characteristic even in matters he knew only slightly, that his interlocutor could not be very well acquainted with Hegel, since how, if he were, could he repudiate a philosopher that gave such a consoling interpretation of religion? For by this time Herzen had come to believe that religion must be rescued from the otherworldly mysticism of the churches and brought completely down to earth. "Namely in this is the question of our century — to reconcile religion with life, Revelation with reason." [18] To this end even more relevant was Herzen's old teacher of idealism, Schelling, whose thought lent itself more readily than Hegel's to poetic and "religious" interpretations; and Herzen read, not just a popularization, but Schelling himself.[19]

From this renewed contact with German idealism Herzen drew the following conclusions. Hegel was moving in the right direction in wishing to make religion rational, and Herzen felt "the most sincere respect, and the same devotion" towards him for this. Nonetheless, he was too "severe" in the "fantastic, unquestioning immutability" he gave to the structure of the ideal world — by which Herzen meant that Hegel's rationalism was too abstract and the political implications of his doctrine were too conservative. Schelling was to be preferred, because his thought held out greater hope for change in the real world.[20] Whether it derived from a superficial contact with Hegel or a superficial contact with Schelling, Herzen's own reconciliation of reason and revelation came down to something like this. The God of revealed religion is seen as corresponding to the "rational" Absolute of world history; and the Father, Son and Holy Spirit are identified with any one of the innumerable dialectical triads of idealism; they become, moreover, symbols of the progressive revelation of Divine Reason in the life of the cosmos, which culminates in the final perfection of mankind — the new, social Christianity. This is only a more metaphysical statement of the views of Leroux and George Sand, and in fact the latter, in her *Spiridion*, had employed the idea of the "three ages" — of the Father, Son and Holy Spirit — of the heretical medieval mystic, Joachim of Floris, a system itself not without parallels with idealism's (particularly Schelling's) philosophy of religion. As at the university, German and French influences, idealism and socialism, fused for Herzen into a single philosophy of history, religious in its symbolism and social in its inspiration.

Again, as at the university, this led him to the study of the past in order to divine the form of the future. No less insistently than he demanded Hegel or the *Revue des Deux Mondes*, he demanded works of history. Among the first he read was the still recent (1835) *De la démocratie en Amérique* of de Tocqueville. Not surprisingly, Herzen missed all the author said on the merits of purely political, or liberal, democracy. Paradoxically, the book turned his attention more toward the hoped-for promise of freedom in Russia than to the existing, though incomplete, accomplishments of America — not, however, without the half knowledge that he was whistling in the dark. "The work of Tocqueville filled me with sorrow and sadness. In conclusion he says: 'two countries bear in themselves the future: America and Russia.' But where in America is the principle of future development? A cold, calculating country. But the future of Russia is unbounded — oh, I believe in her progressiveness." [21] Why he held this belief we are not told; clearly it was founded on an intuition deeper than reason. Was not he himself, together with his friends, the future of Russia? Not to believe in that future would be to destroy the meaning of life, and to mock all his hopes, paid for by suffering and exile. Uncritical belief was the first condition of existence, and all doubts which challenged it must be shut out ruthlessly from the mind.

Similar sentiments were aroused even by David Urquhart's violently anti-Russian *Turkey and Its Resources,* which Herzen read in a French translation, and which provoked the exclamation: "The East is great, but we know it poorly." [22] The sight of the wonderful medieval churches of Vladimir produced the same reflection. "Ancient Greek [architecture] is finished; it has reduced itself to several definite types; the Teutonic [Gothic] is richer, but what can one build after the cathedrals of Reims, Paris, Cologne, Milan? Yet the Byzantine style, born beside the tomb of the Lord, allied with the tranquil contemplative idea of the East, possesses a great future." [23] Since art is simply one expression of the Absolute which expresses itself equally in history, by implication the historical future of Russia is also great. Anything, no matter how remote it might appear from the problems of contemporary Russia, was grist for Herzen's "historiosophical" mill, if it contained so much as a grain of the hope by which he lived.

Above all, however, he preferred reading in works on antiquity, the Middle Ages and the history of religion — all illustrations of the Saint-Simonian theme of the "death" of the classical world and the "birth" of the new hope of Christianity. He returned to the works of Augustin Thierry about the Middle Ages for enlightenment on the history of the church, and to compilations of documents on the rivalry of Burgundians and Armagnacs — again one of those periods of crisis on which he loved so to meditate.[24] He sought for the secret of the ancient world's decline in the work of Arnold-Herman Heeren, *Ideen über die Politik, den Verkehr und den Handel der vornehmsten Völker der alten Welt,* which devoted particular attention to social and economic history.[25] He read the *Iliad* in a Russian translation and at least tried the *Aeneid* in the original; he studied Tacitus' *Annals* and *The Life of Agricola* both in German translation and in Latin.[26] He dug into Georg-Wilhelm Räumer's five volume *History of the Romans,*[27] and to keep in mind the parallels between the crises of the past and those of the present, which was the sole purpose of these investigations, he read Lafayette's memoirs and Wolfgang Menzel's *Geschichte der Deutschen,* which informed him of the activities of "Young Germany" by attacking them.[28]

4

The fruit of all these meditations was a pair of historical plays in verse, entitled *Licinius* and *William Penn.* The first was composed in 1838, not too long after his marriage, and apparently reworked in the following year; the second was entirely the product of 1839. Rather mercifully for Herzen's literary reputation, if not for the study of his thought, the complete verse text of neither play has survived. Tatiana Passek, however, preserved a prose version of the first play as well as large fragments of the original text of the second, while Herzen himself some twenty years later outlined both from memory. From these fragments the structure of his thought is amply clear: it is the familiar theme of the "death" of the "old world" and the painful "birth" of the "new," the drama of historical decadence and regeneration into which he had been projecting his own feelings of frustration and his impatience for change since he first came into contact with Saint-Simonism.

The first play, *Licinius,* is based largely on his reading in Tacitus.[29] Herzen has described how he came to his subject: "One September day melancholy thoughts together with the misty, raw weather filled my soul with sadness." He began to read Tacitus. "Panting, with a cold sweat on my brow I read the terrible tale of how the Eternal City passed away in writhing and convulsions, with the raving speech of the dying. It was not the personalities of the Caesars, or the creatures surrounding them, which impressed me — the terrible personality of the Roman people itself was far more absorbing." He turned for relief from this spectacle of decadence to the *Acts of the Apostles.*

Side by side with dark, bloody corrupt Rome, devoured with passions, I saw the poor society of the persecuted preachers of the Gospel, and I realized that to it was entrusted the regeneration of the world; side by side with a decaying world, whose entire wealth was in memory, in the past, was the sacred repository of good tidings, of faith, of hope in the future.

Then he describes his own deep fascination with this subject.

For a long time I meditated on the period preceding their encounter. There is a special atmosphere of alarm and unrest, of tortured aspiration and fear when the future, pregnant with a whole world, is striving to unfold, to cut away from all that is past, but has not yet unfolded; when a great storm is preparing; when its irresistibility is obvious, but silence still reigns — the present is heavy in such moments, horror and aspiration fill the soul, it is difficult to breathe, and the heart, full of melancholy and expectation, beats more strongly.[30]

Herzen, of course, has here merely transferred to a mythical Rome his own mixed feelings of oppression and expectation in Russia, and dramatized those feelings by associating them with the sweep of history at its grandest.

Indeed the play is not about Licinius in Rome at all, but about Herzen in Russia. The scene is laid during the reign of Nero (or Nicholas); Licinius-Herzen, a brooding, sensitive, and superior young man, is tormented by his inability to believe in the moribund values of the Roman republic. He is equally unable to find consolation in the abstractions of stoicism and epicureanism or in the more spiritualized creed of the Neoplatonists — figures, no doubt, for abstract idealism on the one hand and religious mysticism on the other. Nor can he believe in the virtues of a plot being hatched by his friends to depose Nero and restore the republic, for the republic (or mere liberalism) is dead in men's hearts and thus cannot be brought back to life. Without a spiritual rebirth, by which Herzen means enlightenment, the destruction of one tyrant will simply bring the rise of another. The hatred between plebeian and patrician is such that no political patchwork can cure it, and Licinius paints a picture of slaves, turned into "beasts" by oppression, rising in revolt and destroying civilization — the same picture Herzen was later to paint in his bitterness over the failure of 1848 to regenerate Europe. In rebuttal of his politically minded friends Licinius calls out for a principle vital enough to revive the dying world, "to fuse into one family patriciate and plebs . . . warm them with love . . . and lead them with a proud step into the future centuries." [31] Thus Herzen-Licinius yearns for the coming of the Christ-socialism.

Until He comes, though, the time of waiting is heavy for the sensitive, and Herzen puts in the mouth of Licinius the first draft of the dirge over his own lost generation which was to recur so often in his writings.

You have seen all the horror of the present. What is to be done? In this indeed is the whole riddle of the Sphinx. In all ages, from the troglodytes to the most recent generation, it was possible to do something. Now *there is nothing to be done.* . . . Fate has appointed us to be the suffering witnesses of the shameful death of our father, and has given us no means to help the dying one, has even taken away respect for the corrupt old man. Meanwhile a heart beats in our breast, thirsting for action and high deeds, full of love. Neither Aeschylus nor Sophocles has dreamed of such a tragic situation. Perhaps other generations will come, and they will have faith, hope, the world will be bright for them, happiness will flower, perhaps. But we are an intermediate link, no longer of the past and not yet of the future. . . . Happy descendants, you will not understand our sufferings, you will not understand that there is no more onerous labor, no more bitter suffering than *to do nothing!* The soul suffocates (*dushno*)! [32]

It was painful indeed to be a man of energy in the stagnant Russia of Nicholas I, forced to sit out the best years of one's life in a provincial town with no occupation but the routine of government service. So Herzen has his hero pine away from despair and die. Yet in spite of all, Herzen was buoyed up by belief in the future, and the tale ends on a note of hope. As Licinius's funeral cortege moves along the Appian Way, it encounters St. Paul arriving from the east with the glad tidings of the new faith; he raises the youth from the dead, and abandoning family and friends, Licinius follows the prophet to work for the regeneration of mankind.

Nevertheless, *Licinius* was no more than the first timid step away from idealism. Its socialist symbolism was transparent, but it was still only symbolism, and quite remote from the problems of contemporary Russia; the solution proposed, even though Herzen intended it to be relative to a distant past, was nonetheless put in terms of a purely inward and moral, rather than a social, "regeneration." However, *Licinius* was only the first part of a double "fantasy" to be entitled *Palingenesis* — the term of Ballanche picked up when Herzen was still at the university.[33] Originally, the second part was to have dealt with "Daniel in Babylon," and to this end Herzen began studying the Bible, where he was, appropriately, most attracted by the prophecies of doom leveled by Ezekiel against Tyre and Sidon.[34] It became apparent, however, that this was simply more of the same as *Licinius* — a prophet crying in the wilderness for a purely spiritual rebirth — and under the influence of Sand and Leroux Herzen's religion was becoming increasingly social.

He abandoned the Bible, therefore, and took up a subject nearer to the present, that of William Penn. This idea had no doubt been suggested by his reading of de Tocqueville, who makes much of the importance of evangelical religion for liberal developments in both England and America. The new play was to be accordingly bolder than the first. In April, 1839, he announced its theme to Witberg: "non le christianisme en germe, le christianisme — religion mystique, poétique, orientale, comme il paraît avec l'apôtre Paul . . . mais le christianisme — religion sociale, progressive, le Quakerisme enfin." [35] The "diptych" had assumed final form: *Licinius* was "the manifestation of Christianity in the idea"; *William Penn* its "manifestation in deed." [36] As Herzen's subject became more political, his enthusiasm rose correspondingly. "The beginning [of *Penn*] poured forth with such fire that I am convinced it is good . . . what activity boils again in my breast! *Nein, nein es sind keine leeren Träume*," [37] a (misquoted) verse of Goethe's which Herzen often cited when his hopes were high.

The play opens with Penn's conversion to Quakerism by the "shoemaker-prophet," George Fox. Fox, who is Herzen's principal spokesman in the play, sounds a note which is new in the latter's thinking, and which he owes to Leroux — the oppression of poverty, "of all crosses — the heaviest" to bear.[38] "We [the poor] have no leisure to pray to God; all day long we must work in order to obtain our daily bread. For us there is no knowledge, no books, no leisure to study what we wish; for them [the rich] the whole wide world is open, and from superfluity their desires have grown dull." [39] The idea is trite enough, and a commonplace in the social literature of the day; nonetheless it is the first clear expression in Herzen's writings of an awareness of material — as opposed to intellectual or political — obstacles to the "free flowering of the human personality." Herzen was beginning to develop some of the egalitarian sentiments and the compassion for the masses usually associated with socialism.

Fox combines this thought with more elevated historiographical considerations, however, in the vein of *Spiridion*, which were still nearer to Herzen's heart. "The time of stupid illusions [supernatural mysticism] has passed; now, thank God, we are able to read the Gospels in our native tongue; we now know what Christ wished . . . He wished fraternity, equality, liberty; He wished that there be no rich men at all; He wished that the tears of the poor be wiped away; He wished everybody to love his fellow." [40] Elsewhere it is Penn who declares that the communism of the primitive church, described in the *Acts of the Apostles,* was the true ideal of Christ, and that this ideal had been perverted by the false shepherds of the official church.[41] Both Fox and Penn call for the realization of the promises of Christ, after "fifteen centuries" of superstitious religion, "not through the word alone, but in deed," in "life." [42]

In agreement on this general principle, Fox and Penn clash over the manner of its most effective realization. This clash reveals Herzen's reservations about the purely political democracy of thinkers, such as Tocqueville, whom Penn symbolizes. Penn wishes to use his fortune to found the perfect Christian commonwealth on the "fresh, virgin soil" of the New World. (The idea of national "freshness" was never far from Herzen's mind because of the obvious historical advantages it conferred on Russia.) Fox, however, tries to persuade him to sell all his possessions and preach the true, social Gospel throughout the world, for without a transformation of men's hearts the new community in America would fail. Still, Penn will not be dissuaded; he founds his community, and, true to Fox's prediction, it falls short of "palingenesis" because men are not sufficiently free in their minds from the moral fetters of the old world. The further emancipation of religion from all "mysticism" is necessary, and the play closes with an evocation of the next — but not the final — stage of the world's evolution towards regeneration, with Washington, Benjamin Franklin, and Lafayette assembled in prayer on the tomb of Penn.[43]

5

So much for the past, but what of the future? — as always, the pivot of Herzen's interest in history. Hardly had he finished his two plays when he announced, in October, 1838, that he was "beginning a dissertation about this and that." [44] By the spring of the next year this opus seems to have turned into "an article on the nineteenth century," [45] the subject of which could only have been that century's place in the unfolding of world history. Whatever fragments of this work were written have not survived, but we are informed of its general import by a letter composed at the end of his stay in Vladimir. His theme was no less ambitious than the problem: "What link does our century constitute between the past and the future?" — a question which he described modestly as "very important," and which he had "worked over a great deal." His labors, however, do not appear to have been excessively arduous, for the answer was quickly found. "Suddenly I see something similar has been printed in Berlin, Prolegomena zur Historiographie, I send for it — and imagine my joy, that in all essentials I am in agreement with the author to a remarkable degree." From this agreement he hastily concluded: "Consequently, my theories are correct, and I will take up work on them all the more actively." [46] It takes little to be convinced when one encounters a reflection of the heart's desire.

On the basis of this happy coincidence of opinions it is possible to reconstruct Herzen's own views on the future course of history. The work in question (the correct title of which is Prolegomena zur Historiosophie, not Historiographie) was composed by a Pole named Cieszkowski. The latter, although he considered himself an orthodox Hegelian because he believed in revealed religion, parted company with the master on the subject of the dialectic, which he interpreted very much like the Left Hegelians. He held that although Hegel had admirably worked out the dialectic of change for the past, he had been inconsistent in stopping his analysis with the present, thereby falling into a conservatism incompatible with the ideas of conflict and progress on which his philosophy rested. Cieszkowski boldly maintained that if reason could know the past of the Absolute it could also know its future, since the Absolute was one and the laws of its development the same in all periods.

Accordingly, he divided history into three great phases: the age of irrational feeling; that of rational thought; and that of will, which combines feeling and thought in one harmonious whole. In short, he gives a new variation on the old tripartite spiritual biography of man common to German thought since Goethe and Schiller. The first age, which coincided with classical antiquity, witnessed the reign of polytheism and mythology

— or an intuitive, poetic perception of the world — when human consciousness was as yet undifferentiated from nature. In the second age, stretching from the fall of Rome to the nineteenth century, the human consciousness grew to be distinct from nature and to dominate it; this development was manifested in the reign of self-conscious spirit on the one hand and in mind on the other, embodied respectively in the immaterial religion of Christianity and in rational philosophy. Put more simply, Cieszkowski maintained, like Herzen himself at this time, that revealed religion and rational philosophy were fundamentally one. The final age, the world of the future, would by a dialectical necessity produce the synthesis of feeling with spirit plus mind to give the rational, or moral will. This moral will would at last reconcile nature and man and thereby create the harmonious society, free of all the conflicts and alienations of the past. In other words, in the future men will desire what is good spontaneously, without any coercion by the state — all of which is simply a more contorted and Germanic way of stating Rousseau's old idea of the natural virtue of all human instincts once society has been rationally organized and men properly enlightened. Furthermore, it was obvious to Cieszkowski that this world of harmony would be a socialized one, of which the doctrine of Fourier, in spite of its shortcomings, was the most likely anticipation in the present.[47] It is not difficult to see how Herzen could be in "complete agreement" with this set of ideas. It combined in one harmonious whole all the themes of his thought during the two years in Vladimir. It was Pierre Leroux and George Sand fused with Schelling and Hegel and the themes of *Licinius* and *William Penn*. It was the "scientific" formulation of that hope in the future which had returned to him with renewed vigor following his release from Viatka.

Herzen was not alone in this evolution. As always Ogarev followed him faithfully at heel, in an instinctive synchronization of their developments which is indeed as remarkable as it always appeared to the pair themselves. In the middle of the thirties Ogarev had been even more completely than Herzen given over to his love, to idealism, and to religion. Then, in 1838, the same year as his friend, his interest in politics, which in reality had been submerged more than eradicated, began to revive. For the first time since 1835 he left Penza, on a trip to the watering places of the Caucasus. There he encountered his old friend, Satin, and made the acquaintance of the Decembrist, Prince A. I. Odoevski, both still expiating their crimes in exile. Under their influence, especially that of the "martyr," Odoevski, memories of his own mission returned to Ogarev.[48] Sympathy with Odoevski was all the easier since, like many of the Decembrists, he had turned to religion in exile, and in a form as amorphous and, at bottom, as purely humanistic as that of Ogarev. "Soon I [Ogarev] was able to read Thomas à Kempis with emotion and to remain for hours on my knees before the Crucifix and pray that a martyr's crown would descend upon my brow — for Russian liberty." [49] Under the influence of a local doctor who was close to the exiled Decembrists, Ogarev also read the masonic mystic, St.-Martin, an old favorite of the generation of 1825.[50] At roughly the same time he reworked his "system," over which he had been laboring intermittently since 1834, renouncing the "secular pantheism" of Schelling and replacing it with a "Christian" socialist philosophy of history not unlike that of Cieszkowski.[51] At the beginning of 1839 he was expressing renewed, although not entirely favorable, interest in Fourier.[52] So by the time of their first memorable meeting together with their wives in March, 1839, the pair were in agreement in all their opinions. Both could fall on their knees before the Crucifix, as Ogarev had done in the Caucasus, in a prayer not only of thanksgiving for their friendship and love, but also for the future liberty of Russia.[53]

Once again the two believed in the future with the faith of their youth. In January, 1839, Herzen wrote: "A new year is always a riddle, and the thought of it brings melancholy. We are a year nearer to death! This is true. But humanity is a year nearer to the great epoch of brotherhood and harmony! And this is true." [54] How did he know this was "true?" Because he *felt* that it was. He was still young and full of energy, his ideals were high, and his wishes strong. How could the world long resist the impact of this vitality? Since he refused to accept the limitations imposed on the expansion of his personality by the absurd reality of Nicholas' Russia, these limitations would simply *have to* give way. His belief in the future was the same as his confidence in himself. Besides, he obscurely — and correctly — felt that history was on his side, and not on that of Nicholas. In spite of the blackness of the present the record of the past *did* show that man increasingly dominated nature, that "superstition" gave way to "reason" and tyranny to freedom. He also felt, with the arrival of each new book and pamphlet which echoed his views, that the numbers of those who thought like himself were increasing, while those of the enemy declined. Thus, in his impatience for the age of harmony, and in order to neutralize the frustrations of the present, he generalized his belief in his own destiny and that of his friends into the principle of world history, the essence of the Absolute and the true promise of Christ. All past ages were made to serve as the stepping-stones of his hopes, and the line of humanity's development passed through his wishes to the future of their fulfillment. All this is very similar to his attitude in adolescence; the "historiosophical" scheme of "palingenesis" produced in Vladimir is simply a more mature expression of Herzen's earlier fantasies of self-realization. The exile system of Nicholas had prolonged the confinement of youth beyond its normal term, and by deferring the day of independence perpetuated the necessity of seeking compensation in a life of imagination. The fantasy, however, was becoming increasingly historical and social, and this was new.

By the end of his stay in Vladimir religion for Herzen had been emptied of all supernatural content and had become no more than the poetry of progress. Nevertheless he did not formally break with the church or consider that he had ceased to be a believer, although he was aware that his belief was not what usually passed for orthodox. He considered rather that he had rejected only the outmoded external forms of Christianity and had returned to its true essence. He still felt sufficiently isolated to have a vestigial need for the protection of Providence and the humanitarian symbolism he read into the Gospels; and he was still too infatuated with Natalie to cause her the pain of denying openly the God that had been her sole refuge before she met him. Nor had he cast off idealism; indeed he had returned to it. Still, even this was a step back to earth after the extreme life in fantasy of Viatka. In essence he had returned to a more explicitly social version of his position at the university, with the difference that he retained a tenuous tie with religion. From this reconquered position, in the next two years he was to go on to make a definitive break with his past and to lay the foundations of his new "realism."

6

This process was precipitated by Herzen's release from enforced residence in Vladimir. After several unsuccessful appeals to Imperial clemency, he was finally pardoned in July, 1839, on the intervention of the well-disposed governor of Vladimir. Ogarev had been pardoned in May of the same year, and the other members of the circle who had suffered punishment, such as Satin, benefited from a similar grace. In anticipation of this long-awaited day Herzen had made vague plans. As previously mentioned, he was contemplating a doctoral dissertation in preparation for a university career, a possibility he had already entertained in 1834, before his arrest.[55] He also desired to travel in Europe, again an old dream, to see at last that world of great ideas and fabulous events which he knew only through books. And, significantly for the future, he even seems to have played with the idea of using the liberty of the West to propagandize the "system" of social palingenesis he had worked out in Vladimir.[56]

His father, however, had other plans: now that he had been forgiven Herzen would have to wipe out the sins of his youth by serving loyally in the Imperial administration. And common sense was on the side of Ivan Alexeevich. It would in fact have been imprudent to abandon government service so soon after a pardon, and there was no chance of securing a passport for travel abroad. Other considerations entered into the old man's calculations as well. He was getting on in years and wished "Sasha" to inherit his estates and serfs. According to the law, however, serf-owning was exclusively the right of the gentry, and as an illegitimate son Herzen was not automatically a member of this class. He could enter it only by rising in the bureaucracy to the rank of "collegiate assessor," a position which would soon be his by virtue of seniority, if he continued to serve.[57] Moreover, Ivan Alexeevich wished his son to make a career in Petersburg, where the family had influential connections and where chances for preferment were at a maximum. To secure these advantages for his son the old man was prepared to pay heavily. The governor of Vladimir recommended Herzen for promotion to the rank of collegiate assessor and for transfer to Petersburg some eight months before the normal time. Now, while it was customary to secure such precocious advancement by greasing the palms of appropriate bureaucrats in Petersburg, a single official could not be advanced ahead of those in his province who were senior to him. Therefore Ivan Alexeevich was compelled to purchase the advancement of all the functionaries in Vladimir in line for promotion to the coveted rank before his son, a transaction which involved a considerable sum.[58] Herzen seems to have been in no way distressed by this unsavory, if not uncommon, manipulation, even though its primary purpose was to enable him to become a serf-owner. He acquiesced in all his father's plans, and undertook to do the necessary bribing in Petersburg.

These negotiations occupied Herzen from July, 1839, to the spring of 1840. In their pursuit he made his first direct contact in five years with the intellectual life of the capitals. He made a visit to Moscow in August and September of 1839, and a short trip to Petersburg, his first, in December of the same year. He then returned to Vladimir to wait, until March, 1840, for his appointment to the Ministry of the Interior in the capital. Following this he made a second stay in Moscow, before moving to Petersburg in May.

The Moscow to which he returned was rather different from the one he had left. He arrived at the height of the last and most luxuriant flowering of pure idealism in Russia, and he felt himself distinctly out of step. The university was quiet; there had been no politically minded circles, and no political arrests, since his own group was dispersed in 1834. Nor did his old circle continue to exist as a unit. Ogarev, who since his father's death a year before was the proprietor of four thousand peasant "souls," had returned to Moscow after his pardon and set himself up in a sumptuous establishment, at the same time circulating widely in society; and Ketcher was of course still there. But this was all; the other members of the circle had been scattered. Moreover, Ogarev and Ketcher had taken up with new friends, members of the circle of Stankevich, contemporary with Herzen's own group at the university but with which he had had almost no contact. Stankevich himself was absent studying philosophy at the source in Germany, and though Herzen was never to meet him, his spirit was still very much present in Moscow in the persons of his friends. Through Ogarev and Ketcher Herzen quickly made their acquaintance: the budding literary critic of humble origins, Belinski; the philosopher without precise employment, Bakunin; the future Slavophile, Constantine Aksakov; Botkin, a wealthy tea merchant's son turned dilettante aesthete; and Granovski, who had just returned from two years of study in Berlin, where he had for a time lived with Stankevich, and who was then entering on his career as lecturer in history at the university. The philosophy they propounded was no longer that of Schelling, which had still been the last word in Germanic wisdom at the time of Herzen's exile, but that of Hegel, first introduced into the Moscow circles following Stankevich's departure for Berlin in the fall of 1837, and fed back by him to Moscow from the source.

Herzen's initial reaction to this group, many of whose members were later to become his closest friends and political allies, was cold. He did not like his new position as a relative outsider in his home territory; moreover, he himself had not yet read Hegel and he found it somewhat galling to be thus placed in a position of inferiority.

My old acquaintances received me as one receives *émigrés* and old warriors, people who are just out of prison or who have returned from exile or captivity: with honorable condescension, with a willingness to accept as an ally, but all the same conceding nothing, and hinting that they are *today, whereas we are already yesterday;* meanwhile demanding unconditional acceptance of the *Phenomenology* and the *Logic* of Hegel, and withal, according to their own interpretation.[59]

The most distressing thing about this new development, however, was that their interpretation, in the manner of orthodox or Right Hegelianism, was either apolitical or frankly conservative, a potentiality of the master's thought Herzen had already suspected from afar in Vladimir.[60] Ogarev alone constituted an exception; to him Herzen had communicated Cieszkowski's *Prolegomena* and had met with approval.[61] But aside from this one ally Herzen was an intellectual outcast.

In *My Past and Thoughts* Herzen professed amused contempt for the rampant idealism he encountered on his return to Moscow.

There was not a paragraph in all three parts of the *Logic*, the two parts of the *Aesthetics*, of the *Encyclopaedia*, which was not taken by assault after the most desperate debates lasting several nights. People who were the closest friends broke off relations for entire weeks because they could not agree on a definition of the "all-embracing spirit," or were personally offended by opinions about "absolute personality" and its *an sich* existence." The most insignificant pamphlets appearing in Berlin and the other provincial and country towns of German philosophy in which there was any mention of the name of Hegel were sent for and read to shreds, till they were covered with spots, till the pages dropped out after a few days. Thus, just as Francoeur in Paris was moved to tears when he heard that he was regarded as a great mathematician in Russia, and that all our young generation used his system of notation to solve differential equations, so might they all have wept for joy — all those forgotten Werders, Marheineckes, Michelets, Ottos, Vatkes, Schalles, Rosenkranzes, and Arnold Ruge himself . . . if they had known what duels, what battles they had started in Moscow between the Maroseika and the Mokhovaia [two streets in Moscow], how they were read, how they were *bought*.[62]

His principal quarrel with the Moscow Hegelians was the barren abstraction of their speculations and the concomitant lack of any discernible relation to life as it is lived. Because of the importance of this objection for Herzen's own development — as well as for his talent in describing the intellectual atmosphere of the day — his comments on the current manner of philosophizing bear quotation at some length.

Nobody at this time would have disowned such a sentence as this: "The concrescence of abstract ideas in the sphere of the plastic represents that phase of the self-questing spirit in which it, defining itself for itself, is potentialized from natural immanence into the harmonious sphere of formal consciousness in beauty." . . . Everything that *in fact* is most immediate, all the simplest feelings were erected into abstract categories and returned from thence as pale, algebraic ghosts, without a drop of living blood. . . . A man who went for a walk . . . went not just for a walk, but in order to give himself over to the pantheistic feeling of his identification with the cosmos. If, on the way, he met a tipsy soldier or a peasant woman who tried to strike up a conversation, the philosopher did not simply talk with them, he determined the substantiality of the popular element, both in its immediate and its accidental manifestation. The very tear which might rise to his eye was strictly referred to its proper category: to *Gemüth* or the "tragic element in the heart." And the same thing in art. A knowledge of Goethe, especially of the second part of Faust (either because it is worse than the first, or because it is more difficult) was just as necessary as having clothes. The philosophy of music was paramount. Of course, one did not even speak of Rossini, towards Mozart one was condescending . . . on the other hand philosophical conclusions were drawn from every chord of Beethoven. . . . On the same footing with Italian music French literature was in disgrace, and in general everything French and along with it everything political.[63]

This portrait of the circle of Stankevich is of course overdrawn for satirical effect; nor are the sentiments expressed fifteen years later in *My Past and Thoughts* exactly those Herzen held at the time. He was still too near to idealism himself to see its ridiculous sides as clearly as he does here, and indeed he acknowledges sharing many of the same sins.[64] Nonetheless, at the time he already felt much of what he expressed in his memoirs. He had never been as thoroughgoing an idealist as the friends of Stankevich, and by the time of his return from exile he was becoming increasingly impatient with pure thought. The effect of this encounter, therefore, was to impel him still farther from idealism, and in particular from orthodox Hegelianism.

In Herzen's eyes the worst offenders among the adherents of the new fashion were Belinski and Bakunin, especially the former. It was the period of their famous "reconciliation with reality" founded on Hegel's well-known dictum in the introduction to the *Philosophy of Right* that "the real is the rational and the rational is the real." The pair interpreted this phrase, and indeed the whole of Hegel's philosophy, as meaning that everything which in fact existed was reasonable and hence should be accepted as necessary and just by rational men, whatever their "subjective" feelings might be. Technically speaking they had misunderstood Hegel. His endeavor was to explain the world as the unfolding of the "rational" and necessary life of the universe, or the Absolute. By this he meant that there is pattern, logic and order in the development of all things; that this rational order is inherent in things themselves, and not resident in some transcendent reality; in other words, that reason and the world are one. That this was so did not mean, however, that all existing things expressed reason equally, for reason was also a dialectical development, its forms perpetually changing, although its essence remained constant. All existing historical forms or institutions were only greater or lesser approximations of the rational life of the Absolute, and outmoded forms were on their way to becoming irrational ones. In short, Hegel believed in progress (although for practical purposes this progress turned out to be confined almost exclusively to the past) and Bakunin and Belinski had made the mistake of interpreting him statically. Yet, although they had missed the letter of Hegel's thought, they had caught the spirit very well. In fact, the whole pressure of his later philosophy, which was the version with which they were principally familiar, and of the exegesis of his orthodox followers, was towards submission to the "objective" facts of existence and acceptance of the status quo, absolute monarchy in particular, as the highest form of the "rational" in history. Bakunin's and Belinski's elaboration of this position may have been philosophically crude in a manner which would not have passed in Germany, but their conclusions were in the best tradition of Right Hegelianism.

Working within this framework the pair proceeded to glorify the Russian autocracy, serfdom, and an anti-Western nationalism with a gusto equal to that of the most reactionary supporters of the regime. The explanation of this behavior, so contrary to the rebellious nature of both, lies in the same pressures that had made of Herzen and Ogarev theosophist mystics only a short time before. The stagnation around them was so overwhelming as to induce despair of ever seeing reason and justice triumph in Russia; but despair was an unbearable conclusion to their hopes and so, contrary to all appearances and "subjective" evaluations, the existing situation had to be construed as reasonable, just and necessary. What they could not have in reality they must have in imagination, and they contrived to have it with the aid of the metaphysical legerdemain of Hegel that made black seem white and slavery freedom.

Bakunin had led off the attack by an article in March, 1838, proclaiming on behalf of Russian Hegelianism the folly of struggling against the "objective" reason of existing reality.[65] Belinski was even more vocal and violent. He seized on a rather crudely chauvinistic poem by Zhukovski commemorating the battle of Borodino and used it as a text for expounding his new conservatism. It was at this point that Herzen met him. Belinski read the poem to Herzen with provocative commentaries.[66] It was an insult, not only to Herzen's current convictions, but to his past and to the sufferings of his exile. Violent discussions ensued in the circle, with Ogarev, Bakunin, and Granovski trying to find some middle ground between the extremes represented by Belinski and Herzen, but on the whole "the chorus was for Belinski." Matters were envenomed further when Belinski carried his ideas into print. At the end of 1839 and the beginning of 1840 appeared in rapid succession his notorious conservative articles, two on the theme of Borodino and a third, *Menzel, Critic of Goethe,* attacking the "subjective" malcontent Schiller and extolling the "objective" and rationally reconciled Goethe. The articles were shameless apologias for autocracy and Russian nationalism; they contained, moreover, numerous direct jibes at the radical-minded, in particular Herzen, who are referred to as the "brainless reformers of humankind," productive only of "loud, empty phrases." [67] This passed all bounds, and Herzen broke off relations with Belinski, an action which the latter greeted with a like sentiment of personal hostility.[68] Relations with Bakunin and Granovski continued, but under the circumstances they could hardly be close. Even Ogarev seemed to be making an undue effort at sympathetic understanding of the other side. This experience both shook and angered Herzen. He had the disturbing sensation that the enemy was within the walls; even progressive, Western "science" could lead to obscurantism! For the next year he would have nothing to do with Hegel.

7

Nor were the Hegelians the only menace to enlightenment Herzen found on his return to civilization; by their side a group of religious nationalists, the Slavophiles, was taking shape. Religious nationalism, of course, was not a new phenomenon in Russia. The first radical alarms under

Alexander I had already produced the idea of a return to the old ways of Orthodoxy in order to ward off the contagion of Western revolution. After 1825 such thinking spread and was adopted as the official policy of the government. Count Uvarov, Nicholas' Minister of Education, was its principal spokesman, and his program of "Orthodoxy, Autocracy, Nationality" had long been propagated by the *Journal* of the Ministry. He was seconded in this enterprise by the so-called "reptile" or progovernmental press in Petersburg, presided over by the trio of Bulgarin, Grech, and Senkovski and partially subsidized by the regime. The program of these organs was the subtle deprecation of Western philosophy, literature, and political thought, particularly things French, and the defense of everything national and Orthodox, and thereby of autocracy. But this was the government together with its paid lackeys, and nothing else was to be expected from such quarters.

The Slavophiles were something new, and infinitely more disturbing. They were humane and enlightened men, who had drunk deeply at the font of Western "science," just like the members of the circles of Stankevich and of Herzen and Ogarev. Moreover, they belonged to the same world, the cultivated gentry society of Moscow, and had studied and taught at the university. Constantine Aksakov and Iuri Samarin had been members of the group of Stankevich, and the former was a close personal friend of Belinski, Bakunin, and Botkin. The elder members of the group, Khomiakov and the brothers Kireevski, as well as the professors Pogodin and Shevyrev, had been associated with Pavlov and the "Society of the Lovers of Wisdom," the very beginnings of the development of German "science" in Russia. In addition they were people one saw socially; the *salon* of Madame Elagin (the mother of the Kireevskis by her first marriage) was one of the preferred meeting places of intellectual Moscow, where Herzen and the circle of Stankevich were received as friends. Nor were the Slavophiles on the side of the government; they were independent, thinking men. Yet people such as these were beginning to go the way of reaction!

The change had come in the late thirties during Herzen's absence. In 1836 Chaadaev had published his famous *Philosophical Letter*, damning everything Russian as stagnant and barbaric because it was outside the main stream of history, as represented by Western Europe. For Chaadaev the cause of Russia's lack of true civilization was her conversion to Greek Orthodoxy, and conversely the cause of the flowering of civilization in the West was Roman Catholicism. Chaadaev's contrast between Russia and the West, then, was not that of a political radical — a contrast between liberty and despotism, revolution and reaction — but a contrast of religions, where a real radical would have seen only shades of gray. Nonetheless, the deeper significance of his *Letter* was for the time quite subversive, since to deprecate Orthodoxy and praise Catholicism was in effect to attack the "Official Nationality" of the government and all those who preferred the Russian status quo to Western movement. It was this attack which touched off the Slavophiles; they wanted movement, but within the context of existing institutions and traditions. Chaadaev's assault on everything national, and in particular on Orthodoxy, both offended and alarmed them, for, though less than the government, they feared the corrosive consequences of undiscriminating acceptance of Western models. To ward off this menace they set to work defining the national essence of Russia, extolling those native virtues which they considered worthy of development for the future.

The main lines of the defense were already set by Herzen's return to Moscow. They represented an adaptation to Russian conditions of the various religious currents of thought which had sprung up all over Europe after 1800, and in particular during the Restoration, in reaction to the Enlightenment and Revolution, a movement represented by such figures as de Maistre, Chateaubriand, Schleiermacher, von Baader, and Schelling in his later phases. The reaction of this group to the Enlightenment was far from identical with the related reaction of idealism or, in some cases, with that of literary romanticism. Idealism had said that mere empirical reason was not enough to give true understanding, and that dialectical reason, or transcendental "absolute" reason was necessary. The romantics too, in various ways, held that the reason of the Enlightenment was not enough, and that feeling, poetic intuition, or the voice of "nature" alone could give true insight. The religious thinkers of the Restoration also rejected empirical reason, but offered as a substitute, not another kind of reason or some sort of intuition originating in man or nature, but supernatural revelation and religious faith in the conventional sense. It was this position, more antirationalistic than both idealism and literary romanticism, which was occupied by the Slavophiles.

The cardinal point of their creed was that human reason was a shaky reed, and that the only rock of truth was religious faith. All rationalisms and all philosophy, including German idealism, were a snare. Moreover, since the home of rationalism was the West, the West was corrupt, and its influence on Russia pernicious. Even Western religion, both Catholicism and Protestantism, had been corrupted by the all-pervading rationalism of the Western mind, inherited from the philosophizing Greeks and the legalistic Romans. In consequence Western religion was hardly religion at all, and the only true form of Christianity, unsullied by any contact with rationalism, was Orthodoxy. This was the major innovation made by the Slavophiles in the neo-Christianity they had taken over from that very West. They opposed Russia· and Orthodoxy to rationalism and

Europe in the same way that neo-Christians in the West opposed faith
to reason, the Church to the Revolution. The Slavophiles had added a
geographic and national dimension to the usual Restoration dichotomy
of reason and faith. The Slavophiles, of course, were sincerely religious
men, but their championing of Orthodoxy had a political purpose as well,
which was to preserve Russia from the Revolution by preserving her from
the West. They believed that Western rationalism, penetrating Russia in
an unending stream since the misguided reforms of Peter the Great, was
corroding the pure Orthodox foundations of the national life, and that
the process, if it were allowed to continue, could produce the catastrophes
which they considered had overtaken Europe since 1789. Nevertheless,
this position did not bring them in line with the government, for the
cornerstone of their ideology was not autocracy, as it was for the proponents of Official Nationality, but Orthodoxy, which was a power over
and above the mere earthly might of the emperor, and emperors such as
Peter had sinned profoundly against it. On this ideological difference
hinged important political differences, which, however, will best be discussed later in connection with the full-dress debate between Westerners
and Slavophiles in the middle of the forties.[69]

The only exceptions the Slavophiles were prepared to make in their
rejection of Western influence were for thinkers who, like themselves,
condemned the rationalistic sins of the modern age. Chief among these
thinkers was Schelling, at least in the later expressions of his philosophy.
In the early thirties all of intellectual Moscow had been Schellingian;
and everybody had followed the early Schelling, the philosopher of a
declaredly rationalistic, although highly poetic, idealism. As yet, the
generation which grew up after 1825 had not begun to differentiate
into distinct parties. This occurred only in the late thirties, when most
of the circle of Stankevich abandoned Schelling for the less poetic and
more aggressively rationalistic Hegel, while the future Slavophiles abandoned the early philosophy of Schelling for its later, religious form — or
rather what they had heard rumored of it, for Schelling published little of
his new reflections, and the Slavophiles were in fact inspired more by
his example than his arguments. In this the Russians followed the developing split in German idealism itself. After 1830, as Schelling moved
steadily toward revealed religion and the rehabilitation of mythical forms
of cognition, he renounced absolute idealism and proclaimed the primacy
of faith over reason. This development led to a break with the followers
of Hegel and a lively polemic soon developed between the adherents of
rationalistic and religious idealism in Germany, which did not pass unnoticed in Russia.

The break between the Hegelians of the circle of Stankevich and the
adherents of Orthodoxy grouped around the Kireevskis and Khomiakov

was in part a reflection of the split in German idealism. It was also a response to Russian conditions. The growing impatience of society with the stagnation imposed by the regime produced a corresponding tendency among the intellectuals to think for themselves about where Russia was, or should be, going. As one group groped for a solution in the direction of the rationalist Hegel, the other group in alarm sought a counterweight in the direction of the more mystical Schelling. By 1838 the differentiation of parties was still largely philosophical, but it was on the verge of becoming political, and the first years of the next decade would mark the change.

The position of the Slavophiles had received an initial and rather violently anti-Western formulation from Khomiakov during the winter of 1838–39 in an essay entitled *On the Ancient and the Modern,* in which the author of course defended the ancient ways of Russia. It had received a more moderate expression in Ivan Kireevski's *Reply to Khomiakov,* which took greater account of the fact of Westernization in Russia, while still adhering to the basic principle of Orthodoxy as the foundation of the national life. The Moscow *salons* and the university were still reverberating to these debates when Herzen arrived. Although more absorbed by the menace from Belinski and Bakunin nearer home, Herzen could not have helped hearing about the Slavophiles; Moscow society was too small for such a dramatic novelty to escape his notice. Moreover, Granovski, who was well informed and who was retailing these developments to Stankevich abroad,[70] could not have failed to have told the same to Herzen. Then, too, Herzen made visits to his old friend the Decembrist Orlov and to Chaadaev, and doubtless to the Elagins as well, at whose soirées all the latest ideas were invariably discussed.

Finally, Herzen had an even more painful reminder of the new conservative currents in the person of his old friend Vadim Passek, after Ogarev the closest of his university comrades. Passek had escaped arrest in 1834, but in the interval had succumbed to the regime in more indirect fashion. Not only had he completely shed his early liberalism, he had become an anti-Western chauvinist and an apologist for autocracy, spending his time producing historical studies on the glorious origins of the Russian monarchy — which for Herzen simply meant flight from the real problems of the present into the imaginary greatness of the past.[71]

Thus, by the time Herzen settled in Petersburg in the spring of 1840, the problems confronting him in his new life were clear. In addition to the government, which could not be attacked directly, there were two enemies who could: abstract idealism and religious nationalism, the metaphysics of the circle of Stankevich and the mysticism of the Slavophiles. There was in addition a third, minor enemy in the religious Westernism of Chaadaev, but this for Herzen was a phenomenon more pitiful than dangerous. His intellectual efforts for the next three years were directed toward defining his relation to these menacing tendencies.

8

The atmosphere in Petersburg was at first conducive to this endeavor. If Petersburg was the seat of the despised government, and hence could never be completely congenial to Herzen, it was also the center of Western influence in Russia and consequently a more active stronghold of pro-Western sentiment than Moscow. In particular, Petersburg was the home of the first progressive periodical in Russia since the closing of the *Moscow Telegraph* in 1834 and the *Moscow Telescope* in 1836. After banning these publications the government was determined to grant no new licenses for the founding of troublesome organs of opinion. An enterprising journalist named A. A. Kraevski, however, succeeded in acquiring an existing although minor periodical, the *Annals of the Fatherland,* and proceeded to expand its activities. In January, 1839, it opened its doors under his editorship and began the career which was to make of it the leading Westernizing journal of the forties. Kraevski himself was an aggressive businessman with no strong political opinions one way or the other, and his primary purpose was to make money and acquire personal importance by giving the public the radical fare it could not get elsewhere. But the circle surrounding him and his chief aide, the critic I. I. Panaev, were more sincerely devoted to the cause of enlightenment, and among them Herzen found an atmosphere more sympathetic than the one he had just left in Moscow.

His principal ally in this circle, strangely enough, soon came to be Belinski, by now the chief literary critic of the *Annals.* To assume this position Belinski had settled in Petersburg in the fall of 1839. During the winter and most of the following year he suffered through his famous crisis of revolt against Hegel and all metaphysical "reconciliation," from which he emerged a fiery advocate of humanity, progress, and struggle with "cursed Russian reality." By mid-1840 he was thoroughly ashamed of his recent conservative articles, and the first meeting with Herzen after the latter's arrival, a meeting arranged by Panaev, ended in a rapprochement.[72] From this time on the two grew constantly more close. In December of 1839 (the time of Herzen's first brief visit to Petersburg) Belinski had written of him to a friend: "an intelligent, good, fine person, but if God should grant that we should never meet again it would be all to the good"[73]; and in April, 1840, he had added somewhat more categorically: "I spit on him."[74] By December of the same year, however, he overflowed with enthusiasm for all his qualities. "This man pleases me more and more . . . what a receptive, active nature, so full of interest in life and so noble! . . . I feel free and at ease with him. That he cursed me in Moscow for my *absolutist* articles, this is simply a new right on his part to my respect." [75] The two spent long hours "arguing" ardently over their "convictions"; indeed, no one was closer to Belinski during this crucial year than Herzen, and with no one else did Belinski feel it was possible to have a serious ideological discussion.[76]

As these confidences indicate, Herzen was one of the principal agents in guiding Belinski's conversion from conservatism to radicalism in the course of 1840. Belinski was always very dependent on the learning of his friends for the formulation of his own opinions. He had come to accept Hegel largely through the preaching of Bakunin, and he seems to have been greatly aided in his rejection of Hegel by the preaching of Herzen (a fact which has not always been adequately appreciated),[77] although the degree of personal dependence on Herzen was not as great as on Bakunin. Herzen could not have failed to repeat to Belinski the arguments of Cieszkowski against Hegel's conservatism and to expound his own system of "palingenesis" developed in Vladimir. This influence is demonstrated by the opinions that Belinski began to express when he abandoned Hegel, opinions which smack strongly of Pierre Leroux's "Christian" socialism. In December of 1840 he announced his adherence to "liberalism," as the true realization of the promises of Christ,[78] and by the beginning of 1841 he declared his ideal to be *"sotsialnost"* or socialism. He also renounced his recent hatred of all things French and began speaking of "that noble nation, which has shed its blood for the most sacred rights of humanity." [79] He set about acquainting himself with the teachings of the Saint-Simonians, and he developed a veritable passion for George Sand, referring to her as "an inspired prophetess," "the Joan of Arc of our time," and describing her works, in particular her defenses of the rights of women, as "divine." [80] By the following year he was expressing himself in the idiom of *Spiridion* mingled with that of Hegel. "There will be neither rich nor poor, kings nor subjects. There will be only brothers, men, and, as Saint Paul says, Christ will give his power to the Father and the Father-Reason will reign, but henceforth in a new heaven and on a new earth." [81] All these new enthusiasms were transmitted, in so far as the censorship would permit, to the pages of the *Annals*. This change in Belinski's views derived, of course, primarily from his temperamental inability to remain long a conservative; yet at the same time it is impossible not to detect the hand of Herzen in the form that Belinski's new radicalism took.

Belinski in turn affected his friend's destiny, for through him Herzen was introduced to the columns of the *Annals of the Fatherland,* and thereby at long last acquired the public forum which he had desired since the university.[82] Until his departure from Russia he was to remain a constant contributor. From the beginning his articles appeared under the romantic pseudonym of "Iskander," which was simply the Turkish form of his own name, Alexander. This name soon came to stand for a program, since all of Herzen's contributions, even on the most innocuous subjects, were camouflaged polemics with one or another enemy of "enlightenment" and, ultimately, with the regime. His first productions were already in this vein and very clearly reply to the disturbing currents of thought he had encountered since his return from exile. The conditions of censorship under Nicholas, of course, made it impossible to express directly all that he had on his mind. Much could be said indirectly, however, while ostensibly talking about other things, and Herzen, no matter what his subject, was always talking about politics and the future of Russia. Moreover, he had a ready public in the readers of the *Annals*, for in reaction to the censorship of Nicholas Russian society was already beginning to form the habit of reading artfully between the lines. The public of the *Annals* was looking there more often than not for answers to the social and political problems which every year oppressed its consciousness more heavily.

One of Herzen's first contributions to the *Annals* was an article on the liberal historian, Augustin Thierry. To give the *Annals* the historical rubric it lacked, Belinski suggested that Herzen be approached,[83] and the latter complied by translating and introducing Thierry's *Récits des temps Mérovingiens*, which had already caught his attention at the university and then in Vladimir.[84] His introduction was an attack on those who, like the Slavophiles, were turned exclusively toward the past for their ideals or who, like the orthodox Hegelians, made history into an abstract intellectual investigation divorced from the concerns of the present. He also seems to have had in mind his old friend Vadim Passek, a historian by profession, whom he had seen again in Petersburg shortly before he wrote his article.[85] Thierry was contrasted by Herzen with all these perverters of history. First of all, "in spite of the general infatuation of the young school with theoretical philosophizing in history, he wrote *tales*," in other words he discussed life in the concrete.[86] Moreover, "one should remember that for him the study of history had a contemporary, living, general interest [political interest]: he took up the study of ancient France in order to explain to himself the weighty questions confronting modern France, in which he lived and for which he lived." [87] Finally, Thierry represented that high seriousness in "science," that dedication to enlightenment in the public interest, which Herzen felt should be the inspiration of the educated minority in Russia, and he quotes a lengthy passage from the memoirs of the blind Thierry which sets forth this ideal.

Let it [his work] be a witness against moral exhaustion, that ulcer of the new generation; let it point out the straight road of life to some at least of those who have grown weak, who complain of lack of faith, who do not know where to turn, where to find love and conviction. . . . With it ["science"] life is employed nobly. Blind and suffering hopelessly, I can testify — and my testimony should give faith: there is something more precious in the world than material pleasures, than wealth, than health itself — *the love of enlightenment.*[88]

Let all those figuratively blinded by the reaction of Nicholas, all those of little faith in the future of Russia take note and join in the great work of enlightenment! To make it clear where enlightenment lies Herzen introduces, completely *hors de propos,* several references to the *Encyclopédie Nouvelle* of Leroux, whom he calls the "best speculative brain that now exists in France." [89] The call to intellectual arms was muffled, but unmistakable.

9

A far stronger blast against his ideological foes was contained in a more considerable work, the *Notebooks of a Certain Young Man,* which appeared in two installments, the first in December, 1840, and the second in August, 1841. The young man in question was of course Herzen himself, and the *Notebooks* told in slightly fictionalized form the story of his life to that point. They were, in effect, the first draft of his full autobiography, *My Past and Thoughts,* begun some twelve years later in emigration.

That Herzen should have chosen as the theme of his first important work of propaganda the story of his own life is in part a reflection of his eternal concern with self. The genesis of the *Notebooks* goes back to a time in Viatka when, by harsh necessity, concerns of political propaganda were very far from his mind. One of his chief literary projects at that time had been a work entitled, characteristically, *About Myself,* of which only a fragment has survived.[90] It would even seem that the published *Notebooks* were largely a reworked version of this lost production.[91] Herzen's attitude toward this autobiography is revealed naïvely in a letter he wrote at the time to Ogarev, in an attempt to obtain from him the letters of their youth. "S. [Sazonov] says that you . . . have burned my letters. This is bad; it would have been better to have burned off an inch of the little finger of my left hand. Our letters are the most important document of our development; in them, with the passage of time, are reflected all the modulations, are echoed all the impressions of our souls. Oh, how could you have burned such things!" [92] Ogarev, of course, had destroyed the letters in anticipation of a possible second visit by the police, but for the more flamboyant Herzen such considerations of caution were secondary to the task of eternally memorializing every particle of his extraordinary existence.

He also had, however, propaganda in mind. He was offering his career as a model answer for red-blooded youth to the repression of Nicholas, with an implied reproach to those who failed to rise to the challenge, such as the metaphysicians of the circle of Stankevich or the Slavophiles. This polemical intent is nowhere explicitly stated; it was impossible to proclaim it in the work itself, and time has destroyed the letters giving Herzen's unpublishable thoughts. But the propagandistic import of the *Notebooks* is clear if they are read the way they were written, with as much attention to what is between the lines as to what is on the page.

If the *Notebooks* were composed under any one literary influence it was that of Heine, whom Herzen quotes with approval in the opening paragraphs;[93] but this in itself was a political declaration, for every well-informed reader knew that Heine stood for "Young Germany." The *Notebooks*, in fact, are a long panegyric to a hoped-for "Young Russia," of which Herzen saw himself as the precursor. The main theme of the work is the bursting energy, the divine discontent, and the "hope in the future" of Russian youth. Some of the more lyrical passages in this vein have already been reproduced in the early chapters of this book. In particular, Herzen told of his early literary enthusiasms: his war against classicism in the name of romanticism; his enthusiasm for Pushkin and the new Russian literature (the reader was given to understand that this included the forbidden liberal verses); his reading of Plutarch, which was such a liberal cliché that no one could miss it; and above all his infatuation with Schiller, which was appropriately interwoven with the story of his friendship with Ogarev. This was the most pointed section of the *Notebooks*, for in a country where by Imperial order the opera of Rossini based on *William Tell* had to be given the title *Carl the Bold* and a revised libretto, everyone understood the significance of youthful enthusiasm for Schiller. Herzen, of course, could not openly mention his cult of the Decembrists or his oath on the Sparrow Hills, but through Schiller he was able to hint at them rather unmistakably by speaking of the latter's "sympathy for all that is contemporary" — the word "contemporary" being Herzen's public synonym for "politics" — and by telling how he and Ogarev "swore to sacrifice our existence for the good of humanity," which was the oath on the Sparrow Hills.[94]

Praise of Schiller served another function as well. During the period of Belinski's and Bakunin's "reconciliation with reality" the "dreamy humanitarian," Schiller, had been the enemy, while the hero had been Goethe, the "Olympian" bard of life as it is lived; therefore, to extol Schiller and to put Goethe in his proper place as simply one great writer among many — which Herzen did in the *Notebooks* — was to answer Belinski and all those who thought that discontent with Russian reality was harmful. More precisely, it was an answer to Belinski's final conservative article, *Menzel, Critic of Goethe,* which had appeared in the *Annals* in the spring of 1840, only a few months before Herzen's *Notebooks.* Herzen's praise of Schiller thus was the public prolongation of his quarrel with the circle of Stankevich and the initiate would surely understand it as such.

When Herzen came to the description of his exile he had to be even less direct, but he makes it amply clear that he did not move from Moscow to Malinov (Viatka), "the worst town in the world," of his own free will.[95] He also makes it clear that because of the censorship he is passing over much in silence: "years, versts and quires of paper have been lost between the first and second notebooks" of his young man.[96] "A black dog, by the name of Pluto" has torn out whole pages, "and frankly speaking I don't think they were the worst passages." [97] When he comes to describe the "patriarchal mores of the town of Malinov," he grows bolder, openly satirizing the bureaucracy as he had observed it in Viatka: "a crowd of people . . . up to their necks in mud, who have lost all sense of human dignity, all nobility of sentiment — narrow, petty ideas, coarse, animal desires: it is both horrible and ludicrous." [98] More pointed still was his ridicule of functionaries bowing and scraping before their superiors, of the bureaucrat's petty insistence on rank, and of the degrading effects of power on those who exercise it and on those who are subjected to it.[99]

Another theme is represented by a personage Herzen purports to have met in Malinov, but who in reality reflects a social type he encountered after his return from exile. The personage is described as a "Polish-Prussian" (that is, highly cultivated and Westernized) landowner named Trenzinski, and is given the physical appearance of Chaadaev.[100] He represents all those who, like his model or the Decembrist Orlov, accidentally survived the catastrophe of their generation in 1825 to live on — veritable models of the "superfluous man" — without hope, their abilities and culture unemployed for the good of society and wasted on religion and pure speculation. May these futile, sad specters serve as an example to be avoided by the rising generation! To make his moral even more pointed Herzen again castigates Goethe's "Olympian" detachment from the affairs of humanity during the French Revolution,[101] since the truly complete man cannot live a life of purely personal interests, no matter how rich and absorbing. In Herzen's more veiled formulation, it is impossible "to make the inner world separate from the outer world." [102] This is the moral of the *Notebooks* as a whole: the ineluctable responsibility to Russia of the educated minority. In telling his personal story Herzen was merely giving a particular illustration of this general truth, and painting the portrait of his generation. " 'Each man,' as Heine has said, 'is a universe that is born and dies with him; under each tombstone is buried a whole world history.'" [103] It was a public vindication of his career aimed at the Moscow ostriches with their heads in the sands of a "purely inner life" of idealism or religion, and a call to active propaganda on behalf of reason and the dignity of man.

In a journal that at the same time was printing the prose of Lermontov, Herzen's *Notebooks* could have hardly been expected to create a sensation as literature. They did have some success with the public, however, and in the advanced intellectual circles of the two capitals, where the unpublishable parts of Herzen's story were known, they produced a considerable effect. Botkin was highly offended, feeling quite correctly that he was personally attacked in Herzen's criticisms of socially irresponsible intellectuals.[104] Belinski, who had recommended the work to the *Annals* and had seen it through the censorship, was enthusiastic. In 1839, in the course of their quarrel, he had demolished Herzen's poetic efforts, *Licinius* and *William Penn*, with the salutary effect of persuading Herzen to abandon verse. But of the *Notebooks* he wrote: ". . . a charm, a delight. For a long time I have read nothing that has captivated me so." He was in complete agreement with their polemical purpose: "This is a man and not a fish: men live, but fish contemplate and read books and then live exactly the opposite of what is written in the books." [105] Belinski even predicted, on the basis of this short and youthful work, that polemically slanted autobiography, interspersed with thumbnail satirical sketches, was Herzen's true literary forte.[106] A few years later, in 1846, he wrote to Herzen: "You have your own manner which is just as dangerous to imitate as to imitate the works of a real artist. . . . If in about ten years you write three or four volumes somewhat thicker and broader in scope you will be a big name in our literature and will get, not only into the history of Russian literature, but into the history of Karamzin as well [that is, into Russian political history]." [107] It was one of Belinski's better hits as a critic. It would require only a diminution of sentimentality and an increase in satire, less introspection and more external description (plus of course freedom from censorship), to turn the *Notebooks* into the opening chapters of *My Past and Thoughts*.

Thus, by the end of 1840, Herzen had found a moral equilibrium unknown since his days at the university. He had recovered from the despair of Viatka, and he was beginning to shed the cruder forms of his youthful idealism, of his "religion" and his love. At the same time his return to the world of the living had revealed to him the ideological pitfalls into which those who remained behind had fallen. He had, moreover, already drawn a bead on the enemy and fired his first shots, and in the *Annals* he had acquired the long-desired, if not altogether satisfactory, outlet for his energies. He had begun to realize his old dream of "fame" through his initial, though modest, successes as a writer.

As yet, however, his new position was defined largely in indirect terms; beyond his poetic scheme of "palingenesis" he lacked a positive ideology to oppose to the metaphysics of the orthodox Hegelians and the religion of the Slavophiles. In the following year, during the next great crisis of his life, he was to find this positive answer to the problems of Russia in the hitherto despised philosophy of Hegel.

CHAPTER X

Realism in Philosophy: Hegel

HERZEN had hardly settled into his new life in Petersburg when he was again violently uprooted and sent into exile. To increase the misfortune, the blow coincided with a series of domestic trials, the first to mar the personal happiness he had known since marriage. This double ordeal produced a crisis in his life the like of which he had never before experienced; beside it his first exile was mild in its effect. The latter event had simply called forth an exaggeration of his youthful idealism, but the second exile finally provoked the break with his intellectual past toward which he had been moving since Vladimir. Under its impact Herzen at last matured and became the public figure of his prime, the figure known from the pages of *My Past and Thoughts*.

The cause of his second exile was as absurd as any that the police annals of the reign of Nicholas have to offer, and much more so than that of his first exile. In late November of 1840 he wrote to his father giving the latest small talk of the capital and concluded his letter with a bit of widespread gossip about a policeman who had robbed and murdered several citizens, adding by way of commentary: "from this you can judge what the police here is like." [1] Ivan Alexeevich had warned his son, and relatives in the capital had repeated the warning, against the informers with which Petersburg swarmed,[2] but even the most cautious could hardly have considered that such a remark would attract them. Early in December, however, Herzen was summoned to the Third Section of His Majesty's Own Chancellery to be confronted by its second-in-command, Dubelt, with this letter which "spread false and harmful rumors" about the forces of law and order.[3] Dubelt, and even Count Benkendorf, the Chief of the Gendarmes, were reasonable enough, but the affair had already gone to Nicholas, who, in view of Herzen's dubious past, had decided on exile, and nothing could be done.

At first there was talk of a return to Viatka, but Dubelt and Benkendorf, sensitive to the absurdity of the charge, arranged with Nicholas that the Minister of the Interior, for whom Herzen worked, should choose the place of exile. Fortunately, since the Minister of the Interior, Count Stroganov, headed the regular police, he was hostile to the Third Section and was annoyed that the latter should arrest one of his employees without consulting him. Herzen benefited from this rivalry of jailors, for Stroganov resolved to give him the best provincial opening available, even ahead of senior functionaries, and to promote him to the highest rank compatible with his length of service — all this without bribes. For Herzen, who wanted justice, this simply heightened the absurdity of the affair by adding an arbitrary grace to an arbitrary injury. He indicated as his choice either Tver or Novgorod, the provincial seats nearest to Moscow and Petersburg, and Stroganov named him to the place where the first vacancy occurred, which was Novgorod. Pleading his wife's ill health, through the benevolence of Stroganov Herzen managed to hang on in Petersburg for another six months, but in June, 1841, he was at last obliged to begin his exile.

Under the pressure of these events, Natalie's health, which never was strong, broke down. The nocturnal arrival of the Third Section's gendarme at their apartment, the clanking of his spurs and sabre in their peaceful drawing room, the suspense of waiting, the possible terrors of exile, combined to send her to her bed. She was, in addition, pregnant at the time, and soon gave birth to a child that lived only a few days, while she herself lay in danger of death.[4] In *My Past and Thoughts* Herzen claimed that the birth was premature as a result of Natalie's terror at all that had happened.[5] From letters written at the time by both parents, however, it is clear that the infant arrived in due course, and that its death was probably not caused by Herzen's arrest.[6] Yet it is understandable that in Herzen's subjective reaction Nicholas was the murderer of his child and almost the murderer of his wife.[7] Moreover, throughout their stay in Novgorod and for some time after, Natalie's health continued to be a source of anxiety. In Novgorod they were again visited by tragedy; in December another child was born only to die a few days later,[8] while the same blow fell a third time just a year later, after their return to Moscow.[9] Of their four children only one had survived, and there had been three deaths in two years! Herzen felt that this was more than his portion of misfortune, and almost more than flesh could bear. The bright days of Dante and Beatrice were irrevocably over, and the cares of maturity were upon them, bringing contact with a harsh reality for which the roseate idealism of youth had not prepared them, and from which it was no longer able to rescue them. The same absurd fate reigned in the sanctuary of love as in the realm of Nicholas, and Herzen, reeling under blows from every side, repeated ever more frequently in his letters: *"Fatum! Fatum!"* [10]

2

Nevertheless, Herzen did not resign himself to his fate, and his reaction to the second exile was much more vigorous than to the first. His first exile, for all its hardships, had not been a totally ungratifying experience; it at least offered the excitement of novelty, the interest of new places, and the romance of martyrdom for a great cause. The second exile was simply a chain around his feet. This time there could be no idealization of himself as a Dante wandering through Purgatory, and no heavenly maid to redeem him. He would face the world as it really was — absurd and unjust — and he would protest. At the moment of the blow Ogarev had imprudently written counseling Christian forbearance. "You, Ogarev, preach *resignation* . . . but I think that the whole trouble is that we have *entirely too much of it*. I understand that a man afflicted with consumption would be pitiable to reproach and rage against fate; I understand that a man whose ship has gone down with all his wealth is noble to bear meekly what is outside the sphere of his reason and will; but resignation, when you are hit in the face, I do not understand." In particular he rose up against "*that false monastic passivity* . . . the evil spirit" which only too easily infected the enlightened elite in Russia. The humble acceptance of suffering preached by Christianity might have been a virtue in the past, but Herzen every day was leaving his religion farther behind: "a proud, unbending stoicism becomes us more than a meek forgiveness of reality, indulgence towards all its filth. . . . Oh!! Luther used to say: 'In anger I feel the full might of my being.' Hate is the *superexaltatio* of love." [11] For the first time in his life Herzen had become an angry and almost a bitter man. But this new bitterness implied no loss of faith in the future. Only the facile dreams of youth had been destroyed: "I do not say that, together with my dreams, my hopes have flown away — oh no, no and a thousand times no. On the contrary, in my whole life I have never felt more clearly the '*eppur si muove*' of Galileo. The pain of childbirth is not like the pain of death and yet people die in childbirth." [12] This hope was justified, for out of his sufferings and his will to resist would emerge the new Russia. Once again he curses the late "reconciliation with reality" of his friends and declares that the blow he has received, far from breaking him, has filled him with a new energy to struggle.[13] Certainly one of the reasons Herzen was more radical than the average of his generation was that he had suffered more in his own person at the hands of Nicholas.

Another reason was his more extensive contact with the sordid reality of Russian government, particularly at the lower levels, where it appeared at its worst, for Novgorod meant a return to the despised bureaucratic routine of the provinces. Already in Viatka he had hated it; in Novgorod

it was well-nigh unbearable. There was the same spectacle of the degrading effects of power, of the venality, the ignorance, the crying injustice
familiar to Herzen from Viatka. But this time he reacted much more
violently. In Viatka he had been too preoccupied with his inward anguish
to have much energy left over for indignation at the horrors he saw perpetrated around him, although he could not fail to notice them. In
Novgorod he looked external reality squarely in the face and responded
with the full vigor of his being.

The department over which he presided looked after a miscellany of
affairs. One of these was the supervision of political offenders; and every
three months Herzen had to countersign a report of the chief of police
about his own conduct — farther than this the absurdity of Nicholas'
system could not go.[14] More revolting still was what Herzen learned in
his role as supervisor of abuses of the serf-owners' power: systematic,
sadistic torture of servant girls by their mistresses; whole villages terrorized by drunken, half-demented provincial versions of Paul I. Herzen
was interested in fulfilling his official function conscientiously, at least in
these matters. He did what he could to apply the few laws that existed
for the protection of the peasants; and he succeeded in having one of the
more notorious serf-owners of the province deprived of his estates. But
what was this against the weight of a whole system? The serf-owner could
do what he wished and the administration would close its eyes, or its
benevolence could be purchased if by some rare chance the peasants
made so bold as to lodge a complaint.[15] Right was the exclusive privilege
of the gentry; punishment existed only for the peasants. In fact, there was
no law or justice in Russia; there was only the arbitrary exercise of brute
force, tempered solely by bribery. Memories of all the injustices he had
observed in Viatka and Vladimir revived, but illumined by a harsher light
than formerly. It was in Novgorod that for the first time Herzen came to
reject totally and uncompromisingly the Russian governmental machine
and all its works. Significantly for the character of his radicalism, as in
Viatka it was not the poverty of the masses or the economic inequality
between master and serf which revolted him most, but the absence of all
real law, of any defense of the rights of the individual — or, as he himself
would have put it, the impossibility of being a "human being." As always
it was those aspects of Russian life that offended most his own aristocratic
sense of individual dignity — but not necessarily those that weighed most
heavily on the masses — which were the point of departure for his
"socialism."

In fact, the essence of Herzen's socialism as it began to assume mature
form in this period can be put in a few simple propositions, none of them
economic. All the inhumanity, lawlessness and ignorance of Russian life
must perish utterly; not one cursed stone of the old structure must be left

to stand, not one institution, one tradition, or one memory. In place of the old a totally new world of justice, humanity, and reason, fully realized to the last iota, must be created. Moreover, until this is accomplished, negation of the old must be total and intransigent, regardless of the consequences to oneself in suffering, exile, and wasted years. Anything less is treason and compromise with the forces of darkness, for only such intransigence, however foolhardy it may appear to the prudent, can cleanse the Augean stables of autocracy and Byzantine barbarism. Finally, although the present generation might perish in the struggle, its martyrs would generate new resistance and in the end enlightenment would triumph, if not in the next generation, then eventually, for such was the inevitable march of history.

This was the heart of what Herzen meant by "socialism," and indeed what all nineteenth-century Russian radicals meant by it. Programmatically it more often than not had little in common with what went by the same name in the West; but the kernel was the same: intransigent insistence on the full realization of the promises of the Enlightenment. The intransigence of the Russians, however, was more enduring and steadfast than that of their Western brethren, who tended to slide into reformism and compromise with the existing order at the first opportunity. They, of course, had such opportunities much more frequently than the Russians, for the obstacles to the realization of the democratic dream were infinitely more formidable in Russia and the hope for some sort of satisfaction in the present infinitely less than for radicals elsewhere. It was Herzen's generation, and most clearly of all Herzen himself, that first fully expressed this situation.

It was also in Novgorod that for the first time Herzen's protest began to go beyond himself to embrace somewhat more closely the sufferings of the masses. He had always to a degree generalized his own outraged sense of individual dignity into a universal principle of equality, but this principle had hitherto remained quite abstract. In Novgorod his own new misfortunes led him to participate emotionally in the wrongs of the masses with a feeling of kinship he had never before experienced. For the first time the people, as a reality and not just as an idea, began to play a role in his perception of the world. In his talk of equality and brotherhood he began to think of the Russian peasant and not just of man in general. These new thoughts were not just for the peasant's present misery; they also extended to the peasant's unrealized potentialities, and to hope for the future of the peasant in particular as part of hope for the future of Russia in general. Nor did this transformation go without a considerable idealization of the masses. In short, Herzen began to become something of a populist, if, for the moment, still rather timidly.

Two incidents in particular touched him. In 1842, toward the end of his stay in Novgorod, he was temporarily in need of money and a local merchant advanced him the necessary sum without any written guarantee and without demanding interest. Herzen had never done the man any favors, nor could he do him any in the future since he was then leaving government service. The only explanation was that, "he has appreciated the difference between me and the other functionaries — and for this, thanks." [16] The second case concerned the butler of the local hotel who came to Herzen seeking advice about the education of his son; the boy was already in the gymnasium and wished to enter the university "in order to become a human being." Herzen found the lad intelligent and encouraged him. "The father is someone's liberated serf. *In potentia* there is much in the Russian soul." [17] As is evident, this feeling for the masses was not without its nationalistic overtones.

This line of reflection was stimulated by reading Gogol's *Dead Souls*, which had just then appeared, in 1842.

A wonderful book, a bitter reproach to contemporary Russia but not a hopeless one. Where the glance is able to pierce the fog of impure, dung-born exhalations, there it perceives a daring (*udaloi*) nation, full of strength. . . . It is sad in the world of Chichikov, as it is sad in real life; and both there and here the one consolation is faith and hope in the future. And it is impossible to deny this faith; it is not simply a romantic hope *ins Blaue,* but has a realistic foundation: the blood somehow circulates well in the breast of the Russian. I often look out the window at the barge-haulers, especially on holidays, when they are out in the boats for fun, going by singing, with tambourines — shouts, whistling, noise. Not even in his dreams would a German think of such a good time. And then in storms, what audacity, what daring — fly along and come what may.[18]

The storms on the little river Volkhov could hardly have been as challenging, nor the singing and wild fun (*gulianie*) of the barge-haulers as exceptional as Herzen imagined, but what are such considerations in the face of the heart's desire?

The essence of Herzen's concept of the Russian people's excellence was their "carefree daring" — *udal*, a word which came constantly to his pen — or their instinctively free and expansive nature. It was the classical concept of the "Russian soul," or of the Russians' "broad nature" (*shirokaia natura*), and by no means peculiar to Herzen. At the beginning of the forties it was occurring simultaneously to the most diverse people, Slavophiles as well as Westerners, and Gogol's *Dead Souls*, with its famous image of the Russian troika racing wildly over the limitless plains, had much to do with its popularization. But, in spite of Herzen's aspersions on the dull Germans, the idea itself owes much to their writings; in fact it was little more than a nationalized version of Schiller's free and beautiful soul, of his magnificent and anarchic Moors and Wallensteins. Herzen always needed to believe in his star and his superior virtues in order to overcome the frustrations of the present. As this sense of oppression increased with time, he needed a faith correspondingly more vast: in the star of a whole people, and in the "carefree daring," not only of himself, but of the nation. Communion with the people was a way out of his own isolation in the face of an uncomprehending society and a hostile bureaucratic machine. Yet he was aware how illusory, or rather one-sided, this communion was, for on every hand he met with signs of the peasants' inveterate distrust, bred by centuries of oppression, for all "masters," even the best disposed among them. He was compelled to conclude sadly that he would "bless" the peasant, "if only from the grave," but that for the present the gulf remained unbridgeable and that all his hope for the peasant's future "does not diminish one iota the bitterness of life." [19]

In the end Herzen was always brought back to his own sufferings, and in Novgorod he was constantly oppressed by the feeling that the best years of his life were slipping away unused. In part this derived from the fact that he was growing older. Even in Viatka, when he passed his twenty-fifth year, he began to intone the lament of Julius Caesar, echoed by Don Carlos: "twenty-five years and nothing yet done for immortality!" However, Natalie effectively consoled him by suggesting that whoever had won a friend such as Ogarev and a love such as herself had accomplished something.[20] Two years later this thought appeared less consoling. The accomplishments of friendship and love were simply a "pledge" for the future, "and shall we no more proudly unfold our wings? Twenty-seven years already spent — perhaps no more than another twenty-seven remain. Oh, how much must we labor, toil!" [21] With each birthday the note of urgency became more insistent. In 1842 in Novgorod he passed his thirtieth year, "the half of life." What was there to show for it? The long sleep of childhood, a few bright moments of youth, and eight years of "persecution, oppression and exile . . . at the words thirty years it grows frightening." [22] He wanted to live, to work, to struggle, and the precious time was being consumed in fruitless bureaucratic drudgery. He would try to read or write. "The book falls from the hands, the pen too. I want to live, I want activity, movement, and there is only — only the mute, stupid, absurd position of an exile in this inane provincial hole. . . . It is painful, humiliating, degrading. . . . And to die perhaps in this position!" [23] Visits from Ogarev, Belinski, and Botkin only made matters worse. It was particularly frustrating to compare his lot with that of Ogarev, who had arrived from Rome and Paris, while "I am still here with chains around my feet. I feel the psychic necessity of traveling to some great city; I need people, I am withering; some great unemployed mass of possibilities is roaming around inside of me, which finding no outlet stirs up from the bottom of the soul all sorts of rubbish, pettiness, impure passions." [24] He was brought to the verge of despair.

Lord, what unbearably heavy hours of sadness devour me. . . . Is it possible that I must consider my life finished, is it possible that all that stirs me, all that occupies me so powerfully, all my readiness to work, all the necessity to externalize myself — that all this I must bury, must hold it down under a heavy stone, that I must teach myself to be dumb, until my needs are stifled — and then begin a life of emptiness, of luxury?

In other words, is he to go the way of that classic nineteenth-century Russian type, the superfluous man? To be sure, "there is another life, noble and lofty, purely inward, with the sole end of personal enlightenment; but I feel that among the quiet occupations of the study at times there reigns a frightful boredom. I must live externally as well." [25] This was the cry of a whole generation longing for a life other than that of the mind, or simply longing for life and the freedom to be oneself, after a youth spent in a dreamy flight from the wilderness of Nicholas' Russia.

3

Nevertheless, Herzen's final reaction to the depression induced by his exile to Novgorod was not despair, but the stoic cult of courage to which he had turned when the blow first fell. This stoicism, in whose dignified Roman folds he would drape himself at every crisis for the remainder of his days, was no doubt even more of a poetic stance, without any precise philosophical content, than his Christianity had been. It was a pose, however, which corresponded to a real change of outlook, for it meant that he would no longer look for support in his loneliness to transcendent consolations. Instead, he must find courage in his own unaided human resources, in his individual reason and will. Stoicism was the dramatic expression of his new "realism."

As late as the death of his second child, in 1841, he had been able to write that "religion alone brings consolation." [26] In Novgorod the remnants of this faith abandoned him completely. The occasion of the change was a series of arguments with a mother who had lost three children in rapid succession, and who had found solace in an exalted religious mysticism. In her zeal she disputed with Herzen about the respective merits of the revealed religion of the church and the "rational" religion of German philosophy, attempting to demonstrate that man can never know God by reason but only through faith. To his surprise, under her attacks, Herzen found the case of German "science" for religion less convincing than it had seemed in Vladimir, and he came to agree with his antagonist, though not in the way she had hoped. The proofs of God advanced by philosophy were indeed unconvincing, but this did not mean that faith was any more certain. The only conclusion to be drawn from "science" was that there was no God at all, that faith was an illusion and belief in transcendent consolation simply flight from reality. Man was alone, without any supernatural props, and his only supports were his own courage and will.[27] Just as persuasive as this new view of philosophy was the spectacle of the lady herself, in whom Herzen beheld his own state only a short time before.

Childishly religious people are indeed happy. . . . But as if it were possible to regress from maturity to childishness otherwise than through madness! A certain mother who had lost all her children said to me with a joyous air: "I don't regret them, I have placed them well"; and she would get up nights to attend matins, observed strict fasts and was happy. I am not even able to envy her, even though I marvel at the great secret of curing hopeless grief through subjective, dreamy beliefs. . . . But my shoulders are breaking, yet I still bear up! [28]

No longer would he be able to find "reconciliation" in the ideal or in the supernatural. He must face "reality" directly, and if he failed in the struggle with the real world, then he must recognize failure and live by his courage alone.

A short time later Herzen discovered the perfect rationalization for this rejection of religion. In June, 1842, Ogarev arrived from Germany with the new bible of Left Hegelianism, Feuerbach's *Essence of Christianity,* which had appeared only one year before. It was the work through which Young Germany was completing the break with absolute idealism and belief in a *Jenseits* begun five years earlier with Strauss' *Leben Jesu.* In the *Essence of Christianity* Feuerbach explained religion as an "alienated" projection of purely human needs, a mixture of an imaginary gratification of desire with an equally illusory compensation for frustration. He called for a courageous recognition of this fact as a prelude to any effective action in the real world. This was an explanation calculated to go straight to the hearts of those impatient with idealism. Herzen later recalled in *My Past and Thoughts:* "After reading through the first few pages I jumped for joy. Down with the masquerade attire, away with double-talk and allegory, we are free men and not slaves of Xanthus; we do not need to clothe reality in myths." [29] Feuerbach did not destroy Herzen's religious belief, as has often been maintained; the "reality" of Nicholas' Russia had already accomplished that.[30] But he did supply a wonderfully appropriate set of arguments in justification of Herzen's new mood. Once again Germany had supplied the light to illumine the experience of life in Russia.

But the main agent of illumination was Hegel. Ever since the pernicious "reconciliation with reality" in the circle of Stankevich, Herzen had steadfastly refused to have anything to do with this evil fruit of the tree of "science." His friends, however, subjected him to a ceaseless pressure to abandon his stubborn pride and to go to the school of the master before condemning him. Ogarev wrote:

You laugh at me when you say that I approach him [Hegel] with fear and faith. Just as in former times religion was a mystery which people approached with fear and faith, so in our time is philosophy — and precisely the philosophy of Hegel. Oh, Sasha, in your reading of philosophy you have still not renounced your personal opinion and you have not raised yourself to the level of objective reason . . . the reason of humanity, the reason of God.[31]

Since Hegel inspired such reverence, it was clearly impossible to have any intellectual pretensions and still be ignorant of him. Herzen soon came to realize that if he were to vanquish his enemies he would have to meet them with their own weapons. So in due course he swallowed his pride and set about coming to terms with "objective reason." At the beginning of 1841 he speaks of "continuing to study Hegel and the Germans" and assigns to this project first priority among his intellectual occupations.[32] The change of heart no doubt occurred in Petersburg at the end of 1840 during his discussions with the repentant Belinski, who was seeking from his more learned friend arguments to extricate himself from the toils of conservative Hegelianism. For a year, however, Herzen made slow progress, and it was not until after the blow of his exile to Novgorod and his discussions there with the bereaved mother that he felt impelled to reexamine the foundations both of his faith and his philosophy, and to this end to study Hegel seriously.

The first work he read was, significantly, *The Phenomenology of the Spirit,* Hegel's earliest and most radical major production. The experience was a revelation for Herzen; it was as if the veil of mysticism and subjective idealism had been ripped away from life, leaving him at last face to face with "reality," and holding the key to absolute truth in his hand. He wrote to Kraevski:

Tell Belinski that I have at last read through, *and read well,* the *Phenomenology* and that henceforth he should berate only [Hegel's] followers . . . but that he should not touch the great shade himself. Towards the end of the book it is as if one were entering a great sea: depth, transparence, and the breath of the spirit carries one along — *lasciate ogni speranze* — the shores disappear, one's sole salvation is within one's breast, but suddenly the cry is heard: *Quid timeas? Caesarem vehis,* fear vanishes, the shore is there before you, the wonderful leaves of fantasy are gone but the succulent fruits of reality are there. The water nymph has disappeared, but a full-breasted maiden awaits. Excuse me, I am not completely coherent, but such was my reaction. I read to the end with a beating heart, with a sort of triumph. Hegel is Shakespeare and Homer together, and that is why his Anglo-Greek dialect appears incomprehensible to simple people.[33]

The letter is indeed somewhat incoherent in its mixed romantic and metaphysical jargon, but the meaning behind the confused metaphors is plain enough. They all relate to the transition from ideal fantasy to the real world, from the shore of illusion to the "other shore" of fact (an image to which Herzen would frequently return), from the "water nymph" to the "full-breasted maiden." Religious mysticism and pure idealism are escapes from reality, and the only salvation is to recognize this, no matter how painful such recognition at first might be (this is why Herzen speaks of abandoning all hope), and to face the world as it really is, completely naturalistic and immanent. In this manful recognition there is a better hope than in the dreams of idealism, since the new hope is founded on reality, and man, through his reason, is able to understand the universe and hence to change it. Herzen at long last had gone through the *crise de rationalisme* which most nineteenth-century radicals found necessary to complete their emancipation from the past.

Yet, that he felt compelled to express the transformation in such emotionally colored terms is not without significance. Hegel had given him not just the truth of understanding, but the truth of life; he had not only enlightened him, he had liberated him; reading the *Phenomenology* was as much a political and a moral experience as an intellectual one. Later, in *My Past and Thoughts,* Herzen wrote: "The philosophy of Hegel is the *algebra of revolution;* it frees man to an extraordinary degree and leaves not a stone upon a stone of the whole Christian world, the world of traditions which have outlived themselves." [34] The impact of this discovery was enormous, and long after Herzen ceased to be a Hegelian in any formal sense he still could write: "I even think that a man who has not *lived through* the *Phenomenology* of Hegel and the *Economic Contradictions* of Proudhon, who has not passed through that furnace and that tempering, is not complete, is not contemporary." [35] Again the dramatic, even animistic imagery of suffering and toil — one of Herzen's favorite expressions was "to suffer out the truth" (*vystradat istinu*) — indicate an experience that is more than intellectual. Hegel gave truth not just for the mind, but for the whole man. His philosophy was more than disinterested "science": it was the answer to all the problems created by living in the Russia of Nicholas I.

4

What was the great truth which Hegel's crabbed idiom concealed? According to all the canons of the histories of philosophy, Hegel was no less an idealist than Schelling and the other post-Kantians. Nor would he, of course, have denied the label himself. Yet it is not an accident that he represents the end of idealism, nor that all the doctrines of a "return to reality," both in Germany and in Russia, came out of his system rather than those of Schelling or Fichte. By its very structure, Hegel's thought lent itself to a breakdown of idealism in a way the philosophies of his predecessors did not. Hence the problem of his role in idealism's collapse in Russia is simply a special case of his role in its disintegration all over Europe east of the Rhine. Bakunin, Belinski, and Herzen in their use of Hegel were simply paralleling the similar, although more complex, developments of Strauss, Bauer, Feuerbach, Ruge, Stirner, and ultimately Marx during the same period in Germany. An identical problem is posed by the same development in both countries: why could a turn to realism be effected only through the circuitous path of idealism; why should social radicalism take its origins in metaphysics rather than in direct examination of the ills of society? The relation between the two problems is more than fortuitous; and the fact that social radicalism in both countries had to be sublimated into metaphysics before it could become an active movement left an indelible mark on that movement once it finally emerged.

To understand Hegel's appeal at this crucial juncture it is first necessary to bear in mind what he had in common with the rest of post-Kantian idealism. Basically, Hegel's system is cast in the same pantheistic mold as that of Schelling: the world is a great chain of becoming, developing from inanimate matter through organic nature to self-consciousness in man, in whom the world-process comes to know itself and thereby at last attains to the plenitude of its existence. Moreover, the world-process, or the Absolute, is all there is; there is no transcendent author of the universe, and the Christian God is simply a naïve representation of the Absolute. This, however, does not make the Absolute any the less divine, and since the Absolute attains its fullest realization in the mind of man, man himself becomes quasi-divine, for it is only in his thought that God and the universe ultimately have their being. Hegel does not come as blatantly near as does Schelling to viewing the outer world as a projection of mind; rather he puts the same thought in the proposition that "being" and "consciousness" are one. But in the end this comes down to the same thing: thought is the ultimate reality, and the Absolute is no more than what the ego knows it to be; the knowing subject is the focus of all being and the laws of mind govern the universe. Thus Hegel's pantheism led to the same philosophical egoism as that of his predecessors, and the first function he fulfilled was to provide all the wonderful gratifications to the lonely ego furnished by the whole of absolute idealism.

But Hegel offered other things as well, which in the long run made him more attractive to the age than Schelling. The advantages of Hegel's philosophy relate first of all to what his contemporaries considered to be his greater "objectivity." Schelling's rationalizations of the ego's importance were less satisfactory than Hegel's precisely because they were more transparent. The contact with the external world Schelling offered was, after all, quite "transcendental," or largely in the mind, and the external world tended to vary capriciously from one mind to another, with each individual making up his own universe. While all this was very pleasant, it was also somewhat unsatisfactory when one was in search of absolute truth. In the language of the day, Schelling's Absolute was too "subjective" to be entirely convincing. This is true in spite of the fact that Schelling himself referred to his system as an "objective idealism." By this he meant that his "consciousness" included the external world of nature, in contrast to the more egocentric, almost solipsistic vision of Fichte. In the same way Hegel represents a step beyond Schelling. In fact the line of development of idealism from Fichte to Hegel was to emphasize increasingly the importance of the world external to the individual, whether nature or society, but of course always maintaining its essential unity with mind. Hegel marks the final — and hence most "objective" — stage of this development, as he himself pointed out. Indeed, criticism of the anarchic and "romantic" character of his predecessors' philosophy was one of the principal stimuli to his own thought.

To make his point Hegel insisted on the character of the Absolute as the real life of the real world. He spoke of mind less in terms of subjective, poetic fantasy and emphasized instead its nature as a "subjective" form of reason corresponding to the "objective reason" of the universe. Strictly speaking, of course, this principle was not new; the whole of German idealism had held that the "subjective" and the "objective" are simply two phases of the same development. Yet it was Hegel who, for the first time in post-Kantian philosophy, accorded equal importance in practice to the inner and the outer worlds. Indeed, he insisted endlessly on the complete equation of "being" and "thought": there is no "dualism" in the universe; consciousness inevitably entails existence and existence consciousness. Our knowledge and the reality we know are one and the same thing, and our consciousness is identical with the law of reason which governs the world. Yet for all this deference to the "objective," the fundamental egoism of idealism is in no way diminished. If anything the egoism of Hegel's thought is even more colossal than that of Schelling. The latter at least openly declared that the nature he painted was in a sense a projection of mind, whereas Hegel claimed for his Absolute the value of a fully objective reality, and yet, through the paradox of the dialectic, was able to subsume this "objective" world wholly in the thought (*Begriff*) of the mind.

Yet even this measure of objectivity was important in an intellectual world where everything was so radically subjective. For it led in practice to greater respect for the hard facts of existence external to the self. The tone of Hegel's thought is distinctly less sentimental and romantic, more hardheaded and "realistic" than Schelling's. The external world is accorded, temporarily and dialectically at least, an independence it was never granted by Schelling. Objects are allowed to posit themselves "in and for themselves" before they are negated and reintegrated into the knowing subject. This equivocal recognition of external reality is of course not a goal in itself; Hegel recognizes the external world in all its intractability to subjective wishes only the better to devour it in the end. Schelling's blithe transmogrification of the objective had been too facile a solution. It was much better first to recognize the world in all its concreteness so as eventually to subsume it more convincingly under mind. At bottom Hegel's greater hardheadedness is simply a subtler form of idealist wishful thinking. In order to give his ideal constructs greater plausibility he anticipated the charge of romantic "subjectivity" by recognizing the objective in all its reality. Yet he did so equivocally, or dialectically, and the end result of his method was the same sovereignty of pure thought as in all idealism. On the way to this goal, however, all sorts of things that were not "transcendental spirit" crept in, and Hegel was led to the penetrating insights into the workings of the world with which his writings abound. In effect he had things both ways: the abstract escape into pure thought and the sober coming to terms with objective existence. His system provided the consolations of both approaches; it offered all the usual satisfactions of idealism and added those of a manful realism.

One of the forms Hegel's greater objectivism took was a new emphasis on the historical. Schelling had also professed a philosophy of history, in which the Absolute manifested itself just as it did in nature and art, but, in practice, history played a relatively minor role in his speculations. The emphasis was on subjective mind and its products — art, religion and philosophy — and on nature. This latter emphasis may appear to constitute as significant a homage to the "objective" as does history, but nature is more remote from the individual than is history. It is the most universal and timeless context of man, while history furnishes a setting that is more immediate and concrete. Man is determined only in his most general characteristics by his relations with nature; he is more closely and variously affected by his relations with other men and with society. When this social context is followed backward in time to give history, the image of man changes (which on the whole is not true of man's relation to nature); it grows fuller and richer. Since for idealism a large part of philosophy consists in discovering the laws of mind in the external world of nature or society, history, because it is more human, tells us more about ourselves and consequently about the Absolute than does nature. Nature mirrors only the most abstract forms of man's reason; history fills these forms with all the riches of the concrete, clothes reality with flesh, and hence lends to philosophy a greater "objectivity." Thus, by situating the Absolute more firmly in the human context of history, Hegel brought it nearer to earth and thereby gave to idealism a new aura of "realism."

Another expression of Hegel's objectivism was the fact that, unlike Schelling, he had one system and not many. It was an integral part of Schelling's idealism that there are as many perceptions of the universe as there are minds; philosophy was like a lyric poem — personal, intuitive, subjective. For Hegel there was only one true perception of the Absolute, one reason and one philosophy, since the objective and subjective manifestations of reason were inseparably one. In consequence his philosophy presents a systematic character which Schelling's lacks. It develops, rather than changes, from book to book, and each of its branches is elaborated so as to lead logically to the next. It is fashioned as a structured whole, like the unitary Absolute it pretends to mirror. Because of this structured character it appears more rational and less intuitive than the thought of Schelling, and Hegel in fact talks much of "reason," indeed insisting on his rationalism, whereas Schelling had spoken more readily of insight.

Hegel's hardheadedness appears most clearly, however, in his use of the dialectic. There is a notion of the dialectic in Schelling — the law of polarity — but it is rather weak, and it is far from being the motive force which impels the Absolute along its course. Moreover, it is more an idea of contrast and complementarity, as in the two poles of a magnet, than of conflict and negation. With Hegel the notion of perpetual struggle is raised to the level of the first law of the universe. This innovation fulfilled several functions. It was first of all necessary to link subject and object more closely, and to suppress all vestiges of "dualism" more thoroughly than had been done by his predecessors. If the universe is a seamless whole, embracing God, man, and nature, then all the apparent contradictions and divisions one observes in the world must somehow be "sublated," or "reconciled" (*aufheben* — in Russian *primirit* or *sniat*) in a unity deeper than mere appearances. It is not enough to proclaim the "identity" of subject and object on the basis of a purely passive "polarity" of opposites, as Schelling did. The contradictions of life are too deep to be overcome by such a facile analogy. The unity of the world is found only by facing the contradictory nature of reality in all its seeming chaos, for in this way it becomes apparent that conflict and negation themselves are the links that bind all things in one whole. This dynamic division of reality was the necessary precondition of the ultimate monism of Hegel's universe. It was only by insisting on the instability and the negativity of every finite thing that the solidity of the All he pretended to embrace could in the end be secured. The procedure was paradoxical — or dialectical — and so was its purpose. For Hegel made so much of the mutability of all things precisely because he longed to find at last the immutable, the perfect Absolute, that firm lever of truth above all contingencies, with which the individual mind is able to move the universe.

The psychological functions of the dialectic are perhaps even more

interesting than the metaphysical ones. Hegel surrounds the idea of negation with a cult such as cannot be entirely explained by the logical problem of wedding more closely the inner and the outer worlds. Indeed he
has pushed the dialectic almost to willful paradox, where the negation of
negation becomes the only path to positive existence. Things can be born
only if they first die; nothingness is the matrix of being; negation is the
highest form of affirmation; everything is self-contradictory, and the true
nature of all things is realized only in their imperfections and inadequacies. The reader is more often than not bewildered, the ground seems to
dissolve under his feet (a sentiment Herzen himself had experienced),
and he is lost in a sea of negativity and flux. Such fascination with contradiction can only be explained as the expression of what Hegel himself
called in the *Phenomenology* the "Unhappy Consciousness," or an alienated consciousness, and as the reflection of an exceptionally acute awareness of frustration. It is the consciousness of a self which feels out of joint
with the world and sundered from its desire. Hence the dialectic's insistence on the inadequacy of any one form of being taken in isolation, on the
mutability of all such forms, and on negation as the only means of transcending the limitations of a finite, imperfect nature.

Yet for all this the dialectic is not a pessimistic acknowledgement of
frustration. It makes a cult of negation, but construes negation as a
positive virtue, productive of life and the source of progress. One can
delight in destruction because, as Bakunin said in a famous phrase, it is in
the last analysis creative. Paradoxical to the end, the dialectical consciousness has things both ways at once: the way of hardheaded recognition of
the frustrations that beset all finite being, and the way of optimistic faith
that out of negation and alienation will eventually emerge a higher affirmation and a richer plenitude. It is a device for maintaining hope for the
future in the face of the most disheartening evidence furnished by the
present: the greater the contradictions here and now, the more glorious
will be the eventual harvest of their "reconciliation." It is a device for
making things appear what they are not, or rather of reading into them
"deeper" meanings than external appearances show, for out of the sum
total of all individual inadequacies comes the Absolute. The final message
of the *Phenomenology* is that truth is not to be found in any of the dialectical moments of which experience is composed, but in the dialectical
movement of the whole. Small matter, then, that all is flux and conflict in
the phenomenal world, for the sum of this chaos is the rational life of
the Absolute. Small matter that all concrete forms of being are imperfect
and alienated, for the sum of their imperfections is plenitude, and of
their alienations harmony. Since this is so, the only mature philosophy is
to recognize "realistically" the imperfection of all finite being, the surer
to perceive the rational order of the Infinite All. The philosopher must

even rejoice in the negativity and mutability of all phenomenal existence, for only thereby does he attain to comprehension of the Absolute. He is in the enviable position of being able to indulge without limit in unsentimental awareness of present contradiction, and at the same time to live in unbounded optimism about the life-process of the Great All itself, in short, about the future. In effect, Hegel adjoined to idealism a new and more sober consciousness of "objective reality," and yet, through the dialectic, was obliged to sacrifice none of the "subjective" self-realization in wish of his predecessors.

It might be added that these characteristics of Hegel's thought apply whether he is given a conservative or a radical reading. Indeed, as has already been indicated in discussing Schelling, the conservative nature of idealism, too readily asserted by a simplified Marxism, is open to serious question. Although the political conclusions of Hegel's philosophy, particularly in its later versions, are undeniably conservative, the essence of his position, especially as expressed in the *Phenomenology,* is much more ambiguous. In the first place he thought too much to be truly conservative. The best way to keep things as they are is not to think about them at all, but to accept them without reflecting, and this is what the real conservative always prefers to do. If, through some ill-fortune, the conservative is stirred to reflection by troublesome reformers, his favorite philosophy is an antirationalism which denies the possibility of understanding things and therefore of changing them. Such was the claim, among Hegel's generation, of all the proponents of primordial instinct or divine revelation, from Burke and de Maistre to the Slavophiles. But Hegel and the idealists, particularly in their early phase, held to none of this. Not only did they think, but they set enormous store by thinking, making of thought the highest value which existed. Moreover, to believe in reason means also to believe in the dignity of man and in the supreme value of liberty, and the idealists pushed this belief to the point of a colossal philosophical egoism. Finally, the idealists believed in change and progress; no philosopher has ever made more of a cult of change than Hegel. In short, the idealists believed in all the things the Enlightenment believed in, which to a degree puts them eternally on the Left no matter how conservative their explicit political doctrines may have become under the pressures of the Restoration. Like the men of the Enlightenment they stood for questioning and intellectual ferment. Such activities, no matter how innocent they may appear, are always subversive, as autocratic states well know, and eventually the Prussian government had to forbid even the adepts of its court philosopher, Hegel, from lecturing on any subject but aesthetics.

The idealists stood for all these things with a difference, however: the questioning and the ferment of their thought were exclusively in the realm of the mind. Idealism represents the values of the Enlightenment turned away from the real world and directed toward the abstract. Nonetheless, these values were not abdicated; they were only sublimated. Even when Hegel became overtly conservative he did not abandon them; all his justifications of the absolute state were framed in terms of the values of the Enlightenment: reason, freedom, and human progress — which are very different from the rationalizations of a de Maistre. Idealism, as we have seen, is as much the expression of a frustrated liberalism as the ideology of conservatism; it can even be both at the same time. The tiny class of the enlightened in Germany was in no position to make an assault on absolutism, however cramped it might feel; at the same time the results of unleashing the demos in France suggested that the masses might be more of a danger to civilization than the princes, and consequently that support of the status quo was perhaps the one truly "rational" course. In adopting this practical conservatism, though, idealism lost none of its essential individualism and libertarianism. It was possible for a time to neutralize the latter by maintaining that absolutism represented the highest realization of liberty, but this precarious paradox could not be maintained indefinitely; eventually it was bound to fly apart under the pressure of the "internal contradictions" it had been designed to reconcile. It was Hegel who prepared the way for the disintegration by perfecting the dialectic as the instrument of the reconciliation. Thus, true to its paradoxical nature, the dialectic had the effect of calling attention all the more dramatically to the conflicts and alienations it had been created to remove. It thereby rendered less satisfactory all ideal "reconciliations," and turned the disabused dreamer to a hardheaded recognition of reality in all its imperfections. In the hands of people less patient and less cerebral than Hegel his relative realism and his cult of negation could very easily become revolutionary weapons. For this reason he, and not Schelling, became the philosopher of the rediscovery of reality wherever it occurred east of the Rhine.[36]

In Russia this potentiality became apparent while Hegel's actual role was still a conservative one. The key terms of Russian Schellingianism had been — in addition to nature — "art," "friendship," "love," and "individual genius" viewed as the supreme expression of the nation. The key terms of Hegelianism in the circle of Stankevich were "objective reason," "reality," and something the Russians preferred to leave in the original German, *Allgemeinheit*. With Schelling the emphasis had been on the intuitive and the individual; with Hegel it was on the rational and the general. When the circle of Stankevich broke with its youthful idealism, the great sin of Schelling (and still more of Schiller) was declared to be something called *prekrasnodushie* (*Schönseeligheit*) or a subjective and "dreamy" individualism, while Hegel was held to offer a healthy and objective "reconciliation with reality." [37] Even as a conservative philosophy, Russian Hegelianism appears as a "realism" in reaction to an excessively abstract idealism. From this recognition of reality to criticism of it was only a step, and Herzen, by a bolder use of Hegel than his predecessors, was the first of his generation to take it.[38]

5

The step was made in a series of four articles — actually a short book — published in the *Annals of the Fatherland* and entitled *Dilettantism in Science.* Begun in Novgorod in the spring of 1842 and finished in Moscow during the following winter, they close the crisis of Herzen's second exile and define his new position. Together with his *Letters on the Study of Nature,* composed in the middle of the decade, they have been called the most significant philosophical production of Russian Hegelianism in the forties, an honor which is certainly theirs.[39] Indeed, the only competitors are Belinski's conservative articles — which are hardly serious as philosophy — and Bakunin's more respectable Hegelian writings in German. Neither of these contributions, however, is comparable to Herzen's, either in scope or in philosophical talent, while the rest of Russian Hegelianism was little more than talk in the Moscow salons.[40] Herzen's essays, furthermore, possess an eloquence of style comparable to that of his better known later works, although the aridity of their subject rather hopelessly obscures this quality for readers not thoroughly versed in the arcane language of the day. A final merit of the essays is their contribution to the elaboration of philosophical Russian; more than any other writer of his generation Herzen furthered this development by his inventiveness in adapting the language, still new in the ways of abstract discourse, to the intricacies of German thought.

For all this, however, it would be a mistake to treat Herzen's Hegelian essays primarily as works of philosophy, as has too often been done in the past and as is still done by Soviet historians.[41] As always with Herzen, philosophy was not an end in itself but a vehicle for politics. The censorship, which made the "Aesopian language" of metaphysics the only safe expression of social criticism, was in part responsible for this. Even more important is the fact that by the forties, after almost twenty years of idealism, all aspects of life had become so involved in metaphysics that it was impossible to talk about the world in other terms; the first political battles to be fought were in fact philosophical ones. Idealism could be overcome only from within, by the use of its own categories. Even without the censorship, therefore, Herzen would have expressed his politics first of all as philosophy. This is borne out by his *Diary* for these years. Composed in the privacy of his study, it expresses political opinions which he could not reproduce in print, and accordingly furnishes a useful key to his more hermetic public declarations. Nonetheless, the *Diary* treats of first principles no less than the published writings, and in language hardly less abstract, because the impotence of the opposition in Russia left no other outlet than ideology.

This high level of abstraction makes *Dilettantism in Science,* together with the *Letters on the Study of Nature,* the most difficult of Herzen's writings. To extract the politics from the philosophy extensive transposition, almost decoding, is required. This difficulty is aggravated by the essays' circumstantial character. They give nothing like a systematic exposition of Herzen's Hegelianism, for they were produced in an atmosphere where through long habit the coordinates of the idealist universe were familiar to everybody. They are pieces for the small coterie of the initiate in the circles of the two capitals. In fact, they offer a prolongation in print of the private debates which had occupied Herzen since his return from Vladimir. Accordingly, they are cast as a series of attacks on his enemies in the circles and are comprehensible only in the context of this debate, just as their philosophy is meaningful only as transposed politics.

To examine first this philosophy — and what follows applies equally to the *Letters on the Study of Nature*[42] — we may say that, in a general way, it is the same as that set forth earlier in these pages. It is the naturalistic pantheism of idealism, with its division of the biography of the Absolute into the various stages of the life of nature, the ascending ages of human history, and the final attainment of the universe's self-consciousness in the reason of man. It is the old poem of organic progress that gives to the isolated individual a sense of identification with the invincible power of the World Spirit. But the picture now comes forth from Herzen's pen richer and firmer, with all the logical rigor and precision of detail supplied by Hegel. In particular Herzen traces a more imposing theory of history than had been possible with the relatively feeble means provided by Schelling.

Peoples feeling the vocation to come forth into the area of universal history, having heard the voice proclaiming that their hour has struck, are filled with a double life. Forces appear which no one would have dared to suspect in them. . . . The raw materials of plain and forest are molded into a civilization, the sciences and the arts flourish; gigantic works are accomplished to prepare the caravanserai of the future Idea, but the Idea, a majestic torrent, flows on and on, ever seizing on a greater and greater expanse. Yet these caravanserai are not just the external habitation of the Idea, they are its very flesh, without which it could not realize itself.[43]

This was the culmination of Herzen's youthful ventures in "historiosophy," those magnified projections of his hopes on the wall of the mind.

Much of *Dilettantism* is taken up with similar recapitulations of the idealist world-picture. In this respect Herzen's Hegelianism was the climax of his previous development rather than a new departure. Yet new insights intruded themselves into the old framework and gave it a very different meaning. In Herzen's hands idealism was transformed from a philosophy of withdrawal into a philosophy of action; in the end philosophy itself was declared to be superseded by life, a development which marks the final phase of Russian idealism.

This transformation was achieved from within, by the manipulation of idealism's own categories. It begins with a new perception of the relation the post-Kantians had always seen between the "self-consciousness" of the Absolute and human liberty. Herzen repeats this idea with a very Hegelian emphasis on the painful struggle against illusion involved in mankind's ascent to understanding. "What afflictions the spirit of humanity endured, what sufferings, what despondency it knew, what tears and blood it shed, before it liberated thought from all that is temporary and incomplete, before it began to understand itself as the conscious essence of the universe." [44] For Schelling man's position as the conscious essence of the universe served primarily to exalt the ego's creative genius. But in all idealism "consciousness" was also liberty, and Hegel developed this thought, emphasizing that understanding frees man from blind submission to necessity and makes him the only intelligent agent of progress in the universe. "Science," in consequence, was a "liberation." Hegel had understood this liberation to be purely inward and intellectual; Herzen made it a prologue to action.

The entire past life of mankind, conscious and unconscious, had as its ideal the drive to attain self-knowledge and to raise the will of man to the will of God; in all ages mankind aspired to morally useful, free activity. But such activity did not exist in [past] history, nor could it exist. Science had to prepare the way for it; without knowledge, without complete consciousness there is no truly free action. [45]

Divested of its Hegelian trappings this is the classic rationalist notion that enlightenment liberates man from superstition, thereby enabling him to change the world because he at last sees it as it really is. Herzen had always believed that enlightenment was the high-road of progress; now, with the aid of Hegel's cult of consciousness, he was able to demonstrate its virtues with a new rigor.

Moreover, man's gradual conquest of a rational consciousness became the essence of his ascent to "personality," or that full realization of his potentialities as a "human being" which Herzen had hitherto expressed largely in aesthetic or religious terms. This combination of an aesthetic and a rationalistic view of liberty is best expressed in the *Diary*. One evening in Novgorod Herzen sat by his window overlooking the river Volkhov when a peasant began to sing on the opposite bank.

The time passed, and he sang and sang — sadly, despondently. What forces him to sing? It is none other than the spirit tearing itself free from the stifling, prosaic sphere of the proletariat; by his song he unconsciously enters into the kingdom of heaven, into the world of the infinite, the beautiful. The spirit, which has struggled upward to humanity, sings just as a flower gives off perfume, but it knows that it sings also for itself. After the mere palpitations of unconscious life, after the vague joy in existence of the animal, follows the expansiveness of man. With his song he fulfills his all-embracing unity with others, and he alone is able to satisfy his thirst.[46]

The Idea's striving toward consciousness was the metaphysical lyricism of Herzen's own yearning to escape from the stifling world around him no less than a symbol for the masses' muffled aspiration to become "human beings."

The rationalistic implications of the idea of consciousness were developed further by the use Herzen made of the dialectic. The latter aspect of Hegel's thought had almost totally escaped Belinski and Bakunin in their conservative phase. Herzen was the first Russian to grasp it fully and to popularize it in print within Russia. (Bakunin eventually came to the same conclusions regarding the dialectic as Herzen, and at the same time — 1842 — but he expressed his ideas abroad and in German). His statements on the subject are purple with the enthusiasm of discovery. "The infinite, eternal relationship of two moments, defined one in another, *linked* one in another, constitutes . . . the life of truth. In this eternal play of colors, in this eternal motion, truth lives. This is its inhalation and exhalation, its systole and diastole . . . the universal dialectical beat of a pulse." [47] The Absolute relentlessly evolves from "form" to "form," and from one historical "moment" to another, in a constant dialectical interplay between what is passing away and what is coming into being. With each step the Absolute creates something "higher," which manifests more clearly its own "conscious" essence. The movement of history is from mythological representations of the world, such as religion and art, to rational ones, such as science and philosophy. To lend luster to this idea it is surrounded with the imagery of biological becoming indispensable to idealism since the *Naturphilosophie*. Again and again Herzen insists that the universe is a single, living unit, in a process of constant creative evolution, and that "science" too "is the living organism by which truth develops." [48] This was romantic historicism and organicism in full flower.

The principle of dialectical becoming possessed many meanings for Herzen, but the most important was the notion that all supposedly absolute values or institutions are in reality relative to time and place. Ideas and social forms are never true or false in themselves but only in their relation to the needs of a given historical moment. The only "absolute" truth is the Idea's eternal law of change, or progress. Values and institutions which have been outmoded by the march of progress must be ruthlessly rejected in favor of the coming form of the Idea. "The spirit of mankind, carrying in its depths an immutable purpose, eternally striving towards complete development, cannot rest in any one of its past forms." [49] The implication would be inescapable to the attentive reader that the present state of affairs in Russia could neither last nor be justified as eternally valid in itself. With one stroke the dialectic rendered untenable all the arguments of the conservatives and advanced a revolutionary conception of truth in their place.

In particular, since the march of the Idea was from mythological forms to rational ones, revealed religion and its philosophical surrogates, such as deism, lost their absolute status. They were simply passing manifestations of human needs. Specifically, they were prerational expressions of those needs, and they had been rendered superfluous, indeed noxious, by the advance of "science." Herzen, of course, could not be this explicit in print, but his meaning is none the less clear. [50] A dialectical understanding of life destroyed all the transcendent authorities invented by religion and philosophy; the only authority it left standing was the self-determining reason of man. Thus the mind was freed from the sacred shibboleths of the past and turned toward constructive action in the present. After his fashion Herzen, like Marx, had stood Hegel on his head. For the latter the dialectic had been in large part a device for preserving the partial truths of the past by gathering them into the eternal truth of the Absolute; it accented their positive value — in spite of their ephemeral nature — by accenting their final participation in total truth. For Herzen, by a subtle shift of emphasis, the dialectic became a weapon for demolishing the values of the past in order to prepare the way for the future.

Other functions of the dialectic were psychological more than logical. By relentlessly insisting on flux it turned attention from the hated present to the glorious future. When one knew with certainty that the law of the universe was change ever upwards, frustration paled while hope burned with a brighter light. [51] To a similar end Herzen exploited the animistic imagery provided by the notion of the Absolute as organism. Thus nature: "Not clear in itself, tortured and tormented by this lack of clarity, striving toward an end unknown to itself, but which is at the same time the cause of its restlessness, in a thousand forms it aspires after consciousness. . . . In this is the poetry of life, in this is its inner richness." [52] In these analogies of straining development and burgeoning growth, terminating in the consciousness that is liberty, Herzen was portraying his own restless aspirations.

He was no less sensitive to the dialectic's dramatization of conflict.

Again he speaks of nature, but his thoughts are as much for mankind. "Drawn by a great uncomprehending anguish, nature raises itself from form to form; but passing to what is higher, nature stubbornly maintains itself in its previous form and develops it to the last extreme, as if salvation were in that form. And in fact, each realized form is a great victory, a triumph and a joy; each time it is the highest *which exists*." [53] In this struggle between outworn but tenacious forms of the Idea and the forms of the future still in painful gestation Herzen saw the drama of his own generation. And he found his consolation in the same spectacle, for struggle gave testimony of "life," and the presence of life was the guarantee of the ultimate victory of progress over the dead past. Thus one could consider the most negative evidence as a reason for hope, since all conflicts, no matter how painful, were eventually "reconciled" in a higher harmony by the dialectic. With such a view it was possible to admire the efforts of the autocracy on behalf of enlightenment in the past and for the same reason to combat it all the more vigorously in the present. It was further possible to consider the very strength of the current reaction as a negative sign, but nevertheless a sign, of the vitality of the forces of progress in Russia. Herzen, of course, could not give such an example in print, but he displays an immense fascination for the abstract principle on which it rests. Over and over he repeats the paradox that the contradictions of the present are the matrix of future plenitude, an idea usually framed in incantatory language as if he were grasping in thought what he could not have in life. "In science, as in a sea, there is no ice, no crystal; everything flows, lives. Beneath each point there is equal depth; in it, as in a furnace, all that is solid, petrified, melts when it falls into its eternal, infinite vortex, and as in a sea, the surface is smooth, calm, bright, limitless and it reflects the heavens." [54] The imperfections and the alienations of the present are at the same time their finite selves and part of the infinite harmony of the Absolute. A less abstract form of this intuition is the thought, to which Herzen constantly returns in his *Diary*, that the sufferings of the present are the necessary precondition of the future, humane Russia, and that hence they are already their opposite, or joy.[55] Through the dialectic a negative principle in the present becomes a positive one in the future, and promise is in a sense already fulfillment.

Like all the categories of idealism the dialectic was in part wishful thinking and in part the abstract awareness of something real: frustration did in fact produce explosive energy and this energy would eventually cause change. It reflected too the realization that where action was impossible ideological negation was a positive act, since in the long run it affected the world. The dialectic was the transposition into metaphysics of two conflicting yet related sentiments: the intellectual's consciousness of his impotence to change society, and his equal belief in the dynamic consequence of the discontent this impotence bred. It was because of this very real relation of metaphysics to life that the categories of "science" were so emotionally charged for Herzen. This is particularly apparent in his use of the concept "reconciliation" (*primirenie*), which he evokes with a tireless regularity and an almost religious fervor. Technically "reconciliation" was the dialectical synthesis (*Aufhebung*) of antithetical opposites, but it also meant emotional release from the contradictions of the present, and the harmonious integration of the individual into a rational world after his long pilgrimage through the alienations of life.

Closely related to the dialectic was the notion of the monism of the universe. Subject and object, "consciousness" (*myshlenie*) and "being" (*bytië*), man and nature are united in an indissoluble whole by the organic interplay of the dialectic. Strictly speaking, this idea was not new to Herzen, but the vehemence with which he enunciated it was. Once again his thought is stated in language verging on the oracular. "All that is living is alive and true only as a whole, as an exterior and an interior, as a general and a particular, coexisting together. Life links these two moments; life is the perpetual passage from one to the other." [56] Indeed, Herzen castigates the "dilettantes" for failing to recognize the unity of the universe with such virulence that one might think that "dualism" and not autocracy was the chief impediment to progress in Russia.[57] The reason for this alarm was that dualism furnished the philosophical basis for all retreats from reality into abstract idealism and religion. It separated the real from the ideal, matter from spirit, and the natural from the supernatural. When he attacked dualism, therefore, Herzen was aiming at all forms of belief in a transcendent beyond. By the same token his insistence on the unity of "being" and "consciousness" was a proclamation of the completely immanent character of the universe and its total permeability to human reason. Concretely, this naturalism reinforced the historicism of the dialectic; values and institutions are not only relative to historical situations, they are also the purely natural products of those situations. They do not originate in God or in immutable principles external to man; revealed religions and absolute philosophies are no more than projections of man's terrestrial needs. This was Feuerbach's explanation of the "illusions" of religion, which had struck Herzen when he was composing his essays.[58] The only reality was the life of nature and the dialectical unity of man's consciousness with it; belief in anything else was "mythology" and a hangover from the prescientific past.

In this Herzen was both faithful and unfaithful to Hegel: faithful since the latter had indeed insisted that the universe was completely immanent and rational; unfaithful since he also considered Christianity a symbolic but none the less authoritative expression of the Absolute, which was the same as God. Once again idealism disintegrated into the component parts of rationalism and spiritualism out of which it was composed and which had been momentarily reconciled by the dialectic. Herzen, taking one half of Hegel's ambiguous position, made it the whole of his thought, and this rationalism he felt was his primary debt to Hegel. All transcendent authorities, all values which claimed to originate in a source over and above man, were declared to be overthrown — and this was the great "liberation" conferred by "science."

This rationalism and naturalism constitute the philosophical burden of *Dilettantism in Science.* Hegel in the last analysis represented a form of the Enlightenment for Herzen. Furthermore, he recognized immediately the kinship between his new faith and that of the *philosophes.* Because of their "narrow empiricism" the latter, like all things French, had been in bad odor in Russia since the triumph of German idealism. To own to any admiration for them was to invite intellectual ostracism, and Herzen, ever since his youthful clashes with the "Chemist," had shared this aversion.[59] It was therefore with the surprise of the revisionist that he rediscovered the eighteenth century. In preparing his articles he reread with serious attention some of the *philosophes,* or at least read about them at second hand.[60] He confided to his *Diary* an enthusiasm he could not display in print, expressing a new regard for the witty irreverence of Voltaire and an even greater esteem for the democratic aspirations of Rousseau. Most of all he was drawn to the atheists and materialists, Diderot and Holbach, who destroyed the vestiges of religious myth which had lived on in the "timid deism" of Voltaire and Rousseau. It was this materialism that had been the direct forerunner of 1793, of Robespierre and Saint-Just, and Herzen quotes with approval Diderot's desire "to strangle the [last] king with the entrails of the [last] priest." To be sure these thinkers were mistaken in their deduction of everything from matter, without taking account of that rational force which molds the world and which Herzen calls Idea. Still, by their attribution of man's so-called spiritual faculties to a single, natural source, the materialists were at least on the right track, away from all extra-human authorities.

If all such authorities were overthrown, what then remained to give purpose to life? Herzen's answer was the creative activity of the present moment. In *Dilettantism* this idea was expressed indirectly by a peculiar use of what Hegel calls the "cunning of reason." All historical forms are temporary, incomplete manifestations of reason, serving an end outside themselves, the life of the Absolute. The Absolute, though, conceals this fact from its creatures, in a sense "tricking" them into thinking they are ends in themselves, in order to extract from each the maximum effort of self-fulfillment. "Each stage in the development of nature is at the same time an end and a relative truth . . . a link in a chain, but also a complete ring in itself." [61] Again and again Herzen returns to this idea but always with a slight feeling of scandal that historical periods should be so ruthlessly subordinated to an "unknown future." As a corrective he insists on that half of Hegel's thought which declared that "each phase of historical development contains within itself its end, and consequently its reward and satisfactions." [62] From this he draws the rather un-Hegelian conclusion that action in and for the present moment is in fact the end of life.

If one looks deeply into life one sees . . . that the highest good is existence itself, whatever the external circumstances might be. When men understand this they will understand that there is nothing more stupid in the world than to despise the present in favor of the future. The present is the true sphere of existence. One must seize every minute with pleasure; the soul must be perpetually open; it must fill itself, draw into itself all that surrounds it, and pour out again its own essence into the world. The end of life is life: life in that form, in that stage of development, in which it is situated, i.e., the end of man is human life. [63]

Subordination of the present to the future was simply another form of the subordination of man to transcendent ends outside himself — that source of all tyranny for Herzen. But since man's end is man himself, and not some beyond, either heaven or the future, his goal must be self-realization in the here and now.

6

The philosophy of the present moment led to a position known in Left Hegelian literature as the "philosophy of the deed" (*filosofiia dela*). After liberating man's mind from the transcendent authorities of the past, Herzen felt that "science" had done its work; the next task was to liberate the whole man in life. The vocation of the present generation therefore was no longer abstract speculation but "action." This was an old theme with Herzen, going back to his youthful impatience at Goethe's Olympian aloofness from the affairs of this world. Now, however, it comes crashing through the contemplative harmonies of idealism in a frenzied crescendo. As to the nature of this "action," Herzen was necessarily vague, since it still lay entirely in the future. He could define it only in opposition to various forms of quietism, and this he did with great polemical gusto in *Dilettantism*, growing bolder with each broadside and with each new chapter.

The first attack was leveled against the "dilettantes" properly speaking, a term by which Herzen meant several things at once. In a loose sense he meant people who dabbled in "science" as in an abstract game without any relation to life. In a more precise way he meant people who were either predialectical or dualistic in their thinking. On the one hand they sinned in the direction of the narrow "empiricists" and "materialists" so abhorred by idealism, who rejected everything that did not conform to the classical laws of contradiction. They dissected the "living whole of truth," destroying its "soul" and leaving only "dead abstractions with the odor of a corpse," an idea and an imagery which went back to Herzen's university days.[64] By this refusal to think in terms of contradiction they hindered the progress of "science" and delayed the liberation which it brought. On the other hand the "dilettantes" were those who sinned in the direction of all the transcendent escapisms which Herzen felt paralyzed his generation for action in the real world. Their inability to perceive the organic unity of "being" and "consciousness" led to that dualism which opened the door to religion and the fetish of ideas in themselves. These errors arose in part because the "dilettantes," as their name implies, were amateurs, unwilling to make the effort to penetrate the complexities of dialectical "science," which Herzen insists is a difficult occupation.[65] More important still, the blindness of the "dilettantes" derived from their lack of courage; they were afraid to destroy the comfortable illusion of an Ideal or a God above the contingencies of this world.

After the "dilettantes," who were an intellectual type rather than a political group, came a class which was both: the "romantic dilettantes," by which Herzen meant the Slavophiles. For the benefit of the censorship this attack was framed as a commentary on the debate between classicism and romanticism, terms which Herzen understood in their contemporary German sense. The classics were the heirs of antiquity, men who believed only in the tangible reality of this world and in practical activity; they were the rationalists of history and their most recent incarnations were the men of the Renaissance and the Enlightenment. The romantics, on the other hand, were the heirs of the Middle Ages and Christianity, men who were not at home in the material world but who yearned after some ideal beyond; they were the mystics of history and their final flowering was German romanticism and the religious revival of the Restoration. Herzen presents the two as dialectically complementary: both are necessary moments of past history, yet both are incomplete. Their present destiny is to fuse in a synthesis which will preserve the best of each. This synthesis Herzen feels has been achieved by Hegel, who combined the rationalism of the classics with what was worth keeping of the romantics' sense of man's spiritual dignity. Although Herzen pretends to be rigorously neutral between the two tendencies, in fact all his irony is reserved for the romantics. A "dreamy," otherworldly religion, after the manner of the "senile" later Schelling (the court philosopher of the Slavophiles), is no longer adequate to the "practical" needs of society. He evokes the Slavophiles,

with a black curse for the century on their lips; they see how the castles where
their sweet vision dwelt are crumbling; they see how the new generation scorns
these ruins . . . they hear with a shudder the gay song of contemporary life,
which has not become their song, and gnashing their teeth they look on the
busy century, occupied with material improvements, with social questions, with
science.[66]

Living embodiments of "dualism," the Slavophiles were turned towards
a romantic past and a mystical beyond, and thereby cut off from the
creative "deeds" of the present.

A third enemy was a group Herzen called "the guild of the learned
specialists," the *Fachgelehrten,* by which he meant the ivory tower Germans. Specialists had been a necessary moment in the past development of
consciousness because they supplied the raw materials out of which the
higher "science" of philosophy was built. But they had become dangerous
in the present, since they refused to pass beyond the narrow confines of
their disciplines in order to understand them in the broader context of
universal knowledge. Particularly in Germany the scholars had become
a "caste of the learned," cut off from humanity by a pedantic arrogance
and a barbarous scholastic idiom. Their true place was as servants of
philosophy.

The learned specialists are the functionaries, the subalterns of the Idea; they
are the bureaucracy of science, its scribes, its clerks, its secretaries. Functionaries do not belong to the aristocracy, and the learned specialists cannot consider themselves in the foremost phalanx of humanity, that which is first illumined by the rising sun of the Idea.[67]

This scorn of scholars derived in part from an aristocratic impatience
with what Herzen considered pedantic detail. It sprang even more from
his exasperation with a life of pure speculation and his yearning for
"deeds" in the real world, and his attack on the specialists was another
of his insistent calls for a sense of social responsibility among Russia's
educated minority. The latter failed to see that the "science" with which
they passed their time had at last essentially understood the universe, a
result codified by Hegel, and that in the realm of pure thought nothing
remained to be done. The hair-splitting of the German professors encouraged this error and diverted energies from the task of the present
historical epoch, which was the propaganda of "science" and "action"
to change society. The Russians should imitate the French, perhaps
less original than the Germans, but at least gifted with a great tradition
of popularizing enlightenment. As always, an allusion to France was an
evocation of politics.

The full implications of Herzen's "philosophy of the deed," however,
emerge only in his attack on a group designated as the "Buddhists of
science," to whom he devotes the last and boldest of his essays. The "Bud-

dhists" in question came not from Tibet but from Berlin; they were the Right Hegelians, such as Belinski and Bakunin in the period of their "reconciliation with reality." The orthodox Hegelians were more reprehensible than the other species of "dilettantes" because, unlike the latter, they had understood "science" but failed to follow it to its logical conclusions. They adhered to a dialectical philosophy, yet, while viewing the past as a constant process of evolution, they refused to recognize the equal inexorability of change in the present. More seriously still, they espoused a philosophy which proclaimed the unity of idea and reality, of thought and action, and yet they conducted themselves as if pure philosophy were all that existed and retreated, like Buddhists, into the contemplation of truth in and for itself. They had correctly perceived that "science" gives "reconciliation," or liberation of the understanding, in the realm of "consciousness," but they had failed to grasp that beyond this lies the realm of "being," with which philosophy is organically one. They did not see that abstract reason was simply *"that which underlies reality,"* and that philosophy had meaning only in terms of this reality.[68]

For Herzen the dialectical moment which necessarily followed the possession of abstract truth was a return to reality and action in the world of "being."

Science creates in the world of logic — this is its vocation. But man is called to more than logic; he is also called to the historico-social world, to the world of moral freedom and positive action; he possesses not only the liberating faculty of understanding, but also a will; man cannot refuse to participate in the deeds of humanity which are being accomplished around him; he must act in his place and time — in this is his universal vocation.[69]

The error of the Buddhists was that they "did not understand the necessity of this return, of this exit from science into life, of the realization of the Idea in reality." [70] Philosophy does not exist in and for itself but as a part of living history of which it is the consciousness: ". . . science is a moment, on both sides of which is life; on the one side life — natural and immediate — which is striving towards consciousness, and on the other side life — conscious and free — which flows from it." [71] In the philosophy of Hegel reason had at last attained the goal towards which it had been striving since the dawn of history — the freedom of total self-consciousness; and "when science reaches the highest point, it naturally passes beyond itself," into "deeds." "The world is complete only in action . . . the living unity of theory and practice." [72]

In effect this was the end of philosophy. It was declared to be superseded and propaganda was called upon to take its place. The end result of philosophy was to free the individual from philosophy, to "liberate" him from the toils of pure speculation and from that existence of illusory gratifications in which Herzen felt his generation had too long wasted its energies. Freedom from these illusions was the true "reconciliation with reality" of "science," and not the acceptance of reality which Belinski, following the Buddhists, had once thought. But this very liberation from abstraction could only be achieved by a rigorous education in abstraction, and it was for this reason that Herzen could express his politics only as ideology. The first obstacle to freedom was not autocracy but the metaphysical and religious quietism of the intelligentsia. The revolution in "science" was the necessary first step toward the revolution in "reality." ·

Like all revolutions this break with past illusions was a soul-rending process, which, if in the end it brought "reconciliation," began in anguish. The ecstatic letter whereby Herzen had announced to his Petersburg friends his discovery of the *Phenomenology,* and in which he had compared that event to the perilous yet exhilarating crossing of a sea from the shore of illusion to the "other shore" of reality, was reproduced with new embellishments in the published text of the essays.[73] Again and again he repeats that it is painful to shed one's cherished "subjective convictions" in order to face the "objective reason" of the universe, but that when one has done so he is rewarded a hundredfold.[74] "To suffer through the phenomenology of the mind, to shed the warm blood of the heart and the bitter tears of the eyes, to starve away scepticism, to love, to love much and to give all to truth — such is the lyric poem of one's education in science." [75] The liberation of "science" is even compared to a sacramental death and resurrection. "Thus the individual personality, by losing itself in science does not irretrievably perish. . . . The personality must repudiate itself in order to become the vessel of truth . . . to die to natural immediacy means to be resurrected in the spirit, and not to perish in infinite nothingness as the Buddhists perish." The death of the mind's subjective illusions is its rebirth to reality; he "who loses his soul" in science "saves it." [76] This salvation is "action," itself almost a sacramental value. "Whoever has suffered through to science," for him "the *beatitude* of tranquil contemplation is insufficient; he desires the *fullness of ecstasy* and of the *sufferings* of life; he desires *creative activity,* for only activity can fully satisfy him." [77] The tone rises almost to a scream, and the very heat of Herzen's language betrays the measure of his persisting frustration: in place of the bread of action for which he cries to heaven he is rewarded only with the stones of more ideas. He can come no nearer to deeds than to proclaim their logical necessity in words, and the liberation of "science" is the sole "reconciliation" he is vouchsafed in the present. For the rest he can only live in anticipation, and in the meantime caress his vision of revolutionary action with more burning words.

In print these words could go no farther than hints, but the hints are clear enough in spite of the idealist verbiage in which they are enveloped. His meaning is suggested, first, by the criticism he expresses of Hegel.

The latter, in spite of his genius, had his human weaknesses: "He experienced a panic fear of speaking out directly, just as he feared to go to the last consequences of his principles. He lacked the heroism of logicality, of self-effacement in the acceptance of truth . . . no matter what the cost." [78] He forced his conclusions into an artificial "harmony with that which exists," in other words with political absolutism. Such failings, though, were pardonable in a pioneer whose task was to achieve liberation in the realm of thought. It was for "the younger generation, lightly borne on the mighty shoulders of the thinker of genius," to achieve liberation in the realm of life. The younger generation would become accustomed to the mental heights attained so painfully by Hegel; it "will feel at home there, will cease to wonder at the broad, infinite view and at the freedom it confers . . . then its truth, its science will be spoken out simply, accessible to all; *and this will be*." [79] In his *Diary* Herzen is more explicit, stating that Hegel did not dare be logical in the application of his principles because of his attachment to the status quo, "*das Bestehende*," and that the Young Hegelians by their attacks on the existing order "were truer to him than he was to himself." [80]

Herzen also hints at this revolutionary message in reiterated calls to overcome philosophy by action. At times the hint is muffled and abstract. "In action that is rational, *morally free*, and *passionately energetic*, man attains to the *reality of his personality* and makes himself *immortal* in the world of events. In such action man is *eternal* in temporality, *infinite* in the finite, the representative of his race and of himself, *the living and conscious instrument of his epoch*." [81] "Action" which meets these standards can only be revolutionary, and the careful reader would be sure to understand it as such. At other times Herzen is more direct, descending almost to a discussion of contemporary politics. This discussion took the form of a "historiosophical" effort to determine which nation would first "translate science into life." England was easily eliminated because, although she was gifted with an excellent sense of "activity," she was also too "local" in her interests and indifferent to the fate of humanity. Germany was rejected as the "Buddhist" *par excellence* among nations, who "has taken science as an end in itself and moral freedom exclusively as an inner principle." There remained France, who "following her own path has reached conclusions very near to those of German science," and who therefore might well become "the instrument of the reconciliation of life and science." [82] Given France's revolutionary reputation every attentive reader would understand that the "path" and the "conclusions" in question were political action and socialist theory. But whatever nation was the elect of the Idea — and Herzen suggests that it might even be Russia — the promises of "science" would inevitably be realized. The essays on *Dilettantism* end with a characteristically hyperbolic peroration: "From the temple of science humanity will issue forth with proud, uplifted brow, inspired by consciousness, *omnia sua secum portans* — towards the creation of the kingdom of heaven." The revolutionary cataclysm itself is clearly evoked. "When the time comes, the lightning of events will rend apart the clouds, will destroy, as by fire, all obstacles, and the future, like Pallas, will be born in full armour." In the meantime "science" gives the faith which will eventually bring this future into being. "Faith in the future is our noblest right, our imprescriptible good; believing in it we are full of love for the present. And this faith in the future will save us in heavy moments of despair; and this love of the present will be alive with blessed deeds." [83]

In more abstract form this philosophy of the deed was a vehicle for the same ideal of liberty Herzen had expressed earlier through Schiller's aesthetic vision of personality, Schelling's world-poem, or Saint-Simon's New Christianity. But it was not just a recapitulation. Like the Idea itself, Herzen had evolved from poetic and mythological expressions of his aspirations to philosophical ones, and the result was a great increase in the intransigence of his position. Through the poetry of his youth he had succeeded only in defining his ultimate goal: the full and free personality. By reacting against his former excesses of poetic fantasy, and with the aid of Hegel, he had now defined the present enemy as well: the ideal authorities of the past. This pair of ideas would constitute the *leitmotiv* of his political philosophy for the rest of his days. In particular it would govern his reaction to the failure of the European revolution of 1848, and the elaboration in answer to this of his theory of a superior Russian path to socialism.

7

Marxist commentators beginning with Plekhanov and Lenin, and in their wake all Soviet historians of Herzen, have construed the rationalism of *Dilettantism in Science,* and still more of the *Letters on the Study of Nature,* as an anticipation of dialectical materialism. The argument is that these efforts, although impure with vestiges of idealism, are nonetheless very near to the philosophy — though not to the economics or sociology — of Marx, and great scientific importance has been attached to them in consequence.[84] The narrowly political inspiration of the essays, as well as their highly derivative character, make it difficult to take the latter claim seriously. Nor is it exact to describe Herzen's position as unequivocally materialistic. He was a rationalist, a naturalist, and an atheist to be sure, but all within the framework of idealism, for the law of reason governing the universe was in the last analysis Idea, even though it was wholly immanent in the matter it molded. Even the notion that ideologies are the products of given historical situations was not materialistic with Herzen. Men's transcendent beliefs were not the products of social conditions but the reflection of different stages in the evolution of the "idea" of personality. For Herzen the Middle Ages so revered the Virgin not because of anything to do with the social position of women, but because this belief was somehow necessary at that particular moment to affirm the idea of woman's dignity.[85]

More significantly still, for Herzen it was ideas which made history and not the other way around, a conviction which had important consequences for his political activity. It was because men held erroneous beliefs that they were enslaved to reactionary governments. Revolution was much more the result of enlightenment than of evolving social or economic forces. In consequence, his political efforts would always be directed toward changing men's convictions as the indispensable prelude to changing the conditions under which they lived. When events turned out badly, as in 1848, Herzen's instinctive reaction was to seek the cause in the false ideas the actors held. In this practical sense he remained an idealist even after his conversion to rationalism, and indeed throughout his career. If a philosophical tag must be attached to his position, far better than dialectical materialism is dialectical idealism, with God no longer allowed as one of the ideas.

A better label still is simply Left Hegelianism. Herzen's feeling of kinship with Feuerbach at this time has already been noted. In addition his *Diary* reveals a regular and enthusiastic reading of the principal Left Hegelian organ, the *Deutsche Jahrbücher* of Arnold Ruge; with it "German philosophy comes out of the lecture-room into life, becomes social, revolutionary, takes on flesh and consequently a direct efficacy in the world of events." [86] It is interesting to note that among the articles of the *Jahrbücher* which impressed Herzen most was one by his old foe, Bakunin. The latter had left Russia in 1840, still an orthodox Hegelian, to study philosophy in Berlin. There under the direct influence of the Young Hegelians he had gone through much the same evolution as Herzen, abandoning abstract metaphysics and revealed religion for a philosophy of revolutionary action. In 1842 these conclusions were stated with great dialectical brilliance in an essay remembered chiefly for the anarchist slogan: *die Lust der Zerstörung ist eine schaffende Lust.* Herzen took this "beautifully artistic article" to be the work of a Frenchman, for it was signed with the pseudonym Jules Elisard, and he congratulated himself that the day of revolutionary "action" was about to dawn, since it seemed that the politically minded French had at last begun to understand German "science." [87] In reality, so heavily metaphysical an expression of revolutionary hope could only have been produced east of the Rhine, and in Bakunin's essay Herzen was reading his own typically Left Hegelian views stated more openly because of the milder German censorship.

More important than Herzen's acquaintance with the Left Hegelians' writings is the near identity of his views with theirs.[88] The revision of Hegelianism in Germany had begun in 1835 with Strauss' *Life of Jesus*, an effort to give a naturalistic interpretation of the dogmas of Christianity while still accepting them as symbolically true; the meaning of religion became thereby the individual's strivings toward God-manhood, or the realization of the heavenly kingdom in this world. This was roughly the philosophy behind the "rational" and social Christianity Herzen had expressed in *Licinius* and *William Penn*. With Bruno Bauer's *Critique of the Synoptic Gospels* and Feuerbach's *Essence of Christianity* Left Hegelianism moved to an open rejection of religion, which was now interpreted as a purely mythical expression of human needs. Finally, Ruge and the contributors to his various *Jahrbücher*, including Bauer and later Marx, engaged in a progressively more radical effort to expose belief in absolute ideas, and in the symbols of literary romanticism as well, as a disguised form of religion. This brought the movement down to the conclusions and the date — 1842–43 — of Herzen's *Dilettantism*.[89] In short, Left Hegelianism was the effort of the Enlightenment in more complicated form, refracted through the prisms of the dialectic, and with a new enemy in addition to religious "superstition" — the superstition of ideas in themselves. Herzen's Hegelian essays are a pale northern reflection of this development, less complex and hence less rich in philosophical, historiographical, and psychological insight. He and his compatriots were, after all, no more than provincials in the city of "science."

Why, though, was it necessary to repeat in this fashion and at only a few decades distance the effort of the Enlightenment? The *philosophes* had confronted a religious world-view which had not been substantially refurbished since the sixteenth century; in answer it had been sufficient to explain religion by popular ignorance of nature's workings combined with the unscrupulousness of priests. Since then, however, the world had grown more complex by a revolution and a reaction. In the confusion, a sophisticated religious revival together with the pseudo-science, pseudo-religion of idealism had intervened, renewing theology with all the arguments of dialectical "reason," historicism, and romantic intuition. "Superstition" had assumed new forms, so like "science" as to deceive even the enlightened, and it was necessary to liberate the mind all over again. The simple rationalism of the previous century was no longer adequate to this task; it was now necessary to use the complex dialectical and historical weapons forged by the enemy. In particular, religion could no longer be dismissed as priestcraft; it had to be explained as the result of the myth-making consciousness of the community. This is why Herzen and Feuerbach and Marx felt so near to, and yet so far from, the eighteenth-century materialists: in spite of a common purpose, they were separated from the latter by all the problems due to the intervening rise of ideas in themselves, which had come to constitute an even more formidable obstacle to liberty and "action" than religion.

This heavily ideological approach to liberty poses one final problem. Basically the Left Hegelians, like the more radical *philosophes,* were in revolt against the restrictions on individual freedom imposed by absolute monarchy and a system of legalized class inequality. Nevertheless, both groups made their principal attack, not directly on these institutions, but on religion or its metaphysical substitutes. Liberal or democratic sentiments were considered to be, *a priori,* incompatible with religious belief, and the problem of reform was primarily a problem of enlightenment. This constellation of ideas is peculiar to continental Europe. In England and America the struggle for reform has on the whole proceeded without marked hostility to religion; indeed reformist sentiment has often expressed itself through religion. (The most notable exception to this is the Utilitarians, but their hostility to religion was mild compared to that of the *mangeurs de curé* on the continent.) In some continental countries this difference can be explained in part by the institutional strength of the church, and by the conservative social role the clergy was thereby able to play. This is especially true of Catholic countries, notably eighteenth-century France; it is also true, though to a lesser degree, of Lutheran Germany under the Restoration. For Russia, however, this explanation hardly applies. The church, lacking in intellectual vigor and still more in social influence, was the least of obstacles to reform; the real enemies were unmistakably autocracy and serfdom. Nevertheless, all the leading radicals of the day — Belinski, Bakunin and Herzen — made the destruction of religion-plus-the-Ideal the first step of progress, which would indicate that the heart of the problem lies elsewhere than in the institutional power of the church.

The answer is best sought in the psychological conditions of opposition under an authoritarian regime, an idea already set forth in this book but which bears a special relation to the question of religion. Where power is shared among various groups, no matter how imperfectly, and when the shares are subject to negotiation and readjustment, no matter how gradually, it is what men do and not what they think that is of paramount importance. An aspiring opposition can operate from within the existing order; it can work for the passage of the next reform bill, or prepare for the next parliamentary maneuver. Questions of principle tend to take second place to questions of political efficacy. If a man votes correctly in public it does not make too much difference what private opinions he holds about God or the nature of the universe. The precocious decentralization of power in England and America certainly has much to do with the relative lack of ideological animus in the political life of those countries. Under the old regimes of the continent, however, the concentration of power in one focus, usually bureaucratic and purely administrative in character, and the relative rigidity of such a centralized structure, made the task of reform much more difficult than it was across the Channel. An aspiring opposition lacked any foothold within the system it wished to change; it could only attack from without, which meant it could only attack on the level of first principles. Ideology, therefore, became the touchstone of a man's politics. Such a scheme is no doubt summary, and many other factors would have to be introduced to give a complete picture. But the inflexible resistance of absolutism to a liberal and democratic opposition is, if not the whole story, at least the origin of ideological politics.

Under an old regime, then, ideology is necessary to give faith during the long, impotent wait for change. It is also necessary to provide the unflinching conviction required to make sweeping criticisms of the existing order, and still more to mount the final assault. The resistance of an old regime is rarely broken short of violence, and those who are not totally convinced of their rightness lack the moral strength to make, or advocate, revolutions. In such a context revealed religion easily comes to be regarded as the principal enemy. It minimizes the power of man by subordinating him to God, by reducing history to Providence, and by declaring the natural world to be dependent on some unknown and uncontrollable supernatural. It saps energies required for action and hence is viewed as the chief ideological prop of the status quo. Moreover, God is the universal archetype of all authority, and any attack on authority must first dispose of this ideal sanction. As Bakunin later said, giving a typically extreme statement of this idea, if God exists then man cannot be free. In place of religion the radical must have an ideology which declares man's independence from any authority outside himself and extols his power to change the world; in short, he must have an ideology of natural reason. The liberation of the mind is the necessary first step toward the liberation of the whole man; enlightenment is inseparable from radical politics. This set of attitudes is more doctrinaire in times and places where the frustration of the radicals is greater. As Herzen wrote in his *Diary,* quoting from the *Deutsche Jahrbücher:* "It is necessary to decide once and for all: 'either Christianity and monarchy or science and the republic!' " [90]

Herzen, however, lived not only under monarchy but under the Russian autocracy, and his vision of the future republic was accordingly extreme, indeed to the point of anarchism. Translated into politics, his total war against the transcendent authorities of the past meant rejection of the state and the demand for the total dissolution of the existing social structure. As long as there remained a single institution not freely and rationally consented to by the individual, then man could not be free. This anarchist ideal of the absolute liberty of the individual was, to use the language of the day, the dialectical response to the total lack of liberty under Nicholas. This, of course, was not stated explicitly in *Dilettantism*, nor had Herzen worked out the political implications of his philosophy even in the privacy of his study. Since practical politics were for the moment impossible, he could only proclaim man's total spiritual freedom from all ideological authorities and absolutes. This intellectual intransigence, though, was already the philosophical expression of anarchism, and his career until the death of Nicholas was to be devoted to the elaboration of a corresponding political program. This effort began while he was still in Russia, in the years following the essays on dilettantism; it was completed after his emigration in 1847, when he was at last free from censorship and the more subtle forms of alienation imposed by residence in Russia. But the essential turning point occurred with the anarchist revolt of ideas to which his Hegelianism in the last analysis led.

Some writers on Herzen have pointed out that this intransigent devotion to liberty was in contradiction to his espousal of the historical determinism of German metaphysics,[91] and there is a certain truth in this view. The rejection of all authority external to the individual fits rather poorly with metaphysical schemes of history, including Hegel's, which set up abstract goals for the species independently of the will of men. But even while a Hegelian, Herzen in fact adopted a position which put him outside the system. Yet, though he was eventually to abandon it, he did not do so because of any soul-searching over this contradiction. There was never to be an acute crisis of rejection, or conversion to a new systematic philosophy. His Hegelianism lasted so long as he was confined to inaction in Russia. As soon as he was abroad in the revolutionary "deeds" of 1848 he simply forgot about Hegel, for he at last had something more closely approximating the "fullness of life." In this context the contradiction between determinism and liberty in his thought loses most of its importance. Historicism had never been an end in itself for Herzen but only a device to bolster his conviction in the inevitable triumph of liberty. He was not a philosopher but a political journalist, and he was consistent in his basic aspiration to freedom if not always logical in his rationalizations for it.

Even after Herzen had abandoned Hegelianism as a system, however, much remained of its influence in more diffuse form. There were, first, important vestiges of historicism and organicism; no matter how far Herzen moved from all fixed metaphysical schemes there always lurked in the back of his mind the picture of a growing, evolving universe, and he was never at a loss for an apt "historiosophical" generalization to justify his political hopes. Together with this went another vestige of the metaphysical habit: the drive for the ultimate utopia. Herzen had rejected all ideal absolutes, including that of Hegel, and he would never again seek self-realization in communion with the abstract principles of reason, art, or love. Henceforth he would seek fulfillment only in the life of the world, in the true sense of his "realism." But the fulfillment he sought remained nonetheless total, and, as formerly, he would settle for nothing less than the complete realization of the dream. Having once communed in the "Idea," which conferred "absolute" self-consciousness, or liberty, and raised man to godhead, Herzen continued to ask the same things of "reality." His "translation of science into life" was almost literal; and the socialist version would always be imbued with the maximalism of the idealist original.

CHAPTER XI

Realism in Love: George Sand

ONCE Herzen had disposed of "idealism for the head" the time had logically come to dispatch "romanticism for the heart" as well. This new revolution had far-reaching effects on Herzen's personal life, for it dealt his marriage a blow from which it never fully recovered. What is just as important, in view of the extraordinary significance the age attached to love, it had profound consequences for his thought, adding new shades of red to his notions of morality and, inevitably, to his politics.

The first rumblings of crisis appeared, not in Herzen's *ménage,* but in that of Ogarev. Shortly after the two couples' memorable meeting in Vladimir it became clear that Maria Lvovna was not the lofty creature Herzen at first had thought. She was unconcerned for the fate of humanity, and far from living by "hope in the future of Russia," she wanted to live in the present, and to live well, to the full extent of the fortune and social position her husband had just inherited from his father. Ogarev began to feel an incompatibility of values as early as 1838, in the Caucasus, when he noticed that his wife failed to respond to the exiled Decembrists with appropriate warmth.[1] When the pair moved to Moscow in 1839 the conflict came out into the open. At last free from enforced residence in the provinces, Maria Lvovna wanted to enjoy the high life of the capital: the balls, the dinners, the theatres, and also, it would seem, the men. She was only bored by her husband's political and philosophical cronies, although for a while, out of deference to Ogarev, a pretense of compatibility was maintained by all concerned. Soon, however, Maria Lvovna made clear to Nick her real inclinations, and his friends pronounced her one of the vile "crowd," without "higher interests" and altogether unworthy to be taken into their "circle." [2]

The crisis was major, and by no means the personal affair of Ogarev. Given the ethos of the circle and its intense feeling of cohesion in the face of a hostile world, marrying one of its members meant in a sense marrying the group, and each member reserved the right to pass on the marital choice of his brothers. Bakunin's meddling in the sentimental affairs of

Stankevich, Belinski, and his own sisters is simply the most notorious case among many.[3] Ogarev's problem automatically became the common concern of the circle, and none of his friends hesitated to urge advice on the sufferer. Ogarev soon found himself confronted with the alternative, put almost as an ultimatum, *either* "friendship" *or* "love."

Herzen, as the closest "friend," was particularly active in the struggle. Shortly after his first return to Moscow, in 1839, he volunteered counsels of firmness to Nick in writing, to the great and understandable anger of Maria, who saw the letter. This incident at last made the conflict of loyalties in Ogarev unbearable. His "soul torn in two," he sent Herzen a pathetic plea for a meeting alone where they could seek some solution to the dilemma.[4] Herzen, full of zeal, on his next visit to Moscow scoured the city in freezing weather in search of his friend, only to come away saddened by Nick's continuing "weakness" toward his wife and his begging for a reconciliation between "friendship" and "love." In recounting the incident to Natalie Herzen switched into French (unlike most of the gentry he almost always wrote his letters in Russian) as if to whisper the scandal more confidentially: "Pour en finir avec les nouvelles, Mme. Ogareff est vraiment au dessous de mon opinion; c'est une femme sans coeur, sans esprit de conduite même; déjà il y a des histoires *qu'on raconte* d'elle. Poor, poor Ogarev! And the bandage has not yet fallen from his eyes!" [5]

Out of consideration for his friend, a few days later Herzen effected a reconciliation with Maria Lvovna, but in his heart he stuck to his old opinion: "There is a certain poetry in her, but it is not a lofty poetry." She was a philistine, beyond salvation according to the lights of the circle, and this attitude on Herzen's part, in spite of the truce, had already done much to hasten the collapse of Ogarev's marriage. "The quarrel over me went so far that she proposed a separation." This solution would remain Herzen's hope for Nick's problem until it was, at last, achieved. "It would be better to separate than to sacrifice to pride. . . . Let us turn our glance away — it is as frightening as a scene from Hamlet." [6] Such were the onerous responsibilities of brotherhood in a lofty calling.

The discord in Ogarev's life led Herzen for the first time to revise the theories of sacred love on which his own marriage, no less than his friend's, was founded. The text from which this revision drew its inspiration was a favorite of his youth, Goethe's *Elective Affinities*. A German aesthetician named Retscher had produced a critique of the novel in which he propounded the pseudo-sacramental views of passion which Herzen himself had once seen in it: the triumph of "divine" love over "earthly" egoism and man's union thereby with God. Ogarev in his difficulties found this doctrine consoling. Not so Herzen.

Goethe by no means thought to write a moral fable, but was trying to resolve for himself the excruciating question of the conflict between the formalism of marriage and elective affinity. Marriage did not triumph for Goethe (as Retscher thinks). Is suicide because of jealousy victory over jealousy? No, the contradictions set up by the natural passions, unillumined by the spirit, and the social forms [of marriage] without content [love], entered into a frightful collision and ended in death.[7]

Herzen, indeed, had grasped the true sense of the novel: a naturalistic, almost physiological view of sexual attraction, entailing more often than not a conflict with marriage as understood by society or the church, to which the only "rational" response is freedom to change partners whenever affection changes. His willingness to see all this, however, was new.

Belinski, who as a member of the circle was privy to these debates, with his characteristic impetuosity went further.

For me the bayadere and the hetaera are better than a faithful wife without love just as the Saint-Simonian view of marriage is better and more human than the Hegelian [conventional] view. . . . What is it to me that the state is founded on abstract marriage? It is also founded on the hangman with a knout in his hands. However, the hangman is nevertheless vile. I am even ready to agree with Herzen that Retscher did not understand the novel of Goethe, that it is not an apologia, but rather a protest against a *dog-like gluing together* with the permission of the church.[8]

As usual the question of love raised all other questions; liberation in personal relationships was inextricably interwoven with liberty in general, especially from the state. A few months later Belinski went to the extreme of a doctrine of free love. "When people become human and Christian, when society has at last attained its ideal development, then there will be no more marriages. Away with these frightful bonds. Give us life, freedom!"[9] Quite this far Herzen was not yet prepared to go, but the general trend of Belinski's thought was his own. On all sides the old moral basis of the circle's cohesion, the doctrine of love, was beginning to crumble.

Meanwhile the pitiful object of the group's concern, Ogarev, in a desperate effort to save his marriage, decided to remove himself from the scene of these controversies. In the spring of 1841, after long efforts by Maria Lvovna and with the aid of a bribe, he obtained permission to travel abroad, and in June the pair departed. His hope was that once again alone together they would recover their former ideal affection. The hope, however, proved vain. They were followed to Europe by a minor member of the circle, a young man named Galakhov, whose attentions had been the cause of the earlier rumors about Maria Lvovna's virtue. These attentions continued, and, although they remained purely Platonic, Maria responded to them sufficiently to convince Ogarev that the situation was hopeless. In 1842 he returned to Russia, leaving his wife in Rome, and visited Herzen in Novgorod, where he was subjected to renewed urgings to separate, an idea which he now was ready to accept, albeit reluctantly.[10] Shortly thereafter he returned to Europe; Maria was openly living with a new lover in Rome, and the inevitable separation at last occurred.

But Ogarev did not return home. He stayed in Europe another four years, wandering from country to country unable to forget his old dream of love, writing melancholy letters to Maria and equally melancholy verse for himself, seeking consolation in the art of Italy, the music of Germany, and, on a less elevated plane, in women and wine.[11] Now grown to middle age, he had become the perfect model of the "superfluous man" which the generation of idealism so often produced, and of which such heroes of Turgenev as his *Hamlet of Shchigrovski County* or Lavretski of the *Nest of Gentlefolk* are only the most famous portraits. It was a type for which Herzen felt a mounting abhorrence, since it represented the dissipation by the enlightened elite of talents and energies which would be better expended for the "future of Russia."

Indeed, however much Herzen failed to understand the causes of his friend's "weakness" — and his rather brutal meddling makes it clear that he did not understand — from his own point of view he was right: Ogarev's persisting bondage to an idealistic concept of love and the "formality" of a marriage which no longer corresponded to anything real paralyzed him for all other activity. For over a decade, and long after his return to Russia in 1846, he was still too absorbed in "personal" problems, including two new courtships and a second marriage, to be capable of any sustained work or "general interests." This, moreover, was the decade when the enlightened were at last, for the first time since 1825, taking the ideological offensive against the regime, an attack in which Ogarev could participate with nothing more than good will. Throughout the forties this spectacle of futility was never far from Herzen's mind, and only served to feed his growing revulsion from idealism's cult of the inner, private life.

2

The same spectacle was also before Natalie's eyes, but with very different implications. At the beginning of Ogarev's difficulties, Natalie, unlike her husband, made every effort to see matters through the prism of the old ideal. She wrote to Maria Lvovna that she "loved" her the way they had loved on their first meeting in Vladimir, "because you are one with Nick and Nick is one with Alexander." [12] She was soon forced, however, to see the situation as it really was, and the destruction of her quadrilateral ideal could not but have been painful to her, while Alexander's new hardheaded views of love and marriage must have appeared more menacing still. Indeed, their own life together was beginning to change. Not that Alexander showed any inclination to apply man's newly proclaimed right to separate; on the contrary he flatteringly contrasted his happiness with the misery of Ogarev.[13] The transformation was much more subtle, and proceeded from a fundamental misunderstanding present in their marriage from the beginning.

Natalie had always taken the mythology of Dante and Beatrice more seriously than did her husband; indeed, the divinization of their love had originally been her idea. Moreover, she expected this total love to continue through married life with the same intensity as in courtship. For her as a woman it was normal that the life of the heart and the family should fill the universe more completely than for her husband. Furthermore, as a result of the endless emotional rebuffs of childhood — far more devastating than those which Herzen had experienced — she stood in desperate and unremitting need of reassurance that at last she was loved unconditionally. This need could only have been increased to morbidity, when, during the two years, 1841 and 1842, her three exhausting pregnancies ended tragically.[14] In the roles of wife and mother, which were her whole life, she was wounded almost beyond endurance; she seemed in her own eyes to have failed Alexander and the ideal of their love.

Herzen's needs in marriage were very different. His participation in the cult of absolute love had been both a hyperbolic expression of youthful feelings and a desperate, temporary expedient for overcoming the shock of exile. Once this crisis had passed and the novelty of triumphant passion had worn off, he no longer needed so absorbing a love, but simply a wife, devoted and tender to be sure, but all the same an ordinary, earthly wife. He needed many other things besides — his career, politics, philosophy — to which Natalie was totally indifferent, and which in fact appeared to her as rivals. Thus, though Herzen was not unkind in any overt way, he came to be more and more absorbed in his "general interests" at the very time when Natalie hovered between life and death in fruitless childbearing. She was developing a hysterical feeling of abandonment, while he was feeling increasingly cramped by her clinging affection.

Tension first became acute in Novgorod. The bitterness of Herzen's mood and his intellectual aggressiveness following his second exile seemed to Natalie a reproach to the adequacy of her love. Herzen would often find her weeping beside their son's crib, occurrences she explained as the result merely of "upset nerves" and which he therefore dismissed as of no importance. Then one night, amid hysterical tears, Natalie confessed to a deeper anxiety: she saw Alexander's "boredom," his "feeling of emptiness," the "poverty of his life," and suffered because she could not "cheer him up" — in other words she feared that she was no longer important to him, that he no longer loved her. Herzen was immensely surprised by this revelation. He tried to convince her that she was only imagining things; at length, comforted by the attention her distress had provoked, she grew calm. But about a month later the crisis broke out anew and followed precisely the same course, to Herzen's continuing amazement.[15]

Natalie's fears were scarcely as groundless as her husband asserted. He had always prided himself on his "fiery" nature, and in Novgorod, maddened by the absurdity of his situation, he began to feel the need for more ardent affection than the ill and tearful Natalie could provide. His *Diary* begins to echo a conflict between reason and what "science" termed *Naturgewalt*.[16] This was not a debate in the abstract, for Herzen was beginning to notice the ample and healthy charms of Natalie's chamber-maid, one of his father's serfs. In the summer of 1842, just after he returned from Novgorod to Moscow, he dined out frequently with his friends while Natalie remained home because of her health. On one such occasion, near dawn, Herzen had to awaken the maid in question to admit him to the house, and his resistance to *Naturgewalt* gave way. As he confided immediately to his *Diary*:

I was carried away, could not stop myself — and afterwards cried out my repentance. But in repentance itself is something which defends me in my own eyes. Is it not only those who lack strong passions who hold back? And why was it my passion was full of rapture, of frenzied *bien-être,* which, when I think of it, I cannot curse? A rigoristic morality cannot give me absolution, and indeed I am far from giving it to myself, but a humane judgment must be silent, show forbearance, rehabilitate. In this is the great mission of our century. Let positive law prescribe lashes and chains; we [the enlightened] will not accept it, we must look on a fall, on temptation, from another point of view. Christ did not throw the stone.[17]

The tone is not only self-justificatory; it is almost congratulatory, and at the same time quite pompously ideological. Herzen did not see that to Natalie his indiscretion must appear as the story of Medvedeva all over again and hence as the failure of his "redemption," which it had been her mission in life to achieve. What is more, it never occurred to him that his conduct was strikingly reminiscent of those liberties the Russian gentry traditionally took with their dependents, from which he and Natalie had suffered so much, and which he elsewhere condemns so uncompromisingly.

Trusting that Natalie would see the matter in the same enlightened manner as he did — and also fearing he had been overheard — Herzen confessed to her. He knew that this would be painful on both sides, but he also felt that his escapade should be treated for what it was: an outburst of purely physical desire that in no way destroyed the deeper bonds of their life together — all of which was quite true. He also felt, in accordance with his changing views of marriage, that their union could remain firm only if it were founded on total honesty, and that Natalie would respect him the more for a sincere repentance. Herzen's motives were good enough, and a more mature, less hysterical woman might well have understood, but then if Natalie had been this kind of woman he perhaps would have been less driven to seek consolation elsewhere.

As it turned out the confession was a catastrophe. Natalie (who at the time was pregnant with what was to be her third stillborn child) tried to forgive Herzen, but her most persistent thought was that he had dragged her along with him in his "fall" and that the holy ideal of their love had been irremediably desecrated. Worse still, his act was definitive proof that he no longer loved her; otherwise how could he have succumbed to the very first temptation, and under her own roof! No matter how hard her dismayed husband tried to convince her of his love, Natalie refused to believe him. She became seriously ill, and Herzen seems to have feared for her life.[18]

Even after Natalie recovered from the initial shock the crisis continued. Alexander would find her weeping, a painful explanation would ensue, and all the old wounds would be reopened. Natalie complained unceasingly: "You don't need me; on the contrary, always ill, suffering, I spoil your life; it would be better to get rid of me. You love me, I know, the blow would be painful, but later you would be calmer."[19] Worse still, she revealed that such thoughts had tormented her from the first days of their marriage, that they had been present even since their first meeting: she had always understood that he required someone different, more "energetic" and open to the world. Until now she had hidden these thoughts, but his "fall" at last demonstrated they were only too justified. Herzen was immensely pained by the depth of this distrust, and he was baffled to explain it, for had he not done all that was humanly possible to reassure her, even humiliating himself in endless repentance? "What drives her to torture herself so? An exceptional tenderness and *susceptibilité*, excessive love. But why such a morbid expression of the most simple of principles? The habit of concentration on self, of brooding constantly over painful thoughts."[20]

Such scenes continued intermittently for a whole year. Each time Herzen prayed that he had at last convinced her of his love, but although each time Natalie would seem to grow calmer, after a few days the cycle would begin over again. As a result Herzen, who at first had worn his repentance rather lightly, began to feel real remorse, and finally something approaching despair. Like Natalie, he fell into brooding introspection — referred to as *Grübelei* — which consumed the better part of his energies and for months crowded politics and philosophy from his *Diary*.[21] The whole experience was as painful as any of the persecutions of Nicholas.

At length, however, the crisis began to ease. The family spent the

summer of 1843 alone in the country; rest and isolation improved both
Natalie's health and her spirits. Moreover, she was again pregnant, and
in December a son was born who survived — her fifth child and the
second to live. A year later, in December 1844, her first daughter was born
and also lived. Natalie recovered at least the external appearances of happiness, and Herzen, who had never suffered through doubts of his own
about their marriage but solely because of her doubts, was only too glad
to put the past behind him.[22] Once again politics and "science" take up
the pages of his *Diary*, completely crowding out the *Grübeleien*. To all
appearances the former equilibrium had been restored, and even placed
on a more adult foundation of mutual understanding and tolerance.

For Herzen the meaning of all that had occurred was quite clear: like
the religious superstition and abstract idealism on which it depended, the
old myth of divine love had lived its day. It was time to grow up and seek
only human satisfactions in the life of the heart — and the flesh. Such
terrestrial joys might be imperfect and changeable, but they were also
the richer for being real. In 1843 he serenely surveyed the recent drama:

How much has changed, what trials, in these [last] four years! Yet all that is
essential has survived: friendship, and love, and devotion to the interests of
humanity — but the illumination is not the same; the crimson light of youth
has given way to the bright, northern and cold sun of realistic understanding.
Our understanding is purer, more mature, but the halo surrounding everything
is gone. The period of romanticism has passed; heavy blows and the years have
killed it. Without hesitating we have gone forward, we have achieved much,
but the young forms have taken on the muscular and lean look of a tired
traveler, burned by the sun, who has been tried by all the hardships of the
road and who knows now all the obstacles.[23]

In spite of the rhetoric it was a sensible position: what had happened
should be charged off as a necessary crisis of maturity, and all concerned
should put aside regret and get on with the business of living.

Natalie, compelled by Herzen's greater strength of character and powers of intellect, accepted this evaluation. Not only did she relinquish the
cult of love, she abandoned the consolations of religion and the church as
well. She adopted the whole of her husband's iconoclastic ideology and
became a "contemporary," emancipated woman. In 1846, in one of her
few extant letters of this period, she wrote to him:

Yes, Alexander, romanticism has left us, and we are no longer children but
grown up people; we see more clearly and more deeply, feel more clearly. It
is not the exalted enthusiasm of old, youth intoxicated with life and worshipping
its idols — all that lies far away, behind. I no longer see the pedestal on which
you used to stand, or the halo around your head. I no longer believe that you are
thinking of me and looking at a star at the same moment as I am looking at it
and thinking of you; but I see more clearly and feel deeply that I love you
very much, that my whole being is full of this love, is made up of it, and that this
love is my life.[24]

Yet, in spite of her protestations, it is clear that Natalie was far from sharing Alexander's enthusiasm for maturity; rather her deepest feeling was nostalgia for the lost romance of the past. Nor was her persisting sentiment that love — even enlightened, realistic love — should be the whole of life shared by her husband.

In fact, the old incompatibilities had been repressed rather than resolved, and Natalie remained prey to a nameless restlessness.[25] Although she had grown silent on the subject, she at last knew that Alexander could never give that total love she continued to crave, if now in emancipated form, and which her courtship had once seemed to promise. Herzen was able to mistake her calm for happiness only because he did not understand this. Indeed, in his innate reasonableness, he would never understand so unreasonable a need for love. When the final crisis came during emigration and Natalie made the supreme grasp for her ideal in infidelity, he still would not understand; his only explanation would be that she had been deceived. In defense of his own self-esteem, to the end of his days he would look on their life together as a model of love, and in *My Past and Thoughts* would paint a grotesquely saccharine picture of this suffering woman, whose existence had been dominated by disappointment with what he had been able to give her and with the bonds he mistakenly thought had made them one.

3

Herzen's domestic crisis led him to develop those naturalistic theories of love he first derived from the *Elective Affinities* into the still more radical conclusions of the Saint-Simonians, Pierre Leroux, and especially George Sand. Indeed it is at this time that he first embraced the Saint-Simonian gospel of the "liberation of woman" and the "rehabilitation of the flesh" which in *My Past and Thoughts* he precociously ascribes to his university days,[26] but which even now he caught from Sand rather than the Saint-Simonians themselves. Herzen was first attracted to Sand in Vladimir as the prophetess of Leroux's "social Christianity." [27] During 1842–43, in the midst of his *Grübeleien,* he discovered her views of love, and from this time on he was, together with Belinski, one of her principal propagandists in Russia.

This, of course, is not to say that without George Sand Herzen would have thought very differently. Not only his personal experience, but the whole climate of the age led him in a similar direction. In addition to being the seedtime of modern socialism, the 1830's and 1840's also mark the birth of modern feminism. The liberation of woman and the flesh were slogans common to most circles of the European Left. The ascetic John Stuart Mill felt no less keenly on the subject than did the promiscuous

Sand.[28] Indeed these questions play a surprisingly large role in radical thinking of the day. In Russia this was to remain characteristic of the socialist intelligentsia throughout the century, and in helping to launch this movement Herzen's role was no less seminal than in his later advocacy of the "socialist" peasant commune.

At first glance the prominence in early socialism of feminism and all that went with it is somewhat difficult to explain. Of all forms of inequality, that which exists between man and woman would seem the most "natural" and the easiest to endure. To be sure, in the early nineteenth century there was much about the relations between the sexes which rankled in freer spirits: the prevalence of the *marriage de convenance* and hence of loveless unions; the impossibility or extreme difficulty of divorce and therefore the frequency of unblessed *liaisons;* the authoritarian pattern of family life and the subjection of wife to husband; the legal disabilities of women in matters of property and inheritance. In a society where the old-regime bonds of fixed status were slowly giving way to greater mobility and individual freedom it was logical that women too should wish to benefit. Nonetheless, this problem seems minor when compared to the more basic issues which offered themselves to the energies of reformers, such as the oppressions of property suffrage and absolutism; restrictions on civil liberties, freedom of the press, and freedom of speech; the lack of widespread education; the poverty of the new proletariat in the West; and the degradation of serfdom in Russia. Nor was it feasible to end the enslavement of woman independently of general social reform. But although against a backdrop of serfdom the passion this issue generated in Russia appears a pure luxury, the radicals of Herzen's generation made feminism a paramount concern.

Two partial explanations of this may be offered. The "rehabilitation of the flesh" was a natural reaction to the etherealization of love accomplished by idealism in the thirties. Also, one may invoke the by now familiar explanation that where it was impossible to liberate anyone from autocracy or serfdom, the issue of absolute liberty in personal relations became all the more emotionally charged. Yet it is still necessary to relate these circumstances to the prevalence of a similar mood in Europe as a whole.

In this connection it is appropriate to note that early nineteenth-century feminism, at least as an articulate doctrine, was almost wholly an upper-class movement. It presupposed a relatively high level of education among women, a considerable refinement of sentiment among them and their partners, and freedom from material cares sufficient to permit intensive introspection. The proletariat, and still more the peasantry, could hardly afford such rarefied concerns; of necessity they approached the problem of love either traditionally or pragmatically, but in either case without self-conscious doctrine. It is certainly more than an accident that the only socialist in contemporary France of really popular origin, Proudhon, was quite patriarchal in his views of woman, a circumstance which later shocked the liberal aristocrat Herzen.[29]

Early feminism and all it implied, therefore, was a phenomenon of the same category of professional intellectuals who produced the theories, at least, of socialism. It also sprang from the same ideological source: an intransigent insistence on the dignity of "man," on the right of each and every individual to live life in its plenitude. The demand for the emancipation of woman is simply the logical extension of this right to the larger and better half of mankind, and the demand for the rehabilitation of the flesh is merely the impatient application of the same right to personal morality. Again, it is only logical that these demands should be the especial concern of people for whom the right to absolute individuality played the largest practical role in life, of people who possessed at the same time the relative privilege, the faculties of introspection and the exacerbated sense of their own worth necessary to live on the level of principles — in short an intelligentsia. Finally, it is logical that feminism and the flesh should bulk particularly large in Russian socialism, which was exclusively the affair of such intellectuals, who, moreover, felt especially menaced in their human dignity.

Concretely, Herzen's new realism in love represented a combination of George Sand's views of women with the critique of Christianity and the notion of the historical relativity of ethics he had derived from Hegel. For the bolder statements of this position we must turn to his *Diary*.

We are unable to look freely and broadly on the relations between people — the Christian phantoms hinder us. They were necessary in their time; now they are not needed. Christian marriage was required to teach man to respect in the wife the woman. The jealous love of the Middle Ages, the idealization of the Virgin, surrounded woman with a bright halo; and this will remain. Indeed it will become all the brighter the more morality develops.

But the Christian idealization of woman was achieved only at a price: "Indissoluble marriage on one side and on the other, houses of prostitution, where woman is thrown into filthy corruption, placed lower than an animal." [30] When Christianity had first guaranteed woman's right to personality by instituting monogamous matrimony, it had been progressive, but this historical purpose once accomplished, religion simply became an obstacle to further liberation, and marriage turned into another fetish inherited from the "dead past."

As to the next "form" of the "Idea" in matters sentimental, Herzen thought as follows:

Marriage is not the natural result of love, but its Christian result; it brings with it the terrible responsibility of the education of the children, of life in an organized family, etc. . . . In the future there will be no marriage, the wife will be freed from slavery; and what sort of word is wife anyway? Woman is so humiliated that, like an animal, she is called by the name of her master. Free relations between the sexes, the public education [of children] and the organization of property; morality, conscience, public opinion, and not the police — all this will define the details of [family] relationships.[31]

Like his socialism in general, Herzen's new view of love comes down to a theory of individuality. Love is not some supernatural emanation surrounded by sanctions and responsibilities originating independently of the individual; it is a natural passion to be governed solely by man's free determination of his needs and desires. Love should serve man rather than create obligations for him. It is this, together with mutual willingness to forgive the inconstancy of passion which religion calls sin, that Herzen understood as true morality. Moreover, faithful to this respect for individual freedom, he had to believe that rejection of the family was the desire of woman herself and, as he no doubt hoped, of Natalie in particular. "The Saint-Simonians gave a great example of humility; they waited for the voice of woman in order to decide the question; but since then has not the voice of George Sand proclaimed woman's opinion?"[31a]

Though much had changed for Herzen since the days of Dante and Beatrice, not everything had changed. The old myth of love, for all its celestial paraphernalia, had been essentially the pursuit of self-fulfillment through the limitless cultivation of sentiment. The new realism, if it no longer recognized any immutable obligations, still proclaimed freely indulged sentiment to be among the supreme values, and the quest for passion, though it was no longer central to Herzen's ideology, remained one of the highest forms of self-realization. (It is significant that Natalie, with her sure instinct in such matters, seized on this article as the most consoling aspect of the new faith: George Sand's cult of the full life through passion made her the "Christ of the female sex."[32]) In all this Herzen's realism in love parallels his realism in "science." The old fantasies of an ideal life had been abandoned, but the same thirst for absolute self-fulfillment and total sensation, no less than total self-consciousness, remained.

4

To the general themes of feminism Herzen added a few that were specifically Russian. In searching for an explanation of his difficulties with Natalie, he came to the conclusion that their crisis of maturity would have been much less severe if only she had possessed passions in addition to those of the heart. Exclusive concentration on the "inner life" of love and the family was unnaturally "one-sided"; women as well as men should be concerned with the great world around their little nest. Only the combination of an intense inner and outer life offered the complete realization of human potentialities. Moreover, Natalie's inability to see this appeared to Herzen a particular case of a national malady: the flight of the enlightened elite, as a result of its long immersion in idealism, into all sorts of soul-destroying introspection, while Russia and her problems went begging.

Soon Herzen was expounding these views on the pages of the *Annals of the Fatherland*. In 1843 he wrote:

Love is one moment, and not the whole life of man; love crowns the personal life in its individual significance; but beyond the exclusive personality are great provinces, also belonging to man, or better, to which man belongs and in which his personality, without ceasing to be individuality, loses its exclusiveness.[33]

The really "mature" man is "called" to the "world of general interests, the public, artistic and scientific life." There was "Buddhism" in pure love no less than in pure idealism, with a comparable waste of energy, talent, and education in both cases. "Reverie, romanticism, Platonic love — all this in our epoch is excellent for the transition between adolescence and youth. The soul is washed, spreads its wings in this sea of fantasy. . . . But to remain forever dreamily sighing and hopelessly suffering on *account of it* . . . not seeing what is happening at one's feet or what is thundering over one's head [that is, social questions]!"[34] And this was the nearest that Herzen could come in print to expounding the theories of Sand.

The problem of the relation between the public and the private life continued to be one of Herzen's chief preoccupations throughout the forties. The principal expression of this concern was his major venture into fiction, a novel entitled *Who Is To Blame?* Begun in Novgorod in 1841, it was finished, after interruptions, in 1846, and published by installments in the *Annals* during 1845 and 1846. As literature it is only partially successful; Herzen was an excellent reporter of the Russian social scene, but he could not construct a plot or draw character. Nonetheless the novel is important in the ideological, if not in the aesthetic, development of Russian literature. It is among the more notable products of the "natural school" of the forties, while it is easily one of the boldest bits of social criticism to get published under Nicholas. It made its mark at the time: Belinski raved over it and the Westerners received it as a significant contribution to the cause.[35]

The chief originality of *Who Is To Blame?* is to combine the general socialist theme of the "rehabilitation of the flesh" with the particularly Russian one of the "superfluous man." Soon after he began to write,

Herzen was captivated by a novel of George Sand's called *Horace,* in which he saw himself and his generation depicted: lost in "the transitional period of struggle between two worlds," given over to "egoism," to anarchic and often degrading "passions," without purpose and direction in life.[36] With appropriate adaptations Horace was Herzen during his "fall" or Ogarev wandering aimlessly over Europe — the superfluous man. To this idea Herzen added a setting in Russian life of the day in a manner (roughly) imitated from Gogol's. For the rest, the novel, like all Herzen's fiction, was highly autobiographical, with portions of the author showing up in all the principal characters and the remainder being supplied by his wife and friends.

The novel's subject is the destruction of three lives by "one-sided" romantic love and superstitious attachment to "formal" marriage. In a provincial town a young couple, Dmitri and Liubov (that is, love) Krutsiferski, live in passionate devotion to one another and in isolation from the world, just as Herzen and Natalie had lived in Vladimir. The inadequacy of so "subjective" a life is soon revealed by the arrival of an attractive and restless nobleman named Beltov, whose vast, unused energies — qualities in which he resembles Herzen — lead him to fall in love with Liubov. The lady reciprocates, for Herzen has inverted the roles of real life, giving his own extroverted nature to the wife (perhaps a bit of unconscious wishful thinking) and Natalie's withdrawn character to the husband. Liubov responds to the many-sided Beltov because, like any full-blooded individual, once the romance of early marriage has passed she is no longer able to live for love alone. Yet she also knows that the tender Krutsiferski cannot live without her because he has nothing else in life. So, after a few Platonic exchanges with Beltov, she sacrifices to marital duty and sends her would-be lover away. The tragedy is accomplished: Beltov wanders over Europe lonely and purposeless; Liubov, only half alive, never ceases to pine for him; and Krutsiferski, destroyed by the loss of his wife's affection, takes to drink.[37]

In answer to the question "who is to blame?" Herzen gives the reader to understand that no one is, or rather that the question itself is false, the reflection of an outmoded, "abstract" morality. Though he could not say so openly because of the censorship, for Herzen the only "moral" solution would have been for Liubov to go off with her love and let Krutsiferski find solace in "general interests" until someone else came along. Since neither was capable of such a course, however, the problem of "blame" becomes one of explaining their weakness — and Beltov's restlessness as well — and here the answer lies in the defects of Russian society.

In the first place it is noteworthy that all the principal characters are victims of the gentry's inhumanity. Liubov is the illegitimate child of a coarse landowner and one of his serfs, and she has been raised in his house, though not as his child, only because of a sentimental caprice of his wife — just like Natalie in the house of Princess Khovanskaia.[38] Beltov's mother was born a serf but educated by her mistress so that she could be hired out as a governess. Pursued by the son of the family in which she has been placed, she succeeds in enforcing marriage as the price of her capitulation and thereby gains her freedom. Yet her early humiliations have given her a tormented, unstable character — which Herzen makes her transmit to her son.[39] In both cases, which incidentally furnish the most convincing writing of the novel, the theme is the combination of servile dependence with humanistic refinement, and Herzen in effect is giving an exaggerated picture of his own youth.

Krutsiferski represents a different kind of pariah in the gentry's world. The son of an army physician (*lekar*) turned to civilian practice in a provincial town — an extremely humble position at the time — he has become an *intelligent* by attending the local gymnasium and then the University of Moscow. In Krutsiferski Herzen no doubt meant to portray Belinski's painful beginnings, though not of course his driving energy. All Krutsiferski finds to do with his high-flown education, however, is to become a tutor in the house of Liubov's uncouth father and later a teacher in a provincial gymnasium.[40] Though tutors traditionally appeared ridiculous if not actually contemptible to Russian nobles, Herzen displays a very unaristocratic understanding of Krutsiferski's humiliations, for the situation once again represents the subordination of individual sensitivity to gentry boorishness.

A fourth major character, a Doctor Krupov, though he has not suffered at the hands of the gentry, remains cool and aloof in their midst. Krupov was a very important personage to Herzen. As a man of science he was also a man of sense, the symbol of empirical, skeptical sanity in a world of sentimentalists. His ancestors were the "Chemist" and a hardheaded doctor Herzen had once met in Viatka. Right after *Who Is To Blame?* Krupov was honored with a novelette entitled with his own name in which he went about the countryside diagnosing the romantic, idealist, and religious "madness" of his patients. After 1848 he reappears, though without his name, in Herzen's major philosophical production, *From the Other Shore*, where he again represents the voice of disabused reason in argument, this time, with revolutionary romanticism.[41] Thus for years he was one of his author's favorite spokesmen, in fact Herzen himself in his Voltairian moments. Krupov too is an outsider in the gentry world, a professional man who owes his status to his wits and not to inheritance, but unlike the other characters in the novel he is proud and defiant, not cowed.

Who Is To Blame?, then, is the gentry world seen from a demi-gentry

point of view, and judged very harshly. As such it is strikingly different
from the same world seen at roughly the same time by gentry novelists
such as S. T. Aksakov, the young Tolstoi, or even Turgenev and Goncharov. When these writers were moved to criticize their class — and
the last two were largely occupied with doing so — they did it very much
from the inside and rather tenderly. Rudin, the Kirsanovs, Lavretski,
and even the great symbol of everything that was wrong with the gentry,
Oblomov, for all their vices are presented quite compassionately. But
Herzen's landowners, such as Liubov's father, Negrov, are all viewed with
hostility, when they are not presented as monsters. This characteristic is
pushed even farther in Herzen's other works of fiction. In 1846 in a
story called *The Thieving Magpie* (*Soroka-vorovka*) he returns to the
theme of the cultured slave already exemplified by Beltov's mother, but
this time in the person of a talented serf actress, whose owner demands
more from his puppets than performance on the stage and whose degrading pursuits drive the girl to choose death over dishonor.[42] And in his
unfinished novel, *Duty Before All*, denunciation of the gentry approaches
the point of caricature.[43]

Though Herzen certainly meant to attack the gentry as serf-owners,
it is doubtful that he intended to present creatures of such total depravity
as he did. This welled up from a depth of resentment of which he was
only partially aware, but which indicates the tenacity of his feeling of
difference from the full-fledged gentry. Consciously he was aware only
of the dynamism which set him apart from them, and of which he made
such a cult, opposing it on every possible occasion to their sloth. Nor is
this submerged resentment without significance for his feminism, for the
gentry's most dramatic violation of the "human dignity" of others was
their treatment of dependent women, as both Herzen and Natalie knew
only too well.

A more conscious judgment of his class and generation is given in
the person of Beltov, who is just about an even mixture of Herzen himself
and the futilely wandering Ogarev. By nature Beltov was intelligent,
energetic, and high-minded, but he had been ruined through his mother's
extravagant efforts to compensate for the degradations of her own youth
by giving him an ideal education. He had been brought up in complete
isolation from society by a Genevan tutor, a symbol of Western enlightenment in its most advanced form. Yet this education, excellent in itself,
was hopelessly abstract in a Russian landowner. "[His tutor] made of
him a man in general, as Rousseau did of Emile; the university continued
this excessively general development; a friendly circle of five or six young
men, full of dreams, of hopes, all the more grandiose since life beyond
the walls of the lecture-hall was unknown to them — all this drew Beltov
more and more into a circle of ideas not native, alien to the world in

which he would have to live." [44] This was Herzen's critique of the idealistic education he and his generation had received.

Disillusionment overtook Beltov as soon as he came into contact with Russian reality. Like any full-blooded individual he wished a life of action and public service, and Herzen speaks of this desire with all the feeling born of its incongruity under Nicholas I.

Nothing in the world is more alluring for a fiery nature than participation in current affairs, in history unfolding before one's eyes; whoever has taken dreams of such activity into his breast has spoiled himself for all else. No matter where he turns, everywhere he will be a guest — his real province will lie elsewhere: he will introduce the civic quarrel into art; he will draw his thought if he is a painter; he will sing it if he is a musician. Moving into another sphere he will deceive himself just as a man who has left his native land tries to convince himself that it doesn't make any difference, that his homeland is wherever he is useful . . . yet, within, an importunate voice calls him to another place and reminds him of other songs, another landscape.[45]

Nowhere has Herzen described his own dilemma more eloquently, nor stated better the reasons which eventually led him to emigrate. For where in Russia was such activity to be found? In the bureaucracy? Beltov, like Herzen, tried it and gave up in frustration and disgust.

It was then that Beltov's character began to disintegrate.

He tried medicine and then painting, caroused a little, gambled some, and then traveled to foreign lands. It goes without saying that his affairs there did not arrange themselves in more satisfactory fashion; he studied without system, and studied everything under the sun; he astonished the German specialists by the many-sidedness of the Russian mind; he astonished the French by his depth of thought, and while the French and the Germans accomplished much, he accomplished nothing.

The result of all this was tremendous personal immaturity combined with excessive intellectual development. Beltov "at the age of thirty, like a sixteen-year-old boy, was still preparing to *begin* his life, not noticing that the door to which he was drawing nearer and nearer was not that through which the gladiators entered but that through which their bodies were carried out." [46]

At length boredom drove Beltov home for a final attempt to find a role in life. As the ultimate derision of his hopes, however, all he could find to do was to stand as a candidate for the noblemen's assembly in his native province, a politically meaningless body, to which, moreover, he failed to get elected, for by this time he was as much an alien in Russia as in Europe.

Beltov . . . who loved everything which these gentlemen [the provincial gentry] could not bear, who read harmful books while they played useful cards, a wanderer about Europe; a foreigner at home, a foreigner abroad, an aristocrat by the refinement of his manners, and a man of the nineteenth century by his convictions — how could provincials receive him? He could not enter into their interests, nor they into his, and they hated him, understanding by instinct that Beltov was a protest, a condemnation of their life, an objection against its entire order.[47]

Beltov at last had become the completely "superfluous man"; there remained only the inner life, either of the heart or of the mind, into which to escape. It was because of this deep idleness that he could not resist pursuing Liubov, and it was because of a similar divorce from the real world that she and Krutsiferski had developed into the ineffective creatures they were. In the last analysis it was all the alienations imposed by "cursed Russian reality" that were to "blame" for this triple failure of human promise.

In spite of its literary inferiority, *Who Is To Blame?* is in many ways a more accurate reflection of Herzen's attitude toward his generation than is the portrait of a heroic, defiant Young Russia given in *My Past and Thoughts.* But the original attitude is also one of the reasons why the retrospective portrait is defiant. Herzen felt so near to Beltov that he lived in constant dread of becoming entirely like him. Throughout the forties he had to fight with all his energies not to succumb to the pressures of the society around him, and his decision to emigrate was in large part motivated by this desire for self-preservation. Under these circumstances Natalie and the fruitless *Grübeleien* she represented were as much a menace as Nicholas. In the duel with his wife over the meaning of their marriage which produced *Who Is To Blame?* the stakes were, in fact, enormous: the survival both of himself as a "full human being" and of that "future of Russia" he bore within him. With stakes so high it is understandable that he should become increasingly ruthless in sweeping aside all who stood in his way, first his wife and later, as we shall see, most of his circle.

5

Thus the question of love was by no means peripheral to Herzen's political thought. In fact, as his *Diary* attests, it led him to the problem of socialism much more directly than the question of economic need ever would have. "Why is it that in general woman is rarely able to give herself to living, social interests, but instead leads a purely private life? Why is it she torments herself with personal questions and can be happy only through her personal life? What changes will socialism bring in this respect?" [48] It is noteworthy that this is the first practical question Herzen asked about the "new world" and the only one, before 1848, in terms of which he attempted to visualize concretely the socialist commune. "In communal life, developed on broad foundations, woman will be more involved in general interests; she will be strengthened morally by education, she will not be so one-sidedly attached to the family, and then blows [loss of children or of her husband's love] will be more bearable. Similarly in the past there was consolation in tearing oneself away from the purely personal and raising oneself to God in prayer." [49] Under socialism interest in the community would absorb all of woman's present needs for God, a faithful husband, and the rearing of her children. For all his feminism, Herzen's socialism was decidedly a man's view of the world.

Herzen's new views of love affected his thought in still more sweeping fashion. It may be remembered that one of the favorite themes of idealism, in particular of Schiller, had been the contrast between "egoism" and "love"; the former, which meant isolation and loneliness as much as selfishness, had been the great vice, while the latter, which always implied self-transcendence and sacrifice, had been the great virtue. In the forties Herzen subjected this dogma to a revision that led him to completely new views of personal morality. The process was a gradual one, occurring over the four years following his domestic crisis and paralleling, as will appear in the following three chapters, a general radicalization of his thought that grew to an angry crescendo on the eve of his departure from Russia.

At first, although he advocated the right of separation in cases of incompatibility, Herzen in no way rejected the idea of lifelong fidelity founded on love. With time, however, he came to feel that fidelity under any circumstances was only for the emotionally puny, an abdication of the self, and hence immoral — though it must be pointed out that, as so often, he was more radical in words than in deeds, for he never displayed any inclination to abandon Natalie. This attitude quickly became mixed up with his growing aversion to those "Buddhists" of life, the Germans.

Looking on his [Krutsiferski's] meek face it was possible to guess that he would develop into one of those sweet Germanic natures — quiet, noble, happy in a rather limited but extremely serious learned-pedagogical profession, in a rather narrow family circle, where after twenty years the husband would still be in love with his wife and the wife would still blush at every equivocal joke: these are the lives of small patriarchal towns in Germany, of the houses of ministers, of seminary teachers, pure, moral and unnoticed outside their own circle. But is such a life possible for us [Russians]? I decidedly think that it is not; such a milieu is not native to our soul; our soul cannot quench its thirst with such watery wine; it is either far higher than that life, or far lower — but in both cases broader.[50]

Soon Herzen was describing all wedlock as a loveless prison, or a bourgeois business arrangement, little better than the sale of women to promote family property interests. Marriage took on a nightmarish quality for him. "As I walk down the streets, especially late in the evening, when all is quiet, gloomy, and only here and there a night-lamp flickers, or a dying candle, I am overcome with horror: behind each wall I feel a drama, behind each wall tears appear, tears about which no one knows, tears of disappointed hopes, tears which carry away with them not only youthful beliefs, but all human beliefs, and sometimes life itself." [51]

Under such conditions the old contrast between egoism and love lost all meaning; in fact by 1846 it had been completely reversed. What traditional moralists called love had come to mean for Herzen self-immolation to imaginary moral absolutes, such as fidelity or continence, set over and above the individual by society. Conventional morality had made love an "abstract duty," divorced from the needs of real human beings, and hence had transformed it from a joy into a burden. Such love was no more than another form of slavery to "myth," of superstition before false transcendent values; it was the relic of a "dead" world-view which had once been progressive but had now become an impediment to the humanization of life. The idea of love as "sacrifice" to someone or something outside the self was simply the ethics of those forces of religion and idealism against which Herzen·had been inveighing since Novgorod.

Real love, on the other hand, was a biological function and an emotional need which should be indulged in intelligently so as to give man joy in the here and now. The supreme morality, therefore, was egoism, the indulgence rather than the denial of one's nature, and self-realization rather than sacrifice to something outside the self. In fact, what men call love is no more than gratification of the ego; duty and sacrifice themselves are only a higher form of egoism.

What is egoism? The consciousness of my personality, of its self-sufficiency, of its rights? Or is it something else? Where does egoism leave off and love begin? And in reality are egoism and love contradictory, can one exist without the other? Can I love someone not for myself, can I love if it does not give pleasure to *me*, namely *me*? Is not egoism the same thing as individuality, as that concentration in self, that apartness to which everything that exists aspires as to its final end? . . . And does it not merge with a higher humanism in the educated man? [52]

The dichotomy of egoism and love was now a false one for Herzen, like all forms of "dualism." Man is only himself, an individual and nothing more; his sole duty is to realize fully his own nature, and not the imaginary injunctions of some Absolute or God; only in this way can he love meaningfully and honestly. "How strange people are! Instead of founding sensible and rational relationships between individuals on egoism, on this cryingly obvious basis of all that is human, they try with all their might to annihilate, to blot out egoism, that is, *die feste Burg* of human dignity, and make out of man a weeping, sentimental, vapid do-gooder, begging for voluntary slavery." Correctly understood, egoism is the source of all positive virtue. "The egoism of the civilized, rational man is noble: indeed it is his love of science, of art, of those close to him, of the full life, of the inviolability of others . . . To tear a man's egoism from his breast means to tear out the living principle of his being, the leaven, the salt of his personality (*lichnost*)." And Herzen concludes with rather shrieking paeans to such qualities as "self-will" (*svoevolie*), "originality" (*samobytnost*), and strong "partisanship" in one's convictions (*pristrastie*).[53]

The importance that Herzen attached to this new morality was enormous; for the rest of his days he never wearied of reiterating the call to rational egoism or the condemnation of "abstract duty" and "dualistic morality." One of the principal themes of his unfinished novel, *Duty Before All*, was, as the title indicates, to have been precisely this subject. After he had settled in Europe and could say all that he thought in print, the new morality of egoism was advanced far more prominently than economic equality as the chief goal of socialism.

Indeed, the logical and emotional relationship of Herzen's new morality to his socialism was of the deepest sort: egoism was the ethical aspect of that total autonomy of personality on which all his thought converged. It was the most extreme expression he ever gave to this idea. The secularization of ethics was, of course, not new, but Herzen carried it far beyond most of his contemporaries. He had generalized George Sand's summons to freedom in the life of the heart, which in turn reached back to Rousseau's voice of "conscience," into a theory of absolute "self-will" in all things. In the process any notions of a natural moral law, of a categorical imperative, or of ethical utility — all of which, though non-religious positions, imply objective standards of conduct and hence fixed principles — had been discarded. Morality had become an affair of absolute self-determination without reference to anything outside the individual. This of course did not imply any idea of Nietzschean superhumanity, or the disregard of others and the common good. In some way Herzen never made explicit — save for his vague vision of the fraternal commune — the absolute egoism of each was entirely compatible with the absolute egoism of all. In contemporary thought there was no individualism so extreme except the very similar egoism of Max Stirner.

In all this Herzen's new morality was the pendant to the metaphysical conclusions he had already derived from Hegel. If the naturalistic and dialectical pantheism of Hegel, which brought progress out of destruction and thereby conferred on man absolute freedom from past ideologies, was the metaphysics of anarchism, egoism was the imperative of anarchism's ethics. It was only from this double base, slowly and gropingly, that Herzen would move toward anarchy in politics, during the course of increasingly bitter quarrels both with the Slavophiles and with Westerners more moderate than himself.

CHAPTER XII

The Slavophiles and Nationalism

BY EARLY 1842 Herzen could no longer bear the oppression of government service and the provinciality of Novgorod; he decided on desperate measures to free himself from both, and somewhat to his surprise they succeeded. On the pretext of Natalie's ill health, his father's age, and the disorder of the family's finances, he resigned from government service in the hope of being allowed to live, if not in Moscow, then on one of his father's estates nearby. The step was taken against the warning of friends and not without apprehension about the government's reaction, yet he was ready to accept an additional year of exile if only he could have the free use of his time. The resignation was accepted without penalty, however, and Herzen retired as "court councilor" (*nadvorny sovetnik*), a rank which conferred hereditary nobility — the old dream of Ivan Alexeevich for his son. Still Herzen was not allowed to leave Novgorod, so he again asked permission to live in Moscow, to be refused by Nicholas with the comment: "he has not earned it." [1]

Nonetheless Herzen persisted, bringing rather considerable influence to bear on the government. Ogarev, whose wife was the niece of the governor of Penza, consulted with the Third Section; Herzen's friends from the *Annals of the Fatherland,* the critic Panaev, the poet Nekrasov, and the novelist Count Sollogub, offered the use of their court connections. Finally, it was decided that Natalie should write to the empress, more easily moved to pity than her husband. [2] Herzen felt profoundly humiliated by these appeals — like "prostitutes . . . the first times they sell themselves for money, even though they can plead harsh necessity." Yet he could only "bow the head — there is no struggle where on one side there are no rights, no strength"; he would at least save his "individuality," perhaps to work for Russia. In July Nicholas at last relented; Herzen was allowed to reside in Moscow, but he remained under police surveillance and he was not permitted to visit Petersburg. Herzen reflected bitterly that, except for a few months of freedom in Petersburg in 1840, he had suffered eight years of persecution since his arrest in 1834: "a blighted existence, broken at the very first step." [3] He would remain under police surveillance until the eve of his departure for Europe in 1847 — the whole of his adult life in Russia passed at the mercy of an absurd tyranny!

The worst was over, however, and he would have no more brushes with the paternal despotism of Nicholas. He was at last free to devote all his energies to those "general interests" which had beckoned so long like a mirage. Herzen had just reached thirty at the time of his return to Moscow and he was in the prime of his powers. His father, by now an old man in years as well as in spirit, purchased for him a house adjacent to his own, and from this comfortable base Herzen set out to conquer the Moscow salons. He arrived at a most favorable moment. What the ablest chronicler of the intellectual life of the day, Annenkov, has aptly called "the remarkable decade," had just begun. The forties were the height of the circle-and-salon civilization of gentry Moscow that dominated Russian intellectual life under Nicholas: unquestionably, "this was the most brilliant literary period of Moscow." [4] At the beginning, at least, Herzen frequented everybody: on Monday evenings the house of Chaadaev, on Thursdays that of his old master Pavlov, on Fridays the salon of the Sverbeevs, and on Sundays that of the Elagin's, the home-ground of the Slavophiles. [5]

With equal frequency, more intimate gatherings of the Westerners assembled at Herzen's house or at Granovski's. The latter was now one of the rising young lecturers at the university, and used his courses on history to preach discreetly Hegel, progress, and the inevitable Westernization — and hence liberalization — of Russia. Through Granovski Herzen became acquainted with other liberal Hegelians from the university: P. G. Redkin, professor of jurisprudence, his colleague K. D. Kavelin, and D. L. Kriukov, professor of ancient history, who died in the middle of the decade. Other close members of the circle were the editor of the city's principal newspaper, the *Moskovskie vedomosti*, E. F. Korsh, and the actor, M. S. Shchepkin, who had risen from serfdom to become the chief representative of the new "realism" on the stage. Then there were old friends from the university such as Ketcher, or from the circle of Stankevich such as Botkin, the close friend of Belinski. The latter also occasionally visited from Petersburg, as did Panaev; the gentleman-journalist and European traveler, Annenkov, and of course Ogarev, came as well whenever they were in Russia. [6] It is noteworthy that the Westerners were from diverse social backgrounds and that all were engaged in the liberal professions, especially the university and journalism. The Slavophiles, on the other hand, were exclusively from the landed gentry and were actively concerned with the management of their estates. As will become clear below, this difference of background was certainly related to differences of politics and ideology between the two groups.

At gatherings of the Westerners the intellectual debate was punctuated by copious repasts and libations of all sorts of liquors, of which the favorite seems to have been champagne, especially when Herzen made the choice. The life of the group was a feast of friendship no less than of ideas, in a more adult version of the atmosphere of Herzen's university circle. Often the gatherings did not break up until the small hours of the morning. Summers in the country, where the friends repaired as a group to adjacent *dachas,* were the same: discussion, fraternity, food, drink — all in immoderate quantities. Indeed, alcohol seems to have become an indispensable fuel for Herzen's ebullient activity, for his activity appears almost unnaturally frenetic. A contemporary portrays him arguing far into the night, then walking the streets in agitation until morning, when he would return brimming with energy for the new day in spite of the fact that he had not slept — and it seems this was not an infrequent occurrence. In his conversations in the salons he preferred to talk standing or pacing as if to consume his energy physically as well as intellectually.[7] In all this there was a certain febrility, as though Herzen were trying to make up for the lost years of exile, or as if he were reaching out for some fulfillment he could not grasp. Nevertheless, in spite of this underlying tension, he had a more nearly satisfying life during these five years in Moscow than at any time since the university.

The moment was, on the whole, propitious for the exercise of his new cult of "action." The forties were, relatively, the most liberal period of the reign of Nicholas; the regime had at last recovered from the panic occasioned by 1825 and 1830 and had not yet succumbed to the even greater panic of 1848. There was, of course, no question of open political debate, but indirect discussion through the medium of literature or philosophy was freer than at any time since the beginning of the reign. The various currents of opinion which had begun to emerge toward the end of the thirties, at the time of Herzen's first return to Moscow, now came out into the open. The hitherto more or less united front of Russian idealism had at last differentiated into opposed political tendencies: by 1842 "realistic" Hegelians and "romantic" Schellingians had become Westerners and Slavophiles. Moreover, each group had its periodical to carry the debate, albeit in muffled form, before the public: the *Annals of the Fatherland* for the former and the newly founded *Moscovite* (*Moskvitianin*) for the latter.

It is true that neither journal reflected the debate as well as the contending parties might have wished. The *Annals* was a commercial publication which printed cryptoradical literature only because it sold well with the public, and Herzen, Granovski and Belinski made unsuccessful efforts to secure permission for a publication which would really be their own.[8] On the other hand, the *Moscovite* was controlled by Pogodin, professor of Russian history at the University of Moscow, and his colleague Shevyrev, a literary historian, both of whom stood nearer to the government than did the Slavophiles properly speaking. The latter, like the Westerners, tried several times unsuccessfully to obtain permission for a publication of their own. Only failing this did they fall back on the *Moscovite*, which freely opened its columns to them, since it fully shared their aversion to the West.

Indeed it was the menace of Western liberal thought that had called the *Moscovite* into being. It had been authorized by Nicholas as a special favor to the arch-loyalists Pogodin and Shevyrev as early as 1837, but its editors were moved to begin publication only in 1840 when they were challenged within the university by such Westernizing Hegelians as Granovski, Kriukov and Redkin, and outside it by the appearance in 1839 of the *Annals*.[9] With the founding of the *Moscovite* the polarization of Russian idealism into two hostile camps was completed. By the time of Herzen's return to Moscow it had developed into a lively polemic conducted in print and no longer just in the salons or the halls of the university. The stage was set for the showdown of tendencies which the decade soon produced. In fact, this was the first expression in Russian history of the division of public opinion into something that could be called parties, not of course in an organizational sense, but in an ideological one.

2

Unfortunately, understanding of the issues dividing the two groups has been somewhat obscured by the terms Slavophile and Westerner. On the basis of these labels it is too often assumed that the former were the real nationalists of the day, while the latter were internationalists, antinationalists, or in some way not authentically Russian. Yet the national question was only one of the issues involved, even if a major one. Moreover, as we shall see, devotion to Russia was among the principal traits the two groups had in common. Nor was "Westerner" a title which the group itself chose. The Slavophiles, after assuming so patriotic an epithet for themselves in order to imply a monopoly of the true national spirit, then tagged their enemies "Westerners" to suggest a foreign and unnatural origin. Originally "Westerner" was a "smear" term, which was only eventually taken up by its addressees in a gesture of defiance.[10] Its persistence in historical literature is unfortunate because it implies a conflict between civilizations — which was the Slavophiles' view of the matter — whereas in reality the conflict was between two groups which were equally indigenous to Russia. The concepts of Russia and the West as used by the two sides are simply transpositions into the "historiosophical" language of the day, common to both groups, of a whole series of issues —

philosophical, social, and political — in addition to the more obvious national one. Therefore, since the subject is complex as well as frequently misrepresented, it is necessary to preface Herzen's relation to these debates with a digression on the kindred problems of Slavophilism and Russian nationalism.

As has already been pointed out,[11] the opposition between Westerners and Slavophiles was first expressed, at the end of the thirties, not so much as a question of nationalism as one of religion. The Slavophiles believed in the revealed religion of the church (and accessorily in Schelling's defense of it), while the Westerners, such as Granovski throughout his career, Belinski in his Hegelian phase, and Herzen in Vladimir, believed in the "rational" religion of German "science." At the same time, provoked by Chaadaev's glorification of Western Catholicism and his denigration of Byzantine Orthodoxy, the Slavophiles associated irreligion and rationalism with the West and true faith with Russia. Finally, there was implicit in this dichotomy from the beginning the notion that Western rationalism meant revolution, whereas Holy Russia signified an orderly "organic" development.

By 1842 the differences between the groups had deepened. First, Herzen in his *Dilettantism in Science,* and then Belinski, in his break with Hegel, had gone beyond "rational" religion to outright atheism; what is more, both were growing increasingly eloquent in praise of "socialism" and "*sotsialnost.*" All of this only heightened the Slavophiles' alarm, and led them to ever more violent attacks on the West and more extravagant idealization of Russia. In return, this glorification of godly Russia brought the Westerners to associate progress, freedom, and the life of reason more and more closely with Europe and to identify obscurantism and reaction with Russia. By 1842 the debate between the two groups was becoming increasingly political, which under the conditions of the day meant historical.

Associated with the Slavophiles' rejection of rationalism was their rejection of all Western influence since Peter, cultural, social, and institutional; conversely the Westerners felt compelled to defend Peter's reforms and most of what stemmed from them. But behind the historical issue of Peter's reforms lay more contemporary political concerns. The Slavophiles' rejection of Peter and rationalism signified also rejection of the West's "atomistic individualism," by which they meant political liberalism; of Western "legalism" and "abstract logic," by which they understood a written constitution and formal guarantees for the individual; and of violent "inorganic" breaks with "national tradition" of the sort perpetrated by Peter, by which they meant radical reform or, still worse, revolution. By the same token the Westerners' espousal of reason, Peter, the West, and individualism, signified liberalism, a constitution, legal guarantees of civil liberties and, eventually at least, democracy. Both the philosophical opposition between rationalism and religion and the nationalistic opposition between Europe and Russia meant an opposition between liberals and conservatives, translated into metaphysics and the alienated "historiosophical" terms of the day. As discontent with the reaction of Nicholas grew and as the necessity of change became more apparent, the two groups took positions on how much change there should be and of what sort. In this differentiation of attitudes toward politics the Slavophiles were the "Right," just as they had been in metaphysics, while the Westerners were the "Left." [12]

Nevertheless, the "Slavs" or Slavophiles, as they were variously called during the forties, did not form a homogeneous group. Contemporaries were aware that there was a difference between on the one hand Pogodin and Shevyrev and on the other Khomiakov, the Kireevski brothers, the Aksakovs, and Samarin — the latter being the Slavophiles proper in the subsequent usage of the term. The literature of the day, however, does not convey any more precise sense of this difference than the impression that Pogodin and Shevyrev were somehow nastier people or poorer stylists than the others, together with the more important fact that they were looked upon with greater favor by the government.[13]

In retrospect, however, it is possible to establish a clearer ideological difference between the two types of "Slavs." First of all, Pogodin and Shevyrev accepted Uvarov's famous trilogy of "Official Nationality" — Orthodoxy, Autocracy, Nationality — basically as it stood. More precisely, like the government, they placed special emphasis on the second term, autocracy. Ideologically this meant that they had an immense reverence for Peter the Great and his reforms, which, moreover, they considered eminently national, a view that obviously struck at the heart of the position of the Slavophiles proper.[14] For in the "historiosophical" thought of the day Peter was not only a symbol of Westernization, and hence ultimately of enlightenment and liberalization, but at the same time — paradoxically if also aptly — a symbol of integral autocracy. More particularly, he was a symbol of Nicholas and his policy of strong personal monarchy ruling through an omnicompetent bureaucracy. The emperor had been suspicious of the first estate ever since the "betrayal" of the Decembrists, and his policies were devised in no small measure to limit the *de facto* independence it had acquired under Catherine and during the early years of Alexander. The coupling of Peter and the idea of nationality, then, meant pure bureaucratic autocracy and the total exclusion of the population, even of the most privileged class, from any voice in government. In the shadow-politics under Nicholas, this position, because it meant unconditional defense of the status quo, represented the extreme Right, and intellectual Moscow was quite correct in sensing there was something unsavory about the masters of the *Moscovite,* and still more about the Petersburg journalists Bulgarin, Grech, and Senkovski.

On the other hand, the Slavophiles proper, though generally within the conservative camp, were by no means unconditional supporters of the existing state of affairs.[15] As independent-minded representatives of the gentry they were quite unhappy with the bureaucratic autocracy of Nicholas. They wished instead some measure of participation by "society" in government, at least down to their level if not much beyond. In terms of the terminology just adopted, an appropriate label for them is "Right Center"; more aptly still, within the context of the terminology set by Uvarov, the Slavophiles placed both Orthodoxy and nationality higher than autocracy and gave to all three terms, but especially to the first two, a different and richer meaning than did the regime.

The loosely conservative implications of Orthodoxy as a slogan have already been mentioned; the manner in which the Slavophiles proper assigned pre-eminence to Orthodoxy over autocracy held certain radical potentialities as well. The primacy of religious values meant the primacy of conscience, and hence of human dignity and individual integrity, over unlimited state power. Nicholas quite rightly sensed a significant difference between the Slavophiles and such idolaters of autocracy as Pogodin. There was a cryptohumanism in Slavophilism, as there is in all serious religion, whereas Pogodin's Orthodoxy stood much more unequivocally for the traditional conservative principle that the altar should support the throne in order to secure order and authority.

Even more subversive was the Slavophiles' concept of "nationality," or *narodnost.* In the usage of the day this slippery notion could signify at least two contradictory things. The word itself was of recent coinage, an abstraction based on the word *narod,* people or nation, a term which has roughly the multiplicity of meanings of the German *Volk.* For the government and its apologists, who invented the term, *narodnost* meant primarily "that which is national," in the sense of the distinctive historic institutions of the Russian state, of which the most sacred was autocracy but of which serfdom was by no means the least, even if it could not be extolled so openly as the monarchy. In the Slavophiles' appropriation of the term, on the other hand, *narodnost* meant primarily "that which is of the nation as a whole," a concept which tended to set the people apart from the government. It meant also "that which is of the masses," since the peasants were the only class in Russia which was thoroughly "national" in the sense that they remained undefiled by the Westernization which since Peter had corrupted their masters: they were the only class which still adhered to the pure Orthodoxy of their fathers and the native tradition of old Moscovy. Hence the Slavophiles were in a sense "populists" (*narodniki*), a term which did not yet exist in Russian, but which, when it would come into existence some thirty years later, would be formed from the same root as the conservatives' *narodnost*. Like Herzen, though in a more indirect manner, the Slavophiles had generalized a gentry-bred opposition to autocracy and a sense of their own dignity as individuals into an approximation of democracy. In attacking Westernization, which was an attribute of their own class, and in idealizing the "nativism" of the masses, they were undermining with one hand what they sought to defend with the other.

In spite of such ideological paradoxes, however, as a practical matter the Slavophiles remained well-integrated members of their class, unlike such rootless professors of history or jurisprudence as Granovski and Kavelin, or such plebeian or illegitimate-gentry journalists as Belinski and Herzen, who made up the camp of the Westerners. Thus their feeling for the people did not go beyond what is best termed a paternalistic populism. Concretely, this meant that they desired the emancipation of the serfs, in part because they considered bondage a humiliation for the Orthodox people, but also because they felt that in the nineteenth century serfdom was both politically dangerous and economically unsound. At the same time they did not forget that they were owners of profitable estates, and hence they wished only a reasonable minimum of land settled on the peasants and compensation to the gentry for what was lost, whereas Westerners such as Herzen and Belinski vaguely favored a much more liberal settlement for the peasants. Furthermore, the Slavophiles desired to preserve the patriarchal arrangements existing in the countryside, which meant the peasant commune, or *obshchina*. In this, too, they had mixed motives. The fraternal, charitable sharing of the commune exemplified both the national and the Orthodox virtues of Russia and thereby demonstrated her superiority over the egoistic, divided West. At the same time preservation of the commune would maintain the peasants in practical dependence on the gentry even after emancipation: order and a proper hierarchy would be safeguarded in the midst of progress toward a better Russia.[16] When the smoke of their "historiosophy" is cleared away the Slavophiles emerge as something like a Russian version of enlightened Tories. It is not an accident that, much as they detested revolutionary France and "scientific" Germany, they admired traditionalistic, "organic" England, in spite of her misguided Protestantism.

The social program of the Slavophiles, then, presented prudent openings toward the liberalization of Russian society; their political program was rather more cautious. Briefly, they desired a vague arrangement somewhere between autocracy and a constitutional monarchy. A real constitution with a legislative parliament they held in abhorrence as a rationalistic Western invention. They went further still and maintained that state power as such was an evil, necessitated only by man's fallen condition and something in which God's people, the Russians, did not wish to share, as did the corrupt Christians of the West with their pagan Roman notions of contractual rights and obligations. The only truly Christian society was one based on a community of faith and love, and Russia was the one nation which met this definition. Since, however, Russia was isolated in a corrupt Europe, a strong state power was necessary for protection. Thus, since evil there must be, even in Holy Russia, God had at least limited its scope by granting all power to one person, the tsar, whom He fortified with special graces to resist its corrupting effects.[17]

In spite of the painful necessity of such an arrangement, however, the tsar should have the Christian magnanimity to listen to his Orthodox charges; he should govern, not by coercion, but in harmonious cooperation with the people, who were somehow considered as always unanimous in their desires. This was the Slavophiles' famous notion of the *"sobornost"* of Orthodox Russia, a word usually translated as "conciliarity," and which means roughly a divinely inspired, charitable consensus of the Orthodox community that is at the same time the natural, fraternal consensus of the Russian people.[18] As this heterogeneous choice of terms indicates, the concept falls somewhere between Rousseau's "general will" and a romanticized version of the Eastern Church's dogma of the Holy Spirit's inspiring the seven Ecumenical Councils to a unanimous conclusion. The Slavophiles were influenced by both traditions, and, whatever the ambiguities of their terminology, the import of their message was to run a nationalistic-traditionalistic line and a pseudo-democratic one at the same time. The purpose of this was to fall somewhere — and to fall safely — between the inflexibility of Imperial reaction and the impetuosity of Western-minded reformers.

Concretely, *"sobornost"* meant that "society" should have complete liberty of opinion, and for this freedom of speech, of the press, and of conscience were necessary. Moreover, there should be a consultative assembly — but not a legislative parliament — called by the old Moscovite name of *Zemski sobor,* or "Assembly of All the Land," to express society's opinion to the tsar. In effect, the autocracy would be limited, not by a formal constitution, but by its own good will and the prayers of public opinion. In other words, politics would be the exclusive prerogative of the government, which in turn would refrain from interfering in the "inner life" of its subjects. By this judicious division of functions the Slavophiles hoped both to preserve Russia from division into those selfish parties which in the West led to civil dissension and at the same time to safeguard the rights of the individual. They hoped, furthermore, that these arrangements would eliminate the "German" bureaucracy which since Peter, but particularly under Nicholas, had tended to interpose itself between tsar and people.[19]

Altogether the Slavophiles occupied a strangely equivocal position. They wished some limitation of autocracy and recognition of the rights of society, yet they refused the only effective application of this program — legal guarantees against absolute power — for fear of opening the door to men more reckless than themselves and hence of undermining their own privileged position. They wished to be an opposition party and at the same time to avoid either a second Decembrist revolt or, still worse, another Pugachev uprising, either of which, they feared, might occur if a new revolution broke out in France, in which the Poles would certainly join and thereby perhaps bring a new Franco-Polish Jacobin army to Russian soil, as in 1812. The Slavophiles' fear of the West, and of Westernized radicals within Russia, was not at all groundless, but was founded on the sound historical precedents of the years 1812, 1825 and 1830. Thus, the Slavophiles represent a rather typical aristocratic opposition to absolute monarchy, made cautious, and indeed panicky, by recent experience of revolution. They were both an opposition *and* a reaction — obviously a difficult position. Therefore, to resolve their dilemma, they fell back on the twin fictions of absolutism limited by good intentions and of the natural unanimity of all "true" Russians, or "*sobornost*," as means for achieving discreet participation of society in government without the extremity of a constitution. As a final paradox, this political program was to be realized by the renunciation of politics, since the myth of unanimity and the condemnation of the state as evil meant a refusal to face the realities of power. In this respect Slavophilism has affinities with anarchism, which also rejects the state and politics. It also has affinities with the more utopian forms of socialism, since it maintains that not political forms but social reality (the commune) and the spirit of man are important. Thus, again, the Slavophiles inadvertently supplied ammunition to the radical forces they sought to contain.

In large part because of these contradictions, the Slavophiles expressed their program not so much directly as through a historical mythology about seventeenth-century Moscovy — the "real" Russia — when, they imagined, all those paternalistic relations which they desired had, in fact, existed. At the same time they voiced their opposition both to autocracy and to Western liberalism by castigation of Peter, who, they held, had destroyed the natural Russian harmony between tsar and people and established an absolutism founded on coercion after the European manner. Indeed, the Slavophiles even tended, rather incongruously, to blame serfdom on the baleful influence of Peter and the West. Therefore, in their eyes, the way to a better future for Russia lay in a return to her authentic past rather than in further "unnatural" imitation of the foreigner.

Not only did the Slavophiles declare this to be the only solution for Russia; they held it might also mean salvation for the whole civilized world. As the frightful convulsions which had shaken Europe since 1789 demonstrated, the West was "rotten" or "dying." Turning Chaadaev on his head, the Slavophiles maintained that the seeds of this decline had been sown when the Latin Church, in its Imperial Roman pride, without so much as breathing a word to the East, had unilaterally added the *filioque* and thereby broken the "conciliar" communion of original Christianity. (The Slavophiles were immensely hurt that Europe had not considered Russia important enough to be consulted on common matters either then or since.) From this breach it followed that schism and violence were the principles of the West, although some men mistook Europe's convulsions for movement and progress. Obversely, unity and love were the principles of the East, which alone continued the original Christian community, although some might confuse the serene contemplation of Orthodoxy with stagnation. The initial schism caused by Catholic rationalism and legalism led to the further schism of Protestant individualism, which in turn led to the still more disruptive schisms of the Enlightenment and the Revolution. In the present time the Western principle of disunity had at last borne its full harvest of evil fruit in German "science" and French socialism, which meant that the cycle of European development was completed and that the next word of history belonged to the hitherto silent East, which was still "young" with all the "virgin" forces of its neglected Orthodoxy.

With respect to "science" the Slavophiles shared the Westerners' opinion that Hegel represented the culmination of purely human wisdom, yet they concluded from this not that the millennium of a "rational" world was about to dawn, but that Western philosophy had reached the end of its rope. For Hegel had not accomplished his purpose, which was to establish the truth of Christianity "rationally." Instead, he had transformed religion into a naturalistic pantheism of which the logical conclusion was atheism, as the case of Herzen demonstrated. In this dilemma the only solution for civilization was pure faith, which Russia alone possessed. At the same time, French radicalism had run into a similar blind-alley. The only result of all the upheavals since 1789 was that Europe was menaced by anarchy, while the liberty, equality, and fraternity she sought eluded her more than ever. The measure of Europe's frustration in her efforts to recover her lost "conciliar" harmony was the emergence of the desperate ideal of socialism, the ultimate in rationalistic utopias. Here again Russia already possessed what Europe was vainly striving to achieve, for she had the fraternal principle of *sobornost* and particularly the peasant commune. Furthermore, Russia's preservation of the one true faith was the cause of her preservation of the one truly Christian social system. Thus, by regaining her pristine Orthodoxy and "nationality," Russia in the future would create a civilization far more glorious than any that ever existed in the West; at the same time, she would work the salvation of "old," "dying" Europe. Slavophilism culminated in a grandiose religious-nationalistic messianism, in which the last of civilized nations became the first, and the most humiliated of peoples the most exalted.

3

This messianism brings us finally to the national question *per se*. Thus far in this book much has been said about the alienations suffered by sensitive individuals in a society that failed to provide adequate scope for their energies; little has been said about the frustrations these same individuals experienced in their relations with other cultural groups. Yet, if it was difficult to be a "human being" in Nicholas' Russia, it was almost as difficult to be a Russian, and still hold one's head high, in the community of the civilized nations of Europe. Sooner or later all cultivated Russians were driven to agonies of introspection over the question of their "nationality" no less than of their "individuality." Who were they, not just as manifestations of the universal idea of Man, but as Russians? What was their collective, national destiny in the barbarous land where history had placed them?

It was the Slavophiles who first dramatized these questions. The reason why this was so has already been suggested: it suited their conservative politics to draw a sharp dichotomy between Russia and the West and thereby to make the national question the primordial issue of Russian thought. Moreover, since their politics were Right Center rather than extreme Right, they were driven to develop their nationalism with an intellectual richness and semi-populist overtones capable of appealing to independent minds outside their own camp, a quality which was lacking in the cruder conservatism of Official Nationality. Most of their doctrines have been set forth above; the task of the present section will be to examine the psychology which lay behind them.

Before proceeding to this, however, a word must be said about the basic elements of the problem of nationalism in general.[20] Nor is this a superfluous enterprise, since in so much writing on Russian nationalism the elementary — or what ought to be the elementary —is passed over in favor of such spectacular but misleading metaphysical notions as "innate" national character, immutable "Eastern" destiny, or some similarly disguised form of the "Russian soul" — all of which, incidentally, were originally Slavophile inventions. In particular, the subject of Russian messianism, from the slogan of "Moscow the Third Rome" to the Third International, has been grossly mishandled. So often has this been presented as a monstrously unique aberration of the Russian character that something must be done here to reduce it to human proportions by situating it in a comparative psychology of European nationalism. All of this, more-over, is most pertinent to the understanding of Herzen since, after the Slavophiles, he became the most exuberant and imaginative messianic nationalist that Russia produced in the first half of the nineteenth century.

In a general way it may be said that all men of pride and talent wish that the social, cultural or national community to which they chance to belong should be intrinsically worth belonging to. Men wish to feel that they would have chosen their community if they had not happened to be born into it. This in turn means that their group should in some way be seen as pre-eminent over other communities of which they are aware and, more often than not, with which they are in competition. This desire springs from the same wish for self-fulfillment which animates men as members of social groups within their national community, or as indi-viduals within their class. For no one realizes himself in a vacuum; all men realize themselves only through some group, and usually through several at once, of which they have need both as a context of action and as an audience dispensing approval and glory. If the group to which they belong is in some way inferior or humiliated, acute tensions result which lead to dramatic soul-searching about the group's "deeper" meaning.

In modern, secular societies — at least since the eighteenth century — the most important of these groups is the national community. The nation provides the most all-encompassing context of institutions through which individuals or sub-groups, such as social classes or political parties, must realize themselves. It is the strength of the national state, moreover, which determines whether or not the individuals and sub-groups that live under its protection will preserve an independent context of institutions in which to act. Finally, it is the nation which furnishes the language and cultural tradition peculiar to its members and to them alone (as opposed to older and more universal frames of reference such as Christianity or classical humanism) which are the indispensable vehicles for the expression of the community's higher aspirations, its inner richness and creativity — in short, for the articulation of what its members, in their deeper essence, *are*.

Of the more important nations of Europe at the beginning of the nine-teenth century only England and France present what might be called, inverting Hegel's terminology, a "happy" national consciousness. Their internal institutions provided an adequate arena for the ambitious, or at least for those talented enough to cause trouble if they were excluded. Moreover, in England when the excluded became too numerous or rest-less for safety, the problem could be met by timely reform, which made all concerned more satisfied than before about being English. In France the same result could be achieved by an exhilarating revolution, not only for *la patrie* but for the whole of mankind, which made all but a few losers feel an increased gratification at being French. At the same time, in both countries the armature of the state was of such venerable antiquity and manifest solidity that everyone took its permanence for granted. Furthermore, the level of national success was so high in both countries that any defeat could be viewed as only a temporary setback; or, in the case of France after 1815, the brilliance of the performance preceding defeat was so remarkable that national pride was swelled rather than chastened by the whole experience. Finally, in both countries the national, secular culture, going back to the sixteenth century, was of such universally recognized excellence as to be a model for lesser nations. Consequently, neither people expended great energy worrying about "who they were"; each nation knew very well it was the first in Europe, and a beacon to all mankind. Thus, though there was plenty of nationalism in both places, there was no elaborate nationalistic ideology; in particular there was no metaphysical messianism. Instead there was simply a quiet arrogance, which at bottom was rather civilized and capable of fairly disinterested assistance, or at least of real sympathy, toward oppressed Poles, Greeks or Italians.

Almost everywhere else in Europe, however, early-nineteenth-century nationalism in one way or another was an "unhappy" consciousness, and messianism of some sort resulted. The Italians and the Poles, though they possessed distinctive cultures, lacked a state and hence a context of institutions which was their own. Consequently, the frustrated national consciousness found consolation in viewing its very martyrdom as a source of superior virtue: for both Mazzini and Mickiewicz the lost homeland became the "Christ among nations" which by its sufferings would redeem the world.

In Germany there were independent states (indeed there were too many of them), but no one national state; hence, there was the permanent frustration of national dismemberment, to which was added that of foreign conquest during the short but crucial period under Napoleon. At the same time, all but military and bureaucratic personnel were excluded from a role in most of those states which did exist. Thus, as has already been explained at length, the higher energies of the professional classes could find expression only in the creation of an extraordinarily introspective culture, particularly after 1770. The national idea came to be associated with intellectual superiority: Germany was the mind or soul of the European body, of which other peoples, particularly the successful French and British, were the more vulgar, material members. German messianism was the professorial illusion that the life of the Absolute culminated in the national academic mind and therefore that lack of a national state did not count. But in Germany matters were more complex than elsewhere. In addition to this cultural *Deutschtum*, there existed a state-centered nationalism as well, particularly in Prussia, provoked when the *parvenu* creation of Frederick the Great was almost wiped out by the French after 1806. This new sentiment, however, soon tended to fuse with the old, even obtaining the personal services of such stellar ideologists as Fichte and Hegel.

In spite of important differences of emphasis, however, in all these cases of an "unhappy" national consciousness the underlying psychological mechanism is the same. Whatever was most cruelly lacking in the national existence was rationalized as unimportant, or even construed as a virtue, while those elements of positive achievement which did exist were exalted to the rank of the first principle of life. Nonetheless, since a sense of deficiency resisted these rationalizations, the existing national virtues were also viewed as potentialities which would bear their full fruits only in the future, when they would bring unheard-of benefits, not just to the nation in question but to all mankind. In other words, nationalistic messianism was an ideology of compensation and as such psychologically related to philosophical idealism, which was why, in Germany, Poland and Russia, nationalism was so often associated with idealism.

Russia, unlike the countries of Central Europe, and like France and England, possessed a satisfactory national state, that is, all-encompassing, mighty, and venerable. But the modern, secular culture was weak, and those institutions providing participation for the ambitious in the higher life of the nation — the military or bureaucratic arms of the autocracy — were rudimentary. As we have seen, this situation was satisfactory so long as the only class capable of ambition, the gentry, remained relatively unsophisticated, that is roughly until 1812; thus they could find full satisfaction for their group or national pride in waging the glorious campaigns of Peter, Catherine, and Alexander, since war and "service" were almost all they understood. At the same time, for what secular culture they needed they went to school to France and Germany without any deep feeling of humiliation, since culture was not the center of their values. This comfortable equilibrium, however, broke down under Alexander I.

First of all, for a nation which had known only victories since Peter there was the immense shock of defeat in the war of 1805–07, followed by a humiliating alliance with the victor. Then came the mortal struggle of 1812, capped by the most extraordinary Russian triumph in history — defeat of Europe's greatest captain at the head of her greatest army and the final victorious march over the whole continent to Paris. This dizzy descent into the abyss and the even dizzier extrication made the Russian gentry aware, with a new acuity, of what they represented as a national group.

Simultaneously, the gentry came into contact with a more highly developed national consciousness in Germany and France, and much of what they learned thereby they were forced to adopt, if only in self-defense. In short, the Russian experience in these years was analogous to the Prussian experience of 1806–14, and the result was also similar. After 1812 there was an outburst of chauvinism among the previously cosmopolitan Russian gentry, which, following on the further red, "Western" menaces of 1825 and 1830, culminated in the Official Nationality of Nicholas. This nationalism, however, as its name implies, was fully compatible with ambitions limited to service in the existing institutions of the state, the army and the bureaucracy.

More interesting than this is the nationalism of the opposition. As has already been indicated, the unreflecting good conscience of the gentry began to disintegrate under Alexander I, giving place to a sense of "humanity" and "individuality," at least among the young, who found it increasingly impossible to accept the institutions of what looked more and more like a barbarous military autocracy. But these men — the Decembrists, the idealists of the thirties, the Westerners and the Slavophiles of the forties — were also very much members of the gentry. Like the conservative nationalists, they too had vibrated, either at the time or later, to all the emotions of 1805–1814 (we have seen how clear this was in the case of Herzen); they too wished the group to which they belonged to be pre-eminent. Yet the rationalizations of the state for the superiority of its institutions appeared to them, as free men, to be no more than an apologia for the slavery of autocracy and serfdom. At the same time, as civilized gentlemen, they tended increasingly to exalt culture over the grosser forms of national achievement.

Indeed, after 1825 culture became the crux of the problem of nationalism for the opposition gentry. Since they were alienated from the state there remained only culture to bear the burden of both "nationality" and "individuality." But the frightful fact was that Russia possessed no modern culture of her own; for "enlightenment" she was a mere dependency of France and Germany. Around 1840 the Russians stood roughly in the same relationship to Europe as the Germans stood to France around 1770, and the psychology of the Russian cultural nationalist is very similar to that of his German counterpart. The situation of the Russians, however, was far more desperate than that of the Germans had been. The latter, to become "themselves," had only to cast off (or in Hegelian language "negate") the cultural tutelage of the French. The Russians had to "overcome" the cultural tutelage of the whole of Europe; moreover, they had to do this at a later and more complex stage of European development. Finally, the Russians had to establish their identity following the Napoleonic impact and in an age of exacerbated national consciousness everywhere, whereas the Germans had begun to stake out their claim in the cosmopolitan calm of the eighteenth century, so that when the shock of defeat at Jena hit them, the intellectuals, at least, had something else than the state to fall back on. Hegel, taking his *Phenomenology* to press in Jena in 1806, could serenely assess the world conqueror as the *"Weltgeist* on horseback," because he *understood* whereas Napoleon only *did,* and then get on with his proofs. But the Russian intellectuals could not afford to take Napoleon, or German "science," or anything else that menaced their national identity, so calmly, because they had nothing to fall back on, neither a tolerable state nor a distinctive culture.

The situation only grew worse with time. The Decembrists, in the enthusiasm of inexperience, had believed that by a simple *coup d'état* their "fatherland" would overnight realize the promises of the national and "popular" year of 1812, and become even more glorious than the civilized fatherlands they had observed in France and Germany. But when barbarism was officially sanctified by Nicholas, this hope gave way to despair. By 1836 Chaadaev, provoked beyond endurance by the government's nationalistic bragging, proclaimed that Russia had no past, present, or future, that the national destiny was unrelieved barbarism for all eternity, because Russia by the essence of her culture, Byzantine Orthodoxy, was cut off from the unique source of civilization, Western Catholicism. It was far more difficult to be both a "humanist" *and* a nationalist for the Russians than for any other people of Europe, even the humiliated Italians and Poles. The Poles, and especially the Italians, at least possessed an unmistakable culture, and both had the consolation of being able to blame their national failure on the wickedness of their neighbors as much as on their own deficiencies. In all Europe there was no more profound note of national despair than that sounded by Chaadaev.

But could this be the final answer to the question of what it meant to be a Russian? Obviously not, for such total despair was intolerable. It *must* be possible to be both a "human being" and a Russian; it *must* be possible, in spite of the past and the present, to believe at least in the "future of Russia." It was the Slavophiles who first gave a plausible set of answers to these questions. Herzen, when his turn came, would do little more than reshuffle the pack of ideas originally dealt by his opponents.

The Slavophiles, first of all, introduced a useful distinction between people and government and made these antithetical principles correspond to a "true" and a "false" national past. Concretely, the Slavophiles vindicated the mission of the pre-Petrine state in uniting and protecting the Russian people, thereby securing the national identity against foreign pressure — for the nationalist, no matter how much he is in opposition, must be able to accept some portion of his nation's history. Moreover, the original "popular" character of the Russian state could be restored by purging it of what scandalized free men under Nicholas — the "foreign" Petrine innovations of military autocracy, bureaucracy, and serfdom.

Thus, what was most wrong with Russia in the present was not even Russian at all, and hence nothing a Russian need be ashamed of. In one version or another this scheme could obviously serve "populist" purposes more radical than those of the Slavophiles.

Secondly, the Slavophiles discovered, also in the "true" Russian past, a set of authentically popular institutions which would enable any Russian to hold his head high before the "free" West. For was not the real Russian tradition paternal monarchy founded on fraternal community? Their paternal monarchy would appeal to no one but themselves, but the institutions of fraternal community — *sobornost,* the *Zemski sobor,* and above all the peasant commune — were something for free spirits of whatever camp to conjure with: were they not the pledge of the past that in the future the Russian people would find a humane, democratic home within their state?

Finally, and again in the past, the Slavophiles discovered a national culture which far surpassed that of any Western nation. It was quite true, they admitted, that Russia did not possess a humanistic, rational culture on the model of the West, but she had something which was much better: true faith and all the moral qualities which derived from this — brotherly love, humility, generosity, courage, and a holy simplicity. Thus, though Russia might look culturally poor to someone with corrupted Western vision, *in reality* she was immensely rich. The first item of this culture, Orthodoxy, obviously could not appeal beyond the circle of the Slavophiles themselves. The moral virtues which stemmed from it, however, if secularized as a sense of social community, a daring intrepidity in action (*udal*), a "broad nature," or lack of Western "bourgeois philistinism," offered interesting possibilities indeed for believing in the "hidden" forces of the Russian people. Equally alluring could be the notion that, precisely because Russian culture had achieved little in the past, there were no obstacles to grandiose creativity in the future, of which "old" nations "encumbered" by a long tradition were no longer capable.

In this confused set of rationalizations it is clear that there was far more self-delusion than reality. In the case of the English and the French, their more or less liberal institutions, their reforms, their revolutions, and their culture were all real if also idealized. With the Germans, the Italians, and the Poles reality gave way progressively to myth. With the Slavophiles an enormous ideological structure rested on nothing more substantial (if one leaves aside the question of religion) than the poor peasant commune and certain apolitical traits in the national character, which, however, derived less from Orthodoxy than from the fact that under an autocracy it is by definition impossible for the public to acquire any experience of, or sense for, politics. Yet there was something more real than these wisps in the Slavophile position. Paradoxically what was most real in their ideas was what was most abstract, not in the intellectual German manner, but in the ethical and voluntaristic Russian one. This reality was the act of faith that there was *something* in the Russian people that made it worthwhile for their enormous but enslaved country to exist, an act of faith that by its sheer intensity supplied a measure of the very *something* which was sought.

It was on such an act of faith, or will, that the strength of the Russian intelligentsia, a strength which was moral far more than material, would be built throughout the nineteenth century. Westerners such as Belinski and Herzen later made this same act of faith, and no less intensely than did the Slavophiles. But the latter were the first to articulate it, at a time when the Westerners either despaired or could give no concrete reason why they hoped, when Chaadaev cursed Russia, when Belinski and Bakunin were "reconciled with reality," and Herzen, in Vladimir and Novgorod, thought that "regeneration" could come only from France or Germany. In this way the Slavophiles were the catalysts — though not of course the cause — of a chain-reaction of acts of faith about the "future of Russia" among the Moscow intellectuals which, as the "remarkable decade" unfolded, at last launched the Russian intelligentsia unmistakably on its way.

To this it should be added that in the same decade the modern national culture, until then so cruelly lacking, at last made its appearance in the form of a literature that was both great and uniquely Russian. In fact, the movement went back to Pushkin's first major work in 1820 and to his *Eugene Onegin* and Griboedov's *Woe from Wit* in 1825. The implications of this, however, were not immediately apparent. Belinski had begun his career in 1834, in his *Literary Reveries*, by asking the great question common to both Westerners and Slavophiles — who are we? — and had answered sadly that Russian civilization was still an enigma, since, even though Pushkin was a great and encouraging sign, he was one man and not a culture. Even by 1840 the movement of literary humanism was no more than twenty years old, and contemporaries were still not aware of its existence as a tradition. The turning point in their awareness came sometime early in the new decade. By 1842 there had not only been Pushkin; there had also been Lermontov and, most important of all, Gogol's *Dead Souls*, which bore the imprint of an unquestioned *narodnost*. For the Slavophiles, Pushkin had been somewhat tainted Western fruit, but they acclaimed Gogol as the very voice of the Russian soul and the proof of all their contentions. Belinski acclaimed his *narodnost*, if anything even more enthusiastically, and also asserted that the national cultural tradition did, at last, indubitably exist. By the decade's end the emergence of Turgenev and Dostoevski, indeed of the Westerners and Slavophiles themselves, would confirm the fact. The "consciousness" that

had produced Pushkin and the Decembrists was continuing, in spite of
Nicholas, to bear the fruits of an authentic "humanism." By the time of
Belinski's death and Herzen's emigration in 1847–48 the moral Russian-
ness first proclaimed by the Slavophiles was unmistakably assuming
modern, secular form. No, it was not folly to believe, with these slightly
ridiculous prophets in pseudo-Moscovite dress, the Slavophiles, that there
was *something* in the Russian people which would make everything
come out all right in the end!

4

The foregoing remarks have anticipated somewhat the development
of the Slavophiles' doctrine, as well as the psychology of Herzen's reaction
to it. As of 1842 the positions of Right and Left were by no means as distinct as they have been made above, and the contending factions were still
groping for solutions which only a decade of debates would clarify. The
general trend of these controversies has been indicated at this point
only to make clearer the import of the frequently obscure and fragmentary
evidence which it will be necessary to adduce in this and the following
chapters. At the outset of the forties, however, Westerners and Slavophiles
still thought they could cooperate to a point, for were they not both products of the same idealistic circles and devoted to a better Russia? Moreover, each side thought it could argue the other around to its point of
view, and as the decade began the two groups debated endlessly in the
salons, with a frankness they could display nowhere else, about God and
Hegel, Russia and the West, old Moscovy and Peter.

Soon, however, relations became strained.[21] In 1842 Belinski, who only
the year before had renounced his "reconciliation with reality," was moved
to make a characteristically impetuous declaration of his changed attitude; in the *Annals,* and in the most violent language the censorship would
allow, he attacked the *Moscovite* and the Slavophiles as the high priests of
his late conservative idols. The *Moscovite,* however, because of the nearness of its ideology to Official Nationality, could speak out more freely
than its rival. In answer to Belinski, Pogodin and Shevyrev made published remarks which the Westerners considered thinly veiled denunciations of their liberalism to Nicholas' police, who without such treacherous
help from intellectuals could hardly fathom the radical meaning of the
Annals' "Aesopian" pronouncements.

Then, after two years of muffled recriminations, in 1844 matters came
to a crisis. Granovski had just finished a series of public lectures on the
medieval history of the West, in which he quietly suggested his Hegelian
view of the rational progress of history toward freedom; in conclusion
he spoke with lyric accents of the "future of Russia," by which of course

he meant liberalization on the European model. The lectures, attended by all of intellectual Moscow, produced a tremendous impact; indeed, they were among the great events of the decade and one of the most noteworthy manifestations of the reawakening of public opinion which characterized the forties.[22] Even the Slavophiles were moved by Granovski's patriotic conclusion, which they chose to interpret in a "national" sense. In the midst of this euphoria a banquet was arranged to effect a reconciliation of the two parties. Although Belinski vituperated from Petersburg against such softness, Herzen mobilized his party for the feast, and the reconciliation was sealed in toasts and tears.

The peace, however, proved to be short-lived. Soon it was discovered that the "Moscovites" in the university were intriguing to secure the rejection of Granovski's doctoral thesis demonstrating that the legendary medieval Slavic city of Vineta had never existed. What is more important, by the end of 1844 the political denunciations of the *Moscovite* had resumed. Moreover, the Westerners were outraged by some privately-circulated verses of Iazykov, the brother-in-law of Khomiakov, accusing them of a "traitorous" lack of patriotism. The tension became such that Constantine Aksakov, on seeing Herzen in the street, stopped his sleigh to embrace him and to announce, weeping, that they would meet no more; even more melodramatically, Peter Kireevski and Granovski came to the verge of a duel. Matters, however, stopped short of this bloody extremity, and Westerners and Slavophiles simply ceased all personal relations.

Throughout these turmoils it was Belinski who in the eyes of the public at large was the most prominent figure among the Westerners, and the arch-enemy to the Slavophiles, since he had a monthly occasion to promote the cause of "humanism" before all Russia in the *Annals*. His private role was hardly less important, for in frequent and explosive letters he exhorted his Moscow friends to an ever greater intransigence toward the enemy. In Moscow itself, it was Granovski who was the most conspicuous figure, because of his role as lecturer in the university and before the public. Herzen enjoyed no comparable notoriety. To be sure, a part of his role was public, in the form of contributions to the *Annals*, most of which have been discussed in the two preceding chapters: his philosophical articles indirectly attacked the Slavophiles' religion while his fiction more openly criticized their gentry Russia. But the public on the whole found his Hegelian idiom abstruse, and his fiction enjoyed no more than a modest success.

Herzen's primary role in the controversies of the day was private. He was the most forceful personality among the Moscow Westerners and the best in-fighter in the uncensored debates of the salons. What is more important, although in manner and psychology Belinski was the most authentic democrat of the group, Herzen was intellectually the most radical as well as the most self-consciously political. Hence he was sensitive to populist potentialities in his opponents' position which his friends missed completely. With the other Westerners the relationship to the adverse camp was one of monolithic opposition; with Herzen it was a real dialogue. Fortunately much of what transpired has been preserved, at times almost day to day, in his *Diary*.

Until his return to Moscow Herzen had not been closely acquainted with the Slavophiles. He knew them chiefly as the advocates of an obscurantist return to religion and some reactionary nonsense about the good old times of Tsar Alexis Mikhailovich, all of which he had denounced in his recent essays on dilettantism. When he came to know his foes better, however, he discovered that their position was more complex than he thought. To be sure, Pogodin and Shevyrev confirmed his worst suspicions; accordingly, his hostility toward them was total from the beginning, and he satirized them in the *Annals* as scathingly as the censor would permit.[23] Yet it is significant that, unlike Belinski, these were the only "Slavs" against whom he ever raised a public pen. Toward the Slavophiles proper on the other hand, after an initial period of coolness, he displayed an ambivalence that often verged on softness, and that alarmed not only the "violent Vissarion" but also the more moderate Granovski.

This attraction, no doubt, arose in part from social affinity. For all his radicalism, Herzen was very much the aristocrat in manner and style, and in this respect he stood nearer to such unrepentant noblemen as the Slavophiles than to the more democratic professional types in his own circle, who were at best from the lower gentry. It is clear from comments in his *Diary* and in letters that he found the Slavophiles quite congenial socially. For instance, he was so taken by Samarin as to declare in rather snobbish French: *"c'est un parfait honnête homme* . . . and what is more *très distingué"* — in short, a gentleman, something which Herzen felt from the beginning "by instinct." The plebeian Belinski, on the other hand, judged the same Samarin just as instinctively as a *"barich* (little master), who has studied the people only through his lackey."[24]

But there were more intellectual reasons as well for Herzen's infatuation. He was immensely impressed by Khomiakov's prowess in manipulating the dialectic of "science" so as to demonstrate, more brilliantly even than any of the Westerners, that Hegel led straight to atheism, a result that Khomiakov emphasized only the better to deplore it, but which obviously delighted Herzen. What is more important, Herzen was positively charmed by Ivan Kireevski's indomitable, if somewhat too mystical, faith in Russia's destiny, and he was no less enchanted by Constantine Aksakov's profound, though naïve, belief in the "simple people." In the young Samarin, finally, Herzen found all possible qualities combined. Not only did Samarin understand Hegel, as did Khomiakov, but he used his theories to argue that Russia might be the culmination of the life of the Absolute, thereby giving "scientific" substance to the intuitions of Kireevski and Aksakov; for Herzen there was no more promising and attractive person in all Moscow.[25] In short, Herzen was primarily attracted to the Slavophiles because never before, in all his years of "hoping in the future of Russia," had he heard from anyone such bold affirmations of the virtues of his native land or of its oppressed people; and, gentry child of 1812 that he was, he could not but respond to this glorification of his own Russia. The nationalism which he had absorbed as a boy from tales of the "Great Fatherland War," which had found expression in his youthful essay on Peter the Great, and which had reappeared intermittently in exile, was suddenly stimulated by the challenge of the Slavophiles.

Herzen's great drama was to be both profoundly alienated from and yet very much a part of his class. Until the forties the oppressions of Nicholas had accentuated his sense of alienation to the near exclusion of the other half of his nature. Yet the hope that his world could once again become as glorious as it had been in 1812 was never lost, and it took only the stirrings of public opinion in the forties, and the debate over "nationality" which this produced, to arouse his dormant nationalism. But nationalism, when pushed to its logical conclusion, is inevitably a democratic notion; for, if the nation is to be complete, it must ultimately include all the people as its true sons and the full heirs of the national virtues. Herzen embraced this paradoxical democratic logic of gentry nationalism with exceptional zest and ruthlessness, since, by the taint of his birth and his long exile, he himself was only a half son in the gentry's world. Hence, although the oppositional *narodnost* of the Slavophiles was founded on a paternalistic idealization of the people and only a modest hostility to the state, he could see in it an adumbration of his own more radical desires. Thus at times, and to his own amazement, he felt almost as drawn to their nativism as to the intransigent adherence to Western enlightenment proclaimed by Belinski.

For two years, from 1842 to 1844, he hesitated, alternately attracted and repelled by the Slavophiles: attracted by their faith in Russia and its people, which he demanded nothing better than to share if only he could find "enlightened" reasons for doing so; and repelled by their loyalty to religion and their idealization of what he considered barbarous, retrograde and servile in the national tradition. Yet, sorely tempted though he was by these Slavonic sirens, in the end he drew back. When the final breach between the two camps came in 1844, his verdict was clearly that there was more reaction than progress in the lucubrations of the "Slavs." Nevertheless, in the course of his flirtation he had for the first time come in contact with those populist notions which would permit him to trans-mute the universal ideals of man and reason he had thus far arrived at into the specifically national form of socialism he would hold at the decade's end.

5

Because of the ambiguity of his position, Herzen's comments on the twin problems of the Slavophiles and the national destiny are inevitably confused and even contradictory. Nonetheless, there is a rough pattern to his remarks, and the first element of this pattern is unequivocal rejec-tion of all authoritarian elements in the national tradition. In particular, the undiscriminating patriotism of the Slavophiles and their clamors about Russia's present cultural superiority over the West appeared to him not only unfounded but dangerous.

Why is it [the Slavophiles complain] that foreigners do not understand us? Why is it that they look on us hostilely? Why is it that they pay so little attention to us, etc.? Well then why is it that we have been concerned with our national originality for only the last fifteen years? Why is it that in justifying ourselves we have produced only absurdities? It is possible to pay attention to someone only when he is worth it. Europe is very much interested in our strength, because she sees in it a mighty slave, under the power of the whip and the rod, who is ready at any moment to destroy the great fruits of centuries. Europe tacitly stands under one banner from Königsberg to Dublin. Her differences are private questions, but there is a *labarum* around which all her peoples are ready to unite . . . [In Russia] they see a banner directly contrary to theirs on which is written in flaming letters "Autocracy." They can only hate the camp of their enemies and the one nation which is ready to march to destroy all others.[26]

Herzen's reaction to the sensational book of the Marquis de Custine, *La Russie en 1839*, which the Slavophiles regarded as a libel, was in the same vein. It was "without a doubt the most interesting and intelligent book written by a foreigner about Russia." Custine had understood "the artificiality" of Russian life "which strikes one at every step, the bragga-docio of those elements of European life which exist with us only for display . . . *un empire de façades* . . . *la Russie est policée, non civi-lisée.*" Yet Custine could never fully appreciate the oppressiveness of life in Russia. "One bitterly smiles reading how unlimited power and the total insignificance of the individual reacted on a Frenchman. . . . He, a stranger, merely passing through, nearly galloped away because of the suffocating atmosphere — our lungs are built more strongly." In particular the foreigner could not know what it was like to live year after year in an atmosphere of "lying, dissimulation, and fettered speech."

Custine's condemnation had all the more force since it came from an arch-conservative. "He came to Russia with an *arrière-pensée* hostile to European liberalism, and went away reconciled. He advises sending discontented Frenchmen to visit Russia to cure them." How difficult it was to be a patriot in such a country! "This book has been a torture to me, like a stone crushing against my breast; I do not look at its inaccuracies, for the basis of his view is true. And that frightening society and that country is Russia!" Custine had even understood the bitter frustration of the Russian intellectual. "How truly he spoke: *'La pensée inutile s'envenime dans l'âme qu'elle empoisonne faute d'autre emploi.'* The Slavophiles, believing in a dreamy future, and hoping only in the future although they understand the present, are thus reconciled with the present. They are welcome to such happiness!" [27]

To Herzen the Slavophiles willfully deceived themselves about the frightful reality of the present by turning toward an imaginary future, constructed from the elements of an even more imaginary past. In so doing they blinded themselves to the only hope for Russia — Western enlightenment.

The House of Lords has freed O'Connell. A great country. One can only stand in reverence before this lofty, holy sense of justice. . . . The poor, pitiful Slavophiles! Why is it that England does not just collapse? And how does it happen that in Europe, in the dying West, there remain two or three veins full of healthy blood? . . . The soil of Europe is holy; blessings on it, blessings! [28]

In reality, the moral superiority the Slavophiles claimed for Russia was imaginary, while the contrast between European liberty and Moscovite slavery was an observable fact.

In Paris a Russian is a thousand times more open with a Frenchman than with his compatriots, because out of eight hundred Russians there is a multitude of spies, communicating each word, and the slightest indiscretion — that is everything which is not slavish dissembling — is capable of leading to frightful persecutions which are unimaginable in foreign lands. Thus, we appear more shameful, and still more shameful before Europe; veil after veil falls, and instead of a strong people a grovelling herd is revealed . . . But the Slavophiles, hoping against hope, look on the Europeans with haughtiness and condescension. A childish illusion. [29]

Significantly, Herzen's condemnations of Russia centered on the themes of the lack of individual liberty and of freedom of speech, rather than on social or economic inequality. Unlike the European, the Russian was perpetually debased and humiliated by the impossibility of free expression. At moments Herzen, disgusted by this servitude, went almost to the point of agreeing with the Slavophiles that there was an essential difference of national character between Russians and Europeans, but unlike the Slavophiles, he meant that the Russians were congenitally incapable of rising to the Western concept of the dignity of the individual. As he commented on a play of Calderon:

The Spanish people is great if it possesses such a sense of equity; this is a trait entirely undeveloped with us, not only in the peasant, but in everybody. With us any one who is offended either bears his offense like a slave, or revenges himself like a revolted serf . . . It is evident — as Chaadaev says in his article — that there is something lacking in our nature: we are unable to make the European syllogism.[30]

But such moments of Chaadaev-like despair were rare. Herzen's usual attitude was to search for the cause of his compatriots' inability "to make the European syllogism" in the conditions under which they were obliged to live.

Much of what Herzen thought about the deforming effects of Russian conditions on national character we have seen in his novel *Who Is To Blame?* In his *Diary* he confessed to an even deeper pessimism than he could express in print. Yet, significantly, even when he could write freely, his chief preoccupation was not with the degradation of serfdom but with the plight of people like himself, the Westernized intellectuals, crushed by the "punishment of those who have passed beyond what was really contemporary for their country." "Why did we awake so soon from slumber? It would have been better to sleep, like all around us." Europeanized in a country which was not yet European, cut off from his own people by the acquisition of a humanistic and individualistic culture, the Russian intellectual was condemned to purposelessness and inactivity. "Our position is hopeless . . . because the logic of history demonstrates that we are entirely outside the needs of the people." [31]

This cultural divorce between the elite and the masses and the consequent emptiness of Russian public life, Herzen felt, also explained the psychological deficiencies of the intellectuals.

Either because we have become sharply detached from our environment, or because we have no practical occupation of our own . . . which would absorb all the forces of our souls, we are given to negligence, egoism, laziness and inactivity. The longer and the more deeply one observes our best and noblest people, the clearer one sees that their unnatural divorce from life leads to idiosyncrasies, to subjective fantasies [religion and idealism] . . . In youth it still appears that the future will realize all our dreams, if only we will hasten toward it, but *nel mezzo del cammin di nostra vita* it is impossible to console ourselves — the future promises us nothing, except perhaps redoubled persecutions and then again boredom and inactivity.[32]

The only hope in this situation was that the humanism of the enlightened elite would bear fruit, if not in their own lives, then in the lives of the people in the future.

Will future generations understand, will they appreciate all the horror, the profoundly tragic side of our existence? But, all the same, our sufferings are the bud from which their happiness will blossom forth. Will they understand why we are do-nothings, why we seek out every pleasure, drink wine and the like? Why we do not raise our hands to a great work? Why, in moments of rapture, we never forget our anguish? Oh! may they stand in meditation and in sadness before the stones under which we will sleep — we have deserved their sorrow. Was there ever such an epoch for any nation? [33]

It was by this plight of the intellectuals that Herzen explained the Slavophiles themselves: they were simply one manifestation of the impossibility for civilized individuals to find a role in Russian life. Their return to religion was no more than an escape, and a sign that their characters could not withstand the intolerable pressures of a barbaric society.

Thinking people . . . cast about in all directions. The terrible consciousness of an odious reality, the perpetual struggle, force men to seek reconciliation in anything, reconciliation in all sorts of absurdities, in self-delusion, if only it offers activity for the mind, if only it enables them to tear themselves away from reality and to discover a cause for its vileness. This is the reason for the multitude of parties, of the most incomprehensible sort, in Moscow.[34]

Although the principal of these "incomprehensible" parties was the Slavophiles, another was the small body of Russian Catholics which emerged under Nicholas. Herzen was particularly struck by the action of Prince Gagarin who, putting Chaadaev's theories into practice, became a Jesuit in order to bring civilization to Russia by working for her conversion. For Herzen this was the ultimate aberration produced by the Russian intellectual's *malaise*.[35]

In Herzen's eyes the artificiality of Slavophilism was further demonstrated by the foreign, particularly German, inspiration of its doctrines.

Slavophilism has its counterpart in the modern history of Western literature: the appearance of nationalistic Romantic tendencies in Germany after the Napoleonic Wars, tendencies which found both cosmopolitan philosophy and those currents of thought proceeding from Leibnitz and Lessing to Herder, Goethe and Schiller [that is, the Enlightenment] to be too universal. No matter how natural was the appearance of neo-Romanticism, it was no more than a literary and philosophical phenomenon, without the sympathy of the masses, without any true reality.[36]

Herzen, of course, was right in asserting the kinship between Slavophilism and Western romantic nationalism, just as he was right in insisting on its aristocratic character. "They have no roots in the people. . . . They remember what the people have forgotten, and even about the present they hold opinions which in no way correspond to those of the people." Furthermore, Herzen ridiculed the Slavophiles' praise of the "moral and tender family life of the rural clergy," and of the beneficent "influence of these *patres familias* on the peasants," an "idyll," the chimerical nature of which — he claimed with considerable justification — was known to "whoever has at any time lived in the villages, or who has even so much as spoken with peasants." [37]

The Slavophiles, moreover, were not only wrong in their judgments and ridiculous in their divorce from the true problems of the nation; they were positively harmful because their doctrines impeded progress toward a more humane Russia. In their very efforts to escape from an intolerable situation by preaching a return to the past they succeeded only in making the present more unbearable.

The abhorrent heaviness of our epoch is all the more horrible in that it is necessary for thinking people to struggle not only with the men of power and authority, but also with a portion of the intellectuals. Slavophilism every day bears its luxuriant fruits; open hate of the West is open hate of the whole process of the development of the human race, for the West, as the heir of the ancient world, as the result of all general motion and of all particular movements, is the entire past and present of humanity . . . together with hate and disdain of the West go hate and disdain of freedom of thought, of all guarantees [of individual rights], of all civilization. In this fashion the Slavophiles stand on the side of the government.

No matter how oppositional the Slavophiles were subjectively, objectively their advocacy of a return to historically primitive conditions reinforced the reactionary policies of Nicholas; moreover, this support of the regime was demonstrated explicitly by the political denunciations of the *Moscovite*. Indeed, the realization that in a showdown the Slavophiles would support the autocracy against liberalism was what eventually made Herzen break with them. "Glory to Peter, who repudiated Moscow! He saw in it the hibernating roots of a narrow nationalism which would counteract Europeanism and strive to turn Russia once again away from humanity." [38]

6

Behind these ethical and political objections to Slavophilism was — inevitably — a philosophy of history. For Herzen no watertight divisions existed between civilizations, as they did for the Slavophiles. History was unitary as the Absolute, of which it was the biography, was unitary; humanity had a single line of advance, not several. Moreover, the direction of humanity's advance was determined by a succession of increasingly elevated concepts of the individual, all of which had been worked out on "the sacred soil of the West." Those nations which remained outside this movement did not possess a separate and valid history of their own; they were simply ahistorical, divorced from destiny, like the stagnant despotisms of the Orient. In these views Herzen affirmed the cardinal historiographical principles common to all the Westerners. Furthermore, he tended to agree in particular with Chaadaev that one of the principal

causes of Europe's dynamism and Russia's stagnation lay in their different
religious traditions. The Latin Church from the beginning had been independent of the secular power, and the struggles of popes against emperors and kings had set up a dialectic of progress in the West, whereas
the Greek Church since Constantine had been subordinate to the emperor,
thus breeding autocratic tyranny above and popular submission below, a
tradition unfortunately inherited by Russia.[39]

Before her contact with the West, therefore, Russia had no "real"
history. At best, Herzen was prepared to concede her a half-life, since she
was, after all, a Christian society; this life was a little more vital than the
"slumber" of Asia, but not historical in the full sense. "Of course By-
zantium and Russia possessed life, and a life which was nearer to Europe
than was that of China. Nonetheless, their history was not the complete
realization of all that was implicit in their idea," [40] since the idea of
Christianity for Herzen ultimately meant the sanctity of the individual.
Russia was first really brought into history by Peter, a great "revolutionary," a "man of genius," "with the exterior and the spirit of a barbarian, yet
unshakable in his great intention of uniting his imprisoned country with
the main development of humanity." Herzen, however, by no means
displayed an unequivocal admiration for Peter, and this position set him
apart from the average Westerner. "It is strange to see . . . how with the
knout and the axe humanism was introduced into Russia. These bad means
were inescapably reflected in the results. . . . Europeanism without,
and a complete absence of humanity within — such was the contemporary character from Peter onwards." [41] Indeed, Herzen always had
many extremely harsh things to say about the reformer's work, for it
represented the final development of autocracy and serfdom in Russia.
Yet, in spite of this, there was more good than bad in the Petrine revolution: ". . . all its severity and sorrows were necessary; by those sorrows
our ten-century separation from humanity was redeemed." Moreover,
these sorrows were about to bear fruit in a new Russia. "With us the
Petrine period is brought to an end; we who have abandoned our nationality for a purely European form and essence are completing the great
task of the humanization of Russia. After our time a period of organic, substantial and at the same time human growth will begin for Russia. Then,
her role in the fate of Europe will not be purely negative (as a limit to
Napoleon for example) but positive." [42] This theory of history was at
the same time very Western and very national. Russia never had, and
could not have, a destiny peculiar to her alone, as the Slavophiles
claimed; she could only become a "historical" nation by renouncing her
"narrow nationality" for Westernization. Once she had Westernized,
however, she could become a very great nation indeed, perhaps the very
greatest.

This optimism about Russia's future proved to be the starting-point for Herzen's evolution toward a romantic nationalism very similar to that which he condemned in the Slavophiles. Although it was true that Russian absolutism was much more terrible and enduring than that of any other European nation, nonetheless Peter, by ruthlessly "repudiating the whole past of his country" had demonstrated the Russians' exceptional aptitude for "abandoning their nationality"; but, as we have seen, such readiness to sacrifice the dead heritage of the past was the first revolutionary virtue for Herzen. Likewise he referred to Peter as a monarch who, in contrast to his Western contemporaries, did not "demand feudal adoration," and to the Russian state as one which "does not have the feudal idea as its foundation." [43] In other words, modern Russian society, as molded by the enlightened despotism of Peter, had been purged of its medieval heritage more thoroughly than had Western societies where change had been less brutal. By juggling the categories of romantic "historiosophy" just a little more it might be possible to construe Russia's lack of a "real" history in the past as a revolutionary advantage for the future. This is precisely what Herzen would do after 1848, but the process began in the course of his debate with the Slavophiles.

At times Herzen spoke of Russia's historical "youth" quite directly, as for example in describing Beltov's Genevan tutor.

He wandered sadly about the shores of his wonderful lake, *indignant against Europe*, and suddenly his fancy pointed out to him the north — *a new land*, which, like Australia in the physical sphere, *in the moral sphere* represented something just taking form on an enormous scale, something *young, new, just coming into being* . . . The Genevan bought himself Lévêque's history [of Russia], read Voltaire's *Peter I*, and a week later set out on foot for St. Petersburg.[44]

For this fictional Laharpe Russia was a sort of moral *tabula rasa* on which the conclusions of the Enlightenment might be written with greater facility than on the soul of the West, encumbered with the debris of centuries. The advantages of national "youthfulness" had been a theme of German historicism from Herder onwards, and Herzen here is only making the obvious application of this idea to Russia.

Because of these views on Russia's future Herzen found himself increasingly drawn to the nationalism of the Slavophiles. At the height of his infatuation — in 1843 and early 1844 — the scandal among the Westerners was such as to call forth a violent remonstrance from Belinski against consorting with the "Philistines." Herzen demurred: "I myself do not agree with them, but Belinski does not want to understand the truth in the *fatras* of their absurdities. He does not understand the Slavic world; he looks on it with despair and is wrong. He is unable to hope in *the life of the future ages,* and this hope is the condition of the advent of that future." Herzen was even so reckless as to declare that he occupied a middle position between the two camps. "My position is a strange one — a sort of involuntary *juste-milieu* on the Slavic question: to them [the Slavophiles] I am a man of the West; to their foes, I am a man of the East. From this it follows *hat in our age these one-sided definitions have no place." [45]

The ideology of this middle position is most clearly stated in a note in Herzen's *Diary* early in 1844.

The uninterrupted quarrels and conversations with the Slavophiles have aided much since last year in elucidating the question, and good faith on both sides has resulted in great concessions which have permitted the formation of sounder judgments than did either the pure dreaminess of the Slavs or the proud contempt of the ultra-Occidentals. *"Gottes ist der Orient, Gottes ist der Occident."* Believing (and not without reason) in *the enormous future of the Slavs as that race which is called by its spontaneity to answer the highest logico-historical question worked out by Europe* [socialism], they want to see in its infancy something higher than the European development, as if possibilities for the future meant also superiority over a present that is already developed and has realized its calling. [46]

The Hegelian verbiage of this declaration meant that the Slavs might possibly become the first to translate into "action" the European idea of socialism, since they were still young ("spontaneous") whereas Europe had already reached her full "development" and hence might be played out. Until the Slavs had matured, however, the only possible course for enlightened Russians was to continue to go to school to the West, and not to glory in the imaginary superiority of cultural infancy. In essence Herzen would say little more after 1848. He had only to advance somewhat the time schedule of his scheme of history, to elaborate on the decadence of the West, and to speak more clearly of the peasant commune in order to arrive at his concept of Russian socialism. Russia would play Joshua to Europe's Moses, and lead humanity into the promised land which the aged prophet had been allowed to see only from afar. Merely the shock of contact with Europe would be needed to transform these ideas from a timid hypothesis into an ardent faith.

Another matter elucidated for Herzen in his debates with the Slavophiles was the notion that the great untapped force which guaranteed "the future of Russia" was the "simple people," who had not yet risen to the level of "consciousness" and a meaningful historical destiny. It is at this time, and under the influence of the Slavophiles, that Herzen's previously vague evocations of the Russians' "broad nature" became a worship of the peasants' exceptional and "spontaneous" humanity. "And that simple, good people. I have loved them. A wonderful people — what hope is seen on these intelligent, open, pert faces!" [47] In *Who Is To Blame?* a naïve girl of sixteen declares: "What wonderful faces they [the peasants] have, open and noble! What people it seems that they would turn out to be if they were educated! . . . I cannot at all understand why the peasants of our village are better than all the guests who come to us from the provincial capital . . . landowners and functionaries." [48] This idealization of the masses was one of the sorest points of disagreement between Herzen and the other Westerners, particularly Belinski and Granovski, who both looked on the peasants as mainstays of ignorance and superstition in Russia and hence as obstacles to progress. To the average Westerner the peasants needed to be enlightened from above, not idealized, and Herzen's attitude was as dangerous a form of aristocratic romanticism about his good people as was that of the Slavophiles.

Herzen's growing nationalism found another expression in terms of his general philosophy, particularly with respect to that "passage from science to reality," which in his essays on dilettantism he proclaimed to be the next moment in the life of the Absolute. In concluding these articles he appraised the aptitude of the various nations of Europe for "action," and gave first prize to revolutionary France over Germany and England. Yet he placed almost equal hope in the Slavs.

On the other hand, maybe the lofty vocation to cast our contribution into the great treasury of human understanding is revealed here; perhaps it is we, who have lived only a little in the past, who will be the representatives of the real unity of science and life, of the word and the deed. In our character there is something which unites the best side of the French with the best side of the Germans. We are incomparably more gifted for philosophic thought than the French, and the bourgeois-philistine life of the Germans is definitely impossible for us; in us there is something "gentlemanlike" which is lacking in the Germans, and on our brow stands forth the sign of lofty thought such as does not appear upon the brow of the Frenchman. [49]

Here Herzen has expressed for the first time — the date was 1843 — the momentous idea that the life of the Absolute could possibly come to a culmination in Russia, and that his countrymen, combining the virtues of the active French and the speculative Germans, might be the first to translate the abstract freedom of "consciousness" into the living freedom of socialism.

In essence Herzen's middle position came down to the following. He rejected the Slavophiles' contention that Russia could become the savior of Europe because she had a unique, and specifically religious, national destiny. On the other hand, he hoped, or at least entertained the idea, that Russia's lot might be to crown the single, human destiny she shared with Europe. Yet, in either view, Russia's future would be more brilliant than that of any other nation in Europe. Hence it was possible for Herzen's budding nationalistic messianism of the Left to find inspiration in the Slavophiles' mature nationalistic messianism of the Right.

7

The most momentous point of contact between Herzen and the Slavophiles was the peasant commune (*obshchina* or *mir*), where the idea of nationalism merged most clearly with that of democracy. Herzen's first reference to the commune was in an essay composed in 1836 in Viatka, entitled *Miscellaneous Remarks on Russian Legislation*. Here Herzen mentioned the commune, but only in passing, to show that the Western sense of property was lacking in Russia. "Our legislation accepts possession as a fact and only in this sense preserves it; the best example of this is the ten-year prescriptive right, undisputed land-surveying." Even more significantly, he added in a footnote: "Most important of all is the division of land according to the tax assessment on each peasant household (*po tiaglam*)." [50] As early as 1836, then, Herzen was aware that the absence of private property in the commune distinguished Russia from the West. But he did not associate the periodic redivision of land among the peasants with socialism. He did this only in the forties under the influence of the debate with the Slavophiles.

Herzen's first reference to the socialist possibilities of the commune occurs in his *Diary* in 1843 apropos of the visit to Russia of the Prussian ethnologist, Baron Haxthausen, with whom Herzen had a long conversation.

He [Haxthausen] finds that the peasant commune, which has been preserved since deep antiquity, is very important; it is necessary to develop it in accordance with the demands of the time. He does not consider that individual emancipation, either with or without land, would be useful; it would expose the solitary, weak family to all the terrible pressures of the rural police: *das Beamtenwesen ist grässlich in Russland*.

Now Haxthausen was a conservative, whose enthusiasm for the commune arose entirely from its traditionalistic features; like the Slavophiles, he wished to preserve it after the inevitable emancipation of the peasants in order to insure stability in Russia. Nevertheless, he did suggest as a propaganda point that the commune already afforded that security and fraternal sharing which were the goals of European socialism. Herzen took coolly to this idea. "The position of any commune depends on whether the landowner is rich or poor, whether he is in government service or not, whether he lives in Petersburg or the country, whether he manages his estate himself or through an overseer. Here is that pitiful and disorderly chance which crushes all development." [51]

It is virtually certain, however, that Herzen first heard the idea of the "socialist" character of the commune, not from Haxthausen, but from the Slavophiles. Moreover, it is highly probable that the latter developed the notion around 1840 in reply to Herzen's own advocacy of European social-ism: they wished to demonstrate that Russia needed no such revolutionary innovation since the commune already possessed all the virtues which socialism falsely promised. For example, in 1842, the year before Hax-thausen's visit, Khomiakov wrote in the *Moscovite:* "The peasant is never completely isolated, thanks to the commune. . . . He never has been, and never will be similar to the proletariat of Europe, who offers his arms and his labor from region to region, sought after if he is needed, forgotten by everyone in the contrary case, a starved martyr when he is infirm or sick." [52] Herzen's response to such claims was at first completely negative.

Our Slavophiles discourse on the communal principle, on the fact that we do not have a proletariat, on the division of lands. All these things are excellent *seed-buds,* but in part they are based on a primitive level of historical develop-ment; in the same way with the Bedouins the right of private property does not possess the egoistic European character. Yet, on the other hand, the Slavophiles forget the total lack of any possibility of self-respect for the peasant, they forget his stupid endurance of all sorts of oppression — in a word they forget the impossibility of life under such conditions. Is it to be wondered at that our peasant has not developed the right of property in the sense of personal possession, when his strip of land is not his strip of land, when even his wife, daughter and son are not his? What property can a slave have? He is worse than a proletarian, he is a *res,* a tool for the cultivation of the fields. His master may not kill him, just as under Peter, in certain places, the master could not cut down an oak. Give the peasant the right of trial, and only then will he become a human being. Twelve million people *hors la loi. Carmen horrendum.*[53]

Herzen at first glance rejected the commune because, in spite of its egalitarian and democratic features, it did not safeguard what was for him the most sacred value of all — individual liberty.

Nonetheless, the campaign for the commune continued. Reassured by the consecration that learned Germany, in the person of Haxthausen, had given their theories, the Slavophiles pressed their arguments all the more eloquently. By 1844 Herzen had softened greatly and was writing: "The example of the highest development of the Slavic commune is the Montenegrins . . . they possess the most complete democracy, patri-archal and primitive, but energetic and strong. Europe more and more is turning its attention to this silent world called the Slovenes." [54] If this was true of the Balkan Slavs, might it not also be true of Russia? A few days later Herzen was pondering the problem of the "idea" the Slavs would be called upon to express in history. He was seeking something com-parable to the "idea of the individual, which the Germans brought into the world . . . and which left for the future the *Déclaration des droits de l'homme"* — a destiny already apparent in Tacitus' *Germania.* Although for the Slavs Herzen found nothing so consoling as Tacitus, he did find significant hope in the commune.

But do we have the right to say that the coming epoch, on whose banner is written, not the individual but the commune (*obshchina*), not liberty but fraternity, not abstract equality but the organic division of labor, [in sum, not liberalism but socialism] does not belong to Europe? In this is the whole question. Will the Slavs, fertilized by the West, realize its ideal and unite decrepit Europe to their existence, or will Europe unite us to her rejuvenated life? The Slavophiles decide such questions quickly, as if the matter had long since been settled. There are indications [of a settlement] but we are far from a complete decision.[55]

Thus, for the time being Herzen's conclusion on the question of the national destiny was to wait and see: socialism could come about through a European upheaval, which would also inevitably transform Russia, or it might emerge from the Slavic commune. Yet, on the whole, as of 1844 and with Nicholas on the throne the latter alternative appeared doubtful, and it seemed more prudent to bet on the West where there was open agitation for change and a great revolutionary tradition. For the moment Herzen stopped at this middle position, since no sooner had he reached it than the break between Westerners and Slavophiles ensued; for want of a stimulus his new evolution was interrupted, not to be resumed until 1847 and his first contact with the West.

Nonetheless, Herzen's flirtation with the Slavophiles had gone far enough to leave an indelible imprint, for their glorification of the national group corresponded to his own patriotic preoccupations. This patriotism was the logical extension of his restless quest for "personality," since the national group was the necessary arena for his own self-fulfillment. Personality, in order to be complete, had to be national no less than individual; and the nation in order to be complete had to be democratic, including all of the people as real "persons." Since Herzen was much more impatient and ruthlessly logical in the pursuit of this nexus of values than most of the Westerners, he alone was tempted by the Slavophiles' slogans of the "decrepitude" of Europe, of the "socialist" commune, and of the "simple people" as the great repository of "hope for the future of Russia." Thereby his hitherto abstract patriotism and democracy began to acquire a marked populist content. With the Slavophiles, Herzen had effected another of those transmutation of values from Right to Left which we have already seen in his relations with idealism and romanticism, and which constitute one of the striking traits of the intellectual history of the period.[56] Thus, years later, in *My Past and Thoughts*, in recognition of this ambiguous kinship with his *"ennemis les amis,"* Herzen recalled the quarrels of the forties, not with bitterness but with sentimental tenderness: "We had the *same* love, but we did not love in the *same manner;* we were like the two-headed eagle, or Janus, facing simultaneously in opposite directions, but beneath, in the body, the heart beat as one." [57]

CHAPTER XIII

Socialist and Liberal Westerners

AFTER his disillusionment with the Slavophiles, Herzen's impatience at the confining conditions of Russian life and his restless desire for change became rapidly more acute, and his thought, in consequence, grew increasingly more radical. The middle years of the decade, from 1844 to 1846, therefore, mark the culmination of his struggle against the "idols" of idealism, begun in Novogorod with the aid of Hegel; at the same time they are the final preparation for the anarchistic explosion produced by his emigration in 1847. One aspect of this deepening radicalism we have already seen in his "realistic" views of love and marriage and his new ethics of "egoism." Likewise, his rationalism, although its formal doctrines did not change perceptibly, acquired a more angry and peremptory tone. Finally and most important of all, his socialism began to descend — at least part way — from the empyrean of "palingenetic" visions to a greater concern for the actual state of Europe.

Nevertheless, the socialism of Herzen's middle years, like that of his youth, continued to be founded on a theory of history and a doctrine of ethics. Since socialism was the outcome of a rational historical process, it was inevitable; and since it was the realization of the noblest possible concept of man, it was just. Herzen had by no means renounced the "historiosophical" schemes he had explored in *Licinius* and *William Penn* with the aid of Cieszkowski and Leroux, and which in turn harked back to the New Christianity of his university days.[1] But now this epic of progress was reinforced by all the dialectical rigor and sweep of Hegel and at the same time given a more explicitly secular orientation.

Herzen's theory of history is set forth most fully in his *Letters on the Study of Nature*, composed in 1844 and 1845. Like his old teacher, Pavlov, Herzen here used the natural sciences as a pretext to comment on "science" *tout court*, and his essays are in the form of a history of philosophy from the Greeks to the post-Kantians. In effect, they represent an extremely able popularization of Hegel's *History of Philosophy* and his *Encyclopedia* — of course, in a "Left" interpretation — the philosophy of which has already been examined.[2] In addition, Herzen's *Letters* contains the fullest system of world history produced by any Westerner in the forties. They need to be supplemented only by an essay, *Certain Remarks on the Historical Development of Honor,* finished in 1846,[3] and of course by the *Diary.*

For Herzen, as for Hegel, the pre-history of humanity was the static world of the "Oriental despotisms," where none but the tyrant possessed individuality or freedom. True history, which was the history of the development of freedom, began only with the Greeks, who discovered reason and thereby set in motion the dialectical march of "consciousness." Generally speaking, this march consisted of one great dialectical triad. The thesis was classical antiquity; the antithesis was the "Christian-feudal" world born of the barbarian invasions; and the synthesis was the "new world" of total freedom and reason, which had been adumbrated in the Renaissance and the Reformation, and openly proclaimed by the French Revolution, but which would be fully realized only through socialism.

In antithesis to the monolithic despotisms of the Orient, the classical world first developed a concept of the worth of man. The incarnation of this idea was the citizen of the city-state. His freedom and dignity were limited, however, since the citizen possessed individuality not in himself but only as a member of the *polis;* he had rights solely in terms of his role in the collectivity. Moreover, the mass of the people were not citizens at all but slaves who utterly lacked human status. Thus classical man was not a complete individual, but only the first step upward of the idea of the individual. The imperfection of the classical thesis cried out for a progressive negation, which would lead to a universal concept of man.

This antithesis was supplied by the new religion of the slaves, Christianity, and the "virgin" force of the German barbarians who were to spread the Gospel over Europe. Nonetheless, these new forces did not triumph without that bitter struggle against the tenacious historical forms of the past which invariably attends progress. "The economy of the universe does not permit anything which exists to go down to the grave before exhausting all its forces. Conservatism in nature is just as true to life as is eternal movement and renewal." [4] Indeed the power of the fully developed old order was so great, and its roots in the hearts of men so strong, that the "new world" emerged only through the anguish of generations — a drama which, as always, moved Herzen to rhetoric because of the parallel it presented with the exceptional "heaviness of life for thinking people" [5] in his own time.

The poor intermediate generations . . . ordinarily perish at the midway point, exhausted by their feverish state. Disinherited generations, belonging neither to the old nor the new world, they bear all the weight of past evil yet are deprived of future blessings. . . . Happy are those who have closed their eyes after having seen, albeit from afar, the trees of the promised land; the greater number die either in insane ravings or with their eyes fixed on a heaven that crushes them as they lie on the cruel incandescent sand. The ancient world, in the last centuries of its life, experienced all the bitterness of this cup.[6]

The idea proclaimed by Christianity was that of the individual immortality of the soul; thereby all men, slave and free alike, became equal and the coheirs — in promise at least — of that plenitude of life which the religious call God. In antithesis to the classical world, Christianity affirmed the identity of the individual as a personality separate from the society in which he lived. "The personality of the Christian stood higher than the collective personality of the city; through it was revealed all the infinite worth of man. The Gospel triumphantly proclaimed the rights of man, and for the first time people heard *what they are*." [7] At the same time the German barbarians, organized in the free equality of the *comitatus,* overran the ancient world and eventually established the reign of the individualistic feudal knights. Thus the spiritual individualism of Christianity fused with the aristocratic individualism of feudalism to produce the single "Romano-Germanic" "Christian-feudal" civilization of the West.

Still, this advance was achieved only at a price, namely, the loss of antique rationalism and naturalism and their replacement by an otherworldly, "romantic," and "dualistic" world view. The "Christian-feudal" affirmation of individuality was an alienated one, since Christ's promise of equality was projected into an imaginary life after death while all sorts of barbarous servitude and superstition reigned on earth. This situation inevitably called forth a second dialectical negation and a third phase of history. The general movement of this new period was toward a synthesis between the natural reason of the Greeks and the individual liberty of Christianity, which would eventually make all men free and equal citizens, in unalienated possession of the full life in this world.

This process, however, proceeding through endless dialectical convulsions since the sixteenth century, was as slow and painful as the birth of Christianity. The Renaissance advanced a tentative humanism, and the Reformation stood for a more individualistic form of Christianity than did Catholicism, but religion remained the ideology of the masses. Rationalistic absolutism suppressed the anarchy of aristocracy and feudalism and thereby created for the first time a unified society, but in the process individual liberty was only diminished. Modern science and philosophy, beginning with Descartes and Bacon, commenced an assault on scholasticism and mysticism, a movement which culminated in the "realism" of the Enlightenment; yet the old dualism and "abstract duty" of Christianity lived on disguised as deism or pure idealism. In the political sphere all these developments found expression in the secular individualism of liberalism, which produced first the local revolution of England in the seventeenth century and then the universal revolution of France in the eighteenth, although only a minority of men anywhere, even in the most advanced countries of the West, had in fact acceded to individuality, and society remained almost as undemocratic as before.[8]

Thus — and this was the crucial point for Herzen — a truly "new world," totally antithetical to "Christian-feudal" civilization, had not yet been born.

Many people imagine that the last three centuries are just as separate from the Middle Ages as the Middle Ages are from the ancient world. This is incorrect. The centuries of the Reformation and the Enlightenment constitute the last phase of the development of Catholicism and feudalism. To be sure in many respects they have gone beyond any circle drawn from the Vatican, but nonetheless they represent the organic continuation of the past. All the foundations of Western European society have remained untouched; Christianity has remained the moral foundation of life; the new concepts of right grew up on the same soil of Roman, canon, and barbarian law. . . . Neither Luther nor Voltaire drew a fiery line between the past and the present, as did Augustine.[9]

The third term of the great triad of universal history had as yet only been sketched in; it had not received its full development in the wholly free and rational world of socialism.

The more Herzen brooded, amidst the stagnation of Nicholas' Russia, on the problem of progress, the less seemed to have thus far been accomplished, and the more tenacious appeared the dead grip of the past. "Feudalism survived the Reformation; it penetrated all aspects of the new life of Europe; its spirit took root in that which had risen against it. It is true that it changed, and it is still truer that at the same time something really new and powerful grew up, but that which was new, while awaiting maturity, was under the tutelage of feudalism." Christianity and "feudalism" were even the basis of the contemporary bourgeois order and of modern liberal thought.

The rude, direct feudalism [of the Middle Ages] became a rational, subdued feudalism; feudalism which believed in itself became feudalism which defended itself; a feudalism of blood became a feudalism of money. In philosophy scholasticism occupies the place of feudalism. . . . But the dualism of scholasticism has not perished; it has only abandoned its outward mystico-cabalistic garb and now appears as pure thought, as idealism, as logical abstractions.[10]

By this point, "feudalism" for Herzen meant anything that stopped short of total reason (in his meaning of the term) and of full social democracy; all intermediate, liberal stages between these two extremes he dismissed as meaningless. Thus, the United States became for him the "highest development of feudalism in the post-Reformation world." [11] It was by the persistence of this same "bourgeois feudalism" that a few years later he would explain the failure of the Revolution of 1848.

In his *Diary* Herzen could be bolder than in print about the political struggle against feudalism.

The Reformation gave a shove to childish beliefs; respect was given to the mind and to thought. The French Revolution appears as a completely logical second negation of feudalism. [Under absolutism] the central power had separated itself from the masses and the nobles, thus leaving divine right as its sole prop. The French Revolution was the same movement [against feudalism] on the part of the people; it demonstrated that authority was not of divine origin and thereby closed the *preparatory* stage of the transition to the new world. In our time, in fact, much still stands through force of habit and memory, but it is decrepit and stagnant. [12]

Even the mighty assault of the French Revolution had not destroyed the "Christian-feudal" world. The old dilapidated structure had been patched up again in the Restoration, and, moreover, had survived 1830. None-theless, one more shove and the old world would collapse definitively. Then the Christian, feudal, and knightly concept of the individual, at last stripped of its mystical trappings, would be extended to all men. Moreover, the individual would be reconciled with the state, or society, which had oppressed him ever since the establishment of "anti-feudal" absolutism in the seventeenth century by such monarchs as Louis XIV and Peter the Great. "Individuality" (*individualnost*) and "community" (*obshchina*) would become harmonious rather than antithetical principles, for in the modern world "the worth of the individual is measured by his participation in the *res publica.*" Thus, through self-government, personal dignity would become the endowment of all men, and be transformed from an individual, aristocratic right into a social and democratic one. [13]

The socialist outcome of history, moreover, was linked to the idea of national self-fulfillment; indeed this link was far stronger in Herzen's thought at this time than was any connection between socialism and action by the people. His constant search, therefore, was to find the nation most clearly anointed by the Idea to bring history to its culmination. The signs of this election were two: a deep sense of the idea of personality and the restless energy necessary to transmute "science" into "action." Here Herzen hesitated between France and Germany. (England was simply too "egoistic" and "narrowly national" to be given serious consideration; the chosen nation must have a universal vocation.) Germany was the land of those virtuous barbarians whom Herzen, following Hegel, held to be the first bearers of the Christian idea of the individual; it was also the land where "science" had achieved its greatest triumphs. But

France was the country of the Great Revolution, and more recently it had become the home of socialism, which represented both the highest concept of personality and the translation of "science" into life. The choice, therefore, was a hard one, and for a long time Herzen oscillated between exasperation at the philosophical shallowness of the French and despair over the apolitical contemplation of the Germans.[14] Since "action" was higher than "science," however, by the mid-forties he chose France, even though this was not a completely satisfactory solution.[15] Yet, as we have already seen, at the same time he at least envisaged the possibility that it might fall to Russia's lot to combine the "one-sided" qualities of France and Germany into the ideal revolutionary synthesis, which would also be the synthesis of all previous history.[16]

2

But what could one divine of the socialist forms of the future? As formerly, for light on this question Herzen turned from the philosophical Germans to the political French. What he found in their writings in the mid-forties, however, was rather different from what he had garnered there in the thirties.

Very roughly, in the thirties ideological socialism in France (as distinct from the working-class movement) had been dominated by schemes of "palingenetic" destiny and ethical, humanistic interpretations of Christianity. The predominent school had been that of the Saint-Simonians, of which the tendency of Leroux and George Sand was an offshoot. This movement, moreover, was nonrevolutionary and indeed apolitical, hoping to triumph through education and persuasion. But by 1840, as the regime of Louis Philippe stubbornly held to its franchise of 250,000 moneyed voters and resisted all reform, socialism became more of an active oppositional force. Its representatives addressed themselves less to general theory and more to the specific ills of society; at the same time they drew nearer to the working class with its tradition of republicanism and revolt. As a symptom of these changes, around 1840 the word "socialism" came into general use, and along with it such terms as "communism," "proletariat," "exploitation" and even "bourgeoisie," as a precise economic rather than a loose social category.

Ideologically, the turn of the decade was marked by three innovations that need concern us here. First of all, Fourierism, which throughout most of the thirties had played only a secondary role alongside Saint-Simonism, after the death of its founder in 1837 experienced a new success under the leadership of Victor Considérant, who popularized the original rather fantastic system in more coherent fashion and gave it greater relevance to the economic problems of the day. Thereby the concepts of "association," "right to work," and the fraternal security of "communal living" became common currency. Secondly, Louis Blanc in 1839 in his *The Organization of Labor* first made socialism an integral part of the working-class movement and thereby clearly associated it with political opposition to the bourgeois order defended by Guizot. Finally, after 1840 Proudhon not only heightened the popular flavor of socialism, but added a violence of tone that tended to make it a revolutionary impulse, akin, spiritually at least, to the insurrectionary tradition of Barbès and Blanqui, even though in a literal sense the "revolution" which Proudhon invoked was a revolution in men's minds. Furthermore, Proudhon was a fierce exponent of individual liberty, in the name of which he denied all forms of social organization not based on the fullest mutual consent. Hence he denounced the state in any form, including parliamentary democracy, in favor of the maximum decentralization of power and direct democracy on the local level, principles for which he eventually coined the term "anarchism." It was Proudhon, too, who first completely secularized the idea of socialism in France, vociferously advocating atheism and attacking the principle of God's authority as the first step toward the destruction of social tyranny.

In the forties, moreover, socialist ideas first began to penetrate Russia on a significant scale. As we have seen, the Slavophiles were acutely aware of them. Indeed, as the police later discovered, radical literature from abroad, though its dissemination was forbidden, entered the country in a steady flow throughout the decade and was even sold openly in the bookstores; it was possible to procure the latest subversive work only a few months after its publication in the West.[17] In 1845 appeared the first relatively large socialist group, the Fourierist Petrashevski circle. Herzen's socialism, then, was no longer the exceptional phenomenon it had been in the thirties. He continued to be exceptional, however, in the extremism with which he construed the new ideas.

At the beginning of the forties Herzen was still immersed in the religion-tinted socialism of Leroux, whose various periodicals had long been his principal source of information on French thought. In 1841 he could still praise "the multitude of true and profound ideas" of the Catholic reformer, Buchez. In 1844 he at last read the *Palingénésie sociale* of the mystical Ballanche, the title of which had charmed his youth and in which he still found "many true presentiments," though clouded by "myth" and "fantasy." [18] But this was Herzen's last flirtation with such literature. Beginning in 1843 he embarked on a progressively radical exploration of the newer currents in French thought.

Insofar as he could, Herzen followed the French in their trend toward greater social realism, but he inevitably adapted what they had to say to his own more desperate, and hence more ideological, struggle in Rus-

sia, often with rather hybrid results. He took up all the new catchwords,
"proletariat," "exploitation," "bourgeoisie," etc.; yet, characteristically, he
winnowed out most of their economic meaning and transformed them into
predominantly ethical concepts. Indeed, it is clear that he only half understood what he read, which is not surprising since the social problems
treated by the French were so different from any he knew in Russia. For
example: "Property is an odious thing. Even worse than this, it is unjust;
it is *immoral* and, like a heavy weight, bears man down. It corrupts man,
and he falls to the level of a savage beast when greed throws him from
the pedestal of his historical *Standpunkt*." [19] But these are the sentiments
of an aristocrat waxing moral about bourgeois money-grubbing much
more than of a socialist condemning private property as the source of
inequality and exploitation. They represent a critique of the bourgeoisie
from above rather than from below.

Likewise, Herzen took to noting in his *Diary* horrible examples of
proletarian oppression that he read in the European press. One of these
concerned an unemployed worker in Lyons who was driven to theft in
order to buy food and medicine for a sick wife. When the husband's
identity was discovered, the couple, in despair, attempted to hang themselves but were prevented from doing so by the arrival of the gendarmes.
"Now there will be a trial. . . . It is necessary to note that the French
jury judges murder less severely than *theft*. Such cases, at a stroke, reveal
the contemporary social situation in all its infamy." [20] In Herzen's hands
the French socialists' critique of laissez-faire economics became largely a
critique of bourgeois society's lack of humane sentiment.

Herzen went beyond this elemental moralism, however, to accept
certain important programmatic tenets of his teachers.

But what is the solution? Here is the whole question; yet no complete
theoretical answer can be given. Events will show the form, the flesh, the
strength of the future reformation. But its general sense is clear: the public
control of property and capital, communal living, the organization of labor
and of wages, and the right of private property placed on different foundations — not its complete abolition, but its investiture [in the individual] by
society, so as to give the government the right of determining public measures
and policy.[21]

Here, by 1843, the repertory of Herzen's new sources is complete: Fourier
for "communal living"; Louis Blanc for "the organization of labor and of
wages" and "the public control of property and capital"; and Proudhon
for "the right of private property placed on different foundations." Yet he
refused to make a dogmatic commitment to any one school, since this
would deny man's creative spontaneity in the construction of the new
world.

Of these thinkers, Herzen already had some acquaintance with

Fourier, whom he now studied more closely in Considérant's gloss, *La Destinée sociale*. "Of course, Fourierism has gone into the question of socialism more deeply than other systems. It has given foundations, principles on which it is possible to construct more than phalanxes and phalansteries." [22] The first of these principles for Herzen was Fourier's famous theory of the "passions." A rational and harmonious world could be achieved only by constructing social institutions so as to accommodate man's natural drives and desires rather than to repress them — a theory clearly congenial to Herzen's own morality of "self-will" and "egoism." "Conventional ethics is a lying and pedantic science which for three thousand years has pretended to lead men to virtue and good morals with the absurd dogmas of moderation and the repression of the passions, when it is necessary — not to deny — but to *utilize* and satisfy them." [23]

Even more momentous was the second principle. "The organization of the commune is the cornerstone of the social edifice, no matter how vast and perfect it may be." [24] We have already seen that Herzen hoped communal living would free woman from her present bondage by giving her a means of support other than her husband and by providing public care and education for her children. In fact, this was the only specific function of the commune he envisaged at this time. But he also held a more amorphous though no less compelling notion that the commune meant mutual respect among men, fraternal love and harmony; furthermore, it meant full social equality and the absence of material want. Indeed, it was the nearest that imagination could come to conceiving an institutional embodiment of the socialist virtues. And this was the great legacy of Fourierism to Herzen and all Russian socialism (and in a different sense to the Slavophiles). Henceforth socialism in Russia was inevitably associated with some sort of "commune" or "collective." Still, Herzen did not subscribe to the precise Fourierist formula for the commune. On finishing *La Destinée sociale* he wrote: "It is good, extremely good, but it is not a complete solution to the problem. In their broad, luminous phalanstery things are a bit cramped. It is the organization of one side of life only; no place is left for the others." [25] In other words, the meticulous collectivism of the phalanstery did not leave room for the spontaneity of individual freedom.

From his second source, Louis Blanc, Herzen first derived some sense of the economic aspects of socialism. His guide was the *Histoire de dix ans*, one of the principal sources of information about Western conditions for the Moscow intellectuals in the forties. From it Herzen concluded: "The necessity of a social revolution has now become obvious; the foes of progress, like Guizot, understand this and tremble. . . . The absurdity of the haphazard distribution of such an important instrument of power as wealth, the absurdity of a social order which sacrifices the vast majority, the impossibility of equality in such a society — all this has become self-evident." [26] So down-to-earth and economic a conception of the socialist revolution was quite new with Herzen, and he would never cease to pay lip-service to it in the future, but this was not the most important lesson he derived from Blanc.

The *Histoire de dix ans* was an attack on the July Monarchy in the form of a history of its first decade. It demonstrated how the Revolution of 1830, which had been made by the working people, had been perverted by the "cowardly, selfish and fickle" bourgeoisie, who through deceitful means robbed the masses of their victory and "created a king" out of fear of democracy. Herzen found this account a "revelation." Of course, ever since his youthful commitment to Saint-Simonism he had vaguely held that mere liberal reform was not enough and that some further social transformation was necessary. But he had also vaguely admired Western parliamentarianism and the freedoms that went with it, because they were so much better than Russian autocracy. From Blanc, however, he derived a truly horrendous picture of Western liberalism. The French Chamber now seemed "a muddy marsh in which the mighty stream of the Revolution disappeared," while Louis Philippe assumed the character of a "nightmare, a cynical figure provoking disgust." From this Herzen concluded more clearly than ever before that "political overturns without social changes had become an impossibility." [27] For the first time liberalism and socialism became for him not only separate but irrevocably hostile forces.

Moreover, in Blanc he discovered the cause of liberalism's failure — the "bourgeoisie." Not that Herzen developed any clear idea of what this bourgeoisie was as a class; it was too remote from his own experience for that. Rather, from his half understanding of Blanc he received the impression of some monstrous force of money, vulgarity, and moral pettiness (*meshchanstvo*), far beneath the elegant and "knightly" aristocrats of the old regime and even of the Restoration, whom it had chased out. If so degenerate a group controlled France, how little, in fact, had changed for the better since 1789! Indeed, society was perhaps even more degraded than before 1789, and the rise of the bourgeoisie might be the sign of Europe's "decrepitude" as the Slavophiles claimed. Although at this time — 1843 — Herzen no more than half-perceived such conclusions, he already possessed the elements of the negative judgment he would pronounce on Europe in 1847. Through the reading of Blanc, not only liberalism, but the West as a whole was lowered in his eyes. In Russia, socialism, by its very denigration of European society, could become not only a radical stimulus but a nationalistic one as well.

For the third of his new prophets, Proudhon, Herzen displayed the greatest warmth of all. His debt to Louis Blanc and especially to the

Fourierists was shared by other Russian radicals of the day, chiefly in the Petrashevski circle but also by some Westerners; his high enthusiasm for Proudhon, however, set him apart and distinctly to the left of his contemporaries. Furthermore, this enthusiasm was exceptionally enduring. By the end of the decade Herzen considered Proudhon the greatest European socialist and in later life he placed him on a level with Hegel as one of the two major luminaries of the age. Yet Herzen derived few specific doctrines from Proudhon. Rather he found in Proudhon a spirit, an *élan*, for which he felt an unusual kinship and which served as a diffuse but potent stimulus to the radicalization of his own social thought. "The reading of Proudhon, like the reading of Hegel, gives a special method; it sharpens one's weapons. It does not give concrete solutions, but rather the means for attaining them." [28]

The first aspect of Proudhon's method which impressed Herzen was the incisiveness, the intransigence and indeed the vehemence with which he attacked social problems. Herzen first encountered these qualities in December, 1844, in the famous pamphlet, *Qu'est-ce que le propriété?* (to which the slashing answer was: *la propriété, c'est le vol*). Herzen commented in his *Diary:*

An excellent work, not only as good, but better than what has been said and written about it. Of course, for those who have . . . suffered over similar social questions, the principal thesis is not new; but the development is excellent — to the point, forceful, sharp and full of fire. He completely denies property and admits only individual possession. This is not, moreover, a personal view, but a strict logical deduction, by which he demonstrates the impossibility, the criminality, the absurdity of the rights of property, and the necessity of possession.[29]

Over and above Proudhon's incisive exposition, Herzen was impressed by this middle position on the question of property. Adopting it as his own, he would always be opposed to large accumulations of wealth ("property") which permit the few to oppress the many. On the other hand he would always believe that a minimum of personal wealth ("possession") was necessary to guarantee the independence and dignity of the individual. Hence he would be consistently hostile to complete ownership and control of property by the commune or the nation, such as was advocated by the "communism" of Cabet or by the tradition of Babeuf. Later in life such "communism" appeared to Herzen as an extreme and embittered form of socialism, which was understandable, given existing conditions of inequality, yet which nonetheless menaced individual freedom almost as much as did the monarchic or bourgeois state.

Most of all, however, Herzen was impressed by Proudhon for the rigor of his logic, which again meant intransigence and boldness of thought. He was particularly struck by this quality on reading, in 1845, *De la création de l'ordre dans l'humanité.*

Proudhon decidedly raises himself to speculative thought; he boldly divorces himself from [classical] rationalistic categories; he demonstrates admirably the inadequacy of the principles of causality and substance, and resolves their antinomies by his "series," that is by the concept [the Hegelian *Begriff*] which separates them into all their moments, and reconciles them as a totality through dialectical reason.[30]

This obscure language meant simply that Herzen had found in Proudhon a fellow revolutionary Hegelian — and, of all unlikely places, in France. Now although Proudhon's Hegelianism (the result of tutoring by Marx and Bakunin) was certainly superficial and his use of the dialectic no more than formal, as Marx scathingly pointed out later in *The Poverty of Philosophy*, Proudhon was still the first thinker of the forties to attempt to use the dialectic as an "algebra" of social revolution. The German Left Hegelians that Herzen had hitherto read either addressed themselves exclusively to questions of pure philosophy, as did Feuerbach, or were very abstract in their political radicalism, as was Ruge (or Bakunin in his "Jules Elisard" article), while Herzen simply never made intellectual contact with Marx. Proudhon, therefore, was a unique and precious ally among the European Left and the only one who stood on the highest level of both contemporary "science" and of social thought.

This characteristic of Proudhon, furthermore, made him uniquely ruthless in attacking those dead absolutes of the past against which Herzen also warred. Thus, "the very best part" of *De la création de l'ordre* for Herzen was Proudhon's "proof of the impossibility of religion in the future" — again a rare virtue among the God-fearing French socialists. "His deduction is strong, energetic and bold. He concludes with words of magnificent nobility. 'Let us remember how religion welcomed us with its benediction at our birth and how by its prayers it accompanied our bodies. Let us do the same for it: let us bury it with honor, remembering its benefactions to humanity.'"[31] In addition, Proudhon joined "philosophy" to religion as another victim of the future revolution. His attack on outworn ideal authorities, however, was simply the metaphysical expression of his individualism and of his cult of Liberty and Justice for all. And these principles brought Herzen near to the anarchism that was Proudhon's political program and that would influence him when the two men met during the Revolution of 1848.

Indeed, total negation of existing values and institutions was the final impression Proudhon left with Herzen. As he wrote later in *My Past and Thoughts:*

Proudhon, of course, is wrong in placing at the head of his *Economic Contradictions* [*The Philosophy of Poverty*] the epigraph, *destruam et aedificabo;*

his strength is not in creation but in criticism of the existing order. . . . In this negation, in this annihilation of the social structure is the terrible strength of Proudhon. He is as great a poet of the dialectic as Hegel, but with the difference that the latter remains on the tranquil heights of philosophic movement, while the former is thrust into the hurly-burly agitation of the masses, the hand-to-hand fighting of the parties.[32]

Of Proudhon's numerous economic ideas, however, particularly those of the work extolled here, Herzen hardly ever said a word — either now or later. Nevertheless, Proudhon's bold application of the "poetry of negation" to the criticism of society helped give Herzen's previously abstract revolt of ideas more of a social focus and thereby stimulated his own evolution toward anarchism. This stimulus, in combination with the Fourierist idea of the commune and Louis Blanc's critique of the bourgeoisie, would provide after 1848 the principal Western contributions to Herzen's "Russian socialism," alongside the nationalistic populism of the Slavophiles.

Thus, in the forties as in the thirties, Herzen took from the Western socialists only what was most congenial to his own thought, which was largely what was most general in theirs. Essentially, the socialism of his middle years boiled down to the abstract notion that the new world meant the combination of "personality" with the commune, of individual liberty with democratic equality. Nonetheless, there are degrees of abstraction. His New Christianity of the thirties had been almost pure allegory; the "principles" of "individuality" and "community," which he now emphasized, though still abstract, were more discernibly related to social problems. His use of these new principles, moreover, implied a definite political option: liberty was the end; the commune was only the means — a judgment which, if it is nowhere stated in so many words, is clearly implicit in the contrast between his reservations about the hyper-collectivism of the Fourierists and his enthusiasm for Proudhon's "right of individual possession." At the same time, he paid no more than lip-service to the elaborate economic theories of the French, and he did this much largely because the thinkers he admired insisted that economics was crucial.

And this body of attitudes was quite natural for one in his position, since general principles were the only aspect of socialism that was relevant to Russia. This was true not just for the elite, whose problem was clearly not poverty but civil liberty, but also for the peasants, whose demand was not so much economic equality (of this they possessed an abundance if only in servitude) as, again, personal freedom. Hence Herzen, speaking not only in his own name but also in that of the serfs whose plight he could imagine by magnifying his own, inevitably made individual liberty the first principle of his philosophy. At the same time, in Russia the problem of achieving liberty seemed so staggering to the sensitive and the impatient as to be capable of solution only through a sweeping social transformation and not just a modest political reform. Hence Herzen's demand for individual liberty quite logically found expression as a demand for socialism.

To be sure, the Western socialists also tended strongly to abstraction, but their utopias were constructed out of elements taken from the real world, and their fantasies assumed the form of schemes, often worked out with a profusion of pseudo-realistic detail, for the reorganization of agriculture, industry, finance or politics. But these schemes were related to the conditions under which they lived. In the West, or at least in France and England, even when a man was excluded from the franchise, he still had the freedom to conduct public propaganda, to organize workingmen's associations or mutual credit societies, or to found a trial phalanstery; moreover, these schemes could feasibly be regarded as blueprints or pilot-projects for reform in the relatively near future. In Russia, however, where public action was unthinkable and where even talk was not free, such activities were impossible, while the likelihood of reform was so remote that it was meaningless even to imagine models for the future order. Hence the utopias of the Russians were constructed, not out of elements taken from the real world, but from abstract values. Herzen, therefore, responded only to what was most universal in the thought of the French, and socialism for him became the "principle" that no man could be free unless all men were free and hence also equal.

Nevertheless, abstract as all this was, it was not meaningless. In more concrete language, the idea that socialism signified the "reconciliation" of "individuality" with "community" meant reforming the relation of the individual to the autocratic state and to patriarchal authority, that is, transforming subjects and serfs into citizens. And this, in fact, was the crucial problem of reform and modernization in Russia. The spirit of social radicalism, therefore — though not the precise economic schemes — which had developed in France in the wake of the disappointments of 1789 and 1830, could evoke a profound resonance in Russia, whose specific problems were so different. Indeed, the very backwardness of the Russian old regime and the exceptional obstacles it presented to the recognition of individual dignity and the creation of humane social conditions only made the sweeping principles and the bold *élan* of Western socialism the more attractive to the restless under Nicholas.

A final characteristic of Herzen's socialism must be mentioned. There is a distinct pattern to his borrowings from the French: not only was he insensitive to their economic ideas, but he responded most positively to what was of pre-industrial, and even anti-industrial, inspiration in their thought. We have already seen that he totally ignored the technocratic aspects of Saint-Simonism, but instead seized on its secularized version of Christian ethics and its philosophy of history, both of which represented revised forms of the pre-industrial, eighteenth-century ideas of natural morality and of progress. More revealingly still, Herzen's chief borrowings in the forties — Fourier's phalanstery and Proudhon's "mutualist" utopia of independent peasant proprietors and artisans — are essentially idealized visions of the old village. They represent what is sometimes termed "primitive socialism," or a reaction against industrialization which advocates a return to an agrarian past rather than acceptance and humanization of the new social conditions created by the machine. Louis Blanc, on the other hand, represents acceptance of the new situation, and an attempt to master it by "the organization of labor." Yet Herzen construed even Blanc in an anti-industrial sense by ignoring his positive schemes for the reorganization of industry and responding only to his negative critique of the bourgeoisie. Moreover, it is clear from Herzen's rare comments on industrialization that he considered it a step backward, a new force of human degradation, rather than an impetus to progress which needed only to be socialized in order to produce a better world.

This does not mean, however, that anti-industrialism was the underlying or hidden motive of Herzen's socialism; enough has been said to indicate that he arrived at socialism by universalizing his own aristocratic sense of individual dignity. Moreover, industrialism and capitalism were phenomena which never preoccupied him greatly, not even in later life after he had settled in England in the heart of the new society; and the bourgeoisie always remained for him a moral, aesthetic, or legal category rather than an economic class. Indeed, it is fair to say that he never understood the slightest thing about industrial society, since it was so remote from the conditions he knew in Russia. Thus he was drawn to Fourier and Proudhon because (in addition to the reasons already given) their ideas were vaguely pertinent to the problems of the Russian village, and not because he was struck by a concern kindred to his in their critique of capitalist industry. And he was attracted by Blanc's excoriation of the bourgeoisie as much for nationalistic reasons, the better to humble the West, as for socialist ones.

Nonetheless, Herzen's choice of these guides was not entirely fortuitous. As a landed aristocrat he dimly sensed that industrialism was something alien and menacing to his ideal of life. This sentiment expressed itself more as indifference and incomprehension than as hostility, yet, as his utilization of Blanc shows, active hostility was never far distant. It failed to become important in his thought only because industrialism was never a significant factor in Russia during his lifetime. It fell to later generations of Populists to develop what Herzen had left only as a hint.

By the 1870's industrialization had clearly begun in Russia and Populism, with its cult of the village, began to acquire, not just anti-capitalist, but anti-industrial overtones; by the 1890's, when industrialism had grown to be a major phenomenon, these accents became quite marked. What Herzen had sensed almost by instinct in his borrowings from the French socialists as early as the forties was to become one of the principal articles of the Populist creed. Populism was Russia's "primitive socialism" in the same tradition as its earliest Western models, Fourierism and the "mutualist" anarchism of Proudhon.

3

Herzen's deepening commitment to socialism rapidly led to dissension among the Westerners; indeed, this new crisis developed only two years after their break with the Slavophiles. In 1846 almost the entire circle repaired for the summer to a country place named Sokolovo, where they settled down in neighboring *dachas* for a more intimate feast of friendship and ideas than was possible in Moscow during the winter. To their surprise, however, this atmosphere of almost family-like closeness brought certain latent differences to the point of an open quarrel. Herzen and Granovski were the chief protagonists, but the former enjoyed the loose support of Ogarev and, from afar, of Belinski, while the latter could mobilize a more solid phalanx composed of Korsh, Botkin, Ketcher and the others. Unfortunately the issues involved are not wholly clear, but they may be pieced together approximately as follows.

In *My Past and Thoughts* Herzen presents the quarrel as a philosophical and religious difference growing out of his *Letters on the Study of Nature*, the last of which had just appeared and which marked a more radical development of his rationalism.[33] Back in 1842–43, in his essays on dilettantism, he had only asserted the general principles that "being" and "consciousness" are one and that ideas are wholly immanent in the natural world. These convictions, however, soon led him to explore the material bases of thought, and thus to return to a more hard-headed version of his youthful belief that the natural sciences, and not pure logic, were the key to understanding man and the only sure foundation for philosophy. In 1844–45 he even attended courses at the university on anatomy and in addition read avidly about physiology and chemistry, from which he concluded that all ideas, including religion, were simply emanations of man's nervous system. This, for Herzen, was the true scientific basis for the immanence of thought which Hegel demonstrated by logical principles.[34] This rather crude — and very undialectical — materialism found its way in diluted form into the *Letters on the Study of Nature*, which in fact derived their title from Herzen's growing worship of natural science. And it is to be presumed that he was much more outspoken about his new views in conversation than he could be in print.

It was precisely this materialism which alarmed Granovski, who, although he viewed Hegelianism as a philosophy of reason and progress, also held that it demonstrated the truth of religion. In particular, he defended belief in the personal immortality of the soul, in part because he considered it indispensable to the idea of human dignity, but also because he could not accept the thought that so extraordinary a person as his late and dear friend, Stankevich, should have utterly and irrevocably disappeared, a sentiment that was reinforced when he lost two beloved sisters. Herzen only snorted at these "personal" and "private" reasons which flew in the face of the "objective" truth of science, and, with his impetuous character, he was no doubt less than tactful in his efforts to cure Granovski of his "romanticism." [35] In reply, therefore, at Sokolovo, Granovski declared his frank opinion about his friend's unpleasant "letters" on nature.

Unfortunately, *My Past and Thoughts* is our only firsthand account of the quarrel. It is certainly not complete, for when he wrote it Herzen had every reason to minimize the original tensions, particularly concerning politics, the better to annex the memory of his friends to his own revolutionary cause. Furthermore, since it was impossible to air the subject of atheism in print, the controversy has left no public traces (except for one exceedingly "Aesopian" article by Herzen which will be treated later).[36] Moreover, our usual uncensored sources are lacking: even in private letters it was unwise to discuss the issues at hand with anything more than hints, and Herzen's *Diary* ceases at the beginning of 1845.

These deficiencies are partly remedied, however, by the memoirs of a peripheral member of the group, Annenkov. Though not at Sokolovo himself, he seems to have taken pains to gather information on what occurred there from the participants, for he was extremely curious about the private affairs of public intellectual figures. In his version, Feuerbach's *Essence of Christianity* is presented as playing a major role in polarizing the two parties.[37] Since this is plausible in terms of Herzen's vague account, there is no reason to doubt Annenkov's more interesting statement that Granovski objected to Herzen's socialism no less than to his atheism, an assertion, furthermore, which fits with what we know of the sequel to the quarrel in 1847. Granovski, it seems, argued that socialism was an irresponsible utopianism whose dissemination in Russia would only make the practical task of reform more difficult. He and his partisans, therefore, deprecated all of Herzen's new authorities — Fourier, Proudhon, and especially Louis Blanc — and held up as their ideal the prudent constitutionalism of Louis Philippe and Guizot. Likewise, Herzen was criticized for idealizing the backward and ignorant masses, a penchant he was accused — with some justice — of deriving from the Slavophiles, while Granovski and his supporters placed their hopes in the enlightened elite.[38] From allusions in letters written by protagonists after the event, it is possible to piece together still other differences. Herzen was condemned for "partiality" (*pristrastie*), "intolerance," and "hot-headedness" — in short, extremism — while Granovski and his supporters arrogated to themselves the virtues of "tolerance," "patience," and "skepticism" — in other words, moderation and open-mindedness.[39]

The debate was conducted in relatively civilized tones, much more gentlemanly than those used in the controversy with the Slavophiles. Nonetheless the underlying passion seems to have been great, for the most fundamental principles were at stake. In essence, Granovski's objections to Herzen's position were those of a reformist liberal to a radical revolutionary, and his moderation in matters religious paralleled, and was related to, his moderation in politics. Similarly Herzen's views showed the same association of social radicalism and extreme rationalism displayed in more striking fashion the following year by Belinski's famous *Letter to Gogol*. Hence for Herzen the breach was the confirmation of the necessary link between revolutionary politics and atheistic "science" which he had first proclaimed in his essays on dilettantism. The party of the Westerners, formed at the beginning of the decade in response to the conservative nationalism of the Slavophiles, had, in effect, disintegrated as a result of its own attacks on the latter, for in making clear their differences with the enemy they had also articulated latent differences among themselves. Just as the adherents of Official Nationality were the Right and the Slavophiles the Right Center of intellectual politics in the forties, by 1846 the Westerners had split into a Left Center represented by Granovski and an extreme Left represented by Herzen. Thus, for the first time the ideological spectrum of modern politics was complete in Russia.

Nevertheless, it must be emphasized that the two wings of the Left disagreed over means and not ends. The contrast between the parties of Granovski and Herzen was not a contrast between "individualists" and "collectivists," or between "liberty" and "equality," or between "politics" and "economics," or any of the other dichotomies that are usually supposed to separate liberals from socialists. Enough has been said to indicate that Herzen was as extreme an individualist and libertarian as could exist, and that he had almost no sense of the economic. The difference between the two groups was in the measure of intransigence, impatience, and indeed of violence which each side brought to the same problem of liberalizing and modernizing Russia.

The demand of Herzen (and Belinski) was the total realization of the promises of "enlightenment" and "humanism," the complete destruction of the "old world" and the inauguration of the "new," without any gradual transitions, compromises, or half measures. If pushed to its logical conclusion, this position meant the liberalization of Russia in opposition to the autocracy, by violence and revolution if necessary. The demand of Granovski and his group was "humanism" achieved by peaceful and gradual means, by the slow penetration of education from above. Hence, in practice it meant working with the autocracy, trying to persuade it to grant emancipation of the peasants, civil liberties, and eventually some measure of popular participation in government. This difference between reform *through* the existing government and reform *against* it was to be the principal dividing line between Russian liberals and socialists throughout the nineteenth century, and the quarrel between Herzen and Granovski was the first clear ideological manifestation of this division in Russian history.

Indeed this intransigent maximalism is perhaps what is most fundamental to Herzen's socialism and the chief characteristic which his doctrine had in common with those of the European Left, for such intransigence is the primeval stuff of socialism before it receives any of the programmatic elaborations which local conditions or tactical considerations impose and which create its proletarian or peasant, populist or putschist forms. To be sure, this maximalism had always been Herzen's position, but until now it had remained largely in the realm of abstraction. In his Saint-Simonian and Schellingian days he had sublimated it into a pure poetry of progress and his dream of revolution had been so insubstantial as to be confused with a religious "regeneration." With his conversion to Left Hegelian "realism" this intransigence was for the first time forged into a weapon of combat in the real world, yet it was still a purely ideological weapon. Only through his contact with French radicalism of the forties, and, above all, in the conflict with his friends, did his maximalism at last became all-embracing and clearly social no less than cerebral. But even this ultimate intransigence was not wholly free from abstraction. As of the late forties Herzen must be considered a committed revolutionary because he considered himself to be one; yet, by the very nature of things, his revolutionary commitment could not go beyond words, ideas and sentiment. As a practical matter he could accomplish no more against the autocracy than Granovski could accomplish with it; the socialism of the one was as disembodied as the liberalism of the other. Nonetheless, Herzen had taken the last ideological step toward total intransigence, and it was Nicholas' fault, not his own, if for the moment he could go no further and take the first revolutionary step in the realm of "life."

4

The intellectual differences among the Westerners rapidly led to personal differences as well. Although social relations were not suspended between the two factions, as had happened with the Slavophiles, they did grow perceptibly cooler, especially between Herzen and Granovski. It also seems that personal friction between the wives added to the general acrimony. Only Ogarev, as usual less passionate in his convictions than his friend, preserved the old personal link substantially intact. For Herzen, though, it was the end of the circle, that life of close community which replaced participation in the social body as a whole.[40]

Herzen, in effect, had lost his fight to persuade the group and found himself isolated, with only Ogarev as an ally. Belinski was far away in Petersburg, and anyway he was only in partial agreement with Herzen, sharing his atheism and his general extremism, but condemning the cult of the simple people and even beginning to display a certain skepticism toward socialism.[41] Herzen had experienced a similar isolation in 1839–40, just after his return from Vladimir, when he had also been the lone radical, with only the wavering Ogarev at his side against the conservatism of the orthodox Hegelians. At that time Herzen had reacted by conquering the circle, and in particular by helping to convert Belinski to socialism. The atmosphere then, however, had been one of general reaction against apolitical idealism, and Herzen's reinstatement in the circle had not been too difficult. But now he had pushed beyond what his friends were willing to accept, and he found himself expelled from the circle, morally if not socially. He was deprived of the only sympathetic understanding and the sole forum he enjoyed in Russia. He had lost the role as a moral authority which the circle had afforded him all his life. And there was nowhere else to turn.

To this situation Herzen reacted with the full force of his sensitive pride. Just as he had done in 1839–40, he refused all compromise with the errors of his opponents and retreated into an indignant self-righteousness; in ever stronger terms he denounced the God, the liberalism, and the moderation of his friends. Furthermore, the controversies of the following year suggest that socialism quickly replaced religion as the principal bone of contention.[42] The more Herzen preached Louis Blanc and Proudhon, the more Granovski, and in particular Botkin, made a cult of the bourgeoisie and the July Monarchy. Neither side, of course, had a clear grasp of French problems, nor was either side concerned about Louis Blanc or Louis Philippe *per se*, but in the course of the quarrel, the former for Herzen and the latter for Granovski became emotionally charged symbols of differing attitudes towards reform in Russia. For

Granovski and the moderates the wildest dream of liberty was Westernization in the literal sense of imitating — but only several decades hence — the existing and admittedly imperfect institutions of Europe. For Herzen such caution was despicable, and he understood Westernization only in the figurative sense of seeking inspiration in the perfect socialist institutions of the Europe of the future.

This way of posing the problem, however, made Herzen increasingly suspicious of the imperfect West of the present. After his first flirtation with nationalism in 1843–44, the obscurantism of the Slavophiles and their hostility to European freedom gave him a shove leftward and westward. Yet, once the flagrant errors of the "Slavs" had been disposed of, he for the first time perceived the more subtle "superstition" and political timidity of most of the Westerners. But hostility toward the Westerners inevitably tended to become hostility toward the West they glorified. This second clash, therefore, not only pushed Herzen still further leftward, but for the first time moved him to attack the whole of existing civilization, including its most advanced, liberal and European forms.[43] And from this position a return to nationalism was just one step away.

With such issues dividing the circle, by the end of 1846 Herzen found life in Moscow and Russia intolerable. As early as 1844, at the time of the break with the Slavophiles, he had written in his *Diary* after a summer in the country:

It is time to return to Moscow, but I no more desire to do so than I desire death. Here life is so much more pure and noble; there we have no real activity or vocation: to exhaust oneself in eternal lamentation, in concentrated sorrow, is not activity. What is there for me to do in Moscow? For what reason remain there? Two or three close friends and a stupid, vile herd. When I look at the poor peasants the blood rushes to my heart. I am ashamed of my rights; I am ashamed that I am partly responsible for the misery of their life.[44]

By 1846, even these few close friends were gone. Herzen's sense of divorce from society was total, and his desire to escape from Russia was overwhelming.[45]

Providentially, just at this moment it became possible to depart. In 1846 his father died, leaving him the heir to very considerable wealth. After this change in his fortunes Herzen applied once again for a foreign passport to realize the dream of visiting Europe which he had cherished ever since the university. Thanks to the intervention of friends, on this occasion the police surveillance was lifted and the precious passport granted.[46] In January 1847, Herzen, accompanied by Natalie, their three children, and his mother, finally left Russia en route for the fabled and controversial West.

The little group of his friends, reminded by this departure of their tiny numbers and their isolation from society, drew together for the last time. Both sides forgot their ideological differences, or at least tacitly agreed not to talk about them. The circle accompanied Herzen to the first post-station outside of Moscow, where the parting took place amidst effusions of tears, sentiment, and champagne.[47] Granovski and Korsh in particular were deeply affected. Herzen was forgiving and conciliatory, but more exuberant at the thought of the adventures he obscurely hoped awaited him than moved by leaving his friends: with every nerve he was aspiring *"dahin! dahin!"* [48]

A few days later his coach rolled past the last double-headed eagle marking the limits of the empire of the Romanovs. As he continued on the road to Königsberg he was struck by a novel sight: "There stood a boundary-marker and on it, covered with snow, a gaunt *one-headed* [Prussian] eagle: all to the good — one head less."[49] Although he did not know it, he would never see Russia or most of his friends again.

CHAPTER XIV

The Crucial Year — 1847

WITH Herzen's removal to the West the great adventure of his life began: emigration transformed him from a minor journalist, writing gnarled Hegelian treatises and second-rate social fiction for the Moscow intellectuals, into a major revolutionary figure. If he had not succeeded in escaping from Russia when he did, his place in history would have been modest indeed — that of a more radical Granovski or of a sub-Belinski. A year later it would have been too late, for from 1848 to the death of Nicholas it was extremely difficult to leave Russia, and quite impossible for one with Herzen's past. And if he had left only after 1855 he would have missed the major revolution of the century, and hence have lacked the aura of authority conferred by participation, however modest, in that event. Indeed, what would have been left of his revolutionary ardor after nine more years of frustration in Russia? Among Herzen's friends, only Ogarev kept his radical faith intact under the pressures of the new reaction which began in 1848, the worst of Nicholas' reign; all the others went the way of increasing moderation, and often of frank conservatism.[1]

Escape to the West on the eve of the great upheaval gave Herzen the chance to be the first important Russian figure after Bakunin to pass from radical dreams to a real revolutionary commitment. It gave him the chance, again alongside Bakunin, to be the first Russian spokesman to take his place among the representatives of European "democracy," as all movements to the left of liberal constitutionalism, based on a class suffrage, were called at the time. In this Herzen actually eclipsed his friend. From his conversion to revolution in 1842 until 1848 Bakunin was a minor figure, representing only himself and holding little prestige in European "democracy." He had, moreover, no influence within Russia; even the example of his revolt was unknown except to a handful of his former friends. In 1848 and 1849, to be sure, he experienced a brief burst of revolutionary glory in Bohemia and Saxony, but this had no repercussions in Russia. Then from 1849 until 1861 he was out of the picture entirely, in prisons or Siberia. Herzen was left with the stage to himself as *the* representative of the Russian "revolution," in the eyes of both Europe and his homeland. As a continuous tradition, the Russian revolutionary emigration dates from Herzen's defection rather than from the more spectacular exploits of Bakunin. Finally, because of the freedom of expression afforded by the West, Herzen became the first of his countrymen to elaborate and disseminate a specifically national theory of revolution. With Herzen's emigration the Russian revolution was transformed from an intellectual protest into a living reality, however feeble for the moment, and soon into a tradition and a *mystique*.

It is customary to begin discussion of Herzen's European adventures with the quotation of a few lyric flights from *My Past and Thoughts* or other of his post-1848 writings, where he tells how he hurried across Germany, inattentive to all he saw in his eagerness to arrive at his goal — Paris. "Finally we *arrived* . . . and so I was really in Paris, not in a dream but in reality . . . that moment of which I had dreamed since childhood!" He ran to look at the *Hôtel de Ville*, the moral center of radical Paris, and the *café de Foy* in the Palais Royal, whence Camille Desmoulins had led the mob to the assault on the Bastille — "all those names which had been native to me for so many years." [2] "The name of Paris was wedded with all the noblest enthusiasms of contemporary humanity. I entered it with reverence, as men used to enter Jerusalem and Rome." [3] The impression the reader receives is that Herzen arrived in Paris a convinced Westerner, expecting the imminent overthrow of the existing order and the establishment of socialism. Then begins the sad tale of his disillusionment. The Parisian Beatrice turned out to be no more than a *lorette*, kept by the disgusting bourgeoisie of Louis Philippe and Guizot. This discovery was followed by the far more shattering disappointment of the failure of the Revolution of 1848, not only to create socialism but even liberal democracy. In justifiable fury, therefore, Herzen turned on his former idol, the West, declaring it to be irredeemably reactionary and "decrepit"; he then returned to his native roots and placed all his revolutionary hopes in Russia and its "socialist" peasant commune.

Although this picture contains a grain of truth, it is largely myth. First of all, it distorts the time schedule of Herzen's disillusion with the West, which, as we will see, clearly antedated 1848. Yet the problem of dating is in itself of minor importance, and Herzen's precocious loss of faith in the West has been noticed by all who have read his writings carefully.[4] The date is, however, of much consequence for the light it throws on the more important question of his motivation in rejecting the West, and this has received little attention. The conventional picture possesses the grave defect of making Herzen's evolution appear too rational: a pondered political deduction based on the observation of conditions. In reality his analysis of the Revolution of 1848 was a subjective and visceral reaction, poured forth in torrents of rhetoric which, as so often with Herzen, make difficult uncovering the political sense of what he was trying to say.

In fact, all through his first years in the West Herzen was talking about the constructs of his own mind much more than about European events, constructs he had developed to make life bearable in Russia and which he brought with him when he crossed the frontier: the "new world," the social Incarnation of Christianity, total revolution, and the absolute liberty of man. No conceivable Europe could have satisfied such ideals. Herzen would have reacted much the way he did even if the Revolution had succeeded in establishing good liberal republics everywhere west of Russia, or if there had been no Revolution at all. To be sure, the constructs of his mind were always related to the events transpiring around him, but these events by no means governed his evolution; they were simply one of several catalysts — and perhaps not the most important — which precipitated the development of his new social theories.

2

Much has already been said in previous chapters about certain elements of Herzen's thought which, under appropriate circumstances, could be used for damning Europe and idealizing Russia. A minor theme of his meditations since the university had been that of historical "youth" or "virginity": the German barbarians, "virgin peoples . . . pure and virtuous" had replaced "rotting" Rome.[5] In Viatka he had been struck by the "newness" of Siberia which imparted an "impulse toward progress" lacking in lands burdened by an "aristocratic past."[6] The same idea recurs throughout the forties. Often it is accompanied by the notion of Europe's possible "decrepitude." The hero of *The German Traveler* of Herzen's university days, "weary with the Europe" of the French Revolution, had "gone east to rest from her," just as had Beltov's Genevan tutor, "indignant at Europe."[7] The origin of such thinking, no doubt, is the eighteenth-century idea of the "noble savage" and of the superior virtue of a "state of nature" over "corrupt" civilization. This idea reached Herzen in the nationalistic transposition given it by German historicism, which emphasized the advantage of poor but new forms of the Idea over rich but old ones, exhausted precisely because they had already made their contribution to the development of humanity. Although until he left Russia his talk of historical "youth" was rather abstract and literary, nonetheless preoccupation with this theme reveals an amorphous yet deep nationalism, the full strength of which he himself hardly suspected.

It would require only the shock of contact with something alien to bring it sharply into focus.

A similar hint of latent nationalism is implicit in a more important theme of Herzen's thought before leaving Russia: the incessantly repeated parallels between the end of the ancient world and the dissolution of the "old world" of his own day. Of the three forces of antique civilization — "dying" Rome, the barbarians, and Christianity — only the last possessed a precise modern equivalent: socialism. Rome found a vague counterpart in the old world which socialism would sweep away, while the barbarians were more or less suspended in mid-air without anything in particular to correspond to — altogether a rather untidy historical parallel, whereas idealism liked its parallels neat. Obviously the analogy could be vastly improved by equating Rome with the West and the dangling barbarians with the "virgin" Slavs. Although Herzen's evolution, of course, was not governed primarily by considerations of symmetry, these could help to convince him once he had decided on a position for other reasons, since through long habit he took idealism's pseudo-logic of analogy seriously.

Other elements than nationalism, however, entered into Herzen's rejection of the West. The most important of these was his revulsion at that conglomeration of "Roman," "feudal," and "Christian" values whose continued survival in new guises constituted in his eyes the principal obstacle to the creation of the "new world." Although these were the values of modern civilization in general, and hence common to both Russia and Europe, their place of origin was the West, as indeed their names indicate. Therefore, as Herzen's critique of modern civilization grew in acerbity throughout the forties, his thought inevitably acquired an anti-Western cast. This process was brought to a culmination by his quarrel with the moderate Westerners in 1846. Just how far it had gone by that time may be judged by two articles written shortly before he left Russia, which, though their meaning is more than usually obscured by censorship, still reveal much about his mood on the eve of his encounter with Europe.

The first article, entitled enigmatically *About This and That,* was written at the end of 1845 at a time when tension within the circle, although still latent, was beginning to build up. It began with the note Herzen had been intoning since his *Dilettantism in Science.* "It is not the truths of science which are difficult, but cleansing human consciousness of all inherited rubbish, of all the accumulated silt, the acceptance of the unnatural for the natural, the unintelligible for the intelligible." Yet this process now seemed more difficult to Herzen than it had a few years earlier; the mind was weighted down by the immense force of irrational "habit" — "the thickest chain about the legs of humanity . . . stronger

than convictions, talent, character, passion, intelligence." [8] Because of
the resistance of his friends to that total break with the past demanded
by "science," his position had hardened since the time he wrote his essays
on dilettantism. Then he had spoken sympathetically of the "pain"
involved in shedding the "dear" illusions of the past; now he showed
only impatience at their stubborn survival despite all reason. It was a
change of tone more than of position, but the tone was approaching
that of 1848. Furthermore, the persisting "romanticism" of his friends led
him to doubt the "liberation" of even the most advanced individuals, who,
for all their supposed enlightenment, continued to live by an irrational
mixture of outmoded ethical systems. "One marvels how the mind can
advance to where it simultaneously combines in its moral code the stoic
sentences of Seneca and Cato, the romantic rapture of the medieval
knight, the preachments of self-abnegation of the pious hermits of the
Thebaid, and the self-seeking principles of political economy." [9]

The contemporary world had, in fact, failed to achieve any significant
liberation from the fetters of the past.

Our critical, analytic century, which attacks and dissects all the weightiest
problems . . . calmly permits the grossest, the most stupid superstition to
flourish at its very feet, superstition that hinders humanity's advance and
treacherously covers over the bogs and the pits. The cannon balls shot forth
to destroy the crumbling edifice of Gothic prejudice fly over the heads of the
pre-Gothic huts, because the latter are under the very muzzle. [10]

An amalgam of warmed-over transcendent values above, among the elite,
and the full flower of superstition below, among the masses—these after
1848 would be for Herzen the cause of Europe's decrepitude. This
pessimism about the progress of enlightenment contrasts sharply with
the optimism of his *Dilettantism* a few years earlier.

The tone rises a pitch higher in the second article, appropriately
entitled *New Variations On Old Themes*. Written in large part, if not entirely, at Sokolovo in 1846, it is the only direct document of Herzen's
quarrel with the moderate Westerners, a distinction which, surprisingly,
has not saved it from neglect by historians. [11] With Granovski and his
allies clearly in mind, Herzen wrote: "Turn wherever you will, you
always find in our psychology the same struggle of consciousness with
habit, of thought with legend, of logic with tradition, of mind with immediacy [instinct], of science with history." Even the language of contemporary man impedes liberation: "we constantly lie unwillingly; we
speak in ready-made stereotyped phrases . . . taken from two completely defunct world-views — the Roman and feudal." Moreover, modern
man's refusal to choose between reason and religion led to the direst
political consequences: "from this follows the desire to enjoy all the
blessings of the present and of the future without losing any of the

blessings of the past, despite the fact that recognition of the injustices of the latter is the indispensable condition for the realization of the former." In clearer language, the retention of anything from the past, no matter how good in itself, was incompatible with the creation of a truly new world. Such "cowardly, lying, worn-out tendencies" must be combatted with all the force of one's being. And what was the cause of this moral confusion? "Laziness and habit — these are the two unshakable pillars of authority." Man's bad education was also to blame, but most of all the fault lay in lack of "courage," of "honesty" in "science," and in the fear of taking an independent stand.[12] Never before had Herzen been so violent in denouncing slavery to past beliefs.

He could be more sweeping still in the criticism of his friends. "Whoever does not root out from his breast *everything* that is not justified by reason is not free and is capable of falling so far as to turn away from *all* reason." Herzen had taken the intransigent stand of all or nothing. Anything short of total reason was the grossest superstition; anything short of total freedom was abject slavery. All intermediate — or liberal — stands he rejected as worth nothing. To make the political implications of his position as clear as the censorship would permit he added: "The question does not lie in the width or breadth of military stripes; the question is whether there should be military stripes at all." Yet men were afraid of such total freedom.

From the beginning of time . . . men have talked about moral independence . . . about its charms, yet they never taste these charms because they are incomparably more tied . . . to authority, to external commands and imperatives than to moral freedom. . . . The responsibility of independence (*samobytnost*) is frightening to people; their love of moral freedom is satisfied by eternal waiting, eternal aspiration. They make haste slowly and strive moderately toward the object of their desires, sentimentally believing that their desires will be realized, if not in the present, then in the future. Such a faith consoles and reconciles them with the present — what could be better? [13]

This was Herzen's definition of a liberal: an individual who talks liberty only in order to live his slavery more easily, and who, when the battle lines are drawn between the "old world" and the "new," is afraid to assume the risk of "being himself," and like a "minor" craves the "wardship" of authority.

This definition was designed especially to fit Granovski and his partisans, but it also applied to most of the supposed rebels of modern enlightenment.

The first thing that people who have thrown off one authority do is to accept another, let us say better, but all the same just as oppressive, and, if one forgets its contents, then not better at all, for the simple reason that men have advanced; and so the proportion remains the same. . . . Even such privileged emancipators as Voltaire, although they knew how to scoff at religion, remained simply idolaters before *their own inventions and phantoms.*

The whole of Western enlightenment, down to its last word, German "science," had not really brought freedom from superstition and reverence before authority.

The Votiaks tremble before a stick to which is attached a goat's beard: this is their sacred devil (*shaitan*). The Germans tremble before the terrible phantoms of their science. Of course, from the crude sacred devil of the Votiaks to the sacred devil of German philosophy is a great step; still, it is not difficult to discover a kinship between them.[14]

Nor had all the revolutions since 1789 freed man from authorities outside himself; indeed, they seem, paradoxically, almost to have made matters worse; "the very *love of freedom* has served as an inexhaustible source of moral oppression and servitude." In other words, all constitutional monarchies (such as that of Louis Philippe), and even democratic republics (such as that of the Convention or that dreamed of by the radicals grouped around Ledru-Rollin and *La Réforme*) were morally no better than autocracy. In the same paradoxical manner, even the most emancipated individual had a veritable "love of oppression, of authority, founded on self-contempt, on the annihilation of his own worth." In conclusion to his article, therefore, Herzen apostrophized his pusillanimous friends, paraphrasing grandiloquently Kent's words to the mad Lear: "We can say to many who glory in their intellectual freedom: 'I see on your brow something that makes me call you slave.'"

Taken in themselves these remarks may not appear very startling or bold. But when they are given the full force, and the political implications, of which the censorship deprived them, they become crucial for understanding Herzen's reaction to the West, for they are exactly the same accusations he would level at Europe after 1848. Yet they were first of all his portrait of Granovski and the moderate Westerners, and the two—Europe and his Moscow friends—would remain equated in his mind all through the experience of 1848. Indeed, *New Variations On Old Themes* was already partially an attack on the West, and not just on his friends. In 1858 in a revealing introduction to the second edition of the *Letters From France and Italy*, one of his principal books damning the West, he sought to answer the Russian liberals who criticized him "for speaking of Europe laughingly . . . for destroying faith in her. To these objections I have replied more than once," and *New Variations On Old Themes* was cited as one of these occasions.[15] Before he ever left Russia, then, Herzen had made up his mind that he would not find Granovski's Europe to his liking. Far from entering Paris with a feeling of "reverence," he arrived prepared to be appalled, and in search of ammunition to hurl back at his wayward friends.

3

Like the crucial summer at Sokolovo, the even more crucial year of 1847, when in effect Herzen decided that the West was "rotten" and that the future belonged to Russia, unfortunately is not illumined by the abundance of documentation which most of his career presents. *My Past and Thoughts* offers only a few pages, and these are devoted to his voyage across Germany, while the decisive months in Paris receive only a few paragraphs, as if he did not care to recall them. Instead the reader is referred to *Letters from France and Italy*, but this merely gives his reaction to the West without explaining how he arrived at it.[16] His surviving correspondence for the year is also meager. There is, however, one significant source for his Parisian stay: the memoirs of Annenkov. Fortunately, Annenkov was a more objective, if less brilliant, reporter of men and events than Herzen.[17] Moreover, he was the only person to have seen him both in his Moscow circle while harmony still reigned and immediately after his arrival in Paris; hence he alone observed directly the changes that transplantation produced.

Annenkov, who had not seen Herzen since 1845, was immediately struck by the change in him. After an initial period of reticence, Herzen poured forth his grievances against his friends. Annenkov was surprised by the bitterness of Herzen's tone, and by his determination to break with the past. "After several sincere and confidential conversations . . . I could no longer doubt, to my great amazement, that in the eyes of Herzen and his family Moscow had completely withered, its color had faded, it had lost its appeal to the heart. The whole of their former life there seemed to Herzen and his wife a desiccated steppe." [18] Herzen declared his resolve to shake the dust of an unappreciative Moscow from his feet and begin a new life. He was thirty-five at the time, still young and full of "the strong passions" on which he had always prided himself; the best of life was still ahead of him, and he wished to do something noble and resounding with it. Yet this start of a new existence was hardly accompanied by serenity of spirit; rather his mood was one of pent-up tension restlessly seeking some outlet. For Annenkov, Herzen's quarrel with his friends "shed great light on his conduct in Paris, on all his feverish haste to establish himself in a new life." [19] This very irritability, as well as the febrility of his search for a new life, betrayed the depth of the shock occasioned by the collapse of the circle. Paradoxically, all through 1847, in his efforts to break away from the past he remained very much under its influence.

How did Herzen envisage his new life at this time? His passport had been issued for travel "to Germany and Italy for the health of his wife," and for a period of only six months.[20] Yet in spite of this he went straight to Paris. For the ordinary Russian tourist this would not have been a great imprudence. At the time Russian passports did not officially mention France because Nicholas was still snubbing the "usurper" Louis-Philippe; yet everyone went there just the same, "secretly, like a thief" in Annenkov's words, and the Russian government willingly closed its eyes.[21] For Herzen, though, who only a few months before had been released from thirteen years of police surveillance, such a step was a little reckless.[22] As for the six-months time limit on his European stay, he appears never to have intended to respect it, though it is not clear whether this involved a breach of legality.[23] In all events at no time between his arrival and his final break with the Russian government in 1849 did he display any intention of returning home. When Annenkov first saw him in Paris he had the feeling that, unlike other Russian visitors come to view the radical Babylon as idle tourists, Herzen had come to stay. Although of course he did not consciously decide to emigrate at this time, he set about seeking his new life in directions that were incompatible with a return to Russia.[24]

Even the physical appearances of Herzen and his wife changed, as if to mark by tangible symbols the beginning of their new life. Annenkov portrays Herzen on his arrival "still bearing on all his exterior the sharp imprint of an inhabitant of Moscow," clad in a long frock-coat, which got in the way of his quick movement, and wearing long hair — in short, looking slightly ridiculous and provincial. He was soon transformed, however, "into a complete gentleman of the Western race, with clipped hair, a dandified beard that quickly assumed the correct outlines, and a jacket of free and elegant cut," while Natalie changed "from the quiet, pensive and romantic lady of the [Moscow] circle . . . into a brilliant tourist completely worthy to occupy a place of honor in the great world capital." [25] Herzen and his wife were resolved not to remain behind the much-vaunted West in anything, no matter how trivial. They set about acquainting themselves with the theaters, the restaurants, and the sights of Paris with a vengeance born of years of waiting.

But Herzen had also come to Paris for more serious things. One of his most persistent fantasies had been that of the Russian visitor to Paris during the Great Revolution. He had sketched it first in his youthful tale, *The German Traveler*. It had reappeared intermittently in his preoccupation with Anacharsis Cloots, his hero among the *conventionnels*. Cloots to be sure was not a Russian, but like Herzen he was a man from the outside, and an aristocrat to boot, come to play a role in the great event.[26] During his stay in Paris Herzen worked on his already mentioned novel, *Duty Before All*, of which only the first parts were finished. The hero, the illegitimate son of a great aristocrat of the time of Catherine, bears a striking resemblance to Herzen, and the climax of his adventures is a visit to Paris in 1789, where he plays a glorious role in storming the Bastille.[27] As an illustration of the recklessness of Herzen's mood from the very beginning of his stay abroad, he sent these chapters to Panaev in Petersburg for publication. To the latter it seemed that Herzen had lost his mind in presuming to get such material past the censors, and the manuscript was returned forthwith.[28] Does this mean, as is often maintained, that Herzen came to Paris expecting a revolution, in which he perhaps would play some role? Almost certainly not. At no time before February 1848 did he indicate that he thought a revolution was imminent; in fact, as will be shown later, he thought precisely the contrary.

Instead he hoped for something more limited and personal: a position as Russia's spokesman in the international movement of protest whose center was Paris, to which in the preceding decade malcontents had flocked, literally by the thousands, from all corners of the continent. The revolutionary daydreams of *Duty Before All* were simply the magnified projection of this hope. Herzen's real sentiments are revealed clearly in a short section of *My Past and Thoughts* addressed in 1853 to his Moscow friends, and intended as a justification of his emigration.

I boldly left you with rash self-assurance, with a haughty confidence in life. I hastened to tear myself away from a small knot of people, tightly grown together, so terribly near to one another, bound by a deep love and a common sorrow [for Russia]. Distant, open places beckoned to me, open struggle and free speech; I sought an independent arena, I wished to try my strength in freedom.[29]

Herzen's irritation with his friends was caused not just by his ideological disagreements with them but also by the fact that, through no fault of their own, they symbolized the narrow limits to ambition and activity imposed by existence in Russia. Life with them offered only the tiny arena of the circle or the censored pages of the *Annals of the Fatherland*, whereas Herzen desired a truly full and free life. Like all the more vigorous spirits of his generation, such as Belinski or Bakunin, Herzen had at last come to detest the "*kruzhok*" as an institution.

One of his half-formulated purposes in going to Paris was to replace the paltry circle of his Moscow friends with the great family of European "democracy." This desire was fully as important as that for freedom of speech. The passage last quoted continues: "I found everything I sought, even recognition from the old self-satisfied world [Europe]." His first moment of triumph came in Rome in March of 1848.

Cicerovacchio was on the balcony, brightly lighted by torches and candelabra, and beside him, shielded by the banner of Italy, stood four young women, all *four Russian* [Herzen's wife and three travelling companions]. . . . I see them, as if it were now, on that stone tribune, and below, the swaying, innumerable mass who mingled with their shouts for war [against Austria] and curses against the Jesuits a loud cry of *"Evviva le donne forestiere."* . . . We were accepted by them into the European struggle.[30]

Again, this desire to crash European democracy was only dimly formulated in 1847. Herzen knew he wanted some sort of position in radical society. He was not a man of barricades like Bakunin; the only possibility, therefore, was radical journalism. But it was only gradually that he was to find his way to this.

The desire for radical standing soon added new irritations to those brought from Moscow. The stars of European democracy, of course, were the French, the only people who had made a major revolution and who produced most of the literature on which the radicals of other nations fed. It seems that Herzen at first tried to pay them court, but met with a rebuff. "I confess that at the beginning I was carried away and thought that to speak in a café with the author of *The History of Ten Years* [Louis Blanc] or at Bakunin's with Proudhon was some sort of rank, a promotion; but with me all experiences in idolatry and graven images do not last very long and very soon give way to the most complete negation."[31] His irritation, therefore, quickly came to be directed not only at Granovski's bourgeois West, but at his own socialist West as well. Aristocrat, democrat, and iconoclast that he was, he would kowtow to no one, not even to the reddest. Soviet historians, praising Herzen for his staunch defense of Russian radical dignity against "bourgeois cosmopolitanism," have, in their odd way, something of a point.[32]

The French in particular wounded his pride.

Simply to go to look at celebrities I considered unbecoming. In addition I liked very little the tone of condescending superiority of the French with Russians. They approve, encourage us, praise our pronunciation and our wealth; we put up with all this and act like suppliants toward them, even half excusing ourselves, only too glad when out of politeness they take us for Frenchmen. . . . In order to be on another footing with them one has to *impose*, and for that certain rights are necessary, which I did not then have, but which I made use of once I acquired them.[33]

The rights in question were a radical name and a reputation for revolutionary seriousness; Herzen did not acquire these until he became a political *émigré*, and until the European revolution had failed, thereby giving him the opportunity to extoll the virtues of the coming Russian revolution — his own. Yet even when he attained this position he never warmed to the French, or indeed to any of the major European peoples; the only nationalities he liked were downtrodden ones like the Poles and, especially, the Italians. The reason for this was that the French and the Germans, as groups if not always as individuals, offered the greatest resistance to his crashing of revolutionary society. At the time of his arrival in Paris all liberals and radicals regarded Russia as hopelessly reactionary, the only irretrievably lost soul among the nations of Europe. No one would take seriously a Russian radical, since everyone knew that no such creature existed. To be sure, Bakunin was a good fellow, but at this time no one considered that he represented anything but the eccentricity of a student who had never grown up. Herzen's new mission in life was to accustom the haughty Europeans to the idea of radical Russia's and his own existence. With the French there was a further problem. Ever since the revolutionary and Napoleonic wars they looked on themselves as the destined liberators of mankind — or at least of all oppressed Poles, Italians, and Germans (it never seemed to occur to anyone to talk about *Russian* liberation). Herzen quickly came to find this "revolutionary paternalism" intolerable, and it is fair to suggest that he was not completely displeased the next year by the fiasco of France's efforts to liberate herself.

Unwilling to pay court to the French, Herzen was thrown back for company on foreign refugees, like himself provincials in the capital of revolution. Significantly, he felt most at home with the Germans; in spite of all his scorn for their "pedantry" and "Buddhism," he was nearer to them in education and mentality than to any other European nationality. Indeed no one else could fully understand the idealistic categories in which he continued to express himself, despite his renunciation of all "romanticism." It is not an accident that, although the only Europeans for whom Herzen ever expressed admiration were the "broadnatured" Italians, his closest personal friends were Germans. In 1847, in Paris, he began what were to be lifelong friendships with two intimates of Bakunin, the musician Adolf Reichel and the naturalist Karl Vogt, who was later a radical member of the Frankfurt Parliament, an enemy of Karl Marx, and a noted popularizer of a materialism founded on the then relatively new sciences of physiology and chemistry, a position, as we have seen, to which Herzen himself had come to adhere during the forties.

Herzen's closest European friend, however, soon came to be George Herwegh, to whom he bore a letter from Ogarev and was actually introduced by Bakunin.[34] Herwegh had been a leading poet of "Young Germany," and was now a dominant figure in the colony of German exiles in Paris. He was the only celebrity of international democracy with whom Herzen became close during his first two years abroad, for he was already favorably disposed to Russian radicalism through his friendship with Bakunin and Ogarev and treated Herzen as an equal from the beginning.[35] This relationship was later to have disastrous consequences for Herzen's personal life (of which more will be said later), but at first it helped to fill the emotional void left by the coolness toward his Moscow friends. None of these connections, however, represented much of a change from the intellectual world of Moscow.

This is even more true of Herzen's relations with most of his compatriots abroad, who were his principal companions until the end of 1848. In addition to Annenkov, Herzen saw much of some friends of Ogarev, a gentry family named Tuchkov then making the grand tour of Europe; the father had been connected with the Decembrists and the family's politics were strongly liberal. Somewhat less liberal was another close companion, the novelist Turgenev.[36] These contacts were not important in Herzen's political development since they were too moderate, but like his German friendships they served the negative function of keeping him isolated from French society. In spite of all his efforts, throughout the events of 1848 he remained an outsider in Paris, a fact which is not without significance in understanding his responses to the Revolution.

4

Most important of all during Herzen's first year abroad was his contact with his former foe Bakunin and his old university comrade Sazonov. Bakunin was now the reddest of the red and a full-time political exile, and Sazonov, though less radical and less compromised with the Russian authorities, was still deeply involved in democratic politics. Herzen had previously known Bakunin only slightly, and had not particularly liked him. Since the resounding article of "Jules Elisard" in the *Deutsche Jahrbücher*, however, he had forgiven Bakunin's past and had followed his career, insofar as this was possible, with growing admiration.[37] For Sazonov, in spite of their closeness at the university, Herzen had long since ceased to have any great admiration,[38] but to him, too, much was now forgiven because of his radical interests. Sazonov had been in Paris since 1840 and Bakunin since 1844; both were active in radical circles, principally among the Poles and Germans. Together they constituted the whole of the Russian political "emigration" at the time, if so modest a contingent may be glorified by a title which later became so august. Significantly, these were the first persons Herzen sought out in Paris,[39] and the example they presented was no doubt suggestive to him. At first he was "beside himself with joy" to see them. Relations rapidly soured, however, and this constituted a new source of irritation, which together with those already mentioned finally determined his reaction to the West.

The cause of the trouble is best revealed in a well-known passage of *My Past and Thoughts* describing Herzen's first meetings with his favorite French socialist, Proudhon.

I met him once or twice at Bakunin's, with whom he was very close. Bakunin then lived with Reichel in an extremely modest apartment on the Left Bank in the Rue de Bourgogne. Proudhon often came there to listen to Reichel's Beethoven and Bakunin's Hegel — the philosophical disputations lasted longer than the symphonies. They reminded one of the famous all-night vigils of Bakunin with Khomiakov at Chaadaev's, or at the Elagin's over the same Hegel. In 1847 Karl Vogt, who also lived in the Rue de Bourgogne and often visited Reichel and Bakunin, one evening got bored listening to endless discussions about the *Phenomenology* and went home to bed. The next morning he dropped in for Reichel: the two were to go to the *Jardin des Plantes*. He was surprised to hear, in spite of the early hour, conversation in Bakunin's study. He opened the door — Bakunin and Proudhon were sitting in the very same place before a dead fire, finishing in a few short phrases the discussion begun the night before.[40]

Although Herzen was sensitive to the picturesque aspect of this scene, he was also irked by what he considered to be Bakunin's playing court fool to French celebrity. It offended his sense of that dignity which he felt should surround the heirs of the Decembrists when meeting the heirs of the Mountain. "Fearing from the beginning the humble role of our compatriots and the patronage of great men, I did not try to become acquainted even with Proudhon."

Relations were further envenomed when Sazonov and Bakunin inquired about the progress of democracy back home. Herzen was annoyed by the pair's unrealistic expectation of imminent revolution in Russia, and he was particularly vexed by Sazonov's daydreaming of being "invited" to assume a ministerial post in the new regime. To Herzen such illusions were an insult to the real progress that enlightenment had made in Russia since the two had left. He tried to explain to them the enormous historical significance of Granovski's public lectures, the articles of Belinski, the debate between Westerners and Slavophiles, and the awakening of national consciousness produced by Gogol's *Dead Souls*. Sazonov and Bakunin were unimpressed by such literary trivia, for they had tasted the "activity" of Western radicalism. Herzen was immeasurably irked by this scorn for the progress of Russian humanism. The tension became still more acute when the pair, particularly Sazonov, began criticizing Belinski for writing paltry literary articles in a censored press. Why, they asked, did he not follow their example and seek the freedom of the West, where his talents could be put to some use? Herzen retorted by inquiring acidly what they had done with their precious liberty during seven years in the West: "One critical article of Belinski's is more useful for the new generation than playing at conspiracy and at being public figures."[41] Herzen was right, of course: Belinski's activity had far more historical significance than anything that Bakunin or Sazonov had done until then (or than anything Sazonov would ever do). But a part of Herzen's annoyance undoubtedly came from the fact that their belittling of Belinski's efforts applied equally to his own journalistic activities, which he was flattered to believe were also not without historical significance.

The pair's deprecation of Russian radical achievement had the additional effect of further souring Herzen on the West.

At that time I was especially angered by two criteria used in evaluating people not only by Sazonov but by Russians in general. Their severity in judging their countrymen was matched only by their idolatrous cult of French celebrities. It was vexing to see how our compatriots filed in review before these matadors of rhetoric, who splattered us with words, phrases and commonplaces. . . . And the more modestly the Russians conducted themselves, indeed the more they blushed and tried to cover up the boorishness of the French . . . the more the latter posed and gave themselves airs before these hyperborean Anacharses.[42]

Herzen was particularly repelled by Sazonov's kowtowing to a horde of insignificant Poles, Germans, and Frenchmen, and he was disgusted by Sazonov's patronizing efforts to enroll him in the group, like some provincial newcomer incapable of finding his own way in the great city of international democracy. This brought Herzen back to his grievances against his Moscow friends and to the very principles of his social philosophy. Sazonov's "clientism," like Granovski's rational God, was a pseudo-revolutionary form of modern man's irrational contempt of self, his lack of a feeling of "human dignity," his need of a protective "authority" and his fear of standing alone. The German refugees were to an extent excusable in bowing down before such "truly great" Frenchmen as Pierre Leroux and George Sand, but the Russians' adoration of fifth-rate journalists was beneath contempt; their attitude was an atavistic survival of the "moral Table of Ranks" which the national past had imposed upon their consciousness.[43] In all this it is possible to detect several reactions. Herzen was offended not only in his deepest philosophical conviction — the absolute independence of the individual from all external authority and skepticism towards all "idols" — he was also offended in his personal ambition to play a great role in radical history, in his national pride as a Russian, in his principles as an egalitarian democrat, and finally in his self-esteem as an aristocrat, a point on which he was all the more sensitive since he was not quite the real thing.

It was this accumulation of irritations, beginning in Sokolovo in 1846 and culminating in Paris during 1847, acting in combination with the frustration built up by years of confinement in Russia as well as with his intransigent philosophy of liberty, which determined Herzen's reaction to the West far more than did thoughtful observation of European life or of the events of 1848. From the beginning, Europe was for Herzen a slogan in the battle of Russian political ideologies much more than a society to be understood in itself. The bourgeois France of Louis-Philippe, as the "idol" of the moderate Westerners, had to be demolished. To do this it was necessary to exalt the simple working people and the prophets of socialist regeneration. These very prophets, however, as the examples of Bakunin and Sazonov showed, also presented dangers to an independent Russian radicalism, and so the revolutionary opposition of the West had to be attacked as well. In the last analysis the West had to be rejected *en bloc.* Nevertheless, Herzen knew instinctively that only in the West could he find the new life, the freedom for propaganda, and the chance for fame which he desired. Therefore he was obliged to seek a spiritual home in that European democracy which for other reasons he condemned. It was with this collection of paradoxical attitudes that he would live out the rest of his days. Like the hero of *Who Is To Blame?*, Beltov, he was "a foreigner at home, a foreigner abroad," discontent with both Russia and Europe, with his old friends and his new, yet needing both, loving and hating both at the same time.

Annenkov perceptively summarized these contradictions.

Herzen . . . by his mentality and an inclination towards the energetic beginning of any task, found himself in his native element [in Paris]. He threw himself immediately into that scintillating sea of audacious hypotheses, of relentless polemics, of all possible passions and came out of this a new and extremely nervous man. Thought, feeling, imagination acquired with him a morbid irritability, which expressed itself first of all in indignation against the existing political regime. . . . At the same time he was aroused to no less anger and bitterness by the pretentiousness of the projects of reformers, which falsely promised to put an end to all debates and celebrated the victory even before the battle. Both phenomena seemed equally to him signs of the bankruptcy of society. . . . Yet in spite of this . . . he gave himself over almost unconditionally to that very movement [of protest] which he considered hopeless. . . . There was no man who could have spoken more mercilessly of the failure of European life and who at the same time so decisively attached himself to it, entrusting to it his activity, his material and intellectual being.[44]

The circumlocutions are somewhat heavy (as usual the fault of the censorship), but the portrait is convincing, and much more so than the pose of abused revolutionary confidence struck in *My Past and Thoughts.*

5

Herzen arrived in Paris on March 20, and he undoubtedly did make those pilgrimages to the shrines of the Revolution described in *My Past and Thoughts.* More significantly, however, less than a month later, on April 11, he got off his first blast against the West to his Moscow friends.[45] The attack was rather coy and indirect, since after the tearful adieux of January the rift in the circle was considered by the moderates to be closed. For this reason Herzen chose a somewhat unusual correspondent, the actor Shchepkin, who was not one of his close friends, and took as his subject Shchepkin's speciality, the seemingly innocent topic of the theater. This theme, however, proved to be no more than an opening wedge for politics. The theater belonged to the bourgeoisie (*meshchanstvo*) because that class paid for it. In consequence it represented the "apotheosis of the vulgar, well-ordered life" of the "property owner." The plays were cleverly constructed, but they portrayed no "true passions," and they were utterly closed to the "mighty movement of the waves around and beneath," that is, to socialism. Moreover, the bourgeois was a hypocrite; he pretended to be moral, yet he liked *vaudevilles* which titillated him "by salacious movements, salacious couplets" — a comment that is all the more amusing in that there is ample evidence Herzen enjoyed a good *grivoiserie*, in the best manner of the Boulevards, as much as any bourgeois.[46] He concluded by saying that he often came out of the theater with Annenkov "crushed by sadness," and that to revive their spirits the pair "mournfully," "in affliction" would down a bottle of wine.[47]

This silly letter provoked the reaction Herzen desired: the quarrel with his friends was reopened. Why had he chosen this particular moment to attack? Before he arrived in France he was in a weak position to resume his criticism of the bourgeoisie, since he had no firsthand evidence; arrival in Paris removed this disability and he seized the first opportunity to show that he had not abandoned his socialist guns. Annenkov suggests another motive as well, which he extends to all of Herzen's pronouncements during 1847; they were "in part the product of the usual *fronde*, peculiar to all travelers, to whom it is shameful to submit immediately to a foreign country, without making reservations." [48] Botkin immediately took up Herzen's challenge, for he was an ardent Francophile. On May 14 he wrote to Annenkov, who no doubt showed the letter to Herzen:

I read his [Herzen's] letter to Shchepkin with a feeling of great vexation. Such nonsense he talks! The bourgeois is guilty because the theaters play salacious *vaudevilles*. No joking! It's not for nothing that you wrote that Herzen sets all things upside down in order to have the pleasure of putting them right again. . . . But what can be done! Who does not, the first time he goes to Europe, begin his judgments about it with stupidities? [49]

It should be remembered that Herzen, almost alone of the members of his circle, had never visited Europe before, while most of his friends, Slavophiles as well as Westerners, had spent several years there. For cultured Russians of the age a firsthand knowledge of Europe was normal, and to the circles in which Herzen moved, which for twenty years had lived vicariously the life of Germany or France because they had no "real" life of their own, direct acquaintance with Europe was indispensable. Herzen's inferiority in this respect was no doubt somewhat galling, and Botkin's reminder of his junior status in matters European was as coyly provoking as Herzen's original attack.

From this time on the quarrel resumed with a genteel venom, and Herzen seems to have played the role of aggressor. Most of his letters have not survived, but from a reply of Granovski written some time in the spring of 1847 it is possible to guess their contents. Granovski begins: "'Again romanticism' you perhaps will say on reading this letter" ("romanticism," synonymous with religion and political passivity, had been one of Herzen's accusations against him at Sokolovo). Yet Granovski tries, unlike Botkin, to be conciliatory. He proceeds to call Herzen's *Doctor Krupov*, which had just appeared, a "work of genius" (although when Herzen had read it to him before publication he had not been very impressed). All this, however, was only a diplomatic prelude to the sore subject of their differences.

I have not answered most of your letters because they made a painful impression on me. In them is some sort of hidden reproach, a hostile *arrière-pensée*, which every minute breaks through to the surface. Korsh, it seems, felt the same thing. Your former mockery of your close friends was not offensive, because there was good-natured wit in it, but the irony of your letters offends our self-esteem and our deepest and noblest feelings. It would have been better to write to us directly, even a harsh letter, if you were not content with us, but you scattered hints in your letter to T. A. [Astrakhova, a friend of the circle] etc. and that was hardly decent.

From the mild Granovski these were harsh words indeed. But to underline his desire for conciliation he added, "Your last days [in Russia] could only have shown you . . . that the quarrels of Sokolovo left no traces, and how much love and devotion you left behind. Korsh can joke . . . even when his children are ill, but he wept when you left. Is it possible that you did not appreciate these rare tears?" Granovski then calls for political moderation:

We did not write to you, but did your letters from Paris really call for an answer? What desire have I to quarrel with you about the present meaning of the bourgeoisie? I speak about that enough on the lecture platform. I am a man who is extremely personal, that is, I hold my personal relationships very dear, and my relationship to you was hardly casual these last times. Give me your hand, *carissime!* [50]

Granovski's chief desire was to hold the little group together. Its members were so few and needed each other so much that a breach would be senseless, especially over the bourgeoisie, which did not even exist in Russia and hence oppressed no one. There were enough real forces of darkness in Russia on which the friends could agree. Therefore let them forget their unessential differences and speak only of what they had in common, for only united could they work effectively for enlightenment. In this task, for Granovski, persons were more important than principles. It was a sensible, moderate position, for which much more could be said if Alexander II rather than Nicholas I were on the throne. But it revealed a fundamental miscomprehension of Herzen's position, which also had its logic. Granovski and his friends took Herzen's rantings against the bourgeoisie — which in fact were quite puerile and made no sense in terms of Russian problems — too much at face value. They understood them to be directed against a social class in France, and tried to answer Herzen by talking in calm tones about the historical position of that class. In fact the bourgeoisie was simply Herzen's latest symbol for the status quo in general, and his rantings bore only an adventitious relation to France. They were directed much more against acceptance, no matter how tentative and qualified, by thinking and humane people of the barbarous status quo under Nicholas, and Herzen was willing to split the group rather than abandon his intransigence, no matter how painful this might be personally.

In this unreasonable fury of rejection Herzen, after his fashion, made as much sense as his sensible friend, for Nicholas was not a reasonable sovereign, as Herzen had very personal causes to know and as Granovski did not. Therefore the latter's appeal to good sense had the opposite effect to the one intended. It seemed to Herzen simply another capitulation to barbarism, and hence only hardened his own position and provoked him to still more violent rantings against the bourgeoisie. The fact that Herzen was almost isolated in his intransigence simply made him more unbending. Shortly after Granovski's letter he received another reminder of this isolation. His only real ally, Ogarev, wrote in the polyglot language of "science," also counselling reasonableness: "It seems to me that in spite of so much that is sad and oppressive [in Europe] . . . you have paid too little attention to the *Staat in seiner politiko-oekonomischen Entwickelung*. I am afraid that the *Gesamtheit* of the facts and the wholeness of the development is obscured for you by theoretical dissatisfactions." [51] And Ogarev, too, was very right; however, like Granovski, he failed to see that Herzen was not interested in the *"politiko-oekonomische"* analysis of Europe, but in a courageous rejection of Nicholas and of all authority.

In late July Herzen was subjected to a final provocation from the circle. Belinski arrived in Paris, like Herzen on his first voyage West. It was a different Belinski, however, from the one Herzen had helped convert to *"sotsialnost"* in 1841. In 1846, as a result of a trip through the Russian provinces, Belinski went through the last of his many intellectual revolutions, and decided, in his habitually categorical way, that the writings of the French socialists had no application to Russia, that their theories were abstract nonsense, and that the path of progress for Russia was the development of a bourgeoisie. In July 1847 Belinski wrote from Germany to his close friend Botkin that such war-cries of socialism as "pauperism" and "proletariat" had no meaning in Russia. He then delivered the following pertinent if hyperbolic comment on Louis Blanc's *History of the French Revolution,* which had appeared that year.

What a horse! According to him, from the creation of the world the bourgeoisie has been the enemy of mankind and has conspired against its well-being, when from his own book it is clear that without the bourgeoisie there never would have been that very Revolution about which he is so enthusiastic, and that its very successes are that class's lawful achievement.[52]

Botkin, of course, was delighted by such sentiments and immediately wrote a flattering letter to Paris, addressed to Belinski and Annenkov. He reproached both mildly for believing even a part of the "hothouse doctrinairism" which made people talk nonsense about bourgeois corruption in France, and he congratulated them for taking the moderates' side against Herzen.

You scold me, my dear Annenkov, you whose subtle mind has always remained alien to any kind of doctrinairism (and for this I like you specially), you scold me for defending the bourgeoisie, but for heaven's sake, how can one not defend it when our friends, taking the word of the socialists, present this bourgeoisie as some sort of odious, disgusting, pernicious monster, devouring all that is beautiful and noble in mankind? I understand such hyperbole in the mouth of a French worker, but when it is used by our intelligent Herzen, then it seems to me nothing more than silly. There [in the West] struggle and the spirit of party drive men to such exaggerations — that is understandable; but here [in Russia] instead of an independent view, instead of living, individual thought, all of a sudden one encounters commonplaces. Really it's distressing; and this is why I disliked so his letter to Shchepkin.[53]

The attack continued, the whole contents of which, of course, were communicated to the real addressee. Although geographically dispersed and rent with dissension, the circle was still morally one; from Moscow to Paris the organism was athrob with the great debate over the bourgeoisie. As Turgenev once said, no one who had not lived through the experience could understand the terrible exigencies of belonging to *"ein kruzhok in der Stadt Moskau."* Try as he might Herzen would not escape its grasp, or its mentality, all through the crisis of 1848.

After Belinski arrived in the Paris section of the circle, lengthy discussions ensued between him, Herzen, Bakunin, Sazonov, and Annenkov about the significance of this newly discovered monster, the bourgeoisie — a controversy not without its comic aspects among the subjects of a monarch who gave them much better things to worry about than the "moral" corruption of France. Regrettably, our only source for these debates — which, given the personalities of the participants, must have been colorful — is a long but rather chaotic letter of Belinski to Botkin in

December. Written after his return to Russia, it is directed more toward Herzen's articles on France published in the fall than to the Parisian debates of the summer, of which it hardly gives all the desirable details.[54] Nonetheless, it is fair to assume that Herzen was shocked by Belinski's new views on a subject which by this time had become so explosive for him, and this must have served as a further spur to his denigration of the bourgeoisie and the West. Still, the two retained much in common: namely, their intransigent hate of the "old world" and their atheism, both of which had found volcanic expression in the spring of 1847 in Belinski's famous *Letter to Gogol.*

The line-up in the quarrel was the following. Bakunin, as might be expected, defended the extreme radical position, maintaining that the bourgeoisie must be destroyed root and branch. Sazonov and Annenkov objected that this view was much too sweeping, and argued that there were various kinds of bourgeoisie, the big capitalists being bad, and the rest of the bourgeoisie good, for progress. Belinski, who had a strong dislike for Bakunin since their famous quarrel at the end of the thirties, characteristically found in this personal animosity an added reason for rejecting socialism; indeed he later declared that it was Bakunin's "fanaticism" in Paris which finally turned him away from "idolization" of the masses.[55] Thus Belinksi initially sided with Sazonov and Annenkov, declaring that the "middle bourgeoisie" was a force for progress. Herzen at first was near to Bakunin, although not quite so categorical, but with Belinski in the opposition he had to make concessions and eventually agreed that there was more than one kind of bourgeoisie. That this was only diplomacy on his part is suggested by the fact that in his articles published later in the year he forgot these distinctions and condemned the bourgeoisie *en bloc.* Belinski in turn made concessions, suppressing his dislike for Bakunin enough to deliver over the big capitalists to be devoured by the radical side, but stoutly holding on to his "middle bourgeoisie." [56]

When Belinski returned to Russia he wrote that "the rule of the capitalists has covered contemporary France with eternal shame, reminding one of the time of the Regency . . . and has given birth to an orgy of industry," — a naïvely moralistic view of industrialization which shows how little the debaters understood the phenomenon they were discussing. He even repeated in detail all of Herzen's strictures against the "moral rot" the bourgeoisie was supposed to have caused in art, literature, the theater, the press, and the courts. Nevertheless, Herzen had not really convinced him. Belinski continued to maintain that the bourgeoisie was to be understood first of all as a "historical phenomenon," and to wish for its development in Russia, since experience demonstrated that only where there was a strong middle class was there freedom.[57] It was a paradoxical position, yet it can be explained by the fact that Belinski was defending Herzen's person and his generous intransigence, but not his socialism. This was Belinski's way of preserving an ally against Moscovite moderation while continuing to disagree with that ally's theories. Seemingly substantial as this concession was—and it was the only approbatory word Herzen heard from any of his friends during his first years in Europe — failure to win Belinski back completely must have been a blow, and hence a new stimulus to attack the bourgeois West.[58]

6

These controversies have been rehearsed in detail because it is they, and not the failure of the Revolution, that are the source of Herzen's opinions about the West. Herzen never wrote a line that was not a polemic against someone, and his first productions denouncing Europe were simply his argument with the moderate Westerners carried into print. Called *Letters from the Avenue Marigny,* they appeared in the fall of 1847 in the *Contemporary,* which a few months before had replaced the *Annals* as the principal organ of Westerner opinion. The *Letters* had been composed in Paris between July and September, that is, during the discussions just mentioned.[59] Now that Herzen could speak from firsthand knowledge and not merely from socialist pamphlets, he was telling his friends just what he thought of their marvelous, moderate, middle-class West. Moreover, he wished to attach his *Letters* to a distinguished tradition of patriotic pronouncements of Russian dignity *vis-à-vis* Europe. At the very beginning he contrived to mention the travel *Letters* of Von-Vizin and Karamzin, the first important books (of the end of Catherine's reign) to declare that Russia, with virtues of her own, need not imitate Europe in everything.[60] Herzen's *Letters* were composed in a light tone, so as not to give undue offense to his Moscow friends while still disagreeing with them. This style also suggested that the adverse judgments expressed about the West were not something to be demonstrated but a matter of common knowledge to be discussed in an offhand way — a pose of false detachment intended at the same time to irritate his friends and to camouflage his own involvement. It was the tone of artificial *bonhomie* that marks bitter but half-submerged quarrels between close friends, and which Granovski had already noticed in Herzen's private letters.

The first "letter" described Herzen's voyage across Germany, and was full of seemingly casual banter about bad German cookery, misty German metaphysics, and German pedantry. "In Germany there is nothing to look at. One should read Germany, meditate it, play it on the piano — but ride across it by rail from end to end in one day." [61] Already one

European nation had bitten the dust, and Herzen had served notice that, quick and penetrating like all true Russians, he was unimpressed by anything Germany had to offer. At the same time he began developing "historiosophical" reasons to support this attitude. By the time he reached Cologne he understood that Europe was crushed by the weight of her "feudal" past.

Representatives of each epoch of European life have passed over the banks of the Rhine and have settled there; traces of these peoples, of these epochs have stratified along the course of the river . . . indestructible walls, heavy Romanesque churches, the colossal frame of the Gothic cathedral, the palace of the Templars, those somber warrior-monks, morosely standing on the frontier between feudalism and centralization; the college of the Jesuits, those somber monk-warriors, morosely standing on the frontier between the Papacy and the Reformation; churches of the period of the Renaissance; administration buildings constructed in the period of the Republic, one and indivisible; the new fortifications, recalling the Napoleonic era; and finally the forests of scaffolding around the cathedral, bearing witness to the slow prolongation of the work of the Middle Ages in contemporary Germany. Everywhere memories, everywhere legends.

Herzen generalized from these impressions: "This region has lived much; Europe in general has lived much. Decades of centuries look out from every polished stone, from behind every opinion; behind the shoulders of every European is seen a long succession of majestic personages, like the crowned specters in *Macbeth*." [62]

Then Herzen made the obvious comparison with "virgin" Russia. "At times the gray, blackened monuments of Europe are oppressive; they give it too aristocratic a physiognomy, offensive for one who does not possess such brilliant ancestors and such great traditions. At times, somehow, we Scythians are uneasy among these inherited riches and ruins." Still, this fact need not make the Russian feel inferior. "Is not the motherland of our thought, of our education, here? Did not Peter I, in marrying us with Europe, secure for us the rights of inheritance? Did we not accept them ourselves, assimilating her questions, her afflictions, her sufferings, together with her accumulated experience and accumulated wisdom?" But Herzen did not stop here; for the first time he pursued this line of reasoning to the end, to the conclusion which his historical thinking had prefigured so many times in the past.

Our past is poor; we do not desire to invent heraldic tales, we have fewer memories of our own — but what harm is this, since the memories of Europe, her past, have become our past and our experience? And above all, the European, under the influence of his past, cannot free himself from it. For him the contemporary epoch is a many storied house, for us and North America it is an elevated terrace; his attic is our *rez-de-chausée*. We take up where he leaves off.

He concluded by quoting some verses of Goethe's on America that had
been ringing in his memory at least since 1844:

> Dich stört nicht im Innern,
> Zu lebendiger Zeit,
> Unnützes Erinnern
> Und vergeblicher Streit.[63]

The Russian had the best of two worlds: he enjoyed at the same time
the advantages of backwardness and those of civilization. Herzen was
to say little more after the June Days of 1848.

In the second "letter," describing Paris, Herzen was even more severe
in his judgment of the West. Here he spoke for the first time of the
sorest issue in the debate with his friends — the bourgeoisie. Though
he praised the honesty, the intelligence, the simple human dignity of
the Parisian servants and in general of the proletariat, for the corruption
of the middle classes he could not find words harsh enough. He discovered evidence of this corruption everywhere: in the simple appearance of
the prosperous crowds on the Champs Elysées, in the press, and especially in the theater. Herzen went into great detail on this latter subject,
developing the ideas of his letter to Shchepkin, and attacking particularly
the plays of Scribe, the great success of the day. His criticisms were all
framed in ethical and aesthetic terms: what was wrong with the bourgeoisie was not its economic privilege but greed, hypocrisy, a false sense
of humility, commercialized lust, vulgarity, and a depraved egoism.

> The rich bourgeoisie pays for everything, and the theater more than anything
> else expresses the needs, the interests of the middle classes. . . . Once the
> theater was aristocratic, then later colorless and official, like everything else
> which was touched by Napoleon. During the Restoration it began to come
> under bourgeois control, but then the bourgeoisie truly represented the nation,
> it was sharp, witty, intelligent, considered itself offended, and did not stand
> out, fat and in heavy *haut-relief*, as it does now. The bourgeoisie first appeared
> on the stage in the person of the sly, elusive, sparkling, champagne-like barber
> and steward, in a word, in the person of Figaro! And now it appears on the
> stage as a tender industrialist, the protector of the poor and the defender of the
> oppressed.[64]

All this was intended as a defense of socialism against its Moscovite
denigrators, but in fact it represented much more an aristocrat's reaction
to a world of shopkeepers.

> The bourgeoisie does not have a great past and has no future. It was good only
> for a moment, as a negation, as a transition. . . . The nobility had its own
> social religion; it is impossible to replace the dogmas of patriotism, the tradition
> of courage, the shrine of honor by the rules of political economy. There is a
> truth, a religion, which is the opposite of feudalism, but the bourgeoisie is
> placed between these two religions. The heir of the brilliant nobility and the
> coarse plebs, the bourgeoisie has united in itself the most glaring deficiencies

of both after having exhausted their good qualities. It is rich, like a *grand seigneur,* and miserly, like a shopkeeper. The French aristocracy perished majestically and nobly; like a mighty gladiator, seeing that death was inevitable, it wished to fall with honor; the monument to its heroism is the fourth of August, 1789. No matter what one says there is much that is noble in such a voluntary renunciation of feudalism.[65]

Herzen is as tender to the old aristocracy as he is harsh on the bourgeoisie. Strictly speaking, if he were to take his own scheme of history seriously, the bourgeoisie could not be more wrong, that is anachronistic, than the aristocracy. Herzen's bourgeoisie, however, was not so much a social class as an aesthetic and ethical type. He always had a vast admiration for the haughty and independent *seigneurs* (*velmozhi*) of the time of Catherine and Alexander — before the gentry was tamed by Nicholas — a race from which he himself had sprung. By contrasting this ideal with his reading in French socialist literature he created a "bourgeois-philistine" antithesis to his own vision of the full personality. Then he went to the Parisian theaters seeking examples to support his indignation at people who would settle for less than this vision. It was a curious, but very Russian, example of an aristocratic sense of independence, generalized as the result of frustration, to a democratic concept of universal individual dignity.

In the third "letter" all the aesthetic virtues of the aristocracy were extended to the proletariat. Not that Herzen saw much of the French proletariat — he was too often at the theater, or dining "humanistically" at the *Maison d'or,* or arguing about socialism with his Russian friends. Besides, for Herzen proletariat meant the masses in general rather than industrial workers, and to defend it was simply to challenge the resistance of the moderate Westerners to his own and the Slavophiles' "idolization" of the people. His text was a drama by Félix Pyat, called *Le Chiffonier de Paris,* which glorified the innate virtues of the simple people. For Herzen, now that the aristocracy no longer existed, all nobility and beauty in Western civilization had fled to the proletariat. "Go down the ladder of society — at each step you will find more and more vice and ugliness; but go down to the very botton and you will find as much good and morality as perdition and crime. The most profound corruption is the lot of the lowest level of the bourgeoisie, and not of the people, of the workers." [66]

The last of the "letters," written in September amidst the debates described by Belinski, was the most violent. Herzen dropped his jocular tone and launched into a socialist pamphlet, in the manner of Louis Blanc, with a few traits borrowed from *La Réforme.* He described at length the "corruption" of parliamentary life, of the courts, of the press, of the government and of the opposition. He cited all the scandals of the day, in particular that of the minister, Teste, at the time on trial for bribery. He concluded with a long statement of the irreconcilable opposition between proletariat and bourgeoisie, and with the pessimistic diagnosis that the hold of the latter over France would be difficult, if not impossible, to break. Dramatizing his disillusion he compared Paris to a "beautiful woman" whom one had once loved, but who had since "married basely," and for whom in consequence one "had lost all respect and devotion." France was gravely "ill," and the prospects of cure were slight and distant.[67] Needless to say, such strong statements could get by the censorship only because they appeared to Nicholas' officials as a condemnation of constitutional Europe — which they indeed were.

7

In Russia the *Letters from the Avenue Marigny* provoked the reaction that Herzen had hoped for. Granovski, as usual, was the mildest; he wrote to a friend that the *Letters* "displeased" him, although he found them "in places intelligent": "There is too much *frivolous* Russian superficiality in them. This is how Frenchmen write about Russia." [68] Botkin was much more categorical. On October 12 he wrote a letter to Annenkov, who, gossip that he was, no doubt communicated it to Herzen. He began in the indirectly insulting manner employed by Herzen himself: "By the way, in No. 10 of the *Contemporary* I read the first three of Herzen's *Letters from the Avenue Marigny*, and read them with the liveliest pleasure. The first was worse than the others." Botkin continues, mingling praise of Herzen's wit with condemnation of his views, while at the same time disclaiming any excessive admiration for the bourgeoisie so as to avoid the charge of "partiality."

Herzen has no clear conception of the old aristocracy about which he is so enthusiastic, or of the bourgeoisie which he so despises. . . . God grant that we had such a bourgeoisie! *Cet air de matador* with which Herzen judges everything in France, is very sweet, attractive — I like him for it ever so much, because I know the soft, tender heart of the matador; but really Herzen's judgment explains nothing.[69]

On November 25, after seeing the last and most violent of the "letters," Botkin wrote directly to Herzen, still trying to be conciliatory by talking much of their common animosity toward the Slavophiles, but in the end speaking out sharply: "November 22 we gathered to celebrate your name-day. . . . We drank to . . . the health of the author of *Who Is To Blame?* and *Krupov*, but about the author of the *Avenue Marigny* there was total silence." Having heard that Herzen had written another article (the first chapter of what was to become *From the Other Shore*) with which he was dissatisfied, Botkin added: "But I am convinced that it is very good, convinced because you were very satisfied with your *Letters from France.*" [70] Belinski tried his best to defend Herzen, both in print and in the long letter, already discussed, to his Moscow friends, but in the end he too declared that the bourgeoisie, despite its "vulgarity" and "immorality," was a force for progress.

These expressions of alarm were not just for the sake of contrariness. Herzen's friends felt that in Russia there was enough hatred of Europe, liberty, and enlightenment as it was; they feared that his vituperations against the West — a word which for them had always been as much a symbol for progress as the name of a place — would only make matters worse. They understood the democratic inspiration of Herzen's outpourings, but they feared the public would not. Without knowing it, he was playing into the hands of the Slavophiles and the government, and thereby betraying the "cause." [71]

Herzen, though, was beyond the reach of such objections; his attitude was already all or nothing, both for himself as a "passionate" nature craving "action" and for Russia. He would consequently settle for nothing less than all from Europe. In December he answered Botkin, feigning surprise that his friends should have found *Letters from the Avenue Marigny* objectionable, and making the rather hollow claim that it was half a joke. Then he counterattacked. His friends are disqualified to speak because they are out of date: "There is terribly much that you [the group] don't know. 1847 . . . is extremely important in brutally revealing the moral state of France. Living in Europe, it goes without saying, you would have been able to foresee it; but the eyes of partiality are blindfolded, partiality which springs from an excellent source, but which is all the same partiality." The accusation of "partiality" which had been leveled against Herzen in Sokolovo is here rather unconvincingly turned against its authors. Like "young" Russia with respect to "old" Europe, the junior tourist of the group stands on the shoulders of his predecessors and sees farther than they. Besides why are they blaming him, when he is simply reporting what is obvious to anyone? "I am not guilty if I happened to come here at such a time when there isn't any merit in guessing [the decay of France.]" Even the moderate Annenkov had to admit it; Belinski, "with his marvelous intuition," saw it right away (neither of which statements was exact). "In defense of the substance of my *Letters* I set forth a whole series of convictions and facts. This is a glove which I throw down, a theme which I take upon myself to defend." The tone was polite but categorical.[72]

Then Herzen fired a parting shot, which introduced a new theme into the debate. His friends saw only France in Europe; they had completely overlooked Italy which he, Herzen, had just discovered. He had arrived in Italy in October, 1847, and proceeded to Rome via Genoa and

Livorno. He witnessed first the excitement occasioned by the (very moderate) liberal reforms just granted by Charles Albert of Piedmont, then the more ebullient mood of Tuscany, and finally of Rome, where the political euphoria went back to the election of Pius IX in 1846. Herzen quickly read into these events his own conclusions, and for the next few months Italy was to be the club with which he would beat his friends, the bourgeoisie, France, and moderation over the head. He announced that he was beginning a new series of *Letters,* this time *from the Via del Corso,* his address in Rome. With these, too, he fully expected his friends would be unhappy.[73] But his friends would never read them in print, for the excitement of Italy's awakening pushed Herzen's pen beyond what was publishable in Russia. He had written his last word for the eye of the censor. Tasting freedom of speech for the first time in his life brought him a step nearer the clarification of the goal he was pursuing in the West; it made it all the harder to accept again the fetters of life in Russia. Nonetheless, *Letters from the Via del Corso* was still addressed mentally to his friends and to his old quarrels with them, as was everything else he wrote about the upheaval then beginning.

The purpose of Herzen's new essays is best revealed by a letter of January 1848 to Korsh, Granovski, and Kavelin — all more moderate defenders of the bourgeoisie than Botkin and hence possibly persuadable, if the new Italian evidence were presented properly. "Italy is the only country in Europe which can refresh, calm, make one shed tears of joy and not of indignation and sadness. . . . We did not know Italy, were just as mistaken about her on the minus side as we were about France on the plus side. Actually we always judged by the forms and not the content. . . . The forms of Italy were against her, at least until 1847." The forms which Italy lacked, of course, were a constitution and a unified national state. But Italy possessed something more precious for Herzen than these outward trappings of progress: in her "municipalities" he saw the promise of a real grass-roots democracy. "The city is a personality, the city disposes of its own wealth. It is oppressed, the government quarrels with it (as for instance Piedmont with Genoa before the reform), but all the same the government treats it as a *persona moralis.*" These were the first rumblings of Herzen's political anarchism. His ideal of the autonomous personality was for the first time transferred to a social unit, and all that he said here about the downtrodden but inwardly free Italian city he would later apply to the Russian peasant commune. "France — which in all things loves centralization — France is Paris; you cannot grasp Italy with such simple definitions."[74] For the first time Herzen had designated the centralized state, even when endowed with a constitution, as the principal enemy of individual liberty.

Thus, well before the failure of the Revolution of 1848, Herzen had already sketched in his ideal of an anarchist federation of communes, which are here called "municipalities." His sources for this idea, however, are rather a mystery. It has been suggested that he derived it in the summer of 1847 in Paris during his conversations with Bakunin, who had in turn picked it up from the Poles, in particular Lelewel. Although this is an intrinsically plausible explanation, there is no direct evidence to support it. Just as plausible, and equally incapable of substantiation, is attributing Herzen's budding anarchism to an assiduous reading of Proudhon during 1847, again perhaps under the influence of Bakunin, who was very close to the latter. Yet, even this is not a sufficient explanation, for during his first weeks in Europe, in crossing Belgium on his way to Paris, Herzen seems to have been inspired to anarchist thoughts by the architectural monuments left by the rich "municipal life" of the medieval Flemish towns. Earlier still, however, Herzen had displayed evidence of anarchist sentiments. As far back as 1843 his attachment to Fourierism distinctly implied anarchism, for in a society composed of "communes" formed by voluntary "association" there would be no place left for a centralized authority. Even more explicitly, in the same year he was struck by the arrest of the German "communists" in Zurich and the famous report, *Die Kommunisten in der Schweiz,* published by the cantonal government. There he read with approval of Weitling (who was close to Bakunin at the time) and of his principle: *"Eine vollkommene Gesellschaft hat keine Regierung, sondern eine Verwaltung"* — in other words, in the future society there would exist no coercive state but only an administration. Although it is impossible to prove it directly, it is eminently probable that the combined influence of Fourier, Weitling, Proudhon, and Bakunin did much to suggest to Herzen the idea of the anarchist federation of communes.[75]

Even more than from these influences, however, Herzen's anarchism arose from the fact that, as a libertarian living under Nicholas I, denial of the state was naturally the first problem of politics, and the idea of anarchism was the inevitable antithesis to autocracy. Furthermore, anarchism was the logical extension into politics of the total revolt against ideal absolutes and of the cult of "egoism" which had been Herzen's principal preoccupation through the forties, and which had been brought to a climax by his quarrel with the moderate Westerners; now that he found himself in a world where politics existed, he naturally began to transcribe his revolt of ideas into political terms. Finally, the impact of Italy's example should not be underestimated, for it was there, at the end of 1847, that the repressive European order established at the Congress of Vienna, and of which the regime of Nicholas was simply the most extreme expression, first began to disintegrate. In Italy Herzen was clearly entranced by the spectacle of the growing dissolution of state authority, by the division of the country into largely autonomous units, and by the visible reminders of past municipal independence — all startling novelties to one who had lived under the centralized bureaucracy of Nicholas. Moreover, the Italians seemed to have much in common with the Russians, since they were poor, backward and oppressed. By the same token, they did not give umbrage to Herzen, as did the haughty French. If, then, the most oppressed of Western peoples displayed the greatest revolutionary *virtù*, what hopes might one not have for the most disinherited of all nations, Herzen's own? The principle that the last shall be first was already coming to dominate Herzen's thinking. Although he did not explicitly say so, the image that he constructed of Italy was the rough draft of his post-1848 vision of a revolutionary Russia.

This Italian enthusiasm further hardened his position on France. Once again he defended the *Letters from the Avenue Marigny* against his friends. For "such a light work," what he said about the virtues of the simple people, his "generalizations about Russia in the first 'letter' and about France in the fourth," were enough to pardon any shortcomings. Botkin was accused of an unreasonable "predilection" for France. Even Annenkov was scolded for referring to the French as "dear children" in his own *Letters* from Paris, which had also been published in the *Contemporary*, and which, unlike Herzen's, had elicited the approval of the Westerners. As for himself, "because [the Parisians] are the absurd children of great fathers I go with bared head to *Père Lachaise* but I do not wish to bow down before this rabble, without talent, without energy, without principles, called Frenchmen." Even the simple people — and they for the first time — are included in this condemnation. In France there is only "the sad and deserving *BAS peuple,* but even it has gone no farther than the limits of the sixteenth century in its education." The next year the slavery of the masses to outworn ideologies would be one of the main causes of the failure of the Revolution for Herzen. Indeed he already proclaims that France is so enslaved to past moral values, to the principles of centralization and authority, that her position is almost hopeless.

They live by two or three moral sentences and on the *profession de foi du Vicaire Savoyard,* without noticing that centuries have passed since Rousseau. . . . Oh how well Napoleon understood France and how that Metternich of the Seine, Guizot, understands her now! It is in vain that Botkin thinks the difficulty of understanding European life derives from its real complexity and fullness — no, it is possible to understand what is the matter by the simplest approach to the subject. Just as in general Europe is unable to raise herself to the heights of her own civilization, and the latter remains an abstract ideal, hardly realizable, and just as history, instead of realizing the Roman ideal, realized the Lombard kingdom and papal Christianity, so too France is lower than her past.[76]

The strictures against the half-liberation of his friends spelled out in *New Variations On Old Themes* are here for the first time applied fully to European society. The result was a paradoxical position indeed. Socialism is "hardly realizable," yet Herzen is furious with France for not realizing it. Socialism in practice can only lead to a dowdy compromise, as the ideal of Christianity led only to the medieval Church, yet Herzen continues to believe in it. He is angry at the reformers for being abstract idealists, yet he rejects what they produce when they try to turn their ideals into practice. He vituperates against the European Left, yet he wants to make a place in it for himself. Europe was rotten and finished, and although Italy was encouraging, and so much better than France, still Europe was no good. In this mass of confusions only one thing is clear: for all the frustrations of his past life Herzen was shaking in rhetorical indignation at the whole world, where everyone was wrong but himself, yet at the same time he wanted desperately to belong to something vaster than himself, something lofty, noble, pure — and in this same world.

The final contradiction of all was his ambivalent attitude to his circle. On January 31, 1848, the first anniversary of his departure from Moscow, he appended a postscript to the letter just cited, evoking in homesick tones the leave-taking, and once again holding out the olive branch. He had recently received the issue of the *Contemporary* containing the most violent of the *Letters from the Avenue Marigny*: "Of course, it is God knows what; however, I don't understand why it made you so indignant." [77] — and this when he had written it expressly to annoy them! As with Europe it was a love-hate relationship: he had torn himself away from his friends to seek a new life, yet he could not bear to lose them; he feared alienating them, yet he could not rest until he had demolished their dearest convictions.

8

The four *Letters from the Via del Corso*, written in Italy between the end of December 1847 and the beginning of March 1848,[78] express all these contradictions, and push to their logical conclusion the mixture of anti-Western nationalism, social extremism, and idolization of the simple people which Herzen's friends found so dangerous for progress in Russia. The *Letters* opens with a melodramatic summary of his sufferings in Paris.

Toward autumn the atmosphere of Paris became unbearably oppressive. I could not reconcile myself to the unbelievable moral decadence which surrounded me. I felt accumulating in my soul that resignation, that coldness, that indifference, which is brought by lost hopes, separation from reality, scorn of the present. I was growing stale and only occasionally, stirred by indignation, I still felt my young strength and former anger. Death in literature, death in the theater, death in politics; the walking dead man, Guizot, on the one hand and the childish babble of the opposition on the other — it was frightful! There, somewhere down below, far away [among the masses] were heard from time to time heavy groans; it seemed as if they rose from a strong and healthy breast, but on the surface Paris was an extinct crater, which had turned into dirt and mire. . . . To Italy! I had need of rest, of the sea, warm air, lush greenery, and of people less worn out, less weary of heart.[79]

The kindest word Herzen could say for Paris was "that there . . . was the only place in the dying West where one could perish grandly and properly," by which he meant that one was free to protest, as did the socialists, against the frightful state of civilization.

For the rest Herzen abandoned himself to the blackest pessimism. On passing through Lyons, he was filled with horror by the fortifications of the city, erected, not against an external enemy, but against the restless proletariat of the Croix Rousse. Here was a fitting example of the irreformable nature of European, and in particular of French, society. With all its might Europe was striving to crush any possibility of change. "Cannons are also to be found in the middle of the city itself. Suddenly in an alley-way you come upon two or three yawning muzzles, turned down a corresponding number of streets, covered with the tricolor and surmounted by the ironic inscription: *Liberté et ordre public.*" [80]

In Provence, amidst his "joy" on first discovering the South, Herzen did not fail to remark the signs of an ingrained sense of property alien to the Slavs.

One thing offends the eye and wrenches the Slavic soul: high stone walls, encrusted with broken glass, separate the gardens, the *potagers*, and sometimes even the fields. They represent a certain immortality of exclusive possession, a certain insolence of the right of property. For the poor man the dusty road, the cruel and offensive wall, remind him constantly that he is a pauper, that he is not even permitted to possess an uninterrupted view of the countryside. It is impossible to imagine the sinister character which these walls give to the land and the fields; the trees, like prisoners, look through them; the most beautiful landscapes are spoiled.

Even more significantly, Herzen made the comparison between this enclosed landscape and the open fields of Russia.

The Russian village does not exist in Europe. The rural commune in Europe has meaning only in terms of the police. What is there in common between these scattered houses fenced off one from another? For them everything is particular, they are joined only by common boundaries. What can there be in common between hungry workers, to whom the commune accords *le droit de glaner*, and the rich landlord? Gentlemen, *long live the Russian village* [*selo*]! *Its future is great.*[81]

This remark is capital for understanding Herzen's development. Here for the first time he adopted as his own the idea that the Russian peasant commune could serve as the foundation for socialism. The date was December 1847, fully six months before the June Days and only seven months after his arrival in Europe. Nor was this an isolated reflection. In the next "letter" from the Via del Corso, dated 4 February, 1848, he elaborated this idea in a discussion of the Italian peasant.

In spite of all efforts, of the foreign yoke, of the lack of moral freedom, the Italian has never been ground down to the same degree as the Frenchman or the German. One must not forget that the Italian governments are exceedingly ill-organized, that the bureaucrats are as negligent as the landlords. But the principal cause is that the Italian has not linked his entire existence to the government: for him the government has always been a form, a condition, and not an end, as for the Frenchman. *The peasant of central Italy no more resembles a downtrodden herd than the Russian muzhik resembles property.* Outside of Italy and Russia, I have nowhere seen that poverty and hard work have passed over the face of man with so little effect, deforming nothing in his noble and courageous features. *Such people possess a hidden idea, or more precisely, not an idea, but an untapped force which they themselves do not understand until their hour has struck,* and which enables them to endure the most crushing misfortune, even serfdom.[82]

Trait for trait, this was the portrait that Herzen would paint after 1848 of the hidden virtues of peasant Russia.

Moreover, the Italians, like the Russians, were "real persons," although they might not yet, legally, be "citizens" rather than "subjects." "Respect of self, of the personality, is particularly developed in the Italians; they do not feign democracy, as do the French; it exists with them in their *mores,* and by equality they do not mean equal slavery." At the same time the anarchist note grew stronger:

In Genoa I saw my first *"civica,"* il populo armato. In general I like neither arms nor soldiers, but if it is necessary to have an armed force, then a home guard composed of the citizens, but not dressed in a fool's uniform, is the least offensive. Fortunately the Tuscan *civica* has not yet had time to sew itself a new uniform. . . . You cannot imagine how much the absence of a uniform ennobles a simple soldier. *The uniform is a chasuble, a sacerdotal vestment;* the soldier is not a simple citizen, he is a priest of death, of human sacrifice.[83]

The Italians lacked that innate respect for authority founded on divine or ideal sanctions which for Herzen was the source of all slavery.

Italy, surprising though it may seem, was even relatively "young" and "virgin." To be sure she had something of a "past," as monuments such as the Coliseum and a few other ruins attested, but she had no "Gothic" (religious) past, and this was what caused all the trouble in France and

Germany. Italy's past was pagan, humanistic, and worldly. Even the Papacy, in spite of a mystic reaction after the Council of Trent (largely of Spanish and Austrian inspiration and hence not the Italians' fault) was essentially an ancient pagan and humanistic institution, as one could learn simply by looking at Michelangelo's frescoes.[84] Most of all, Italy was free of the past because since the sixteenth century she had lived under foreign domination, and hence had not known the period of centralized state-building and the growth of a pernicious bourgeoisie experienced by the other nations of Europe. This in a sense wiped the historical slate clean and gave Italy an inestimable advantage over her supposedly more advanced neighbors.[85] The "historiosophy" here was more than usually complex, but it was a tight squeeze to make Italian conditions fit the future forms of Russian "youthfulness." Nevertheless Herzen had accomplished his chief purpose: he had established anarchic Italy vs. despotic France as an antithesis, which after 1848 would become the antithesis of revolutionary Russia vs. conservative Europe.

CHAPTER XV

The Revolution of 1848

J UST as Herzen was on the point of victory in his Italian campaign, news of the February Revolution in Paris reached Rome. From this time on he began reacting more to events than to his friends; or rather he began manipulating his symbols more in terms of the new happenings than of the old quarrels of Sokolovo. The essence of his preoccupations, however, remained the same: to score certain ideological points against both his Moscow circle and the vaster world of European democracy.

From the beginning his reaction to the February Revolution was ambivalent. On the one hand it gainsaid everything he had maintained during 1847, and Herzen was not a man who swallowed his pride easily. Yet on the other hand he had been waiting for the Second Coming of the Revolution during most of his life, and he did not wish to be left out if something were really going to happen. At first he allowed himself to hope. On March 3 he recorded: "Today the editor of *The Epoch* came to see me with the news that Paris has remembered she is Paris, that the barricades have gone up and that men are fighting." [1] His enthusiasm clearly was subdued and tentative. On the following day he learned that the Republic had been proclaimed in France. "Is this happening in a dream or am I really awake? Events each day move faster, gather force, gain importance; the quickened pulse of history beats feverishly; personal views and feelings are lost in the magnitude of what is happening." Herzen was almost ready to abandon his "personal views" and admit that his first judgment of Europe had been hasty. "My hand trembles as I pick up the newspapers . . . either a glorious resurrection or the last judgment is at hand. New forces have awakened in my soul, old hopes are reborn and a certain courageous readiness for anything has come to the fore." [2] As is evident, some effort was necessary to summon up even this half-despairing "courage." This was Herzen's enthusiasm for the Revolution of 1848 at its most delirious.

Then doubt began to get the upper hand. The March uprisings in

Austria and Prussia, where nothing revolutionary or democratic had ever occurred before, seem to have left Herzen totally unimpressed. Moreover, he showed no undue haste to return to Paris, which was paradoxical in terms of his own values. In France there was at least a republic, recognizing universal suffrage and even allowing socialist participation in the government — an unheard of constellation of qualities at the time. In Italy, however, there were still such "progressive" forms of sovereignty as kings in Naples and Piedmont, a grand duke in Tuscany and a pope in Rome, and nowhere was there a constitution more radical than Louis-Philippe's *Charte*. Yet Herzen tarried in Rome until April 13. In a letter to Annenkov at the beginning of March, just after he had learned of the February Revolution, Herzen was already pouting about the improbable French Republic, and bragging up his Russian-Italians more than ever. "The Italians are very near to a republic, and the Romans and the Tuscans are in the van. Here the republic will be different [from that in France] — not centralized, but federal, municipal and democratic." Herzen's anarchist ideal of a loose federation of self-governing communes or municipalities had taken almost definitive shape. He went on to argue that Rome was not a capital in the same sense as Paris, but a "moral center," which could group around it the sovereign cities of Italy, yet could not oppress them by centralized force.[3] Already his goal was not just a reformed state, but the abolition of the state. Experience with the French Republic would only confirm this view, but it did not create it.

While still in Rome Herzen had practically made up his mind he would not like the Second Republic when he saw it. "In Rome when I read the list of members of the Provisional Government fear came over me. The name of Lamartine forbode no good; Marrast had previously been known as a great intriguer; and those lawyers, those unknown names! Only Ledru-Rollin seemed to represent something; Louis Blanc and Albert stood apart — what was there in common between these people?"[4] From the start Herzen sensed that this republic would not be his republic. On leaving Rome he even anticipated the coming reaction.

What will come of all this? The sky is not without clouds; from time to time a cold wind blows from funeral vaults, bringing the odor of a corpse, the odor of the past; the historical *tramontana* is strong, but come what may I am thankful to Rome for the five months I spent there. What I experienced will remain in my soul, and all that has happened will not be blown away by the reaction.[5]

Herzen's pessimism deepened as he moved northward to Paris. On first setting foot in France he "read about the frightful pacification of the [proletarian] uprising in Rouen; this was the first blood shed after February."[6] He arrived in the French capital on May 5 and immediately began a new series of "letters," entitled *Again in Paris,* in which he chronicled his impressions almost day by day for his absent friends.[7] The newly elected National Assembly had just opened. It was noteworthy as the first European parliament since the Convention to be chosen by universal suffrage, and precisely because of this — since the majority of the electors were small peasant proprietors — the Assembly was moderate republican in complexion, and not the least bit socialist. It was only the Parisian radicals and their proletarian followers who were socialist, but they constituted no more than a small minority in the country. Herzen took violent exception to the moderate republican results of the elections, in spite of their democratic nature. For him, the Assembly was the cowardly reflection of the frightened bourgeoisie, not the "real" expression of the needs of the "masses." He had made one of the great discoveries of so many radicals during 1848: that the "formalistic" democracy of universal suffrage, applied in the framework of the old state and the old social order, and among a population that was still largely illiterate, simply returned the notables of existing society and thereby perpetuated it more successfully than did the class suffrage of the liberals.

Herzen's confidence in the Revolution collapsed completely just ten days after his arrival in Paris, when the Parisian populace failed to unseat the Assembly in the semi-insurrection of May 15.

May 15 tore the bandage from my eyes; the Revolution is defeated; and next it is the Republic that will be defeated. Three full months have not yet passed since February, "or ere those shoes were old" in which men built the barricades, and France is crying out for slavery; her freedom weighs heavy on her. Once again she has made a step forward, for herself, for Europe, and again she has grown fearful, after seeing the reality of that which she had only known in words, that for which she was ready to shed blood.[8]

For Herzen, May 15 was a revolt of the people against the state in any form, whether republican or monarchic, "the great protest of Paris against the obsolete pretention of law-making assemblies to absolutism, behind which always and everywhere has hidden monarchy, reaction and the old social order." [9] The defeat of the populace was the defeat of "true democracy," that is, anarchy.

For Herzen May 15 meant that the representatives of Europe's "feudal" past, frightened by the unexpected incursion of the forces of the "new world" in the last days of February, were beginning the reconquest of the territory they had momentarily lost.

The *Royalists* took up arms to defend the Republic and the National Assembly. By saving the Assembly they saved the monarchic principle, they saved a timid authority, they saved the constitutional order of things, the misuse of capital, and, of course, of interest. The alternative was not the republic of Lamartine, but the republic of Blanqui, a republic, not in words, but in actual fact; the alternative was a revolutionary dictatorship, serving as a transitional state between monarchy and the [real] republic; the alternative was *suffrage universel,* not in its present absurd form, where it is used only to choose a despotic assembly, but as applied to the whole administration; the alternative was the liberation of man, of the commune, of the department, from subjection to a *strong* government, which persuades by bullets and chains. The Assembly, upheld by the National Guard, conquered, but morally it was conquered on May 15; it maintains itself, like all outworn institutions, solely by the force of bayonets.[10]

In this precocious pessimism Herzen was in a small minority with such figures as Proudhon, Blanqui, Barbès, and Lamennais — all of whose newspaper articles or parliamentary speeches he read with avidity throughout 1848. Most socialists in France, with Louis Blanc at their head, still had some hope that their ideals might triumph. The mass of republicans and radicals all over Europe continued to believe that some sort of democratic order was at hand; not only was there a republic in France, but Italy, Prussia, and Austria were still at the height of their revolutionary effervescence. Under these circumstances Herzen's reaction to the inconclusive *journée* of May 15 seems premature and exaggerated. Although in other circumstances he showed a remarkable faculty for hope despite great odds (for example his belief in the "socialist" peasant commune), he abandoned his faith in the European Revolution without the semblance of a struggle. To be sure, there was an element of prescience in Herzen's gloom about the outcome of the Revolution, but it loses most of its intellectual interest because of the excessively visceral reasons he advanced for his predictions.

One reason for this easy surrender to despair lay in his now heady nationalism: it was almost as if he did not want the Revolution to succeed, so as to avoid European patronage of Russian democracy. More fundamentally still, his pessimism derived from his now fully ripe anarchism, worked out in the long quarrel with his friends and revealed for the first time in all its details in the passage just quoted. Democracy for Herzen no longer meant something so simple as a centralized republic based on universal suffrage; this was no better than the most absolute of monarchies. In such a state the people in their ignorance and slavery to past prejudices delegated their power — that is, surrendered their liberty — to an absolute assembly, which then assumed all the sovereign rights of the old monarchy. The new republic, like the monarchy, represented a body of law, a system of property rights, and a power of coercion above and outside the individual. Indeed, the political republic must be considered worse than a monarchy, because it masks its authority with such slogans as universal suffrage, liberty, equality, and fraternity. A monarchy frankly proclaims it is an authority over and above individuals; the centralized republic, with its pseudo-democratic trappings, dupes the people, and thus retards their real liberation.

The *true* republic, on the other hand, would apply the principle of universal suffrage on every level, and not just to create a despotic assembly. Each village and commune would elect all its own officials, its courts, militia and police; all would be subject to popular recall. The central government, insofar as there would be one, would be the creature of the communes, and not their master. It would be the moral center of a loose federation and not the sovereign law-making and executive summit of a state. The true republic would be as near as possible to every individual citizen. Only in this way could the individual have that total freedom which was Herzen's ideal. Anything less was slavery. As in "science" and ethics, his stand was all or nothing. In politics there was no meaningful middle term between the regime of Nicholas and the anarchist federation of communes.

For Herzen, after May 15 the Second Republic was a lost cause. Thus when a second and far more serious rising of the proletariat was suppressed with great bloodshed in the June Days, Herzen felt that his worst prognostications were confirmed, and his tone rose to a crescendo of rage. This was expressed in the "letters," *Again in Paris;* it was given voice even more forcefully in a second set of essays begun in Italy, but written mostly in France after the June Days, and eventually entitled *From the Other Shore.* It is in one of the latter, called "After the Storm," that Herzen gave his most eloquent reaction to the bloody suppression of the Parisian workers.

Paris! How long did that name burn as a lodestar for the nations; who did not love it, did not bow to it? But now its time is past; let it disappear from the stage. During the June Days it entered upon a great struggle which it lacked the strength to finish. Paris has grown old, and youthful dreams no longer become her. In order for Paris to rouse herself, she has need of a great shock; nights of St. Bartholomew, September Days. But the June Days did not revive Paris; and so the decrepit vampire draws still more blood, the blood of the just, that same blood which on June 27 reflected the fire of the torches lighted by the exultant hands of the bourgeoisie. . . . What will come of this blood? Who knows, but no matter what the issue, it is enough if in this paroxysm of madness, of revenge, of discord, of retribution that world perishes which oppresses the new man, preventing him from living, keeping the future from being born — and this would be magnificent, and so I say: long live chaos and destruction!
Vive la mort!
And let the future be born.[11]

Herzen's theory of revolution is here complete. That substitute for monarchy, the centralized bourgeois republic, could not last. He saw two alternatives to it. The "forces of order" could triumph, either openly establishing a new monarchy, or setting up a pseudo-revolutionary strong man such as Cavaignac or Louis Napoleon, with or without the support of a "despotic assembly." In this case the "old world" of social inequality and irrationality would be saved for a while, but eventually the masses would rise and destroy all civilization, thus signaling the definitive demise of Europe. If, on the other hand, this catastrophe were to be avoided and the Revolution saved, then the only recourse was a second popular uprising, more violent than that of June, which would utterly destroy the existing order and establish a dictatorship of the people. In the general carnage and ruin, which Herzen evokes in endless pages of rhetoric, the "new world" of free, democratic communes *might* be born. At least this was Europe's only chance; so Herzen called for universal destruction, even at times suggesting that Nicholas might intervene with his cossacks in order to make the holocaust of civilization more complete.[12] Insofar as Herzen's rantings had political meaning, he was in effect advocating *la politique du pire:* the worse the reaction became, the nearer would Europe be to the volcanic, democratic explosion of the masses. But Herzen was not very optimistic about the triumph of democratic anarchy, even with the aid of these desperate measures. Either the strength of the gathering reaction would be too great, or the antidote to it — the destruction of civilization — would be too barbarizing in its effects for "humanism" ever to develop in Europe. Western society would most probably "perish" in an orgy of reaction, hopeless proletarian revolt, and cossack intervention. In all likelihood Europe was too far gone to do anything more than "die."

After the June Days, Herzen in essence had nothing new to say about the Revolution. He stood by and watched the "writhings" of the Republic — first the final absurdity of universal suffrage in producing the election of *Prince* Louis Napoleon as *president* in December 1848, then the would-be insurrection of the "Mountain" in June 1849, and finally the *coup d'état* of December 2, 1851. At each of Europe's "steps toward the grave" Herzen repeated his imprecations of June in numerous "letters" from one place or another, to a total of fourteen in all, and in essays *From the Other Shore.* His worst predictions had come true: reaction had triumphed everywhere in Europe. Herzen finally became convinced that the workers would not rise to the universal holocaust for which he hoped. Even his faith in the popular masses — at least those of Europe — abandoned him. The proletariat, no less than the bourgeoisie, loved its slavery; it too was afraid of the responsibilities of freedom and individuality; it too was enserfed to the principle of authority. Europe would never create the "new world" of democratic socialism; the burden of her past precluded all future development. She would linger on, preserved for a while by reaction, and then go down in "barbarism." [13]

2

As might be expected, Herzen's explanation of the failure of the
Revolution was not economic, or even political, but ideological. The
point of departure of his analysis was to reiterate endlessly the critique
formulated in 1846–47 of the "feudal" values by which modern society
still lived. The Revolution had failed because Europeans were slaves to
the transcendent principles of past authority. "Conservatism and reaction
are slumbering in the heart of anyone who wishes to keep anything, no
matter what, of the Christian, feudal and Roman foundations of our
civilization." [14] These familiar ideas, however, were now stated much
more clearly and categorically than before 1848. Moreover, the accusation of "feudalism" was now directed, not so much against the bourgeoisie as against the popular masses and, most violently of all, the
European Left. Indeed, for Herzen the socialists came to be quite as
much the villains of the revolutionary fiasco as was the party of order.

All the criticisms he had originally addressed to the Moscow moderates he now hurled at the supposedly enlightened elite of Europe. "The
French have never freed themselves from religion. Read George Sand,
Pierre Leroux, Louis Blanc and Michelet — everywhere you will find
Christianity and Romanticism, done over to fit our mode of life; everywhere dualism, ideology, abstract duty, obligatory virtues, official rhetorical morality, without any link with real life." [15] At times, in the paradoxical manner now habitual with him, Herzen considered that even he
himself shared these failings.

No matter how much we may object, how much we may rage, we, too, by our
way of life, our habits, our language, belong to that same literary and political
milieu which we have rejected. It is not in our power to turn our theoretical
break with it into a practical one. . . . Our great creative act is exactly,
precisely this [theoretical break]; it cost us much labor and effort . . . but
we are strong only in the struggle with other readers of books, and with the
pharisees of the conservative and revolutionary worlds.[16]

Herzen once again evoked his parallel between the crisis of the nineteenth century and the end of the ancient world. Since he and his kind
lacked the total faith to be "new Christians" (real socialists), and since
by their education and class privileges they were too much part of the
"old world" to be "barbarians" (the masses), the only position left for
them was that of individually enlightened but ineffective Stoics. The
members of the emancipated elite might welcome the new morality of
democracy from afar, yet they had no useful role to play in its implementation; their only recourse was to retreat into their individual integrity,
and, with stoic dignity, to await the end of existing civilization and the

possible triumph of socialism by "barbarian" methods.[17] Such was Herzen's dramatic image of himself in the midst of the shipwreck of 1848.

The inadequacies of the radical elite and of their abstract ideals were the principal theme of *From the Other Shore,* Herzen's philosophical commentary on the Revolution, just as the *Letters from France and Italy* was his political commentary. Of all Herzen's writings (except *My Past and Thoughts*) this is perhaps the most brilliant literarily; and it is certainly the most original philosophically. Yet it is also the most confused, and indeed paradoxical. This is reflected in the form of the book, much of which is written as a dialogue opposing a believer in humanity and progress to a skeptic and an iconoclast, with Herzen himself torn between the two. On the one hand he demolished as "romantic" delusions all revolutionary utopianism, all "sentimental" belief in humanity and in the necessity of progress, and all optimistic rationalisms, since there was no empirical, "scientific" basis in the experiences of 1789–1848 to justify such ideas; it was precisely because the leaders of the Revolution had lacked the hardheaded courage to recognize this that they proved so ineffective in the face of events. Yet on the other hand he was clearly drawn to the values he attacked; and he continued to believe, even though he had deprived himself of all rational reason for doing so, that somehow the "new world" would be born; and in the end, for all his pessimism, he reaffirmed more strongly than ever his faith in man, freedom and socialism, as existential if no longer as rational values.

Essentially, *From the Other Shore* takes up the conclusions of *Dilettantism in Science* and the *Letters on the Study of Nature* and pushes them to the *nec plus ultra* of philosophical anarchism, which is now for the first time explicitly related to politics. Herzen's starting point is his familiar war against "dualism."

The basis of the world-view which insures so well man's moral servitude and the humiliation of his personality is to be found almost entirely in dualism. . . . [Dualism] divides into supposed opposites what in reality is inseparable — for example body and soul — and hostilely opposes these abstractions, unnaturally reconciling what by nature is one, in an indivisible unity. This is the evangelical myth of God and man, reconciled by Christ, translated into the language of philosophy.[18]

Strange conclusions indeed to draw from the failure of a revolution! But, for each page in Herzen's writings on 1848 criticizing the West from the point of view of political anarchism there are ten expressing his horror at European dualism, Christianity and "feudalism." In spite of the fact that he was now a free man living in the midst of real politics and not just dreaming of "action," the old abstract emphasis continued.

Nevertheless, this critique of dualism had a real political content as well. "Just as Christ, redeeming human kind, tramples on the flesh, so in dualism, idealism takes the side of one phantom against the other, giving the preference to spirit over matter, to the species over the individual, and thus sacrificing man to the state, and the state to mankind." In other words, the duality of spirit and matter meant the existence of abstract principles — whether of the Left or of the Right — independent of concrete, individual men; such principles were the basis of authority, and for Herzen all authority was indistinguishable from tyranny. It was for this reason that the dualism introduced into the world by Christianity was the root-cause of the revolutionaries' failure, since even their ideals were tainted with it. "Our language is the language of dualism, our imagination possesses no other images, no other metaphors. During a millennium and a half everyone who taught, preached, or wrote, or who was active in any way, was imbued with dualism; no more than a few men toward the end of the eighteenth century began to doubt in it, yet even they continued to speak its language for propriety's sake, and in part through fear." [19]

More particularly, in attacking dualism Herzen had in mind the state and the principles of sovereignty, civic "duty," obedience to "abstract" law, and coercive right on which it rested.

Monarchy is founded on dualism. Government never should, never must, be separate from the people. The state as it now exists, however, is Providence, Holy Orders, the creative spirit, while the people is the passive mass, the obedient herd of the Good Shepherd. Monarchy is largely theocracy founded on divine right; it has always supported religion, and religion has always supported monarchy. [20]

These criticisms applied equally to a democratic republic. In a republic the sanctions of religion are secularized as the "will of the people," "popular sovereignty," or "parliamentary supremacy," but they remain nonetheless absolute sanctions for the tyranny of the state and society over the individual and hence, as a practical matter, are the same as divine right. While in Russia, Herzen had attacked religious and idealistic dualism as the justification for moral or intellectual absolutes which enslaved man in his private life; he now extended this notion into a critique of all public authority as well.

Although the whole of Europe was guilty of the sins of dualism and reverence for authority, France presented by far the worst case in Herzen's eyes, and one last diatribe against that country must be included for the sake of its new anarchist note.

You will never knock the monarchic principle out of the heads of the French — they have a veritable passion for police and authority. Every Frenchman is at heart a police sergeant; he loves parade and discipline. Everything that is independent or individual enrages him; he understands equality only as leveling, and he submits only on the condition that everyone else submit as well. Place any sort of military insignia on a Frenchman's cap and he becomes an oppressor, he begins to persecute the simple man, that is, the man without insignia; he demands *respect* for authority.[21]

And this vice was a national, not a class phenomenon, shared by the mass of the people as well as by the bourgeoisie.

Included in this condemnation of things French were all phases of socialist thought from Saint-Simon to Louis Blanc. The only exception was Proudhon, the prophet of anarchism and author of the formula, *"Dieu, c'est le mal."* All socialist thought before him was mere utopian daydreaming, which for this very reason could not be ruthlessly lucid in criticizing the existing order; like idealism, it was an escape from reality, not a weapon of attack against it. Moreover, all socialist thought before Proudhon was system-building, but a socialist system is a contradiction in terms, since its very structured character perpetuates the religious and authoritarian principles of the "old world" that socialism is supposed to replace. "As soon as the problem of building socialism actually presented itself, Saint-Simonism and Fourierism vanished and socialist communism [Herzen's civilization-destroying dictatorship of the masses] appeared, that is, a struggle to the death, the socialism of Proudhon, who said himself that he offered no system but only criticism and negation." [22] After 1848 Proudhon alone continued to influence Herzen's thought, although, of course, this influence was not the source of his own very independent anarchism.[23] Among the men of action only Blanqui continued to enjoy Herzen's esteem. "Blanqui is the revolutionary of our epoch; he has understood that it is useless to patch things up, *that the primary task today is to destroy what exists."* [24] Anything short of this total destruction would only permit the survival, in some new disguise, of dualism, authority and the state.

Herzen had no doubt fallen into contradiction in accepting simultaneously (and even confusing) Proudhon's grass-roots anarchism and Blanqui's "communist" dictatorship of the proletarian minority, a policy which could only produce authoritarian results. But this advocacy of "communism" was no more than a temporary exaggeration of Herzen's thought, and a measure of his fury against the "old world," rather than a real adherence to "Blanquist" methods. In reality Blanqui, like Proudhon, meant for Herzen not the positive authority of dictatorship but the negative force of destruction.

A final victim in this holocaust of Herzen's late idols was German "science," particularly the Hegelian tradition. To be sure, these abstruse subjects did not preoccupy Herzen greatly amidst the excitement of the Revolution; in one sense he freed himself from Hegelianism simply by forgetting about it when he crossed the Russian frontier. Yet in view of his past commitment he could hardly fail to react in some more direct manner to the Hegelian world-view, and *From the Other Shore* (the title itself recalls his discovery of Hegel) is in large part an anti-Hegelian tract. The master himself is mentioned no more than episodically as another crypto-Christian and dualist, and in the turbulence of his rhetoric Herzen does not stop to spell out further details. Nevertheless, he is in fact renouncing his own former Hegelianism, since he is denying all rationalistic system-building. In this view, Hegelianism, in spite of its pretentions to be a monistic naturalism, can only be considered a monstrous secular cosmology, governed by the laws of a rigid logic, and hence just as much a figment of the mind as Christianity. It, too, therefore could provide sanctions for an "objective" order of law and authority existing independently of the individual.

Included in these strictures, again largely by implication, were the "half-emancipated" Left Hegelians, whose "religion of humanity" and "abstract man" Herzen castigated as still other disguises for the principle of an ideal authority external to the individual; subordination of man to "humanity" was just as much slavery as subordination of man to a supernatural Deity. God, the Idea, humanity were all unreal abstractions; the only reality was man, in the sense of individual men. The only true "humanism," therefore, was recognition of the individual as an end in himself, as a completely autonomous person accepting no authority but his concrete needs and desires. In a new and more sweeping fashion Herzen had declared anarchic "egoism" to be the supreme value and the only true freedom.[25] He had come out of Left Hegelianism philosophically, not by the side of Marx, as Soviet historians claim, but by the side of Max Stirner. Although it is doubtful that he read Stirner until much later, his conclusions at this time are strikingly similar to those of *The Ego and Its Own*.[26]

By the same token, the March of History was also sacrificed, because belief in inevitable progress, in some organic logic of historical development, once again signified subordination of the individual to "objective" law. It meant the "abstract" sacrifice of present life to an ideal future — a future that, in fact, did not even exist. Herzen's rejection of such "slavery to the future" led to a redoubled emphasis on that "philosophy of the present moment" which, since Novgorod, had lived in his mind in peaceful contradiction with Hegel's determinism. But now it broke completely free from its Hegelian moorings.

If progress is the end, for whom are we working? What is this Moloch who, as the toilers approach him, refuses to reward them, but instead only draws back, and as a consolation to the exhausted, doomed multitudes crying *"morituri te salutant,"* can only return the mocking answer that after their death all will be beautiful on earth? Do you really wish to condemn all human beings alive today to play the role of caryatids supporting a floor for others some day to dance on . . . or of wretched galley slaves, up to their knees in mud, dragging a barge filled with some mysterious treasure and with the humble words "progress in the future" inscribed on its bows? . . . An end that is infinitely remote is not an end, but, if you like, a trap. . . . Each age, each generation, each life had and has its own fullness.[27]

Again Herzen had adopted a paradoxical attitude, for he hardly possessed the "fullness of life in the present" which he now declared was the only acceptable end for man; yet at the same time he had abandoned his old rationalizations for "hoping in the future." Still, he accepted this dilemma because more than anything else he feared the servitude of self-delusion, which diminished the dignity of the individual by undermining his inner integrity. Although he could do nothing about the servitudes imposed by society, he at least had it in his power to break the fetters of fantasy; therefore, he sacrificed his cherished belief in inevitable progress, because 1848 had convinced him that it was simply another surrogate for freedom. In *From the Other Shore* Herzen rejected the ideal substitutes for liberty of French socialism and of the Hegelian idea of history, just as in Novgorod he had rejected the abstract "reconciliation" of religion and of the "Buddhistic" forms of "science." No matter how painful it might be, he preferred to face the world as it really was, for only in this way could he be truly himself, an emancipated and autonomous individual: this much at least he could grasp of the "fullness of life in the present."

Furthermore, nature, like history, now became for Herzen a blind, chaotic force. To be sure there were patterns of development in nature which loosely governed the evolution of species, and thought remained as much as ever a derivative of man's physical make-up, but there was no one overall pattern in the life of the world leading harmoniously from inanimate matter to the "consciousness" of mankind. Man, for Herzen, was no longer comfortably buoyed up by the teleological world-process of Hegelianism; he had ceased to be the purpose and end of nature, who dominated the universe by his understanding. Instead, the universe was a meaningless anarchy, in which man and his consciousness were no more than a happy biological accident, and nature was a hostile force arbitrarily granting life or death to the individual, permitting or denying the development of personality. By the same token the historical development of humanity and the emergence of freedom were equally patternless and accidental. It was precisely because the men of 1848 had failed to realize this, and instead had trusted to their unreal schemes of "progress" and "reason," that the elemental force of reaction had crushed them. With these strokes Herzen had cast down the last idols of dualism and idealism: this was the bitter wisdom he found on "the other shore," after traversing the "storm" of the Revolution.

Nevertheless, his new philosophy did not end in despair, for it had rent asunder the last veils of illusion which had obscured his consciousness and for the first time conferred on him total inner freedom, which was the prerequisite for all other freedoms. Moreover, if anarchy were the law of the universe, then man was also limitlessly free. Since the world was governed by chance, the fundamental law of life was "possibility" rather than "necessity." [28] Although necessity no longer guaranteed the triumph of liberty, it also did not stand in its way. Men, acting with their concrete, individual desires on the various "possibilities" provided by history, would create their own future, which would be good or bad depending on the quality of their action. The key to the future, therefore, became the "active will" of individuals. Liberty might yet be born through the intelligent intervention of this will in the interplay of historical contingencies, and the future could still be socialistic if individuals were sufficiently enlightened and energetic. Herzen had abandoned the consolations of inevitability, but had made up for their loss by a more extreme affirmation of individual dignity and freedom and a new, though more circumspect, "hope in the future."

The moral independence of man is the same immutable truth as his dependence upon his environment. . . . Around us everything changes, everything shifts. We stand on the edge of an abyss and see how it caves in [as in the failure of the Revolution] . . . yet we do not seek a haven anywhere but in ourselves, in the consciousness of our *unlimited* freedom, of our autocratic independence.[29]

In making this bold affirmation Herzen was no doubt less than logical, for it is hard to see how man can be "autocratically" free if he is at the same time "dependent" on the blind forces of his natural and historical environment. Herzen, however, had deliberately placed himself beyond ordinary consistency, and had instead founded his faith on radically new principles. On the one hand, *From the Other Shore* dissolved all rational values and schemes, whether of "science" or of socialism, since such beliefs now constituted in Herzen's eyes a "dualistic" and "abstract" separation of man from his desires; thereby his philosophy ended in universal negation and the world became in a sense absurd. Yet on the other hand, he salvaged one value — belief in human freedom — which he founded on what would now be called a form of existentialism. Although rationally the world may be meaningless, the individual is existentially aware of the force of his will, of the reality of his choices, and of his capacity to act; and therefore he is free.

If Herzen's ethical anarchism recalls Max Stirner, this existentialist

note recalls another contemporary rebel against Hegelianism — Kierkegaard.[30] To be sure, Herzen did not develop his position with anything
like Kierkegaard's philosophical sophistication or richness of insight.
Still, the fact that he held this position at all is remarkable enough, for
it places him in a tiny minority among contemporary thinkers who not
only went beyond the traditional values of religion and metaphysics, but
also transcended the new value systems of utilitarianism, positivism, or
materialism which were dominant among the *avant-garde* by 1850.
Herzen's position was annunciatory of values which would become
prominent only toward the end of the century, and hence confers on him
an originality possessed by none of his contemporaries in Russia and by
few in the West. In the short span of years between 1841 and 1848
Herzen had moved from the conventional religious and social idealism
of his generation to an almost unique existential egoism; and thereby
he had at last developed the perfect philosophic counterpart to his
political anarchism.

3

By 1849 the crisis of negation which had begun in 1846 during
Herzen's quarrel with the moderate Westerners was completed. The
question naturally arises: how seriously should one take his declarations
about Europe? Hyperbole was habitual with Herzen, and a certain
skepticism is in order when approaching his more flamboyant pronouncements. A part of what he said was simply rhetoric, which would pass
when the crisis was over; another part was more substantial, and would
remain as the basis of his political philosophy. The problem is to distinguish the two.

In general, the more apocalyptic aspects of Herzen's declarations
were largely verbal, and hence temporary; his aspiration toward the total
freedom of the individual, and its political expression in anarchism, was
more real, and hence enduring. In particular, the dream of a holocaust
of civilization did not last very long. The acquiescence of the French
proletariat to the regime of Napoleon III, and finally the poor showing
of Nicholas and his cossacks in the Crimean War, effectively put an end
to his visions of a socialist "barbarism." But Herzen continued to
employ anarchist standards in judging Europe, and consequently to find
all European governments wanting, including the most liberal, such as
those of England and Switzerland.[31] Certainly none could serve even as
a partial model for the "new world." With time, however, his practical
judgment of Europe softened, even if his theoretical declarations did not:
there existed, particularly in England and Switzerland, at least "some
respect for the individual and freedom of speech."[32]

In the last analysis, even his thunderous declarations that Europe was "dying" should not be taken completely literally. Like all things for Herzen after 1848, these statements came under the category of "possibility" rather than of "necessity." On the whole, he thought — and even hoped — they were true, but, like everything else, this idea was inflated by the metaphorical habit of idealism. There was, nevertheless, a kernel of conviction to which he held fast. Beneath all the *fatras* about "Roman," "Christian," and "feudal" survivals, about "dualism" and the "monarchic" republic, there was an intuition which was true. Translated out of Herzen's idealistic idiom, his declarations meant that too many groups in Europe had a vested interest in preserving society basically as it stood, and that these groups were too strong for society to be swept away completely. The Revolution of 1848 had "failed" because Europe was fundamentally conservative, and Europe was conservative because the majority of Europeans felt they had something worth conserving. Most elements of European society desired, or would accept, moderate reform, but they would not accept total revolution. Only an unorganized minority — the proletariat — acting out of desperation rather than any clear view of its goals, had a real interest in radical change. This minority was strong enough to frighten the rest of society into a highly unpleasant, though by no means "mortal" reaction, but it was not strong enough to destroy the "old world."

If Herzen understood the essentially conservative character of European society — and it was the chief object of his irritation from the beginning — why then did he react with such fury to the "failure" of the Revolution? The frustrations of his previous life and the intensity of the quarrel with his friends have already been evoked as explanations. But there were other reasons as well. Throughout his first years in Europe Herzen was a lonely and isolated man, cut off from any society in which he could occupy a meaningful position. He had begun by voluntarily renouncing his native milieu, the Moscow circle. After June 1848, he lost contact with it almost completely. Annenkov and the Tuchkovs, fearing they would be compromised in the eyes of the Russian government if they remained even to witness the red scenes transpiring around them, returned home; somewhat later Turgenev followed their example. Until the end of the Crimean War in 1856, except for occasional letters smuggled through by travelers, Herzen remained virtually cut off from Russia, the only world where his name meant anything.

In addition, from the fall of 1847 to that of 1849 there was no place to publish either in Russia or in Europe the prolific productions which were piling up in his valises. For the first time in a decade he lacked an audience and public attention, yet never before had he burned so to speak out his anger to the world. At the same time he was a complete outsider in Europe, needed by no one and with no role to play in the events around him. Before 1849, only his friend, George Herwegh (himself, after the fiasco of his expedition into Baden in April, 1848, a revolutionary failure and a figure of decreasing account), took him seriously as a spokesman for Russian radicalism. Of all the revolutionaries roving the continent, Herzen was just about the only one without a real movement, without even a noble failure, to back him up. Bakunin at least had been able to annex his minor Slavic brethren at the Pan-Slav Congress in Prague, in June 1848.

Herzen was left an idle spectator of the Revolution, one from whom no sacrifices were asked, and to whom no rewards or punishments would be meted out. This position of total irresponsibility gave him the freedom to set his demands as high as he wished. He could demand orgies of anarchy, "regeneration," and "palingenesis," cataclysms of destruction and resurrection from the French proletariat because his responsibility was not involved; Ledru-Rollin, Louis Blanc, even Proudhon, had to be, and were, more circumspect, because they played a role in events. They were trying, in varying degrees and in various ways, to accomplish something in the real world; Herzen's only stake in the Revolution was to dramatize certain principles of intransigence and generosity. This put him in the same camp with men in reality much more reckless than he, such as Bakunin and Blanqui, who were prepared to assume responsibility in fact for a program to which Herzen committed himself only in words. Proudhon, anarchist though he was, did not advocate the total violence Herzen subscribed to in ink, and which Bakunin and Blanqui were willing to transcribe in blood.[33] Life in Russia, where Herzen had been totally cut off from the reality of power, had been one long lesson in political irresponsibility; his role as spectator during the Revolution only prolonged this education. Anarchism, therefore, came easily to him, since it is a doctrine which categorically rejects everything that exists. In essence, it is a refusal to assume any responsibility within the limits of an actual political situation; instead it places itself outside the possibilities offered by the real world and demands a new heaven and a new earth.

This is why Herzen's comments on the Revolution have such an abstract ring. In his isolation from responsibility he turned the Revolution into a gigantic melodrama into which, with the habitual egoism of idealism, he projected his own frustrated aspirations. Yet with Herzen (unlike Bakunin, whose motivation was analogous) the violence was largely verbal, à la Karl Moor, and one senses behind all the bloodthirsty rhetoric a man who is much too humane to act on a quarter of what he said. This impression would be borne out after the death of Nicholas, when at last Herzen would be able to play a real role in Russian politics.

Then he would settle for much less than *all* from Alexander II — co-operating to a point with an autocrat to obtain the most satisfactory possible emancipation of the peasants, agitating for such a half measure as a constitutional monarchy, and showing an extreme reluctance to support the Polish revolt of 1863 because he understood, as he did not in 1848, that premature revolution bred reaction. But while Nicholas was on the throne Herzen knew he could get nothing. So what would be lost by demanding all? — especially when the addressee of the demand was a bystander, not a party to his dispute with Nicholas, and not listening to him anyway. Thus Herzen hurled his indignation against Nicholas and against his own confined existence at the unheeding heads of the French proletariat, of the "cowardly" Western socialists, and of Europe in general; then he threw what can only be described as an ideological tantrum when he did not get what he wanted, as he had known all along he would not — all of which helped fill the "emptiness of life," and convinced him of his own impeccable redness in the teeth of Nicholas, of his "slavish" Moscow friends and of doubting European democracy.

4

A final reason for the exceptional violence of Herzen's revolt immediately after 1848 was personal, for in the wake of the Revolution he was visited by a shattering series of family tragedies. In 1851, his mother and his second son, a deaf-mute since birth, were drowned in a shipwreck in the Mediterranean. This loss, however, was overshadowed by a still more staggering blow which fell at almost the same time — the infidelity of Natalie and her death. The story of this affair is told in *My Past and Thoughts* with great detail and frankness, as well as with Herzen's usual self-dramatization;[34] an even fuller and more balanced account has been given in English by E. H. Carr in *The Romantic Exiles*.[35] Therefore, although the early phases of Herzen's marriage have been examined in detail in previous chapters, the *dénouement* will be touched on only briefly here.

The tragedy occurred primarily because Natalie had never been able to reconcile herself to the changes wrought in her life by her husband's earlier infidelity and his consequent view that love was not the whole of life but only a part, subordinate to "general interests." [36] She never ceased to hope that she would live again the total love that "Dante" once had pledged to "Beatrice," and the more Herzen neglected her for politics and revolution the more intense this hope became. In her maturity, however, she viewed this love through George Sand's ideas on the natural rights of passion rather than through the religious idealism of her youth: this much, at least, she had accepted of her husband's ideology.

For Natalie, escape to the West meant a second chance to find this all-consuming passion. In 1849 she thought she found it in the embraces of the family's closest European friend, Herwegh. Although she kept this liaison a secret from her husband, it was by no means a vulgar adultery in her eyes. On the contrary, she persuaded herself that when the appropriate time came to reveal her love to Alexander, he would respect and indeed revere it, since the sincerity of her passion was clearly higher than the bonds of conventional marriage. To this principle of Sand's she joined her old notion of the unity of "friendship" and "love": Herzen and Herwegh were "friends" and she was "sister" and wife to them both, but since Herwegh was the weaker of the two he had the greater need of her "love." Surely Alexander would understand that these multiple bonds were compatible, and that the three of them could live together in harmony!

Herzen, however, when he accidentally discovered the truth, did not understand. Although he never claimed his "rights" as a husband in so many words, he in fact behaved in what strongly resembled a "bourgeois" manner toward the lovers. Of course, he could not contest their freedom to love, but he did give vent to indignation at their deceit, a practice which was not in the canon of Sand. Moreover, in order to assuage his pride, he maintained that Natalie had never truly loved Herwegh at all (though her letters clearly indicate she did); the latter had simply taken unscrupulous advantage of her exceptional tenderness in order to seduce her, and he alone was responsible for the deception. The affair, therefore, was not a "true" passion as understood by the new morality, but a "treacherous" abuse by Herwegh of the friendship the Herzens had accorded him. In making this point Herzen was inadvertently aided by Herwegh himself, who, once he had been found out, rapidly lost his ardor, thereby confirming all of Herzen's accusations. As for Natalie, separated from her lover and disillusioned by his conduct, she had no choice but to accept her husband's assurances of renewed affection (of bourgeois "pardon" there was never any question) and to return to her old life. The ordeal of this second failure in love, however, was too much for her frail constitution. Early in 1851, exhausted by two pregnancies which had occurred during the crisis as well as by nervous strain, she took to her bed and died.

With this, Herzen's isolation in the world was complete. He had long since lost his Moscow circle, and now his only close European friend, Herwegh, whose family had lived with his almost as one household since 1848, had betrayed him in the most despicable manner. Not even Natalie was left to him, and with her disappeared all family life and the last fixed point in his universe. Yet for all this his will to fight back did not abandon him. Of course, he could not admit to himself that Natalie's infidelity had perhaps arisen from dissatisfaction with her marriage; nor could he confess to any failure to achieve the fullness of personality or the ethics of "egoism" in their life together. Herzen's domestic drama led him to question none of his principles; rather it moved him to reaffirm them all. Natalie became in his eyes the "dear martyr" of Herwegh's villainy, and her memory was surrounded by a love and reverence that recalled the days of "Dante" and "Beatrice." But she also became a "martyr" to the cause of the emancipation of woman, of the "new marriage," and of the new morality. Herwegh was no more than the agent of her ruin; fundamentally she had been destroyed by the "corrupt" and "rotten" West that had created her seducer, and that had also destroyed the Revolution: she was a sainted victim in the national no less than social struggle against the "old world."

This is not to suggest, however, that Herzen's conjugal drama was the hidden cause of his bitterness against society after 1848, as has at times been maintained.[37] Enough has been said about the roots of his anarchism to demonstrate the contrary. Moreover, a simple examination of dates removes all possibility of doubt; Herzen learned of Natalie's infidelity only at the beginning of 1850, but his diatribes against the existing order had already attained full volume by the summer of 1848. Still, it would be a mistake to omit entirely his personal tragedy from a discussion of his anarchism. For those raised in the Russian idealist circles personal and social self-fulfillment were one, and society was judged primarily by the possibilities it offered for the free development of the individual. If he and Natalie were unable to realize in their private lives the ideal of the "new marriage," it was because Western society was still too imperfectly emancipated to permit this. Thus the conclusions he drew from his domestic drama reinforced those he had already drawn from the failure of the Revolution.

It is this situation which explains, in part at least, the violence of Herzen's anarchism immediately after 1848, as contrasted with its milder character both earlier and later. During these years he had his back to the wall, with little defense against a world that was more than ever alien. How else could he reply, indeed how else could he continue to live, than by denying without compromise a society that denied all his own values? How else could he continue to "hope in the future" than by seeking refuge in a political, philosophical and ethical anarchism more violent than the forces that menaced his own beliefs? Given Herzen's values, personal as well as social, total negation of the existing world, and at the same time unlimited affirmation of the ego's autonomy, in spite of all that oppressed it, was the only way out of the crisis, both political and personal, to which his new life in Europe had brought him.

CHAPTER XVI

Russian Socialism

BY 1849, as the fires of the Revolution died out all over Europe, Herzen at last began to acquire that role as Russia's deputy to European democracy which he had sought in vain since 1847. The two events were not without a close connection. When the Revolution failed, its leaders became *émigrés* in the few remaining islands of liberalism: England, Switzerland, or Piedmont's Nice. This fact completely changed Herzen's relation to his fellow radicals. They were no longer the haughty entrepreneurs of a going revolution, with no time or need for him; like himself they were outcasts, men who lived on past memories and future hopes. For the first time he was on a footing of equality with them. Moreover, they were failures, no longer entitled to speak with the old galling authority on matters red. Herzen, in consequence, felt that he had every right to be listened to as an equal.

It was in this society of malcontents that Herzen made his home for the rest of his days. Until the death of Nicholas, when he would once again be able to make his voice heard distinctly in Russia, it was to be almost his whole world. The relation, as formerly, was an ambivalent one. Except for a few, such as Proudhon and the Italians, he half-despised the *émigrés* of 1848 as phrase-mongers lacking the courage of their flaming words; most of the portraits of them in *My Past and Thoughts* are ironical and even condescending. At the same time, however, he admired them for having dared to act, and he eagerly solicited their good opinion of himself and of Russian radicalism. He had an absolute need of them as audience, even, in the last analysis, as patrons of his own efforts; and his irony toward them may well have been partly an antidote to his need of their approval.

Herzen's first step toward integrating himself into this world was to become an *émigré* himself. It is not completely clear when he decided to do this, but it seems to have been sometime during 1849, for by then the Russian consular services in Europe were trying to catch up with him.[1] They finally succeeded in doing so at Nice in 1850; Herzen was presented with a summons to return home, which he flatly refused to do, thus making the break open, and, at least for the life of Nicholas, irrevocable.[2] In taking this drastic action Herzen seems not to have known even a moment's hesitation; indeed, he most probably drifted into it under the pressure of events more than he came to it through any thoughtful deliberation.

This step, however, still did not make of Russian democracy in exile a very considerable movement. Bakunin by now was back in Russia and in prison; Herzen's only fellows were Sazonov and a landowner named Golovin who, in 1844, had embroiled himself with Nicholas largely by accident and had therefore decided to remain abroad. After 1850 the group was joined by a picturesque but highly unstable young man named Engelson, who had been converted to "general interests" by an old article of Herzen's in the *Annals* and who later had been implicated in the Petrashevski affair.[3] Until the arrival of Ogarev in 1856 Herzen was the only important Russian democrat in exile.

When he decided to remain abroad, Herzen also instituted measures to withdraw his considerable fortune from Russia. In 1849 his property had been sequestered at the personal order of Nicholas, but in 1850 Herzen circumvented this move with the aid of Baron James Rothschild of Paris — while the "old world" still stood Herzen felt there was no point in refusing its services in a crisis. He made a fictitious sale of his property to Rothschild; the latter in turn menaced Nicholas with refusal of a loan then pending in order to obtain removal of the sequester and transfer of the value of the property to Paris.[4] It was a brilliant *coup* which Herzen, as well as Rothschild, enjoyed immensely — and quite understandably.

With the aid of Rothschild, Herzen even increased his fortune in the West. A part of the money he invested in Parisian real estate, which during the building boom under the Second Empire increased greatly in value. Another part he invested in various American bonds, which were also both solid and lucrative. Finally, in the conditions of general insecurity which prevailed in Europe after the Revolution, there were many profitable opportunities for speculation, in which Herzen, still with the aid of Rothschild, did not disdain to engage.[5] In spite of his extremism, Herzen in many ways was a very sensible man. Not only did he think of the personal security of himself and his children; he also knew that Russian democracy in exile would have need of money if it were to be effective — an idea which never occurred to Bakunin. This substantial capitalization of the Russian revolution began to pay political dividends immediately. To cover himself against any possible extradition proceedings, Herzen in 1851 became naturalized as a citizen of the Swiss canton of Fribourg. The Swiss, in spite of their liberalism toward political refugees, did not extend the favor of naturalization to any and all revolutionary wanderers; this required money, and Herzen was one of the few exiles with enough to obtain such a coveted protection.[6]

At the same time that he secured his material position in the West, Herzen set about with equal diligence creating a moral position for himself in European democracy. Until the election of Louis Napoleon as President of the Republic at the end of 1848 Herzen remained ignored and unpublished in France. It was at the beginning of 1849, when the affairs of the Left were entering into their definitive decline, that he made his first conquests. He was briefly associated with an effort, led by Mickiewicz and the Poles, to create a newspaper devoted to liberation movements outside of France (only summarily treated by the French press) and called *La Tribune des Peuples*. But Herzen, who was to have held the Russian rubric, was put off by Mickiewicz's Bonapartist and messianistic sentiments, and soon dissociated himself from the venture.[7] He next engaged in the only revolutionary "action" of his career: on June 13, 1849, he participated in the abortive street revolt of the radicals led by Ledru-Rollin. Herzen marched with the rest, but without believing for a minute in the success of the enterprise; he went home rather early in the day, as soon as the troops appeared, to write more "letters" about the "hollow rhetoric" and the "cowardice" of the European Left.[8] Unlike Bakunin, Herzen's weapon was the pen, not the sword, and henceforth he would do all his fighting with the former instrument.

In July he fled to Geneva to avoid possible reprisals by the French government for his participation in the *journée* of June 13. The alarm, however, turned out to be largely imaginary, and he returned to Paris in 1850, unmolested, to negotiate the financial affairs already mentioned. Then, on the request of the Russian government, he was expelled from France — a happening which only confirmed his suspicions about the lack of any essential difference between bourgeois republics and autocracies.[9] But he was never in any danger of arrest and extradition (the fate of Bakunin at the hands of the Saxon authorities after his participation in the Dresden uprising of 1849), and the interdiction on residence in France did not survive his acquisition of Swiss citizenship. Still, the precedent of Bakunin was disquieting; and Herzen understandably did not wish to place his new freedom at the mercy of a caprice of Louis Napoleon's Prefect of Police. So he stayed abroad — in Geneva during the second half of 1849, and then in Nice, at the time still a part of Piedmont, from 1850 to 1852.

There were other reasons for this choice, no less important than considerations of security. Geneva and Nice contained large colonies of refugees from the Revolution, principally Germans, Frenchmen, and Italians; and in their company Herzen at last fully found his place. In Geneva he was taken up by James Fazy, the leader of the canton since the liberal uprising of 1847, and was treated for the first time by an important radical figure as an equal, without patronage. He also received a favorable reception from the German colony, to which he was introduced by Herwegh (it was before the discovery of the liaison with Natalie); but this meant less to Herzen, for in his eyes the Germans as a nation were the biggest talkers and the worst actors of the whole European Left.[10] Most gratifying of all, however, he was taken very seriously by the great Mazzini and his lieutenants, Orsini (the future would-be assassin of Napoleon III) and Saffi, all freshly arrived from the collapse of the Roman Republic. Although Herzen disagreed with their politics, especially with Mazzini's "superstition" of a humanitarian religion, he respected immensely their "spirit" and "audacity" — almost worthy of Russians. The cult of Italy continued in spite of the failure of the Revolution there as elsewhere. In 1850 Mazzini paid Herzen the supreme honor: at a secret rendezvous in Paris the patriarch of European conspiracy offered him the position of Russian representative in his latest international organization, to be called the Central European Committee. Herzen, however, declined because, although the Committee stood for the independence of oppressed peoples and for republicanism, it was neither socialist nor sufficiently "new-worldly." [11] Nonetheless, Herzen was immensely flattered, both for Russia and himself; it was at last recognized that he represented a force in European democracy.

Shortly before this he had received a similarly august consecration, though on slightly less flattering terms. In 1849 he at last entered into close relations with Proudhon, but of a business as much as of a political nature. Through the efforts of Sazonov, Herzen was invited to put up the police bond (24,000 francs) for Proudhon's last attempt to keep an anarchist press operating in France, a newspaper named *La Voix du Peuple*, which Proudhon edited from his cell in the prison of Sainte Pélagie. In return for his money Herzen insisted, with the full dignity of his growing importance in European democracy, on certain terms: he was to be foreign editor of the paper and to have full freedom to express all his opinions about Europe and Russia. This venture, however, was short-lived. The paper lost money from the beginning; then, in 1850, it was closed by the police, and Herzen forfeited his entire bond.[12] But the loss was worth it, both for what editorship by the side of Proudhon meant in prestige for the Russian Left, and for the first taste, however brief, of that free forum for his ideas which Herzen had desired all his life.

A similar gratification was accorded him shortly thereafter. In 1850, through his German connections, Herzen succeeded in publishing in Hamburg abridged translations of his *Letters from France and Italy* and *From the Other Shore,* and both enjoyed some success among disillusioned German democrats. Needless to say, they also aroused opposition. In particular, Marx could never abide Herzen for what he felt were his stupidities about "dying" Europe being regenerated by "young" Russia.[13] But at least controversy was started over Herzen's ideas; Europe was paying attention to his opinions. By 1850 he occupied a position in European democracy more important than that held by Bakunin before the latter's brief moment of fame in 1848–49. In fact, Herzen incorporated Bakunin's exploits into his own propaganda. He was willing to produce an article defending Bakunin's record for any radical journal that would uphold his friend's oft-maligned memory.[14] He slowly acquired the reassuring feeling that he was accustoming the haughty European "matadors of rhetoric" to the idea of Russia's radical potentialities. Translations from his articles even appeared in French, German and Irish *émigré* publications as far away as New York.[15]

Satisfying as all this was, however, it was not enough. Herzen wished most of all to convince the Russians, and in particular his timorous Moscow friends, of their own radical potentialities, and from them he remained almost completely cut off. His two principal books on the West, the *Letters from France and Italy* and *From the Other Shore,* had been written for them; and they are liberally punctuated with the formula "you, my friends," by which Herzen meant, not just readers in general, but specifically his Moscow circle. Still, except for the chapters on Paris written in 1847, these books had never been published in Russia, or even in Russian. In July 1848, when Annenkov and the Tuchkovs returned home, Herzen sent with them manuscript copies of his writings to date; and in the ensuing years a number of letters were smuggled back and forth. But until 1856 he received only one visit: from Shchepkin in 1853 — who came chiefly to reproach him in the name of the circle for the perils his reckless propaganda created for liberty at home.[16]

And, indeed, Herzen soon began to feel some guilt about the consequences of his own conduct for his friends. Eighteen-forty-eight had begun another period of reaction in Russia, the most ferocious of Nicholas' reign. In 1849 a new "revolutionary conspiracy" was uncovered in Petersburg, that of the Petrashevski circle, which was punished by Nicholas with a harshness second only to that he had meted out to the Decembrists. In these circumstances, Herzen's emigration automatically compromised all of his friends, already sufficiently suspect as it was. Belinski had had the good fortune to die early in 1848, since he certainly would have been one of the first victims of the new repression. But others, such as Kavelin, and especially Granovski, were badgered and at times seriously harassed; Ogarev, Herzen's old friend Satin, the Tuchkovs, and Turgenev were for a time placed under house arrest on their estates. And Herzen eventually learned of all this. He, of course, was not directly responsible for what had happened; Nicholas hardly needed prompting to be severe. Still, Herzen felt a share of responsibility for the sufferings of his friends, as he had not in the case of the European proletariat. As conditions grew worse in Russia, he experienced an increasingly acute need to justify his own conduct and his opinions.[17] This justification took the form of insisting ever more strongly on the revolutionary potentialities of Russia, which, he also maintained, could only be fought for in freedom abroad. He needed a red homeland, not only to enhance his and Russia's prestige in European democracy, but also to defend himself before his friends and his own conscience.

He finally acquired the means of conducting the Russian half of his campaign in 1852. After his domestic tragedy and the death of Natalie in 1851, Herzen found Nice, the scene of these events, an increasingly unbearable place of residence. Besides, in the midst of the growing reaction, one could not be certain of the continued benevolences of the Piedmontese authorities. Therefore, he decided to move. He had at least talked from time to time of emigrating to the United States as the nearest thing to a "new world" the planet had to offer. But America was really too far from the center of the revolutionary activities that interested him; furthermore, in spite of its newness, the very success of the American republic made it the epitome of "bourgeois" civilization.[18] So Herzen decided on England. By the summer of 1852 he was settled in London, which, in addition to freedom of speech, presented the advantage of being now the chief center of his new family, European democracy in exile. Though he did not know it at the time, he was to spend most of his remaining years there.

Herzen would become even less integrated into English life than he had been into French, but not for the same reasons. He had a certain respect for the English, in particular because of their proud independence both as individuals and as a nation; in *My Past and Thoughts* their practical sense of human dignity is always flatteringly contrasted with French revolutionary rhetoric and German humanistic pedantry.[19] But, for Herzen personally, there was nothing in these English virtues beyond the right of political asylum. He never made the connection between English liberty and English liberalism, while English radicalism seemed to him an unimpressive movement not worth any strenuous courting. Hence he largely ignored the English, as they did him. Instead, he made his life among revolutionary *émigrés* of all nationalities, men whose interests and experience he shared, equals among whom he could play a role. Not surprisingly, he was closest to the Italians and the Poles.

It was the latter who finally gave him the opportunity to make his voice heard once again in Russia.

The Poles, old hands at conspiring against Nicholas, since 1831 had maintained various publishing enterprises in Western Europe, the current center of which was London. Their example crystallized an idea which had been in the back of Herzen's mind for a long time.[20] To replace the defunct *Voix du Peuple* — which had never been his anyway and which was not a Russian publication — he would found a press of his own. In 1852–53, with Polish technical aid and the use of the weak but still existent Polish underground to distribute his publications within the empire, he established the Free Russian Press (*Volnaia russkaia tipografiia*).[21] The event was a momentous one: this was the first uncensored published "word" in Russian history,[22] and in addition the ancestor of a long and distinguished line of free Russian journals abroad. The operations of the new Press were at first modest. There was almost nothing to publish but Herzen's own productions, and very little got through to Russia before 1856. Still, the essential had been accomplished: a free forum for Russian opinion had at last been established, and it would grow into a major political force under the more liberal conditions of the next reign. Of course, all this was made possible not only by the freedom of "bourgeois" England; it also presupposed Herzen's personal fortune. Gentry Russia not only supplied the ideas and the talent to launch the Russian revolutionary movement; it also supplied the capital, as if in repayment to the serfs. Indeed, under Herzen's administration, Russian democracy, if the tiniest, was also the best heeled emigration in all London.

The first major enterprise of the new Press was the partial publication of a work which has already been referred to many times in these pages, *My Past and Thoughts.* From the time of Herzen's arrival in London until the end of the Crimean War, managing the affairs of Russian radicalism in exile was hardly a full-time occupation. To employ his ever-restless energies, as well as to fill the void created by Natalie's infidelity and death, Herzen undertook to write an *apologia pro vita sua.* In reality it was an enterprise in which he had been engaged through all his "fiction" since he wrote the *Notebooks of a Certain Young Man.*[23] The new memoirs had several aims. Herzen was first of all telling his story for its own sake, a story he characteristically felt was very important since it was about himself. He was also writing an intellectual history of the reign of Nicholas, which at the same time was the story of the birth of Russian radicalism — incidentally the first major essays on both subjects. Finally, he was analyzing the wonderful potentialities of the Russian national character, which at every opportunity was contrasted with the bourgeois degradation of the Europeans. He was at the same time creating his own myth and that of the Russian revolution.

Needless to say, under such conditions *My Past and Thoughts,* in spite of all its brilliance and wit, is as much *Dichtung* as *Wahrheit,* a model he had in mind when he wrote.[24] It is this which gives rise to the numerous problems in interpreting his career of which frequent examples have already been presented. Certain things are omitted, others are in part invented, and everything is edited in one degree or another, usually to give whatever is being discussed the most radical possible slant. Finally, in every controversy and incident, whether in Russia or Europe, Herzen always has the *beau rôle* and the last word. But then the book was as much a work of propaganda as an autobiography. As such it was addressed to his Moscow friends and intended as a justification of his life in their eyes, an intention which is demonstrated in various prefaces entitled "To My Brothers in Russia" or "To My Friends." But it was also addressed to Europe; and on every occasion which presented itself Herzen published partial translations in French, German, or English.[25] In spite of his declared scorn both for his Moscow friends and for Europe, he had a tremendous need of the approval of both — and expended tremendous energies to obtain it.

2

Herzen's chief justification for his career and for the revolution he represented, however, came in a series of essays and books composed between 1849 and the Crimean War in which he at last set forth in fully developed form his famous theory of a native Russian socialism, founded on the peasant commune. To be sure, Herzen did not discover the idea of the "socialist" *obshchina,* although he was closely associated with it from the beginning. As we have seen, it first occurred to the Slavophiles early in the forties; stimulated by Herzen's and Belinski's socialist preachings, they answered that the *obshchina* already expressed in reality the ideal toward which Europe was still vainly striving in theory.[26] This idea was then taken up and exploited systematically by the Prussian, Haxthausen, in a work famous in the history of Russian social thought: *Studien über die inneren Zustände, das Volksleben und insbesondere die ländlischen Einrichtungen Russlands,* the first two volumes of which appeared simultaneously in German and French in 1847, and the third in the same languages in 1852 and 1853. The purpose of the Slavophiles and Haxthausen, of course, was conservative: to demonstrate that Russia needed neither socialism nor revolution because she already had the benefits which both were supposed to confer. But Haxthausen's book revived interest in the commune in Russia and for the first time gave it sociological standing with the Left no less than with the Right. After 1847 everyone from Belinski to Khomiakov, including of course Herzen, was reading it, even though its translation into Russian had been forbidden.[27]

Haxthausen also helped naturalize the idea in Europe, especially among the Germans and the Poles, and again as much with the Left as with the Right. In particular, Herwegh and the Germans whom Herzen frequented in Geneva were impressed by the possibilities of a bucolic socialism. Simultaneously, and it would seem independently of both Germans and Russians, various Polish exiles, notably Lelewel, arrived at the same idea from the study of general Slavic history (Lelewel was a historian by profession), for contemporary Poland itself had no commune. By 1847 Bakunin had caught the idea from the Poles and had begun to expound it in 1848 — that is before Herzen — with Pan-Slav overtones.[28]

The ground, then, was already well prepared when Herzen took up the cause. Nor was this idea difficult to come by. Given the interest of the Right all over Europe in national folkways and of the Left in egalitarian communes, someone was bound to make the Russian connection sooner or later; and, as is obvious, many people did so simultaneously. Herzen's role, therefore, was not that of inventor but of chief exegete and popularizer of this idea in its radical version. He developed and disseminated a whole theory to support what Bakunin had left only as a suggestion. And in doing so he added much that was specifically his own.

As we have seen, Herzen first intimated his faith in the commune in 1847.[29] But from this to its systematic defense was a step which he approached gingerly. The Slavophiles and Haxthausen were bad references, and he did not wish to be discredited by a misalliance. On November 5, 1848, in one of his rare letters to Moscow, after an unusually violent diatribe against Europe (in which the French electorate was compared to orang-outangs), he took the following cautious stand on the commune.

But if this is so then you have become a Slavophile? No; just because Europe is dying it does not follow that the Slavs are not in their infancy. And infancy, for a healthy, full-grown man is the same as senility. Europe in dying wills to the world of the future, as the fruit of its last efforts, as the summit of its development, socialism. The Slavs *an sich* possess the ingredients of socialism in a primitive form. It is very possible that, if in our day they had not encountered socialist Europe, their communal life would have disappeared, as did that of the Germanic peoples. The nature of the Slavs, in those cases where it has had a chance to develop, is rich and strong . . . these examples of development give promise of a brilliant future, but the present is poor. The task of Russia is more difficult than that of Europe — she must revise and renounce two pasts: the pre-Petrine and the post-Petrine [that is, native nationalism and Orthodox religion as well as imported Western "feudal" values].[30]

At first glance this looks like no more than a repetition of the skepticism Herzen had expressed toward the commune in 1843 in his discussions with the Slavophiles. But he protests too much for true skepticism; in reality he was simply covering himself against possible association with the Slavophiles — an old accusation of his friends. Then, too, in November 1848 the Revolution was not yet completely dead. It might be safer to wait for Europe's final groan before crying victory for Russia.

By the second half of 1849 the Revolution was unmistakably dead, and Herzen unmasked all his batteries. The unmasking occurred in an essay-letter to Herwegh entitled *La Russie: à G.H.*, first published in November 1849, in French, by Proudhon's *Voix du Peuple*. Soon afterward it was translated into Italian for Mazzini's *L'Italia del Populo* and in 1850, under Herwegh's patronage, into German, which edition bore the melodramatically grim signature "A Barbarian." [31] This essay was followed the same year by a shorter but essentially similar *Lettre d'un Russe à Mazzini*, which appeared both in the latter's journal and in *La Voix du Peuple*, and then later in German.[32] In the course of the next few years Herzen repeated his views in four other productions. In 1851 in Paris he published a book, *Du développement des idées révolutionnaires en Russie*, which was both a history of the awakening of the intelligentsia since the Decembrists (like *My Past and Thoughts*) and a defense of the socialist peasant commune; in the same year this work received a German abridgement.[33] Again in 1851 and in French, he appealed to the cosmopolitan generosity of another influential European democrat with *Le peuple russe et le socialisme, Lettre à M. Jules Michelet*, which also was soon translated, this time into English.[34] After his removal to London, Herzen first carried his ideas directly to the Russian public in *Baptized Property*, first published by the Free Press in 1853 and the same year reproduced almost literally in English.[35] Finally, in 1854 he made a direct attack on the English public (which he felt was too exclusively preoccupied with slavery in America) in *The Old World and Russia. Letters to the Editor of "The English Republic," W. Linton,* Linton being one of his few radical contacts in Britain.[36] Herzen left no stone in European democracy unturned. But if this was the first public he wished to convince, he did not forget his friends at home. Many of the works listed here were later published in Russian by the Free Press; and the ideas they contain were repeated endlessly in *My Past and Thoughts*.

The form of Herzen's argument in all these productions is the same: that of a contrast between "young" Russia and "old" Europe. From the time of his arrival in Europe, each of his negative judgments of the West had implied a positive judgment of Russia; already in 1847 and 1848 each attack on Western "feudalism" was an indirect encomium to Russian "virginity." Indeed, Herzen had made these attacks all along, not so much to say something about Europe, but in order to talk about *his* Russia. In the midst of an alien revolution, he could maintain his "hope in the future" of that ideal radical Russia which had been his life ever since the Sparrow Hills only by destroying hope in the present of Europe. All that changed in 1849 was that the "historiosophical" symbols for this faith became direct rather than indirect. He at last stated explicitly what had been implicit from the day he set foot in Europe. As if to demonstrate this continuity, both the *Letter to Herwegh* and *Du développement des idées révolutionnaires en Russie* had as their epigraph the verses of Goethe on America which had first struck him in 1844 and which he had already quoted in the *Letters from the Avenue Marigny*, verses which will be repeated here since the use of incantatory repetition — an old habit of idealism — was one of Herzen's principal traits both as a writer and as a thinker:

> Dich stört nicht im Innern,
> Zu lebendiger Zeit,
> Unnützes Erinnern
> Und vergeblicher Streit.[37]

By Russia's "youth" Herzen meant several things at once. First of all, he intended the analogy with the life cycle of an organism quite seriously; Russia was "young" because, historically speaking, she had experienced less and created less than Europe. But Herzen also meant that Russia, unlike Europe, was not conservative, since almost no group in Russian society had a vested interest in the preservation of the status quo. Virtually the entire population was fundamentally discontented with things as they were. The educated minority chafed under the lack of freedom imposed by the autocracy, as the revolt of the Decembrists demonstrated. Above all, the peasantry was radically opposed to the whole existing structure. An entire population had nothing to lose but its chains, unlike Europe, where numerous and powerful segments of society had a great deal to lose besides their chains, and hence wore them all the more lightly.

Russia is in a completely different position [from Europe]. The walls of its prison are of wood; raised by brute force alone, they will give way at the first blow. A part of the people [the Westernized gentry], denying its entire past like Peter the Great, has shown what power of negation it possesses; the other part [the peasantry], remaining estranged from the present state structure, has submitted, but it has not accepted the new regime [the autocracy as instituted by Peter], which has the look of a temporary bivouac. People obey because they are afraid; but they do not believe.[38]

Unlike Europe, Russia presented a truly revolutionary situation because no one, other than the autocrat and the insignificant minority that profited from autocracy, had a vested interest in the preservation of the existing state of affairs. Again unlike Europe, none of the institutions or values created by Russia's past was dear to any but the same minority. "We are free from the past because our past is empty, poor, and narrow. It is impossible to love such things as Moscovite tsarism or the Empire of Petersburg." [39] Europeanized minority and peasant majority alike rejected both Russia's past and its present uncompromisingly. They were held in subjection by brute force alone, by a state power external to them, and not by the self-imposed moral servitude to the past characteristic of Europe. "We are independent [of the past] because we have nothing, because there is nothing for us to be attached to; bitterness and resentment are in every memory." [40] The Russians were born anarchists and revolutionaries, and this for Herzen was the essence of their "youthfulness."

Behind this perceptive analysis of the basic instability of the nineteenth-century autocracy lay a more dubious theory of Russian history, of which we have already seen the antecedents. The purpose of this theory was twofold: to justify the idea of Russia's youthfulness in the face of the long historical existence of the Russian state; and to vindicate the essentially revolutionary and democratic nature of the Russian people in the face of their centuries-long submission to autocracy. The solution to both problems was found by claiming — in a manner reminiscent of the Slavophiles — that the Russian state was of another essence than the Russian people, thereby rejecting the autocracy as not really Russian at all. By establishing a convenient distinction between the "true" Russia of the people and the "false" Russia of the state, Herzen abolished with one stroke the undemocratic aspects of the national history. Reassured by this feat of metaphysical legerdemain, he was able to substitute his wishes for reality and to write in all tranquillity that: "The true history of Russia dates only from 1812; before that there had been only the introduction. The vital forces of the Russian people have never been effectively absorbed by their development, as have those of the Germano-Latin peoples." [41] By eliminating the disagreeable aspects of the past as, in a sense, an illusion, the way was prepared for seeing only what he wanted to see.

The vision ran as follows. Originally, before the appearance of the state, the Slavs had lived a life of primitive democracy and socialism in the peasant commune, which of all forms of social organization was the one most natural to them.

In all the world there is perhaps no situation more compatible with the *Slavic character* than [that which existed] in the Ukraine from Kievan times to the period of Peter I. Here was a Cossack and agricultural republic, ruled with military discipline, but on the basis of democratic communism, without any centralization, without any state power, subject only to ancient custom, submitting neither to the tsar of Moscow nor the king of Poland. There was no aristocracy; each individual who was of age was an active citizen; all offices, from sergeant to hetman, were elective. . . . In the Ukraine, in Montenegro, and even in the case of the Serbs, the Illyrians, and the Dalmatians, everywhere the Slavic genius manifested its nature and aspirations but did not develop a strong political form.[42]

The state, when it appeared, was an alien force imposed by harsh necessity. The pressure of other peoples, the Mongols first, then later the Polish-Lithuanians and the Swedes, made necessary the creation of a strong central government. Otherwise the Russians would have known the fate of the Balkan Slavs at the hands of the Turks, or of the Czechs at the hands of the Austrian Germans — loss of independence and of national character. Later the mission of the state was to bring enlightenment and the influence of the West to Russia.[43] With this act Russia became a part of the main stream of human development. Still, in spite of these services, the autocracy always remained an alien force in Russia, unlike the deified Roman state of the West, which was a native phenomenon. The "true" life of Russia withdrew into the peasant commune, crushed under the weight of an imported Byzantine autocracy and a German bureaucracy, yet still tenacious and vigorous.[44]

The Slavic peoples, properly, like neither the state nor centralization. They prefer to live in scattered communes, as far removed as possible from all interference on the part of the government. They hate military organization, they hate the police. A federation would be the most authentically national form of organization for the Slavic peoples. The Petersburg period was a terrible ordeal, a painful education in state life. Forcibly it performed a useful function for Russia, uniting her scattered parts and welding them into a whole, yet it must pass.[45]

But this state had never tapped the vital forces of the people, those forces hidden in the democratic commune and unused since the dawn of time. This was another reason why one could say that the "real" history of the Russian people had not yet begun. Again Herzen's mythological terminology expressed a true intuition: the human resources of Russia were in fact the most underexploited in Europe; serfdom is not an efficient way to develop human potentialities.

The "true" beginning of Russian history was heralded by signs that the age of the Russian state was drawing to a close. Since the time of Catherine the state had no longer served any useful purpose, either of national self-preservation (since the "armed people" could defend themselves if need be, as the peasant partisans had done in 1812), or of enlightenment. "The state, having separated itself from the people in the name of civilization [under Peter], soon [in Catherine's last years] renounced enlightenment in the name of autocracy." With Nicholas the state definitively lost its historical mission; it became a parasite, a dead weight around the neck of the Russian people:

It [the autocracy] renounced civilization as soon as through its aspirations began to appear the tricoloured sign of liberalism; it tried to return to its national roots, to the people [with Official Nationality]. But . . . people and state no longer had anything in common: the former had become alienated from the latter, and the state seemed to see in the depth of the masses a new specter, a still more terrible specter — the *red* symbol of the *pugachevshchina*.[46]

From this point on the preservation of state power became an end in itself. But "autocracy for autocracy's sake in the end becomes impossible. It is too absurd, too sterile." [47] Repression at home and reactionary intervention abroad represented the only possible future for such a regime, until the day a new Pugachev revolt would finally sweep it away. "For such a regime there remains nothing but to conduct foreign war," to become the gendarme of international reaction.[48] This was the essence of Nicholas' government; and in the very violence of the current reaction Herzen saw, dialectically, the end of the "old world" for Russia. "The Winter Palace, like the summit of a mountain toward the end of autumn, is being covered more and more with snow and ice. The life-giving sap, artificially raised to the governmental heights, is little by little freezing into immobility; there remains only force and the hardness of the cliff, still holding back the pressure of the revolutionary waves." [49] Though Herzen's rhetoric led him to overestimate the size of the revolutionary waves, his fundamental idea was sound: a policy based on the purely negative principle of repression in the long run simply made the opposition more radical, as his own case amply demonstrated.

The peasant masses were rumbling with discontent, and sooner or later the autocracy would have to face the alternative of liberation or revolt. But Nicholas hesitated, knowing that emancipation meant the beginning of the end of the entire "old world." "He has understood that emancipation of the peasants is linked with emancipation of the land, and that emancipation of the land in its turn is the beginning of a social revolution, the proclamation of agrarian communism." [50] Again, though the case was overstated, the basic idea was correct: if we leave aside the apocalypse of the "new world," the real and immediate problem confronting Russia was the crisis that would be created even by a legal emancipation, which was now only a question of time. This crisis would arise inevitably from the contradiction between the *de facto* possession of half the land by the peasants and the *de jure* ownership of all of it by the nobles. On the one hand, if the peasants received no land on emancipation, their disappointment might well produce a revolutionary explosion; on the other hand, if they were allotted the land they used, even with compensation to the gentry, this would involve compulsory alienation of private property on a revolutionary scale unthinkable elsewhere in Europe. The peaceful preparation of "socialism" through adoption of the latter course would be the burden of Herzen's politics during the opening six years of the next reign. For the first time the ethical and subjective inspiration of his vision had come fully into contact with the objective conditions in Russian society that made Populism a plausible and potent doctrine. Yet how late, and after what meanderings through the abstract, had he at last hit the bedrock foundation of his "communism" in the relatively mundane question of a landed vs. a landless emancipation!

By "agrarian communism" Herzen did not mean simply the primitive democracy of the Slavic peoples before the appearance of the state, the "Cossack republic" of the pre-Petrine Ukraine. The existing "communism" and "democracy" of the commune would be only a beginning, the culmination of which would be the rationalist and libertarian utopia that Herzen called socialism. "The commune saved the Russian people from Mongolian barbarism and from imperial civilization, from the gentry with its European veneer and from the German bureaucracy. Communal organization, although strongly shaken, withstood the interference of the state; it survived, fortunately, *until the development of socialism in Europe*." [51] Herzen carefully continued to distinguish his revolutionary nationalism from the conservatism of the Slavophiles.

But it was nationalism none the less; for the Russian commune represented everything that he maintained Europe was not, and was vainly striving to become. The commune by its very nature was incompatible with the Roman and Western notion of the state. "Centralization is contrary to the Slavic spirit; federalism is far more natural to its character." [52] Distrust of all authority coming from above and claiming to transcend the free association of individuals in the commune had been made second nature to the Russian because of his long and bitter experience with state power. The Russian would never deify the state as did the European. The proof of this was in the whole of Russian history; in the innumerable peasant revolts, from Bolotnikov to Pugachev, and in the Cossack republics of the past;[53] in the uncompromising hostility of the Old Believers to the state and the established church;[54] in the people's ingrained distrust of all formalized administration by bureaucracy in the German manner. "The Russian people even today does not like paper dealings between equals — close the deal with a hearty handshake and a swig of vodka, and make an end to it." [55] Since state power and a complicated administrative machinery, as such, were incompatible with freedom, Russia presented far more favorable conditions for a true revolution than did Europe.

The same contrast could be seen in the Russian's attitude to the traditional Western means for maintaining public order — the law, the courts, and the police. The European made a fetish of these institutions; the Russian had nothing but hatred for them, submitting only under the compulsion of force. The Russian's instinctive reaction to the law and the courts was not respect, but evasion and noncooperation. "The sentence of a court does not blacken a man in the eyes of the Russian people: exiles and convicts are called by them the *unfortunate*." [56] A conspiracy of an entire people existed against the official law and its agents. Conversely, the people settled through the commune such legal problems as the state left in their hands peacefully and justly, by the free cooperation of equals. Judges, like all peasant officials, were freely elected; in the submerged world of the commune there was no distinct judicial class any more than there was a distinct bureaucratic class.[57] All the commune's affairs were administered and its members judged by elected equals, as in the old days before the coming of the state. The use of force or any formal constraint by the commune on its members was unknown. Likewise deceit was nonexistent in personal dealings between peasants: "between them reigns almost unlimited confidence; they know no formal contracts or written understandings." Moreover, the peasant's mentality was deeply democratic and egalitarian, formed as it was by this state of affairs. "The Russian peasant knows no morality which does not arise instinctively and naturally from his communism; and this morality is deeply rooted in the character of the people." [58] Here indeed — or so at least it might seem with the application of a little good will — was an embryonic form of the socialist ideal of equality through fraternal cooperation.

The same was true in questions of property. The European made an idol of the right to private property. The Russian peasant knew neither the institution nor the idea. His understanding of property was profoundly "communist." [59] The noble's private right to the land had never been recognized by the peasant. Land belonged to the whole community, and each member had an equal right to its use, but never to absolute ownership of it in the Roman and Western sense. Of course, the irrefutable proof of this was the practice of periodic redivision of the land among the members of the commune. Insofar as they were left to their own devices, the peasants determined the uses of property in the same democratic manner as they administered justice or decided questions of communal government — by election on the basis of the equality of all members of the *obshchina*. With property, as with all questions relating to the public order, everything was harmony and cooperation in the commune; nowhere was there coercion or constraint.

Now the periodic redistribution of land is obviously what made possible Herzen's belief in the commune; without this he could not have made the association with Western socialism. Yet it is significant that in his finished theory the collective right to the land bulks no larger than communal self-government, administration of justice by elected officials, and the psychological characteristics of the peasants — distrust of the state, of bureaucracy, and in general of all authority. Herzen writes of all these things with even more enthusiasm and at greater length than of the periodic redistribution of land. Moreover, even in the matter of communal property, he was more impressed by the fraternal harmony with which repartition was carried out than by the principle of collective ownership itself. "[The peasant] has preserved only his insignificant, modest commune; that is, the possession in common of the land, the *equality* of all members of the commune without exception, the *fraternal* division of the fields according to the number of workers, and the autonomous direction by the commune of its affairs." [60] Or again:

The problems of marking off the boundaries of fields are necessarily very complicated in the constant redivision of land according to the number of households; nevertheless the process is carried out without complaints or lawsuits. . . . Minor disagreements are submitted for judgment to the elders or to the assembly of the commune, and their decisions are accepted unconditionally by all. The same is true in the *arteli* [producer cooperatives of peasant artisans].[61]

Furthermore, it should be borne in mind that Herzen's commune was in no sense a collective farm; never once did he mention communal living or group labor, since neither of these institutions existed in the *obshchina*. It is clear from his silence on these points that he thought that the primary economic function of the future commune would be to effect a periodic redistribution of land between households so as to guarantee their continuing equality and their individual self-sufficiency. After the redistribution, however, each household would presumably live as a separate economic unit, and the commune would be largely an association of independent peasant producers. Thus, despite all his talk about the "communism" of the *obshchina*, Herzen's Russian socialism was in fact much nearer to Proudhon's "mutualist" utopia of individualistic smallholders, each enjoying the "possession" of his plot, than to such collectivistic ideals as Fourier's phalanx, which supplied Herzen with little more than the symbol and the slogan of "community."

Yet for Herzen what was most essential in the commune was not even this "mutualist" ownership of land but rather the absence of constraint and authority imposed from above. Although he was first drawn to the commune by the parallel it presented with the collectivist schemes of Western socialism, in the end he idealized it much more for his own anarchist principle of the voluntary association of equals, which he felt it embodied in all aspects of life: in administration, in justice, and in the antiauthoritarian mentality of the peasants. Herzen's ideal *obshchina*, for all its "communism," was primarily a means for fostering the development of "individuality."

This is further borne out by the reservations he entertained concerning the commune, reservations very similar to those we have already seen him express in his discussion with the Slavophiles in the early forties. Even now he feared somewhat that communal organization, by its nature, might be a fetter on the free development of the individual, who risked being "swallowed up" by the group. The commune as it stood was far from adequate; it would become truly socialist only when some way were found to combine it with individual freedom in the Western sense. "To keep the commune and give freedom to the individual, to spread that self-government now existing in the villages and the districts to the cities and to the whole country, while at the same time preserving national unity — in this consists the question of the future of Russia." [62]

For Herzen, history revealed that the peasant commune by itself does not lead to socialism. All peoples knew the commune in their "youth." Western Europe had once possessed it, but had lost it in the development that led through "feudalism" and Roman notions of private property to a one-sided and "antisocial individualism." [63] The Asiatic peoples, too, had once possessed the commune, but it had led to nothing because they had been unwilling to renounce a narrow self-sufficiency and enter into the main stream of history as represented by Europe.[64] Russia, unlike Europe, was "young" in that she still possessed the commune; moreover, unlike Asia, she had a remarkable capacity for renouncing her own narrow past, as the "antinational" revolution of Peter and the Westernization of the educated classes demonstrated. Russia, then, found herself in an extraordinarily favored historical position. "Fortunately, we arrive with our commune in an age when anticommunal [liberal] civilization has run up against the absolute impossibility of resolving, on the basis of its principles, the contradiction between individual right and social right." [65]

In less Hegelian language, socialism would result from the fusion of the democratic equality of the Russian commune with the Western principle of the dignity of the individual. Young Russia, awakened at last to a truly historical existence by the "West, which alone could still illumine the abyss of Russian life," carrying on where the European creative effort left off, would lead mankind on to a "future henceforth common to the Orient and Occident." [66] Far from turning its back on Europe and withdrawing into its Moscovite past, as reactionaries such as the Slavophiles desired, Russia should seek salvation by assimilating the heritage of the West — scientific enlightenment and the idea of the individual — and in developing the peasant commune to accommodate these principles.

To do this it was not necessary for Russia to retrace Europe's evolution. Russia could simply appropriate for her own uses the historical conquests of the West. "Russia has gone through her revolutionary embryogeny in the European class. . . . The Russian people does not need to begin from the beginning this heavy labor." [67] Indeed, to retrace the bourgeois development of the West would be fatal to the one advantage which Russia's "youth" conferred on her — the commune — and was therefore something to be avoided at all costs. In particular, the bourgeois notion of private property would destroy the "communism" of the *obshchina,* and turn the peasantry into the same defenseless rural proletariat that existed in the West. Since the historical form of the future was socialism, repetition of the Western development would be historical suicide for Russia:

The Russian people has suffered everything, but has retained the commune; the commune will save the Russian people; to destroy it would be to hand the people over, tied hand and foot, to the *pomeshchik* and the police. And to touch the commune at a time when Europe is bemoaning the parceling out of her countryside and is striving with all her strength toward some sort of communal social order! [68]

For Herzen the Russians were by nature an agricultural people, and he never envisioned the possibility of an urban, industrial development among them. When he proclaimed that it would be unnecessary for Russia to retrace the European development, he was not thinking of bourgeois industry but of bourgeois legal forms — private property and Roman law. "Imagine the European agricultural situation with Petersburg autocracy, with our bureaucrats, with our rural police. Imagine twenty million proletarians seeking work on the gentry's lands, in a country where there is no legality, where all government is venal and aristocratic, where the individual is nothing and influence is all." [69] When Herzen said that Russia need not repeat the historical development of Europe, he meant, as usual, not only something "historiosophical," but also something concrete — in this case, no individual emancipation without land. Landless emancipation would mean forfeiting Russia's historical chances for a socialist future; still worse, it would be inhuman in the present. Never before had Herzen envisaged in such practical terms the problem of "humanizing" Russia.

3

How, in Herzen's view, was the principle of individuality to be united with that of the commune? Through the intermediary of those members of the Westernized minority who, like the Decembrists and the radicals of his own generation, were in revolt against the existing order. Like the peasantry, this group was "young" and "free of the past" in that its only inheritance was slavery and degradation. Unlike the European intellectual, the educated Russian could afford to be ruthlessly revolutionary; already a gagged slave, what could he lose, since he had nothing, not even the "half-freedoms" of the West?

Thrown into an oppressive world, armed with a clear view and an incorruptible logic, the Russian quickly frees himself from the faith and ways of his fathers.

The thinking Russian is the most independent man in the world. What can stop him? Respect for the past? But what is the starting point of modern Russian history if not a negation of nationality and tradition [Peter]?

Or, perhaps, the tradition of the Petersburg period? This tradition, this "fifth act of a bloody drama transpiring in a brothel," binds us to nothing; on the contrary, it unbinds us definitively.

On the other hand, the past of the Western people serves as a lesson for us and nothing more. In no way do we consider ourselves the executors of their historical testament.[70]

The Russian could be absolutely logical in his criticism of inherited ideas and institutions, since the Russia of Nicholas I was so obviously absurd and inhuman that no civilized person could feel any attachment to it, or want to preserve any part of it. Nor was the Europeanized Russian moderated in his revolt by his European education. It did not mean the same thing to him, an outsider, as it did to a European. On the European his civilization conferred tangible, if imperfect, benefits; it meant parliaments, free speech, partial enlightenment, and a decent life, at least for some. On the Russian, contact with European civilization conferred no benefits; it simply furnished a corrosive comparison that inflamed his hatred and fanned his revolt, leading him to demand revolution where the European was content with reform. A European education, far from inspiring in the Russian any sentimental loyalty to a past which was not his, made him equally discontent with the barbarism of Russia and the pusillanimity of Europe. In short, it made him the ideal revolutionary, unafraid to follow ideas through to their logical conclusion. "We share your [Europe's] doubts, but your faith does not warm us. We share your hate, but we do not understand your attachment to what your ancestors have bequeathed to you; we are too oppressed, too unhappy to be content with half-freedom. You are bound by scruples, you are held back by arrière-pensées. We have no arrière-pensées, no scruples. We lack only strength." [71] There could be no clearer statement, nor a better explanation, of the traditional maximalism of the Russian radical than this.

The existence of this revolutionary "middle gentry" in Russia was as much the source of Herzen's hope for the future as was the commune. To be sure, he constantly said the commune was the more important of the two, and he always deferentially ceded the place of revolutionary honor to the peasant. "We Russians who have passed through Western civilization, we are no more than a means, a leaven, no more than intermediaries between the Russian people and revolutionary Europe. The man of the future in Russia is the *peasant,* just as in France he is the *worker*." [72] Still, the revolutionary gentry was as essential as the peasants. Without it the commune could never become socialist. Indeed, Herzen speaks quite as much of the intellectuals as he does of the peasants. The bulk of *Du développement des idées révolutionnaires en Russie* is devoted to tracing the awakening of the radical gentry from Radishchev to the Petrashevski circle. Half of the *Letter to Michelet* is concerned with the same. The peasantry alone, without the "leaven" of the radical gentry, could never advance beyond a primitive stage of development, just as the "communism" of the *obshchina*, without the full development of the individual, would never produce socialism. Europe and Russia, collectivism and individualism, peasantry and radical gentry were equally necessary for the creation of the "new world."

This, then, was the context of revolutionary hopes in which Herzen situated his belief in the peasant commune. These hopes were not tied exclusively, or even primarily, to the collectivist property arrangements prevailing in the *obshchina*. They arose much more from the structure of Russian society as a whole. For Herzen the socialist revolution had to be maximalist, or it would not be a real revolution at all. And Russian society presented a unique set of conditions for the realization of such a revolution. No appreciable group in Russia was tied either by interest or by sentiment to existing institutions or values; an alien state, standing for nothing more positive than blind preservation of the status quo, was holding in subjection, by brute force alone, both peasant mass and educated minority, whose every instinct demanded a revolutionary reversal of the status quo.

Too many chains lay upon us for us voluntarily to lay on more. In this respect we are on a footing of complete equality with our peasants. We submit to brute force. We are slaves because we do not have the possibility of freeing ourselves, but we accept nothing from our enemies.

Russia will never be Protestant [moderate].

Russia will never be *juste-milieu*.

Russia will never make a revolution with the aim of getting rid of Tsar Nicholas and of replacing him with tsar-representatives, tsar-judges, tsar-policemen.[73]

In essence Herzen's Russian socialism comes down to one proposition, which is neither economic nor "collectivistic" in nature: that the Russians could never be moderate in their rejection of authority imposed from above. His view of the commune fits in quite logically with this. For the commune symbolized in three essential respects the negation of all authority external to the individual: negation of the "Roman" idea of a sovereign power (that is, simply the state) which transcends the sum of the individuals who compose it; negation of the "Roman" principle of law as something existing over and above the freely expressed will of the members of the community; negation of the sacred right of private property as something transcending the humane purposes for which material wealth ought to exist. The commune was socialist because it was the living negation of all authority not based on the voluntary association of autonomous individuals; Russia as a whole was revolutionary because the enlightened elite could give voice to what the peasants expressed instinctively through their way of life — in other words, because both masses and elite were natural anarchists.

As usual, Herzen had overstated his case, particularly with respect to the supposedly seething discontent of the "middle gentry." He, of course, knew this very well; indeed a half of his purpose in writing was to convince his Moscow friends of their own unsuspected revolutionary potentialities. Yet with the aid of time and distance, and in his eagerness to persuade Europe, the gentry world from which he came understandably took on redder and redder hues. Who in Europe knew enough to contradict him? Or who in Russia had the liberty to put the whole picture into print? So he was free to project into his class as a whole the reckless discontent of a minority: himself, the dead Belinski, the imprisoned Bakunin, and the silent Ogarev, not all of whom were from the gentry. Nonetheless, in spite of these exaggerations, what he said was basically true: Russian society contained the greatest explosive potential of any society in Europe, and he was the authentic spokesman of this titanic discontent. His picture would be completely in focus if for "middle gentry" one substituted "radical intelligentsia" in general, originating in any class whatsoever. And this substitution was taking place in real life as he wrote, in the persons of those still obscure Chernyshevskis and Dobroliubovs, formed by his own and Belinski's writings during the last seemingly dead years of Nicholas, who would emerge on the scene in the late fifties and sixties. By the seventies, it was men of similar stamp, seeking in every way to make contact with the desperate discontent of the peasantry, a type that de Maistre at the beginning of the century had baptized by anticipation *un Pougatchev d'université,* who at last would incarnate the total revolutionary of a purely Russian nature that Herzen thought he wanted. Indeed, it is fair to state that he would have been more than a little appalled had he really known the exceptional qualities of the revolutionary article he was trying so eloquently to sell both East and West.

4

The question again arises: how seriously should one take Herzen's pronouncements about the socialist "future of Russia"? On the whole they should be read more literally than his jeremiads over Europe, but still not completely so. His theory admitted of several significant reservations. First of all, the socialist flowering of the commune was by no means a foregone conclusion. Herzen maintained categorically: "I do not believe that this is *necessary,* but that it is *possible.* Nothing is ineluctably necessary." [74] This caution was a product of the collapse, after 1848, of his belief in Hegel's March of History. The future would depend on the energy of the enlightened elements of Russian society, in preventing, for example, emancipation without land. It would also depend on what happened in Europe.

It does not follow that we should believe blindly in the future. Every seed has a right to development, but not every one develops. The future of Russia depends not on her alone. It is linked with the future of Europe. Who can predict the fate of the Slavic world if reaction and absolutism should definitively conquer the revolution in Europe? [75]

Herzen's optimism regarding the commune depended also on circumstances at the moment of writing. For example, the *Letter to Michelet* had been provoked by the addressee's deprecatory comments about Russia in an article on the Polish revolutionary hero, Kosciuszko. Herzen began his reply with a categorical assertion of faith in the commune. In the course of composition, however, the second installment of Michelet's article appeared, in which he spoke more sympathetically of Russian sufferings. Immediately Herzen's tone became less confident. "For us the hour of action has not yet struck; in justice France may still be proud of her forward position. Until 1852 [the theoretical date for the election of Louis Napoleon's successor] to her belongs an onerous right. Europe without doubt will reach the grave or a new life before us. The hour of action for us perhaps is still far off." [76] Herzen never maintained, in the old manner, that his theory was "scientific." In the last analysis the "socialist" future of the commune was presented only as an impressive plausibility; it was an expression of desire more than of certitude.

Nor was Herzen definitely claiming Russian superiority over the West, or subscribing unequivocally to a nationalistic messianism, as any real Slavophile must. In spite of certain hints in these directions, what his glorification of the commune really proclaimed was Russia's equality with the West; but in order to make this point he often overstated it: In less polemical moods, however, he knew how to moderate his claims. "Europe . . . has not resolved the antinomy between the individual and the state, but she has set herself the task of resolving it. Russia too has not found the solution. Before this question begins *our equality.*" [77]

Or again, in still more revealing terms:

It is painful and ugly to live in Russia, this is true; and it was all the more painful for us in that we thought that in other countries it was easy and agreeable to live.

Now we know that even there it is painful, because there too that question upon which the whole energy of mankind now centers has not been solved — the question of the relations of the individual to society and of society to the individual. Two extreme, one-sided developments have led to two absurdities: to the Englishman, proud of his rights and independent, whose independence is founded on a form of polite cannibalism [Blanqui's definition of capitalism], and to the poor Russian peasant, impersonally swallowed up in the village commune, delivered into serfdom without rights and, in virtue of this, become the "victuals" of the landowner.

How are these two developments to be reconciled, how is the contradiction between them to be resolved? How is the independence of the Englishman to be kept without the cannibalism, how is the individuality of the [Russian] peasant to be developed without the loss of the communal principle? Precisely in this lies the whole agonizing problem of our century, precisely in this consists the whole of socialism. [78]

Here Herzen is saying, "we *too* have something to offer," much more than, "we *alone* have anything to offer"; and this was the final import, at least for the European public, of his propaganda for the commune.

He wished to reply to European arrogance about Russia by demonstrating that the latter was potentially as socialist as the West, if not even more so, and hence deserving of respect from the European Left as a fellow sufferer instead of contempt as the enemy of all progressive mankind. [79] Indeed, to some extent Herzen was attempting to mobilize European liberal opinion — which for polemical purposes he pretended to despise but for which, particularly in England, he really had a certain esteem — against autocracy and serfdom in order to bring pressure on the Russian government to reform. In England he was particularly impressed by (and a little jealous of) the extent of sympathy for the American slaves, and he saw the possibilities of exploiting this for the benefit of the Russian serf. [80] In short, he wished to do for Russia what Mazzini had done (also in England) for his people: to advertise his nation's cause, both by the example of his own emigration and by propaganda, and to educate the European public about the difference between the Russian government and the Russian people. This desire, certainly, was another reason for the especial kinship he felt for Mazzini and the Italians.

Yet Herzen wished to do this with dignity, without appearing to solicit compassion. Therefore, as in the passage last quoted, he declared England and Russia to be equal despite all appearances. Both were backward and both progressive, but in different ways, and fundamentally there was little choice between the two. The Russian need not feel any inferiority toward the West, just as the latter's airs of superiority were uncalled for. Russians at least realized their inadequacies; they were willing to learn from the West. Europeans might well imitate this humility and recognize that they had something to learn from Russia, in particular that the commune might prove to be the salvation of both in the crisis in which they found themselves *together*. It is the contradiction between Herzen's desire to win Europe over and yet not to beg that explains much of his chauvinistic hyperbole. But underneath, as Botkin had perceptively observed, "the heart of the ferocious matador was tender";[81] Herzen had in him much of the Mazzinian ideal of Young Europe, with the universal brotherhood of free peoples as his goal — a fact which is made evident particularly by the extreme solicitude he always displayed for the Poles. But if only Europe would recognize that there *was* a Young Russia, and that the Russian was a legitimate brother! Since Europe on the whole was recalcitrant, this internationalist note was sounded less frequently than were Herzen's more strident patriotic measures.

5

More interesting than the intentions of Herzen's propaganda with respect to Europe were his intentions with respect to Russia. Herzen always said he was a revolutionary, and so far we have taken his word for it. In Europe, in 1848, he had clearly called for a volcanic revolt of the masses, but, as has already been pointed out, there he had not been involved directly and his blood-thirstiness had been largely a polemical exercise. As regards his theory of "Russian socialism" the question of revolutionary methods is oddly the one point on which he was imprecise. To be sure he brandished the banner of the *pugachevshchina* on occasion, but he did not insist on it; nor did he ever call explicitly for a mass uprising. Instead he placed his principal hope for "regeneration" in the enlightened minority, who, by means he left vague, were supposed to render the commune socialist.

Before 1855 he broke this silence on the question of means only once, in a short article for the Free Russian Press that does not bulk very large beside the more apocalyptic pieces outlining his vision of Russian socialism. The article, published in 1853, was entitled *St. George's Day*. It took its title from a practice which had existed in the sixteenth century, before the definitive establishment of serfdom, when, on one day of the year, the peasants had the right to change masters freely; this day, St. George's Day, had remained in the popular consciousness as a symbol of freedom. The article was addressed "To the Russian Gentry." It was an appeal to that class, as the one free group in the country — who had produced the Decembrists, the creators of Russian "humanism," Pushkin and Lermontov, and the radicals of Herzen's own generation — to liberate the serfs voluntarily while there still was time, before the latter took up the "axe" and destroyed all civilization in Russia. This, however, was an appeal to the tradition of the Decembrists rather than of Pugachev, to the tradition of the humanitarian *coup d'état* by the gentry rather than that of the peasant *jacquerie*. Yet was even a *coup d'état* necessary? Might not the gentry liberate the serfs peacefully, in agreement with the government? Or might not even the autocrat, in his unlimited power, simply decree emancipation? Herzen envisaged this last possibility, too, though he much preferred to have the task accomplished in one way or another by his own "radical" gentry.[82]

All this is a far cry from the red dreams in which Herzen habitually dwelt. His ends are radical enough: a completely democratic and liberal Russia in which all wealth (by which he meant primarily land) would be collectively owned. But his means can only be called moderate: cooperation with the representatives of the status quo, the gentry, and even possibly the autocracy; persuasion and not violence; and inevitably, although he did not explicitly say so, gradual change rather than a sudden overturn. It may seem strange at this late date to discover seeds of moderation in Herzen's political philosophy. Nevertheless, behind his flaming invocations of total revolution this was his practical program. In order to save civilization, enlightenment, and humanism in Russia, of which the gentry were the bearers, Herzen hoped for the introduction of socialism from above. The *pugachevshchina* was a last desperate resort, which he was willing to embrace only if the enlightened elite failed to act. Thus his practical program was not completely different from Granovski's, who also wanted peaceful reform from above. The principal difference, and it is an important one, was that if Granovski had to choose between the *pugachevshchina* and waiting out the autocracy and the gentry, he would take the latter course.

Herzen's theory of Russian socialism, then, if not actually moderate, was amorphous and ambiguous; it was less a political program than a vision designed to serve as an exhortation and a goad in order to stir enlightened society into some sort of action on behalf of the peasants. In reality Herzen's confused rhetoric concealed two distinct positions, which may be called, in later socialist fashion, a program maximum and a program minimum. The program maximum was his full-blown vision of the anarchist federation of communes, and this was his ultimate hope for Russia. The program minimum, hinted at before 1855 only in *St. George's Day*, was the more mundane goal of emancipation of the peasants with land but with little or no compensation to their masters — a program under which socialism would come only in the fullness of time.

The underlying ambiguity of Herzen's position became even more apparent under Alexander II, when for the first time since the beginning of the century practical politics existed in Russia and it became possible for the opposition to achieve something in the real world. Under these circumstances Herzen began thinking less about general ends and more about particular ways and means; for several years he put aside his program maximum of social revolution to concentrate on his program minimum of a decent emancipation. For a while he even thought, as he had done once before during a brief moment in Viatka,[83] that the autocracy might return to its former role as the bearer of enlightenment to Russia, and he expressed to the new emperor his willingness to cooperate in a famous article, *You Have Conquered, Oh Galilean!* [84] He was, of course, soon disabused, for Alexander had no intention of granting anything remotely approaching the "socialist" emancipation that Herzen sought. When this expedient failed, Herzen then took a cue from the constitutional opposition and agitated for a *Zemski sobor* which would give the supposedly radical "middle gentry" a chance to mold the new Russia. It was only when this, too, had failed, and when the emancipation turned out to be unsatisfactory in his eyes, that, in 1861–62, he returned to his old demand for total revolution, and his Free Press issued a call to radical youth to "go to the people" with the great word of socialism. Nevertheless, for seven years he had flirted with the idea of gradualism; underlying his extremism, there was always a certain readiness to abandon theoretical maximalism, if a really suitable occasion presented itself to achieve a significant social transformation by cooperation with the Establishment.

Nor was he alone in this desire. All the radicals of his generation at one time or another expressed it. Belinski in his last days adopted the utopian idea that Nicholas was about to become a radical Peter the Great who would force emancipation of the peasantry, enlightenment, and progress down the throats of the reactionary landowners.[85] (Belinski, unlike Herzen, did not come from the gentry and hence never shared his friend's high opinion of that class.) Bakunin in prison in 1851 wrote his famous *Confession* to Nicholas, in part to excuse his conduct during his years in Europe, but in part also to enlighten the emperor in the hope of bringing him around to the side of progress — all in a manner reminiscent of the famous interview of Schiller's Carlos with Philip II.[86] In exile in Siberia it seems that Bakunin dreamed similar dreams of enlightened despotism with his cousin, Muraviev-Amurski, Nicholas' Governor-General for the Far Eastern Provinces.[87] The same idea was expressed later as one of three possibilities, together with the gentry *coup* and the peasant revolt, in a pamphlet, *Romanov, Pugachev or Pestel?* [88]

This catholicity in the choice of means for regenerating Russia was one of the principal traits distinguishing the radicals of Herzen's generation from their successors, the men of the sixties and seventies. Neither Chernyshevski and his student followers nor the members of *Land and Freedom* would have anything to do with the autocracy, the gentry, or the status quo in any form. They believed only in unilateral action by an enlightened minority, which they resolutely distinguished from the gentry, or, later, in peasant revolt and terrorism. Herzen represented only the first degree of radical desperation in Russia. As with most of his generation, the embryonic desire for peaceful cooperation with the existing order was present in him even at his reddest. The Soviets, therefore, are quite right to speak of his "liberal waverings," and to feel that he is not so pure a diamond of "revolutionary democracy" as the *raznochintsy,* or commoners, who came to dominate the scene after 1855.

And these "waverings" were only natural, for Herzen and his contemporaries represented no more than the first generation of socialist thought in Russia. Because they were pathfinders their energies were of necessity absorbed by the elaboration of general principles rather than the refinement of strategy. At the same time they lacked the cumulative experience of struggle with the regime which produced in later generations that acute sensitivity to revolutionary means which precluded any form of cooperation with existing society as half-heartedness or betrayal. Herzen's Populism belongs roughly to the same stage of development of socialist thought as that represented by Saint-Simon and Fourier in the West — the phase of eschatological prophecy rather than of political program-making — for as of 1855 Russian conditions, like those of Europe before 1830, hardly permitted the development of anything more precise.

Yet the amorphous quality of Herzen's socialism is due to more than his priority in time in the development of Populism. It is due equally to the fact that he was a democrat by choice, out of a lordly generosity, rather than by necessity, because of the lack of other means than revolt to secure his vital interests. Revolution was his *point d'honneur,* not his social destiny. As later radicals never tired of pointing out, such freedom of choice tends strongly to foster a certain lack of democratic logic and even dilettantism, characteristics which are certainly manifest in Herzen's "middle gentry" Populism and his weakness for red rhetoric that went beyond his real intentions. But this raises the question of the general nature of his position, and thus brings us to the problem with which this book began and which will also be its conclusion — his character as a "gentry revolutionary."

CHAPTER XVII

The Gentry Revolutionary

As of 1855 and the death of Nicholas I the modern Russian political tradition was scarcely fifty years old, yet in that relatively short space of time it had undergone a remarkably swift process of radicalization. Matters had begun mildly enough at the start of the century with Alexander I and his advisors, who first seriously proposed eliminating the twin scandals of autocracy and serfdom, but who considered attacking them with no more than the means of enlightened despotism — peaceful and gradual reform from above leading to a *Rechtstaat*. In the 1820's with the Decembrists the idea of reform became the idea of revolt, and the goals envisaged became correspondingly more daring — either a constitutional monarchy or a Jacobin republic. In the thirty years of repression under Nicholas the idea of revolt became the ideal of revolution, and the goal was no longer a change in the political regime or the legal status of the citizenry but a total social and moral renovation of the nation. Indeed, this "socialist" goal had assumed the form of the most extreme and uncompromising theory of revolutionary liberation — anarchism. Throughout this whole process of radicalization, however, there is one remarkable element of continuity: with each shift leftward the impetus came predominantly from men of the same social group — the gentry.

As of 1855 Herzen certainly stood at the extreme Left of this movement. He was distinctly more politically minded and more of a Populist than Belinski; he was more dynamic and dedicated than such lesser figures as Sazonov, or even Ogarev; and he was more radical than the relatively plebeian friends of Petrashevski, who, although socialists, were not advocates of revolution. The only one of his contemporaries who matched his radicalism was Bakunin, and in order to elucidate fully the character of Herzen's anarchism it is necessary to make the inevitable comparison with this other giant among "gentlemen revolutionaries."

In discussing Herzen's reaction to 1848 the opinion has already been expressed that anarchism is an irresponsible doctrine since it places itself outside the political possibilities offered by the real world. It may be added that anarchism is less a serious political program than an abstract fantasy of negation; it is quintessential intransigence, pure protest. It is the politics of someone whose politics is above all compounded of his refusals; or who is unable, because of the situation of practical impotence in which he finds himself, to formulate his positive goals except as fantasy. All this, moreover, is almost the inevitable consequence of intransigent opposition to a rigid old regime such as that maintained by Nicholas. By 1848 the progressive humanization of the gentry had produced the radicalization of political thought already noted, but this development had not been accompanied by the slightest reform of the regime, which on the contrary had grown more rigid still. During the fifty years of its existence Russian political thought had failed to make any impact on the real world; it was like a machine turning ever more furiously in a void. It is precisely this widening gap between thought and life that explains the rapidity of the evolution of opposition opinion toward that total rejection of existing society and that disembodied ideal of freedom which constitute anarchism. And certainly all these traits are characteristics of Herzen's position no less than of Bakunin's.

Nevertheless, there are important nuances which separate the two, and these may be categorized briefly as positive anarchism in the case of Herzen and negative anarchism in the case of Bakunin. With Bakunin the chief, indeed almost the sole, emphasis was on disorganization, destruction, and negation; the dominant theme of his thought was the anticipated exultation of a new, universal *pugachevshchina*. The order that would emerge from this holocaust, however, he hardly mentioned, and the ideals of man and freedom in the name of which this total negation was invoked he left vague and abstract, a question of philosophical principle rather than of concrete human needs. Herzen, on the other hand, only rarely — such as in 1848 — chose to revel in the drama of destruction. To be sure, he called unequivocally for a clean sweep of the past, but he spelled out the anarchist poetry of negation much more readily with respect to ideas than to social institutions. Nor does one have the feeling with Herzen, as one does with Bakunin, that destruction was an end in itself. Instead, Herzen emphasized the positive, if vague, values the socialist cataclysm was expected to promote — human dignity, reason, freedom and "the full flowering of personality." In particular, when discussing the peasants, Herzen never gave descriptions of mass upheavals but instead portrayed the peaceful virtues and the humane fraternity of the future commune. Finally, Bakunin, when discussing the role of the intelligentsia, dwelt on techniques of conspiracy and insurrection, whereas Herzen reserved his most fulsome rhetoric for the tradition of Russian "humanism" and "enlightenment."

Nor are these ideological differences without practical consequences. To be sure, in a literal sense Herzen's commune was as idealized, and indeed as unreal, as were Bakunin's peasant brigands à la Stenka Razin. Nonetheless Herzen was at least constructing a mythology of human and social fulfillment rather than of destruction. His emphasis on the positive, moreover, meant that, for all his hyperbole, he was basically attempting to accomplish something in the real world: to promote humanitarian sentiment in Russia, to advance education, to hasten the abolition of serfdom and to establish civil liberties. Herzen's abstractions always bore some relation, no matter how remote and inverted, to the real problems of Russia. In particular, his vision of an anarchist federation of communes, for all its utopianism, represented a real effort to imagine how maximum local self-government, individual initiative, and a guaranteed minimum of material well-being for all might be achieved quickly in Russian agrarian society. In a sense Herzen's Russian socialism was the idea of the Swiss federation of self-governing cantons extended to the scale of the Russian empire, a fantastic scheme no doubt as matters stood under Nicholas, yet still not an intrinsically impossible arrangement. Bakunin's anarchism, on the other hand, appears as an intrinsically fantastic game of philosophical negation, conspiracy, and insurrection, conducted for the adolescent delight of seeing how thoroughly one could transpose a ruthless logic into life; and his idea of freedom appears more as an abstract antithesis to the principle of authority than as a serious plea for human dignity. Likewise, it is difficult to see what, if anything, Bakunin was trying to accomplish in the real world, other than to blow the whole place up for the sheer fun the bang of the explosion would produce.[1]

Thus, Bakunin's anarchism could easily lead to the exploitation of popular discontent for any demagogic end whatsoever; Herzen's anarchism could serve more readily as a gadfly to the humanitarian conscience of society. At his most irresponsible Bakunin wound up in alliance with Nechaev; Herzen was able, for a time at least, to play a positive role in inflecting the Great Reforms in a more liberal direction. Because of the sincerity of his devotion to individual freedom Herzen was later regarded not only as the author of Russian socialism but also as one of the first great Russian liberals; Bakunin, on the other hand, because of his emphasis on the techniques of insurrection has been primarily associated with a tradition of revolutionary opportunism where anything goes so long as it helps unleash chaos. Herzen, in short, was later claimed by the full range of opposition opinion to be the prophet of what was most humane and civilized in Russian politics; almost no one, however, has been eager to own to any moral debt to Bakunin.

These differences are all the more worth pointing out since the utopian form in which Herzen's ideals, no less than Bakunin's, were expressed is alien and even disturbing to the empirical, pragmatic Anglo-Saxon mind. It is only too easy for the insular or transatlantic critic of continental ideologies to demonstrate that in a literal sense such utopian extravagances are unreal or untrue; and the present book in particular has not neglected this enterprise of "de-mythologizing" and of ideological deflation. Nonetheless, the world is moved as much by visions as by reasoned reflection on reality. To be sure, grandiose schemes such as Herzen's never are, or can be, applied literally. Yet, just as surely, utopias are "over-ideologized," or inflated, statements of possible solutions to real problems, statements that are inflated in response to the pressure of staggering obstacles to action; and the more refractory these problems are to reasonable resolution, the more exaggerated the utopia becomes. In short, utopias arise in situations where, in order to make a point at all, it is necessary to overstate it. Indeed only in this way can the psychic energy be generated that permits the beginning of action under oppressive conditions; for utopias are effective not as pondered social blueprints, but as dramatizations of nascent ideals and catalysts of new values.

Of course (as the "reasonable" critic never fails to point out), visionary exaggeration can be highly dangerous to the very values it purports to foster, as the dubious figure of Bakunin by Herzen's side illustrates. And, in fact, Bakunin represents a caricature, the *reductio ad absurdum,* of the democratic dream. What is more, he incarnates the ever-present menace of maximalist revolutionary means to those humanitarian ends that revolution is supposed to promote — a menace that is born precisely of the original maximalist definition of these ends. This paradox thus is inherent in the Populist apocalypse as such, and hence, to a degree, in Herzen himself: Cain, as much as Abel, was the true son of the one Adam; and Ishmael, no less than Isaac, was a blood-son of the man of the Promise. Still, disturbing as this fact is, we must also recognize that in many of the world's less fortunate nations an apocalyptic goal is necessary if a sluggish society is to be moved at all; and that great risk attends every bold enterprise. In any case, the historical problem utopianism poses for us is not to demonstrate that its visions are "misguided," but to explain how and why men are driven to embrace them.

The urge to utopia, surely, was the lot of any democratic idealist under Nicholas, for the possibility of a humane life for all was so remote and the obstacles to its attainment were so great that one could express the problem only as myth. Nevertheless, despite Herzen's mythopoeism and the alarming comrade at his shoulder, and no matter how banal his ideal of universal human dignity now seems (at least as an ideal), we should not forget that his goal was a startling novelty in a society still based on autocracy and serfdom, nor that he carried on his crusade in the face of obstacles that were, in truth, immense.

Certainly one reason for the difference between the two founders of Populism is that Herzen always remained closer to the real problems of Russia whereas Bakunin, roving over all Europe and equally at home everywhere, moved toward an ever more universal and abstract idea of revolution. Herzen's nearness to national concerns, further, meant a closeness to his roots in gentry culture which his cosmopolitan ally gradually lost. Of course, Bakunin was initially no less a gentry product than Herzen; indeed, the very extravagance of his politics evokes the caprice of a *grand seigneur* who can allow himself anything, no matter how outlandish. Yet this extravagance expresses gentry culture only superficially. Herzen reflects the same background in far richer fashion; in motivation and values he is nearer the "ideal type" of the gentry rebel that appears with the Decembrists and fades with his own generation.

2

We have already seen the simplest and most explicit expression in Herzen's socialism of his gentry roots: his preference for a "middle gentry" revolution and his reverence for gentry "humanism." For all his democratic sentiments he could believe without any feeling of contradiction that, although the coming revolution must be made for the people, it need not necessarily be made by them. It is for this reason that the Soviets classify him as a "gentry revolutionary," who looked backward to the tradition of the Decembrists as much as forward to that of the full-fledged Populists of the seventies. And in fact he did not push the Populist position to its ultimate conclusion, which is to believe that a truly democratic revolution can be made only by the people. Nor did he adopt the corollary dogma that all progressiveness and authentic humanity reside in the masses and in them alone. For Herzen the people shared these qualities with the enlightened elite — which in his eyes invariably meant the gentry — in a single national communion of revolutionary virtue.

As this view indicates, another gentry trait he shared with the Decembrists and which set him apart from the men of the sixties and seventies (but which the Soviets mention less often) was his overt nationalism. Although wholly alienated from the Imperial government, its bureaucracy, and the average boorish, conservative landowner, Herzen had been very well treated by the more refined and independent-minded segments of the Moscow aristocracy. Hence he always felt very close to an idealized "middle gentry" world of intellectual Moscow, of memories of 1812, of Pushkin and the Decembrists, and of the palmy aristocratic days before Nicholas. It was the patriotism fostered by this background which made him consider socialism primarily as a problem of national rather than of class destiny, of Russia vs. the West rather than of the peasantry vs. the gentry. Indeed, it is no exaggeration to state that he advanced his theory of socialism as much to vindicate Russian national honor before Europe and to assuage the patriotic pride of his class as to dramatize the cause of democracy.

But the gentry character of Herzen's socialism also expressed itself in more profound and pervasive ways, namely, in the human values it sought to promote and in the type of ideology by which these were articulated. By now it should be amply clear that Herzen's socialism was — to adapt a later slogan — collectivistic in form but individualistic in content. It should also be clear that the latter trait was distinctly the more important of the two. This priority of values, moreover, may fairly be considered as the expression of a gentry mentality, a situation that can be explained by recalling the process through which Herzen arrived at socialism.

It has been the major thesis of this book that the democratic ideal arose in Russia, not by direct reflection on the plight of the masses, but through the introspection of relatively privileged individuals who, out of frustration, generalized from a sense of their own dignity to the ideal of the dignity of all men. This is not to claim that such individuals must inevitably come from the top, or near the top, of society; or that the masses are intrinsically incapable of developing a sense of individual dignity and independence. Rather it is meant that in a relatively closed society the most fertile breeding-ground for great democratic theories is in an intermediate area between the serene privilege of the Establishment and the mute servitude of the masses, an area where some measure of dignity and education make possible the self-confidence, the acute sense of moral scandal at social injustice, and the ideological talent to formulate generalized demands. As modern societies grow more diversified and complex, the intermediate area from which such individuals come grows broader and increasingly more democratic. But in Nicholas I's empire this area was largely coterminous with the gentry, which was why — and not because of any innate merit — the democratic ideal in Russia was born among that class.

Broadly speaking, the evolution of Herzen and his generation was in two stages. The first was the affirmation of the individual's autonomy and dignity against the forces, both of family and state, that oppressed the ego's free creativity. In the barren world of Nicholas, however, this affirmation could only take the abstract form of exalting art, love, and above all rational "self-consciousness," which, since this permitted the isolated individual to dominate a hostile world through his sensibility and his intelligence, also conferred on him freedom and "personality."

Thus an aristocratic sense of individual dignity, thwarted in the real world, was absolutized as the repository of universal reason. This was the role of idealism, of the combined impact of Schiller, Schelling, and Hegel, in the evolution of Herzen and his generation.

Still, for the more impatient spirits this purely ideal self-realization failed to remove the original sentiment of frustration; a second stage, therefore, ensued, this time under the aegis of the Left Hegelians and the French socialists. Idealism's introspective and lonely ideal of man was generalized to the external world; the cult of "individuality" was socialized as the quest for "community." And idealism's absolute concept of personality, when translated into politics, could only result in the idea of the right of all men to the full life, or democracy, and eventually in the most impeccably logical concept of democratic equality, socialism. Indeed, so intransigent is idealism's concept of individuality that its application to society could readily give rise to what, intellectually speaking, is the most pure and uncompromising ideal of liberty — anarchism. Thus the imperfect moral perquisites of the gentry in the present were made perfect by being universalized and promised to all the people in the future: it was in this manner that an aristocratic ideal of honor became the psychological source of revolutionary Populism. Such, in brief, was the overall movement of Herzen's thought and the deeper meaning of the necessary link between reason and revolution, between "science" and socialism, to which he always subscribed.

In this pattern of evolution, moreover, the experience of Herzen and his generation repeated in general outline that of the development from Enlightenment to Revolution in eighteenth-century France and from idealism to social democracy in pre-1848 Germany. Likewise, this experience has an archetypal value in the history of the Russian revolutionary movement. In each successive phase of its development the same passage from the self-affirmation of the thinking individual to social revolution is to be observed: the "rational egoists" and "critically-thinking realists" of the 1860's became the Populists of the 1870's; the critical and analytical Marxism of the 1880's and 1890's gave rise to the actively revolutionary Marxism of the new century. Indeed, one may say that this progression from universal reason to democratic revolution, in one guise or another, represents the life-course of any radical intelligentsia striving for self-realization under an unbending old regime. And it was Herzen and his generation who first lived through this cycle in Russian history.

In each such cycle, moreover, the character of the politics which results is largely determined by the quality of the rationalism which precedes. A socialist theory which takes its values from a romantic idealism does not have the same emphases as a socialism which originates in a hard-headed positivism or materialism. Similarly, a democratic theory produced by an aristocrat does not have the same tone as theories produced by men farther down on the social scale, whose background of privilege is correspondingly less secure. Herzen's background, both social and intellectual, is apparent in every detail of his socialism.

On the one hand he was an unimpeachable democrat since he would settle for nothing less than a Russia where each and every individual would enjoy the fullness of life; yet on the other hand he had an extraordinarily exalted, individualistic and indeed elitist concept of what the full life was. It meant absolute personal freedom, total "egoism," and the plenitude of "consciousness." To be a full "human being" it was virtually necessary to have assimilated all the world's classics from Homer to Hegel. Herzen's socialism meant total enlightenment as much as total democracy; it signified the acme of civilized sensitivity no less than a ruthless egalitarian leveling. Thus socialism for him did not mean the triumph of the people in a state of nature; rather it meant raising the people to a life of civilized refinement and a haughty, indeed lordly, sense of individual independence. In effect, Herzen's utopia of the socialist commune is a projection into the world of peasant Russia of his own aristocratic and idealist education, its extension from the Moscow salons and lecture halls into the humble huts of the village.

This aristocratic view of socialist values is already apparent in Herzen's idealism. The principal legacy of his idealism has already been described as an aesthetic concept of personality and the goal of the absolute ethical freedom of the individual. This legacy might also be characterized as an intransigent form of personalism, or an exclusive preoccupation with the essence of man considered in rarefied abstraction from the concrete social or economic situations in which real men exist. In particular, the communist Russian peasant of his writings was a shadowy and insubstantial creature, especially when compared, for instance, with the peasants of Turgenev. (Significantly, the concrete social aspect of personality to which Herzen devoted the greatest attention and which he described most convincingly was national character, a concern which again was a reflection of gentry rather than of peasant sensitivities.) Such exalted preoccupation with the essence of man, however, is the appanage of one who enjoys great security of social status, complete freedom from material want, and the leisure for endless self-refinement, of one who has never experienced the cruder forms of struggle to make his way in the world, and who has been exempt from the crueler types of personal humiliation — in short a gentleman. Men who have experienced the harsher degrees of human degradation tend to be less general in their demand for social justice and more concerned with the liberation of specific categories of men from equally specific social ills. Herzen, however, despite his illegitimacy and his exiles, knew no such humiliation.

Hence he could see his needs mirrored in the unalloyed personalism of idealism, and he could transpose this concern into politics so as to make the problem of personality the cornerstone of his socialism. It was first of all in this sense that he was a "gentry revolutionary."

It is from this root-cause that the more obvious political reflections of his background follow: his preference for a "middle gentry" regeneration rather than a mass revolt in order to preserve "humanism" in Russia; his emphasis, when describing the commune, on the individualistic, libertarian spirit of that institution rather than its collective property arrangements. It is for this reason also that, when under Alexander II opposition politics lost the monolithic simplicity it possessed under Nicholas, Herzen for a time allowed his devotion to civilization and enlightenment to impede his revolutionary *élan* and succumbed to "liberal waverings." It is for this reason, finally, that he has enjoyed an ambiguous reputation in Russian history: despite his Populism, by the end of the century he could be plausibly claimed as a precursor by Russian liberals no less than by socialists, since he had always made the dignity and freedom of the individual, or the problem of civil rights, the inspiration of his politics.

This liberal image of Herzen, however, is secondary, and the primary image remains that of the revolutionary Populist; nor should we confuse his personalist concept of the civilized life with crypto-moderation. In the last analysis, under Alexander II as under Nicholas I, if Herzen had to choose between the accomplishments of existing civilization and democracy — as in 1848 — he took democracy. And there was great logic to this precisely in terms of his aristocratic concept of civilization. Given the intransigent ideal of "humanism" he entertained, he could not but believe that true civilization would exist only when all men became "human beings." Moreover, in terms of practical politics he felt that in the modern world even existing civilization would be destroyed by the barbarous methods the privileged minority would have to employ to resist democracy. The choice of the modern world, therefore, was not between popular savagery and civilized decency, as the moderate liberals of the period maintained, but between democracy and "death," or an authoritarian reaction which would snuff out all sense of human dignity among elite and masses alike.

The nationalistic elaborations of Herzen's socialism fitted quite logically with the foregoing. It was Europe's historical failure not to have realized the necessity of democracy in 1848, since her upper classes, who knew some measure of freedom and of the humane life, were afraid to risk the blessings they already enjoyed by embarking on the adventure of equality. Conversely, it was Russia's historical chance to possess none of Europe's half-freedoms, for in a society where everyone was enslaved, it was clear that no one could be free unless all were free, and until those abominations of servitude — autocracy and serfdom, and indeed any class hierarchy — were utterly done away with. Only at this revolutionary price could civilization anywhere be saved. It was invariably to this ruthlessly democratic conclusion, despite all his "liberal waverings," that Herzen's gentry sense of humanism — forever prodded by his gentry patriotism — ultimately led.

Or at least this is the conclusion which a literal reading of his writings imposes. Yet even if one makes full allowance for his tendency to hyberbole and his gentlemanly dilettantism, the verdict remains roughly the same. Driven to desperation by thirty years of frustration under Nicholas, Herzen no doubt said somewhat more than he meant, at least in a literal sense; but what he said acquired a life and a momentum of its own and soon became the great democratic myth of the century in Russia. Therefore, whatever mental reservations he as an individual may at times have entertained about his more flamboyant pronouncements, he must stand, *tel qu'en lui-même enfin l'éternité le change,* as the progenitor of that ultimate in democratic pathos — revolutionary Populism.

3

Herzen's impact on Russian political life may be summed up in a few simple propositions. Together with Belinski (who, despite his humble origins, had also derived his values by universalizing the "humanism" of the dominant gentry culture around him), Herzen was the first in Russia to assert with absolute intransigence the ideal of man as an end in himself and of the free individual as the purpose for which society should exist. Together with Bakunin, he was the first in Russia to proclaim, and with the same intransigence, the necessity of rapid, revolutionary democratization. His theory of Russian socialism was the *mystique* which combined these two ideals; which first plausibly related them to the particular conditions of Russian society; and which thereby dramatized the hope of their realization for the young, the ardent, and the angry who made up the swelling ranks of the radical intelligentsia.

But exalted utopias of this stamp, by a perverse yet classic logic, invariably end in politics that are far less pure than the original vision. The modern history of all countries, and in particular of Russia, demonstrates that the practical problem of combining individual liberty with revolutionary democratization is one of immense difficulty and that both ideals inevitably become tarnished in their application. The immensity of this problem in Russia began to become apparent in Herzen's lifetime, as soon as Alexander II started to reform and when the radical opposition began to act on Herzen's own theories. He himself, because of the very purity of his principles, never satisfactorily adapted to the new situation, either in the camp of the reformers or in that of the radicals. When in the sixties a younger and more hard-headed generation of the intelligentsia moved to the front of the stage, he was first alarmed, then rebuffed, and finally rejected. He was among the first to be dismayed by the acerbity of the politics of Russian socialism and by the enormity of the tasks its implementation posed.

The politics of Russian socialism, however, is another story, as is Herzen's growing ambivalence toward the revolutionary movement he had helped call forth. Therefore we may take leave of him at a time when his vision was at its brightest, as yet uncompromised by the exigencies of revolutionary struggle, and on a day when there was good reason to believe that the "future of Russia" would be better than the past, and after which it was in fact to be so for many years. To put matters in a manner that is (roughly) his own, it was a day in March, 1855, during the Crimean War, when Herzen learned the news that after thirty years the Tyrant had at last passed from the scene amidst the ruin of all his policies; the man who, only less than that other tyrant, Ivan Alexeevich Iakovlev, had made him what he was; who more than any other tsar was the perfect embodiment of autocracy; whom he had seen only once, at the coronation in 1826, when as a boy of fourteen he had beheld the Imperial hands "still red with the blood of the Decembrists," but who had dominated his whole life since the Sparrow Hills, first as a symbol, then as a reality. When Herzen learned this news, with a truly Russian "broad nature" (for it was not yet eleven o'clock in the morning), he summoned in his *émigré* friends, uncorked his best champagne, and to the London urchins who gaped at this scene through the garden gates he threw pieces of silver, calling to them to shout through the streets the tidings that meant a new and more "human" life for all Russia: "Hurrah! hurrah! Impernikel is dead! Impernikel is dead!" [2]

Bibliography

At present the most complete edition of Herzen's works is Aleksandr Ivanovich Gertsen, *Polnoe sobranie sochineni i pisem*, edited by M. K. Lemke (22 vols.; Petrograd, 1915–1925). It is this edition that has been used principally for the present book.

A new edition of Herzen's writings is now in the process of publication by the Soviet Academy of Sciences: A. I. Gertsen, *Sobranie sochineni v tridtsati tomakh* (30 vols.; Moscow, 1954–). When this edition is finished it will replace that of Lemke as the definitive collection of Herzen's writings.

The only other edition of Herzen's works still of interest — because it contains both sides of his correspondence with his wife — is *Sochineniia A. I. Gertsena i perepiska s N.A. Zakharinoi* (7 vols.; St. Petersburg, 1905).

In addition there exist two editions of individual works of Herzen which are of special interest because of their notes and commentaries: A. I. Gertsen, *Byloe i Dumy*, edited by L. B. Kamenev (3 vols.; Moscow-Leningrad, 1932) and A. I. Gertsen, *Pisma iz Frantsii i Italii*, edited by L. B. Kamenev (Moscow-Leningrad, 1933).

It is indispensable to supplement these general editions by several collections of materials devoted in whole or in part to Herzen and his circle. The most important of these are *Literaturnoe nasledstvo* (Moscow), vols. VII–VIII, 1933; vols. XXXIX–XL and XLI–XLII, 1941; vol. LXI, 1953; vol. LXII, 1955; vol. LXIII, 1956; vol. LXIV, 1958. Also important are *Zvenia* (Moscow-Leningrad), vols. III and IV, 1933; vol. VI, 1936; vol. VIII, 1950; *A. I. Gertsen: novye materialy*, edited by N. M. Mendelson (Moscow, 1927); "Some Unpublished Letters of Alexander Herzen," edited by E. H. Carr, *Oxford Slavonic Papers*, vol. III, 1952; *Neizdannye pisma A. I. Gertsena k N. I. i T. A. Astrakovym*, edited by L. L. Domger (New York, 1957).

Several of Herzen's works have been translated into English: *My Past and Thoughts: the Memoirs of Alexander Herzen*, translated by Constance Garnett (6 vols.; London, 1924–1927); Alexander Herzen, *Selected Philosophical Works* (Moscow, 1956); A. Herzen, *From the Other Shore and The Russian People and Socialism*, translated by M. Budberg (London, 1956).

A full list of works on Herzen or pertinent to his career would constitute a small book in itself. However, much of this material is either too old or too directly the expression of partisan purposes to be of scholarly interest, and therefore to warrant mention here. For the rest, the more valuable literature on Herzen and related subjects is given at appropriate points in the notes, by chapters, below. The following list, then, represents only a selection of the most important general works on Herzen. For a fuller listing the reader is referred, in addition to the notes, to the comprehensive bibliography of B. Ia. Bukhshtab, *A. I. Gertsen, ukazatel osnovnoi literatury* (Moscow, 1945); this should be supplemented by "Materialy k bibliografii proizvedeni A. I. Gertsena i literatury o nem, 1936–1947 gg," in *Uchenye zapiski Leningradskogo gosudarstvennogo pedagogicheshkogo instituta imeni A. I. Gertsena*, vol. 78, 1948, and by A. G. Fomin, "Bibliografia o Gertsene," in Ch. Vetrinski (V. E. Cheshikhin), *Gertsen* (St. Petersburg, 1908).

The most important old-regime studies of Herzen are the work of Vetrinski, just mentioned, and V. Ia. Bogucharski (Iakovlev), *Aleksandr Ivanovich Gertsen* (Moscow, 1912), both of which were composed before any reasonably full edition of Herzen's works was available. The only full-length Soviet biography of Herzen is Ia. Elsberg, *Gertsen* (3rd ed.; Moscow, 1956) which, though informed and highly readable, is needless to say very official in its point of view. The principal Soviet study of Herzen's thought is L. Piper, *Mirovozzrenie Gertsena* (Moscow-Leningrad, 1935). Of particular value are two specialized studies of Herzen's activity: Z. P. Bazileva, *"Kolokol" Gertsena* (Moscow, 1949) and I. M. Beliavskaia, *A. I. Gertsen i polskoe natsionalno-osvoboditelnoe dvizhenie 60-kh godov XIX veka* (Moscow, 1954). Other specialized works are, N. S. Derzhavin, *A. I. Gertsen. Literaturno-khudozhestvennoe nasledie* (Moscow-Leningrad, 1947); L. Ginzburg, *"Byloe i Dumy" Gertsena* (Leningrad, 1957); I. Novich, *Dukhovnaia drama Gertsena* (Moscow, 1937); N. Pirumova, *Istoricheskie vzgliady A. I. Gertsena* (Moscow, 1956); V. A. Putintsev, *Gertsen pisatel* (Moscow, 1952). The chief non-Russian work on Herzen is Raoul Labry, *Alexandre Ivanovic Herzen* (Paris, 1928), exhaustive but rather ponderously philosophical in its approach. In English there is the brilliant if somewhat excessively ironical study of Herzen's private life by E. H. Carr, *The Romantic Exiles* (New York, 1933).

Notes

CHAPTER ONE

Introduction

1. V. I. Lenin, "Chto delat?" (What Is To Be Done?), *Sochineniia* (4th ed.; Moscow, 1946) V, 347, and (quoted from Karl Kautsky) *Sochineniia*, V, 355, henceforth referred to as Lenin, *Sochineniia*.

2. The best study of the ideology of the Decembrists remains V. I. Semevski, *Politicheskie i obshchestvennye idei dekabristov* (St. Petersburg, 1909); henceforth Semevski, *Idei dekabristov*. The most recent and exhaustive history of the movement is M. V. Nechkina, *Dvizhenie dekabristov* (2 vols.; Moscow, 1955).

3. Henry de Man, *The Psychology of Socialism* (New York-London, 1928), p. 228. In spite of the author's collaboration with National Socialism at the end of his life certain of his earlier comments on socialism, which he knew from the inside, remain interesting.

4. The literature on the problem of the intelligentsia is too vast to mention here. A good bibliography is given by N. M. Somov, *Bibliografiia russkoi obshchestvennosti: k voprosu ob intelligentsii* (Moscow, 1927–1931). Those comprehensive treatments of the intelligentsia which do exist are both old and heavily ideological in approach, ignoring almost entirely the social aspect of the problem. A few of the most notable of these works are: P. V. Ivanov-Razumnik, *Istoriia russkoi obshchestvennoi mysli* (2 vols.; 4th ed.; St. Petersburg, 1914), henceforth referred to as Ivanov-Razumnik, *Obshchestvennaia mysl;* T. G. Masaryk, *The Spirit of Russia,* translated from the German by Eden and Cedar Paul (London, 1919); and D. N. Ovsianiko-Kulikovski, *Istoriia russkoi intelligentsii*, vols. VII–IX of *Sobranie sochineni* (St. Petersburg, 1910), henceforth Ovsianiko-Kulikovski, *Russkaia intelligentsia*.

5. To mention once and for all Lenin's contribution to the historiography of the revolutionary movement in general and of Herzen's career in particular the appropriate references, cited unfailingly in all Soviet works on both subjects, are given here. Lenin, "Pamiati Gertsena," *Sochineniia*, XVIII, 9–15; Lenin, "Rol soslovi i klassov v osvoboditelnom dvizhenii," *Sochineniia*, XIX, 294–296; Lenin, "Iz proshlogo rabochei pechati v Rossii," *Sochineniia*, XX, 223–225. All of these pieces are short journalistic efforts of no great value as historical analysis, unlike some of Lenin's longer and more pondered works. The article "Pamiati Gertsena" (To the Memory of Herzen) was written for the newspaper *Sotsial-Demokrat* (April 25, 1912) to commemorate the hundredth anniversary of Herzen's birth. It is no more than an attempt to annex

Herzen to the tradition of Lenin's own party against the claims of the Socialist Revolutionaries, which in reality were much more substantial. Yet this chance article has been the basis for Herzen's great fortune in Soviet historiography. Without it Herzen might well have been spurned as an aristocrat, an anarchist, and Marx's foe — which was the fate of Bakunin. But Lenin's blessing has not been an unmixed one, for the same "remarkable" article (as it is inevitably described) has also been the strait jacket into which all Soviet scholarship on Herzen has had to fit since the 1930's, and it is a narrow one indeed.

The general sense of Lenin's position on the revolutionary movement is given most succinctly in the third of the pronouncements mentioned above. In an analysis which is quoted too often by the Soviets to be ignored Lenin divides the history of the movement into three class phases: "the gentry (*dvorianski*) period, approximately from 1825 to 1861; the period of the commoners (*raznochinski period*) or the bourgeois-democratic period, approximately from 1861 to 1895; the proletarian period, from 1895 to the present time" (Lenin, *Sochineniia*, XX, 223). The Decembrists and Herzen are held to be the chief representatives of the gentry period, which means that although they were revolutionary and democratic in spirit they could never arrive at a realistic formulation of their aims — which would be "scientific" socialism — because they lacked roots in the people.

6. The early years of Bakunin have been reconstructed by A. A. Kornilov in *Molodye gody Mikhaila Bakunina* (Moscow, 1917), henceforth referred to as Kornilov, *Molodoi Bakunin*, and those of Belinski by V. S. Nechaeva in *V. G. Belinski: nachalo zhiznennogo puti i literaturnoi deiatelnosti, 1811–1830* (Moscow, 1949). The enterprise has not been undertaken for Ogarev, and the attempt will be made here while discussing Herzen's own youth.

7. Aleksandr Ivanovich Gertsen (Herzen), *Zapiski odnogo molodogo cheloveka* in *Polnoe sobranie sochineni i pisem*, edited by M. K. Lemke (22 vols.; Petrograd, 1915–1925), II, 380–406, 437–467. Since the Lemke edition of Herzen's works is at present the most complete it will be used here whenever possible, that is in the majority of cases. Henceforth reference to it will consist simply of the mention "Lemke." This will be preceded by the title of the individual work of Herzen in question (which after the first reference will, when convenient, be given in an abbreviation) followed by the volume and page number from Lemke. In this way it is hoped that cross-referencing with other editions of Herzen, particularly that now being published by the Soviet Academy of Sciences, will be facilitated. For the same reason all letters of Herzen will be referred to by correspondent and date. When editions of Herzen other than Lemke are used this fact will be indicated each time.

8. *Byloe i Dumy*, Lemke, XII–XIV, henceforth referred to as *B. i D.* Written over a period of years, *Byloe i Dumy* is as much a series of chapters or sketches as a single, integrated work. Herzen himself never gave a definitive version of his memoirs; indeed, certain sections were published for the first time only long after his death by Lemke. The structure of *Byloe i Dumy*, then, is in part the work of Herzen's editors, and editions vary. That given by Lemke has since been improved upon twice in authoritative fashion: by L. B. Kamenev, ed., *Byloe i Dumy* (3 vols.; Moscow-Leningrad, 1932), henceforth referred to as Kamenev, ed., *Byloe i Dumy;* and in the current unfinished edition of Herzen's works by the Soviet Academy of Sciences, A. I. Gertsen, *Sobranie sochineni v tridtsati tomakh* (30 vols.; Moscow, 1954–   ), vols. VIII–XI, henceforth referred to as Herzen, *Sochineniia v tridtsati tomakh*. The last of these

editions is the most painstaking and probably the nearest to the author's intentions, in so far as the latter were fixed. Nonetheless the differences between editions are relatively slight, and none of them is significant as regards substance. Therefore Lemke's has been preferred both because it is complete — although perhaps not always in the right order — and to make all references, in so far as possible, to the same edition of Herzen's works.

9. Isaiah Berlin in "Introduction" to A. Herzen, *From the Other Shore,* translated by M. Budberg (London, 1956), pp. xii, xiii.

CHAPTER TWO

Family and Childhood

1. Down to Herzen's departure from Russia in 1847 dates will be given according to the "old style," or the Julian calendar, in the nineteenth century twelve days behind the Western calendar. After his removal to Europe dates will be given according to the "new style," or Gregorian calendar.

2. Article "Iakovlevy," in *Entsiklopedicheski slovar,* XLI (Brokgaus-Efron, St. Petersburg, 1904), 611; note of ed., Lemke, I, 4–6.

3. Some material about the Iakovlev family was published by Herzen's cousin, D. D. Golokhvastov, in *Russki arkhiv* (1874), I, 1053–01095. The more relevant parts of this material are quoted by Lemke in "Kommentarii" of ed. to part I of *Byloe i Dumy,* Lemke, XII, 158–170.

4. T. P. Passek, *Iz dalnikh let* (3 vols.; 1st ed.; St. Petersburg, 1878), I, 2.

5. *Ibid.,* and cf. Herzen's portrait of his cousin, D. D. Golokhvastov, *B. i D.,* Lemke, XIII, 156–183.

6. D. N. Sverbeev, *Zapiski Dmitriia Nikolaevicha Sverbeeva, 1799–1826* (2 vols.; Moscow, 1899), I, 169.

7. *Ibid.,* 170.

8. Passek, *Iz dalnikh let,* I, 2–3.

9. Mme. Passek, née Kuchina (the *Korchevskaia kuzina* of *My Past and Thoughts*) is not always the most reliable of witnesses, and various critics, in particular Lemke (I, 8, 14), have tended to discount her testimony. These strictures are certainly merited for the latter portions of her memoirs, devoted to Herzen's mature years, where much of what she says is reported at second hand or simply invented. However, she was very close to Herzen and his family until her cousin was around twenty, and here she did not have to embroider the truth in order to have a story. What she tells of Herzen's youth is intrinsically plausible; moreover, all that she says checks with hints in writings and letters of Herzen, a good part of which she had not seen and which hence could not have guided her own writing. There is every reason, therefore, to credit her testimony for Herzen's early years.

10. Passek, *Iz dalnikh let,* I, 4–5, 12.

11. *B. i D.,* Lemke, XII, 22, 101; Passek, *Iz dalnikh let,* I, 56; Golokhvastov, in *Russki arkhiv* (1874), I, 1080.

12. Passek, *Iz dalnikh let,* I, 3; *B. i D.,* Lemke, XII, 24–25.

13. "Kommentari no. 15" of ed. to part I of *B. i D.,* Lemke, XII, 172; Passek, *Iz dalnikh let,* I, 3–4.

14. *B. i D.,* Lemke, XII, 80.

15. This is made apparent every time Herzen discusses the gentry of his father's generation, as for example *B. i D.,* Lemke, XII, 79–96; the portrait of

Olga Alexandrovna Zherebtsova, *B. i D.*, Lemke, XIII, 56–65; or in his story *Elena*, Lemke, II, 45–72.

16. *Dolg prezhde vsego*, Lemke, VII, 409–464.
17. Passek, *Iz dalnikh let*, I, 37–38.
18. *Ibid.*, 36.
19. *Ibid.;* note of ed., Lemke, I, 6–7.
20. *B. i D.*, Lemke, XII, 11–18.
21. Tolstoi, *War and Peace*, book IV, part II, chap. 9.
22. *B. i D.*, Lemke, XII, 24.
23. *Ibid.*, 79.
24. *Ibid.*, 81.
25. *Ibid.*
26. *Ibid.*, 79.
27. *Ibid.*, 86.
28. *Ibid.*, 27
29. Herzen to Herwegh, 23 May, 1850, "Pisma k Georgu i Emme Gervegam," in *Literaturnoe nasledstvo*, LXIV (Moscow, 1958), 195.
30. *B. i D.*, Lemke, XII, 82.
31. *Ibid.*, 44–48.
32. *Ibid.*, 81.
33. *Ibid.*, 19–20.
34. Passek, *Iz dalnikh let*, I, 78–79.
35. *Ibid.*, 77–78.
36. *B. i D.*, Lemke, XII, 82, 95.
37. Passek, *Iz dalnikh let*, I, 114.
38. According to his own admission, *Zapiski odnogo molodogo cheloveka*, Lemke, II, 387.
39. *B. i D.*, Lemke, XII, 30–41.
40. *Ibid.*, 30.
41. *Ibid.*, 82.
42. The exact age is in doubt. Herzen's own testimony is understandably vague. He makes the crisis of discovery span three years, from "around the age of ten" to thirteen (*B. i D.*, Lemke, XII, 27, 29). Lemke dates it 1820, when Herzen was eight (*ibid.*, note, p. 29). Tatiana Passek places it "around the age of twelve" (Passek, *Iz dalnikh let*, I, 156). Labry's deduction is also twelve: Raoul Labry, *Alexandre Ivanovic Herzen* (Paris, 1928), pp. 37–40, henceforth referred to as Labry, *Herzen*. Given the tension that reigned between Herzen's parents his curiosity was probably aroused earlier rather than later, or nearer to the age of ten than of twelve.
43. *B. i D.*, Lemke, XII, 27–28.
44. *Ibid.*, 29.
45. *Ibid.*, 28.
46. *Ibid.*, 30.
47. *Ibid.*, 29.
48. *Ibid.*, 30.
49. Passek, *Iz dalnikh let*, II, 61–62.
50. *Dolg prezhde vsego*, Lemke, VII, 409–464. An earlier version of the same, together with a good statement of the importance Herzen originally assigned to this novel, is given by Iu. Krasovski in *Literaturnoe nasledstvo*, LXI (Moscow, 1953), 27–88.
51. Herzen to Natalie, 21 Nov., 1837, Lemke, II, 502–503.

52. *B. i D.*, Lemke, XII, 90.
53. Passek, *Iz dalnikh let*, I, 157. Italics added.
54. *B. i D.*, Lemke, XII, 18.
55. Labry, *Herzen*, p. 24.
56. *B. i D.*, Lemke, XII, 18.
57. *Zapiski odnogo molodogo cheloveka*, Lemke, II, 384.
58. Passek, *Iz dalnikh let*, I, 115–116.
59. Labry, *Herzen*, pp. 24–26.
60. *B. i D.*, Lemke, XII, 19–20.
61. *Zapiski odnogo molodogo cheloveka*, Lemke, II, 388.
62. *Ibid.;* Passek, *Iz dalnikh let*, I, 140.
63. *Zapiski odnogo molodogo cheloveka*, Lemke, II, 388.
64. *Ibid.; B. i D.*, Lemke, XII, 41.
65. *Ibid.*, 42.
66. *Ibid.*
67. *Ibid.*, 47–48.
68. *Ibid.*
69. Labry, *Herzen*, p. 27.
70. Passek, *Iz dalnikh let*, I, 239–240; Herzen to T. Passek, autumn 1827, Lemke, I, 21.
71. Passek, *Iz dalnikh let*, I, 160, 249.
72. *B. i D.*, Lemke, XII, 62.
73. Passek, *Iz dalnikh let*, I, 204, 286; *Zapiski odnogo molodogo cheloveka*, Lemke, II, 394.
74. Passek, *Iz dalnikh let*, I, 246.
75. Herzen, "Ranni avtobiograficheski nabrosok" (1833), in *Literaturnoe nasledstvo*, LXI, 11–12: Passek, *Iz dalnikh let*, I, 246, 305–306.
76. Passek, *Iz dalnil·h let*, I, 278–279.
77. *B. i D.*, Lemke, XII, 49.
78. Passek, *Iz dalnikh let*, I, 195, 213.
79. *Ibid.*, 214.
80. *B. i D.*, Lemke, XII, note, p. 55. First published for the thirtieth anniversary of the uprising of the Decembrists by Herzen's *Poliarnaia zvezda* in 1855.
81. *B. i D.*, Lemke, XII, 54.
82. *Ibid.*, 56.
83. *Ibid.*, 54.
84. Passek, *Iz dalnikh let*, I, 242; Herzen to T. Passek, Oct. 1828, Lemke, I, 27.
85. *B. i D.*, Lemke, XII, 57.
86. *Zapiski odnogo molodogo cheloveka*, Lemke, II, 389.
87. *B. i D.*, Lemke, XII, 57.
88. *Ibid.;* Passek, *Iz dalnikh let*, I, 219–222.
89. *Zapiski odnogo molodogo cheloveka*, Lemke, II, 396.
90. A good analytical classification of the various schools of romanticism, together with a full bibliography, is given by Paul van Tieghem, *Le romantisme dans la littérature européene* (Paris, 1948). For the penetration of French romanticism into Russia see V. Sadovnik, *Ocherki po istorii russkoi literatury XIX–go veka* (2 vols.; 7th ed.; St. Petersburg, 1911), vol. I, chap. xiii, "Russkaia literaturnaia kritika v pervoi polovine XIX-go veka"; for a more extended treatment see I. I. Zamotin, *Romantizm dvadtsatykh godov XIX stoletiia v russkoi literature* (2 vols.; St. Petersburg-Moscow, 1911).

91. "Neskolko myslei o poezii," in *Syn otechestva*, 1825.

92. For the cultural role of Polevoi and of the *Moskovski telegraf* in the twenties see N. K. Kozmin, *Ocherki iz istorii russkogo romantizma. N. A. Polevoi, kak vyrazitel literaturnykh napravleni sovremennoi emu epokhi*, published as *Chast LXX* of the *Zapiski istoriko-filologicheskogo fakulteta Imperatorskogo S.-Peterburgskogo Universiteta* (St. Petersburg, 1903), henceforth referred to as Kozmin, *Polevoi*.

93. *Zapiski odnogo molodogo cheloveka*, Lemke, II, 390–391.

94. Passek, *Iz dalnikh let*, I, 221.

95. *Zapiski odnogo molodogo cheloveka*, Lemke, II, 391.

96. *Ibid.*, 391–392.

97. *Ibid.*, 396.

98. *Ibid.*, 399.

CHAPTER THREE

Schiller and Ogarev

1. *Zapiski odnogo molodogo cheloveka*, Lemke, II, 400.

2. *B. i D.*, Lemke, XII, 76.

3. *Ibid.*, 72.

4. *Zapiski odnogo molodogo cheloveka*, Lemke, II, 400–401.

5. N. P. Pavlov-Silvanski, "Materialisty dvadtsatykh godov," in *Sochineniia* (3 vols.; 2nd ed.; St. Petersburg, 1909–1910), II, 239–288, henceforth Pavlov-Silvanski, *Sochineniia*.

6. For the penetration of German literary influence, and in particular of Schiller, into Russia, see N. V. Gerbel, *Liricheskie stikhotvoreniia Shillera v perevodakh russkikh poetov* (St. Petersburg, 1857); Otto P. Peterson, *Schiller in Russland, 1785–1805* (Deutsche Akademie of Munich, New York, 1934); H. Raab, "Die Lyrik Schillers in früher russischer Uebersetzung," in *Zeitschrift für Slawistik* (Greifswald, East Germany, 1957), Band I, Heft I, pp. 40–60. The most valuable general treatment of this subject is Marcelle Ehrard, *V. A. Joukovski et le préromantisme russe* (Paris, 1938), especially part I, chap. vi, and part III, chap. iv.

7. For Richter see Lemke, I, 65, 127, 261, 501; II, 119, 126–127. For Hoffmann see Herzen's enthusiastic article of 1834, *Gofman*, Lemke, I, 138–154.

8. For a more extensive development of this interpretation of Schiller see M. E. Malia, "Schiller and the Early Russian Left," *Harvard Slavic Studies*, vol. IV (The Hague, 1957). The fullest possible case for the essentially aesthetic import of Schiller's message and for the influence of this aspect of his work in Russia is given by D. Chizhevski, "Schiller v Rossii," in *Novy zhurnal*, vol. XLV (New York, 1956). The importance of an "aesthetic humanism" in Russia deriving from Schiller is perhaps most forcibly stated by V. V. Zenkovski, *Istoriia russkoi filosofii* (2 vols.; Paris, 1948–1950), vol. I, part II; henceforth referred to as Zenkovski, *Russkaia filosofiia;* translated by E. Kline as *History of Russian Philosophy* (New York-London, 1953). On Schiller himself see Reinhard Buchwald, *Schiller* (2 vols.; 2nd rev. ed.; Wiesbaden, 1953); Robert D'Harcourt, *La jeunesse de Schiller* (3rd ed.; Paris, 1928). For the interpretation of Schiller's art and thought see H. A. Korff, *Geist der Goethezeit* (4 vols.; Leipzig, 1927–1953), especially vol. II; Franz Schultz, *Klassik und Romantik*

der Deutschen (2 vols.; 2nd ed.; Stuttgart, 1952), part II; Benno von Wiese, *Die Dramen Schillers. Politik und Tragödie* (Leipzig, 1938); Werner Busch, *Die Selbstbetrachtung und Selbstdeutung des jungen Schiller* (Doc. dissertation, Univ. of Bonn; Würzburg, 1937). A convenient summary in English is F. W. Kaufman, *Schiller, Poet of Philosophical Idealism* (Oberlin, Ohio, 1942). For Schiller's philosophy in the more technical sense of that word see Kuno Fischer, *Schiller als Philosoph* (2nd ed.; Heidelberg, 1891); Robert Petsch, *Freiheit und Notwendigkeit in Schillers Dramen* (1st vol. of *Goethe-und-Schillerstudien;* Munich, 1905); Emil C. Wilm, *The Philosophy of Schiller in Its Historical Relations* (Boston, 1912). The relation of Schiller's philosophy to Kant has not been considered here since, although it is important for understanding Schiller himself, it is not particularly germane to his influence in Russia. Needless to say, although the opinion of Schiller expressed in this chapter derives indirectly from the commentaries listed here, the opinion itself, and the implications deduced from it, are not to be laid at the door of any of the above authorities.

9. For the exiguous social basis and individual isolation which produced this aesthetic "alienation" in Germany see W. H. Bruford, *Germany in the Eighteenth Century: The Social Background of the Literary Revival* (Cambridge, 1935).

10. *Zapiski odnogo molodogo cheloveka,* Lemke, II, 392.

11. Passek, *Iz dalnikh let,* I, 240; Herzen to T. Passek, June 1828, Lemke, I, 25.

12. Schiller, *The Robbers,* Act I, Scene 2. Citations from Schiller's dramas are taken, with minor revisions, from the translation of Charles J. Hempel, *Schiller's Complete Works* (2 vols.; Philadelphia, 1870).

13. *The Robbers,* Act I, Scene 2.

14. *Zapiski odnogo molodogo cheloveka,* Lemke, II, 402.

15. Schiller, "Philosophical Letters" in *Aesthetic Letters, Essays and the Philosophical Letters of Schiller,* translated by J. Weiss (Boston, 1854), p. 366.

16. *B. i D.,* Lemke, XII, 72.

17. *Zapiski odnogo molodogo cheloveka,* Lemke, II, 403.

18. *Ibid.* The passage from Schiller is not reproduced literally but paraphrased; therefore it probably was quoted from memory, in 1838–1839, which would indicate the profound impression made by the original event.

19. The sources of Ogarev's early life are as follows: the very short and disappointing "Zapiski russkogo pomeshchika," in *Byloe,* no. 27–28 (1924), written in 1873 for Tatiana Passek (Passek, *Iz dalnikh let,* I, 259–264); the longer and more illuminating "Moia ispoved," in *Literaturnoe nasledstvo,* LXI, 659–700, written between 1856 and 1861 at the urging of Herzen; a third short autobiographical fragment, in reality an introduction to "Moia ispoved," published as "Iz publitsisticheskogo naslediia Ogareva," in *Literaturnoe nasledstvo,* XXXIX–XL (Moscow, 1941), 357–358. In addition there is some autobiographical material in Ogarev's poems, the most recent and complete edition of which is N. P. Ogarev, *Stikhotvoreniia i poemy* ("Biblioteka poeta"; 2nd ed.; Leningrad, 1956).

20. Ogarev, "Zapiski russkogo pomeshchika," in *Byloe,* no. 27–28 (1924), p. 16.

21. Ogarev to Herzen, 29 Aug., 1836, "Iz perepiski nedavnikh deiatelei," in *Russkaia mysl* (1888), book IX, p. 3.

22. Ogarev, "Moia ispoved," in *Literaturnoe nasledstvo,* LXI, 693.

23. *Ibid.*, 683–684.

24. *Ibid.*, 681, 693–694.

25. *Ibid.*, 686.

26. In another place Ogarev stated that his first deep ideological impressions were, like Herzen's, "Schiller, Rousseau and the fourteenth of December": "Iz publitsisticheskogo naslediia Ogareva," in *Literaturnoe nasledstvo*, XXXIX–XL, 358.

27. *Zapiski odnogo molodogo cheloveka*, Lemke, II, 402.

28. *B. i D.*, Lemke, XII, 75.

29. *B. i D.*, Lemke, XIII, 4.

30. M. O. Gershenzon, *Istoriia Molodoi Rossii* (Moscow, 1908), pp. 294–295, henceforth referred to as Gershenzon, *Molodaia Rossiia*.

31. Herzen to Ogarev, 19 July, 1833, Lemke, I, 117.

32. *B. i D.*, Lemke, XII, 73.

33. Herzen to Natalie, 21 Nov., 1837, Lemke, I, 502.

34. *Zapiski odnogo molodogo cheloveka*, Lemke, II, 403.

35. *B. i D.*, Lemke, XII, 76.

36. *Don Carlos*, particularly Act I, Scene 9, and Act IV, Scene 21.

37. *B. i D.*, Lemke, XII, 76–77.

38. *Zapiski odnogo molodogo cheloveka*, Lemke, II, 403.

39. The exact date is in doubt. Indeed, given the limited evidence available, it cannot be fixed more precisely than a hesitation between the summer of 1827 and that of 1828. For the best discussion of the problem, see the notes of M. V. Nechkina to Ogarev's "Moia ispoved," in *Literaturnoe nasledstvo*, LXI, 673. Mme. Nechkina concludes for 1827.

40. *B. i D.*, Lemke, XII, 74.

41. *Ibid.*

42. For example, Labry, *Herzen*, p. 70.

43. Ogarev to Herzen, 7 July, 1833, "Iz perepiski nedavnikh deiatelei," in *Russkaia mysl* (1888), book VII, pp. 4 and 6. A corrected version of this letter is published in *Literaturnoe nasledstvo*, LXI, 713–714. These passages are quoted by Herzen in *B. i D.*, Lemke, XII, 75. Most, although not all, of Ogarev's early letters have been republished in M. T. Iovchuk and N. G. Tarakanova, eds., N. P. Ogarev, *Izbrannye sotsialno-politicheskie i filosofskie proizvedeniia* (2 vols; Moscow, 1952–1956), vol. II, part II; henceforth referred to as Ogarev, *Izbrannye*.

44. Ogarev to Herzen, 1837 or early 1838, "Iz perepiski nedavnikh deiatelei," in *Russkaia mysl* (1888), book IX, p. 7.

45. Ogarev to Herzen, 20 Feb., 1840, "Iz perepiski nedavnikh deiatelei," in *Russkaia mysl* (1889), book I, p. 6.

46. *B. i D.*, Lemke, XII, 59; *Zapiski odnogo molodogo cheloveka*, Lemke, II, 391.

47. *B. i D.*, Lemke, XII, 76. The line "Was I such, unfolding like a flower?" (*Takov li byl ia, rastsvetaia?*) is from Pushkin's *Otryvki iz puteshestviia Onegina*.

48. Lemke, I, 89–90.

49. *Gofman*, Lemke, I, 138.

CHAPTER FOUR

University and "Circle"

1. *B. i D.*, Lemke, XII, 97–98.

2. *Ibid.*, 98; Passek, *Iz dalnikh let*, I, 312.

3. Nicholas A. Hans, *History of Russian Educational Policy (1701–1917)* (London, 1931), chaps. i–iii; S. V. Rozhdestvenski, *Istoricheski obzor deiatelnosti ministerstva narodnogo prosveshcheniia, 1802–1902* (St. Petersburg, 1902), Introduction and chaps. i–iii.

4. *Istoriia Moskvy* (6 vols.; Moscow, 1952–1958), vol. III, chap. i, section 4; chap. x; chap. xi, section 4. Although this work makes the social atmosphere of early nineteenth-century Moscow somewhat too plebeian, it nonetheless furnishes the elements for a more balanced view. The best picture of gentry Moscow around 1825 is given by M. O. Gershenzon, *Griboedovskaia Moskva* (2nd rev. ed.; Moscow, 1916).

5. *Ocherki po istorii russkoi zhurnalistiki i kritiki* (one vol. now published[?]; Leningrad, 1950), vol. I, part iii.

6. For the atmosphere of the university at this time see Ia. I. Kostenetski, "Vospominaniia iz moei studencheskoi zhizni, 1828–1833," in *Russki arkhiv* (1887), nos. 1–3, 5–6, and I. A. Goncharov, *Vospominaniia* in *Sobranie sochineni* (8 vols.; Moscow, 1952–1955), VII, 193–233.

7. Goncharov, *Vospominaniia, Sobranie sochineni*, VII, 214. For more on university life at this time see K. I. Aksakov, *Vospominaniia studenchestva* (St. Petersburg, 1910), as well as the selections from other memoirs in *Moskovski universitet v vospominaniiakh sovremennikov*, edited by R. A. Kovnator (Moscow, 1956). A good analysis of the university milieu and its relations with society is given in Labry, *Herzen*, pp. 95–114.

8. *Istoriia moskovskogo universiteta*, edited by M. N. Tikhomirov (2 vols.; Moscow, 1955), vol. I, chap. iii; Rozhdestvenski, *Istoricheski obzor*, chaps. iii–iv.

9. *B. i D.*, Lemke, XII, 141.

10. *Ibid.*, 107.

11. Passek, *Iz dalnikh let*, I, 317.

12. *B. i D.*, Lemke, XII, 107–108.

13. *Ibid.*, 99–101; Kostenetski, in *Russki arkhiv* (1887), nos. 1–3, p. 5; Goncharov, *Vospominaniia, Sobranie sochineni*, VII, 193–223; Aksakov, *Vospominaniia, passim*. For a good discussion of this point see Labry, *Herzen*, pp. 85–95.

14. *B. i D.*, Lemke, XII, 108.

15. *Ibid.*, 109–113.

16. *Ibid.*, 114.

17. Passek, *Iz dalnikh let*, I, 324. Lemke disputes this assertion on the basis of very fragmentary evidence ("Kommentari no. 45" of ed. to part I of *B. i D.*, Lemke, XII, 186). Nonetheless Tatiana's testimony checks with Herzen's own account, as well as with the character of Ivan Alexeevich.

18. Herzen to Ogarev, 19 July, 1833, Lemke, I, 118.

19. *B. i D.*, Lemke, XII, 140–141; Herzen to friends, May 1833, *Literaturnoe nasledstvo*, XXXIX–XL, 189.

20. Herzen to Natalie, 5–6 July, 1833, Lemke, I, 115–116.

21. Herzen to friends, May 1833, *Literaturnoe nasledstvo*, XXXIX–XL, 189.

22. Herzen to Ogarev, 5 June, 1833, Lemke, I, 114–115.

23. Herzen to T. Passek, June–July 1833, Lemke, I, 109–110.

24. *B. i D.*, Lemke, XII, 118–120.

25. The most perceptive approach to the phenomenon of the *kruzhok* is that of Gershenzon, *Molodaia Rossiia*, Introduction and chaps. iii–iv (especially pp. 210–214). See also P. N. Miliukov, *Iz istorii russkoi intelligentsii* (St. Petersburg, 1908), chaps. iii–iv, henceforth referred to as Miliukov, *Russkaia intelligentsiia;* Kornilov, *Molodoi Bakunin;* E. H. Carr, *Michael Bakunin* (London, 1937), henceforth Carr, *Bakunin;* V. S. Nechaeva, *V. G. Belinski. Uchenie v universitete i rabota v "Teleskope" i "Molve," 1829–1836* (Moscow, 1954), chap. viii.

26. The purest exemplar of the mentality of the *kruzhok* is Stankevich. See A. Stankevich, ed., *Perepiska N. V. Stankevicha* (Moscow, 1914), henceforth, *Perepiska Stankevicha;* P. V. Annenkov, "N. V. Stankevich," in *Vospominaniia i kriticheskie ocherki* (3 vols.; St. Petersburg, 1881), vol. III, henceforth Annenkov, *Vospominaniia.*

27. Belinski to Botkin, 13 June, 1840, *Belinski, Pisma,* edited by E. A. Liatski (3 vols.; St. Petersburg, 1914), II, 129.

28. *B. i D.*, Lemke, XII, 127–135; Passek, *Iz dalnikh let*, I–II, *passim.*

29. *B. i D.*, Lemke, XIII, 204–233; "Kommentari no. 42" of ed. to part I of *B. i D.*, Lemke, XII, 188–191; note of Kamenev, ed., to *Byloe i Dumy*, III, 436–438.

30. B. Kozmin, ed., "Iz literaturnogo nasledstva N. I. Sazonova," in *Literaturnoe nasledstvo*, XLI–XLII (Moscow, 1941), 178–187; *B. i D.*, Lemke, XIII, 572–589; "Kommentarii nos. 41–51" of ed. to part V of *B. i D.*, Lemke, XIV, 128–151.

31. Note of Kamenev, ed., to *Byloe i Dumy*, III, 554–555.

32. N. M. Satin, "Iz vospominani N. M. Satina," in *Pochin* (Moscow, 1895), pp. 232–250; N. M. Satin, "Iz literaturnykh vospominani," in *Russkie propilei*, edited by M. O. Gershenzon (6 vols; Moscow, 1915–1919), I, 195–204; "Kommentari no. 15" of ed. to part II of *B. i D.*, Lemke, XII, 355–357.

33. Ogarev, "Kavkazskie vody," in *Izbrannye*, I, 396–413. This article also contains information on Satin.

34. The small-gentry status of Savich and Lakhtin is more to be inferred from the manner in which Herzen and Ogarev speak of them than from any direct evidence available.

35. That the majority of students at the university in the thirties and forties were of non-noble, or *raznochinski*, origin, but that the tone of the university and of its intellectual life was none the less set by the gentry has been amply illustrated by V. R. Leikina-Svirskaia, "Formirovanie raznochinskoi intelligentsii v Rossii v 40-kh godakh XIX veka," *Istoriia SSSR*, no. 1 (Jan.–Feb. 1958), pp. 83–104.

36. *B. i D.*, Lemke, XII, 141–142.

37. *O sebe*, Lemke, II, 163.

38. *B. i D.*, Lemke, XII, 143–149.

39. *Ibid.*, 143.

40. *Ibid.*, 108.

CHAPTER FIVE

Schelling and Idealism

1. *B. i D.*, Lemke, XIII, 10.

2. Semevski, *Idei dekabristov, passim;* Pavlov-Silvanski, "Materialisty dvadtsatykh godov," in *Sochineniia*, II, 239–288. The personal character of the Decembrists is admirably contrasted with that of "the men of the thirties" by Gershenzon in his portrait of M. F. Orlov, *Molodaia Rossiia*, pp. 1–74; see also his *Dekabrist Krivtsov i ego bratia* (Moscow, 1914).

3. Among the many studies of the beginnings of idealism in Russia the best are Alexandre Koyré, *La philosophie et le problème national en Russie au début du XIXe siècle* (Paris, 1929), henceforth referred to as Koyré, *La philosophie*, and Wsewolod Setschkareff (Vsevolod Sechkarev), *Schellings Einfluss in der russischen Literatur der 20er und 30er Jahre des XIX Jahrhunderts* (Leipzig, 1939), henceforth referred to as Setschkareff, *Schellings Einfluss*. See also P. N. Sakulin, *Iz istorii russkogo idealizma. Kniaz V. F. Odoevski*, (2 vols.; Moscow, 1913); Ivanov-Razumnik, *Obshchestvennaia mysl*, vol. I, chap. vi; Zenkovski, *Russkaia filosofiia*, vol. I, part II, chaps. i–ii.

4. For details see Labry, *Herzen*, pp. 95–106.

5. For the description of German idealism given here the following works have been utilized, although obviously by no means exhausted. Needless to say, none of the authorities mentioned below is to be held responsible for the interpretation of idealism set forth in this chapter. The classical, though old-fashioned, compendium of information on the history of idealism is Kuno Fischer, *Geschichte der neuern Philosophie* (10 vols.; 3rd rev. ed.; Heidelberg, 1878–1908), especially vol. VI (Fichte), vol. VII (Schelling) and vol. VIII (Hegel). Of the numerous "Kant to Hegel" books perhaps the most valuable is Richard Kroner, *Von Kant bis Hegel* (2 vols.; Tübingen, 1921–1924). Also useful are Julius Ebbinghaus, *Relativer und absoluter Idealismus. Historisch-systematische Untersuchung über den Weg von Kant bis Hegel* (Leipzig, 1910) and Nicolai Hartman, *Die Philosophie des deutschen Idealismus* (2 vols.; Berlin-Leipzig, 1923–1929). Old (first published 1857) but still useful as an introduction is Rudolf Haym, *Hegel und seine Zeit* (Leipzig, 1927). Specialized studies which are particularly valuable for understanding idealism as a whole are Jean Wahl, *Le malheur de la conscience dans la philosophie hégélienne* (Paris, 1929), Jean Hyppolite, *Genèse et structure de la Phénoménologie de l'Esprit de Hegel* (Paris, 1946) and Herbert Marcuse, *Reason and Revolution. Hegel and the Rise of Social Theory* (2nd ed.; New York, 1954). Perhaps the best popular introduction to German idealism in English is Josiah Royce, *Lectures on Modern Idealism* (New Haven, 1919). For the romanticism so closely allied with idealism see Rudolf Haym, *Die romantische Schule* (5th ed.; Berlin, 1928) and Ricarda Huch, *Die Romantik* (2 vols.; Leipzig, 1922). Extremely helpful for understanding the spirit behind the formal doctrines of idealism and for recreating the mood of the period is Wilhelm Dilthey, *Leben Schleiermachers* (one vol. published; Berlin, 1870), and his *Die Jugendgeschichte Hegels* (Berlin, 1905) (see also notes 7–10 below).

6. The view of the egocentrism of idealism given here derives first of all from reading in the idealists themselves, both German and Russian, where after a time it simply becomes obvious. It also emerges, in one way or another, in

Dilthey and some of the other authors mentioned in the preceding note. It is stated more accessibly, if also much more crudely, by George Santayana, *Egotism in German Philosophy* (London-Toronto, n.d.), and, in the same vein though even less satisfactorily, by John Dewey, *German Philosophy and Politics* (New York, 1915). The chief virtue — and the sole innovation — in the approach of both authors, especially of Santayana, and one which has been found suggestive here, is their common-sense Anglo-Saxon way of taking the Germans at their word and spelling out literally the practical implications of the latter's much more subtle metaphysics. This quality is also to be found at times in the German romantic tradition itself, in particular in Heine, who (to quote Dewey, p. 83), "with his contempt for technical philosophy . . . had an intimate sense of its human meaning." See his ironical but penetrating commentary on idealism, Heinrich Heine, *De l'Allemagne depuis Luther*, in *Revue des Deux Mondes*, 1 Mar., 15 Nov., 15 Dec., 1834; German text, *Zur Geschichte der Religion und Philosophie in Deutschland*, in *Sämtliche Werke* (11 vols.; Munich, 1925–30), vol. V.

7. See Friedrich Schelling, writings collected as *Schriften zur Identitäts-philosophie, 1801–1806*, in *Schellings Werke*, edited by M. Schröter (12 vols.; Munich, 1927–1954), vol. III; Fischer, *Geschichte der neuern Philosophie*, vol. VII, book II, parts I and III. On Schelling in general see Hermann Zeltner, *Schelling* (Stuttgart, 1954) and Emile Bréhier, *Schelling* (Paris, 1912). On the origins and character of his thought see Kurt Schilling, *Natur und Wahrheit. Untersuchung über Entstehung und Entwicklung des Schellingschen Systems bis 1800* (Munich, 1934) and especially Ernst Benz, *Schelling. Werden und Wirken seines Denkens* (Zurich, 1955). On Schelling's connections with literary romanticism see Hinrich Knittermeyer, *Schelling und die romantische Schule* (Munich, 1929). See also the illuminating commentaries of Paul Tillich, *Die religions-geschichtliche Konstruktion in Schellings positiver Philosophie, ihre Voraussetzungen und Prinzipien* (Phil. Diss.; Breslau, 1910) and *Mystik und Schuldbewusstsein in Schellings philosophischer Entwicklung* (Theol. Diss.; Halle, 1912).

8. See Schelling, writings collected as *Schriften zur Naturphilosophie, 1799–1801*, in *Werke*, vol. II; Fischer, *Geschichte der neuern Philosophie*, vol. VII, book II, part II. See also Carl Siegel, *Geschichte der deutschen Natur-philosophie* (Leipzig, 1913), chap. iv, and Alexander Gode-von Aesch, *Natural Science in German Romanticism* (New York, 1941).

9. See Schelling, *System des transzendentalen Idealismus*, in *Werke*, vol. II, and *Philosophie der Kunst*, in *Werke*, vol. III; Fisher, *Geschichte der neuern Philosophie*, vol. VII, book II, part III; Bréhier, *Schelling*, part II, chaps. iii, iv.

10. Schelling's philosophy of history has been pieced together by Georg Mehlis, *Schellings Geschichtsphilosophie in den Jahren 1799–1804* (Phil. Diss.; Heidelberg, 1906).

11. The background information on which this generalization is based is given most succinctly and accessibly in Bruford, *Germany in the Eighteenth Century*. The mode of analysis — or rather the style of thinking — employed here, as indeed throughout this chapter and in much of the rest of the book, is obviously akin to that which a Left Hegelian, including Marx, would have deemed appropriate for analyzing the world in which he lived (e.g., Marx's *German Ideology*). To indicate here as completely as possible the intellectual foundations — not to say "sources" or "documentation" — on which this book

is constructed, suffice it to point out that the approach employed represents an amalgam of the Hegelian-Marxist tradition itself with important hints and suggestions from the types of materials mentioned in notes 5, 6, and 7 above, together with such obvious modern classics of the "sociology of knowledge," as those — diverse in their aims yet related in their preoccupations and often in their methods — of Karl Mannheim, *Ideology and Utopia*, translated by Louis Wirth and Edward Shils (New York, 1936), Georg Lukács, *Geschichte und Klassenbewusstsein* (Berlin, 1923), and Max Scheler, *Die Wissensformen und die Gesellschaft. Probleme einer Soziologie des Wissens* (Leipzig, 1926). Finally, it should be equally obvious that this whole Central and Eastern European tradition has been transposed here into a more pragmatic, Anglo-Saxon mode.

12. I. S. Turgenev, *Rudin,* translated by Alex Brown (London, 1950), pp. 161–162.

13. N. P. Ogarev, "Profession de foi," in *Russkie propilei,* II, 123.

14. *B. i D.,* Lemke, XIII, 11. Chap. xxv of *Byloe i Dumy* contains Herzen's most extended discussion of his early idealism.

15. For example, V. Ia. Bogucharski (Iakovlev), *Aleksandr Ivanovich Gertsen* (St. Petersburg, 1912), chaps. i–ii, and Ivanov-Razumnik, *Obshchestvennaia mysl,* I, 255, 270–271. Among the Soviets see L. Piper, *Mirovozzrenie Gertsena* (Moscow-Leningrad, 1935), chaps. ii–iii, which is perhaps the best Soviet analysis of Herzen's philosophy; D. I. Chesnokov, *Mirovozzrenie Gertsena* (n.p., 1948), chaps. i–ii; Ia. Elsberg, *Gertsen* (Moscow, 1956), part I, chaps. ii–iv, henceforth Elsberg, *Gertsen.* All these works greatly play down the role of idealism in Herzen's youth.

16. So as not to claim the discovery of an America everyone knows is there, it should be pointed out that the role of idealism in Herzen's development has been examined in detail before, notably by Labry, in his *Herzen*. Though Labry has assembled most of the pertinent information, he takes Herzen's philosophical efforts far too literally, commenting as gravely on his "doctrine" as if it were that of Aristotle or Kant, and treating it largely out of any living political and social context. That this is a fundamental error of perspective, which distorts the significance of Herzen's intellectual career, has been ably pointed out by someone who is at the same time a philosopher and a connoisseur of Russian history, Alexandre Koyré, in an essay-review of Labry, "Alexandre Ivanovitch Herzen," in *Le monde slave*, 1931, nos. 3–4; republished in A. Koyré, *Etudes sur l'histoire de la pensée philosophique en Russie* (Paris, 1950), pp. 171–223, henceforth referred to as Koyré, *Etudes.* The most sophisticated approach to Herzen's philosophy is that of Zenkovski, *Russkaia filosofiia,* vol. I, part II, chap. vi, but Zenkovski, like Labry, tends to view Herzen too much as a technical philosopher, complete with epistemology, metaphysics, ethics, etc. The treatment which best conveys the psychological sense of Herzen's philosophy is that of George Florovski, "Iskaniia molodogo Gertsena," *Sovremennye zapiski* (Paris, 1929), XXXIX, 274–305, and XL, 335–367; however, this covers only Herzen's early years and tends too much to make of Herzen a "religious" philosopher *manqué* — as indeed does Zenkovski. For the origins of this tradition of interpretation see S. N. Bulgakov, *Dushevnaia drama Gertsena* (Kiev, 1905).

17. Herzen to T. Passek, Oct. 1828, Lemke, I, 29.

18. For Cousin's role in Russia see Labry, *Herzen,* pp. 110–111, and Koyré, *La philosophie,* pp. 131–132, 168–169.

19. Herzen to T. Passek, June 1828, Lemke, I, 25.

20. *B. i D.*, Lemke, XII, 101–104.

21. *Ibid.*, 104–105.

22. *Ibid.*, 104.

23. *Ibid.*, 106.

24. *Ibid.*, XIII, 10.

25. Herzen to T. Passek, June–July 1833, Lemke, I, 109.

26. *O zemletriaseniakh*, Lemke, I, 48–55. See also note of ed., Lemke, I, 524–525.

27. *Analiticheskoe izlozhenie solnechnoi sistemy Kopernika*, Lemke, I, 92.

28. For Cuvier see Lemke, I, 77; for de Candole see *O nedelimon v rastitelnom tsarstve*, Lemke, I, 55–60; for Linnaeus see Lemke, I, 76; for Darwin see Lemke, I, 56; for Oken see Lemke, I, 76–77.

29. *O meste cheloveka v prirode*, Lemke, I, 71–82.

30. *Ibid.*, 80.

31. *Ibid.*, 78.

32. *Ibid.*, 75.

33. *Analiticheskoe izlozhenie*, Lemke, I, 92.

34. *O meste*, Lemke, I, 81.

35. This suggestion, it seems, was first advanced by the leader of the *Liubomudry*, Prince V. F. Odoevski.

36. Heine, *De l'Allemagne depuis Luther*, in *Revue des Deux Mondes*, 15 Dec., 1834, p. 668.

37. *Ibid.*, pp. 667–668.

38. Herzen to Ogarev, 1 Aug., 1833, Lemke, I, 120–121. Almost a year earlier Ogarev, in writing to Herzen, had expressed identical sentiments about Fichte, Spinoza, and Schelling, which would indicate the persistence of the pair's preoccupation with finding one all-embracing philosophy: Ogarev to Herzen, 9 Sept., 1832, *Literaturnoe nasledstvo*, LXI, 710.

39. Herzen to N. I. Astrakov, 14 Feb., 1839, *Neizdannye pisma A. I. Gertsena k N. I. i T. A. Astrakovym*, edited by L. L. Domger (New York, 1957), p. 37, henceforth Herzen, *Pisma k Astrakovym;* these letters are also published in *Literaturnoe nasledstvo*, LXIV, 461–538.

40. See especially Setschkareff, *Schellings Einfluss*, chap. iv.

41. Koyré, *La philosophie*, especially chaps. iii–v.

42. Herzen to Ogarev, 5 June, 1833, Lemke, I, 114; 19 June, 1833, Lemke, I, 118; 1 Aug., 1833, Lemke, I, 121; 7–8 Aug., 1833, Lemke, I, 127.

43. I. V. Kireevski, "Deviatnadtsaty vek," in *Polnoe sobranie sochineni*, edited by M. O. Gershenzon (2 vols.; Moscow, 1911), I, 85–108. See also Koyré, *La philosophie*, chap. vi, and N. Dorn, *Kireevski. Opyt kharakteristiki ucheniia i lichnosti* (Paris, 1938), chap. iii. For Herzen's enthusiastic comments on Kireevski's article several years later see his *Dnevnik*, 21 Dec., 1843, Lemke, III, 148.

44. *28 Ianvaria*, Lemke, I, 85.

45. *Ibid.*

46. *Ibid.*, 86.

47. *Ibid.*, 87.

48. *Ibid.*

49. *Ibid.*, 87–88.

50. *Ibid.*, 88.

51. *Ibid.*

52. *Ibid.*, 90.

CHAPTER SIX

Saint-Simon and Socialism

1. "Kommentari no. 15" of ed. to part II of *B. i D.*, Lemke, XII, 347.
2. *B. i D.*, Lemke, XII, 196–202.
3. *O meste cheloveka v prirode*, Lemke, I, 71. Herzen says *B.* Rodrigues. This is doubtless a mistake for *Eugène* Rodrigues, one of the more mystical of Saint-Simon's followers, who was also influenced by German idealism.
4. *B. i D.*, Lemke, XII, 125.
5. *Ibid.*, 151.
6. *Ibid.*, 151–152.
7. *Ibid.*, 152.
8. This would explain why Herzen's first mention of the Saint-Simonians comes in late 1832 (see note 3 above). Moreover, it checks with the rather vague passage already cited in *B. i D.*, Lemke, XII, 151. On Herzen's Saint-Simonian period in general see especially P. N. Sakulin, *Russkaia literatura i sotsializm* (2nd rev. ed.; Moscow, 1924), pp. 106–117, henceforth referred to as Sakulin, *Literatura i sotsializm*, and G. V. Plekhanov, "A. I. Gertsen i krepostnoe pravo," in *Sochineniia* (24 vols.; Moscow-Leningrad, 1923–1927), XXIII, 269–353, henceforth Plekhanov, *Sochineniia*.
9. Herzen to Ogarev, 19 July, 1833, Lemke, I, 117.
10. This is true notably of older writers such as Sakulin, *Literatura i sotsializm*, and Ch. Vetrinski, *Gertsen* (St. Petersburg, 1908). Rather more imaginative treatments of Herzen's social thought are given by Iu. M. Steklov, *A. I. Gertsen* (2nd ed.; Petrograd, 1923) — which exists also in a German version, *A. I. Herzen: eine Biographie* (Berlin, 1920) — and by M. O. Gershenzon, *Sotsialno-politicheskie vzgliady Gertsena* (Moscow, 1906). See also V. I. Vodovozov, *A. I. Gertsen* (Petrograd, 1920).
11. For example, most of the standard histories of socialism, such as Harry W. Laidler, *Social Economic Movements* (New York, 1944, originally entitled *A History of Socialist Thought*, 1927); Alexander Gray, *The Socialist Tradition* (London, 1946); G. D. H. Cole, *A History of Socialist Thought* (5 vols.; London, 1953–1960), (for purposes of the present discussion see especially vol. I, *The Forerunners, 1789–1850*); Max Beer, *Allgemeine Geschichte des Sozialismus und der sozialen Kämpfe* (6th ed.; Berlin, 1929), especially part IV, 1750–1860. An interesting and thoughtful attempt to define socialism is by Emile Durkheim, "Définition du socialisme," in *Revue de métaphysique et de morale*, XXVIII (July–Sept. and Oct.–Dec., 1921), 479–495, 591–614.
12. The genealogy of the idea that revolutionary socialism reflects economic backwardness begins implicitly with Bernstein and the German revisionists, who discovered that a parliament and trade-unions can make violence unnecessary. This trend became more apparent in the Russian "Legal" Marxists, such as Struve, and the Mensheviks, such as Martov and Plekhanov, who had to explain, first the appearance of socialism, and then the success of Bolshevism, in Russia in spite of the fact that according to Marxism the country was not yet ripe for a proletarian revolution. See in particular Iu. O. Martov, *Istoriia rossiiskoi sotsial-demokratii* (3rd ed.; Petrograd, 1923); Iu. O. Martov, *Zapiski sotsial-demokrata* (Berlin, 1922); F. I. Dan (Gurvich), *Proiskhozhdenie bolshevizma* (New York, 1946); or for a similar tradition reflected in English, Selig Perlman, *A Theory of the Labor Movement* (New York, 1928). The idea

of backwardness is also strong in Lenin's theory of "imperialism" and Trotsky's "law of combined developments."

13. For the theory of Marxism and anarchism expressed here see Adam B. Ulam, "The Historical Role of Marxism and the Soviet System," in *World Politics*, VIII (Oct. 1955), 20–45; for the remarks on Saint-Simonism and related tendencies see Alexander Gerschenkron, "Economic Backwardness in Historical Perspective," in B. F. Hoselitz, ed., *The Progress of Underdeveloped Areas* (Chicago, 1952), pp. 3–29.

14. So far as I know the idea that socialism is the reaction to an old regime has been suggested (but not elaborated) only by Louis Hartz in *The Liberal Tradition in America* (New York, 1955), though it may well appear elsewhere.

15. Gerschenkron, "Backwardness," in *The Progress of Underdeveloped Areas*; Emile Durkheim, *Le socialisme; sa définition, ses débuts, la doctrine saint-simonienne* (Paris, 1928); Maxime Leroy, *La véritable vie du Comte Henri de Saint-Simon* (Paris, 1925); Sébastien Charléty, *Histoire du saint-simonisme 1825–1864* (2nd ed.; Paris, 1931).

16. See Hubert Bourgin, *Fourier* (Paris, 1905) and Charles Gide, *Fourier, précurseur de la co-opération* (Paris, 1923).

17. The best general survey of the beginnings of socialism in France is Maxime Leroy, *Histoire des idées sociales en France* (3 vols.; Paris, 1946–1954), especially vols. II and III. See also George Weill, *Histoire du parti républicain en France de 1814 à 1870* (Paris, 1900); Célestin Bouglé, *Socialismes français* (Paris, 1932); Gaston Isambert, *Les idées socialistes en France de 1815 à 1848* (Paris, 1905); J. P. Plamenatz, *The Revolutionary Movement in France, 1815–71* (London, 1952); O. K. Hertzler, *History of Utopian Thought* (New York, 1923); D. O. Evans, *Social Romanticism in France, 1830–1848* (Oxford, 1951).

18. Carl Grünberg, "Der Ursprung der Worte 'Sozialismus' und 'Sozialist,'" in *Archiv für die Geschichte des Sozialismus und der Arbeiterbewegung*, II (1912), 372–379; A. E. Bestor, Jr., "The Evolution of the Socialist Vocabulary," in *Journal of the History of Ideas*, IX (June 1948), 259–302.

19. Lenin, *Sochineniia*, V, 347.

20. In addition to the works on socialism mentioned in notes 11 through 18 above, see the useful manual by D. D. Egbert and S. Persons, eds., *Socialism and American Life* (2 vols.; Princeton, 1952); vol. II is taken up entirely with an excellent bibliography which includes Europe as well as America (see especially part I). Yet little of the vast literature on socialism goes beyond rather superficial description. Some of the more sophisticated analytical works devoted wholly or partially to socialism are: Werner Sombart, *Sozialismus und soziale Bewegung* (6th rev. ed.; Jena, 1908), translated by M. Epstein as *Socialism and the Social Movement* (London, 1909); Werner Sombart, *Der proletarische Sozialismus* (2 vols.; Jena, 1924), an extended reworking of the preceding; Gustav Schmoller, *Die soziale Frage* (Munich-Leipzig, 1918); Ferdinand Tönnies, *Gemeinschaft und Gesellschaft* (3rd rev. ed.; Berlin, 1920), translated and supplemented by C. P. Loomis as *Fundamental Concepts of Sociology* (New York-Cincinnati, 1940) and as *Community and Society* (Ann Arbor, 1957); Vilfredo Pareto, *Les systèmes socialistes* (2 vols.: Paris, 1902–1903); Karl Diehl, *Ueber Sozialismus, Kommunismus und Anarchismus* (4th rev. ed.; Jena, 1922), especially parts I and II; the already mentioned Karl Mannheim, *Ideology and Utopia*, and Henry de Man, *The Psychology of*

Socialism. However, these works are for the most part concerned with socialism as it developed under industrial conditions in the West, and hence are only of indirect relevance to Russian Populism. Among the numerous works on the latter, by far the most comprehensive and impressive is Franco Venturi, *Il populismo russo* (2 vols.; Turin, 1952), translated by Francis Haskell as *Roots of Revolution* (New York, 1960). Venturi's approach is to present all Populist thought, including Herzen's, as the result of reasoned reflection on objective social and political conditions, both in Europe and in Russia, and in particular on the plight of the Russian peasant. The approach of the present book is clearly the opposite: that is, to seek the source of Populism in the subjective reactions of the intelligentsia to the pressures generated by its own — not the peasants' — position in Russian society. For still another point of view which accords greater significance than is done here to external, particularly economic, factors in the intelligentsia's motivation, see Alexander Gerschenkron, "The Problem of Economic Development in Russian Intellectual History of the Nineteenth Century," in E. J. Simmons, ed., *Continuity and Change in Russian and Soviet Thought* (Cambridge, Mass., 1955), pp. 11–39.

21. Ogarev to Herzen, 3–4 Sept., 1832, *Literaturnoe nasledstvo*, LXI, 706.

22. *Ibid.*, 706–708.

23. *Ibid.*, 709.

24. Herzen to Ogarev, 1–2 Aug., 1833, Lemke, I, 121.

25. *Ibid.*

26. Ogarev to Herzen, 3–4 Sept., 1832, *Literaturnoe nasledstvo*, LXI, 708.

27. For a full account of Herzen's ambivalent reactions to America see David Hecht, *Russian Radicals Look to America 1825–1894* (Cambridge, Mass., 1947), chaps. ii–iii and M. M. Laserson, *The American Impact on Russia — Diplomatic and Ideological — 1784–1917* (New York, 1950), pp. 205–236.

28. Herzen to Ogarev, 19 July, 1833, Lemke, I, 117.

29. Ogarev to Herzen, 29–30 July, 1833, *Literaturnoe nasledstvo*, LXI, 716–717.

30. Herzen to Ogarev, 1–2 Aug., 1833, Lemke, I, 120–121.

31. For the influence of Guizot and the French historical school of the Restoration in Russia during the thirties see P. N. Miliukov, *Glavnye techeniia russkoi istoricheskoi mysli* (3rd ed.; St. Petersburg, 1913), pp. 294–342.

32. See Koyré, *La philosophie,* chaps. v–vi.

33. Herzen to Ogarev, 7 or 8 Aug., 1833, Lemke, I, 126–127.

34. *Ibid.*, 127.

35. *Ibid.*

36. Herzen to Ogarev, 31 Aug., 1833, Lemke, I, 128–129.

37. Ogarev to Herzen, 29–30 July, 1833, *Literaturnoe nasledstvo*, LXI, 716. See also note to same, p. 704; Lakhtin's only surviving letter to Ogarev on the philosophy of history is in *Literaturnoe nasledstvo*, LXIII (Moscow, 1956), 294–296.

38. "Kommentari no. 15" of ed. to part II of *B. i D.* (the proceedings of Herzen's trial), Lemke, XII, 346–347.

39. *B. i D.*, Lemke, XII, 153. See Kozmin, *Polevoi*, pp. 467–490 for Herzen's full relations with Polevoi.

40. *Plan izdaniia zhurnala*, Lemke, I, 135.

41. *Ibid.*, 135, 137.

42. *Ibid.*, 135.

43. *B. i D.*, Lemke, XII, 429–430; Passek, *Iz dalnikh let*, I, 460–463, this time rather untrustworthy; *3 avgusta 1833*, Lemke, I, 122–124, dedicated to Liudmila and a specimen of Herzen's most romantic prose.

44. "Kommentari no. 15" of ed. to part II of *B. i D.*, Lemke, XII, 347 (proceedings of Herzen's trial).

45. *Pisma iz Frantsii i Italii*, Lemke, VI, 99.

CHAPTER SEVEN

Arrest and Exile

1. The Kritski affair was first discussed publicly by P. A. Efremov in Herzen's own *Poliarnaia zvezda* (1862), book VII, no. 1; it was set forth in detail on the basis of archival material by M. K. Lemke, *Byloe* (1906), book VI. For Herzen's knowledge of Polezhaev, see *B. i D.*, Lemke, XII, 154–157.

2. Ia. I. Kostenetski, "Vospominaniia iz moei studencheskoi zhizni, 1828–1833," in *Russki arkhiv* (1887), nos. 1–3, 5–6; B. Eikhenbaum, "Delo Sungurova," in *Zavety* (1913), books III–IV; I. A. Fedosov, "Revoliutsionnye kruzhki v Rossii kontsa dvadtsatykh i nachala tridtsatykh godov," in *Istoricheskie zapiski* (1957), no. 59. See in general, V. I. Orlov, *Studencheskoe dvizhenie moskovskogo universiteta v XIX stoletii* (Moscow, 1934), chap. ii.

3. *B. i D.*, Lemke, XII, 136–137.

4. "Kommentari no. 15" of ed. to part II of *B. i D.*, Lemke, XII, 334–335.

5. "Kommentari no. 1" of ed. to part II of *B. i D.*, Lemke, XII, 322–328.

6. *B. i D.*, Lemke, XII, 214–215.

7. *Ibid.*, 210, 219–220, 223;· Herzen to Natalie, 8 Feb., 1835, Lemke, I, 166.

8. "Kommentari no. 15" of ed. to part II of *B. i D.* (record of Herzen's trial), Lemke, XII, 357.

9. *Ibid.*, 335.

10. *B. i D.*, Lemke, XII, 228–229.

11. "Kommentari no. 15" of ed. to part II of *B. i D.*, Lemke, XII, 335–351.

12. *B. i D.*, Lemke, XII, 230; "Kommentari no. 15" of ed., Lemke, XII, 354–355.

13. *Ibid.*, 357–359; 366; *B. i D.*, Lemke, XII, 235–236.

14. *Ibid.*, 432–433.

15. The chapters of *My Past and Thoughts* devoted to Herzen's exile are more than usually distorted in the light of his later role as spokesman for the Russian revolution. This has been admirably demonstrated by one of the few close checks made of the memoirs against earlier material. See Monica Partridge, "The Young Herzen: A Contribution to the Russian Period of Herzen's Biography," in *University of Nottingham, Renaissance and Modern Studies*, I (1957), 154–179. Miss Partridge shows conclusively that Herzen, far from acting the rebel during his government service in exile, on the whole played the game according to the rules. However, she goes too far in implying that a brilliant government career became his chief professional goal. That this was not the case is demonstrated by the social radicalism of his writings in Vladimir, discussed in Chap. IX below. For further details on Herzen's government service in exile, see *Zvenia* (Moscow-Leningrad), VI (1936), 313–337, and VIII (1950), 61–86.

16. *B. i D.*, Lemke, XII, 263–264, 285, 309, 318–319.

17. Herzen to Ketcher and Sazonov, 18 July, 1835, Lemke, I, 189–190. See also "Statisticheskie raboty Gertsena v Viatke," *Literaturnoe nasledstvo,* XXXIX–XL, 172–184.

18. *Otdelnye zamechaniia o russkom zakonodatelstve,* Lemke, I, 368–371.

19. This is hinted at in his *Ispoved* (Confession), M. A. Bakunin, ed. Iu. Steklov, *Sobranie sochineni i pisem* (only 4 vols. published; Moscow, 1934–1935), IV, 99–207, henceforth referred to as Bakunin, *Sochineniia* (Steklov). This idea is stated openly in his *Narodnoe delo. Romanov, Pugachev, ili Pestel?* (London, Free Russian Press, 1862).

20. Belinski to K. D. Kavelin, 22 Nov., 1847 and his letter to P. B. Annenkov, beginning of Dec. 1847, *Belinski, Pisma,* edited by E. A. Liatski (3 vols.; St. Petersburg, 1914), III, 297–303, and 313–321, henceforth referred to as Belinski, *Pisma.*

21. *Pismo iz provintsii,* Herzen, *Sochineniia v tridtsati tomakh,* I, 132.

22. *Ibid.,* 133.

23. Herzen to Ketcher and Sazonov, 18 July, 1835, Lemke, I, 190.

24. *Vtoraia vstrecha* (written 1836), Lemke, I, 233.

25. *B. i D.,* Lemke, XII, 256.

26. *Ibid.,* 269.

27. *Ibid.,* 259–260.

28. *Ibid.,* 311. For the full career of Tiufiaev told on the basis of documentary material see "Kommentari no. 21" of ed. to part II of *B. i D.,* Lemke, XII, 367–380.

29. *B. i D.,* Lemke, XII, 269.

30. *Ibid.,* 268.

31. *Ibid.,* 314–315.

32. *Ibid.,* 271.

33. *Ibid.,* 263–264.

34. *Ibid.,* 270–293, *passim,* and 252–253.

35. Herzen to Natalie, 6 June, 1835, Lemke, I, 179.

36. *B. i D.,* Lemke, XII, 269.

37. *Ibid.,* 253.

38. *Ibid.,* 249–251; *Vtoraia vstrecha,* Lemke, I, 230–237.

39. *B. i D.,* Lemke, XII, 263–264.

40. Herzen to Natalie, 5 Dec., 1836, Lemke, I, 357.

41. Herzen to Natalie, 24–26 Feb., 1838, Lemke, II, 98–99.

42. Herzen to Natalie, 20–22 July, 1836, Lemke, I, 308.

43. Herzen to Natalie, 24–26 Feb., 1838, Lemke, II, 96–97.

44. *B. i D.,* Lemke, XII, 263 ff.; Herzen to Natalie, 12 Nov., 1835, Lemke, I, 203; Herzen to Ketcher, 22 Nov., 1835, Lemke, I, 205–206.

45. The aristocratic character of Herzen's outlook was first emphasized by Kirik Levin, *A. I. Gertsen, lichnost-ideologiia* (2nd ed.; Moscow, 1922). This is also a theme of Peter Scheibert, *Von Bakunin zu Lenin* (3 vols. planned; Leiden, 1956–), vol. I, chaps. vii, xiv, xviii. Indeed, Scheibert essentially derives Herzen's politics, as well as the utopian temper of the nascent intelligentsia in general, from the distortion of this aristocratic mentality by the gentry's alienation from the masses and the state alike. He does so, however, in a manner that is far more sweeping and direct than that followed in this book.

CHAPTER EIGHT

Love and Religion

1. Herzen to Natalie, 5 Dec., 1835, Lemke, I, 209.

2. *Pervaia vstrecha* (original title *Germanski puteshestvennik,* written 1835, revised 1836), Lemke, I, 286–300.

3. *Ibid.,* 297, 295, 299–300. Similar sentiments are expressed in an untitled essay of 1833, Lemke, I, 110–113. All this is in part a reflection of the attacks of "Young Germany" against its apolitical elders. See Lemke, I, 142, 294 for reference to the controversy aroused by Wolfgang Menzel's praise of the "Olympian" Goethe together with his attacks on Schiller and especially on such younger poets as Heine and Börne.

4. For Pascal see *Pervaia vstrecha,* Lemke, I, 297, and Herzen to Ketcher and Sazonov, 22 Sept., 1836, Lemke, I, 325. Imagery from the Gospels is scattered throughout Herzen's letters for this period, e.g., Herzen to Natalie, 21 Feb., 1835, Lemke, I, 167.

5. Dante indeed was his preferred author in prison and exile, and reference to the poet is well-nigh constant down to Herzen's marriage in 1838. See especially an autobiographical fragment on his arrest and exile, Lemke, I, 180–186, later largely incorporated in *B. i D.,* Lemke, XII, 239–245. This example, among others, shows that in writing the sections of *Byloe i Dumy* relative to his exile Herzen had before him a number of his youthful letters and essays and hence that what he says is not just the product of memory with all its distortions. Compare, for example, his joke about the "horror" he felt when his provincial landlady in Perm "suspected him of being capable of keeping his own cow," *B. i D.,* Lemke, XII, 247, with a similar remark in his letter to Natalie, 29 April, 1835, Lemke, I, 176.

6. Herzen to Natalie, 10 Dec., 1834, Lemke, I, 160.

7. *Ibid.*

8. *Legenda* (1836), Lemke, I, 237–259.

9. *Ibid.,* 248.

10. *B. i D.,* Lemke, XII, 264.

11. All this is passed over in silence in *Byloe i Dumy.* But Herzen's despair and his frustrating efforts to find companionship in Viatka are clear from his letters at the time. See Herzen to Natalie, 6 June, 1835, Lemke, I, 178–179; 25 June, 1835, Lemke, I, 186; 24 July, 1835, Lemke, I, 187; 7 Aug., 1835, Lemke, I, 192; 12 Nov., 1835, Lemke, I, 203; Herzen to Ketcher and Sazonov, 18 July, 1835, Lemke, I, 188–189.

12. Herzen to Natalie, March 1835, Lemke, I, 170. For similar chronic daydreaming a few months later in Viatka see Herzen to Natalie, 6 June, 1835, Lemke, I, 178–179.

13. For example, Herzen to Natalie, 28 February, 1836, Lemke, I, 228.

14. See above Chap. VI, fourth section.

15. For example, Herzen to Natalie, 1 Oct., 1835, Lemke, I, 195; 5 Dec., 1835, Lemke, I, 209. In the first of these letters Herzen reproaches himself rather theatrically for his abandonment of Liudmila.

16. *B. i D.,* Lemke, XII, 433–441.

17. *Ibid.,* 418–430. Herzen's account here is not to be seriously questioned

since it is based, not only on what Natalie told him of her childhood, but also on her letters to him during the thirties, which Herzen kept and from which he quotes in *Byloe i Dumy*. All of Natalie's letters to Herzen are published in an early edition of his works, *Sochineniia A. I. Gertsena i perepiska s N. A. Zakharinoi* (7 vols.; St. Petersburg, 1905), vol. VII, henceforth referred to as Herzen, *Sochineniia* (1905).

18. *B. i D.*, Lemke, XII, 420.

19. *Ibid.*, 424.

20. Natalie to Herzen, 24 Sept., 1835, Herzen, *Sochineniia* (1905), VII, 34–35.

21. *B. i D.*, Lemke, XII, 202–203.

22. *Ibid.*, 238; Herzen to Natalie, 10 April, 1835, Lemke, I, 173.

23. Herzen to Natalie, 12–14 Oct., 1835, Lemke, I, 201.

24. Natalie to Herzen, 27 Oct., 1835, Herzen, *Sochineniia* (1905), VII, 40–41.

25. Herzen to Natalie, 25 Dec., 1835, Lemke, I, 212.

26. Herzen to Natalie, 12 Nov., 1835, Lemke, I, 204. The same sentiments and the same verses (from Victor Hugo) are repeated in his letter to Natalie, 5 Dec., 1835, Lemke, I, 209.

27. Herzen to Natalie, 19 June–1 July, 1836, Lemke, I, 300–301.

28. *Ibid.*, 302.

29. Natalie to Herzen, 8–26 May, 1836, Herzen, *Sochineniia* (1905), VII, 90. Herzen adopted the idea of "saving Medvedeva" in his letter cited in the previous note.

30. Herzen to Natalie, 6–9 April, 1838, Lemke, II, 157.

31. *Ibid.*

32. *B. i D.*, Lemke, XII, 447. Herzen here even had the tasteless reaction, more than twenty years after the affair, to note with flattered astonishment that Medvedeva had been buried in the New Monastery of the Virgin (*Novodevichi monastir*, one of the most important cemeteries of Moscow), almost where he had buried her in his tale *Elena*.

33. *Elena*, Lemke, II, 45–73; *B. i D.*, Lemke, XII, 447. In his memoirs Herzen gives the story a happy ending, no doubt to make himself feel better about the whole affair: "From the windows of the convent words of prayer are heard; soft feminine voices sing of absolution — the young nobleman is cured." The psychological analysis of Herzen's love given in this chapter owes a significant debt to F. Seeley, "Herzen's 'Dantean Period'," *The Slavonic and East European Review* (Dec. 1954), pp. 44–74.

34. Natalie to Herzen, 24–25 March, 1834, Herzen, *Sochineniia* (1905), VII, 531.

35. Herzen to Natalie, 9–14 April, 1837, Lemke, I, 407–408.

36. Herzen to Natalie, 21–23 Sept., 1836, Lemke, I, 327.

37. Herzen to Natalie, 14–16 Aug., 1836, Lemke, I, 312.

38. Herzen to Natalie, 25–26 Aug., 1836, Lemke, I, 318.

39. Herzen to Natalie, 18–28 Oct., 1836, Lemke, I, 244; the remark on Judas is in *Otdelnye mysli* (1836), Lemke, I, 341.

40. *B. i D.*, Lemke, XII, 239; Lemke, I, 182, 184; Herzen to Ketcher and Sazonov, 18 July, 1835, Lemke, I, 191.

41. Herzen to Natalie, 29 Sept., 1836, Lemke, I, 329.

42. Herzen to Natalie, 13–20 Jan., 1837, Lemke, I, 381–382.

43. Herzen to Natalie, 17–21 April, 1837, Lemke, I, 411.

44. Herzen to Natalie, 9–14 April, 1837, Lemke, I, 408.
45. Herzen to Natalie, 30 March–3 April, 1838, Lemke, II, 144–145.
46. *Ibid.*, 143.
47. Herzen to Natalie, 25 Aug., 1836, Lemke, I, 318.
48. Herzen to Natalie, 10–14 Oct., 1836, Lemke, I, 336.
49. Herzen to Natalie, 10 Feb., and 14–17 Feb., 1837, Lemke, I, 386 and 388.
50. Herzen to Natalie, 19 Jan., 1838, Lemke, II, 27; and 25 Nov., 1835, Lemke, I, 208.
51. Herzen to Natalie, 9–14 April, 1837, Lemke, I, 408–409.
52. Herzen to A. L. Witberg, 7 April, 1838, Lemke, II, 156.
53. Herzen to Natalie, 20–22 July, 1836, Lemke, I, 309.
54. Herzen to Natalie, 24–26 Feb., 1838, Lemke, II, 98–99.
55. *B. i D.*, Lemke, XII, 295, 299.
56. *Zapiski A. L. Vitberga,* in Herzen, *Sochineniia v tridtsati tomakh,* I, 380–451.
57. *B. i D.*, Lemke, XII, 295.
58. "Akademik A. L. Vitberg i ego pisma k A. I. Gertsenu," in *Russkaia starina* (Nov. 1897), pp. 477–495.
59. Herzen to Ketcher and Sazonov, Oct.–Nov., 1836, Lemke, I, 339.
60. Herzen to Ketcher and Sazonov, 22 Sept., 1836, Lemke, I, 325.
61. *Ibid.*
62. Herzen to Ketcher and Sazonov, 18 July, 1835, Lemke, I, 191.
63. Herzen to Natalie, 4–11 Oct., 1837, Lemke, I, 479.
64. Herzen to Natalie, 30 April–5 May, 1837, Lemke, I, 416–417.
65. Herzen to Natalie, 5 Jan., 1838, Lemke, II, 8.
66. Herzen to Natalie, beginning of Sept. 1837, Lemke, I, 460–461.
67. Herzen to Natalie, 5–8 March, 1838, Lemke, II, 114. In another place he says that he has bid goodbye to his "dreams of fame, of a career, of [political] activity," in other words all that he had lived for at the university; Herzen to Natalie, 5 Jan., 1838, Lemke, II, 8.
68. Herzen to Natalie, 7–8 Jan., 1838, Lemke, II, 10.
69. Herzen to Natalie, 29 Sept., 1836, Lemke, I, 327–328. Herzen also at times expressed the wish that at the moment of their marriage the two of them might die before the altar, to be reunited in eternal if immaterial bliss.
70. *Ibid.*
71. *Eto bylo 22-go oktiabria 1817,* Lemke, I, 482–485.
72. Herzen to Natalie, 4–11 Aug., 1837, Lemke, I, 452–453.
73. See Annenkov, "Stankevich," in *Vospominaniia,* vol. III; Miliukov, "Liubov u idealistov tridtsatikh godov," in *Russkaia intelligentsiia,* pp. 73–81. Miliukov's discussion of Herzen's romance (pp. 116–168) is less successful since he takes the latter's rationalizations of his sentiments too literally.
74. For the triangle involving Belinski, Bakunin, and the latter's sister see Miliukov, *ibid.*, pp. 81–116. But the best account is Carr, *Bakunin,* chaps. iv–vi.
75. Ogarev to his wife, 23 April, 1836, in M. O. Gershenzon, "Liubov N. P. Ogareva," in *Obrazy proshlogo* (Moscow, 1912), p. 341, henceforth referred to as Gershenzon, *Obrazy proshlogo.* "Liubov N. P. Ogareva" is composed chiefly of excerpts from Ogarev's correspondence with Maria Lvovna. It is the principal source for Ogarev's life in the late thirties and the early forties, and together with Herzen's letters to Natalie the most noteworthy — as well

as the saddest — romantic correspondence of the age. The story of Ogarev's love has been told in English by E. H. Carr in *The Romantic Exiles* (London, 1933), chap. vii, henceforth referred to as Carr, *Romantic Exiles*. For this reason fuller discussion has been omitted here.

76. See Charles Quénet, *Tchaadaev et les Lettres Philosophiques* (Paris, 1931); M. O. Gershenzon, *P. Ia. Chaadaev. Zhizn i myshlenie* (St. Petersburg, 1908).

77. See Annenkov, "Stankevich," in *Vospominaniia*, vol. III; Miliukov, "Liubov u idealistov," in *Russkaia intelligentsiia*, pp. 73–81.

78. *B. i D.*, Lemke, XII, 310.

79. *Ibid.*, 448–457.

80. Herzen to Natalie, 26 Feb.–1 March, 1838, Lemke, II, 100.

81. *B. i D.*, Lemke, XII, 458–474. See also Herzen's letters for early 1838.

82. *B. i D.*, Lemke, XII, 475, 480–481.

83. Herzen to N. I. and T. A. Astrakov, 15–19 March, 1839, Lemke, II, 234. Almost twenty years later Herzen was still so moved by the memory of this scene that he did not shrink from reproducing it in his memoirs; *B. i D.*, Lemke, XIII, 6.

84. Herzen to Ogarev, 21 March–27 April, 1838, Lemke, II, 261.

85. *B. i D.*, Lemke, XII, 75.

86. *Ibid.*, XIII, 6.

87. *Ibid.*, 11.

88. Herzen to T. Passek, Oct. 1828, Lemke, I, 26–30.

89. See the description of the aged functionary in *Elena*, Lemke, II, 45–49. The duality of Herzen's intellectual style has been noted by one of the most perceptive critics of Russian literature to write in this century, Dmitri Mirski: "Though the content of his [later] ideas was materialistic and scientific, their tone and flavor always remained romantic." *A History of Russian Literature From the Earliest Times to the Death of Dostoevsky* (New York, 1934), pp. 273–274.

90. *Zapiski odnogo molodogo cheloveka*, Lemke, II, 381.

91. *B. i D.*, Lemke, XII, 1.

CHAPTER NINE

Quest for Reality

1. Bakunin, *Sochineniia* (Steklov), III, 369. See Benôit-P. Hepner, *Bakounine et le panslavisme révolutionnaire* (Paris, 1950), parts III and IV for one of the best accounts of the philosophical aspects of Bakunin's and Belinski's revolt against idealism. See also D. I. Chizhevski, *Gegel v Rossii* (Paris, 1939), chaps. v. and vi, henceforth referred to as Chizhevski, *Gegel*. This work exists also in a German version, *Hegel in Russland* (Prague, 1934).

2. *Ocherki po istorii russkoi zhurnalistiki i kritiki* (Leningrad, 1950), p. 290; A. G. Dementev, *Ocherki po istorii russkoi zhurnalistiki 1840–1850 gg.* (Moscow-Leningrad, 1951), p. 61, henceforth, Dementev, *Russkaia zhurnalistika*.

3. Herzen to A. L. Witberg, May 1838, Lemke, II, 196.

4. Herzen to Ketcher, 4 Dec., 1838, Lemke, II, 226.

5. Herzen to A. L. Witberg, 8 Dec., 1838, Lemke, III, 228.

6. Herzen to Ketcher, 4 Oct., 1838, Lemke, II, 223.

7. Herzen to Ketcher, 20 Aug., 1838, Lemke, II, 203.

8. *Ibid.*

9. Herzen to Ketcher, 7 Feb., 1839, Lemke, II, 239.

10. Herzen to Ketcher, 28 Feb., 1839, Lemke, II, 243.

11. Herzen to Ketcher, 7 Feb., 1839, Lemke, II, 239–240.

12. *Ibid.*, and Herzen to Ketcher, 28 Feb., 1839, Lemke, II, 242.

13. *Ibid.*, and Herzen to Ketcher, 16 March, 1839, Lemke, II, 245.

14. Herzen to Ketcher, 7 Feb., 1839, Lemke, II, 240. See Barchou de Penhoën, *Histoire de la philosophie allemande depuis Leibnitz jusqu'à Hegel* (2 vols.; Paris, 1836).

15. Herzen to Ketcher, 28 Feb., 1839, Lemke, II, 242.

16. Herzen to A. L. Witberg, 24 Nov., 1838, Lemke, II, 223.

17. Herzen to Ketcher, 16 March, 1839, Lemke, II, 244.

18. Herzen to A. L. Witberg, 23 March, 1839, Lemke, II, 258.

19. Herzen to N. I. Astrakov, 14 Feb., 1839, Herzen, *Pisma k Astrakovym*, p. 37.

20. *Ibid.*

21. Herzen to Ketcher, 20 Aug., 1838, Lemke, II, 203.

22. *Ibid.*

23. Herzen to A. L. Witberg, 8 Dec., 1838, Lemke, II, 227.

24. Herzen to Ketcher, 7 Feb., and 27 June, 1839, Lemke, II, 239, and 273. The documents in question were those published by Pierre Fenin as *Mémoires relatifs à l'histoire de France*.

25. Herzen to Ketcher, 28 Feb., 1839, Lemke, II, 243.

26. Herzen to Ketcher, 16 March, 1839, Lemke, II, 246; Herzen to N. I. Astrakov, 14 Jan., 1839, Herzen, *Pisma k Astrakovym*, p. 35.

27. Herzen to Ketcher, 7 Feb., 1839, Lemke, II, 240; Herzen to T. A. Astrakov, 18 April, 1839, Lemke, II, 260.

28. Herzen to Ketcher, 16 March, 1839, Lemke, II, 244–245.

29. *"Litsini"* i *"Viliam Pen." Scenario dvukh dramaticheskikh opytov,* Lemke, II, 205–208. *Litsini* (*otryvok*), Lemke, II, 211–222. The Licinius theme (without, of course, the political use that Herzen made of it) was fairly frequent in eighteenth century literature, both Western and Russian. Pushkin also has a poem on the subject, and this may well have been one of Herzen's models.

30. *Litsini* (*otryvok*), Lemke, II, 211–212.

31. *Ibid.*, 221.

32. *Ibid.*

33. Herzen to Ketcher, 4 Oct., 1838, Lemke, II, 223.

34. Herzen to Ketcher, 28 Feb., 1839, Lemke, II, 243.

35. Herzen to A. L. Witberg, 18 April, 1839, Lemke, II, 258.

36. Herzen to Ogarev, 21 March–27 April, 1839, Lemke, II, 262.

37. *Ibid.*

38. *Viliam Pen* (*Stseny v stikhakh*), Lemke, II, 277.

39. *Ibid.*, 279.

40. *Ibid.*, 279–280.

41. *Ibid.*, 304.

42. *Ibid.*, 302–303.

43. *"Litsini"* i *"Viliam Pen." Scenario dvukh dramaticheskikh opytov,* Lemke, II, 211.

44. Herzen to Ketcher, 4 Oct., 1838, Lemke, II, 223.

45. Herzen to Ogarev, 21 March–27 April, 1839, Lemke, II, 262.

46. Herzen to A. L. Witberg, 28 July, 1839, Lemke, II, 274.

47. See August Cieszkowski, *Prolegomena zur Historiosophie* (2nd ed.; Posen, 1908. First published, Berlin, 1838); Walter Kühne, *Graf August Cieszkowski, ein Schüler Hegels und des deutschen Geistes* (vol. 20 of *Veröffentlichungen des Slavischen Instituts an der Friedrich-Wilhelms-Universität Berlin* (Leipzig, 1938); Gustav Shpet, *Filosofskoe mirovozzrenie Gertsena* (Petrograd, 1921), appendix I, pp. 76–80; Labry, *Herzen*, pp. 202–206.

48. Ogarev, "Kavkazskie vody," in *Izbrannye*, I, 406.

49. *Ibid.*, 407.

50. *Ibid.*, 410.

51. Ogarev to Herzen, 1838, probably toward the end of the year, "Iz perepiski nedavnikh deiatelei," *Russkaia mysl* (1888), book IX, pp. 11–15; partially reproduced in Ogarev, *Izbrannye*, II, 294–299. This letter in effect is a new version of the "system," first set forth in Ogarev's "Profession de foi," *Russkie propilei*, II, 111–142.

52. Ogarev to Herzen, 7–8 Jan., 1839, "Iz perepiski nedavnikh deiatelei," *Russkaia mysl* (1888), book X, pp. 10–11.

53. See above, Chap. VIII, seventh section.

54. *Dnevnik*, Jan., 1839, II, 266.

55. See above, Chap. VI, fourth section.

56. Ogarev to Herzen, 1838, "Iz perepiski nedavnikh deiatelei," in *Russkaia mysl* (1888), book IX, p. 16; also Ogarev, *Izbrannye*, II, 299. Ogarev says: "You have written your system and want to go abroad and proclaim it to men, because at home you are not allowed to speak." This is the first hint in Herzen's life of the idea that later developed into the Free Russian Press and *Kolokol*.

57. Note of ed., Lemke, II, 343.

58. *B. i D.*, Lemke, XIII, 38–39.

59. *Ibid.*, 11.

60. See above, Chap. IX, third section.

61. Ogarev to Herzen, late 1839, "Iz perepiski nedavnikh deiatelei," in *Russkaia mysl* (1888), book XI, p. 5.

62. *B. i D.*, Lemke, XIII, 11–12.

63. *Ibid.*, 12–14.

64. *Ibid.*, 12.

65. "Gimnazicheskie rechi Gegelia," April 1838, Bakunin, *Sochineniia* (Steklov), II, 166–178.

66. *B. i D.*, Lemke, XIII, 15–16.

67. V. G. Belinski, "Borodinskaia godovshchina," in *Sobranie sochineni V. G. Belinskogo* (*iubileinoe izdanie*), edited by P. V. Ivanov-Razumnik (3 vols.; St. Petersburg, 1911), I, 495, henceforth referred to as Belinski, *Sochineniia*.

68. Belinski to Botkin, 30 Dec., 1839, Belinski, *Pisma*, II, 18.

69. On the religious thought of the Slavophiles see especially A. Gratieux, *A. S. Khomiakov et le mouvement Slavophile* (2 vols.; Paris, 1939), henceforth Gratieux, *Khomiakov;* George Florovski, *Puti russkogo bogosloviia* (Paris, 1937). For their "historiosophy" see Nicholas V. Riasanovsky, *Russia and the West in the Teaching of the Slavophiles* (Cambridge, Mass., 1952), henceforth Riasanovsky, *Slavophiles*.

70. A. Stankevich, *T. N. Granovski i ego perepiska* (2 vols.; 2nd ed.; Moscow, 1897), Granovski to Stankevich, 27 Nov., 1839, II, 369–370. Volume I of this work is a biography of Granovski; volume II contains his correspondence, henceforth referred to as Granovski, *Perepiska*.

71. Passek, *Iz dalnikh let*, II, 310–316; and numerous remarks in Herzen's letters, e.g., Herzen to Ketcher, 7 Feb., 1839, Lemke, II, 239, and Herzen to Natalie, 9 Dec., 1839, Lemke, II, 345.

72. *B. i D.*, Lemke, XIII, 20–21; I. I. Panaev, *Literaturnye vospominaniia*, (Moscow-Leningrad, 1950), pp. 291–292, henceforth referred to as Panaev, *Vospominaniia*.

73. Belinski to Botkin, 30 Dec., 1839, Belinski, *Pisma*, II, 18.

74. Belinski to Botkin, 24 April, 1840, Belinski, *Pisma*, II, 121.

75. Belinski to Botkin, 11 Dec., 1840, Belinski, *Pisma*, II, 190.

76. *Ibid.*, 191.

77. Perhaps the best case for Herzen's influence on Belinski is made by Labry, *Herzen*, pp. 222–228.

78. Belinski to Botkin, 11 Dec., 1840, Belinski, *Pisma*, II, 187.

79. *Ibid.*, 186.

80. Belinski to Botkin, 28 June, 1841; Belinski to Bakunin, 7 Nov., 1842; Belinski to Botkin, 9–10 Dec., 1842; Belinski, *Pisma*, II, 249, 318, 328.

81. Belinski to Botkin, 8 Sept., 1841, Belinski, *Pisma*, II, 268.

82. To be sure, Herzen had published before this time (his article *Hoffmann* in the *Moscow Telescope* in 1836 and his scientific pieces at the university), but these efforts hardly made him a real author and public figure such as Belinski.

83. Belinski to Botkin, 11 Dec., 1840, Belinski, *Pisma*, II, 190.

84. See above, Chap. V, ninth section, and Chap. IX, third section.

85. Herzen to T. Passek, 11 Oct., 1840, Lemke, II, 373–374.

86. *Razskazy o vremenakh merovingskikh* (1841), Lemke, II, 410.

87. *Ibid.*, 411.

88. *Ibid.*, 412.

89. *Ibid.*, 410. Herzen also managed to slip in a reference to Buchez, *ibid.*, 411.

90. *O sebe*, Lemke, II, 163–174.

91. In a letter on 24 Nov., 1840, Natalie referred to the soon to be published *Zapiski* as "a fragment of *O sebe*" (note of ed., Lemke, II, 493). Thus it is clear that what was printed had been revised from an earlier and presumably franker text written in exile; but censorship precluded full publication. See also "*O sebe*," in *Literaturnoe nasledstvo*, LXIII, 9–55.

92. Herzen to Ogarev, 11–20 Feb., 1841, Lemke, II, 416.

93. *Zapiski odnogo molodogo cheloveka*, Lemke, II, 381.

94. *Ibid.*, 400, 403. To indicate his meaning more clearly Herzen adds after hinting at his oath and as if he were editing the text of his young man: "(Here again two or three pages are missing)."

95. *Eshche iz zapisok odnogo molodogo cheloveka*, Lemke, II, 437.

96. *Ibid.*

97. *Zapiski odnogo molodogo cheloveka*, Lemke, II, 402.

98. *Eshche iz zapisok*, Lemke, II, 447.

99. *Ibid.*, 449.

100. *Ibid.*, 453. The phrase "*chelo kak cherep goly*" — Pushkin's description of Chaadaev — would seem to establish this conclusively. Lemke, however, disputes the fact on the basis of Herzen's fourth *Pismo budushchemy drugu* (see note of ed., Lemke, II, 495). Still the identification with Chaadaev seems probable.

101. *Eshche iz zapisok*, Lemke, II, 459–466. For *The German Traveler* see above Chap. VIII, first section.

102. *Eshche iz zapisok*, Lemke, II, 455.

103. *Zapiski odnogo molodogo cheloveka*, Lemke, II, 381.

104. Belinski to Botkin, 30 Dec., 1840–22 Jan., 1841, Belinski, *Pisma*, II, 207.

105. Belinski to Ketcher, 3 Aug., 1841, Belinski, *Pisma*, II, 258.

106. In 1863 referring to *Byloe i Dumy* Herzen wrote: "This is my true literary genre, and Belinski guessed it in 1839." Lemke, XVI, 566.

107. Belinski to Herzen, 6 April, 1846, Belinski, *Pisma*, III, 109.

CHAPTER TEN

Realism in Philosophy: Hegel

1. Note of ed., Lemke, II, 375.

2. *B. i D.*, Lemke, XIII, 39–40.

3. *Ibid.*, 46. The full story of Herzen's second arrest occupies pp. 43–55.

4. Herzen to Ogarev, 11–20 Feb., 1841, Lemke, II, 417.

5. *B. i D.*, Lemke, XIII, 47.

6. Herzen to Iu. F. Kuruta, 17 Jan., 1841 and note of ed., Lemke, II, 407–408.

7. *Dnevnik*, 9 Dec., 1842, Lemke, III, 61.

8. Herzen to Ketcher, 25 Dec., 1841, Lemke, II, 473.

9. *Dnevnik*, 9 Dec., 1842, Lemke, III, 60.

10. Herzen to Ketcher, end of Dec., 1841, and 25 Dec., 1841, Lemke, II, 473.

11. Herzen to Ogarev, 11–20 Feb., 1841, Lemke, II, 414–416.

12. Herzen to Ketcher, 1–4 March, 1841, Lemke, II, 422.

13. *Ibid.*, and Herzen to Ogarev, 2–4 March, 1841, Lemke, II, 426.

14. *B. i D.*, Lemke, XIII, 68.

15. *Ibid.*, 69–78.

16. *Dnevnik*, 27 June, 1842, Lemke, III, 31.

17. *Ibid.*, 31–32.

18. *Ibid.*, 11 June, 1842, Lemke, III, 29.

19. *Ibid.*

20. Herzen to Ogarev, 21 March–27 April, 1839, Lemke, II, 261–262.

21. *Ibid.*

22. *Dnevnik*, 25 March, 1842, Lemke, III, 17.

23. *Ibid.*, 23 May, 1842, Lemke, III, 28.

24. *Ibid.*, 10 June, 1842, Lemke, III, 28.

25. *Ibid.*, 4 April, 1842, Lemke, III, 20.

26. Herzen to Ogarev, 11–20 Feb., 1841, Lemke, II, 417.

27. *B. i D.*, Lemke, XIII, 17–20.

28. *Dnevnik*, 4 April, 1842, Lemke, III, 20–21.

29. *B. i D.*, Lemke, XIII, 20.

30. On the basis of the just quoted passage from *My Past and Thoughts* it has often been maintained that Herzen's rejection of idealism and religion in Novgorod was produced by the "influence" of Feuerbach. This view has been demolished twice in detail, first by Gustav Shpet, *Filosofskoe mirovozzrenie Gertsena* (Petrograd, 1921), appendix II, pp. 81–100, and then by Labry, *Herzen*, pp. 230–240; consequently it was not felt necessary to do more than touch on the subject here. However, certain differences of opinion with Shpet and especially Labry should be pointed out. First of all, Labry insists

that it was not Feuerbach but Hegel who induced Herzen's new mood; the burden of the present chapter is that it was neither, and that Herzen's intellectual crisis was not produced by any mere book but by the circumstances of his life in Novgorod. Secondly, though Herzen framed his rejection of religion primarily in terms taken directly from Hegel, the result was inevitably near to Feuerbach — who. after all had done the same thing — and there are even traces of the latter's influence in Herzen's writings during the forties. Thus it is not incorrect to consider Herzen a *"Feuerbachianer,"* though not in a doctrinaire sense. This has been pointed out by Boris Jakowenko, *Geschichte des Hegelianismus in Russland* (one vol. published; Prague, 1938), pp. 90–102, henceforth referred to as Jakowenko, *Hegelianismus*. It is Jakowenko's view which will be followed here.

For Feuerbach's thought and its general impact see Albert Lévy, *La philosophie de Feuerbach et son influence sur la littérature allemande* (Paris, 1904); Simon Rawidowicz, *Ludwig Feuerbachs Philosophie; Ursprung und Schicksal* (Berlin, 1931), an outgrowth of his more limited *Ludwig Feuerbachs philosophische Jugendentwicklung und seine Stellung zu Hegel bis 1839* (Berlin, 1927), both of which present interesting parallels with Herzen's development. Also illuminating for the disintegration of German idealism in general is Friedrich Engels, *Ludwig Feuerbach and the Outcome of Classical German Philosophy,* no translator (New York: International Publishers, 1935).

31. Ogarev to Herzen, end of 1839, "Iz perepiski nedavnikh deiatelei," in *Russkaia mysl* (1889), book I, pp. 2–3.

32. Herzen to Ogarev, 11–20 Feb., 1841, Lemke, II, 416.

33. Herzen to A. A. Kraevski, 3 Feb., 1842, Lemke, III, 7.

34. *B. i D.*, Lemke, XIII, 16.

35. *Ibid.*

36. Needless to say this very limited discussion of Hegel is intended to illuminate, not so much the endless complexities of the man himself, as the reasons for his impact in Russia. For the literature on which these remarks are based, see first of all the titles listed above, Chap. V, notes 5–11. See also Willy Moog, *Hegel und die Hegelsche Schule* (Munich, 1930); Herbert Marcuse, *Hegels Ontologie und die Grundlegung einer Theorie der Geschichtlichkeit* (Frankfurt-am-Main, 1932); Hermann Glockner, *Hegel* (2 vols.; Stuttgart, 1920–1940). For the *Phenomenology* in particular see the already mentioned Jean Hyppolite, *Genèse et structure de la Phénoménologie de l'Esprit de Hegel,* and Alexandre Kojève, *Introduction à la lecture de Hegel, leçons sur la Phénoménologie de l'Esprit* (collected and published by Raymond Queneau; Paris, 1947); for one not to the manner of idealism born, it is helpful to have the whole subject transferred into a more direct idiom.

37. See especially letters of Belinski, 1839–1841, Belinski, *Pisma,* II, *passim;* his article *Mentsel, kritik Gete,* in *Sochineniia,* I, 538–582; letters of Bakunin 1837–1840, *Sochineniia* (Steklov), II, *passim.*

38. For Russian Hegelianism in general see Chizhevski, *Gegel* (especially parts A and B); Jakowenko, *Hegelianismus,* which complements rather than duplicates the work of Chizhevski; Koyré, "Hegel en Russie," in *Etudes,* pp. 101–170; Zenkovski, *Russkaia filosofiia,* vol. I, part II, chaps. v, vi.

39. Chizhevski, *Gegel,* p. 195.

40. Certain writings of such Slavophiles as Constantine Aksakov and Iuri Samarin constitute a partial exception to this statement. See Chizhevski, *Gegel,* pp. 166–182 and Jakowenko, *Hegelianismus,* pp. 260–286.

41. This is the besetting sin of Labry; see especially his *Herzen,* chap. ix. It

of course applies to the Soviets; see note 84 below. Chizhevski and Jakowenko have the best grasp of Herzen's philosophy *qua* philosophy; however they do not attempt to situate it in its social context, which is the purpose of the present chapter.

42. *Diletantizm v nauke*, Lemke, III, 163–233, published 1843, henceforth referred to as *Diletantizm; Pisma ob izuchenii prirody*, Lemke, IV, 1–182, published 1845–1846, henceforth referred to as *Izuchenie prirody*.

43. *Diletantizm*, Lemke, III, 232.

44. *Ibid.*, 175.

45. *Ibid.*, 230.

46. *Dnevnik*, 28 June, 1842, Lemke, III, 32.

47. *Diletantizm*, Lemke, III, 172–173.

48. *Ibid.*, 207; see also 172–173.

49. *Ibid.*, 231.

50. This idea is made explicit at several points in the *Diary; e.g. Dnevnik*, 11 Nov., 1842, Lemke, III, 56. See also an essay written at the end of 1843, but not published until 1848, *Neskolko zamechani ob istoricheskom razvitii chesti*, Lemke, V, 210–232 (discussed below in Chap. XIII).

51. *Diletantizm*, Lemke, III, 233.

52. *Ibid.*, 230.

53. *Ibid.*, 230–231.

54. *Ibid.*, 169.

55. For example, *Dnevnik*, 11 Sept., 1842, Lemke, III, 41.

56. *Diletantizm*, Lemke, III, 207.

57. The word "dualism" is actually used more in the *Izuchenie prirody* than in the *Diletantizm;* however, it has been employed here as the term most appropriate to Herzen's meaning throughout.

58. The formulation of Herzen's position given here is much more explicit than he could make it himself, but translated into a less abstract mode of thought, this is the import of his message.

59. See above, Chap. V, seventh section.

60. In Abel-François Villemain's *Leçons sur la littérature du XVIIIe siècle. Dnevnik*, 13 April, 1842, Lemke, III, 22–23.

61. *Diletantizm*, Lemke, III, 230–231.

62. *Ibid.*, 232.

63. *Dnevnik*, 28 June, 1842, Lemke, III, 32.

64. *Diletantizm*, Lemke, III, 173. This idea is developed at much greater length in the first chap. of the *Izuchenie prirody*, Lemke, IV, 1–28. For its origins in Herzen's youthful Schellingian phase see above, Chap. V, sixth section.

65. *Diletantizm*, Lemke, III, 167.

66. *Ibid.*, 192–193.

67. *Ibid.*, 205.

68. *Ibid.*, 212–213.

69. *Ibid.*, 222–223.

70. *Ibid.*, 223.

71. *Ibid.*, 217.

72. *Ibid.*, 218.

73. See above, Chap. X, third section, and *Diletantizm*, Lemke, III, 174.

74. *Ibid.*, 175.

75. *Ibid.*, 215.

76. *Ibid.*, 216.

77. *Ibid.;* italics added.
78. *Ibid.,* 210.
79. *Ibid.,* 211.
80. *Dnevnik,* 22 Sept., 1842, Lemke, III, 43; italics added.
81. *Diletantizm,* Lemke, III, 218.
82. *Ibid.,* 218–220.
83. *Ibid.,* 233.
84. This tradition begins with Plekhanov in his various articles on Herzen; see especially "Filosofskie vzgliady A. I. Gertsena," Plekhanov, *Sochineniia,* XXIII, 354–413, and "O knige V. Ia. Bogucharskogo," Plekhanov, *Sochineniia,* XXIII, 446–452. It is continued by Lenin; see above, Chap. I, note 5. It has been repeated infallibly by all Soviet commentators on Herzen's philosophy since the 1930's; see especially Piper, *Mirovozzrenie Gertsena* and D. I. Chesnokov, *Mirovozzrenie Gertsena* (n.p., 1943). For a polemical criticism of this position see V. V. Zenkovski, "O mnimom materializme russkoi nauki i filosofii," *Institut po izuchenii SSSR. Issledovaniia i materialy,* series 1, *vypusk* 27 (Munich, 1956), especially pp. 39–44.
85. For example, *Dnevnik,* 30 June, 1843, Lemke, III, 118–119; *B. i D.,* Lemke, XII, 481–482.
86. *Dnevnik,* 15 Aug., 1842, Lemke, III, 37–38.
87. *Ibid.,* 7 Jan., 1843, Lemke, III, 88.
88. In terms of formal doctrines this is not entirely true, as Chizhevski has pointed out; see his *Gegel,* p. 204. However, it is true in terms of the spirit and the practical implications of Herzen's position, and this is what counts.
89. There are no really satisfactory histories of Left Hegelianism as a whole. The movement is usually approached either as an appendage to Hegel or as the context of Marx's early development. In addition to the studies of Feuerbach mentioned in note 30 above see Karl Löwith, *Von Hegel bis Nietzsche* (Zürich, 1941), especially part I, chap. ii, and part II, chaps. iv, v; the Marxist-oriented but informative studies of Auguste Cornu, *Karl Marx, l'homme et l'oeuvre. De l'hégélianisme au matérialisme historique 1818–1845* (Paris, 1934) and *Karl Marx et Friedrich Engels* (one vol. published; Paris, 1955), vol. I, *Les années d'enfance et de jeunesse, la gauche hégélienne 1818/1820–1844,* both of which contain very good bibliographies on Left Hegelianism in general; Sidney Hook, *From Hegel to Marx* (London-New York, 1936); and most valuable of all for a deeper understanding of the movement, Maximilien Rubel, *Karl Marx, essai de biographie intellectuelle* (Paris, 1957), especially parts I and II.
90. *Dnevnik,* 15 Aug., 1842, Lemke, III, 38.
91. George Florowskij (Florovski), "Die Sackgassen der Romantik," *Orient und Occident. Blätter für Theologie und Soziologie,* IV (1930), 14–27. This in general represents the religious critique of romantic idealism.

CHAPTER ELEVEN

Realism in Love: George Sand

1. Ogarev, "Kavkazskie vody," in *Izbrannye,* I, 411–412.
2. Passek, *Iz dalnikh let,* II, 104–107. The story of Ogarev's married life as seen through his letters to Maria Lvovna is given by Gershenzon, "Liubov N. P. Ogareva," in *Obrazy proshlogo,* pp. 347–493. It has been told in English by Carr, *Romantic Exiles,* chap. vii.
3. See Kornilov, *Molodoi Bakunin* and, in English, Carr, *Bakunin.*

4. Herzen's letter has been lost but the sharpness of its contents is clear from Ogarev's melancholy reaction; Ogarev to Herzen, Nov. 1839, "Iz perepiski nedavnikh deiatelei," in *Russkaia mysl* (1888), book XI, p. 11, and Nov. or Dec. 1839, *ibid.* (1889), book I, pp. 1–2. See also Herzen to Natalie, 11 Dec., 1839, Lemke, II, 346.

5. Herzen to Natalie, 8 Dec., 1839, Lemke, II, 341–342.

6. Herzen to Natalie, 18–20 Dec., 1839, Lemke, II, 353.

7. Herzen to Ogarev, 11–26 Feb., 1841, Lemke, II, 417–418; see also Herzen to Ketcher, 1 March, 1841, Lemke, II, 423.

8. Belinski, *Pisma*, II, 188.

9. *Ibid.*, 220.

10. *Dnevnik*, 10 June, 1842, Lemke, III, 28.

11. Gershenzon, "Liubov Ogareva," in *Obrazy proshlogo*, pp. 493–545.

12. Natalie to Ogarev, Maria Lvovna and friends, Dec. 1839, "Iz perepiski nedavnikh deiatelei," in *Russkaia mysl* (1889), book X, p. 12.

13. Herzen to Natalie, 18–20 Dec., 1839, Lemke, II, 353.

14. See above, Chap. X, first section.

15. *B. i D.*, Lemke, XIII, 84–85.

16. *Dnevnik*, 10 and 12 June, 1842, Lemke, III, 28–29, 30.

17. *Dnevnik*, 29 July, 1842, Lemke, III, 34.

18. *B. i D.*, Lemke, XIII, 85–87.

19. *Dnevnik*, 16 Jan., 1843, Lemke, III, 91.

20. *Ibid.*, 92.

21. *Dnevnik*, Jan.–June, 1843, Lemke, III, *passim.*

22. See especially *Dnevnik*, 30 and 31 Dec., 1843, and 14 and 16 Dec., 1844, Lemke, III, 149 and 363–366.

23. *Dnevnik*, 19 March, 1843, Lemke, III, 102.

24. E. S. Nekrasova, "A I. Gertsen, ego khlopoty o zagranichnom pasporte i posledniaia poezdka v Peterburg," in *Russkaia mysl* (1904), book IX, pp. 161–162.

25. This is apparent from her "*dnevnik*," of which there exist a few entries for 1846–47; *Russkie propilei*, I, 233–238. See also her letter of Dec. 1846 to Ogarev, *ibid.*, 239–240.

26. *B. i D.*, Lemke, XII, 152. Also see above Chap. VI, first section.

27. See above, Chap. IX, third section.

28. On feminism in general and the role of George Sand in particular during this period see especially Marguerite Thibert, *Le féminisme dans le socialisme français de 1830 à 1850* (Paris, 1926); Célestin Bouglé, "Le féminisme saint-simonien," in his *Chez les prophètes socialistes* (Paris, 1918); Lucien Buis, *Les théories sociales de George Sand* (Aix-Marseilles, 1910); D. O. Evans, *Le roman social sous la Monarchie de Juillet* (Paris, 1930); Wladimir Karénine (Mme. Komarov), *George Sand, sa vie et ses oeuvres* (4 vols; Paris, 1899–1924); Ernest Seillière, *George Sand: mystique de la passion, de la politique et de l'art* (Paris, 1920).

29. *B. i D.*, Lemke, XIII, 464–473.

30. *Dnevnik*, 30 June, 1843, Lemke, III, 119.

31. *Ibid.*

31a. *Ibid.*

32. Natalie's "*dnevnik*," Nov. 1846, *Russkie propilei*, I, 238.

33. *Kaprizy i razdume, I. Po povodu odnoi dramy*, Lemke, III, 261–262. The drama in question was *Huit ans après* by Arnould and Fournier. For the origin of Herzen's article see *Dnevnik*, 13 Sept., 1842, Lemke, III, 41–42.

34. *Po povodu odnoi dramy,* Lemke, III, 265.
35. Belinski to Herzen, 2 Jan. and 6 April, 1846, Belinski, *Pisma,* III, 91 and 108–109. For Belinski's public praise of the novel see his *Vzgliad na russkuiu literaturu 1847 g.,* in *Sochineniia,* III, 962–972.
36. *Dnevnik,* 13 Aug., 1842, Lemke, III, 37.
37. *Kto vinovat?,* Lemke, IV, 194–376.
38. *Ibid.,* 203–215. It is interesting to note that Herzen reflects that Liubov (Natalie) might well have been better off if she had grown up as an uncomplicated serf instead of becoming "humanized" in her ambiguous status as a "ward" in the gentry's world (pp. 213–214).
39. *Ibid.,* 260–267.
40. *Ibid.,* 215–223.
41. The doctor first appears in 1836 in *Vtoraia vstrecha,* Lemke, I, 233, then in 1841 in *Eshche iz zapisok odnogo molodogo cheloveka,* Lemke, II, 445–446. The story *Doktor Krupov,* whose hero is a much more caustic and skeptical version of the doctor of the novel, was written in 1846 and published in 1847 in the *Contemporary* after Herzen had left Russia; see Lemke, V, 59–107. The doctor's principal subsequent appearances are in 1849 in *S togo berega,* "Consolatio," Lemke, V, 450–468; 1851, *Povrezhdenny,* Lemke, VI; and 1868–1869, *Skuki radi,* Lemke, XXI.
42. *Soroka-vorovka,* Lemke, V, 185–204.
43. See above, Chap. II, first section, and below, Chap. XIV, third section.
44. *Kto vinovat?,* Lemke, IV, 297. The best discussion of Beltov as a type of *intelligent* is that of Ovsianiko-Kulikovski, *Russkaia intelligentsiia,* in *Sochineniia,* VII, 117–124.
45. *Kto vinovat?,* Lemke, IV, 285.
46. *Ibid.,* 298–299.
47. *Ibid.,* 299.
48. *Dnevnik,* 26 May, 1843, Lemke, III, 112.
49. *Dnevnik,* 28 March, 1844, Lemke, III, 321.
50. *Kto vinovat?,* Lemke, IV, 220.
51. *Kaprizy i razdume, II. Po raznym povodam,* Lemke, IV, 402.
52. *Kaprizy i razdume, III. Novye variatsii na starye temy,* Lemke, V, 22. The roots of this "egoism" go back farther than 1846, however. The idea follows logically from Herzen's "philosophy of the present moment," which had been formulated by 1842 in Novgorod; see above Chap. X, fifth section. Perhaps the first use of the word "egoism" in the new sense is in *Dnevnik,* 15 April, 1843, Lemke, III, 106.
53. *Novye variatsii na starye temy,* Lemke, V, 23, 25.

CHAPTER TWELVE

The Slavophiles and Nationalism

1. *Zvenia,* VIII, 78–81; *Dnevnik,* 6 April, 1842, Lemke, III, 21; note of ed., Lemke, III, 67.
2. Note of ed., Lemke, III, 68–69.
3. *Dnevnik,* 8 April, 3 and 9 July, 1842, Lemke, III, 21 and 33; note of ed., Lemke, III, 70.
4. *Vospominaniia B. N. Chicherina,* S. B. Bakhrushin, ed. (4 vols.; Moscow, 1929), II, "Moskva sorokovykh godov," 6. After Annenkov's *Zamechatel-*

noe desiatiletie, this is one of the best firsthand accounts of intellectual life in the forties.

5. *B. i D.,* Lemke, XIII, 42. Chizhevski (*Gegel,* pp. 60–61) appropriately adds the house of Pavlov, whose memory Herzen boycotts in his memoirs, to the list of those frequented by both Slavophiles and Westerners, including Herzen.

6. *B. i D.,* chap. xxix, Lemke, XIII, 99–119.

7. A. P. Panaeva, *Vospominaniia* (Moscow-Leningrad, 1933), pp. 130, 136, 166, 210, 212.

8. Nikolai Barsukov, *Zhizn i trudy M. P. Pogodina* (22 vols.; St. Petersburg, 1888–1911), VII, 439–442, henceforth Barsukov, *Pogodin.* This monumental labor of conservative and nationalistic love is a mine of information for the narrative aspects of social and intellectual history under Nicholas I. For the present and following chapters see especially vols. V–IX. Herzen's reaction to Granovski's failure to obtain permission for a periodical is given in his *Dnevnik,* 27 Dec., 1844, Lemke, III, 368.

9. Barsukov, *Pogodin,* V, 107–117, 486–492, and VI, 5–9; Dementev, *Russkaia zhurnalistika,* pp. 185–187.

10. Elsberg, *Gertsen,* p. 135.

11. See above Chap. IX, seventh section.

12. See in particular Gratieux, *Khomiakov,* vol. II, "Les doctrines"; Riasanovsky, *Slavophiles,* chap. iv; Jakowenko, *Hegelianismus,* chaps. on Slavophiles and Constantine Aksakov; P. Sakulin, "Russkaia literatura vo vtoroi chetverti veka," in *Istoriia Rossii v XIX v.* (Izdatelstvo "Granat"; Moscow, 1910), II, 443–508.

13. For example, Herzen's *"Moskvitianin" o Kopernike* and his *Putevye zapiski g. Vedrina,* Lemke, III, 269–272 and 273–274.

14. Nicholas V. Riasanovsky, "Pogodin and Shevyrev in Russian Intellectual History," *Harvard Slavic Studies,* IV, 149–167.

15. The explanation of Slavophilism given in this chapter does not derive directly from any of the studies of the movement mentioned in the notes. Rather it represents an attempt to reinterpret the findings of these works in the terms of the approach to Russian politics used throughout this book.

16. For the Slavophiles' views on emancipation see especially Boris Nolde, *Iuri Samarin i ego vremia* (Paris, 1926).

17. This discussion of the Slavophiles' political program is based primarily on Constantine Aksakov, *Zapiska o vnutrennem sostoianii Rossii,* in L. Brodsky, *Rannie slavianofily* (Moscow, 1910).

18. Nicholas V. Riasanovsky, "Khomiakov on *sobornost,*" in Simmons, ed., *Continuity and Change in Russian and Soviet Thought.*

19. An interesting though over-simplified attempt to interpret Slavophilism in terms of gentry class interests is N. Rubinshtein, "Istoricheskaia teoria slavianofilov i ee klassovye korni," in *Trudy Instituta Krasnoi Professury, Russkaia istoricheskaia literatura v klassovom osveshchenii,* edited by M. N. Pokrovski (Moscow, 1927), I, 53–117.

20. It would be idle to attempt to set forth here any reasonably full listing of works on nationalism in general or on Russian nationalism in particular. The remarks in this chapter are not intended as a learned discussion of either question; they are no more than an effort to explore in terms of common-sense categories the elements of the problem.

A few useful or suggestive titles on nationalism in general are: Koppel S. Pinson, *A Bibliographical Introduction to Nationalism* (New York, 1935);

Carlton J. H. Hayes, *Essays on Nationalism* (New York, 1928) and *The Historical Evolution of Modern Nationalism* (New York, 1931); Hans Kohn, *The Idea of Nationalism* (New York, 1944) and *Nationalism, Its Meaning and History* (Princeton, 1955); Walter Sulzbach, *National Consciousness* (Washington, D. C., 1943); Boyd Shafer, *Nationalism, Myth and Reality* (New York, 1955); René Johannet, *Le principe des nationalités* (2nd. ed.; Paris, 1923); George Weill, *L'Europe du XIXe siècle et l'idée de nationalité* (Paris, 1938); Waldemar Mitscherlich, *Nationalismus: Die Geschichte einer Idee* (Leipzig, 1929); Roberto Michels, *Der Patriotismus: Prolegomena zu einer soziologischen Analyse* (Munich, 1929); J. Fels, *Begriff und Wesen der Nation: eine soziologische Untersuchung und Kritik* (Münster, 1927); Heinz Ziegler, *Die moderne Nation: ein Beitrag zur politischen Soziologie* (Tübingen, 1931); Eugen Lemberg, *Geschichte des Nationalismus in Europa* (Stuttgart, 1950).

The bibliography of Russian nationalism is unfortunately both sparse and, on the whole, of poor quality. The best general historical treatment remains that given by P. N. Miliukov in his *Ocherki po istorii russkoi kultury* (Jubilee edition, 3 vols.; Paris, 1930–37). See also the writings on Russian nationalism of Vladimir Soloviev, *Sobranie sochineni* (2nd ed.; 10 vols.; St. Petersburg, 1911), vol. V. Of more specialized — and for present purposes peripheral — interest are Hans Kohn, *Pan-Slavism, Its History and Ideology* (Notre Dame, Indiana, 1953) and Michael Petrovich, *The Emergence of Russian Panslavism, 1856–1870* (New York, 1956). Much writing on Russian nationalism in Western languages, however, is marred by dubious metaphysical and polemical considerations. Prominent examples of this approach are Jan Kucharzewski, *The Origins of Modern Russia,* English translation sponsored by the "Polish Institute of Arts and Sciences in America" (New York, 1948), and Alexander von Schelting, *Russland und Europa im russischen Geschichtsdenken* (Bern, 1948). Both these works dwell at length on Herzen as one of the more horrific exemplars of an inveterate Russian imperialism inspired by hate of Europe and of all civilization, a phenomenon these writers hold to be all the more insidious in Herzen's case because it was disguised as a social messianism and hence foreshadowed Bolshevism. The remarks in this chapter are designed in part to substitute a more analytical view for the emotionalism of such works. (Two important studies germane to the present discussion appeared after this book was completed and hence could not be utilized: Hans Rogger, *National Consciousness in Eighteenth-Century Russia* (Cambridge, Mass., 1960), and Nicholas Riasanovsky, *Nicholas I and Official Nationality in Russia, 1825–1855* (Berkeley and Los Angeles, 1959).)

21. Herzen's rather conciliatory version of the quarrel between Westerners and Slavophiles is given in *B. i D.,* chap. xxx, Lemke, III, 138–155. See also *Dnevnik,* Nov.–Dec., 1844, and Jan.–Feb., 1845, Lemke, III, 358–369 and 440–449, *passim.* For other accounts of the quarrel see Panaev, *Vospominaniia,* part II, chap. v.; Annenkov, *Zamechatelnoe desiatiletie,* in *Vospominaniia i kriticheskie ocherki,* vol. III, chaps. xvi, xviii–xx, also published in Annenkov, *Literaturnye vospominaniia* (Leningrad, 1928); Barsukov, *Pogodin,* vol. VII, chaps. xvi-xx.

22. For Herzen's assessment of Granovski's impact see *Publichnye chteniia g. Granovskogo,* Lemke, III, 279–282 and 403–407; *Dnevnik,* 24 and 28 Nov., 1 and 21 Dec., 1843, and 7 March, 1844, Lemke, III, 143–147 and 315–316.

23. For example, *Um — khorosho, a dva — luchshe* and *"Moskvitianin" i vselennaia,* Lemke, III, 287–291 and 465–470.

24. Herzen to Ketcher, 2–3 Dec., 1843, and 27 April, 1844, Lemke, III,

286 and 394; A. Pypin, *Belinski, ego zhizn i perepiska* (2nd ed.; St. Petersburg, 1876), p. 481.

25. Herzen's favorable remarks about the Slavophiles begin at the very end of 1842 and continue through the middle of 1844. See especially *Dnevnik*, 23 Nov., 1842, 21 Dec., 1842, 8 Jan., 1843, 5 April, 1843, 10 Nov., 1843, and 18 Jan., 1844, Lemke, III, 57–58, 62–64, 88–90, 104, 141–142, 302.

26. *Dnevnik*, 10 Dec., 1844, Lemke, III, 363.

27. *Dnevnik*, 26 Oct. and 10 Nov., 1843, Lemke, III, 138–139, 142.

28. *Dnevnik*, 15 Sept., 1844, Lemke, III, 352.

29. *Dnevnik*, 1 Feb., 1844, Lemke, III, 305.

30. *Dnevnik*, 9 July, 1844, Lemke, III, 336.

31. *Dnevnik*, 9 Nov., 1844, 10 and 21 April, 1843, Lemke, III, 359, 106 and 107–108.

32. *Dnevnik*, 17 Sept., 1844, Lemke, III, 354.

33. *Dnevnik*, 11 Sept., 1842, Lemke, III, 41.

34. *Dnevnik*, 8 Jan., 1843, Lemke, III, 88.

35. *Dnevnik*, 8 Jan., 1843, and 2 Nov., 1844, Lemke, III, 89 and 358.

36. *Dnevnik*, 10 Dec., 1844, Lemke, III, 362.

37. *Ibid.*, 362–363.

38. *Dnevnik*, 2 Nov., 1842, Lemke, III, 53–54. For similar sentiments at the time of the break see *Dnevnik*, 20 Nov. and 17 Dec., 1844, Lemke, III, 360–361 and 367.

39. *Dnevnik*, 4 and 10 June and 20 July, 1844, Lemke, III, 330–331 and 338–341.

40. *Dnevnik*, 17 Feb., 1844, Lemke III, 309.

41. *Dnevnik*, 16 July, 1843, Lemke, III, 128.

42. Herzen to Ketcher, 1–4 March, 1841, Lemke, II, 424.

43. *Dnevnik*, 16 July, 1843, Lemke, III, 128.

44. *Kto vinovat?*, Lemke, IV, 271.

45. *Dnevnik*, 17 May, 1844, Lemke, III, 328.

46. *Dnevnik*, 24 Jan., 1844, Lemke, III, 303.

47. *Dnevnik*, 25 Aug., 1843, Lemke, III, 133.

48. *Kto vinovat?*, Lemke, IV, 233.

49. *Diletantizm*, Lemke, III, 220.

50. *Otdelnye zamechaniia o russkom zakonodatelstve*, Lemke, I, 370.

51. *Dnevnik*, 13 May, 1843, Lemke, III, 111.

52. Khomiakov, *On Rural Conditions*, as quoted by Labry, *Herzen*, pp. 274–275.

53. *Dnevnik*, 26 June, 1843, Lemke, III, 117.

54. *Dnevnik*, 17 Feb., 1844, Lemke, III, 310.

55. *Dnevnik*, 21 Feb., 1844, Lemke, III, 311–312.

56. Herzen's ideological debt to the Slavophiles was perhaps first explored by D. Ovsianiko-Kulikovski, "Zapadnichestvo i slavianofilstvo Gertsena," "Natsionalizm i sotsializm Gertsena," and "Russki messianizm Gertsena," in *Nasha zhizn* (1905), nos. 129, 146, 168, and his *Gertsen* (St. Petersburg, 1908). Herzen's "Russian socialism" is seen almost as a direct borrowing from Slavophilism in Bogucharski, *Gertsen*. The Soviets have always objected violently to such efforts to derive revolutionary Populism from "reactionary" Slavophilism. Nonetheless, an examination of Herzen's *Diary* for 1843–44 makes the conclusion inescapable that he first heard of the ideas of the "socialist" commune and of Russian messianism from the Slavophiles. Although Herzen later developed these ideas with a radical spirit alien to their authors, the formal

doctrines of Populism do in large part originate in Slavophilism. This debt, however, no more impugns Herzen's honor as a "revolutionary democrat" than does the very similar debt of Marx to the conservative Hegel diminish the revolutionary quality of Marxism, and it is difficult to see why the Soviets get so upset about the whole matter.

57. *B. i D.*, Lemke, XIII, 120.

CHAPTER THIRTEEN

Socialist and Liberal Westerners

1. See above, Chap. IX, fourth section.
2. See above, Chap. X, fifth section.
3. *Neskolko zamechani ob istoricheskom razvitii chesti*, Lemke, V, 210–232. Written in 1843, revised in 1846 and published in 1848. The subject of this essay is the historical development of the duel as an expression of the "feudal" idea of individuality. For this reason on certain points it gives a more concrete statement of Herzen's theory of history than does the philosophical discussion of the *Pisma ob izuchenii prirody*.
4. *Izuchenie prirody*, Lemke, IV, 101.
5. *Diletantizm*, Lemke, III, 163.
6. *Izuchenie prirody*, Lemke, IV, 104–105.
7. *Ibid.*, 114.
8. *Dnevnik*, July 1843, Lemke, III, 120–131, *passim*.
9. *Izuchenie prirody*, Lemke, IV, 113–114.
10. *Ibid.*, 134.
11. *Dnevnik*, 18 June, 1843, Lemke, III, 116.
12. *Dnevnik*, 10 July, 1843, Lemke, III, 124.
13. *Istoricheskoe razvitie chesti*, Lemke, V, 217, 220–221, 231.
14. *Dnevnik*, 15 Aug., 1842, Lemke, III, 38.
15. *Diletantizm*, Lemke, III, 219.
16. See above, Chap. XII, sixth section.
17. "Vospominaniia Liprandi," *Russkaia starina*, June 1872, pp. 66–68.
18. *Rasskazy o vremenakh merovingskikh*, Lemke, II, 411; *Dnevnik*, 14 March, 1844, Lemke, III, 316–317.
19. *Dnevnik*, 28 Aug., 1844, Lemke, III, 347.
20. *Dnevnik*, 18 Feb., 1843, Lemke, III, 96–97.
21. *Ibid.*, 97.
22. *Ibid.*
23. *Dnevnik*, 17 June, 1844, Lemke, III, 332.
24. *Dnevnik*, 12 June, 1844, Lemke, III, 331.
25. *Dnevnik*, 26 June, 1844, Lemke III, 334.
26. *Dnevnik*, 28 June, 1843, Lemke, III, 118.
27. *Dnevnik*, 4, 18 and 28 June, 1843, Lemke III, 113–114, 116, 117–118.
28. *B. i D.*, Lemke, XIII, 447.
29. *Dnevnik*, 3 Dec., 1844, Lemke, III, 361–362.
30. *Dnevnik*, 28 Feb., 1845, Lemke, III, 448.
31. *Ibid.* For a fuller discussion of Herzen's reading of Proudhon at this time see Raoul Labry, *Herzen et Proudhon* (Paris, 1928), chap. i, henceforth Labry, *Herzen et Proudhon*.
32. *B. i D.*, Lemke, XIII, 447–448. The works of Proudhon mentioned here and the most important for understanding his impact on Herzen — *Qu'est-ce*

que la propriété? (1840), *De la création de l'ordre dans l'humanité* (1843) and the *Système de contradictions économiques, ou philosophie de la misère* (1846) — are most conveniently found, with admirable annotations, in his *Oeuvres*, edited by C. Bouglé and H. Moysset (Paris, 1923–). On Proudhon's life and thought see the old but still very valuable Sainte-Beuve, *P. J. Proudhon, sa vie et sa correspondance* (Paris, 1875) and Karl Diehl, *P. J. Proudhon, seine Lehre und sein Leben* (3 vols; Jena, 1888–1896). More recent studies are E. J. Droz, *Proudhon* (Paris, 1909); C. Bouglé, *La sociologie de Proudhon* (Paris, 1911); Edouard Dolléans, *Proudhon* (Paris, 1948); E. Dolléans and J. L. Puech, *Proudhon et la Révolution de 1848* (Paris, 1948); Shi Yung Lu, *The Political Theories of P. J. Proudhon* (New York, 1922); Henri de Lubac, *The Un-Marxian Socialist: a Study of Proudhon,* translated by R. E. Scantlebury (New York, 1948).

33. *B. i D.*, chap. xxxii, Lemke, XIII, 184–193.

34. *Dnevnik*, 3 Oct., 1844, Lemke, III, 356; Herzen to Ogarev, 1/13 Jan., 1845, Lemke, III, 433–437; Herzen to Ketcher, 3 March, 1845, Lemke, III, 463; *Dnevnik,* 17 March, 1845, Lemke III, 444.

35. Tension clearly began to build up over these issues in 1844–45, more than a year before the quarrel at Sokolovo. See Herzen to Granovski, 9 June, 1844, Lemke III, 410–411; Herzen to Ogarev, 1/13 Jan., 1845, Lemke, III, 437; Granovski's comments in Gershenzon, *Molodaia Rossiia*, p. 230; *Dnevnik*, 14 March, 1845, Lemke, III, 450.

36. See below, Chap. XIV, second section.

37. Annenkov, *Zamechatelnoe desiatiletie* in *Vospominaniia*, vol. III, chap. xxvii, especially pp. 130–131.

38. *Ibid.*, chaps. xxv–xxvii; Panaev, *Vospominaniia*, part II. chap. v. For the origin of disagreement on the question of the "simple people" see Herzen to to Ketcher, 19 June, 1844, Lemke, III, 397.

39. Echoes of these accusations come through in Herzen's letters of 1847, discussed in the following chapter, and in an article of 1846, *Kaprizy i razdume, III. Novye variatsii na starye temy,* Lemke, V, 22–28. See also "Pisma Ogareva k Gersenu. Akshenski period," in *Literaturnoe nasledstvo*, LXI, 746–762; Granovski, *Perepiska*, II, 445–446; and Passek, *Iz dalnikh let*, II, 330–332.

40. *B. i D.*, Lemke, XIII, 193. The full extent of Herzen's feeling of isolation and dissatisfaction in 1846 cannot be documented directly from his writings at that time. But it can be inferred with a high degree of certainty from his actions and writings in 1847, discussed in the following chapter. See in particular Annenkov, *Zamechatelnoe desiatiletie*, in *Vospominaniia*, vol. III, chaps. xxi, xxxiii.

41. See below, Chap. XIV, fifth section.

42. See especially the letters of Botkin to Annenkov in *P. B. Annenkov i ego druzia. Literaturnye vospominaniia i perepiska 1835–1885 godov* (2 vols.; St. Petersburg, 1892), I, henceforth Annenkov, *Druzia*.

43. *Novye variatsii na starye temy*, Lemke, V, 13–28. See also below, Chap. XIV, second section.

44. *Dnevnik*, 4 Sept., 1844, Lemke, III, 350–351.

45. Natalie's *"dnevnik,"* *Russkie propilei*, I, 233–238; Annenkov, *Zamechatelnoe desiatiletie*, in *Vospominaniia*, vol. III, chap. xxxiii; notes of ed., Lemke, IV, 428–429, 441–442.

46. *B. i D.*, chap. xxxiii, Lemke, XIII, 194–203; note of ed., Lemke, XIII, 275.

47. *Ibid.*, 202–203; Herzen to Granovski, 20 Jan. 1847, Lemke, V, 5–6; Granovski to Herzen, 1847, Granovski, *Perepiska*, II, 445–446.

48. *B. i D.*, Lemke, XIII, 184, 193.

49. *Ibid.*, 203.

CHAPTER FOURTEEN

The Crucial Year — 1847

1. Granovski became increasingly moderate until his early death in 1855. His chief spiritual heir, Kavelin, under Alexander II was one of the principal proponents of gradual, liberal reform through cooperation with the autocracy. Ketcher and Botkin after 1855 became downright conservatives, fearful even of emancipating the peasantry. Herzen's criticism, then, that the "logical" consequence of his friends' moderation was *de facto* support of autocracy had a certain foundation in fact.

2. *B. i D.*, Lemke, XIII, 289.

3. *Pisma iz Frantsii i Italii*, fifth letter, June 1848, Lemke, VI, 65, henceforth referred to as *Frantsiia i Italiia*.

4. This was first pointed out by N. N. Strakhov, *Borba s zapadom v russkoi literature* (St. Petersburg, 1882), p. 31. It is of course insisted upon by Soviet writers, anxious to demonstrate how quickly Herzen saw through Western capitalism; e.g., Elsberg, *Gertsen*, part IV, chaps. i–iii.

5. See above, Chap. VI, third section.

6. See above, Chap. VII, second section.

7. See above, Chap. VIII, first section, and Chap. XII, sixth section.

8. *Kaprizy i razdume. II. Po raznym povodam* (written end of 1845, published 1846), Lemke, IV, 396–397.

9. *Ibid.*, 398.

10. *Ibid.*, 397.

11. *Kaprizy i razdume. III. Novye variatsii na starye temy*, Lemke, V, 13–28. This essay is divided into four sections. The last two are specifically dated "Sokolovo, July, 1846"; the first two were presumably written earlier in the same year, before the debates at Sokolovo. The whole was published in a censored version during the spring of 1847 in the *Sovremennik*, that is after Herzen had left Russia.

12. *Ibid.*, 15–21.

13. *Ibid.*, 16–17.

14. *Ibid.*, 18–19.

15. *Frantsiia i Italiia*, introduction of 1858, Lemke, V, 110.

16. *B. i D.*, part V, chap. xxxiv, Lemke, XIII, especially p. 283.

17. In spite of the fact that he was acquainted with such figures as Marx, Bakunin and Herzen, Annenkov was only the mildest of liberals; hence he describes his radical friends somewhat from the outside. For this reason his testimony on Herzen during 1847 has been called into question, notably by Lemke (V, 12); and the same caution towards him has been observed on the whole by the Soviets: see introduction to Annenkov, *Literaturnye vospominaniia*, B. M. Eikhenbaum, ed. ("Academia"; Leningrad, 1928). Nonetheless the very fact that Annenkov was an observer rather than a participant, without emotional involvement in what he saw, made him sensitive to — and honest about — many things that Herzen in his polemical zeal either omitted or distorted to create the desired revolutionary image of his motives and activities.

18. Annenkov, *Zamechatelnoe desiatiletie,* in *Vospominaniia,* III, 174.
19. *Ibid.*
20. "Kommentari no. 1" of ed. to part V of *B. i D.,* Lemke, XIV, 1.
21. Annenkov, *Zamechatelnoe desiatiletie,* in *Vospominaniia,* III, 153.
22. *Ibid.*
23. This is only a supposition based on Herzen's actions during 1847–48. Our only source for the matter, Lemke, produces no documents between the original grant of the passport in late 1846 and the first measures taken against Herzen in Sept. 1849; see Lemke, XIV, 1, 9–15 and VI, 146–148. On the assumption that it would take the Russian government several months to react to Herzen's loss of contact with the consular authorities his break would occur sometime in the second half of 1848 or at the latest in the early months of 1849.
24. Annenkov, *Zamechatelnoe desiatiletie,* in *Vospominaniia,* III, 174–175.
25. *Ibid.,* 152–153.
26. See Lemke, I, 228; III, 13; V, 415, 464.
27. *Dolg prezhde vsego,* Lemke, VII, 409–464. The original text is given, with a useful commentary on the circumstances of its composition, in *Literaturnoe nasledstvo,* LXI, 27–88.
28. Annenkov, *Zamechatelnoe desiatiletie,* in *Vospominaniia,* III, 164–165.
29. *B. i D.,* Lemke, XIII, 297–298.
30. *Ibid.,* 299–300.
31. *Ibid.,* 582.
32. For example, Elsberg, "Satira-pamflet protiv kosmopolitizma," in *Literaturnoe nasledstvo,* LXI, 89–94.
33. *B. i D.,* Lemke, XIII, 307.
34. *Ibid.,* XIII, 500; Ogarev to Herzen, 3 Jan., 1847, *Literaturnoe nasledstvo,* LXI, 748.
35. The original, chiefly French, text of all Herzen's letters to the Herweghs (with a copious selection, in Russian translation, from Natalie's letters) is given in *Literaturnoe nasledstvo,* LXIV, 9–318. The manuscripts of the full correspondence are in the British Museum, Add. MSS. 47664–8.
36. Tuchkov and daughters accompanied the Herzens to Italy in 1848–50; see Carr, *Romantic Exiles.* Herzen frequented Turgenev in Paris in 1848–50.
37. See above, Chap. IX, sixth section, and Chap. X, seventh section.
38. Herzen's very negative portrait of Sazonov is given in *B. i D.,* Lemke, XIII, 572–589. Lemke makes a defense of Herzen's attitude towards Sazonov in his "Kommentarii nos. 41–51" to part V of *B. i D.,* Lemke, XIV, 128–149. A more balanced treatment is that of Kamenev, ed., *Byloe i Dumy,* III, 255–262.
39. *B. i D.,* Lemke, XIII, 289.
40. *Ibid.,* 453.
41. *Ibid.,* 579–580.
42. *Ibid.,* 580–581. The "Anacharses" in question were named after the Scythian (i.e., by extension, Russian) philosopher in ancient Greece; Herzen was no doubt also thinking of Anacharsis Cloots.
43. *Ibid.,* 582.
44. Annenkov, *Zamechatelnoe desiatiletie,* in *Vospominaniia,* III, 161–162.
45. Herzen's letters to his friends while crossing Germany had been jocular and reportorial, with no direct attacks against the West, since he had not yet seen the idol of the moderates, liberal France. Still he manages to drop offhand remarks about the "narrow-mindedness, the philistinism, the low,

petty point of view and aspirations" of the German merchants and about the weight of the West's past as observed in the monuments of Cologne. He even declares that: "In all encounters I have shown myself . . . a proud Russian [*Russ*] . . . and indeed the Germans understand the broadness of our nature." This was to be the gist of his criticism of the West for the rest of his life, and it was formulated before he ever saw Paris and less than a month after he had crossed the Russian frontier. See Herzen to friends, 8/20 Feb., 1847 and 12–19/24–31 March, 1847, *A. I. Gertsen. Novye materialy,* edited by N. M. Mendelson (Moscow, 1927), pp. 27–34, henceforth referred to as Herzen, *Novye materialy.* (Hereafter, whenever it is pertinent, letters will be cited simultaneously according to both the Russian and the Western calendars, as in the example just given.)

46. For example, the quite scabrous puns about Turgenev's amatory adventures in Paris, Herzen to Herwegh, 16 April, 1850, "Pisma Gertsena k Gervegam," in *Literaturnoe nasledstvo,* LXIV, 165.

47. Herzen to M. S. Shchepkin, 11/23 April, 1847, *Literaturnoe nasledstvo,* LXI, 208.

48. Annenkov, *Zamechatelnoe desiatiletie,* in *Vospominaniia,* III, 163.

49. Botkin to Annenkov, 14/26 May, 1847, Annenkov, *Druzia,* I, 540.

50. Granovski to Herzen, second half of 1847, Granovski, *Perepiska,* II, 445–446. The letter of Herzen to T. A. Astrakov to which Granovski alludes is that of 29 May/10 June, 1847, Herzen, *Pisma k Astrakovym,* pp. 99–102.

51. Ogarev to Herzen, 7/19 June, 1847, *Literaturnoe nasledstvo,* LXI, 764.

52. Belinski to Botkin, 7/19 July, 1847, Belinski, *Pisma,* III, 244–246.

53. Botkin to Annenkov and Belinski, 7/19 July, 1847, Annenkov, *Druzia,* I, 542.

54. Belinski to Botkin, Dec. 1847, Belinski, *Pisma,* III, 321–333, especially 325–332.

55. Belinski to Annenkov, 15/27 Feb., 1848, Belinski, *Pisma,* III, 338. This, Belinski's last pronouncement on the bourgeoisie, is also his strongest. He "spits" on Louis Blanc and the socialists, declares that the simple people always and everywhere has been incapable of liberating itself and asserts that the "internal process of civic development in Russia will not begin sooner than when the Russian gentry turns into a bourgeoisie." *Ibid.,* 339.

56. At least these are the positions that can be deduced from the letters cited in the two previous notes.

57. Belinski to Botkin, Dec. 1847, Belinski, *Pisma,* III, 326, 331.

58. That Herzen says nothing of these rebuffs in *My Past and Thoughts* by no means indicates that he did not feel them as deeply as is maintained here. His editing of his quarrel with the Slavophiles and with the moderate Westerners shows that he tended to suppress his failures to win over important Russian figures in a political discussion. This is no doubt why the frustrating year 1847 is hardly discussed in his memoirs.

59. In 1854 the *Pisma iz Avenue Marigny* were included in slightly revised form as the first four chapters of the *Pisma iz Frantsii i Italii,* by which title they have generally been known since. They are cited here under the latter name but from the text of 1847 as given by Lemke. For the dating of their composition see note of ed., Lemke, V, 507.

60. *Frantsiia i Italiia,* first letter, Lemke, V, 115.

61. *Ibid.,* 116.

62. *Ibid.,* 119.

63. *Ibid.*, 120; *Dnevnik*, 18 Jan., 1844, Lemke, III, 302.

64. *Frantsiia i Italiia*, second letter, Lemke, V, 131–132.

65. *Ibid.*, 133.

66. *Ibid.*, third letter, 145.

67. *Ibid.*, fourth letter, 155–161.

68. Granovski to Frolovs, 7/19 Nov., 1847, Granovski, *Perepiska*, II, 424.

69. Botkin to Annenkov, 12/24 Oct., 1847, Annenkov, *Druzia*, I, 550–551. Herzen at the time was in Italy and Annenkov in Paris, but the two were in correspondence. Unfortunately, however, the latter's letters have not survived to show just what news he passed along to Herzen; see Herzen to Annenkov, 5/17 March, 1848, Lemke, V, 205, where he speaks of receiving letters from his friend.

70. Botkin to Herzen, 25 Nov./7 Dec., 1847, *Literaturnoe nasledstvo*, LXII, 40.

71. Annenkov, *Zamechatelnoe desiatiletie*, in *Vospominaniia*, III, 164.

72. Herzen to Botkin, 31 Dec., 1847/12 Jan. 1848, Herzen, *Novye materialy*, pp. 40–41.

73. *Ibid.*, 41.

74. Herzen to Korsh, Granovski and Kavelin, 30 Jan./11 Feb., 1848, Lemke, V, 178.

75. For the possible influence of Bakunin and the Poles, see Boris Nikolaevski, "Za vashu i nashu volnost — stranitsy iz istorii russko-polskikh otnosheni," *Novy zhurnal* (New York), no. 7, 1944; for Proudhon see, Labry, *Herzen et Proudhon*, where the author concludes that Herzen's anarchism was an independent development; for the hint on the Flemish towns see *Frantsiia i Italiia*, first letter, Lemke, V, 121; for Fourier see above, Chap. XIII, second section; for Weitling see *Dnevnik*, 4 Nov., 1843, Lemke, III, 140–141.

76. See Herzen to Korsh, Granovski and Kavelin, 30 Jan./11 Feb., 1848, Lemke, V, 178–180. A similar defense of Herzen's *Letters* from France concludes the first of the *Letters from the Via del Corso*, Lemke, VI, 19–20.

77. Herzen to Korsh, Granovski and Kavelin, 31 Jan./12 Feb., 1848, Lemke, V, 181–182.

78. The *Pisma s Via del Corso* were begun for publication in the *Sovremennik*. In the course of writing Herzen realized they could never pass the censorship; however, he continued them, but only for circulation in manuscript among his friends. Never published under their original title, they first appeared in German and in a slightly revised form as the opening chapters of *Briefe aus Italien und Frankreich (1848–1849), von einem Russen* (Hamburg, 1850). They were published in Russian for the first time in 1854 as letters IV–VIII of *Frantsiia i Italiia*, by which title they are generally known. Since the original version has not survived in entirety, citations are made here from the text of 1854 used by Lemke; however, only those passages are quoted which definitely date from 1848. See note of ed., Lemke, VI, 540–542; what remains of the original text is given in Lemke, VI, 564–613.

79. *Frantsiia i Italiia*, fifth letter, Lemke, VI, 1.

80. *Ibid.*, 3–5.

81. *Ibid.*, 6–7. The expression "rural commune" is a translation of "*derevenskaia kommuna*," a Russianized form of the French term *commune* and only approximately the equivalent of *obshchina*.

82. *Ibid.*, sixth letter, 32. Italics added.

83. *Ibid.*, fifth letter, 9–11. Italics added. In the original version these

passages are worded in slightly more moderate fashion, but the sense is the same; see Lemke, VI, 570 and 574.

84. *Frantsiia i Italiia,* fifth letter, Lemke, VI, 14–15, 18–19.
85. *Ibid.,* sixth letter, 28–30.

CHAPTER FIFTEEN

The Revolution of 1848

1. *Frantsiia i Italiia,* eighth letter, 3 March, 1848, Lemke, VI, 49.
2. *Ibid.,* 50.
3. Herzen to Annenkov, 5 March, 1848, Lemke, V, 208.
4. *Frantsiia i Italiia,* ninth letter, June 1848, Lemke, VI, 58.
5. *Ibid.,* eighth letter, April 1848, VI, 57.
6. *Ibid.,* ninth letter, June 1848, Lemke, VI, 58.
7. Like the *Pisma s Via del Corso* (see above Chap. XIV, note 78) the articles *Opiat v Parizhe* could not be published in Russia at the time of their composition in 1848. Hence they too were first published in German and in revised form in 1850. They appeared in Russian only in 1854, still further reworked, in particular condensed, as a part of the final chapters of *Pisma iz Frantsii i Italii,* by which title they are generally known. What remains of the more extensive text of 1848 has been given by Lemke (VI, 613–668) and in Herzen, *Novye materialy,* pp. 112–129. Since the text of 1854 is the best known and the most readily available, quotations here will be taken from it, however only when they correspond to the spirit, if not always to the exact wording, of the original.
8. *Frantsiia i Italiia,* ninth letter, June, 1848, Lemke, VI, 57.
9. *Ibid.,* 62.
10. *Ibid.,* 62–63.
11. *S togo berega,* "Posle grozy," Lemke, V, 417–418.
12. In 1849 in *Lettre d'un Russe à Mazzini,* Lemke, V; in 1850 in *S togo berega,* "Donoso-Cortes," Lemke, V; and especially in 1854 in *The Old World and Russia. Letters to W. Linton,* Lemke, VIII.
13. See especially *Frantsiia i Italiia,* fourteenth letter, Dec. 1851, Lemke, VI, 128–131.
14. *Frantsiia i Italiia,* eleventh letter, June 1849, Lemke, VI, 98.
15. *Ibid.,* tenth letter, Sept. 1848, 96–97.
16. *Ibid.,* thirteenth letter, June 1851, 124.
17. *Ibid.,* 125–127; *S togo berega,* "Omnia mea mecum porto," Lemke, V, 469–484.
18. *Ibid.,* 478–479.
19. *Ibid.,* 479.
20. *Frantsiia i Italiia,* eleventh letter, June 1849, Lemke, VI, 101.
21. *Ibid.,* tenth letter, Sept. 1848, 94–95.
22. *Ibid.,* eleventh letter, June 1849, 106.
23. This has been demonstrated in detail by Labry, *Herzen et Proudhon.*
24. *Frantsiia i Italiia,* tenth letter, Sept. 1848, Lemke, VI, 90. Italics added.
25. These themes run throughout *S togo berega.* See especially "Consolatio" and "Epilog 1849," Lemke, V, 467 and 488.
26. Herzen's first reference to Stirner does not come until 1858, and even then it is not clear how much he read. See Lemke, XVIII, 367. In any event Stirner was not a significant "influence" in any stage of Herzen's development.

27. *S togo berega,* "Pered grozoi," Lemke, V, 405. This passage, as the title of the chapter from which it is taken — "Before the Storm" — indicates, was written prior to the Revolution, in 1847; hence the full development of the philosophical aspects of Herzen's anarchism, like the first stirrings of his political anarchism and of his belief in the "socialist" Russian peasant commune, dates from before the June Days. Thus we have another indication that the ideological break marked by his emigration was due less to objective "disillusionment" with Europe than to the subjective repercussions of his quarrel with the moderate Westerners. Indeed, the passage quoted is one of Herzen's speeches in an imaginary dialogue with a minor figure among them, I. P. Galakhov.

28. This theme is especially prominent in *S togo berega,* "Pered grozoi," Lemke, V, 406–407. It recurs in subsequent chapters of *S togo berega,* especially in Herzen's second imaginary dialogue with Galakhov, "Vixerunt!," *ibid.,* 429–450, "Consolatio," *ibid.,* 450–469 and "Omnia mea mecum porto," *ibid.,* 469–484.

29. *Ibid.,* "Omnia mea mecum porto," 473. The philosophical views set forth in this and similar passages of *S togo berega* are best discussed by Zenkovski, *Russkaia filosofiia,* I, 291–304. Zenkovski's position is that after 1847 Herzen reverted from the logical determinism of Hegel to the more anarchistic poetry of Schelling, or from the view of a universe ruled by rational progress to that of one moved by the blind impulse of *Naturgewalten.* Though there is some truth in this, it underemphasizes those elements of pattern and logic with which Schelling endowed nature, or at least which Herzen, following Pavlov, had seen in the *Naturphilosophie* in his youth. What is more important, so philosophical an approach to *S togo berega* obscures the fact that, for political and psychological reasons which had nothing to do with Schelling or Hegel, by 1847–48 Herzen needed to believe in a universe of anarchic forces which explained the absurd contingencies of history (such as the reaction after 1848) and yet left the individual free of any ·necessity outside himself. Thus man could be crushed by external forces and still remain inwardly, morally free — which was Herzen's view of his own position and of that of all progressive men after 1848.

30. Herzen's anticipation of existentialism was first pointed out by Shpet, *Filosofskoe mirovozzrenie Gertsena.*

31. *B. i D.,* Lemke, XIII, 362.

32. Introduction to *S togo berega,* Lemke, V, 386–388.

33. Labry, *Herzen et Proudhon,* especially chap. iii.

34. See chaps. xliv–l of *B. i D.,* Lemke, XIII, 500–561.

35. Carr, *Romantic Exiles,* chaps. iii-iv; also Chap. XIV, note 35, above.

36. See above, Chap. XI, second section.

37. For example, Carr, *Romantic Exiles,* pp. 210–211; P. Guber, *Kruzhenie serdtsa: semeinaia drama Gertsena* (Leningrad, 1924).

CHAPTER SIXTEEN

Russian Socialism

1. See above, Chap. XIV, note 23.

2. *B. i D.,* Lemke, XIII, 419–423; Herzen to Count Orlov, 23 Sept., 1850, Lemke, VI, 145–148.

3. On Engelson see *B. i D.,* Lemke, XIII, 590–623 and "Kommentarii" of

ed. to same, XIV, 91–161, *passim;* on Golovin see *B. i D.,* Lemke, XIV, 347–368, and M. K. Lemke, "Emigrant Ivan Golovin," in *Byloe* (1907), nos. 6, 7.

4. *B. i D.,* Lemke, XIII, 398–411.

5. Herzen's good business sense, even in the midst of his anguish over 1848, is demonstrated by his regular and full letters to the overseer of his affairs in Russia from 1847 to 1850, when at last the Imperial government sequestered his property. See "Pisma A. I. Gertsena G. I. Kliucharevu," in *Literaturnoe nasledstvo,* XXXIX–XL, 195–243. For his willingness to reap a speculative profit with the aid of Rothschild by taking advantage of the scarcity of capital after 1848 see especially his letter of 15 Feb., 1849, *ibid.,* 230. This, of course, was only good sense, even revolutionary good sense, and it would be difficult to reproach Herzen for it. Nonetheless, his action contrasts in democratic purity with that of Ogarev, who on his father's death a decade earlier had liberated the majority of his serfs with land, for a price to be sure, but still at a significant loss, which eventually made of him a relatively poor man whereas he had started richer than Herzen.

6. *B. i D.,* Lemke, XIII, 437–445; "Kommentarii nos. 13 and 14" of ed. to part V of *B. i D.,* Lemke, XIV, 20–25. Herzen had to deposit 25,000 frs in the Bank of the Canton of Fribourg, which were to remain there until his children became of age (*ibid.,* 24).

7. *B. i D.,* Lemke, XIII, 306–313.

8. *Ibid.,* 314–323.

9. *Ibid.,* 323–326; 405–411; "Kommentari no. 16" of Kamenev, ed., to *Byloe i Dumy,* II, 522–523.

10. *B. i D.,* Lemke, XIII, 361–381.

11. *Ibid.,* 326–360.

12. *Ibid.,* 446–463; Labry, *Herzen et Proudhon,* chap. iv; letters of Sazonov to Herzen, June–July 1849, *Literaturnoe nasledstvo,* LXII, 532–539.

13. Herzen's numerous printed clashes with Marx (the two never met) are mostly conveniently summarized in "Kommentarii" of Kamenev, ed., to *Byloe i Dumy,* II, 584–613. Herzen's acid comments on Marx — whose followers are referred to as "Marxids" — are given in *B. i D.,* Lemke, XIII, 303–307.

14. *Michel Bakounine,* written in 1851 for Michelet, Lemke, VI, 466–474; *The Russian Agent Bakunin,* written in 1853 for the London *Morning Advertiser,* Lemke, VII, 303–304. Bakunin is also treated in most of Herzen's longer pieces published in Europe, which are discussed below.

15. *Le républicain de New York,* Dec. 1854; *New-Yorker Abend-Zeitung,* Sept. 1850; *The Citizen,* Dec. 1854.

16. Letters of Herzen to friends, Lemke, V and VI, *passim;* Herzen, *Novye materialy,* pp. 45–80; letters of Granovski to Herzen, July 1849 to June 1855, *Literaturnoe nasledstvo,* LXII, 94–104; "Arkhiv N. P. Ogareva," *Russkie propilei,* IV, *passim;* "M. S. Shchepkin," *B. i D.,* Lemke, XIV.

17. For example, the introduction to *S togo berega* of March 1849, "Proshchaite!," Lemke, V, 386–391; the announcement of the founding of the *Volnaia russkaia tipografiia* in 1853 entitled *Bratiam na Rusi,* Lemke, VII, 186–187.

18. For example, *B. i D.,* Lemke, XIII, 426–427.

19. The English come off rather well in the comparisons that Herzen makes between them and the French or the Germans. For example, see *B. i D.,* Lemke, XIV, 269–271 or his letter to M. K. Reichel, 26 Aug., 1852, Lemke, VII, 126.

20. In embryo at least since 1839; see above, chap. IX, note 56. Herzen

first actively considered publishing in Russian abroad — naturally his own articles — in Paris in 1849; see *Literaturnoe nasledstvo*, XXXIX–XL, 165–171.

21. For details see Z. P. Bazileva, *"Kolokol" Gertsena* (n. p. 1949), chap. i.

22. Actually Herzen's productions were not absolutely the first uncensored political literature in Russian printed abroad. This honor probably belongs to a pamphlet published by Herzen's fellow emigrant, Golovin, in Paris in 1849. Nonetheless, Herzen's efforts represent the first significant Russian publication abroad and the real beginning of a tradition.

23. For the genesis and composition of *Byloe i Dumy* see Zh. Elsberg, A. I. *Gertsen i Byloe i dumy* (Moscow, 1930); the introduction, entitled "Istoriia sozdaniia, soderzhanie i izdaniia 'Bylogo i dum'," by Kamenev, ed., *Byloe i Dumy*, vol. I; and L. Ginzburg, *"Byloe i Dumy" Gertsena* (Leningrad, 1957).

24. Herzen to M. K. Reichel, 5 Nov., 1852, Lemke, VII, 157. The memory of Rousseau's *Confessions* was no doubt also an influence.

25. "Bibliograficheski kommentari" of ed., *B. i D.*, Lemke, XIV, 787ff.

26. See above Chap. XII, seventh section.

27. Herzen's first mention of reading Haxthausen's book is in 1849, in the essay where he first developed his own view of the "socialist" significance of the commune. See *La Russie: à G. H.*, Lemke, V, 306, 308–318.

28. Boris Nikolaevski, "Za vashu i nashu volnost — stranitsi iz istorii russko-polskikh otnosheni," in *Novy zhurnal*, no. 7, 1944, pp. 252–276. Nikolaevski develops the thesis that it was the Poles, in particular Lelewel, who first propounded the idea of the "socialist" peasant commune, that Bakunin picked it up from Lelewel in Brussels in 1843–44 and then transmitted it to Herzen in Paris in 1847. The hypothesis is interesting, but there is no direct evidence to support it, while Herzen's contact with the same idea expressed by the Slavophiles and Haxthausen is beyond doubt. But more important than any of these direct "influences" is the fact that this idea was a logical one for any Russian with socialist leanings and was, moreover, in the air at the time.

29. See above, Chap. XIV, final section.

30. Herzen to Moscow friends, 5 Nov., 1848, Lemke, V, 243–244.

31. *La Russie: à G. H.*, Lemke, V, 299–329, and note of ed., p. 528.

32. *Lettre d'un Russe à Mazzini*, Lemke, V, 366–371 and note of ed., p. 529.

33. *Du développement des idées révolutionnaires en Russie*, Lemke, VI, 197–297 and note of ed. p. 670.

34. *Le peuple russe et le socialisme, Lettre à M. Jules Michelet*, Lemke, VI, 433–461 and note of ed., pp. 685–686. Lemke gives only the Russian version of this work; the original French text is in Herzen, *Sochineniia v tridtsati tomakh*, VII, 271–306.

35. *Kreshchenaia sobstvennost*, Lemke, VII, 263–288; *Russian Serfdom*, Lemke, VII, 339–360.

36. *The Old World and Russia. Letters to the Editor of "The English Republic,"* W. Linton, Lemke, VIII, 25–57. This article is a translation from the French original of Herzen, which appeared separately the same year in *L'Homme*, the newspaper of the French exiles from Napoleon III grouped around Victor Hugo on the island of Jersey. This text is given in Herzen, *Sochineniia v tridtsati tomakh*, XII, 134–166. Since all these works say roughly the same things in only slightly different form there is no point in distinguishing between them. Consequently, in the notes below the usual practice of giving

short titles will not be followed; citations will be made simply by the volume and page numbers from Lemke. For a fuller discussion of the questions treated here see M. E. Malia, "Herzen and the Peasant Commune," in E. J. Simmons ed., *Continuity and Change in Russian and Soviet Thought*.

37. Lemke, V, 300 and VI, 232; see above Chap. XIV, note 63.
38. Lemke, VI, 279.
39. *Ibid.*, 280.
40. *Ibid.*, VI, 456, and VIII, 25.
41. *Ibid.*, VI, 209.
42. *Ibid.*, VIII, 32.
43. *Ibid.*, 32–33.
44. *Ibid.*, VI, 297.
45. *Ibid.*, VIII, 45.
46. *Ibid.*, VI, 448.
47. *Ibid.*
48. *Ibid.*, VIII, 34.
49. *Ibid.*, VI, 448–449.
50. *Ibid.*, 449.
51. *Ibid.*, 447.
52. *Ibid.*, 440.
53. *Ibid.*, VII, 278.
54. *Ibid.*, VI, 446.
55. *Ibid.*, VII, 267.
56. *Ibid.*, VI, 445.
57. *Ibid.*, VIII, 51.
58. *Ibid.*, VI, 445–446.
59. See *La Russie: à G. H.*, Lemke, V, 308–318 and "Annexe" to *Du développement des idées révolutionnaires en Russie*, Lemke, VI, 293–297, for the fullest and most compact exposition of Herzen's ideas on the commune.
60. Lemke, VII, 279. Italics added.
61. *Ibid.*, VI, 446.
62. *Ibid.*, VIII, 49.
63. *Ibid.*, VI, 296.
64. *Ibid.*, VIII, 47.
65. *Ibid.*, VI, 296.
66. *Ibid.*, 282.
67. *Ibid.*, VIII, 46.
68. *Ibid.*, VII, 277
69. *Ibid.*, 267, 276–280; quotations on p. 276.
70. *Ibid.*, VI, 455–456.
71. *Ibid.*, 456.
72. *Ibid.*, 450.
73. *Ibid.*, 457.
74. *Ibid.*, VIII, 38.
75. *Ibid.*, VI, 457.
76. *Ibid.*, 458.
77. *Ibid.*, 450.
78. *Ibid.*, VII, 279–280.
79. See Gershenzon, "Gertsen i zapad," in *Obrazy proshlogo*, pp. 175–282.
80. See notably *Russian Serfdom*, Lemke, VII, 339–360.
81. See above Chap. XIV, seventh section.

82. *Iurev den! Iurev den! Russkomu dvorianstvu,* Lemke, VII, 248–254.

83. See above Chap. VII, second section.

84. *Ty pobedil, O Galileianin!,* Lemke, IX.

85. Belinski to Kavelin, 22 Nov., 1847, and Belinski to Annenkov, beginning of Dec. 1847, Belinski, *Pisma,* III, 297–303, and 313–321.

86. *Ispoved,* in Bakunin, *Sochineniia* (Steklov), IV, 99–207.

87. See Carr, *Bakunin,* chap. xviii.

88. Bakunin, *Romanov, Pugachev ili Pestel?*

CHAPTER SEVENTEEN

The Gentry Revolutionary

1. For a fuller comparison of Herzen and Bakunin see Isaiah Berlin, "Herzen and Bakunin on Individual Liberty," in E. J. Simmons, ed., *Continuity and Change in Russian and Soviet Thought.* For Herzen's own awareness later in life of what separated him from his friend see his *Pisma staromu tovarishchu,* Lemke, XXI, 433–449.

2. "Engelsony," *B. i D.,* Lemke, XIII, 616.

Index

DATE DUE

			Printed in USA